1295
JP

THE PREPARATION OF THIS BOOK
WAS SPONSORED BY THE
Minnesota Historical Society

*Theodore C. Blegen

MINNESOTA

A HISTORY OF THE STATE

with a new concluding
chapter, "A State That Works,"
by Russell W. Fridley

UNIVERSITY OF MINNESOTA PRESS

Printed in the United States of America at the
North Central Publishing Company, St. Paul

 3

Published in Canada by
Burns & MacEachern Limited, Don Mills, Ontario

Library of Congress Catalog Card Number 75–6116

ISBN 0–8166–0754–0

✳
Acknowledgments

THROUGH more than four decades I have been interested in the history of Minnesota, its sources, and the hundreds of articles and books written about the state. For many years I have wanted to try my hand at writing the Minnesota story for the "general public" — citizens of Minnesota and people elsewhere who may be interested.

Now that the book has been finished, I want to record my gratitude to all who have influenced my work — colleagues, other scholars (some of whom I have never met), students, friends, institutions. Since a listing of names would go beyond even the limits of the bibliographical references that follow my narrative, let me just say thanks to the many who have made contributions in this field.

I must add a few names, however. Several critics have read chapters of this book in its various stages: Bertha L. Heilbron, Russell W. Fridley, Lucile M. Kane, Elwood Maunder, and Professors E. W. Davis and Elden O. Johnson, among others. For their helpful comments I am grateful. Dr. John Q. Imholte of the University of Minnesota at Morris served as a research assistant in the summer of 1961 and aided me particularly on problems relating to the Civil War period. Most of my chapters were typed (in successive versions) by Mrs. Gladys Upham; Mrs. Zephyra E. Shepherd prepared the index; Mrs. Mary Nakasone drew and lettered the maps; Mrs. Helene Thomson of the Minnesota Historical Society helped to find illustrations and Eugene D. Becker, curator of pictures, did most of the photocopy work. Staff members of the University of Minnesota Press were so encouraging to me and so generous in competent advice and help that I thought of them as partners in the making of the book. Dr. Theodore L. Nydahl's contributions to the Minnesota reading guide that he and I published in 1960 helped me to organize material on the more recent history of the state. My wife read the manuscript, chapter by chapter, and gave me many good suggestions.

I am indebted to the Minnesota Historical Society for sponsoring the Research Fellowship that I held for more than two years (September 1960 through December 1962) and for providing me with an office. The members of the society's staff were unendingly helpful in giving me access to the resources of the institution in its several divisions. The funds for my fellowship were generously supplied by the Elmer L. and Eleanor J. Andersen Foundation of St. Paul, to which I am deeply grateful. For more than a decade Mr. Andersen has been voicing the need for a one-volume history of the state designed for general reading. Many months before I retired in 1960 from the deanship of the Graduate School of the University of Minnesota, he asked me to consider the feasibility of such a project. I was happy to do so, and the result is this book.

T. C. B.

Table of Contents

TABLE OF CONTENTS

party, 576–78. The Freeman administration, 578–83. Andersen's administration, 583–85. The election of 1962, 585–90. Problems facing the state, 590–97. "History is people," 597.

Illustrations

TABLE OF CONTENTS

between pages 226 and 227

Minnehaha Falls about 1868. Early leaders in Minnesota politics, industry, and education: Alexander Ramsey, Ignatius Donnelly, Henry H. Sibley, and John S. Pillsbury. Two noted governors of the twentieth century: Floyd B. Olson and Luther Youngdahl. The Minnesota House of Representatives in session. The Minneapolis Symphony Orchestra. The Rochester Art Center.

between pages 418 and 419

South St. Paul stockyards. An early cooperative. Whitefield's view of the Mississippi near Maiden Rock. Red River carts. The first airplane flight over Minneapolis. A forerunner of the Greyhound Bus Company. A research balloon.

between pages 578 and 579

The skylines of Minneapolis and St. Paul. The Round Tower at Fort Snelling. The Sibley House at Mendota. The port of Duluth. Main Street, Sauk Centre. A modern Minnesota farm. Contour farming in Minnesota.

between pages 708 and 709

The Minneapolis skyline in the 1970s, dramatically changed by the freeway and the IDS tower. St. Paul's Osborn Building. The Guthrie Theater in 1974. The old Duluth railway depot, now the St. Louis County Heritage and Arts Center. One of the demonstrations that marked the 1960s and early 1970s — a peace march on the state capitol, May 9, 1970. Hubert H. Humphrey, Eugene J. McCarthy, Warren E. Burger, Wendell R. Anderson, and Elmer L. Andersen. Fishing remains an important industry on the Red Lake Indian Reservation. Snowmobiles on a winter trail. Charles A. Lindbergh, Jr., at Rainy Lake in 1969, part of the future Voyageurs National Park.

MINNESOTA · A HISTORY OF THE STATE

Land, Water, and Time

EVENTS "take place." They occur somewhere and sometime. Consequently, historians, from the Greeks to our own day, have had to take into account geography and its connections with human affairs.

Geography means many interrelated things. It involves location, proximity to seas and to other lands or areas, climate and seasons, soil, and minerals. It has to do with mountains, hills, valleys, prairies, lakes and streams, water power and supply, and animal and plant life. It looks at nature's resources in their abundance or lack of abundance — and at what people have thought about resources and done with them.

According to a geologist, "Minnesota's history could have been enacted in just one place, and that is Minnesota." This is obvious, and with changes in geographical designations, similar statements could be made about Egypt, Greece, England, indeed any inhabited area, large or small, in the world. Human living has scene and setting and can be neither imagined nor interpreted in a vacuum. The "important determinant of any culture," writes the poet and novelist Lawrence Durrell, is "the spirit of place." This may or may not be true, but no divorce between history and place is possible, just as time, from beginnings through growth and change, is basic to history.

If the historian must have the sense of "place," he must also be sensitive to the truth that one place can be part of another. Boundaries can

3

be superimposed upon other boundaries, with one extending far beyond another. An American state is an integral part of the national whole, just as its own localities are integral parts of the state. Minnesota's once-thriving fur trade was part of a vast theater of trading operations west of the Great Lakes. The political boundaries of the American states are fixed by historical circumstance and law, but the nation has economic "states" that pay scant attention to such boundaries. These include metro-politan areas, which represent the nonpolitical orbits of economic and cultural centers.

The sense of place, its recognition, and its treatment in the literature of America are important, but they in no way commit a writer or an art-ist to parochial or provincial views. Such views imply a blindness to interrelations, a failure to understand boundaries beyond boundaries, an unawareness of what is of broad concern. Interrelations with region, na-tion, and world have been vital to the ongoing life of people in every state of the Union.

Interconnections with other areas and with national and international forces are important, but it remains true that the state at the Mississippi's headwaters is the central setting for Minnesota history. In reviewing that history, one is tempted to take as a text the dictum of the famous Ellen Semple that "What is today a fact of geography becomes tomorrow a fac-tor of history." Certainly facts of geography — and of geology reaching back millions of years — have been significant and even decisive factors in Minnesota's history.

Geographic factors are so interwoven, one with another and with the human story of Minnesota, that it is difficult to single out a very few that dwarf the others in significance. The central geographic position of the state, however, is fundamental to its history. Occupying the Lake Su-perior highlands, a portion of the prairie plains, the very apex of the Mississippi Valley, looking eastward through the Great Lakes and south-ward along the great river, serving as the northern gateway to the West, and meeting central Canada at the north, Minnesota is not only the "Star of the North," as its official motto proclaims. It is the crest of the Middle West and just about the geographic center of the continent.

It was "place" — the central position of Minnesota — that led Senator William H. Seward of New York in 1860 to predict that the "last seat of power on the great continent" would be found in this region "at the

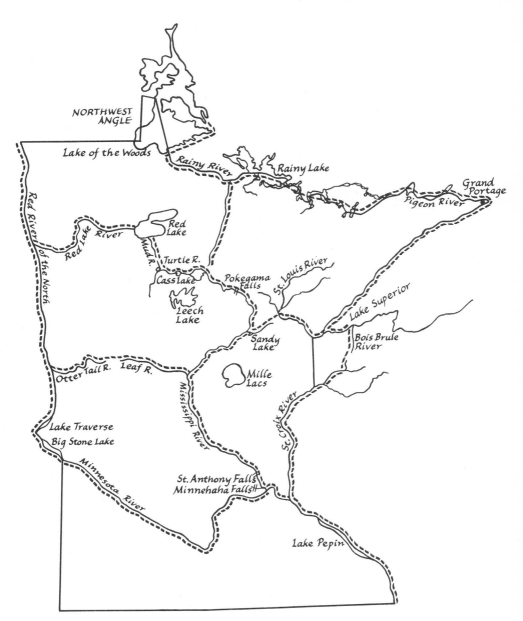

The waterways of Minnesota (adapted from Robinson's *Early Economic Conditions and the Development of Agriculture in Minnesota*)

head of navigation on the Mississippi river, and on the great Mediterranean Lakes." Place accounts for the American occupation of this area at the particular period of the westward movement when it occurred. Position and the historical forces of expansion are keys to the birth of Minnesota Territory in 1849 and the State of Minnesota in 1858, as, indeed, they are to many other chapters in the story of this commonwealth.

The prodigal waters and water highways of Minnesota attest its centrality and constitute another and related geographic factor of immense importance to its history. The total area of the state in square miles has been measured as 84,068, and of this, water occupies 4059 square miles — a greater water area than that of any other state. Its more than eleven thousand lakes are the state's most distinctive feature, and its intricate system of water highways has profoundly influenced the course of its history.

Minnesota's waters flow out into three great systems — north, east and south. Hudson Bay, with the Red and Nelson rivers as its tributaries, drains about 34 per cent of the state's area. The Great Lakes and the St. Lawrence system are outlets for about 9 per cent; and the many-branched Mississippi, which starts in picturesque Lake Itasca, about 57 per cent. Thus lines from the Minnesota watersheds run to Hudson Bay and the Arctic, to the Atlantic, and to the Gulf of Mexico. Minnesota is in some sense "the mother of three seas."

The lines are both of ingress and egress. They are thoroughfares which, with all their interlacings, offered the white man a network of routes for transportation. From Lake Superior the "grand portage" led the traveler to the Pigeon River and the boundary-water route to the west. The St. Louis River with connecting portages and lakes opened the way to the upper Mississippi. The Brule offered a water path to the St. Croix and the Mississippi. And the Mississippi itself wound into (and out of) the very heart of Minnesota, with numerous tributaries, including the Minnesota River bending south and then west, having portage and lake connections with the north-flowing Red River.

Explorers, fur traders, voyageurs, missionaries, and early settlers knew and used the waterways provided by geological forces through eons of time. They were travel routes. Supplies were brought in, furs sent out, in canoes, barges, boats, steamboats. Water linked frontier Minnesota with nation and world; and within the area it connected community

6

with region. On the rivers, logs were floated to mills in a great lumber industry. Lakes and streams, easy of access, had much to do with the location of cities and towns and the exploitation of the soil. Falls and rapids offered water power for industry, large and small. It is no chance circumstance that the leading city of the state grew up alongside the Mississippi and the eternally plunging (but now harnessed) Falls of St. Anthony, or that St. Paul, the capital city, was the head of steamboat navigation on the great river.

Waterways decisively influenced the diplomatic and legal architects of Minnesota's boundaries. At the north most of the border with Canada is the old canoe route from Lake Superior to Lake of the Woods. On the northeast and east, Lake Superior, the St. Louis and St. Croix rivers, and the Mississippi form the significant dividing lines. And on the west the boundary follows the strategic path of the Red River and Lakes Traverse and Big Stone. At some spots the state does indeed have straight lines drawn by surveyors. These are the boundary at the south with Iowa (the 43° 30′ parallel); the line running south from Big Stone Lake to the same parallel, separating Minnesota from part of South Dakota; the forty-ninth parallel heading westward straight below the northwest point of Lake of the Woods; and a line from the St. Louis River to the St. Croix. With these exceptions, Minnesota is water-bounded, a fitting circumstance for a state dotted with lakes that drain to seas north, east, and south. Within its boundaries, the state stretches some 400 miles from north to south, with varying width — 367 miles at the greatest and an average of about 225.

Early white men took Minnesota as they found it, with little thought of the sculpturing hand of time. But the historian of today must have an awareness of an awesome past. It is a past with a time span embracing hundreds of millions of years. One is appalled at the thought of more than five hundred million years in the range from Paleozoic to Mesozoic and Cenozoic times, but the charts of geologists carry the story into a Pre-Cambrian era so deep in the past that the measuring unit of years becomes the billion instead of the million. To this remote time, long before human life emerged on the planet, we must look for the origins of many of the natural phenomena characteristic of Minnesota, including the red earth which man, at our turn of the time cycle, transforms into steel.

From the dim age of greenstone at the earth's crust through eons, geologists trace a story of profound change. They block out eras that would seem like fantastic inventions if it were not for the dependable evidence of the rocks in their successive layers. The record tells of volcanoes and spreading lava; of ancient oceans across the Minnesota surface; and of vast ranges of mountains thrust up, and then worn away — or nearly away — by erosion, with reminders to modern man in the granite hills that still lift their faces along the north Superior shore. New expanses of water with all their deposits played their part. Sediments of sand and mud somehow got mixed with silica and iron oxides to form, with the play of time, iron deposits of great richness. There was a succession of seas and mountains. Long ages passed in which life, first in water, then on land, began to appear. There came a reptilian era across some sixty millions of years when strange beasts, possibly including dinosaurs, roamed whatever surface the seas did not cover, and ancestors of modern plant life developed where soil and climate were favorable, where shores or islands offered needed sanctuary. Mammals in strange forms appeared. And somewhere along the chronological line the seas receded.

Even this far vista of time does not include the state's "geological yesterdays," for it omits the age of glaciers. That age, extending across about a million years, comes up to some ten or twelve thousand years in the past — much nearer our time than scientists of only a few decades ago understood. The region was visited by four great invasions of ice, with intervening periods of melting.

The glaciers, in their advances and withdrawals, profoundly and visibly marked and altered the Minnesota surface, as indeed they did all Canada and much of the northern area of the United States. The four glacial periods bear modern names derived from states because of characteristic deposits: Nebraskan, Kansan, Illinoian, Wisconsin. The first two of these glaciers moved down from the northwest, the third from the northeast, and the final one, apparently, from various directions in a series of stages.

The glaciers spread southward, as one geologist puts it, "like pancake batter in a skillet." In this instance the batter was a river of ice, sometimes as deep as a mile, and the skillet was a broad area of the continent. The geologists know what glaciers were, roughly when they came (through a mere matter of ten thousand centuries), and how they

8

influenced the geography of the regions they touched. But nobody seems to know precisely why climatic conditions were such as to usher in the glacial age. Whatever the reasons, certainly the glaciers did come. The real Blue Ox that left footprints on the land was not the fabled animal of a mythical Paul Bunyan, but snow and ice, forming, moving, melting.

Such gigantic movements remodeled the landscape. The enveloping ice, plus the cold that preceded and accompanied it, drove off animal and plant life. It carried in its grasp stones and immense boulders, sometimes hills and mountains. It scooped out hollows as large as the Great Lakes and as small as thousands of Minnesota's little lake basins; and it swept away thick crusts of rock above the sleeping iron giant of the range country. Wherever the ice went, it left its marks. Where it did not go, as in southeastern Minnesota and adjoining Wisconsin (the so-called drift-less area), one finds valleys and hills that preserve, to some extent, the land character of preglacial years. Even in some areas visited by the glaciers, like northern Minnesota, there are a few lake basins carved by erosion in the dim ages before glaciation.

The glaciers did not simply glide down from the frigid north and then return to the arctic region. The batter did not run back to its original pan. The ice carried the arctic breath with it — and then it melted. Its melting meant plunging glacial rivers that sought outlets and dug paths for Minnesota's river system. It created lakes wherever there were hollows to contain them. It meant the deposit of rocks ground fine to make fertile soils. It piled rocks and debris in mounds and hills. And it carved out, among other lakes, Glacial Lake Agassiz, so vast that its area exceeded that of all the Great Lakes rolled into one. Lake Agassiz disappeared in postglacial years, but its outlet was what we now call the Minnesota Valley and a part of its ancient bed is the flat, fertile Red River Valley. Sand ridges marking the shore lines of what is now a gigantic ghost lake are still discernible in western Minnesota.

Thus glacial influences helped to fashion the geography inherited by life — animal, plant, and human — as that life developed in areas freed of the ice that once enveloped the region. When one turns to the resources of climate, soils, and forests and other vegetation, the glacial background is again part and parcel of the story. These factors are closely related not only to one another but also to all the surface features to which the glaciers gave distinctive character.

The state has a continental climate. Its winters are cold, its summers warm. It has a mean annual temperature of about 44° and a growing season running from about 100 to 160 days. Its average precipitation is some 25 inches, with variations in different parts of the state. All these factors have been primary in Minnesota's history. The winters, in conjunction with rivers, lakes, forests, and open lands, were basic to Minnesota's first industry — the fur trade. Lumbering, the second great industry, centered in the evergreen forests of the north, age-old products of climate and soil. And agriculture, in a state ranked second in the United States in its resources of good farming land, has found in the climate a great boon, notwithstanding the misgivings of pioneers that the growing season might prove too short to produce fully grown crops and despite alarms because the frozen rivers closed transportation routes to the outer world. Experimentation proved that good, vast, and varied crops could be raised, and transportation problems were eased by roads, railroads, and other modern means.

Not only have early fears about the climate been dissipated, but the very factors that caused apprehension have been turned to man's advantage. The winters, however long and severe, have provided virtually ideal conditions for winter sports and recreation; and in the summers, the plenitude of lakes has made the state a playground for its people and a resort for visitors whose numbers undergird what is now known as the "tourist industry." This industry is not quite so recent as some assume, for in pioneer days southerners came up the Mississippi to Minnesota to escape from excessively warm areas in summer months. The climate generally, through a century and more, has proved an attraction to health seekers. As early as the 1850s an exuberant Minnesota editor addressed a special invitation to the "Sunburned denizens of-the torrid zone," and said, "Come and bask in the cooling breezes that intensify the delights of our lovely lakes. Come to Minnesota all ye that are roasting and heavy laden and we will give you rest."

State history has been affected not only by the richness and variety of soils which, with rainfall and an adequate growing season, provided the basic resource for agriculture as one of the great industries of Minnesota, but also by the natural variety of vegetation that characterized the region. Here two outstanding features, when white men appeared on the scene, were the coniferous and deciduous forests and the generous expanse of prairie country. Northern Minnesota was blessed with a wide

10

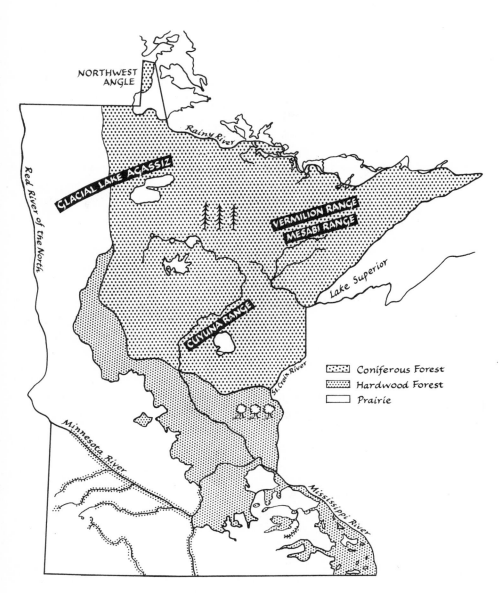

The major land areas of Minnesota (adapted from
Folwell's *History of Minnesota*)

and deep stretch of evergreen forests. They constituted an original paradise for lumbermen because of their fabulous wealth of white pine, spruce, fir, tamarack, and cedar. This was the land of ax and saw, of lumberjacks and logging camps, and of huge crops of timber carried on streams and rivers to the mills and markets of America. The deciduous area ran from the northwest down to the southeast, deepening into what the pioneers called the "Big Woods." These were in the central and southeastern parts — a region, a hundred miles long and forty wide, of hardwood, chiefly oak, maple, ironwood, and basswood. Here was ample wood for building and fuel. To the farmer, however, the area offered difficulties in clearing the land for crops. West, southwest, and south was the prairie, treeless grassland and flower-land, inviting in its promise to farmers, not needing to be cleared of forests, but nevertheless also presenting hard frontier problems. These involved the plowing of the tough turf and everyday living in primitive sod shanties. Pioneers in Minnesota faced the stern realities of wind and weather in the kind of country that caused the disconsolate Beret Hansa, in Ole E. Rölvaag's novel *Giants in the Earth*, to mourn because she could find no tree to hide behind.

Geological time, with all its sculpturing of the landscape — especially in the million-year glacial period — furnishes essential clues to Minnesota's soils, residual and transported; to its mineral riches, building stone, sands, and gravels; its lakes and rivers; its vegetation; its topography; and indeed much of the world of nature that has been the theater of human life in this region. The writings of geologists and geographers catalogue and describe the natural resources in informing fullness of detail, but even a quick sketch would be incomplete if it did not include factors that do not lend themselves to a scientific geographic record. Thus a Minnesota poet sings of "the stream that bends to sea," "the pine that seeks the blue," of "woods and waters fair," and of "prairies waving far." The Minnesota song is a paean to geographic factors interwoven with the human history of the state. The very name of "Minnesota," signifying the "land of sky-tinted water," dramatizes one distinctive aspect of its geography.

Minnesotans, if asked to point out characteristic features of the state's geography, might speak first of its thousands of lakes, with special mention of Red Lake, Mille Lacs, Leech, Vermilion, and picturesque Minnetonka. They might also include the international Lake of the Woods and express their joint pride with Canada, Wisconsin, and Michigan in majestic Lake Superior. They would give special attention to the state's rivers and the picturesque valleys of the St. Croix and the Minnesota. They would point to the iron country of the northeast — the Vermilion, Mesabi, and Cuyuna ranges — and the beauty of the north shore and Arrowhead region.

Many dancing waterfalls would claim affectionate attention, especially the storied Minnehaha Falls, which still "flash and gleam among the oak-trees, laugh and leap into the valley." Minnesotans would speak of the valleys and hills of the unglaciated southeast, and of that widening of the Mississippi known as Lake Pepin, with its legend-encrusted hills and rocks. They might invite a look to the southwest at the pipestone quarries with their Indian traditions of tobacco and peace. And they would not forget the state's far-stretching and fertile acres, its north country of primitive beauty, its summer days, its snow-mantled earth in the deep of winter.

Modern Minnesotans, however, while accepting the realities of geographic backgrounds, might take as their theme, not what Minnesota was when man took over its lands and waters, but what people have done to alter its geography.

Geography is not static. Minnesota has had and still has a "changing geography." Nature itself, through immemorial ages, has "operated unspent" as the architect of change, but modern man has not been content to leave the state's geography unaltered by his handiwork. The redmen, it is true, did little to change conditions, though they adapted themselves to the environment in which they lived. But when civilized men invaded the Minnesota arena, they set in motion processes of change that went forward every year and every decade and have by no means come to a stop.

Much of the Minnesota story centers in man-made geographic change. Forests were cut down — and desolated areas later reforested. Farmers turned sod and cleared land for fields of waving grain and gardens of fruits and flowers. Plants and trees previously unknown to the Minnesota soil were introduced. Waterfalls were harnessed and rivers bridged and deepened. Roads and railroads crisscrossed areas that once were wilderness. Towns and cities were built, including a great metropolitan center with wide-stretching suburban filaments. Throughout the state its differing regions — fields, ore lands, valleys, and prairies — were taken in hand for man's use, carved, landscaped, altered. Men and their machines created their surroundings, as a scientist has said, "without regard for natural heat or cold, or light or darkness."

Human will and purpose modified the face of Minnesota. Geography, through time's sculpture, is fundamental to the state — but the history of the region turns on what men have done with and to the resources they have found at this central and richly endowed spot of the American continent.

Buffalo hunt, from an oil by John Mix Stanley

The Redmen through Many Moons

No one knows when Asiatics, in the pre-dawn of history, crossed over a land bridge to the North American continent, but the finds of archaeologists point to a very early time indeed. The dispersion of these Mongoloid people and the emergence of American Indian races antedate the pyramids of Egypt by long ages.

Ancestors of the redmen almost certainly were in Minnesota in late glacial times. The domination of the scene by them and their descendants went unchallenged by white men until the seventeenth century. The era of the redmen, therefore, has a sweep of ten thousand or more years.

In 1931 a skeleton was unearthed in Otter Tail County, together with a dagger shaped from an elk antler, and a conch-shell ornament, some nine or ten feet below the surface in a deposit of layers of glacial lake silt. The particular glacial lake (Pelican) was somewhat earlier than Lake Agassiz. Archaeologists regard the finds as proof not only of man in Minnesota some ten or twelve thousand years ago, but also of primitive aboriginal southern contacts, since the conch shell presumably could not have come from a source nearer than the Gulf of Mexico. "Minnesota Man" is the designation of this ancient skeleton, though the "man" was a girl of some fifteen years — a girl presumably drowned in a glacial lake (had she been out fishing?). A monograph on these archaeological remains employs the title *Pleistocene Man in Minnesota: A Fos-*

sil Homo Sapiens, but laymen have referred to the find as the "Lady in the Lake."

Yet another skeleton, that of "Browns Valley Man," has been found in a gravel bar of a once great river flowing out of Glacial Lake Agassiz. Here too other objects came to light: flaked stone points, knives, and sandstone abraders. A few thousand years later than "Minnesota Man," this nameless *Homo sapiens* of the Indian past probably lived and hunted in primeval Minnesota some seven or eight thousand years ago. By that time the region had cast off the cold of the glaciers. Men were in the upward climb — the age-long process of adjusting their ways to an environment that may not have differed much in essential character from that of historic times.

Archaeologists, using evidence from excavations, have pictured people in this region through many scores of generations living on game and fish, gathering wild rice, and finding further nourishment in fruits and berries and nuts. At a very early time they discovered ways of shaping stones to their use by grinding stone against stone, pecking, or pounding both hard and soft materials. Among the latter were pipestone, slate, and even copper — a metal they mined to depletion in that charming island of Lake Superior later known as Isle Royale.

Evidences of early modes of transportation are difficult to find, but one assumes that the marvel known as the birchbark canoe did not lack predecessors of primitive workmanship that enabled men to keep afloat on lakes and streams while harvesting rice, fishing, and moving from place to place. As centuries passed, human intelligence and ingenuity, here as elsewhere in the history of man, showed itself in increasing skill in the making of weapons, utensils, and ornaments — bowls, mauls, axes, gouges, knives — and even more fundamentally in the development of speech and the building of ideas and customs that raised men far above the level of the animals they mastered in the wilderness.

As one moves into what scholars call the Woodland era — from about 1000 B.C. to the coming of the white men in the seventeenth and eighteenth centuries — Indian mounds help to elaborate the story of primitive life. Modern man, transforming Minnesota, has dealt roughly with the mounds. Originally there must have been more than ten thousand in the state; an actual count in the 1880s, with several counties omitted, ran to 7773. But if many have been plowed under or opened by casual curio hunters, many others have survived, and not a few, along with various village sites, have been excavated with scientific care. Largest of the state's prehistoric mounds is one at Laurel, near International Falls, where interesting finds of bone and copper have been made from a culture that was in existence some ten to twenty centuries ago. This "Grand Mound" is more than a hundred feet long, nearly as wide, and forty-five feet high.

Into the mounds went gifts to accompany, solace, and serve the dead. Excavations, including those of village sites, have brought up pottery, pipes, arrowheads of different kinds (among these, some stemmed or notched), shell ornaments, necklaces of pearls, copper pieces, pins, awls, armbands. Many kinds of stone tools and implements have been found from what was basically a stone age, notwithstanding some use of copper for such items as fishhooks and breastplates. The bow and arrow, emblematic of Indian life, did not appear until the Hopewell phase of Woodland culture (from about 300 B.C. to 1000 A.D.). The natives adored tobacco, and their pipes, equally emblematic, were made first of stone or clay and later of catlinite from the Pipestone quarries.

The Indians took an earnest interest in the dead, as witnessed both by the multitude of mounds and by their so-called bundle burials, in which the wrapped bodies of the dead were hoisted onto platforms. To these places people came to offer gifts, to dance, and to recite late news, as if the dead were still alive to hear, see, and enjoy. Minnesota in the 1880s had a dozen or more effigy mounds, shaped in the form of birds, buffaloes, bears, or snakes, with symbolic religious meanings, but these unhappily have since been plowed under by farmers who cared more about crops than about archaeology.

The effigy mounds have disappeared, but the Pipestone quarries still exist in southwestern Minnesota, where Indians traditionally mined red stone (catlinite). It was easy to work and beautifully adapted to pipemaking. The quarries remain as a natural memorial and now have status as a national monument. Here, as we are reminded by Longfellow, the mighty "Gitche Manito," the Great Spirit, called on tribes to lay aside their animosities:

> Break the red stone from this quarry,
> Mould and make it into Peace-Pipes.

Widely dispersed throughout the country, the calumets dug from quarries here and in other areas were used in the ceremonial smoking so much venerated in Indian councils.

The two great Indian "families" of major importance in Minnesota history were the Sioux or Dakota and the Chippewa or Ojibway. The Sioux occupied most of Minnesota when white explorers and traders first saw the region in the seventeenth century.

Just how long the Sioux had lived here or what their relationship was to the primitive folk of the postglacial era, no one can say, but probably the Sioux had been in this mid-American region for a fairly long time. They were a tall, vigorous, gifted, warlike people organized in seven tribes or "council fires": Mdewakanton, Wahpekute, Wahpeton, Sisseton, Yankton, Yanktonai, and Teton. The largest of these, the Tetons, and also the Yankton and Yanktonai, were people of the plains stretching out to and beyond the Missouri. The four tribes first named (the Santee Sioux) were primarily Minnesotan, and of these the Mdewakanton — meaning the "people of the spirit or holy lake" — occupied a place of central importance.

The Siouan people were a widely dispersed linguistic family of redmen, a tribal group in a loose kind of confederacy with a vast geographical spread north of Mexico. This family or group included, in addition to the seven council fires, such tribes as the Winnebago, Iowa, Oto, and Missouri — the latter three known as the "Chiwere" tribes. Though the names "Sioux" and "Dakota" are often used interchangeably, the Dakota Indians are usually thought of as the Siouan peoples who spoke the Santee, Yankton, Assiniboin, and Teton dialects. The word "Dakota" means "allies," but the alliance was tenuous. The Assiniboin of the north country and adjacent Canada, for instance, spoke a Dakota dialect, but at some time, perhaps early in the seventeenth century, they had broken away from the Yanktonai of western Minnesota and Dakota. Thereafter they were enemies of all other Sioux Indians. Despite geographical dispersion and such divisive moves as that of the Assiniboin, the "spirit or holy lake" of the Dakota Indians — Mille Lacs — was long regarded as the very center of an allied Dakota world. Common usage has endorsed "Sioux" for designation of the Dakota Indians of the Minnesota region.

Studies made by archaeologists show that at some time in the past — perhaps about 1000 A.D. — there was an intrusive move into the Upper Mississippi Valley, and into Minnesota, of people representing the "Mississippian culture" — a culture distinct from the Woodland. Its remains have been found in village sites near Red Wing and Mankato.

For storing products of the soil these people built underground pits, bell-shaped and like the pits of the modern Mandan Indians. They used hoes made from the skulls of bison or elks. Some of their villages were even palisaded. They were built on river terraces, and farming was done in the alluvial river bottoms.

It seems likely that the redmen of this Mississippian culture, in historic times, are represented by the Mandan, by the Cheyenne, and by other tribes. There can be no doubt that the Oto, Omaha, and Iowa Indians were in southern Minnesota in late prehistoric times; and the Mandan and Cheyenne probably were here. These early inhabitants carried on farming to supply the wants of their villages; and in the summers they engaged in communal hunts on the prairies for bison. Probably because of geographical limits to the cultivation of maize, the Mississippian culture did not extend farther north than a line drawn from the Twin Cities to Lake Traverse at the west.

Generally the Mississippian cultures had some influence on the Woodland cultures of the North. An example is the change from the elongated cone-shaped pottery of the Woodland peoples to the round, globular form that was typically Mississippian. The trade pottery of the South has not infrequently turned up in excavations of northern sites.

The Sioux were dominant in the Minnesota region in the seventeenth century, but their dominion soon came under stern challenge from the east. Just as there was a westward movement of white Americans, so also there were westward migrations of redmen, and some of them had wide geographical scope. Such was the continental spread of the Algonkian family westward from the St. Lawrence in part under the fierce impact of Iroquois power. They were a distinguished nation that included, in the western area, the Chippewa, Sauk, Fox, Cheyenne, Ottawa, Potawatomie, Cree, and Menominee tribes. Of this many-branched Indian nation, it is the sturdy, stocky Chippewa that are of special Minnesota interest, for their westward advance extended into this region, first along the border waters of Lake Superior and then, in the 1730s and 1740s, in a head-on challenge to the Sioux farther toward the south and west, from Lake Superior to Mille Lacs.

Decisive were battles fought in the 1740s when the invading Chippewa drove the Sioux out of their northern villages, including the strategic Dakota center at Mille Lacs. The contest was uneven, for the Sioux fought in their immemorial fashion, with arrows, spears, and clubs, whereas the Chippewa, who in their migration westward to the Great

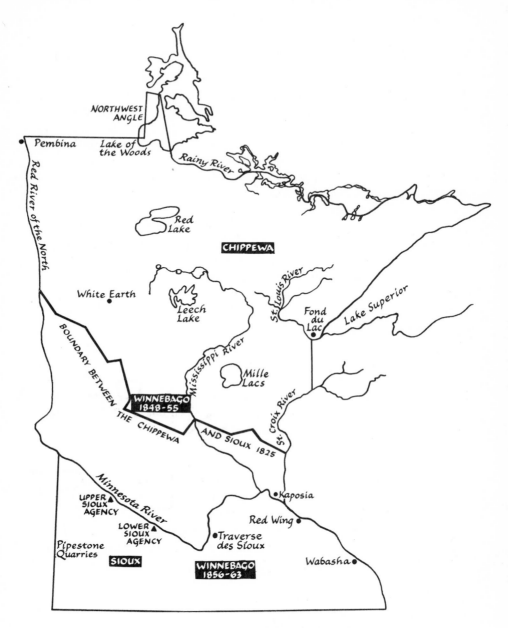

The Indians of Minnesota (adapted from Folwell's
History of Minnesota)

Lakes region had long been in contact with white people, had firearms
and may even have had counsel and leadership from French officers.
Thereafter Minnesota was divided — the Chippewa north, the Sioux
south, Chippewa in the canoe country, Sioux in the hills and valleys and
plains of south and west.

There was no going back for the Sioux. There was no reconquest,
though deep hostility continued between them and the Chippewa, with
frequent raids from one side or the other, sometimes campaigns and
pitched battles. In 1825 the United States brought about an agreement
on a boundary line between the two tribes, with pledges of peace that
were broken again and again as young warriors thirsty for glory hunted
for scalps. The very name "Sioux" reflects the traditional enmity between
the two tribes, for it is shortened from "Nadouessioux"— a French version of a Chippewa name meaning a "snake." To the Chippewa the Sioux
were reptiles, and if the Sioux had any epithet for the Chippewa, one
may assume that it was not less contemptuous.

What manner of people were the Sioux and Chippewa whose destiny
was to be interwoven with the thirty-second state?

The Sioux, when the whites first came, were of the stone age. "There
is nothing but cryes," wrote a Frenchman of the seventeenth century who
entered a midwestern Indian village where the inhabitants never before
had seen a white face. Cries, certainly, of wonder at a white face — perhaps, too, at seeing strange and unimagined "trade goods" out of an
unknown world. Cries, really, of astonishment by stone-age people meeting civilization.

Primitive as was Sioux life, it was packed with wisdom out of the
wilderness past. Stone, wood, bones, and horns were workaday materials
from which they shaped implements and weapons: axes, knives, arrows,
spears and blades, hammers, scraping instruments. They knew how to
start fires by friction. They made pottery, not highly decorative, but serv-
iceable for pots and jars. With open fires, they boiled or roasted foods
and prepared soups flavored with berries or rice. They were clever hunters
of bears, buffaloes, elk, deer, and small game; and they knew the fisher-
man's art of spear and hook. If sometimes they failed to store sufficient
food for cruel winters, yet they were skilled in sun-curing meats of their
favorite animals and fish. One of their prized foods was pemmican, dried
and pounded buffalo meat flavored with cherries or berries and preserved in skin bags. The idea of the wheel, most important of man's

23

inventions, had eluded them, but like peoples the world over they had developed a language (how far rooted in the past we do not know) which served their needs in practical living and in the realm of ideas. They did not have an alphabet or writing, but they talked. And they conveyed messages in rough pictographs. They have left rock drawings, some of which have not been worn away by the tooth of time.

Because of tribal wars and clashes with whites, the Sioux are portrayed as fighters and scalp hunters. These they were. Fighting was bred in the Indian bone, an integral part of stone-age culture. But they also were gregarious, lovers of feasts and councils and of games and jokes and betting. Eloquence among them was an art and its exercise by men of wisdom singled them out for leadership in their pipe-smoking councils. Tribes divided into bands, each with its chief, and decisions hinged upon the band council, whose approval and consent had to be won by debate. The office of chief might be hereditary, but often natural leadership, wisdom, renown, and eloquence determined the choice. Chiefs bore such names as Wabasha, Little Crow, Big Thunder, Cloud Man, Good Road, Shakopee, and Sleepy Eye.

The Sioux were a singing and dancing people, their chanting songs expressing curiosity and wonder at nature and the spirit world:

> The owls hooting softly, the owls hooting low,
> In the passing of the night, the owls hooting low,
> In the gray dawn of the morning, the owls hooting low,
> To whom are they calling? I wish I could know.

In summer the nomadic Sioux lived in bark-covered lodges, in winter in conical skin-covered tipis. They gave an important place to marriage and family, though a brave might have several wives. As children were born and grew in strength, boys learned to hunt and fight, girls to do humdrum work of sundry kinds. Marriage carried explicit obligations, including care of the wife's parents for a time by hunting and other services. Some people assume that an Indian girl's own wishes had no relation to marriage, but one of the revered Indian legends of Minnesota is the Sioux story of Winona, a chief's daughter who, rather than marry the man chosen against her will, threw herself to her death from Maiden Rock on Lake Pepin.

Like primitive peoples the world over, the Sioux had a pervading sense of the supernatural. Nearly everything mysterious in nature was to them "wakan"— a spirit. The wonder of the Sioux about a future life, about

24

the might of unseen forces, and about things in nature they could not fathom found expression in dance, in other forms of worship, and in superstitions and beliefs. Their dances were a lively element in their lives — medicine, sun, thunder, elk, bear, scalp dances, among many, with the accompaniment of chanting and drum-thumping. These dances were not merely savagely exuberant, but serious in spirit. They were designed to express gratitude and rejoicing, avert evil, gain supernatural support. The Sioux worship seemed to envisage a Great Spirit, a Gitche Manito, creator of earth and man, but like the Greeks they were prodigal in finding or inventing gods. Nature generously supplied them: sun, moon, stars, birds, stones, and many more. Some gods even reflected a curious humor — Heyoka, for instance, the contrary and anti-natural god, the god of paradox, who cries when he is happy, laughs when melancholy, lies when he wants to tell the truth, wraps himself in buffalo robes in summer, and goes naked in snow and cold. Thunder was the terrible cry of the thunderbird, lightning the blinding flash of his eyes. The Sioux doctors were "medicine men" who exorcised evil spirits from a sick body by incantations and ceremonies, and also used medicines from plants and roots, some with, most of them without, therapeutic value. Death was a translation to happy hunting grounds, the survivors supplying the dead with provisions and tools, bundling their bodies onto scaffolds, burying them in mounds.

The Chippewa Indians, as they worked and fought their way into the Minnesota country in the eighteenth century, were already under marked white influence and not only in possessing firearms. They used kettles of tin and iron and brass, and many of their tools were of steel or iron, traded to them for skins and furs. The long-flowing blanket, highly prized by all American Indians, was already among their possessions. Even in their eating and drinking habits they were in transition, for alongside their use of the foods of the north country they had flour and pork and molasses — and even drank tea, though their taste ran to firewater when supplies of rum and whisky were made available to them.

One of the admirable achievements of the Chippewa was the birch-bark canoe, sleek in lines and fine in workmanship, perfectly adapted to facile use on the rivers and lakes of the northern regions. And these people, with their long Algonkian backgrounds, were as skilled and graceful in the use of the paddle as they were adept in the art of canoe-making. Here we touch a marked difference between Chippewa and

Sioux, for the latter, in early times, used clumsy wooden dugouts or buffalo-skin boats. Because of the open country in which they lived, however, the Sioux became as expert on horseback as the Chippewa were at paddling.

Other differences emerge as one compares the two groups, notably in their dwellings, with the Chippewa making beehive wigwams or lodges of birchbark over frames of poles, whereas the Sioux, as has been noted, built skin tipis, easy to set up or move and therefore adaptable to a nomadic manner of life. But it is easy to exaggerate differences. The truth is that Indian life from tribe to tribe had more likeness than difference. Both the Sioux and the Chippewa hunted, fished, fought, scalped, played, enjoyed feasts, told stories and legends, recognized chiefs, loved feathers and paint, and lived a hard, exposed, primitive life with advantage to the robust. Modifications came through contact with white men, but the stone age was still near. Both tribes faced an extraordinary revolution in a period infinitesimally brief compared with the centuries of their occupation of primeval lands. Their own wars and raids continued, but once the Chippewa won the north country, these were mere episodes compared with the disruption, dispossession, and complex ordeals brought on by engulfing waves of civilization in the eighteenth and nineteenth centuries.

Difficulty and ordeal have not been on one side only. The Americans who took over the Indian lands had no easy or simple task. And it was made more difficult because of misconceptions of Indian character and life popularly entertained through much of our national history. These ideas have tended to obscure the truth that the Indian (including both Sioux and Chippewa) was a thoroughly human being, but of a culture vastly different from that of the civilized European. Even for perspective on Minnesota natives it is helpful to note a few misconceptions of the American Indian that have been listed by Stanley Vestal, the biographer of Sitting Bull and author of many other works on Indian life and history. They are that the Indian was a simple Child of Nature, a Noble Savage, a Worthless Degenerate, a Red Devil of the Plains, a Vanishing Race.

The Indian was intimate with the natural world he knew and his life in many ways was as simple as it was primitive, but the romantic concept of nobility was an echo of eighteenth-century revolt against civilized decadence. It overlooked faults and foibles that characterized the Indians as humans. The real Indian was neither the idealized savage of Rousseau nor the cardboard hero of James Fenimore Cooper. The "Red Devil" view was born of war and understandable fear — and spread by wild West shows and stories. Its slogan was that "the only good Indian is a dead Indian," and the fear was not allayed by an understanding that the redman, fighting for hunting grounds and food, employed ways traditional and acceptable to his warrior culture. As to degenerate Indians, this view commonly was recorded by observers who did not get very far away from white settlements, saw beggars and drunkards, and perhaps forgot that many people in civilization beg and drink. The "Vanishing Race" concept fitted the seductive idea that remorseless destiny was shoving the redman out of the way, but in fact the race, though pushed, crowded, and moved, is not vanishing but increasing in numbers.

The Indian population of the country seems to be less than it was when Jamestown and Massachusetts were settled, but it has been growing in recent times. Today there are some 18,000 Indians, mainly Chippewa, in Minnesota, living in eight reservations and about a half dozen Indian communities. What the population was early in the nineteenth century we do not know with precision — the Indians took no census — but the number of redmen in Minnesota then probably ran from 10,000 to 15,000, though the proportion of Sioux to Chippewa was of course much greater before the Indian war of 1862 than after the removal of the Sioux.

History tends to dramatize conflict, and the story in Minnesota of Indian-white relations is not lacking in conflict, notably the bloody Indian outbreak and war in the 1860s. But history should also recall Indian contributions, both in aid given the white man in early stages of exploration, trade, and settlement, and in products and ideas that have merged with the American heritage. Indians were guides to white men unraveling the mysteries of the hinterland beyond the Great Lakes. Their canoes, food, knowledge of woodcraft, portages, and furs were vital to explorers and traders. The Indian economy, as one views the total American scene, made basic contributions to the national substance. Some years ago an agricultural historian, E. E. Edwards, declared that "four-sevenths of the total agricultural production of the United States, measured in farm values, consists of economic plants domesticated by the Indian and taken over by the white man." He reminded readers of corn, squash, tomatoes, pumpkins, potatoes, and tobacco; of food methods involving maple sugar, corn pone, baked clams, planked beef, turkey. And we should not forget the native pemmican, cherished by the Indians and of crucial importance to white fur traders through a long period.

Edwards also told of medicines and dyes, toboggans and birchbark canoes, even Indian games, including lacrosse, which the Sioux passionately liked to play. Such lists can be expanded in the realm of ideas. One remembers that hundreds of words and phrases of Indian origin have enriched the common speech, such as "Father of Waters," "pipe of peace," "war paint," "Indian summer," "bury the hatchet," and "Great Spirit." Indian legends, Indian music, and Indian themes in American literature are creative reminders of the native past. Much of this total contribution runs far beyond Minnesota, with its Sioux and Chippewa, but even here, as illustrated by the poetic tale of Hiawatha and Minnehaha, the heritage is rich. And as Walt Whitman sings, the "red aborigines" have charged "the water and the land with names." The Minnesota map is dotted with mellifluous names out of the Sioux and Chippewa past. "Minnesota" itself is a Sioux name, and others are Minnetonka, Waseca, Wabasha, Winona, Mendota, Mankato, Minnehaha, Dakota; and from the Chippewa: Pokegama, Mahnomen, Bemidji, Chisago, Winnibigoshish.

So prodigal and far-reaching are the Indian contributions that the historian encounters embarrassment in reversing the coin to view the white man's contributions to the Indian. Here one thinks of material things: tools and implements wrought of metal, traps, guns, blankets and clothing, plates and cups, mirrors, and the many ornaments and useful objects poured into barter for beaver skins, buffalo robes, and other furs. A darker side is the story of firewater and of diseases against which the Indian had no protection and from which he suffered misery and death. Over the run of decades there is the still more somber record of peoples thrust aside, removed from lands they once occupied and controlled, and faced with the challenge of living as wards next to, but not really a part of, an alien civilization nurtured through centuries of the Old World.

The Indians, with roots in an unfathomable past, move through Minnesota history from explorer to trader, from land cessions to war, from migration to reservation, from the stone age to the twentieth century.

Whether or not Europeans had contacts with the aborigines of Minnesota before the arrival of the French in the seventeenth century is one of the conundrums of history. An inscribed stone unearthed in western Minnesota in 1898 bears an inscription in runic characters, with the date 1362, telling of a journey of exploration from Vinland westward by twenty-two Norwegians and eight Goths. For more than a half century this document — the "Kensington Runestone" — has been the subject of controversy. The authenticity of the inscription has had its defenders, but it has been critically challenged by runologists. It may fairly be said that no one has proved beyond doubt its genuineness and no one has demonstrated, finally and conclusively, that it is a hoax. The stone merits mention as a fascinating problem and a curiosity. The weight of scholarly authority is against acceptance of it as an authentic record of a Scandinavian expedition into the American interior in the fourteenth century. If Goths and Norwegians stood on Minnesota soil in the 1300s, their imprints have been effaced save for an artifact of dubious authenticity. Possibly one could apply to the inscribed stone the words once used by Winston Churchill in a somewhat different context: "It is a riddle wrapped in a mystery inside an enigma."

Montreal canoe, from an oil by Frances Anne Hopkins

The French Look West

T H E water route from Montreal to Lake Superior and beyond was long and toilsome in times when paddles and muscles furnished the motive power for transportation. The wonder is, not that it took much time for white men to establish control over the wilderness, but that they made their way into the "savage country" as early as they did. Only a decade after the initial settlement of Quebec in 1608, and before the *Mayflower* landed at Plymouth Rock in 1620, Frenchmen reached the waters of Lake Superior, westernmost of the inland seas.

Fourteen years after the *Mayflower*, Frenchmen stepped onto the western shore of Lake Michigan. By the 1650s they were lifting the curtain of mystery on the Middle West and tapping its wealth of furs. And by the 1670s and 1680s the French, with only some nine thousand people in the St. Lawrence Valley, had discovered the Upper Mississippi. They had pushed expeditions into Minnesota and proclaimed a mid-American empire for Louis XIV. They had carried on far-reaching missionary enterprises, exploited a trade in furs international in scope, and trained a corps of voyageurs. They had mapped much of the hitherto uncharted wilderness, and written books about the new country which piqued their curiosity and tried their courage.

The French opened the gateways to the American West in the first half of the seventeenth century and passed through them in the second half. In the first half they explored the domain of the Great Lakes and in the second, the imperial Mississippi Valley.

31

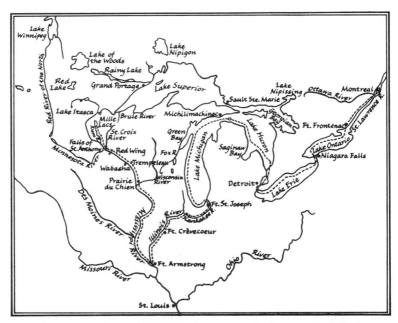

The water routes from Montreal west, with the course of Father
Hennepin's journey in 1678–80 traced

A buoyant, confident, adventurous people, the French! And the seventeenth century — the age of Richelieu and of Louis XIV and Colbert — was one of exuberance and magnificence, particularly during the reign of the Grand Monarch. Far in the interior of America, French explorers, traders, and missionaries never forgot the might of France, to their minds the greatest power on earth. They constantly sought ways to impress that might on the minds of natives who had no conception of the French homeland across the Atlantic. "What shall I say of his wealth?" exclaimed the missionary Father Claude Allouez at Sault Ste. Marie in 1671, speaking of Louis XIV to Indians. "You count yourselves rich when you have ten or twelve sacks of corn, some hatchets, glass beads, kettles, or things of that sort. He has towns of his own, more in number than you have people in all these countries five hundred leagues around; while in each town there are warehouses containing enough hatchets to cut down all your forests, kettles to cook all your moose, and glass beads to fill all your cabins."

32

The missionary's interpretation of French power to the Indians in terms they could understand is a reminder that the early Minnesota story echoes bold and far-reaching international ambitions. The impact of events a long way from the lakes and rivers of the north country was decisive for Minnesota's political destiny. England and France, stirring with expansive energy, were competing in the seventeenth century — and the eighteenth, too — for nothing less than the North American continent. Spain, also, though its imperial power was on the decline after the defeat of its proud Armada, was important in the New World picture, drawing wealth from Central and South America, and concerned with the West Indian centers to which Columbus had sailed on the great discovery, and with the southern area where De Soto and other Spaniards early planted their flag. Here, too, both the French and the English were interested.

The English colonists after Jamestown and Plymouth Rock were moving by many approaches into the rich interior of the land. And the seventeenth century would also witness English advances and claims from Hudson Bay to the south. France made its major approach by way of the St. Lawrence to which Jacques Cartier had come in the first half of the sixteenth century, and to which Samuel de Champlain, typifying French discovery and exploration at its most magnificent, followed early in the seventeenth century. Thus on a continental stage national interests moved toward clash and decision over great stakes, with the rumble of recurring European wars in the background.

In this setting Minnesota must be viewed as a region that has been ruled under four flags — French, English, Spanish, American — at times with two or three claims extending concurrently over the same areas. The wars and treaties of European powers, as well as colonial controversies and struggles, played major roles in the fate of the hinterland west of the Great Lakes. The drama ran across the seventeenth and eighteenth centuries, and even into the nineteenth. Climaxes came in the Treaty of Utrecht (1713), when France lost Hudson Bay to the English; in the Treaty of Paris (1763), when New France itself bowed to the British; and in the War of Independence, with the emergence of the United States (1783). Still later was President Jefferson's purchase from France of Louisiana in 1803 — after a lapse of nearly forty years (1762–1800) during which the little-known empire between the Mississippi and the Far West had been under the sovereignty of Spain.

If national ambitions and the clash of arms in Europe had far-reaching effects on the political future of the wilderness country, it is no less true that the Minnesota story was influenced by leadership and the progress of events in eastern Canada. It was also touched by dreams of the silks and spices of Cathay, by curiosity about what lay beyond the inland seas, and, as realistic Frenchmen learned of sleek inland treasures, by their avid hunt for furs. Frenchmen were early aware of the potential wealth the New World might open for them — not in jewels and gold, but in fishing and trapping. Their own sailors from Brittany, unnamed to history, were in Labrador waters fishing cod in the fifteenth century; and Champlain, on his first trip to New France, was backed by a nobleman and a group of merchants who had secured a monopoly of the trade in furs. Furs and daring men are the very stuff of early Canadian history.

The sixteenth-century voyagings of Cartier were two generations in the past when Champlain, soldier, sailor, geographer, and explorer, emerged as the creator of Canada and as a major figure in the backgrounds of the American West. His achievements, despite repeated discouragements, were monumental. He founded Quebec, explored the St. Lawrence, and discovered Lake Champlain and Lakes Huron and Ontario. In a grand sense Champlain was the discoverer of the Great Lakes, though his own eyes did not see the greatest of them at the west. But he trained and inspired others to carry forward his ideas and aims. Evidence is convincing that he knew of a "Grand Lac" beyond Ontario and Huron. Geographer by training, he even ventured to map it roughly in 1632, probably on the basis of information supplied by Etienne Brulé who, it is believed, saw Lake Superior before 1620, perhaps as early as 1618. Champlain even heard vague reports about a great river out in the western country whose waters ran to some sea — and these suggested the possibility that the unknown river was a path to the fabulous lands Marco Polo had visited in the days of Kublai Khan.

School textbooks bemoan the misfortune or blunder of Champlain in making enemies of the Iroquois Indians. As early as 1609 he made war on these fierce natives, and he did so in alliance with the Algonkians and Hurons, the latter from the Georgian Bay region. As the historian A. L. Burt writes, "The Iroquois had never seen a musket, but now they saw it spit fire and kill by magic." The time came when the Iroquois, who were later supplied arms by the English and Dutch, took grim

34

revenge on both the French and the Algonkians and Hurons. Their revenge proved a dreadful check to the French and it was one factor in driving the Algonkians to the west. But it is easy to judge men in the light of events of a later time. Champlain was trying to protect the fur trade and the waterway westward, and it seemed natural to him to make friends with the Indians who lived along that way and to fight the natives who threatened its use. Whatever the troubles of later years, Champlain never abandoned his interest in furs and the western country. From 1627 to his death in 1635, except for a short period when the British took and held Quebec, he was governor of New France. This position deepened his natural authority over the colony he had fathered. And he gave aid and encouragement to younger men.

One of these was Jean Nicolet, brought to New France from Cherbourg and trained for fifteen years in wilderness lore by living among Indians — a hard schooling that prepared him for a major assignment. Champlain had heard rumors not only of vast lakes and a great river, but also of the "People of the Sea" somewhere toward the west. And the minds of Europeans were still captivated by the thought that the way to Cathay might be open to them. They wanted to find out who the "People of the Sea" really were. In 1634 a new stage in the westward advance was heralded by Nicolet's journey by way of the Ottawa River, Lake Huron, and the Straits of Mackinac.

This journey led to the discovery of Lake Michigan and Nicolet's dramatic landing at Green Bay clad in a robe of damask and carrying "thunder in both hands," as the frightened natives described his pistols. Whatever the Indians were (actually they were a Winnebago tribe), they were not men of Cathay, though certainly "people of the inland sea." The modern reader finds it difficult to escape the impression that Nicolet, notwithstanding his gorgeous Oriental costume, harbored no illusion that he was landing in China. He made an alliance with the natives and returned to the East, and he seems to have told his story firsthand to Champlain. What Nicolet accomplished was a major discovery that would open the way to the Mississippi Valley and lands beyond, though he himself evidently did not go much farther than the Wisconsin shores. It is likely that he heard reports from the natives of a great river somewhere in the interior.

If the period after Nicolet was one of inactivity in French exploration of the West, it saw great missionary enterprise that reached as far as

Sault Ste. Marie by 1641, with the Jesuits Isaac Jogues and Charles Raymbault. Meanwhile Montreal was becoming a busy mart, receiving Indian fur fleets each spring from Ottawa tribesmen, and bartering kettles, blankets, and supplies of many kinds for the furs. One senses an increasing French awareness of a kingdom of furs that might surpass the imagined riches of the Orient.

When Iroquois-Huron hostilities cut down the native traffic to Montreal, Frenchmen more and more pushed westward by themselves to collect furs. Some were duly licensed, some were without official authorization. The class of wood rangers — *coureurs de bois* — emerged. They were daring and vigorous young Frenchmen who, as independent traders, blithely risked the hazards of Indian attack and of hardships for the rich profits from furs. And it is in the period of the 1650s that the story moves toward the Minnesota region with the travels, adventures, and observations of two Frenchmen, Pierre Radisson and his brother-in-law the Sieur des Groseilliers.

It is Radisson's name that has the most familiar ring to Minnesotans, but the two men were closely associated. The fame of the one has been enhanced because he told of his adventures in a priceless account written as early as 1669 but unknown to historians until late in the nineteenth century. Originally penned in French, it was translated into curious English in Radisson's own day, and the translation has survived in the Bodleian Library at Oxford University. In 1885 it was published for the first time. Through many decades scholars have been quarreling more or less amiably about the "voyages" the Frenchmen made to the West — just where they went, and how to interpret the language of the manuscript.

The autobiography unfolded by Radisson tells of the incredible experiences and hardships of a Frenchman who went out to Three Rivers in New France as a boy. He was captured by the Iroquois, tortured, and had adventure after adventure. After a time he fell in with Groseilliers, who had married his sister. But the great and dramatic importance of the narrative for western history lies in its account of two journeys to the Great Lakes region and beyond, between 1654 and 1660. We now know that Radisson could not have gone on the first, in 1654, though he describes that journey, taken by Groseilliers and a companion, as if he himself had been the companion. He and Groseilliers certainly went together on the second trip, probably begun in 1659.

36

On the 1654 journey Groseilliers went to Lake Michigan, and then he traveled into Wisconsin beyond Green Bay, possibly reached the Mississippi, and he may even have penetrated into Minnesota. The language of Radisson's narrative is too obscure to permit conclusive identifications of places, but the evidence leaves no doubt that Groseilliers was in the western country, lived among the Indians, and engaged in trade. With a fleet of fifty canoes loaded with furs and paddled by Indians, he returned in triumph to Quebec. He received a welcome that celebrated the success and the daring of his enterprise, and his highly prized furs — in a period of fur famine in eastern Canada — were shipped off to European markets.

The next expedition to western waters, in 1659, was furtive. Radisson and Groseilliers could not get official authorization without pledging a very large share of their fur profits to the governor of New France. This they would not do, and so, secretly, they slipped away from Three Rivers and made their way to Sault Ste. Marie. Having arrived there, instead of pushing south to Lake Michigan, they entered Lake Superior and went along its southern shores.

At Chequamegon Bay (near present Ashland) they built what some have surmised was the first white man's house in the Middle West. Then they made their way inland in Wisconsin to an Ottawa Indian village, where they spent a hard winter. This miserable village was a scene of starvation among the Indians, and their strange white visitors suffered, too. "Good God, have mercy on so many poore innocent people!" exclaimed Radisson. After agonizing months, deer were caught on melting lakes and the famine came to an end. The Frenchmen met with the Sioux Indians — "the nation of the beefe" — in the spring, and Radisson described the Indian dress and the ceremony of a council, to which the white men added excitement by tossing gunpowder on a fire and discharging what they called their artillery. They gave gifts to the Sioux and told of their interest in the Indian country. Such primitive scenes inspired one of Radisson's most famous utterances: "We weare Cesars, being nobody to contradict us." Radisson and Groseilliers were indeed like some visiting royalty. Precisely where and how far the Frenchmen went in the western country before their return in 1660 to Quebec is difficult to say, but it is probable that they canoed up along the north shore of "the delightfullest lake of the world" and from the lips of Indians learned about Hudson Bay as a water route to the unknown lands beyond Lake Superior.

Escorted by a fleet of Indian canoes packed with furs, the Frenchmen returned to the East and were greeted with a salute of cannon at Montreal. Soon they were disappointed and bitter, for they were arrested for illicit trading, and their profits were largely confiscated. "Was not he a Tyrant," wrote Radisson of the governor, "to deal so with us after wee had so hazarded our lives?" The resentment of these fur-gathering explorers led them to turn to the English, and after sundry adventures that reinforced their desire to exploit the fur trade via Hudson Bay, they reached England in 1666. There they were given an audience by Charles II and interested both the king and his cousin Prince Rupert, as well as various noblemen, in the potential riches of furs from the far north. This interest led to an expedition of two ships, one under Radisson and the other under Groseilliers, to Hudson Bay in 1668. Radisson's vessel was battered by storms and barely managed to return to England, but his brother-in-law reached the bay of the north, collected furs, and brought them back to England as proof of the claims advanced. This success led to the founding of the Hudson's Bay Company in 1670 — "The Governor and Company of Adventurers of England Trading into Hudson's Bay" — a fur company that has survived to the present day and has been important in Minnesota as well as in Canadian history.

It is difficult to exaggerate the historical importance of Radisson and Groseilliers. They added much to geographical knowledge. Apart from what they saw with their own eyes, it was their representations that caused men of business to open the region between Lake Superior and Hudson Bay. The two Frenchmen were quick to understand the key to the fur trade. It was the idea of going north for the choicest beaver skins. The direction is foreshadowed by their own travels — Wisconsin, Lake Superior and especially its north shore, then Hudson Bay. Theirs is no simply local story. It is international not only in their travels but in long-flowing consequences, especially in the great fur-trading company of nearly three hundred years of enterprise. The international importance is underlined by the fact that these men strengthened the British in the race of nations for the domination of the continent. They were not unaware of the European interest in finding a Northwest Passage, and they used this theme in their efforts to enlist English support. But the records they left emphasize furs and the wilderness that could produce them.

Explorers they were indeed, but implicit in their exploring was the drive of trade.

There are other ways, too, in which their story is of historical interest. Radisson was a prophet of the coming glories of middle America, though his prophecies did not reach the ears of the European world of the seventeenth and eighteenth centuries. The vast lands that he and his brother-in-law saw were, to him, a potential "labyrinth of pleasure" for millions of people in old Europe, for the poor and miserable folk of many countries that engaged in wars over a mere "rock in the sea." Finally, the story Radisson told, though as tortured in translation as he was by the Iroquois, is still an original and vivid description of primitive life and pristine nature, of white men in contact with the stone age, of things seen and heard in interior America more than a century before the American Revolution and the birth of the United States.

It was no coincidence that only a few years after the Radisson journey of 1659–60 Father Claude Allouez, a celebrated Jesuit missionary, built a mission station on Madeline Island, not far from the place where Radisson and Groseilliers had landed on Chequamegon Bay. Allouez typifies the Jesuits of the seventeenth century and later. They were educated men of infinite curiosity about the new lands and their people, careful observers and recorders, explorers and map makers, servants of the Society of Jesus who faced the perils of wilderness and even cruel martyrdom with courage. If Allouez had small success in Christianizing the natives, he played an important role in the advance of geographical knowledge and the expansion of New France. His work contributed to the Jesuit map of 1670 on which Lake Superior (also called Lake Tracy) appeared with a detail quite lacking in earlier maps. And he himself explored the western and northern shores of that great lake.

Gradually, with the efforts of many contributing to the sum total of knowledge, the French familiarized themselves with the newer New France. Their mapping and advance on several lines of approach were forerunners of occupation and high claims of possession. Expanding geographic knowledge as disclosed in a long succession of French maps, from Champlain on to Franquelin (1688) and still later, often seems to outrun the information written in diaries, books, and other sources. This testifies to a kind of pooling of verbal information as travelers returned and told about what they had seen. The makers of maps, if not explorers themselves, talked with explorers and probably with obscure traders who left no diaries or books. Often items appear that pique one's curiosity, as instanced by a note on a French map of Lake Superior in 1658 with the words: "Some people have told me of having gone for 20 days about Lake Superior without having circumnavigated half of it." What people? And when?

There is a pageantry of events in the story of the French envelopment of the West. One finds a line here, a thrust there — new discoveries, new knowledge, adventurers, fur-laden canoes, martyrs, narratives, maps. And there is actual pageantry of a kind dear to French hearts, such as the scene enacted on a June day in 1671 at Sault Ste. Marie.

Louis XIV in 1663, abetted by his chief minister Colbert, had set out to strengthen New France by making it a royal province and building its population and military resources. Two years later he sent out Jean Talon as "intendant," a high official having authority over commerce, finance, and justice, to serve alongside the governor, the king's representative in matters of state. Talon soon struck down the hostile Iroquois and cleared the path for renewed Indian trade. He reached out toward continental empire for the glory of Louis XIV. At some strategic spot, closing his eyes to Spanish and English claims, Talon wished to take formal possession of interior America. The spot he chose was Sault Ste. Marie, Great Lakes junction, crossroads of white and Indian travel, site of a Jesuit mission established in 1668 by Father Jacques Marquette, a village of the Chippewa (called the Saulteurs). He acted through the nobleman Daumont St. Lusson and redmen were invited from the far interior. Salutes were given and speeches were delivered, one by Father Allouez. There were prayers and hymns, a bonfire, and shouts of "Vive le Roi!" Then St. Lusson made formal claim, in the name of Louis XIV, to "all these lakes, straits, rivers, islands, and regions lying adjacent thereto, whether as yet visited by my subjects or unvisited, in all their length and breadth, stretching to the sea at the north and at the west, or on the opposite side extending to the South Sea." In later years similar ceremonies were enacted. They were pageants, but underlying the pageantry — the gold and braid and flashing swords of officers — was the ambition of the master in faraway Versailles. His dream was one of annexation and sovereignty from ocean to ocean of a royal domain including the mysterious lands one day to be known as Minnesota. Great claims and exciting dreams! But the Grand Monarch and his ministers would soon have to think more of European mastery than of control in the New World. Wars at home would dim French aspirations in the West.

Those aspirations for a time were at high tide. The energetic Talon would not rest content with far-reaching claims. In maps and reports the French were answering questions about the lakes and lands to the west, but they had not yet found their way to the great river. The time had come to test rumors current since the days of Champlain. Before Talon returned to France in 1672 he had selected a young man named Louis Jolliet to find the Mississippi. His commission came not from Talon, however, but from that greatest governor of New France after Champlain, Count Frontenac, just arrived from France. Frontenac directed him to "discover the south sea . . . and the great river Mississippi, which is believed to empty in the California sea." Jolliet, the Canadian-born son of a French cartwright, was a skilled cartographer. He had hunted for copper in the Lake Superior country, had witnessed the Sault Ste. Marie pageant, and knew at first hand the Great Lakes region. Trained and daring, he was qualified for a great assignment.

The story of the journey in 1673 has been told and re-told, notably and dramatically by Francis Parkman. It need not be reviewed here except to emphasize the significance of the route from Green Bay by way of the Fox and Wisconsin rivers to the Father of Waters. This opened another gateway to Minnesota, though Jolliet pushed far southward on the great river, settling once and for all the direction of its flow. The search for elusive Cathay was not lost sight of by the French, but Jolliet's achievement pointed to empire and wealth in the vast valley to which he had come, and his successors would soon strike both north and south in that valley.

A dramatic part of the traditional accounts of Jolliet relates to Father Marquette, who is believed by most historians to have been Jolliet's companion on the famous journey and whose role has been thrillingly described by Parkman. Recent research has cast doubt, however, on the authenticity of the much-used narratives ascribed to Marquette which in turn have been the chief basis for the traditional tale. This doubt has even extended to the claim that Father Marquette was a participant and partner in the enterprise. It seems not unlikely that further research will throw new light on the question, and it is possible that the traditional view of Marquette will be re-established. Meanwhile one thing is certain. The French, with Jolliet in the van, proved the truth of the rumors of a great river in the West beyond the Great Lakes. The river was the Mississippi, a majestic stream running down through the continent as in fact it runs through the course of American history.

Pity that Jolliet, returning to Quebec to report to Frontenac, had a canoe accident not far from Montreal and lost his precious papers and maps in the swirling Lachine rapids. Like the French original of Radisson's *Voyages*, his records are among the lost manuscripts of history. Luckily he saved his own life, later met the governor, and told his story. Before his career came to an end he was the royal cartographer of New France. This was an accolade, but his fame does not rest on position. It rests on his own hard-wrought achievement.

Father Hennepin at the Falls of St. Anthony, from an oil by Douglas Volk

Minnesota and New France

THE vibrant leadership of Frontenac, the curiosity of traders and missionaries, the gaudy proclamation of the aims of Louis XIV at Sault Ste. Marie, and the discovery by Jolliet of the upper waters of the great river gave impetus to the westward advance of the French in the 1670s and 1680s. This brought Minnesota within the orbit of French exploration and royal control.

Other forces also made themselves felt. The great company sponsored by England's Prince Rupert, chartered only a year before the Sault Ste. Marie ceremonies, served notice of coming competition reaching downward from the north. And the French in the next decade would challenge the claims of the British by capturing their trading posts on James Bay. From the Atlantic side the English, with spreading settlements and increasing populations, were sensitive to trade and lands and to the strategic importance of the inland chain of lakes. By the 1680s their trading interests had touched the crossroads post of Michilimackinac. The Iroquois were friendly to the English, ready at an instant to contest with the French on and near the waterways to the West, as they did when France and England went to war in 1689. But, whatever the rumblings of trouble and challenge, New France was in a mood of achievement inspired by good leadership.

Some part of that achievement is recorded in maps. There was unending curiosity about Lake Superior by the great and the humble. Again and again it was mapped — remarkably well by the Jesuits in 1670, and

45

a few years later by an engineer, Hugues Randin, commissioned to explore the vast lake in 1676 and to win Indian friendship and trade. Others added maps in the 1680s, each usually filling in new details, including more and more of the country beyond Superior's western shores.

That country in 1679 and 1680 was entered by explorers who approached it both by way of Lake Superior and up against current on the Mississippi. One of the dramatic episodes of western history is the meeting of the two French groups in the heart of the Minnesota country, at a Sioux village on the shores of Mille Lacs.

In view of the early French interest in Lake Superior it seems historically appropriate that the first of these expeditions to reach Minnesota made use of the lake approach. Its leader was Daniel Greysolon, Sieur du Luth, a native of Lyons, a French soldier of an old family of the lesser nobility, and a member of the select King's Guard. He went to Canada when he was thirty-six and returned to France to fight in the battle of Seneffe, in Flanders, under the Prince of Condé. Then he struck out again for the New World with a younger brother known as the Sieur de la Tourette. Thirsting for adventure and the glory of blazing a way to the Pacific, he left Montreal for the West in 1678, with seven companions. This move opened a career that marks Duluth, to use the more common form of his name, as one of the most helpful lieutenants of Count Frontenac and New France. A singular frustration characterized Duluth's career. Time and again when about to set out for the "Sea of the West," he found himself obliged to return to deal with crises in Indian and civil affairs. Thus he did not win for himself the transcontinental glory of Alexander Mackenzie or of Lewis and Clark.

With others, Duluth wintered (1678–79) near Sault Ste. Marie, seeking to strengthen the friendly relations of New France with the Chippewa. Then, fearing "not death, only cowardice or dishonor," he set out for the western shores of Superior to urge the fierce Sioux to keep peace with the Chippewa. A council was held not far from the site of the city that now honors Duluth in its name, after which he and his men pushed into the interior, to the Mille Lacs Sioux village. There Duluth asked for friendship for the French and named the sacred lake "Buade," the family name of Count Frontenac. This was material for a stirring narrative recording a visit by the first white man known to have entered the Sioux central village on the shores of that beautiful inland lake. Duluth, a man

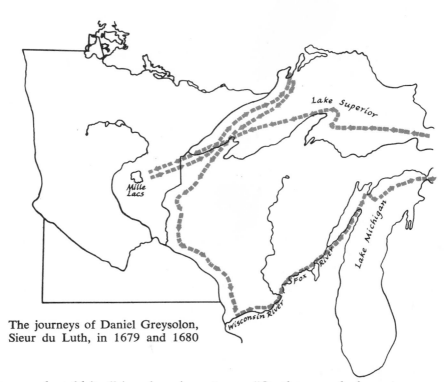

The journeys of Daniel Greysolon,
Sieur du Luth, in 1679 and 1680

of few words, told it all in a laconic sentence: "On the second of
July, 1679, I had the honor to set up the arms of his Majesty in the
great village of Nadoucioux called Izatys, where no Frenchman had
ever been, nor to the Songakitons and Ouetbatons, distant 26 leagues
from the first, where also I set up the arms of his Majesty in the same
year 1679." Thus he referred to the Sioux, the Sisseton, and the Wahpeton Indians. The ceremony of affixing the royal emblem to a tree was
a claim of possession for Louis XIV.

Duluth sent three of his men farther to the interior beyond Mille Lacs.
Later they reported that "it was only twenty days' journey from where
they were" to the "great lake whose water is not good to drink." Was
this a hint of Great Salt Lake? Or perhaps of the western ocean? How
far the men actually went is not known. Perhaps it was not beyond western Minnesota, but their information may account for the appearance on
later maps of the edge of the Teton country. In the absence of a specified
record from Duluth, it is impossible to say what he thought the report
of salt water meant. He had no knowledge of the Great Salt Lake or of
the appalling breadth of the continent — and it is a fair conjecture that

47

to him the water "not good to drink" was the western ocean, the goal of French dreams of continental exploration. Meanwhile he set aside dreams, retraced his steps, arranged a peace council of Sioux and Assiniboin, and wintered at Kaministikwia. The next summer, June 1680, he set out upon a new adventure.

This time he traveled with several companions down the lake shore to the Bois Brule River, paddled up that Wisconsin stream, then portaged to the St. Croix, and canoed to its junction with the Mississippi. This trip opened a new route deep into Minnesota. At the Mississippi Duluth received the surprising news that somewhere down river the Sioux, who only the summer before had pledged friendship with the French, held three white men as prisoners. Without any delay, taking an interpreter and two companions with him, he set out to find them and uphold the authority of France. On July 25 he came upon the three captives of the Sioux. They turned out to be Michel Accault, Antoine Auguelle, and Louis Hennepin.

They were emissaries of La Salle. Earlier in the year they had been sent north on the Mississippi from Fort Crèvecœur on the Illinois River. Thus Minnesota enters the saga of the imperious Frenchman whose aim was to bind the Mississippi Valley to New France. The Minnesota journey was collateral to La Salle's larger plans. Though Accault, an obscure voyageur, was the leader of this expedition, it is Father Hennepin, Recollect friar, traveler, and adventurer, whose fame has reached down to our day.

Hennepin, native of Ath, Belgium, and army chaplain under the Prince of Orange, had been intrigued by tales of the New World, and in 1675 had sailed for Canada with La Salle and Bishop Laval. He acquired schooling in frontier ways at the newly established Frontenac seignory, where La Salle was the commandant. La Salle himself shared some of the great ambitions of Frontenac, and by 1678 he was ready for a novel venture. La Salle invited Hennepin to accompany him, first across Lake Ontario to Niagara. There La Salle's chief lieutenant, the Italian-born Henri de Tonti, a cousin of Duluth, built a sailing vessel, the *Griffon*, for navigating the lakes. And there Hennepin saw and described, for the first time, the greatest waterfall in America. To him Niagara was "a vast and prodigious Cadence of Water."

La Salle's expedition is famed in history. The explorer voyaged through Erie, Huron, and Michigan. He landed at Green Bay and there

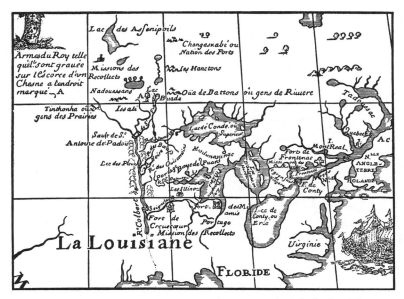

The map by Father Hennepin in his *Description de la Louisiane*,
published at Paris in 1683

the *Griffon* was loaded with furs to be carried back to the East. It sailed
away to unknown disaster and has never been heard of since. La Salle
went on to Illinois and there built a fort, early in 1680, on the shores
of Lake Peoria. Leaving a lieutenant in command, he made his way
east once more. Later he returned to the Mississippi country, traversed
the great river to the Gulf, and was murdered in 1687 in the lower valley.

The ambitions of La Salle furnish the background for the journey
northward of Hennepin and his companions. Starting at the end of
February 1680, they went down the Illinois River and then turned north
on the Mississippi, struggling against current and ice. On April 11 they
were captured by a war party of Sioux Indians, who spared their lives
but took them up to the Minnesota country as prisoners. With the Sioux
they had a series of remarkable adventures before the stern-faced Duluth
came on the scene to rescue them.

It is one of the extraordinary facts of western history that only three
years later a book ascribed to Father Hennepin appeared in Paris. This
was his *Description de la Louisiane* (1683), in which he related his
adventures in detail. The work won wide fame, became a best seller,

49

and was translated from French into many other languages. With its successors, the *Nouveau Voyage* of 1696 and the *Nouvelle Découverte* of 1697, it is a classic of American western history and in fact of greater importance historically than the Hennepin travels themselves. Hennepin's writings were a novel disclosure about the interior New World, and they were read with lively curiosity by people in Europe. The significance of Hennepin is not much lessened even though modern research indicates that he himself wrote only a part of his famous *Description*. Much of the book apparently was drafted by someone else to forward La Salle's efforts to secure royal support for a great expedition across the Atlantic to build a colony in the lower Mississippi country and thus solidify Louis XIV's expanding empire.

Whatever the mysteries of authorship, the experiences revealed by Hennepin were manifestly his own. In vivid phrase one reads of his journey up river, his capture by Indians sweeping down in a flotilla of thirty-three canoes, the naming of the "Lake of Tears" (now known as Lake Pepin), and the nature of Indian life at Mille Lacs, where Hennepin was given "a robe made of ten large dressed beaver skins, trimmed with porcupine quills" and adopted into the family of a chief. After an overland journey the weary Hennepin was treated to a steam bath and massaged with wildcat oil. He baptized a sick child, and he tried to work out a dictionary of Sioux words. In a kind of flexible captivity Hennepin and his companions accompanied the Sioux on a hunting party. With Auguelle, the friar discovered and named for his patron saint the Falls of St. Anthony. His *Description* contains a map showing the Mississippi — he calls it the "Meschasipi" — from the Illinois fort to Mille Lacs and the region farther north to Lake of the Woods, with many familiar places indicated and even a drawing of the arms of the king affixed to a tree at Mille Lacs.

Possibly Hennepin has had "a fame beyond his deserts." In his books claims are advanced that have not been corroborated. Charges of exaggeration and falsification have been made against him, and he has been called an imposter. How much weight can be attached to such aspersions and to inconsistencies in his writings is difficult to say. One must remember that the very authorship of the drafts as printed is open to question and Hennepin's own part uncertain. Certain conclusions are undeniable, however. Hennepin did make the Minnesota journey in 1680. His own record of it somehow got into the narratives published under his name.

The record bears the marks of truth, not of plagiarism or fiction, though it is ungenerous both to Accault, the leader, and to Duluth, the rescuer.

Meanwhile, on that summer day in 1680, an indignant Duluth took Hennepin and his companions under his protection, forced the Sioux to return to their Mille Lacs village, there scorned the pipe of peace, and gave the Indians a tongue lashing. He well knew that if a single Frenchman received unfriendly treatment from the Sioux, all French visitors might expect similar hostility. He demanded the release of the three prisoners, and he postponed his plans for finding the salt sea of the West. He then guided the little party to the Straits of Mackinac, following the route by way of the Mississippi, the Wisconsin and Fox rivers, and Lake Michigan. Hennepin himself got back to France by 1682 and soon found himself famous with the publication of his book — the first about Minnesota.

Duluth, after troubles over securing a license to trade, journeyed to Minnesota again in 1683. He used the Fox-Wisconsin-Mississippi route, secured a new pact of friendship from the Sioux, then pushed up the St. Croix to the Brule River (the Bois Brule) and Lake Superior. He built forts or posts in the St. Croix region and at Kaministikwia (Fort William of today) and instructed his brother, the Sieur de la Tourette, to build one farther north, at Lake Nipigon. Recalled to enforce French authority at Mackinac, he set out yet again, in 1688, for Minnesota and beyond to challenge the British in the Hudson Bay area. This might have been the occasion for a great expedition to the West, but the Iroquois were on the warpath in the East, and a disastrous attack on the French settlement of Lachine near Montreal brought him east once again. Later for a while he was commandant of Fort Frontenac. He died in 1710, and of him a historian writes, "He had added to New France an empire in the Northwest, had explored the routes from Lake Superior to the Mississippi, had ventured farther west than any of his confreres, and had made French alliances with the greatest and most populous of the northwestern tribesmen." Truly he was a "nobleman of Old and New France."

French enterprise in the final decades of the seventeenth century seemed headed for occupation and settlement of the Mississippi Valley from north to south. Explorers and traders were filling out the map, correcting errors, expanding knowledge, and the stage was ready for a colonization which, had it not been for wars in Europe, the vigor of the

English, and the thinness of population in the Canadian East, might greatly have altered the history of the continent.

Valiant efforts were indeed made. Nicolas Perrot, a trader experienced in wilderness life, was named commandant of the West in 1685. He led an expedition to the Upper Mississippi country and established posts on the Wisconsin side of the river. At the second of these, Fort St. Antoine, on May 8, 1689, he took formal possession of the Sioux country — the Upper Mississippi — in the name of Louis XIV, with ceremonies not unlike those at Sault Ste. Marie eighteen years earlier, which he had witnessed. These outposts, far up the river from the spot where Jolliet first saw the Mississippi, gave promise of establishments still farther north, and another trader, present at the 1689 ceremonies, carried the fleur-de-lis to posts built on Minnesota territory.

This was Pierre Charles le Sueur, a native of Artois, who already knew the Superior region and had traded with the Sioux. After the events at Fort St. Antoine, he ranged the western country to forward trade along the Superior-Mississippi route and in 1693 established a post on Madeline Island. He evidently made use of the Brule–St. Croix water paths, and seems to have built a post, perhaps in 1694 or 1695, on Prairie Island at the mouth of the St. Croix. A restless, ambitious man, Le Sueur went back to Montreal with a chief of the Sioux and arranged an audience with Frontenac. Then he was off to Paris to apply to the king for a ten-year monopoly of the fur trade of the Upper Mississippi and also for a mining authorization. A skeptical view of Le Sueur's mining intentions was expressed by a French official, who said, "The only mines that he seeks in those regions are mines of beaver skins." After various adventures Le Sueur succeeded in his errand, but he was instructed to make his approach, not from eastern Canada, but from Louisiana. He sailed for America with the Sieur d'Iberville, the founder of the French colony at Biloxi, in 1699.

This was a prelude to a curious chapter in Minnesota's early history — and a commentary on the lure of trade. Le Sueur, with nineteen men, a small sailing vessel (a "shallop"), and two canoes, set out in April 1700 to ascend the Mississippi from its mouth very nearly to its source. The journey took until the following September. A boat builder named Jean Pénicaut, one of the party, told of the trip in a letter. After long and hard months the Frenchmen reached the Falls of St. Anthony, which Pénicaut described as "the entire Mississippi falling suddenly from a height of sixty feet, making a noise like that of thunder rolling in the air." They then went up the St. Peter's, or Minnesota, River to the mouth of the "Makato," now called the Blue Earth. Not far from it they built a small post called Fort L'Huillier. Indicative of the fact that many men unknown to history roamed the West was the sudden appearance at the fort one day of seven French traders, doubtless *coureurs des bois,* who stayed on through the winter.

From writings of Le Sueur and Pénicaut the experiences of the men at the fort can be pieced together: the killing of four hundred buffaloes as winter provisions, gifts of guns and powder and balls as well as axes, tobacco, and pipes to the Sioux, and the mining of alleged copper ore. What Le Sueur mined was not copper but only colored clay, yet when he left in the spring of 1701 on the long return journey he loaded two tons of this "ore" into his boat and the next year carried it off to France. Is this some joke across the ages? Was it a mere nominal fulfillment of the commission to work mines? Were the "mines" originally just a pretext? We do not know, but we do know that Le Sueur also carried out furs, and they were far more precious than the "ore." On a single occasion the Sioux brought in for trade "more than four hundred beaver robes, each robe being made of nine skins sewed together." Le Sueur left a dozen men at the fort, and they held it until 1702, when they abandoned it as a consequence of a surprise attack by Fox Indians, then on the warpath against the Sioux. Before the Frenchmen left they buried their trade goods, a cache that, so far as is known, has never been found by archaeologists. In 1702, a map, probably drawn by Le Sueur, added still more to known knowledge of Minnesota. The Brule–St. Croix route is there, lands and streams west of Lake Superior, the approximate source of the great river, Lake of the Woods, and not a few names of places, chiefly Sioux.

With this forest drama, the curtain drops on French Minnesota for a time. New France was in decline and western occupation was delayed. Louis XIV in his later years was embroiled in great wars. The Iroquois were a continuing menace to eastern Canada and the western trade. Frontenac died in 1698. The English were competing for the Ohio Valley, and the licensed trade out of Canada was thwarted by that of the wood rangers. So the passing of Fort L'Huillier marks a transition from the era of hope and achievement. The challenge of the French to the Hudson's Bay Company had given them control of the major part of that great area by treaty at the end of King William's War (1697), but the peace between France and England was only a breathing space. Sixteen years later, when Queen Anne's War ended in the Treaty of Utrecht, Hudson Bay went back to Britain (Newfoundland and Nova Scotia, too), a portent, perhaps, of things to come. And yet New France still had a half century of existence before it bowed to British supremacy.

Decline there assuredly was, but in due time there came a swing. Mackinac was reoccupied within a year or two after Utrecht, Kaministikwia in 1717, and La Pointe the next year. Three years later Father Charlevoix, the early Jesuit historian of New France, went on a quest that had persistently intrigued and frustrated the French. This was the finding of a northern way to the Sea of the West. He learned no more than Duluth had known, that there were two ways of heading toward the far Pacific. One was the route of the Great Lakes, to Superior and then by stream and portage westward. The other was to ascend the great river to the Sioux country and then turn west, probably by way of the Minnesota River. This was the route that Lamothe Cadillac, commandant at Mackinac in the 1690s and founder of Detroit, had advocated in a famous *Memoir*.

It is possible that Cadillac in turn had been influenced by the Baron Armand Lahontan, one-time associate of Duluth and the genial author of a book of travels entitled *New Voyages to America*. This work, published in France in 1703, contained an elaborate description of the "Long River," a mighty western arm of the Mississippi which he claimed to have discovered. Some writers have contended that the Long River was in fact the Minnesota and that the baron did explore it, but most historians regard it as fictitious, the airy product of an ingenious imagination. An interesting defender of Lahontan was the Canadian scholar and humorist Stephen Leacock, who ranked the clever Frenchman with La Salle and other great explorers. Lahontan, he wrote, was "a man of honor" who "would not lie, and could not lie."

Charlevoix made a concrete and practical suggestion: that of seeking again the friendship of the Sioux and of building somewhere on the Mississippi a strong fort to serve as a wedge between the Sioux and their enemies to the south, the Fox Indians. The French government in 1723 countenanced an expedition with such purposes, but the problem of financing, combined with continued Fox hostilities, delayed it. It was not until 1727 that, with financial support from Montreal merchants who were given a three-year monopoly of the fur trade, a new expedition set out from Montreal for the Indian country of the Upper Mississippi.

Its leader was Réné Boucher, Sieur de la Perrière. The Sioux had indicated that they would welcome "black robes," and La Perrière took with him two Jesuit missionaries, Michel Guignas and Nicolas de Gonnor. With a flotilla of canoes he set out in June 1727 from Montreal, spent about five weeks before reaching Mackinac, reloaded supplies in large canoes, then paddled along the Michigan shores to Green Bay. He had a pleasant welcome from the Winnebago, and then made his way to the Mississippi, there turning northward. In September the party reached Lake Pepin and landed at its upper end on the Minnesota side.

Here they established Fort Beauharnois, a palisaded enclosure one hundred feet square, with several large buildings and also small cabins, its name honoring the governor of New France, Charles de Beauharnois. The missionaries built a small chapel and called it the Mission of St. Michael the Archangel. Like the Jesuits generally, they had both Christian and scientific purposes. They were soul seekers and map makers, and their equipment included, alongside the Bible, a quadrant, a telescope, and other instruments. In November a celebration was held in honor of the governor's birthday. Rockets were fired and the air resounded with shouts of "Long live the king!" One of the Jesuits, telling of this glamorous event, writes that when the stars fell from the sky, "women and children took flight." The visiting Sioux Indians asked for an end to the play of "this terrible medicine."

The fort, strategic in its location, might have served as a base for an expedition to the Pacific, but this dream faded out. La Perrière returned to Montreal in 1728 with one of the missionaries. Some twenty soldiers and traders left at the fort were in a precarious situation because the Fox were again on the warpath, attacking French outposts in Illinois. Beauharnois, determined to administer a severe lesson, sent a little army of four hundred men out from Montreal in 1728 to carry war to the Fox, but the wily natives retreated and avoided pitched battles. The French soldiers, after destroying abandoned villages and burning fields of corn, went back to the East. The garrison on Lake Pepin was advised to give up Fort Beauharnois, and some of its men tried to slip away. They were captured by allies of the Fox, held prisoners, and ultimately released. Off and on, in troubled times, the fort was maintained for a decade. It was abandoned in 1737 after the Sioux, who had struck a blow at Frenchmen on the international waterways, appeared at the Lake Pepin post to brandish before the garrison the bloody trophies of their sally against white intrusion in the north. Beauharnois was then left unoccupied until the 1750s, when under new leadership it had another period of activity before the final curtain fell on the French regime.

The French had by no means lost their interest in the waterways and furs of the hinterland beyond Lake Superior. Nor had they put aside their ideas of a northern passage to the western rim of a continent whose vast width was hidden from their understanding. From Radisson to Duluth and later, the north country had stirred French imaginations. Stray bits of information on maps and little items in other records point unmistakably to the early presence of Frenchmen on the international waterways. A voyageur, Jacques de Noyon, seems to have spent a winter on the "Ouchichiq River," or Rainy Lake, as early as about 1688. Lake of the Woods appears on early maps; and some evidence indicates that French traders, perhaps including De Noyon, had in fact been at that western lake before 1717. There is reason to believe that voyageurs, including Zacherie Robutel, Sieur de la Noue, had occupied a post at Rainy Lake about the same time (the dates are around 1717 and 1720). La Noue, a soldier of the colonial wars, had been sent as commandant at Kaministikwia in 1717. He served there for four years and was notably successful in drawing in furs from the north country in competition with the Hudson's Bay Company. A shadowy figure in Minnesota history, he deserves a larger place than has been accorded him.

Casual glimpses of little-known Frenchmen in the "savage country" recall the sudden appearance at Le Sueur's lonely post on the Minnesota river of wandering French traders in 1700. The desire for beaver skins and the spirit of adventure may well have drawn many Frenchmen far into the interior with only faint traces in surviving records. The fact that a post at Kaministikwia on the Superior shore was occupied makes it a fair inference that Frenchmen made their way into the regions from which their precious furs came. They were not a breed of men content to sit at water's edge, and they knew how to handle canoes on streams and inland lakes.

While Frenchmen were struggling for a foothold on the Upper Mississippi, a Canadian-born Frenchman, Pierre Gaultier de Varennes, Sieur de la Vérendrye, was maturing plans for an expedition beyond Lake Superior. He was interested in exploration, trade, and the finding of a route to the Sea of the West. La Vérendrye, born at Three Rivers in 1685, was the son of the governor of that community. As a youth he went to France and fought and was wounded in the battle of Malplaquet (1709). He returned to New France, became an officer in a colonial regiment, married, and had four sons — Jean Baptiste, Pierre, François, and Louis Joseph — all of whom were to figure in the western saga.

La Vérendrye was made commander of the French post at Lake Nipigon, and there listened to tales told by Indians, notably by a certain Auchagah, of a western river that flowed into a salt sea, of strange mounted men clad in armor, far to the west. Auchagah drew a crude map on birchbark that embodied such ideas and rumors, and La Vérendrye was fired with ambition to head a move westward. He carried his plans to Beauharnois in 1730, with a request for supplies and funds and a hundred men. The governor approved and asked for official authorization from Louis XV. The response from Versailles was affirmative, but no grant was forthcoming, save that both king and governor pledged a monopoly of the fur trade to La Vérendrye.

Once again, as in the case of La Perrière, the motive of trade and the financial support of Montreal merchants turned plans into actuality. In June 1731, La Vérendrye set out from Montreal with three of his sons, a nephew (La Jemeraye), and fifty soldiers and voyageurs. Guiding the party was the Nipigon Indian, Auchagah, and at Michilimackinac a Jesuit priest joined the expedition. On August 26 the flotilla of canoes came into the sheltered and picturesque bay at Grand Portage, landing on Minnesota soil at a spot destined for historical fame in fur-trading annals.

Larger plans were deferred until the next year, and La Vérendrye took most of his men north to spend the winter at Kaministikwia. La Jemeraye, however, with one of the La Vérendrye sons, a voyageur, and a guide, crossed the portage of some eight or nine miles to the Pigeon River, then went on to the western end of Rainy Lake and built a post called Fort St. Pierre. Here, the next summer, La Vérendrye and his followers joined La Jemeraye. With a brigade of canoes, they pushed westward to Lake of the Woods, where they established Fort St. Charles in what later became known as Minnesota's Northwest Angle. This fort of 1732 was palisaded, an enclosure one hundred feet by sixty, with two

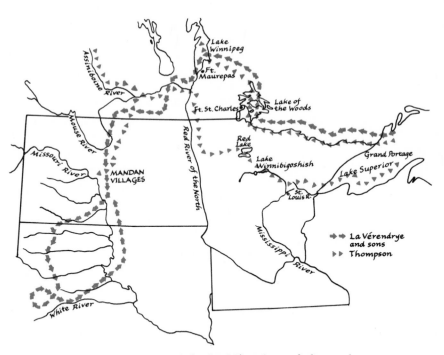

Exploration routes of the La Vérendryes, father and sons,
in 1732–43, and of David Thompson in 1797–98

gates, a watchtower, four main buildings, powder magazine and store-house, chapel, and houses for the commandant and the missionary.

One might imagine such a post as buried in the deep wilderness, without human contacts. The truth, however, is that it was a busy place on an open water route. In the spring of 1733 La Jemeraye departed with furs and made his way the long distance to Montreal and Quebec — and was back by August. In a single day as many as 150 canoes arrived at the fort, Indians bringing foods for trading. One day some 300 Sioux dropped in on their way to attack the Chippewa at Madeline Island, and the next day about 500 other Sioux paused there on a foray against the prairie Sioux. There was incessant trading. Councils were held, one with Cree and Assiniboin Indians, and there were volleys of salutes, speeches and replies, and gifts to the Indians of tobacco, knives, ramrods, powder and shot, awls, beads, needles, vermilion, axes, cloaks.

La Vérendrye, trader and negotiator, was also a farmer and hunter. Corn and peas were planted, wild rice was gathered, and his men fished and hunted. That there was danger from forest fires in the north country,

58

then as now, is known because a Jesuit priest, Father Aulneau, coming out in 1735 to replace the first priest at the fort, wrote, "I journeyed nearly all the way through fire and a thick stifling smoke, which prevented us from even once catching a glimpse of the sun."

La Vérendrye himself made several journeys back to the East, for he was deeply concerned about his mounting debts and was seeking further support. Meanwhile the fort was held, notwithstanding danger of attack by wandering Sioux war parties, one of which in 1736 massacred a group of Frenchmen sent out from the fort to meet an incoming brigade of canoes loaded with provisions and trade goods. The explorer's son Jean, the missionary Aulneau, and nineteen voyageurs were surprised on an island in Lake of the Woods by Sioux seeking revenge because the French were friendly with their own enemies the Cree and Assiniboin. To the last man the French were killed and beheaded. When La Vérendrye learned of this dreadful tragedy, he said, "I have lost my son, the Reverend Father, and my Frenchmen, misfortunes which I shall lament all my life." But he did not give up the fort. Instead he rebuilt and strengthened it, though it was this roving assault that led, as we have seen, to the abandonment of Fort Beauharnois on Lake Pepin in 1737.

Fort St. Charles, however interesting, colorful, and heroic on its own immediate account, is important historically as a base for further exploration westward and for a veritable chain of forts built far beyond Lake of the Woods. Back at Montreal in 1737 the governor, himself under pressure from the colonial minister in France, insistently urged La Vérendrye to carry his explorations farther into the interior. If the merchants were interested in furs, the high officials were concerned about power and expansion. So, too, was La Vérendrye, but trade was his financial foundation and he could not neglect it. Yet he and his sons used Fort St. Charles as a kind of western capital for an empire of the Northwest. La Vérendrye journeyed in 1738 to the Mandan country of the Missouri and wrote a detailed and fascinating account of the relatively advanced culture of that strange tribe of Indians. A more ambitious expedition headed by two of his sons went still farther west in 1742 toward the lake or sea whose water "is not good to drink." How far they got is uncertain. "On January 1st 1743," wrote one of the sons, "we were in sight of the mountains." They pushed on to the foothills — but did they reach the Rockies or the Black Hills? No one seems to have a final answer, though the problem has invited much conjecture. What is known is that when they returned to the Missouri they inscribed and buried a lead plaque as a record, and this was found a hundred and seventy years later by a schoolgirl playing on a hill above Fort Pierre, South Dakota.

These pioneering thrusts westward are only a part of the French exploits, for new forts were built in the Canadian Northwest — one near Lake Winnipeg, one where the city of Winnipeg now stands, one up the Assiniboine River, and yet others in the Saskatchewan country. The chain of establishments gave promise of greater achievements to come — save for the impact of events in the East and across the Atlantic. In the late 1740s, La Vérendrye himself, once more in eastern Canada, had every intention of pursuing his explorations and of raising up still more posts in the western country. But his dreams were closed by death in 1749.

The time would come when the very site of old Fort St. Charles, deep in the north country, would be forgotten. More than a century and a half after the fort was built a party of Canadians discovered its site and excavated it. Under the chapel they unearthed the skeletons of La Vérendrye's son and Father Aulneau and the skulls of the voyageurs who were massacred with them in 1736.

La Vérendrye is remembered and honored as a major figure in the history of the continent. His death, however, by no means marked the end of French trade, forts, and occupation in the upper western country. His surviving sons continued their interest and activity. The posts stretching westward from Lake Superior seem to have been maintained, and there was a new spurt of trade and exploration in the Upper Mississippi country. Paul Marin had long been active in the western trade and had been on the Upper Mississippi as early as 1729. He was there again at mid-century and built a Minnesota fort on Lake Pepin, evidently not far from the older Fort Beauharnois. His son Joseph succeeded him at this post after a long journey among Indian tribes in the West, including those in the Sioux country. Recent research has disclosed the interesting fact that in the 1750s there were three important posts in or near Minnesota as well as several lesser establishments. The major posts were La Jonquière, the one built by the elder Marin on Lake Pepin; Duquesne, somewhere near the present site of Brainerd, Minnesota; and Vaudreuil, in Iowa, opposite the point where the Wisconsin joins the Mississippi.

The minor posts were on the St. Croix and at or near the junction of the Mississippi and Minnesota rivers.

Several collateral expeditions were sent west and north; efforts were made to learn more about the Sea of the West; and the Marins carried on a vigorous trade in furs. Mercenary clashes in claims and authority took place between the younger Marin and the youngest son of La Vérendrye, Joseph — the "Chevalier" who participated in the exploring expedition that buried the lead plate of 1743. The competition for trading advantages was not just between the two men. It was a contest between the Wisconsin and Fox river route and that of Grand Portage and Lake Superior. In the period of spreading Chippewa occupation of northern Minnesota, Joseph la Vérendrye was making a bid for the Sioux trade, while Marin was trying to control that trade by promoting peace between the Sioux and Chippewa.

The full detail of the posts both on the Upper Mississippi and in the border country of the north is not clearly revealed for the final years of French dominance, but it appears that they were held longer than was once supposed. If the final chapter of the western French regime has its heroic aspects, there is also evidence of no little venality among higher officials and on the part of some of the traders who employed dishonest means of profiting under the French grants of monopoly.

As the French and Indian War neared its climax on the Plains of Abraham above Quebec, the talent and daring of French officers trained in the rigors of life beyond the Great Lakes were tapped by New France to bolster defense in the East. This obviously meant a loss of leadership in the western areas remote from the St. Lawrence and Ohio valleys. The drama at Quebec in 1759 was greater than that of the two heroic generals who died, the one in victory, James Wolfe, only thirty-two years old, reciting Gray's "Elegy" and remarking that he would rather have written its lines than have taken Quebec; the other Louis Joseph de Montcalm, veteran of Fort Ontario and Ticonderoga, killed with his British conqueror. The historic drama, capped the next year by the English triumph at Montreal, was the climax of nearly three-quarters of a century of what has been called "a single war with interruptions." This was the series of French-Indian-British colonial wars and their European counterparts from 1689 to the 1760s. The Treaty of Paris in 1763, by which France gave up all its claims to North America east of the

Mississippi (except for the island of New Orleans), marked the end of a prolonged struggle in the Old and New worlds for domination. Its prize was in effect the North American continent, though France in 1762 had secretly ceded to Spain its possessions west of the great river. Behind the colonial wars there were those of Britain and France and various coalitions: King William's War (the War of the Grand Alliance), Queen Anne's War (the War of the Spanish Succession), King George's War (the War of the Austrian Succession), and the French and Indian War (the Seven Years' War). All these wars on the colonial side had in fact been French and Indian wars, with interludes of semi-peace. The record is one of conflict and treaties — a closing in on New France as Britain, with commanding sea power, and its New World colonies fought for the seaboard and interior valleys and lakes of America. English settlements of more than a million people were matched against thinly occupied New France, much of its vigor routed to trade.

The lilies of France were hauled down on a regime that reached back to Cartier and Champlain, and the Union Jack was raised up over the western posts. The French never achieved their dream of reaching the beckoning Sea of the West, but they accomplished much. They opened routes to the West. They explored mid-America. They made new discoveries, enlarged the map, and reported their findings to the people of the Old World. They expanded the empire whose brilliant center was Versailles, and pioneered the trade in beaver skins and other furs. They learned the ways of the wilderness and trained the gay voyageurs who would play a skillful, important, and colorful part in the new regime to come. They scattered French names on the maps of Minnesota, Wisconsin, and other states — names that have lingered to the present day. Through all their regime, they produced leaders of courage, imagination, and hardihood. They left a legacy of buoyancy and curiosity in mid-America and on a state whose official seal designates Minnesota as *L'Etoile du Nord.*

Grand Portage, from a scratchboard drawing
by Francis Lee Jaques

The British and a Lakeside Emporium

BRITISH control of the lands given up by the French was not achieved by any easy transition. The French, it is true, readily abandoned their western posts, but the change of regimes was no simple matter of the French stepping out and the British stepping in.

Even before peace was proclaimed, British troops and traders tried to occupy posts in the frontier region. Their purposes centered particularly in Mackinac and Green Bay, with Detroit as a strategic point of defense. The brilliant Robert Rogers, a "ranger" of distinguished exploits, was sent out to take over these establishments, but he encountered the bloody obstacle of Indian war at its worst.

A storm of native protest against the British broke out in the spring of 1763. This was the Pontiac War whose fury extended the long way from Niagara to Mackinac. Some places were captured by the Indians, including Mackinac, but certain key posts, among them Detroit, withstood Pontiac's guile, siege, and assault. In the end the natives were forced to accept the sovereign authority of George III.

The British dominion over the Minnesota region lasted well over a half century after 1763. Wars were fought and treaties negotiated, but they were remote from the beaver country. The British held on despite the Treaty of Paris in 1783 at the end of the Revolutionary War. They clung to the West in the face of Jay's Treaty of 1794. And they ignored the Spanish claim to Minnesota West from 1762 to 1800. Indeed, even the Louisiana Purchase in 1803 did not immediately change the picture of British control. British occupation, British management of the fur trade, British operating posts, British enterprise — these were carried forward decade after decade.

That the British clung to some of their western fur-trading posts after the achievement of American independence is understandable in the light of the circumstances of the time. For one thing, they had reason to believe that a quick release of the posts might foment Indian troubles. They had ample incentive to protect as long as possible their big and long-cycled financial interest in the trade. Moreover there were uncertainties and developing disputes about the precise lines of the international boundary. And the British were well aware of the fact that diplomatic maneuvers followed every war and every treaty. With respect to the Minnesota country, it is also true that Americans did not contest British control until the early 1800s and even then only in a tentative fashion. Not until after the War of 1812 did the United States enforce with troops and a strategic fort the rights which, in its view, had been legally American ever since the Treaty of 1783.

The British regime carried forward the French tradition of Indian trade, without the planting of agricultural settlement. Obviously the time was not ripe for farming in a region so remote from the eastern agricultural frontiers as Minnesota. And Britain recognized realities in its statesmanlike Proclamation of 1763. This organized Quebec and other provinces, but forbade grants of lands in the West or private purchases of such lands from the Indians. In effect it created a vast interior reservation that white settlement could not encroach upon. Though issued while Pontiac's forces were raging, it was no suddenly improvised plan but a considered policy to conciliate natives and control abuses that had long fed Indian antagonism. Eleven years later, in 1774, the Quebec Act extended the province to the Mississippi, and the Ohio at the south, shutting off the interior from the spread of institutions from the Atlantic colonies. This has been described as the "first constitution nominally in effect in Minnesota," but actually it was not in operation in this region.

Exploration under the British went hand in hand with trade. The old dream of finding a route to the Pacific, if not a Northwest Passage, was turned into reality. The barter for furs and the drive of exploration were continental in scope, but the British did not overlook the potentialities of

66

Minnesota. Before their domination came to an end, they had literally dotted this region with trading posts. The period also witnessed a resumption of competition between trading interests centered in Montreal and those reaching down from Hudson Bay. This was not a French-English struggle, but one almost equally sharp and fierce between rival groups of British merchants.

As the British initially exploited the lucrative trade of the Great Lakes and beyond, they issued licenses, under the Proclamation of 1763, and they centered the trade in large posts, with awards to traders of exclusive rights, not unlike the monopolies of the French. One of these traders, Alexander Henry, only two years after the Treaty of 1763 was granted broad rights in the Superior country. Working out from Chequamegon Bay and the Sault, this native of New Jersey, who had miraculously escaped butchery at Mackinac when it was captured by Indians in 1763, developed trade that reached the Chippewa beyond Lake Superior, hunted for ores, and made himself familiar with the lake region. Other traders, too, journeyed in that region, even on the waterways westward from Grand Portage.

Western trade in 1767 was released from the rigidities of exclusive grants, and from that time onward many expensive consignments of trade goods went out to Lake Superior and to trading posts far to the west. Small partnerships emerged, and as increasing competition pointed to larger organization, it took form, by several stages, in the North West Company, famous in Minnesota and western business history.

Meanwhile Robert Rogers, commanding the garrison at Mackinac, a man of action and imagination, conceived the idea of sending an expedition to the Pacific Coast to search for the river "Ourigan" and to discover a Northwest Passage from the Pacific to Hudson Bay. Everybody now knew that Cathay was not within easy reach, but the British government, alert to national glory, had offered a prize equivalent to a hundred thousand dollars to the man who should discover a Northwest Passage. Rogers believed that an expedition might cross the continent and then go northward until it found a water passage that would lead back to Hudson Bay. The facts of geography, as later ascertained, did not sustain his hypothesis, but Rogers' willingness to give it a trial accounts for the adventures and writings of a major figure in the colonial history of Minnesota, Jonathan Carver.

A Massachusetts-born colonial, Carver had served as an officer in the

French and Indian War. In the spring of 1766 he made his way from Boston to Mackinac, where Rogers commissioned him to go to the Sioux country. His assignment was to win over the friendship of the natives and to invite them to send representatives to a great peace council at Mackinac. Then he was to join, as surveyor, a planned expedition to the Pacific and the "Ourigan" under the leadership of Captain James Tute, with James Stanley Goddard second in command. So Carver set out for the Northwest, using the Green Bay–Fox and Wisconsin route to the Mississippi. He stopped at Prairie du Chien, a trading village that he found thronged with some two hundred Indian warriors. Then, with a Frenchman and an Indian, he went north on the river, paused in November 1766 at a great Minnesota cave now known by his name, proceeded to the Falls of St. Anthony, and wintered some distance up the Minnesota River. The next spring he started southward, held a council near the cave he had visited in the autumn, invited the Sioux to send tribesmen to the Mackinac council, and went down river to meet Tute.

On May 21, 1767, Tute, Goddard, and Carver, with a Chippewa guide and a crew of workers and interpreters, started north on the Mississippi. Originally they intended to push across Minnesota to the Red River and then make their way to the distant Canadian Fort La Prairie, where they expected to find supplies sent by Rogers via Grand Portage. This plan Captain Tute changed, perhaps because his Chippewa guide was apprehensive of Sioux attacks. Instead the explorers journeyed to Lake Superior, paddled to Fond du Lac, the Chippewa village at the mouth of the St. Louis River, and then moved up the north shore to Grand Portage. Here to their bitter disappointment they learned that Rogers had not sent any supplies. The party returned to Mackinac, where Carver dolefully recorded the end of this attempt "to find out a Northwest Passage."

These travels, prosaic and marking no real advance on Duluth and Hennepin, afford scarcely a hint of the historical importance of Carver. This rests instead on his book, *Travels of Jonathan Carver through the Interior Parts of North America in the Years 1766, 1767, and 1768*, published in London in 1778. Containing a narrative of his travels and an account of American Indian life and customs, this was the first book of travel in this region by an English writer. It was a lively, interesting, and informing account that won wide and long-continued popularity. Through nearly two centuries it has been reprinted forty times in English,

French, German, Dutch, even Greek, and its story therefore has reached readers in many lands.

Carver's descriptions are vivid and his outlook is broad. Like Radisson, he had the vision of a prophet. When he saw the Minnesota country he let himself go in soaring prophecy: "There is no doubt that at some future period, mighty kingdoms will emerge from these wildernesses, and stately and solemn temples, with gilded spires reaching the skies, supplant the Indian huts, whose only decorations are the barbarous trophies of their vanished enemies." As Hennepin was the first of Europeans to make a drawing of Niagara Falls, so Carver for the first time in history pictured the Falls of St. Anthony, which Hennepin himself had discovered nearly a century earlier.

Carver and his book have been the subject of controversy in modern times. Carver's narrative is alleged to be ungenerous, egotistic, exaggerated. It omits Major Rogers, the inspiring mind behind the expedition. Some critics have believed that even Carver's personal narrative was penned by another. And the second half of his book is largely plagiarism. But Carver's fame has not been much dimmed. New light on his veracity has been shed by his diaries, preserved in the British Museum and not yet published. Scholars know that the reason for the failure of the Tute expedition to receive supplies to sustain it on a westward trek was that Rogers was in disgrace. He had been imprisoned on trumped-up charges that led to a military trial for treason — and his acquittal. Carver, after the expedition, was in England seeking support for another effort to find the Northwest Passage. One may reasonably assume that he suppressed the name of Rogers and detail on the Tute expedition to avoid prejudicing his case.

The unprinted Carver diaries tell about Rogers and Tute and attest the truthfulness, in the main, of the Carver story. The book does indeed have exaggerations. And at times it departs from details as set down in the diaries, but here again history is friendly to the man. It is probable that when he wrote the manuscript of the book, he did not have his own diaries at hand, and so it seems likely that he wrote his narrative from memory. If so, it was a good achievement even if, like Homer, he occasionally nodded. The second part of his book — really a separate work — drew much upon Charlevoix and other writers without acknowledgment, but modern critics sometimes forget that borrowings from other writers were common in the travel literature of the eighteenth century. The custom of the time, as a noted historian has remarked, was to quote without quotation marks. Carver was one of many who indulged in the practice.

Controversy of a more malodorous kind trailed Carver after his death in 1780. A new edition of his book included a fantastic account of a vast grant of lands alleged to have been made to him at the spring conference in 1767. He himself had made no mention of any such grant in his book or diaries, and he had advanced no claims in relation to it. Later claimants produced a document intended to substantiate their petitions for great stretches of land. The document was patently forged. Had there been such a transaction, it would have been an impudent violation of the Proclamation of 1763. Many years later the claim was rejected by Congress, but even in the twentieth century it has reared its absurd and spurious head many times in Minnesota and Wisconsin.

As to Carver, if he merits no high place in the galaxy of western explorers, yet the travels narrated were his own. And his book was a readable contribution to the literature that revealed the Middle West to the minds of curious Europeans.

Early and late in Minnesota history, Yankee influence has been important. It was another colonial Yankee, colorful and shrewd, who came up the Mississippi and spent two years in Minnesota trading with the Indians just before the American Revolution. This was Peter Pond, whose diary for those years was miraculously rescued from a Connecticut kitchen stove long after Pond's death. The diarist recorded his adventures in words spelled by him exactly as he pronounced them, and the result is a quaintness that does not mask the clarity and acuteness of a good writer and remarkable man. Before his journeys to the West, he was a soldier in the French and Indian War, having enlisted when he was only sixteen. "One Eavening in April," he wrote, "the Drums an Instaments of Musick ware all Imployed to that Degrea that thay Charmed me." At Detroit he had a duel with a man who had abused him in a "Shameful manner." This episode came to a quick end: "We met the Next Morning Eairley & Discharged Pistels in which the Pore Fellowe was unfortenat."

Pond engaged in a partnership for trade on the Upper Mississippi, loaded his trading goods into twelve large canoes, and set out from Mackinac in 1773. At Prairie du Chien, by this time a lively center, he delegated nine agents to trade on different streams flowing into the Mississippi, while he himself went to the mouth of the Minnesota and built a cabin some distance up that river. Here Indians brought in beavers and other skins and furs, and Pond said, "Thay ware Welcom, and we Did our bisnes to advantage."

In the spring Pond returned to Prairie du Chien to find that his agents had been highly successful. He records the sight of 130 canoes at the Prairie du Chien water front, from Mackinac and even from as far away as New Orleans, and the village was crowded with traders and Indians. He then went back to Minnesota for another year (1774–75) and collected furs valued at close to $20,000. His adventures on the Upper Mississippi attest the colonial and British exploitation of its wealth of furs, but for Pond they were a minor episode in a career that won him lasting fame. Like Radisson he sensed that the essential clue to the best beaver skins was "north." He journeyed to Grand Portage and in later years went far into the Canadian Northwest, to the Athabasca region and even as far as Great Slave Lake. Skilled as a trader, he became one of the founders of the North West Company, and he also figures in western history as a clever map maker.

As the British regime established itself west of the Great Lakes, the name of "Grand Portage" appeared with increasing frequency in the contemporary records. The place was strategically located at the Lake Superior edge of the trail to the Pigeon River and the water road to the vast interior. It fronted on a picturesque bay guarded by an island which has been likened to "an emerald on a lady's hand mirror." A beautiful spot, Grand Portage was a meeting place for trade and travel from Montreal and from the rivers and lakes of northern America. That the French had occupied a post at this "great carrying place" seems certain. It is equally certain that from La Vérendrye's day onward they had made much use of the portage. The British were not slow in exploiting Grand Portage. Carver, referring to his visit in 1767, hoped to meet the traders "that annually go from Michilimackinac to the northwest," a clear confirmation that the British were sending traders and canoes packed with trade goods to the place of rendezvous. Carver in fact reported that several hundreds of Indians were there awaiting the arrival of traders. He makes no mention of buildings or a stockade, but evidence indicates that beginnings were made the following year on a major post that grew progressively in importance during the next decade and blossomed into its great period of the 1780s and 1790s. This was the era of the North West Company, an alignment of copartnerships formed at Montreal in 1779 and reorganized under a new agreement in 1784. It changed in the constituency of its partners from time to time and dominated the trade via Grand Portage as it expanded in its capital and power.

Grand Portage was an emporium for an international trade based on capital and credit. The cycle of this trade was one of three or more years between the placing of orders for goods in London by Montreal merchants and the return of profits from sales in the markets of England. The business was potentially big — but slow. Orders sent from Montreal in the fall were filled and the goods dispatched from England the next spring. Then came the laborious task of making up packs at Montreal (of ninety pounds each) before they were sent, after the following winter, to the post on Lake Superior. Here in the summer, after repacking, the goods were taken up by traders who went off to the interior for a year of trading. Then furs were brought to Grand Portage, shipped on to Montreal and to London, where, after further delays, they were marketed. No wonder that such procedures led first to combinations and then to a kind of organized monopoly, fashioned by businessmen, not, as with the French, by governmental assignment.

How rapidly the Grand Portage post was built up by the British after beginnings in the 1760s is not clear, but its trade in 1778 was measured at 40,000 pounds sterling, and 500 persons took part in it. By that time there were buildings enclosed in a stockade. A small military fort was erected to accommodate a few British troops (a dozen soldiers) sent out for protection — the only military operation during the American Revolution that touched Minnesota soil. By the 1790s the stockaded (and bastioned) post, nestling near the bay and in the lea of a high hill called Mount Rose, had sixteen buildings, including a great mess hall where a hundred men could foregather for meals, storerooms, and houses for partners and clerks.

Outside the enclosure was a canoe yard where each year as many as seventy "north canoes" were built. Wharves for landing were on the lake shore — at some time also an L-shaped dock — and in the gala period the company even had a schooner (of ninety-five tons) to facilitate transportation to and from the Sault. The tents of Indians and of voyageurs, ground for a few cattle, a vegetable garden, and the dark opening of the portage path were features in the Grand Portage scene. At the terminus of the portage, some nine miles away on the Pigeon River, was another post, Fort Charlotte — a travel station for arrivals and departures, where canoes of the northern rivers and lakes were loaded and unloaded.

The West was not untouched by the American Revolution. George Rogers Clark in the Illinois country, with his captures of Kaskaskia and Cahokia in 1778 and his defeat of General Hamilton, menaced the western trade of the British, but throughout the war years they kept their hold on Mackinac and Detroit, essential to the trade from Montreal. Thus, though a new nation was rising in the storm of war, and portentous events were happening in the outer world, Grand Portage, summer after summer from the 1770s through the next two decades, was crowded with people concerned solely with furs and the exploitation of the wilderness.

Life at Grand Portage was especially exciting in July, that busiest of months for the traders. At the lakeside emporium, when organization of the trade gradually took shape, the magnates of the business, "the Gentlemen of the North West Company," met to assign tasks and to consider the problems and policies of an enterprise that had a commercial sweep from Grand Portage to the Rockies and beyond, and eastward to the Montreal center and across the waters to London.

Grand Portage was the Great Lakes base from which Alexander Mackenzie and his voyageurs pushed out to Lake Athabasca (over streams and a hundred portages) and then (in 1789) to the great northwestern river that bears his name and on to the rim of the Arctic Ocean. And from Grand Portage in 1792 he once more set out for the distant West, this time making his way up the Peace River, finally crossing the Rockies and catching a thrilling view of the Pacific Ocean. Not indeed the Northwest Passage that Rogers sought, but a dream come true — an overland expedition across America to the Salt Sea of the West!

Mackenzie was a man of iron will and resolute courage, but he was only one of many in the Grand Portage chronicle whose names and careers are well remembered in Canadian and American history. There are David Thompson, Simon Fraser (Vermonter in origin), the phonetic Peter Pond, the Alexander Henrys, the Jean Baptiste Cadottes, and Dr. John McLoughlin, who knew Grand Portage and Vermilion and Rainy lakes long before he won renown in the pioneer history of Oregon. And there were able traders and organizers who bore such Scottish names as McLeod, McKay, McGillivray, and McDonald, as well as other Mackenzies, and the great Simon McTavish himself, partner of Benjamin and Joseph Frobisher and a founding magnate, with them and others, of the North West Company.

Alexander Henry the Elder continued his activity in the Superior and western region for many years. In 1775, accompanied by the experienced French-Canadian Jean Baptiste Cadotte as a partner, he left Sault Ste. Marie with a fleet of sixteen canoes loaded with goods worth about $15,000 and manned by voyageurs. They paddled around Lake Superior to Grand Portage, then carried their goods across the trail to the Pigeon River, and were off for Lake of the Woods and the Canadian Northwest to trade for furs and hunt with the Indians. Some idea of the wealth of the trade is suggested by the fact that during the winter twenty to thirty Indians arrived at the white men's camp every day bringing in packs of skins and furs. From a single group Henry and Cadotte bartered for "twelve thousand beaver skins, besides large numbers of otter and marten."

Cadotte's son, also Jean Baptiste, voyageur and trader like his father, made a daring expedition into the Minnesota Sioux country in 1792, with a party of sixty men, including his brother Michel. They ascended the St. Louis River and made their way by stream and portage to Sandy Lake and the Mississippi, built a winter camp in the interior, and the next spring reached the Red River. They then went north to the border waters and traveled east to Grand Portage. Cadotte urged the North West Company to develop trade with the Sioux by building new trading posts, and soon several such establishments were set up, based on one built in 1793 at Fond du Lac, not far from the site of the later city of Duluth, by Jean Baptiste Perrault, a French-Canadian who had traded in the region for several years.

In developing the trade with Chippewa, Sioux, and other Indians, the North West Company planted many trading posts at strategic spots on Minnesota rivers and lakes and in areas far to the west and northwest of Minnesota. There were such posts at Vermilion, Sandy, Leech, Cass, Red, and Rainy lakes, and on the St. Croix and other rivers — and in fact at a score of other Minnesota places. Some were large and substantial, such as that at Sandy Lake, others more modest. Usually the buildings erected — storehouse, shop, powder magazine, houses for the clerk in charge and for the men — were given the protection of a stockade. Ordinarily the flag-decked posts were called "forts," as in fact they were,

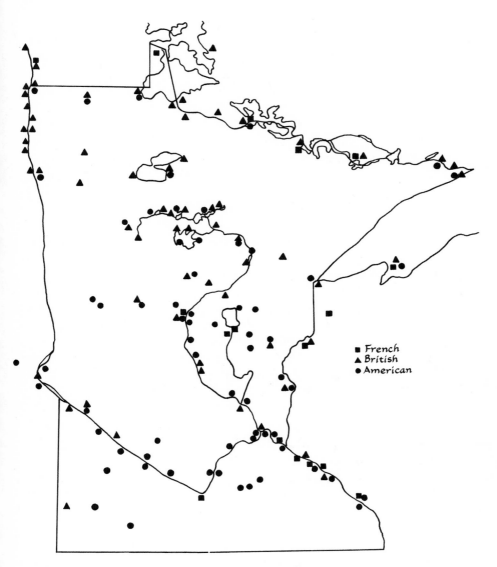

Trading posts under three flags, French, British, and American (adapted from a wall map at the Minnesota Historical Society, which was based on Grace Lee Nute's map in *Minnesota History*, December 1930)

serving both as trading centers and as defense against attack, if any, by hostile natives. A survey made some years ago of the fur trade in the Minnesota area for the French, British, and American periods listed more than 130 trading posts, and researches have since brought to light still others. For the British period Grand Portage was central to the trade of the border waters and beyond, but it was only one of many business stations exploiting the riches of woods and waters for the world of fashion.

The cartography of the Northwest advanced as trade intensified, for not a few traders were skillful at map-making. In 1797 at Grand Portage Mackenzie — by then Sir Alexander — and other officials appointed David Thompson as surveyor and astronomer for the North West Company.

No choice could have been happier, for Thompson was a self-taught master of sextant, compass, and telescope. He was a meticulous recorder of travels and a map maker extraordinary. As a boy he had been apprenticed from England to the Hudson's Bay Company, which he served for thirteen or fourteen years, learning trading techniques and perfecting his knowledge of instruments and skill as an observer in uncharted regions. Indians nicknamed him the "Star Man" before he offered his services to the rival of the Hudson's Bay Company; and he was quickly commissioned to join a brigade of traders heading west in August 1797. His assignment was to survey the forty-ninth parallel and a route to the headwaters of the Missouri, and also to map the trading posts of the North West Company. He journeyed to Lake of the Woods, northwest to Lake Winnipeg, then southwest across the Dakota plains to the Mandan villages on the Missouri. He faced peril from storm and Sioux attack with self-reliance and courage. He recorded carefully the unusual level of culture of the Mandan community and then trekked eastward, passing through northern Minnesota. He came close to discovering the source of the Mississippi, reached Lake Superior at the mouth of the St. Louis, followed the south shore of the lake to the Sault, and journeyed back to Grand Portage along the north shore. When he arrived at its friendly harbor, he had been gone ten months and had surveyed four thousand miles of wilderness. He made detailed notes of his travels then as later when, in 1809, he crossed the Rockies and went down the Columbia to the sea. After the War of 1812 he helped to mark out the boundary between the United States and Canada. He lived to be a very old man, his lifework culminating in a map of the West on such a prodigious scale that he could not get it published. But his achievements won for him a recognized place in the history of the two neighboring countries as a "land geographer."

Another engaging figure of Grand Portage and the West is Alexander Henry the Younger, a nephew of the Alexander Henry whose exploits touch the earlier history of the region. The fame of the younger Henry rests both on his adventures and on one of the most vivid and detailed diaries ever kept in the western country. In 1800, after crossing the portage, he started with a fleet of canoes for the Red River Valley, where he had already spent a year and was to devote eight more seasons trading for the North West Company. Into his canoes were packed sugar, flour, tobacco, knives, tools, guns, powder, cloth, looking glasses — and firewater (ten kegs of liquor in each canoe). In the Red River country Henry first built a post at the junction of the Park and the Red rivers, then moved to the mouth of the Pembina. Here he built a stockade enclosing a few buildings and raised a flagpole seventy-five feet high. He was ready for business, and business developed. One year he sent back to Grand Portage furs and pelts in these numbers: 1621 beavers, 125 black bears, 49 brown bears, 4 grizzly bears, 862 wolves, 509 foxes, 152 raccoons, 322 fishers, 214 otters, 1456 martens, 507 minks, 45 wolverines, 469 moose, and 12,470 muskrats.

Henry's diary tells of buffalo hunts, prairie fires, a journey to the Mandans and Cheyennes, and annual returns to Grand Portage. He also records the degrading effects of liquor on the natives, "the root of all evil," as he wrote, "in the North West" — but still he dispensed it in appalling quantities. Henry traveled by canoe, cart, dog sled, and horseback in his many journeys. Toward the end of his career he went out to Astoria, famed trading post on the Columbia River. There in 1814 he was drowned, along with Donald McTavish and a group of voyageurs when their boat capsized. Fortunately his diary was not lost in the swirling waters of the Columbia.

In a typical summer in the 1780s and 1790s Grand Portage, especially in July, was swarming with people — as many as a thousand white men, and hundreds of Indian braves, squaws, children — and dogs. Noise, excitement, feasting, fun, news and gossip were crammed into the precious days when hard-bitten men from lonely winter posts met friends from other wilderness places and also traders and voyageurs newly arrived from Montreal.

There was much hard work to do. The trade goods brought in great canoes from the East had to be repacked in accordance with varying needs at the interior posts, and the skins and furs had to be sorted and baled for shipment east. Many kinds of furs came to Grand Portage, as Alexander Henry's list for one season illustrates, but prime beaver pelts were the very basis of the trade — pelts from which felt could be made and then turned into the great (and expensive) beaver hats that were immensely popular in the European world.

The trade had an even greater international sweep than that from wilderness posts to London by way of Montreal. Great fur auctions were held every year in London and also in Germany, at Leipzig, with fur buyers from far and near. There are records of furs out of the north country bought by Russians, transported across Siberia, and marketed in Canton and other Chinese cities. The beaver not only supplied the demands of fashion but, for special reasons, contributed hugely to the high success of the North West Company. These reasons were that the company exploited northern areas which produced the finest pelts and it pushed relentlessly its search for new territory that had not been raided by other ruthless fur hunters. With large capital and assured credit, the company had the resources for big business. It also received from England trade goods, including blankets, of superior quality. The full western trade of the British involved furs valued annually at considerably more than a million dollars.

Beavers were so highly prized, it may be noted incidentally, that the social organization of the North West Company magnates in Montreal was called "The Beaver Club." It was founded in 1785 and its membership was restricted to men who had wintered in the north country.

Grand Portage in summer dress, at the heyday of the trade, was colorful. Here assembled many of the partners, the overlords of the trade; clerks from distant posts; interpreters and guides; and the dashing French-Canadian voyageurs. These French-speaking voyageurs, celebrated in western lore, were the canoemen of lakes and rivers, tough, hardy, gay, insouciant, skilled in wilderness travel. They were basic contributors to the success of the trade. There were two classes, the "pork eaters" (*mangeurs de lard*) and the "winterers" (*hivernants*). The pork eaters were the canoemen of the Great Lakes, voyageurs who had not been toughened and experienced by life in the interior but who nonetheless were splendid canoemen capable of paddling the long way out from Montreal and back. They also helped to carry the ninety-pound packs of traders' goods across the portage to Fort Charlotte, not infrequently loading two or even more at a time on their backs. Their customary food was hominy boiled in pork fat. The winterers, or "Nor'westers" (as they were called if their careers had taken them over the Height of Land beyond Superior), were men of the interior, experienced in every kind of travel from canoe to dog sled, workers in the trade under the clerks through the long winters, adventurers ready to face any hazard.

The voyageur was as colorful in dress as he was individual in speech and custom. He wore a bright capote, brilliant in blue, and often a red cap. He had a braided sash, leggings and deerskin moccasins, and, if he had achieved the proud status of a "Nor'wester," a plume. He was gay, tough, voluble, and a great smoker (equipped with clay pipe and a beaded pouch). He had strength and endurance for strenuous portages, long stints of paddling, and life in the open amid every condition of weather. The historian of the voyageurs quotes one French-Canadian who for twenty-four years had been a canoeman, could sing fifty songs, had saved ten lives, and had twelve wives. To him no life was "so happy as a voyageur's life."

Not the least interesting aspect of the life of the voyageurs who wintered in wilderness posts was their food supply. One of the major items was pemmican. This remarkable food, made of pounded buffalo meat, was vital to survival through the long winter months. It was so important, in fact, that its production and distribution became an organized and big business. Forts far out in the buffalo country served as manufacturing centers, and other posts, including Grand Portage, were used as distributing places. Some posts stored supplies of pemmican in hundreds of packs of the customary size.

At Grand Portage the partners, or *bourgeois*, and clerks (*commis*) in charge of distant posts were housed within the stockade and ate their meals in the great dining hall. The voyageurs were outside the enclosure. The pork eaters usually slept under their overturned canoes and the winterers in tents. The latter were given rations of meat and bread and wine instead of the hominy of the pork eaters.

Sometimes long-protracted balls were held in the big mess room inside the palisades, to which the voyageurs might be invited — violins, flutes, and bagpipes furnishing the music for squares and reels, Indian girls and women the dancing partners. But perhaps the most dramatic moments were those when great Montreal canoes (the *canots du maître*), thirty-five feet to forty feet long, propelled by fourteen paddles, came sweeping in brigades into the harbor from the curving Point de Chapeau, red-bladed paddles flashing in rhythm with spirited voyageur songs, the men dressed in their very best finery. Then came the graceful landing, shouts of welcome, and quick interchange of news from the faraway world and from forts deep in the wilderness. The "north canoe" (*canot nord*) was smaller than the craft from Montreal, perhaps twenty-five feet in length, yet it could carry some three thousand pounds of baggage in addition to its crew, usually eight men.

These men out of French Canada were people who worked, played, and laughed, and they were also singing men. Their songs were many, but their great favorite was "A la claire fontaine," a chanson of a love lost all for an undelivered bunch of roses. Many of the songs were drawn from the folk melodies and verse of the valley of the Loire, brought to Canada by the French in the seventeenth century. Not a few were plaintive, but many were vigorous and rollicking. One of these was "En roulant ma boule," "A-rolling my ball," which runs on for a dozen or more stanzas about ponds, three bonnie ducks, and a prince "on hunting bound" who carried a gun "with silver crown'd."

The voyageur songs were adapted to singing in rhythm with the strokes of paddles on lakes and rivers. They were also used on trudges across winter trails behind dog sleds or in camps or sheltered posts. Not many songs seem to have been created out of the wilderness experience. The voyageurs loved ballads of nightingales, cavaliers, springtime, rosebuds, fair ladies, and gallant captains. A collection of voyageur songs made in the early 1800s in the far north by a North West Company clerk who played the fiddle has disappeared. It is believed that the songs he collected were destroyed because many of them were offensive to good taste, even obscene. One wonders if they were inventions, possibly parodies, produced by the voyageurs themselves, who were not precisely averse to indecorous ways.

The expanding trade of the North West Company in the 1790s was not without competition. To what extent independent traders or other partnerships were active is not entirely clear, but in 1791 the British abandoned the traditional system of governmental licenses for traders and trade goods sent from Montreal to the interior. This action encouraged greater freedom for the fur trade. Not a few traders and groups of traders, working out from Mackinac, explored the Wisconsin and Upper Mississippi trade. For instance, Robert Dickson, Scottish in background and a member of the elite Beaver Club of Montreal, formed a partnership, including French traders, that operated northward on the Mississippi from, Prairie du Chien, with posts on the Rum River, at Sauk Rapids, at the mouth of the Minnesota, and even as far north as Leech Lake, in the 1800s. This was British trade carried on with both Sioux and Chippewa. And a dissenting group of traders, about 1797–98, formed the competing XY Company, which also built a post at Grand Portage and one on the Pigeon River, but after much rivalry was absorbed by the North West Company, some seven years later.

More serious was the developing competition of the Hudson's Bay Company which had found it impossible to sustain its old policy of drawing the Indians and their furs up to the posts on or near the Bay. Even before the 1790s the older company was building posts toward the south, some, but not many, in or close to the Minnesota country. This competition would flare into bloodshed and veritable war after the Earl of Selkirk in 1811 obtained a vast grant of land from the Hudson's Bay Company for a colonization plan that threatened the fur domain of the North West Company.

Meanwhile, however, the western headquarters of the company were removed from Grand Portage to Fort William, about 1804. Jay's Treaty in 1794 had specified that the British were to give up their western posts on American territory in 1796, and as a result many important ones were relinquished, including Detroit, Oswego, Mackinac, and Green Bay. Although the agreement was not observed in the Minnesota country, the treaty was a sign of transition that the North West Company took under careful consideration. A change, if not imminent, was inevitable. The treaty did indeed permit foreign traders to do business on American territory, but this did not mean British forts and posts flying the Union Jack.

The removal from Grand Portage to Fort William was more than a precaution spurred by Anglo-American diplomacy. It developed in part from a British rediscovery of the Kaministikwia water route to Dog Lake and the international channel that traders had approached by way of the Pigeon River. This rediscovery of a way familiar to the French meant an all-British approach to the boundary waters. The removal was also, in some sense, an anticipation of American legal action that actually did not come until after the War of 1812 — the rescinding in 1816 by the American Congress of the privilege agreed upon in Jay's Treaty. No one yet knew, when the company was planning its move north, precisely where the international boundary line would be drawn, but the partners were clear that a new depot was called for. In fact Simon McTavish clearly saw the advantages of Fort William over Grand Portage as early as 1799, when he was apprised of the Kaministikwia route by its rediscoverer, Roderick McKenzie.

Perhaps the definitive mark of transition in the northern hinterland was the merging of the North West Company into the Hudson's Bay in 1821 — two years after the American flag was raised over a military fort at the confluence of the Mississippi and Minnesota rivers. The saga of Grand Portage and the British regime had run its course through more than five decades, a trading prelude to the American regime. The record is one of trading posts, the collecting and marketing of furs in a wide-ranging business, diplomatic maneuvers, a succession of forceful personalities of British (to a great degree Scottish), French, and Yankee backgrounds, and the lives and services of the voyageurs, who enlivened the period with their vivacity and color. The British regime in Minnesota forms an interlude between the French and the American regimes. Louise Phelps Kellogg has said of the British in Wisconsin that they "developed no institutions, assumed no governmental functions, built up no settlements." Theirs was certainly a "wilderness regime" devoted to the fur business. It must fairly be added that their business was one of extraordinary efficiency in organization and method. The British contributed to the expansion of geographical knowledge of Minnesota and the West, leaving a rich legacy of maps, diaries, narratives, and other records.

Grand Portage subsided into a quiet little village of Indians and a few whites, including in later times fishermen and missionaries. The buildings and palisades of the once flourishing emporium crumbled and disappeared, although even today the portage trail on which thousands of feet trudged in the eighteenth century is still clearly marked. The island emerald shines at the outer edge of the harbor; and a few decades ago the L-shaped dock, the palisades, and the central building of the old trading post were reconstructed. In 1958 Grand Portage was accorded historical recognition by Congress as a national monument, and a new fur-trade museum is being planned for the old center.

A modern and dramatic sequel to the story is the Underwater Research Program of the Minnesota Historical Society. This institution has sent skin-divers to certain spots in the north country — on the water trail of the voyageurs — where, because of dangerous rapids, canoes laden with trade goods were suspected of having capsized in early days. The idea resulted in the recovery in 1960, on Saganaga Lake, of a nest of seventeen copper and brass kettles, and in 1961, on the Basswood River, of thirty-five trade axes and twenty-four spears and chisels, along with buttons, beads, musket balls, knives, and even a small piece of Indian face paint. The discoveries, made after studies of journals and other records of early traders and travelers, are of interest intrinsically and as evidence of the perils faced by men on the turbulent streams of the interior in the gala period of the wilderness trade. The voyageurs were expert canoemen, but now and then they struck rocks as they dared dangerous waters and, with their canoes broken, their cargoes went to the bottom. Now, by methods of which they never dreamed, their lost goods are being recovered as artifacts of a vanished era, that of the 1780s or 1790s, when Grand Portage was the capital of an industrial western empire.

Fort Snelling about 1851, from an oil by E. K. Thomas

The Americans Build Fort Snelling

THE transfer of the North West Company's emporium from Grand Portage to Fort William came none too soon. National and international movements early in the nineteenth century led to American control of the Minnesota country. That control meant that the British would have to move north to be under their own flag, and such a change coincided with their own fur-trade interests.

One major influence on events was the organization of the American fur trade under John Jacob Astor. He was a native of the Duchy of Baden who emigrated to America in 1783 at the age of twenty after he had learned of the treaty of peace establishing the independence of the United States. As a shopkeeper and trader in New York, Astor took a lively interest in furs. He ventured into the China trade, buying North West Company furs that he imported from London before reshipping them to far-off China. After Jay's Treaty, which legalized direct commerce between Canada and the United States, he made furs his overweening interest.

By the early 1800s this astute and energetic merchant was wealthy. The Louisiana Purchase stirred his interest in the fur riches of the Far West and the further development of Oriental commerce. The plans and activities of John Jacob Astor may seem remote from Minnesota, but his American Fur Company, which was chartered in New York in 1808, was destined to exploit the Minnesota fur region. His earlier fur interests encountered difficulties that came to a head in the War of 1812 and the collapse of Astoria, the trading post he had established at the mouth of the Columbia River. But the reverses he suffered proved only a prologue to his invasion of the Middle West. And this enterprise he turned the more to his advantage because he secured the passage of the American law of 1816 which excluded aliens from the fur trade on American territory (except as employees or by special executive authorization).

American interest in the fur trade and related Indian affairs was not confined to private business enterprise. Concurrently with the rise of Astor's fur empire, the United States government was conducting its "factory system," a chain of government fur-trading posts or stores. With a background of colonial precedent, it was established in 1795 on the recommendation of President Washington and continued until 1822, when, under bitter attack by Astor and his company, it was swept away by congressional action. Government-owned fur establishments, each under a "factor," functioned at various places at different times, including such centers as Prairie du Chien, Green Bay, Mackinac, and Detroit. The governmental motive was not profits, but a check on the incursion of foreign traders, mainly English and Spanish, the forwarding of peaceful Indian relations, the bolstering of western military policy, and the sheltering of the natives from impositions by private fur traders. Little success was achieved and opposition was widespread, but the system was an assertion of official American concern over problems centering in the fur trade.

Meanwhile political changes destined to have far-reaching consequences were taking place. Thomas Jefferson, acting through his diplomatic emissaries Robert R. Livingston and James Monroe, bought nearly half a continent from Napoleon in 1803, only three years after Spain's retrocession of Louisiana to France under the secret treaty of San Ildefonso. Dreamer, philosopher, and democrat turned imperialist, President Jefferson made a tremendous advance toward the goal of a United States extending from ocean to ocean. In due time transfers of the vast lands of Louisiana were made to the United States. Thus that portion of Minnesota lying west of the Mississippi was officially made American territory by a ceremonial transfer in St. Louis in 1804. The boundary at the north, however, had not yet been defined by diplomatic agreement; and Minnesota was still, for all practical purposes, the fur domain of the North West Company.

Jefferson was not content with acquiring title for the United States to the expanse of lands from the Mississippi to the Rockies, great as that achievement was. Even in the 1780s and 1790s his agile mind and imagination had been excited by the idea of having the farther West explored. Indeed, some months before the Louisiana Purchase, he had transmitted to Congress a plan for a transcontinental expedition and had even taken steps to secure from the French the necessary passports for an exploring party.

After the treaty of cession (April 30, 1803), the road was cleared for an expedition that needed no passports. This was the exploring thrust of Meriwether Lewis and William Clark, under instructions from Jefferson — up the Missouri, west to the Columbia and to the Pacific Ocean, the American counterpart to Mackenzie's pioneer achievement of the 1790s. The start was made from old St. Louis in May 1804. Eighteen months later, on November 7, 1805, the explorers reached the shores of the western sea, the goal of the early French trail blazers. On February 19, 1806, President Jefferson was able to announce to the world the news of the successful outcome of this tortuous and hazardous expedition. Its details do not form a part of the Minnesota saga, but it is interesting to know that on the autumn day of 1805 when Lewis caught his first view of the Pacific, another exploring expedition was in the wilderness of Minnesota, tasting the flavor of an early northern winter. This expedition was led by an army officer, Lieutenant Zebulon Montgomery Pike.

Lieutenant Pike received his orders, not from the President, but from General James Wilkinson, then stationed at St. Louis, commander of western forces and governor of Louisiana. Jefferson's initiation of the Lewis and Clark expedition and his interest in the western lands were, of course, a part of the background of the Pike expedition, but it was made without the President's explicit authorization. He was later informed about it and gave it his "approbation."

Some historians have questioned the underlying motives of Wilkinson, perhaps in part because his reputation is sullied by intrigues and association with Aaron Burr, but the instructions he gave Pike were comprehensive and well conceived, without any trace of intrigue. Pike was to go up the Mississippi to its source if possible. He was to conciliate the Indians and "attach them to the United States." He was instructed to learn about their population and lands as well as the quantity and kinds of skins they bartered and the people with whom they traded. He was told to confer with the natives about building military posts and "trading houses" as part of the "factory system" at certain critical points, which included the Falls of St. Anthony and the mouth of the Minnesota River. And he was to keep a diary recording his observations. That the young officer (he was twenty-six) observed his instructions faithfully, including the keeping of a diary, adds to the historical significance of this first American military expedition into the Minnesota country.

The expedition was unpretentious. The officer, whose fame is recorded in the naming of Pike's Peak, and who died a hero's death as a brigadier general in the War of 1812, was only a subaltern when, on August 9, 1805, he started north from St. Louis in a seventy-foot keelboat. With him were a sergeant, two corporals, and seventeen private soldiers. In his later report, dedicated to the President, he said that he himself performed the duties of astronomer, surveyor, commanding officer, clerk, spy, guide, and hunter, and that every evening, by firelight, he recorded the events of the day. He was as hard-working as he was versatile.

Exchanging the keelboat for two bateaux near Prairie du Chien (a village then of five to six hundred white people), Pike went up river for seventeen days to the mouth of the Minnesota River. There he encamped (September 21) on Pike Island and raised the Stars and Stripes (probably for the first time on Minnesota soil). He achieved one of the major objectives of the expedition by holding a council with the Sioux on the 23rd. In an eloquent speech he urged them to keep the peace with their traditional enemies, the Chippewa. He asked them to abandon their trade with the British; promised government trading "factories"; and secured the cession by the Sioux (under Chief Little Crow, grandfather of the Little Crow who led the Sioux revolt in 1862) of two tracts of land for American military posts. One was at the mouth of the St. Croix; the other along the Mississippi from below the mouth of the Minnesota to above the Falls of St. Anthony, nine miles on each side of the river. This "treaty," duly signed (and in 1808 ratified by the United States Senate), had no immediate consequences, but it was important, fourteen years later, in the fixing of the site of Fort Snelling, the first military post established in Minnesota. Ceremonies were concluded with gifts and apportionments of rum, plus the promise of $2000 or its equivalent in merchandise.

88

The first American military expedition through the Minnesota country, in 1805, under the command of Lt. Zebulon Montgomery Pike

Much of Pike's mission had been accomplished, but he still faced the problems of dealing with British trading posts on American soil and searching for the source of the great river. He therefore started north, soon encountered snow and cold, built a stockaded camp in the interior (four miles from the present city of Little Falls); and then, with sleds and a pirogue, pushed north with his men. He celebrated Christmas near present Brainerd (issuing extra meat, flour, rum, and tobacco to each man), and finally got to the British trading posts at Sandy and Leech lakes. Though the move of the North West Company to Fort William had just about synchronized with the American acquisition of Louisiana territory, the company had continued to operate its Minnesota posts.

At Sandy and Leech lakes, Pike and his cold and tired soldiers were given a warmly cordial reception by the North West Company officials (and treated to roast beaver and boiled moose head). In order to symbolize American sovereignty, Pike had his men shoot down the British flag flying above the post at Leech Lake and raise the American flag. He addressed a formal letter to Hugh McGillis, the proprietor of the post, sternly setting forth the American position and reminding the British of their legal obligation to pay duty on trade goods used in their business.

To this McGillis, with suave courtesy, replied, promising compliance with Pike's demands and assuring him of esteem and regard.

Probably the British flag went up again soon after the American "army" departed, but Pike had done what he could to enforce American authority. He termed Leech Lake the "main source of the Mississippi," though he also saw Cass Lake, which he called the "upper source." Later exploration designated Lake Itasca as the source, but Pike was not far away from that spot. So he left Minnesota, but not until he had spoken in council with the Chippewa and admonished them, as he had the Sioux, to maintain peace with their enemies, and also told them that they must return their British medals and flags. By April 30, 1806, he was back at St. Louis after nearly a nine months' journey of five thousand miles or more.

The most significant result of Pike's expedition was the land agreement with the Sioux. The time was not yet ripe for the building of a fort or indeed for American management of the fur trade. The British managed their posts and neglected to pay duties on their goods; and the Indians went on with their feuds and scalping raids. The Minnesota situation remained much as it had been before the little "army" arrived. Pike's diary and observations were published in 1810 and in due time appeared in French, Dutch, and German translations — another contribution to the world's store of firsthand knowledge of the American West.

The picture of the Minnesota country from Pike's visit to the close of the War of 1812 is shadowy and confused. The fur trade was carried forward, but it was in a stage of uncertainty and change. British trade via Prairie du Chien employed for some years the Michilimackinac Company in joint agreement with the North West Company. Under the arrangement, the North West Company prevailed north of established lines through Wisconsin and Minnesota, the Michilimackinac Company south. In 1811, three years after Astor formed the American Fur Company, he bought out, in part, the Michilimackinac Company, working with British merchants in joint ownership of the South West Company, which succeeded to the boundary arrangement. This was a preliminary move by Astor looking toward a monopoly of the Great Lakes and Upper Mississippi trade, but it ran afoul of the Non-Intercourse Act and the War of 1812. By and large, the North West Company continued its domination of the Minnesota trade until after the War of 1812. Throughout the earlier 1800s, Robert Dickson, working with the South West Company, and other fur traders, as has been noted, established posts at various points in Minnesota and operated them until the disruption of the War of 1812. Though the governmental "factory system" reached as near Minnesota as Prairie du Chien, the factories envisaged for Minnesota by Pike never became a reality.

The War of 1812 on its left flank was one of defense by American forces that were swept off their feet in the early stages of the conflict. Throughout the war years, the British maintained their control of the Northwest. Dickson, who smuggled $50,000 worth of trade goods into the West by the Mackinac route in 1811, was a leader in recruiting Indian warriors to fight on the British side. His Indian troops were among the forces that closed in on Mackinac in 1812 and took it without a blow, catching by surprise an American commander who had not yet learned that Britain and the United States were at war. This capture led to the bloody massacre at Fort Dearborn and in turn to General Hull's surrender of Detroit, and it proved a decisive factor in keeping the western natives allied to the English. Dickson continued vigorous work as the British agent for the Indians of the Northwest. Wabasha, hereditary Sioux chief in Minnesota, was quick to join forces with the British. To him the Americans were a cloud "approaching over the heads" of his people, and his tribal lands, he believed, were in peril. Another Minnesotan who aided Dickson in the War of 1812 was Joseph Renville, son of a French father and a Sioux mother, a noted guide and interpreter who had earlier served Lieutenant Pike. He was commissioned as a captain in the British Army and took part in the siege of Fort Meigs (on the Maumee River in Ohio) in 1813.

Americans, attempting to regain strength in the West, tried to retake the western posts, and Prairie du Chien was in fact briefly occupied in 1814. Fort Shelby was built there, but the British and their Indian allies soon recaptured that strategic center. This event, and the failure of American forces to retake Mackinac, seemed to ensure continuing British control of the Northwest. But the end came with the Treaty of Ghent, signed December 24, 1814, and ratified February 17, 1815; this was followed by British withdrawal from the American western posts.

The success of the British forces in holding the Upper Mississippi country to the war's end had encouraged some British hopes that in the peace settlement new boundary arrangements would be made through which a neutral Indian domain could be created. Allied to these hopes was the idea that the British would be free to continue their trade via Mackinac in regions that were American by the Treaty of 1783. Once again, however, forces far removed from the fur regions were decisive.

The British negotiators at Ghent wanted peace. England was still in the shadow of the Napoleonic wars, to which its great energies had been devoted. Certain proposed conditions presented by the British diplomats at the outset of negotiations were withdrawn when they threatened the success of the Anglo-American conference. The treaty as agreed upon did not disturb the retention by the United States of its sovereignty over the American Indian tribes and their territory. The noted Wisconsin historian Louise Phelps Kellogg writes that the treaty "forever laid at rest the plan for a neutral Indian state," and she adds that it "broke the monopoly of the British traders" in the Wisconsin-Minnesota area. The path was opened for military occupation of the Minnesota frontier and American exploitation of its resources.

The drive for profits from the fur trade was sharp and bitter wherever competition reared its head. This was illustrated by a frontier war, not of Britons versus Americans, but of British against British. While the War of 1812 was going on, the rivalry of the North West Company with the Hudson's Bay Company erupted in the Red River region. This was a prelude to the disappearance of the North West Company and the founding of Manitoba, and its repercussions were of historical importance to Minnesota. As the richest sources of furs moved northwestward, the North West Company, working out from Montreal and from its Fort William emporium, faced increasing difficulties in transportation and travel, while the Hudson's Bay Company, operating south and southwestward from the Bay, had certain advantages. The rivalry deepened in 1811 when the Scottish Earl of Selkirk, impelled not by motives of trade but by philanthropy, secured from the Hudson's Bay Company (in which he had a controlling interest) a grant of millions of acres of land in the West — "Assiniboia," in what became Manitoba but also was assumed to include American territory in Minnesota and Dakota (since the international boundary south and west of Lake of the Woods had not yet been defined). Selkirk had in mind an agricultural colony for evicted Scottish crofters and in fact had already experimented with the idea on Prince Edward Island and in Upper Canada. In the period 1811–13 he brought out to the West his first contingents of colonists, who settled around the junction of the Red and Assiniboine rivers. This move infuriated the magnates of the North West Company, to whom it meant an invasion by farmers of the regions their traders had to cross to the rich fur lands of the West, a menace to their vital supplies of pemmican for the trade, perhaps the ruin of their business.

The North West Company partners determined to remove or destroy the colony by one means or another, drew bands of French-Indian half-breeds (métis) to their aid, made life miserable for the settlers, forcing them to move east or, for a time, to take refuge far to the north. After the colony had been re-established, with additional recruits, the Montreal merchants sanctioned what in effect was a war — an invasion by a force of métis under a Scot-Indian trader. A bloody massacre took place in 1816 — the Massacre of Seven Oaks — in which the governor of the colony and more than a score of his men were killed. The earl then came to the rescue with a force of soldiers, captured Fort William, and brought in additional settlers to Manitoba, including Germans and Swiss, some of whom in due time established themselves at Pembina to the south.

Selkirk did everything in his power to rebuild the colony, but he suffered bitter reverses in court actions brought by the North West Company, and in 1820, broken in health by his many troubles, he died. While he lived, he would not countenance any move toward conciliation or union with the North West Company, but after his death action came quickly. The North West Company had had its day, and the Hudson's Bay Company took over its great rival in 1821. The importance of these events lies less in the fur-trade rivalry itself than in the emergence of the great Canadian settlement to the north which became the province of Manitoba, neighbor and friend of Minnesota through all later decades. Yet other results were the coming of some of the Selkirk settlers as pioneers to Minnesota and the spur that these events of the north country gave to American defense and control of its own wilderness lands.

The uncertainties with respect to the southern limits of Selkirk's "Assiniboia" and the northern boundary of Minnesota West were removed during the final years of Selkirk's activities. Much had been learned about the geography of the country west of Lake Superior in the French and British periods. But when diplomats fashioned the Treaty of 1783, at the end of the American Revolution, no one knew precisely where the Mississippi River took its rise. Unquestionably, the British had historical claims to vast areas in the north, but there was uncertainty as to the northern limits of Louisiana, ceded to Spain in 1762, and as to the southern limits of British sovereignty. The Treaty of 1783 provided that the boundary to the west of Lake Superior should follow the line of water communication to the Lake of the Woods, run through that lake to its northwestern point, and then proceed due west to the Mississippi. That one could go due west from Lake of the Woods and across the continent without touching the Mississippi was wisdom after the diplomatic event. Americans were eager to secure precise knowledge, however. A provision in Jay's Treaty, nearly a decade before the Louisiana Purchase, called for a survey of the Upper Mississippi to its source. This provision was not carried into effect.

In Jefferson's day efforts were made to effect a settlement of the northern boundary, and Americans knew then that the Treaty of 1783 had committed a geographical blunder. As early as 1802 James Madison, then secretary of state, calling for a reopening of the boundary discussions, pointed out that it was impossible to intersect the Mississippi by a line drawn due west from Lake of the Woods. After the Louisiana Purchase the question became even more plainly one of national interest (and of very special interest for the Minnesota future).

Following the War of 1812 a boundary commission tackled the conflicting British and American claims in the area from Lake Superior to the Lake of the Woods, but no change was made in the Treaty of Ghent with respect to the boundary beyond the Lake of the Woods. In 1818, however, diplomats settled this western line, adopting the forty-ninth parallel as the boundary as far west as the Rockies. Since no line could be run straight west of Lake of the Woods to the Mississippi, the Convention of 1818 hit upon a simple solution (one that had been discussed in early negotiations), namely, to run a line due south from the northwest point of Lake of the Woods to the forty-ninth parallel. This action was decisive. Apart from the important matter of fixing the long line westward, the agreement of 1818 gave to the United States (and to the coming state of Minnesota) that curious projection of land known as the Northwest Angle — American territory separated from the rest of the land area of the United States by Buffalo Bay, a southwestern arm of the Lake of the Woods.

Early governmental jurisidictions in the Minnesota area before military occupation and pioneer settlement were largely nominal. Up to 1784 the

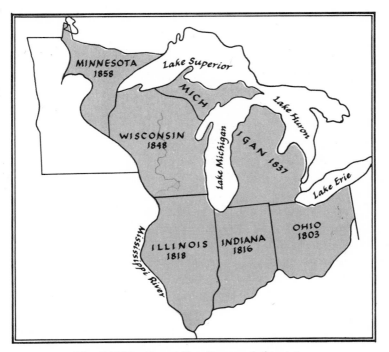

The Old Northwest Territory and the states
successively carved out

land claims of Virginia extended to Minnesota east of the Mississippi. Then for three years Minnesota East was unorganized, but in 1787 it was made a part of the Northwest Territory. Thus Minnesota shares in the heritage of the Northwest Ordinance, the Magna Carta of the West. In the state's background is the pledge by the nation of states dedicated to the "fundamental principles of civil and religious liberty." The state inherits guarantees of freedom of religious worship, jury trial, common law, habeas corpus, due process; the interdiction of slavery or involuntary servitude (save as punishment for crime); and the pledge of encouragement of schools and education through all time.

Minnesota is one of six great states carved out of the Northwest Territory: Ohio (1803), Indiana (1816), Illinois (1818), Michigan (1837), Wisconsin (1848), and Minnesota (1858). Officially Minnesota East was part of Indiana Territory from 1800 to 1809, of Illinois Territory from 1809 to 1818, and of Michigan Territory from 1818 to 1836. Min-

95

nesota west of the Mississippi was part of Louisiana (District and Territory) from 1803 to 1812 and of Missouri Territory from 1812 to 1821, after which, for thirteen years, it was "unorganized."

The establishment in 1819 of Fort Snelling (first called Fort St. Anthony) at the junction of the Mississippi and Minnesota rivers marks a significant historical turning point. In a sense it is the beginning of the modern, American period of Minnesota.

Interweaving forces explain the emergence of this frontier fort toward the end of the second decade of the nineteenth century. Among them were the termination of the War of 1812 and the exploitation of the fur trade by Americans. National interest had been alerted to the need of frontier protection from external hazards and from hostile Indian action; and this interest involved also the desirability of promoting peace among the Indian tribes. Spurred by the Louisiana Purchase and Jefferson's policies, Americans wanted to extend their knowledge of the relatively unknown lands of the West; and there was a growing awareness of the likelihood of westward expansion in the years ahead — the coming "tread of pioneers." The past demonstrated that treaties of themselves, especially if boundaries were ill defined, could not extend American authority into the wilderness. Only occupation could turn authority into actuality.

Frontier defense developed as a significant part of national policy after the War of 1812. In the formation of that policy American fur-trading interests undoubtedly played a role. They did so especially through the machinations of the American Fur Company and the skill of the business genius at its head. Astor's will prevailed, as has been noted, in the law of 1816 which in effect restricted the fur trade on American territory to American ownership and control. Only a year later the fur magnate bought out the remaining British interest in the old South West Company and thenceforth had in his hands the former posts, on the American side, of both the North West and the South West companies. In the reorganization of the American Fur Company he gave attention to the trade of the Middle West, alongside his many other commercial and financial operations. In this same period he used every effort to bring about the dissolution of the "factory system," which meant governmental competition, minus the profit motive, with the privately owned fur trade. Not so well known is the fact that Astor played a part in the movement to accord official military protection to the fur traders. He was informed about the Selkirk war and disturbed by the news of Lord Selkirk's capture of Fort William. He was particularly irked by reports that Selkirk had carried confiscated trade goods into American territory in contravention of American laws. In 1816 Astor appealed to the secretary of state, James Monroe, for the dispatch of an American military expedition to take by force the goods Selkirk was believed to have seized.

Such an expedition was not sent, but the American government, after the War of 1812, embarked upon a broad policy of frontier defense. As early as the summer of 1815 a treaty of peace was negotiated with the lately hostile Sioux Indians, who pledged friendly relations and acceptance of American authority. Mackinac, the same summer, was taken over by American forces. The next summer Prairie du Chien was occupied by American infantry, and a new fort — Fort Crawford — erected. This was no single action unrelated to a wider plan, for the same year — 1816 — saw the emergence of Fort Armstrong at Rock Island and Fort Howard at Green Bay; and also the building of the second Fort Dearborn at Chicago. The larger strategy was aimed at a chain of military posts supplementing to the north and west the forts stretching from Detroit to St. Louis and southward. In 1816 and 1817 Monroe and John C. Calhoun, the latter secretary of war, studied the problem of frontier defense. Calhoun set up a board of officers to "examine the whole line of our frontier" and to recommend appropriate sites in a range from Minnesota to the Missouri country.

Even before Calhoun announced this plan, a military expedition was made from St. Louis, in the summer of 1817, to the Falls of St. Anthony. This was led by Major Stephen H. Long, an experienced topographical engineer who, earlier in his career, had taught mathematics at Dartmouth College. He went north under instructions from the War Department to examine the portages of the Fox and Wisconsin rivers and to ascend the Mississippi to investigate the sites acquired by Lieutenant Pike twelve years earlier and to make recommendations to the department concerning their suitability for military posts. Long duly carried out his assignment. He spent seventy-six days going up the Mississippi in a six-oared skiff, examined the earlier sites, and at the mouth of the Minnesota chose a "high point of land, elevated about one hundred and twenty feet above the water, and fronting immediately on the Mississippi." This, he believed, was the place best suited for a "military work of considerable magnitude," a choice confirmed by Calhoun in 1818. Realistic in his

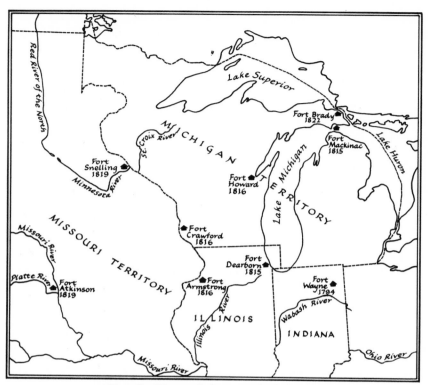

Fort Snelling and sister sentinels in the
frontier defense program

judgment of the site, Long was a romantic at heart, and his diary describes the place as "the most interesting and magnificent of any" he had ever seen. He took occasion to explore Carver's Cave, also Fountain Cave, and he recorded, from the lips of an Indian — "Shooter from the Pine Tree" — the romantic legends of Maiden Rock on Lake Pepin and of the Falls of St. Anthony.

Events now began to move at a faster pace. Plans were announced in the spring of 1818 for a fort to be built at the mouth of the Yellowstone, far up in the Missouri country. In December Secretary Calhoun reported that a fort would soon be established in the Minnesota area favored by Major Long. Both these forts, he said, were to be erected "for the protection of our trade and the preservation of the peace of the frontiers." The plans afoot made it clear that the two forts, and yet others designed for the Missouri, were parts of a grand program of frontier defense. As things turned out, the Yellowstone plan did not materialize, though Fort Atkinson was built in Nebraska, a military post strategic in the early history of that state. The Minnesota fort was established, however, and it took on added importance because, in the absence of the intended fort at the Yellowstone, its sphere of influence extended to the Missouri country.

Fort Snelling, like Rome, was not built in a day. The Fifth United States Infantry at Fort Gratiot (Detroit), under Lieutenant Colonel Henry Leavenworth, a veteran of the War of 1812, was entrusted, under an order dated February 10, 1819, with the job of building it. Characteristic of American negligence in its Indian relations was the fact that nobody had ever paid the Sioux the $2000 promised by Pike in the treaty of 1805. The government suddenly realized that in order legally to build the fort on land acquired by Pike, it must first make good its fourteen-year-old promise. As a result the Indian agent at Rock Island, Major Thomas Forsyth, was sent north concurrently with the troops. He divided the payment (in goods) among a half dozen chiefs, including Wabasha and Little Crow (grandfather of the Sioux War leader), liberally lubricating the transactions with liquor.

Colonel Leavenworth did not arrive at the mouth of the Minnesota until late in August (the 24th). With him came a detachment of 98 soldiers, and in September the post was augmented by an additional 120. Thus some 200 soldiers, with their officers, initiated the frontier post, building first a temporary cantonment (New Hope) on the south side of the river, near present Mendota. Then, after a miserable winter marked by a disastrous attack of scurvy, in which it appears that no fewer (perhaps more) than 40 soldiers died, a summer camp of tents was occupied on the west side of the river (Camp Coldwater). Leavenworth made plans for a permanent fort some distance north of the site finally chosen. Before its building was launched, however, he was transferred, and his place was taken by Colonel Josiah Snelling.

It was the vigorous and competent Colonel Snelling, Boston-born veteran of the War of 1812, who designed and built Fort Snelling while serving as commandant (from 1820 to 1827). Snelling promptly selected the present site of Fort Snelling at the crest of the bluff above the river junction. Precisely when the various structures were erected is difficult to say, but by the summer of 1824 the colonel was able to report that that year would witness the completion of the fort; and it was in the same year that General Winfield Scott inspected the post and was so deeply impressed that he recommended to the War Department the dropping of the old name, Fort St. Anthony, and its renaming as Fort Snelling, a change richly merited and made official in 1825.

The job of fort-building, done by the soldiers under Snelling's supervision, was laborious and praiseworthy. The men cut pine logs in the Rum River region, floated them down the Mississippi, and built a sawmill at the Falls of St. Anthony that was doing business by 1822. Gradually the fort took shape — a diamond shape, completely enclosed by stone walls ten feet in height. Encrusted with Minnesota historic lore are the limestone hexagonal and round towers, each with loopholes for musketry, the one bastion overlooking the Minnesota Valley, the other "standing like the prow of a ship at the prairie end" of the area, both structures still in existence. At other corners were a pentagonal tower and a battery and lookout. Within the enclosure were officers' quarters, barracks, commandant's house, shops, hospital, parade grounds, guardhouse, commissary and quartermaster's store, magazine, a well, and even a schoolhouse. At the Falls of St. Anthony were both a gristmill and a sawmill plus additional barracks.

The frontier fort has been described as "an isle of safety" in the wilderness, impregnable to Indian assault (though not to artillery). It would be difficult to overestimate the importance of Fort Snelling in the development of Minnesota. It was not, indeed, the scene of battles — even in the 1860s when the Sioux Outbreak occurred — but for more than three decades it was the northern military outpost of the Mississippi Valley. Fort Snelling was a strategic center for encircling settlement, and in the course of time the two greatest cities of Minnesota grew up only a short distance above and below the Mississippi from the fort. Symbol of American authority, the fort was the focus for negotiations with the native tribes. Under the protection of the fort the fur trade flourished. Its soldiers were farmers as well as carpenters, masons, and builders, millers, and sawyers. Snelling saw to it that wheat and corn were planted. A visitor in 1823 noted that more than two hundred acres of land were under cultivation for wheat, oats, corn, and garden vegetables — guarantees against the return of the fearful scurvy that assailed the soldiers in their first year. In 1824 Snelling reported 4500 bushels of potatoes stored from the previous summer and said that he expected a larger crop in 1825. The fort was the Minnesota center to which, as the years went by, just about all visitors to the region came — explorers, missionaries, travelers. It was the objective of steamboat travel on the Mississippi after navigation pioneered the northern course of the river in 1823. And through more than a century and a quarter the fort (save for a short period before the Civil War) was a military center serving region and nation in successive wars as well as in peace.

Important as is its local story, Fort Snelling must be interpreted in the larger setting of the services of the United States government in the forwarding of the westward movement. The government "guided, directed, and protected the movement." As a historian of American frontier forts has written, the Army "surveyed rivers and lakes; it improved harbors and built fortifications; it surveyed routes and built roads and bridges; it protected mail routes, government stores, roads, and ferries; it ejected squatters and established legal claimants; it protected agents and commissioners; it restrained and regulated hunters and trappers; it assisted officers of the law; it protected whites against Indians and Indians against whites; and finally it fought those occasional battles which seemed to be inevitable."

Even these varied categories do not tell the full story of such forts as Snelling and the Army's contributions to the building of the West. The frontier posts were not merely "isles of safety," not merely hubs around which vast growth and development would come with the passing decades, but also communities of civilized people whose own lives and activities were a part of the unfolding culture of the Middle West.

Fort Snelling, once it emerged from its initial ordeals, was a center not only for military duty and work, but also for reading, dances, theatricals, hunting, schooling, family life, adventure, and the formalities of reviews, the daily ceremony of flag raising, and entertainment of visiting dignitaries. The fort's history reveals interesting personalities. Colonel Snelling himself, peppery red-haired commander, affectionately nicknamed "The Red Hen" by his soldiers, was an officer of the old school, stern in discipline, hard-driving, hard-drinking, efficient in getting things done; and his wife was a lady of acknowledged charm. After Snelling's departure in 1827, the fort was commanded for a year (from the summer of 1828) by a future President of the United States, Zachary Taylor. But life at the fort proved an unhappy experience for "Old Rough and

Ready," who was not impressed by the glories of Minnesota. A "most miserable and uninteresting country," the southern-born officer wrote before his transfer to Fort Crawford.

In 1823 Snelling brought out to his fort as a tutor for the children of the officers a Harvard graduate, John Marsh, who studied medicine under the fort's surgeon, Dr. Edward Purcell, and also served as mail carrier between the fort and Prairie du Chien. One of Marsh's pupils was the colonel's eldest son, William Joseph Snelling, wayward, adventurous, and a near genius. Then and later the pupil took a lively interest in the Sioux Indians, and in 1830 published a book of stories, *Tales of the Northwest*, a portrayal of Indian life marked by authentic realism and not in the Cooper cardboard tradition — a minor frontier classic.

Life at the fort seems to have been a spur to writing, for many other records were produced, one entitled *"Three Score Years and Ten"* by Charlotte Ouisconsin Van Cleve, daughter of a lieutenant and born at Prairie du Chien (1819) as the family was on its way to the frontier. Mrs. Van Cleve wrote late in life, looking back with nostalgic eyes at the scenes of her childhood.

In the 1830s the physician of the fort was Dr. John Emerson, who brought to Minnesota (in 1836) his slave, Dred Scott. Later Scott, who married his wife Harriet at the fort, was taken to Missouri by the doctor. After Emerson's death Scott sued for freedom because, he alleged, the fact that he had lived at Fort Snelling, in the Missouri Compromise area on which slavery was prohibited, had emancipated him. So the story of the frontier fort is entwined with one of the most famous of legal cases in the background of the Civil War. Commandant for a brief period in 1837 was Captain Martin Scott, Vermont Yankee, famed as a hunter who kept a pack of twenty or more dogs, deadly marksman, ready for a duel at the slightest insult, at the end killed in battle in the Mexican War. Dr. Edward Purcell, Irish-born surgeon who accompanied Leavenworth in 1819, administered in his post quarters the first hospital in Minnesota and was himself the pioneer practitioner of medicine in the region. He struggled with the problems of scurvy during the first year, but after that ordeal there were relatively few deaths among the soldiers during the years of Dr. Purcell's services, which continued until his death at the fort in 1825.

A commander of Fort Snelling in the 1840s was Seth Eastman, a scenic artist whose many paintings have enriched the regional lore. His wife Mary recorded in a very popular book the legends of the Sioux as she heard and collected them in the Minnesota country. Not a few officers who attained high rank in the Civil War saw frontier service at the Minnesota fort. These included Thomas W. Sherman, wounded at Port Hudson in 1863 and later breveted brigadier general; Major General Edward R. S. Canby, who had charge of federal troops in New York City after the draft riots of 1863 and who captured Mobile in 1865; and Eastman, who was breveted brigadier general in 1866 after Civil War service. The Confederate general, Simon Buckner, who surrendered Fort Donelson to General Grant in 1862 had also been stationed at Fort Snelling.

The lot of officers and their families was lightened by many amenities, but that of the men was one of drills and routine from reveille to tatoo, roll calls, fatigue duties, parades, hard work on assigned jobs, care of horses and cattle, special errands, a cash income of six dollars a month, severe punishment for infractions of rules (including floggings sometimes adminstered personally by the commandant with a cat-o'-nine-tails). There were not infrequent desertions, and there are some evidences of occasional near-mutinies. For all at the fort, life in wintertime meant isolation, the river highway closed to transportation. But for the officers and their families there was the post library, and there were diversions in cards, chess, checkers, dominoes, balls, and frequent amateur plays — the post records tell, for instance, of a performance of *Monsieur Tonson*. In summer there were picnics and rides or walks to Minnehaha Falls and nearby lakes. Frequently there was the excitement of visiting Sioux and Chippewa, with their dances and violent games of lacrosse. And the feuds of the inveterate enemies sometimes erupted within the very shadows of the frowning walls of the fort. Now and then animosities among the officers found vent in duels — once Colonel Snelling himself was challenged, as commanding officer declined, and his place was taken by his son William. The son was wounded slightly and the officer with whom he fought was court-martialed.

An enclosed little world, this diamond post north in the Mississippi Valley. It was remote from, yet an extension of, the centers of civilization. Its officers and men were alert to the importance of their military mission but they probably were little aware of their role as pioneers of a coming state whose people would look back to Fort Snelling as to a shrine. Its memories would be collected and preserved and the time would come in the twentieth century when the very site would be excavated to expose foundations of buildings long since destroyed and to bring to light artifacts as of some ancient culture.

Far in the past Fort Snelling may seem to modern eyes, but it is linked with the modern commonwealth, not merely through cherished lore, but in the evolution of the state. From earlier to later times it played a role significant, colorful, influential, and worthy of the traditions of the American Army. In its earlier years, it had scarcely been established before it began to function as host to a succession of exploring expeditions that spanned the length and breadth of Minnesota, while the same early period witnessed a new chapter in the exploitation of the fur trade under American control and management, with the center of that trade established across the river from the fort. Old Fort Snelling was the nucleus of life and enterprise in Minnesota as it emerged into its American period. It may fairly be said to have "set in motion the transformation of a vast Indian territory into an American state." In view of the role played by Fort Snelling through close to a century and a half, it is appropriate that in 1960 it was given status as a national historic landmark. This emphasized its importance in the history of the American West and of the United States. The enduring Minnesota interest in the fort was in turn given recognition in 1961 when its original site was turned over to the state by the federal government. The area thus transferred is known as the Fort Snelling Historical State Park, and it is expected that in time it will be greatly expanded.

Schoolcraft landing at Lake Itasca, from a
water color by Seth Eastman

Under the American Flag

F ORT SNELLING was a frontier sentinel. The interests that brought it into being found expression in a pageant of exploration, moves to direct American relations with the Indians, the reorganization of the fur trade, the coming of missionaries, and trickles of settlement.

Much had been done to reveal the nature of the lands beyond the Great Lakes. Explorers, traders, and travelers had pushed north on the Mississippi. The waterways beyond Superior had long known the flash of paddles and the strains of lilting songs. Pike had carried the American flag to northern posts; and soldiers had occupied a fort at a commanding spot above the Mississippi and the Minnesota.

The time was now at hand for explorations that would reveal the source of the great river; delineate lakes and streams; yield information about resources for lumbering, farming, perhaps mining; marshal information about fertile valleys, such as those of the Minnesota and Red rivers; deepen knowledge of the Indian tribes and their traditions; fill out the map, and clarify puzzles related to the northern boundary.

These problems invited many and diverse talents — those of naturalists, cartographers, engineers, writers, artists, men of the cross, and even observant tourists. Such talents and skills appeared in the 1820s and ensuing decades. There was a galaxy of explorers and travelers — not a concerted series of moves under a master plan, but explorer and expedition, one after another, each contributing to the total of information.

107

And the personalities of the pathfinders lent color to the record of what they did.

The finding of the precise source of the Mississippi was no longer a matter of vital diplomatic importance but it intrigued explorers as a matter of geographical interest. The land geographer David Thompson, traversing the region between Red and Cass lakes in 1798, had mistakenly assumed that Turtle Lake was the source. Pike went as far as Leech and Cass lakes in 1806. And it seems very likely that a fur trader, William Morrison, saw Lake Itasca — officially *the* source — as early as 1804, but he made no report or claim of discovery until decades later. If he did see the little lake, the event ranks as a *finding*, not a *discovery* in the historical sense of making known to the world what was seen.

Fort Snelling was only a year old when, in 1820, the governor of Michigan Territory, Lewis Cass, led an expedition to the Minnesota country. In 1819 he had secured governmental authority to explore an outlying portion of his own Michigan Territory. He set out from Detroit with a party of experts including as topographer a professor of mathematics at West Point (Captain David B. Douglass); a popular writer and mineralogist (Henry R. Schoolcraft); a physician, the Indian agent at Chicago (Dr. Alexander Wolcott), witty, clever, ironical; a secretary and official recorder (James D. Doty), who later became governor of Wisconsin Territory; and a private secretary to Cass, Robert A. Forsyth. The party also included ten voyageurs, an equal number of Indians, a squad of seven soldiers, a guide, an interpreter, and other assistants. In assembling such a company, Cass displayed the energy and ambition that later characterized his national career (twenty-eight years later he was a candidate for President of the United States). When he proposed this expedition to Minnesota, he wrote to Secretary of War Calhoun, "It has occurred to me that a tour through that country, with a view to examine the production of its animal, vegetable, and mineral kingdoms, to explore its facilities for water communication, to delineate its natural objects, and to ascertain its present and future probable value, would not be uninteresting in itself, nor useless to the Government." But this was by no means all. He also had in mind land cessions from the Indians, the counteracting of British influence, and other objectives. He wanted a large expedition befitting the authority of the national government and his own dignity as governor.

On a May day in 1820 the expedition got under way in large canoes,

Route of the 1820 expedition to the Minnesota country led by Governor Lewis Cass of Michigan Territory

the voyageurs "chanting one of their animated songs," the Indians and French-Canadians at once engaging in a spirited race. This was picturesque, but after skirting the south shore of Lake Superior, the party thrust its way into Minnesota from Fond du Lac (first stopping at a post of the American Fur Company), and soon its members, crossing swamps and portages, found themselves up to their knees in mud — a posture somewhat less than picturesque or romantic. From Sandy Lake the expedition went on to the sheet of water Pike had called Upper Red Cedar Lake. Young Schoolcraft, honoring the governor, named it "Cassina," and this name, shortened to "Cass," still stands. To Governor Cass the lake was the source of the Mississippi, but Schoolcraft, the skeptical chronicler of the expedition, and Captain Douglass took note of the fact that the lake had two inlets. Whence came the water — where its origin? Neither Schoolcraft nor his secretary, Doty, regarded Cass Lake as the source, and it remained for Schoolcraft a dozen years later to satisfy his curiosity by finding the little body of water that proved to be in fact the ultimate source. Meanwhile the exploring party made its way to Fort Snelling (not yet so named), and there Cass met the commander, was greeted with a "national salute," and feasted on fresh vegetables from the fort's gardens.

A young man of Detroit, Charles C. Trowbridge, interested in the French-Canadian and Indian languages, had been invited to accompany the Cass expedition. He said he "would rather black boots than miss it" — and he did not miss it. Through the entire journey he kept a detailed diary which did not, however, come to light and find publication until nearly a century and a quarter later. But Schoolcraft published at Albany in 1821 his *Narrative Journal*, a lively, popular account which is at the same time a solid record of the journey. If the larger aims of the pomp-loving governor were not fully achieved, his expedition was nevertheless not an inauspicious opening — only a year after Fort Snelling was founded — of the pageant of American exploration.

The same summer that saw Cass's triumphant appearance at the fort witnessed the arrival of another expedition, a military force that came up from Council Bluffs under Captain Matthew J. Magee, seeking to establish a "practicable route" from the Nebraska fort to Fort Snelling. The laborious trip is not of any special historical importance, but with Magee came a young lieutenant named Stephen Watts Kearny, whose journal recorded the journey and who himself would reappear in Minnesota a decade and a half later.

The precedent set by Cass for a large expedition was observed only three years later by another enterprise under the command of Major Stephen H. Long, the same officer who had ascended the Mississippi in 1817 as a preliminary to the founding of Fort Snelling and who in 1820 explored the Rockies. This expedition of 1823 was virtually a circumnavigation of Minnesota. It headed for the Minnesota and Red River valleys and included a visit to the Pembina region. Thereafter it crossed the north country from Lake Winnipeg to Fort William on Lake Superior. Its purposes involved a survey of the Selkirk settlement to determine whether or not, as its colonists had moved southward, they had occupied American territory below the forty-ninth parallel.

The nature of Long's exploring party emphasized a wide range of fundamental information about the land and its resources, natural life, the natives, the trade in furs, and border relationships. Long was himself a topographical engineer, and his party included Thomas Say, entomologist and conchologist, at the time a professor in the University of Pennsylvania, and so distinguished in his specialty that he has been called "the father of descriptive entomology in America." Long also had the

110

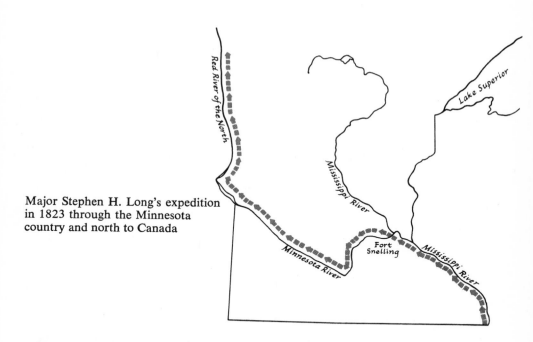

Major Stephen H. Long's expedition in 1823 through the Minnesota country and north to Canada

assistance of a landscape painter, Samuel Seymour; a young astronomer, James E. Colhoun; and an escort of soldiers under the noted hunter Martin Scott. William H. Keating, like Say a member of the Pennsylvania faculty, was a mineralogical chemist, and he played also the role of historiographer. Drawing on his own observations and those of his colleagues, he kept notes, and only a year after the trip he published a two-volume narrative of the expedition.

Long and his companions, coming up the Mississippi from Prairie du Chien, paused at the Indian villages of Wabasha and Red Wing. They later enjoyed the hospitality of the officers at Fort Snelling, where the noted half-breed trader Joseph Renville joined the party as a guide and interpreter, and the colonel's son, "Joe" Snelling, also became a member. The expedition then made its way up the Minnesota River, some of the travelers going by canoe, others by land. In western Minnesota Long turned northward, saw herds of buffaloes on the plains, encountered some hazard of Indian attack, and reached Pembina, which he found to be south of the forty-ninth parallel. The settlement of sixty cabins and some 350 people — Scottish, Swiss, and other nationalities that had freely intermarried with the native Indians — was American except for a single cabin north of the line.

The major marked the border, raised the American flag, had a salute fired, and proclaimed the area United States territory. Having thus performed with éclat one important part of his assignment, he pushed north to the Canadian forts in the area of later Winnipeg, went to Lake Winnipeg, thence to Lake of the Woods, and made his way out by the international waters. He followed the route beyond Rainy Lake via Lac La Croix and the Kaministikwia to Fort William on Superior instead of the waterways leading to the Pigeon River and Grand Portage. At Rainy Lake, visiting a post of the Hudson's Bay Company, Long had the pleasure of meeting its factor, Dr. John McLoughlin.

Long, Keating, and their associates rank as major explorers in the American period, notably because of Keating's narrative report of the expedition. This work, published in America, England, and Germany, gave to the world its first accurate knowledge of some of the richest agricultural lands of the continent. It included an almost encyclopedic account of the Indians, particularly the Sioux and Chippewa, and Say supplied descriptions of Minnesota fishes, shells, leeches, and insects.

Before Major Long's expedition started west from Fort Snelling in July 1823, an Italian traveler intent on discovering the source of the Mississippi joined the party. This was the romantic Giacomo Constantino Beltrami. He was a native of Bergamo, lawyer, student of language, and political exile who had arrived at Fort Snelling as a passenger on the *Virginia*, the first steamboat to ascend the Upper Mississippi.

The *Virginia*, which came up from St. Louis, has been called the *Clermont* of the Upper Mississippi. Beltrami made no allusion to Robert Fulton's memorable voyage on the Hudson River in 1807, but he understood that the trip of the *Virginia* was epoch-making, and he described in his own style the astonishment of the Indians when they saw the vessel land at Fort Snelling. "I know not," he wrote, "what impression the first sight of the Phoenician vessels might make on the inhabitants of the coasts of Greece; or the Triremi of the Romans on the wild natives of Iberia, Gaul, or Britain; but I am sure it could not be stronger than that which I saw on the countenances of these savages at the arrival of our steam-boat. When they saw it cut its way without oars or sails against the current of the great river, some thought it a monster vomiting fire, others the dwelling of the Manitous, but all approached it with reverence or fear."

After journeying with Long to Pembina, Beltrami broke away from the expedition, whose commander he did not like, and set out, with a guide and two Indians, toward the southeast. He was intent on discovering the "sources of the king of rivers." Deserted by his lone guide, he found himself somewhere on the Red Lake River, but engaged a half-breed who led him to a small, heart-shaped lake that he named Lake Julia. This to him was the goal of his American travels, the source of the great river. He described the lake as the source both of the Mississippi and of the Red River — actually it empties its waters into the Red River's basin and is not the originating spot of the Mississippi. Beltrami had no doubts, however, and he went into ecstasy, imagining that the shades of Marco Polo, Columbus, Vespucii, and other famous Italian explorers of the past were at his very side, rejoicing with him. He made his way out of the wilderness to Fort Snelling and in 1824 published at New Orleans a book in French telling of his discovery and adventures. Four years later his narrative was brought out in London in an English version.

The exuberant Italian had a story to tell and he did it with rhetorical flourishes — but he did not realize that the area he had traversed was familiar ground to fur traders and had been covered a quarter of a century earlier by David Thompson. Faced later with criticism, Beltrami in 1825 addressed to the public an impassioned defense of his travels and writings and denounced his "calumniators." His claims are not upheld by history, but his books are authentic in the detail they give of the travels he made. Beltrami faced hardship with fortitude; and his personality adds a touch of color to the history of Minnesota exploration. As a commentator has said, "He rode across the Minnesota horizon like some old armored knight clad in the mental panoply of the Middle Ages, to which period he really belonged." Incidentally it should be noted that Beltrami was not the first Italian to touch Minnesota soil, for a compatriot of his, Count Paolo Andreani, remembered chiefly for a pioneer balloon ascension in Italy in 1784, had made observations in the lake region as early as 1791 and had visited Grand Portage and described its lively commerce in furs.

It was no fortuitous circumstance that Major Long came out on the shores of Lake Superior at the end of his Minnesota travels, though his interest was less in the big lake than in the boundary country to its west. The interest of the French and British in Superior was succeeded in the American period by continuing exploration and charting. In the 1820s there was much activity in the lake country. The ubiquitous David Thompson, serving the British on boundary surveys, traveled up the Superior shore in 1822 from Fond du Lac to Grand Portage, recording his observations. And he was in the region again the next summer, this time with Dr. John J. Bigsby, who journeyed on the north shore down to Grand Portage. As early as 1825 Bigsby contributed to a London scientific journal an essay on the geography and geology of Lake Superior that included a detailed map of the lake drawn by David Thompson; and at mid-century he published in England a two-volume travel narrative entitled *The Shoe and Canoe.*

Yet others, in the same year as Long's expedition, were in the Superior region, including Joseph Delafield, an American investigator of boundary problems, and Henry W. Bayfield, an English naval officer who charted the lake a few years later and has been described as its "first modern cartographer." Thus men observed, recorded, wrote reports, and drew maps, amplifying knowledge of the lake, its beautiful (and treacherous) shores, its beckoning hinterland.

The year 1826 witnessed a gaudy governmental expedition to Fond du Lac under two commissioners, Thomas McKenny, head of the Bureau of Indian Affairs (in the War Department), and the enterprising Governor Cass. Its purpose was to negotiate a treaty with the Chippewa bands supplementing treaty negotiations at Prairie du Chien in 1825. The Americans — a party of nearly seventy men, including officers, soldiers, musicians, a surgeon, and Henry Schoolcraft — came up the St. Louis River to the American Fur Company post at Fond du Lac on a July day, with flags flying and a band playing "Yankee Doodle" and "Hail Columbia." British medals and flags were surrendered by the Indians, and a treaty was negotiated (August 5, 1826) under which the Chippewa granted to the United States "the right to search for, and carry away, any metals or minerals from any part of their country." For this right, the Chippewa were given gifts and promised an annuity of $2000. The treaty betrays an early awareness of potential mineral riches in the Chippewa country, though many decades would go by before the opening of the iron-ore industry. McKenny, the leader of the official party, published in 1827 a long account, *Sketches of a Tour of the Lakes*, that enriched the pioneer literature of the north country especially through his sensitive appreciation of scenery and natural life, and his sympathetic understanding of the Indians.

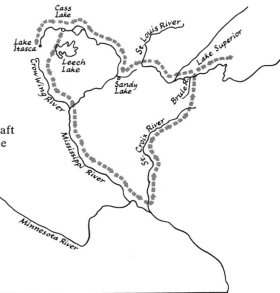

Route of the Henry Rowe Schoolcraft
expedition of 1832 during which the
source of the Mississippi River
was discovered

It fell to the lot of Henry Rowe Schoolcraft in 1832 to achieve the historic goal that Thompson, Pike, Cass, and Beltrami had narrowly missed. Schoolcraft, already indebted to Cass for the opportunity to take part in the expedition of 1820, was sponsored by the Michigan governor in 1831 when he was sent on a visit to the Lake Superior Chippewa. The authorization of a new expedition to the Upper Mississippi in 1832 also emanated from Cass, by that time secretary of war in Andrew Jackson's Cabinet. The instructions to Schoolcraft centered in the Indians of the region. Schoolcraft was to concern himself with their welfare, and with the curbing of Chippewa-Sioux antagonisms. An important assignment to combat smallpox fell to Dr. Douglass Houghton. A minister, William T. Boutwell, was invited to join the expedition to study the spiritual needs of the natives. And there was an escort of ten soldiers under Lieutenant James Allen, a topographer. The instructions contained nothing about the source of the river, but this was uppermost in Schoolcraft's mind. He had not forgotten his curiosity twelve years earlier about waters flowing into Cass Lake. That he intended to solve the question was made clear by a conversation he had with Boutwell while the party was on the outward journey. For the anticipated discovery, he felt he must be ready with a splendid name. Rusty in Latin, he asked the minis-

115

ter to suggest some classical words meaning the headwaters or true source of a river. Boutwell (almost equally rusty) wrote down Latin words for truth and head — *veritas* and *caput* — and Schoolcraft struck out the first syllable of the one and the last of the other, joined what remained, and announced that the name would be "Itasca."

The name was and still is Itasca, though its origin was in doubt until a modern scholar some years ago discovered a contemporary letter by Schoolcraft confirming the Latin story. A writer in the 1850s (Mary H. Eastman) believed that the name came from that of an Indian princess, daughter of Nanabozho, who was carried to the underworld by Chebiabo and whose eternal tears supplied the waters that flowed out into the great river, a legend that Schoolcraft himself for some unexplained reason sponsored in later years. But research has dried the tears of "Itasca."

Equipped with the name, Schoolcraft went on to Fond du Lac, Sandy Lake, then Cass Lake, "the *ultima Thule* of previous discovery." He called on natives for canoes, guides, and aid in mapping. Thus prepared, he started with a party of sixteen on the final stage of the hunt. He passed Lake Bemidji, turned south — and came to the lake called "Elk" by the Indians. The "cheering sight of a transparent body of water burst upon our view," he wrote. "It was Itasca Lake — the source of the Mississippi." Schoolcraft did not exult in the manner of a Beltrami, but he had thoughts of the great La Salle. Many years later he turned to verse. He hailed the "truant of western waters" and the sources, "discovered to the eye in crystal springs that run, like silver thread, from out their sandy heights, and glittering lie within a beauteous basin. . . ." His lines ended thus: "I quaff the limpid cup at Mississippi's spring." At the time of discovery, July 13, 1832, Schoolcraft and his party landed on an island near the northwest end of the lake (known since as Schoolcraft Island) and raised the American flag. Later, he presented to his very helpful Chippewa guide, Ozawindib, a presidential medal and a flag, the emblems of a chief.

Eager to report his discovery, Schoolcraft hurried back to the Sault. He stopped briefly for a visit to Fort Snelling, and his colleagues headed by different routes for Fond du Lac. The versatile Dr. Houghton — the physician, geologist, and botanist — had taken seriously his assignment to deal with the health problems of the Indians. Over a period of about two months he vaccinated no fewer than 2070 Chippewa in the Superior and Upper Mississippi areas (nearly 900 of them children under ten). The Indians submitted cheerfully to his ministrations, and he learned why. They had suffered at least five epidemics of smallpox (in 1750, 1770, 1784, 1802, and 1824) and, with this sorry tribal experience, they trembled at the very name of the disease. To Dr. Houghton small-pox seemed one of the greatest scourges (next to alcohol) that the whites had visited on the natives. The energetic doctor ranks as a pioneer of medicine in Minnesota and the Northwest, but his medical services were performed alongside botanical and mineralogical studies. Lieu-tenant Allen duly reported on the topography of the region he had visited — a crisp, informing record plus an excellent map; and both Boutwell and Dr. Houghton kept diaries which have since appeared in print. Schoolcraft's own official report omitted the Itasca story since it had not been embraced by his instructions. In 1834, however, he published an extensive *Narrative of an Expedition through the Upper Mississippi to Itasca Lake*, the title of which touches what, to him, was the heart of the expedition. All in all, the enterprise was successful and well documented, and its historical significance goes beyond the identification of the charm-ing lake that starts the Mississippi on its journey to the Gulf of Mexico.

The discovery of Lake Itasca was a genuine geographic advance, but the 1830s and 1840s witnessed not a few other expeditions that sought out new detail about the Minnesota country, lengthened the roll of ex-plorers, and added to the shelf of narratives, reports, diaries, and maps.

Two men of special interest and importance emerge — George Catlin and Joseph Nicolas Nicollet — but many others, some obscure, some well known, figure in the sequence of events. Catlin was a self-trained artist whose imagination was touched when he saw in Philadelphia, where he had opened a studio, a group of Indians in their gaudy native dress. His aim was to make a record in pictures of the North American Indians — in his view a vanishing race without "historians or biographers of their own to portray with fidelity their native looks and history." How well he per-formed this task is demonstrated in his writings, including a great two-volume work on the manners, customs, and conditions of the Indians of North America; in his paintings — many hundreds of portraits and scenes of Indian life; and in exhibits presented in England and the European world.

Minnesota interest in Catlin's career is based on two visits, made in

117

1835 and 1836, when he studied and recorded the Sioux Indians and a variety of scenes. Impressed by the West, he suggested as a "Fashionable Tour" a steamboat trip north from St. Louis on the Mississippi to the Falls of St. Anthony — an idea that soon took hold. On his second visit, faithfully recorded, Catlin — undeterred by native threats — explored the Pipestone quarries, Indian sacred ground and a place of "medicine." He described the quarry as "a perpendicular wall of close-grained, compact quartz," made a drawing of the scene, and carried away samples of the pipestone. He is popularly regarded as the discoverer of the famed quarries — but fur traders had long been familiar with the place and had even (as in the case of one Philander Prescott) dug out stone to make pipes themselves. Catlin was not the first white man to invade the precincts of the red stone, but unlike the traders he reached out to the public with his story.

Nicollet, a gifted French mathematician and astronomer and author of a treatise on the mathematics of life insurance, ranks as a colorful and significant Minnesota explorer. He appeared at Fort Snelling in 1836 and won friends because of his modestly worn learning, his geniality, and his charm of manner. Though he carried letters of introduction from the War Department, his was a private expedition, with some financial aid from a St. Louis fur-trade magnate. His first objective was Lake Itasca. Giving honor to Schoolcraft and his associates for the discovery of the lake, he explored it with great care and determined its latitude and longitude and height above sea level. He was not unconscious of the spectacle he presented while trudging across a portage: "I carried my sextant on my back, in a leather case, thrown over me as a knapsack; then my barometer slung over my left shoulder; my cloak, thrown over the same shoulder, confined the barometer closely against the sextant; a portfolio under the arm; a basket in hand, which contained my thermometer, chronometer, pocket-compass, artificial horizon, tape-line, &c., &c. On the right side, a spy-glass, powder-flask, and shot bag; and in my hand, a gun or an umbrella. . . ." The burdened explorer, stumbling over rough paths and "bogged in marshes," occasionally regretted "the rashness" that led him to make his journey. But he met its ordeals with steadiness and courage — and his listing of instruments affords a measure of the care with which he equipped himself for observation.

The Itasca adventure was a prelude to long services by the French scholar. He spent the winter at Fort Snelling, and later, in 1838, the

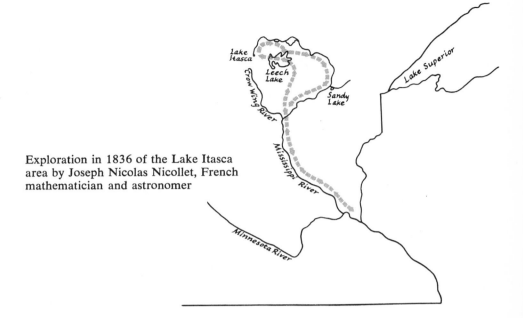

Exploration in 1836 of the Lake Itasca area by Joseph Nicolas Nicollet, French mathematician and astronomer

United States government commissioned him to explore and draw maps of the country between the Missouri and the Mississippi, with a young lieutenant, John C. Fremont, as an assistant. The Frenchman's unpublished journals have come to light only in recent years, but in 1843, the year of Nicollet's death, his official report was published as a Senate document. It took the form primarily of a great map, with a relatively brief narrative supporting and illustrating it. Nicollet was a scientific cartographer, and his majestic map, drawing on his explorations and the records of earlier observers and mappers, is the fundamental map of the West, from the Mississippi to the Missouri and in particular of Minnesota, with meticulous explications of geographic details and names, and with masterly execution. Nicollet's American career was a climax to earlier and brilliant achievements in France, where he had won election to the Legion of Honor and then fled his native land after financial disaster. In modern Minnesota his contributions are remembered, not through emblems, but in numerous place names in his honor.

Various other travelers and explorers contributed to knowledge and public understanding of the Minnesota region in its earlier American period. One was a crotchety English-born scientist, George W. Featherstonhaugh, who was appointed United States geologist in 1834 and the next year undertook a geological excursion to the Minnesota Valley and the southwest as far as the Coteau des Prairies. He was not without a gift for observation, as is disclosed in an official report and in a two-volume work published in London in 1847 under the curious title *A Canoe Voyage up the Minnay Sotor*. He added relatively little to what was known, but he emerges from the records of the time as a curious character: a person whose aversion to tobacco led to embarrassment when he was asked by Indians to share in the pipe of peace; a fastidious individual who, whatever the circumstances of travel, never failed to have his daily tea and bath; a man of sharp pen who could describe a certain missionary-farmer as an "odd, long-legged, sharp-faced, asparagus looking animal"; and a man not overgenerous, as is evidenced by his failure to give any credit to Lieutenant William W. Mather, who accompanied him and rendered highly competent assistance.

Kearny, the army officer who traveled east to Minnesota in 1820, led a detachment of United States dragoons from Fort Des Moines to Wabasha's village on the Mississippi River in 1835. Chief interest in this expedition centers, not in Kearny, however, but in a lieutenant named Albert Miller Lea. Lea's claim to fame resides in the fact that he kept a journal and field book and after the trip drafted a map and wrote a narrative. He managed to get his work published in Philadelphia. A third of the edition was "lost on a sand bar in the Ohio," as the author explained later; another third fell into irresponsible hands; and only five hundred copies "got into market." One distinction of the book was that it applied, for the first time, the name "Iowa" to the region that later became the state of Iowa. "Albert Lea" is now the name of a city in southern Minnesota.

The international flavor of Minnesota travel, to which Beltrami, Featherstonhaugh, and Nicollet made contributions, was sharpened in the 1830s and 1840s. Thus an Italian nobleman, Count Francesco Arese, passed through the Minnesota region in 1837, following a route from the southwest, visiting Traverse des Sioux, and thereafter Fort Snelling. His French narrative, recently made available in an English translation (*A Trip to the Prairies*), is a travel account of only mild interest. Though his route was unusual, the story bears no comparison with the robust *Diary in America* (1839) written by the author of *Mr. Midshipman Easy*, Frederick Marryat, a traveler out to see the sights, who took the fashionable tour to Fort Snelling in 1838. There was increasing interest in scientific work in the wilderness. A Saxon botanist, Charles Geyer of Dresden, who met Nicollet on a Missouri River steamboat, journeyed with the Frenchman in Minnesota, studying New World plant life. And in 1846 another Frenchman, Auguste Lamare-Picquot, also a naturalist, collected Minnesota specimens for a museum. A traveler reported that his American museum included a buffalo head, elk, deer, otter, beaver, fox, and wolf, as well as beetles, butterflies, reptiles, wild swan, pelican, eagle, partridge, and "scarlet bird."

By the 1840s the Minnesota scene was shifting. Exploratory expeditions turned westward toward the Red River and plains country. Panoramists and others, successors to Catlin, interested themselves in the wonders of the Mississippi Valley and the pictorial recording of native life. The Red River country seems to have had appealing interest to artists, and their sketches and paintings are a part of the saga. As early as the 1820s a gifted Swiss artist, Peter Rindisbacher, did water colors of the Pembina and Red River region; and in the 1840s Paul Kane, Irish-born painter, made impressive recordings of the half-breeds of the region and their picturesque buffalo hunts. He went there in 1846 and executed hundreds of sketches in the valley country. Scientific observation continued in various Minnesota sections, notably in the Superior country, where such figures as Louis Agassiz, the great Swiss-American geologist and zoologist, and the gifted Le Conte cousins (John and Joseph), appeared during the 1840s.

Thus much was done to enlarge knowledge about Minnesota. The Army must be said to have played a leading role. Explorers, cartographers, engineers, scholars, artists, and casual travelers came and went, amid changing scenes. They reveal not only an alert American curiosity but also a European interest in the wilderness. The tradition of curiosity about the virginal lands, given impetus in the days of the French and British, was kept alive.

A problem of importance was brought to a settlement in 1842. This was the boundary line at the north, from Lake Superior to the Lake of the Woods. It is one of the curiosities of history that the northern boundary was not "reduced to intelligible terms" until nearly six decades after the Treaty of 1783. Abortive efforts were made in early years to bring about some kind of understanding, but the matter languished until the end of the War of 1812, when the Treaty of Ghent provided for a commission to study the boundary from the St. Lawrence to the Lake of the Woods and to take into account the "true intent" of the Treaty of 1783. The western boundary beyond Lake of the Woods, as has been noted, was fixed in 1818, but the eastern line became enmeshed in negotiations and unconscionable delays. The disputes seemed near settlement in the 1820s when surveyors — Joseph Delafield and James Ferguson for the Americans and David Thompson and Dr. Bigsby for the British — made reconnaissances of the water routes to Lake of the Woods.

But diplomacy, like the mills of the gods, works slowly. A puzzling question was that of locating "the Long Lake" designated by the Treaty of 1783 as the boundary starting point from Lake Superior to the west. Where was this "Long Lake"? The famous Mitchell map used by the early treaty makers indicated that it was the mouth of a river some miles southwest of the Kaministikwia. Was this the Pigeon River? If so, the name "Long Lake" seems not to have been applied to it by explorers and early traders. Three theories emerged, centering in the Pigeon River, the St. Louis, and the Kaministikwia. In 1823 Delafield, the American, learned that the British, advised by the experienced David Thompson, would claim that the Long Lake was the estuary of the St. Louis River (if sustained this claim would have put the iron range and the future city of Duluth under the British flag). Delafield knew nothing about mineral riches or an unborn city, but he set to work to prove that the mysterious lake was the mouth of the Kaministikwia, far north on the Superior shore in what is now Canada.

Compromise was inevitable between these two extreme positions. In 1827 agreement on the Pigeon River appeared to be at hand, but the British contended that, if the Pigeon was adopted, the line should be diverted to run through certain portages, including the old Grand Portage. As a means of meeting this contention, the Americans suggested that, retaining the Pigeon River as the boundary, both nations should be granted free use of the portage path to the river. Once more long delays ensued. Under the Ghent treaty, the boundary commissioners were called on to submit their findings to a neutral umpire — a sovereign or state — but such action was not taken. Years went by, and it was not until 1842 that Britain and the United States, through Daniel Webster (secretary of state) and Lord Ashburton, settled the issue. The Minnesota-Canadian question was but one of many problems dealt with in the Webster-Ashburton Treaty. On this particular problem agreement was reached on the Pigeon River and the customary line of water communication with the West. An interesting proviso was that the usual portages and water routes from Superior to Lake of the Woods, including Grand Portage, should be "free and open to the use of citizens and subjects of both countries."

If in later times there have been grumblings from Americans about the details of the line worked out from the Pigeon River westward, it is salutary to recall the contemporary verdict of Lord Palmerston in the House of Commons. "A good treaty," he said, "but a very bad bargain." The treaty settled a major question. But boundaries, mile after mile, are not easy to work out, even after treaties. Negotiations dragged on until the twentieth century with respect to the specific details of this northern boundary. As late as 1908 a new boundary commission was created which set in motion surveys that carried into the 1920s, with a final report in 1931. It is all of a piece that some of the early records did not reach the public until very late. Thompson's remarkable maps were not made public until 1898 and Delafield's important diaries did not come out until 1943.

Wisdom after the event is easy. We now know that the stakes in the boundary dispute were great. From an American point of view, it is well that, whereas Webster was firm for the Pigeon River boundary, Lord Ashburton regarded it "as of little importance to either party how the line be determined through the wild country between Lake Superior and Lake of the Woods." Some line, he believed, "should be fixed and known." What the baron was talking about, though the future veiled it from his eyes, was the fate of the Minnesota north shore, the "Arrowhead country," the iron mines, and the proud cities of the northeast, including Duluth at the head of the Great Lakes. These inestimable prizes, which might have been lost by a diplomatic misstep, were won for the United States and for the state of Minnesota.

Interior of a Hudson's Bay Company store, from Robert M.
Ballantyne's *Hudson Bay* (London, 1876)

Tribal Feuds and a Fur Barony

AMERICAN wisdom was challenged by the job of superintending the wilderness, governing frontier lands, and dealing with people recently out of the stone age.

Treaties, laws, soldiers were essential, but they were not enough. This the War Department realized. Its policies involved not only defense, the building of forts, and the sending of expeditions in search of information, but also a frontier civilian administration. This centered in the management of Indian relations. It meant agreements with native tribes; law enforcement; the prevention, if possible, of intertribal wars; control of the use of liquor in the fur trade; payments of annuities; administrative arrangements for Indian removals and reservations; and guidance for the Indians on the paths to civilization.

A singular feature of American Indian policy is the role long played by formal treaties. This system, bulwarked by colonial and pre-constitutional precedents, functioned under the War Department from 1789 to 1849 and was continued thereafter, under different auspices, until as late as 1871.

The national experience of the United States, which negotiated hundreds of Indian treaties, was reflected in the Minnesota story. Treaty-making, with its formal ceremony and Senate ratification, implied that the United States was in fact dealing with independent nations. But our treaties with England and France establishing national boundaries car-

125

ried no limitation on American sovereignty over the lands acquired. Agreements with the Indians were needed, but the treaties were a diplomatic kind of pretense. In the aftermath, promises were disregarded or forgotten or delayed in fulfillment (as illustrated by Pike's treaty of 1805). The natives were eager to receive gifts and compensation, but they had little conception of what their promises meant. Tribal practice did not accept chiefs' signatures as commitments that individual tribesmen had to honor. Dishonest agents found ways to cheat the Indians; and honest agents were frustrated in their work to protect them. When the tide of settlement came, pioneers paid little or no respect to the limits of land cessions agreed on in solemn treaties.

Before Fort Snelling was founded, indeed as early as 1815, General Clark, the superintendent of Indian affairs at St. Louis, urged the stationing of a United States Indian agent at the junction of the Mississippi and Minnesota rivers, but action was not taken until 1819. In the spring of that year, before Colonel Leavenworth established the fort, President Monroe appointed Lawrence Taliaferro to be the Indian agent at St. Peter's (the junction of the Mississippi and Minnesota rivers). At first directed to accompany the troops, Taliaferro was later ordered to report to Clark at St. Louis, and he did not arrive at Fort Snelling until the summer of 1820.

A Virginian of a patrician family, colonial Italian in origin, and a friend of President Monroe, Major Taliaferro had served in the War of 1812 and continued in the Army until Monroe had him resign his commission in order to accept a civilian appointment. He was an unusual Indian agent, courtly and dignified, a gentleman of integrity whose nearly twenty years of Indian service were marked by an understanding attitude toward the Sioux and Chippewa; an aristocrat's appreciation of the natives' love of pomp and ceremony; and an honesty which, according to Dr. Folwell, made him "cordially hated by all who could neither bribe nor frighten him to connive at lawbreaking to the harm of Indians."

In a priceless diary Taliaferro recorded his experiences from 1820 until he resigned in 1839 — day-by-day occurrences, primitive scenes, councils, solemn orations by the Indians, some of his own replies, and the many problems that made his position one of difficulty and, in the end, frustration and discouragement. The spirit of the man is reflected in a speech to the Sioux midway in his service. He did not fail to praise their leaders of the past —"the old branches which have fallen from the

Trunk of the old oak of your Nation." He urged the tribesmen to ab-
stain from war with their traditional enemies, and he alluded to American power: "Your Great Father has had much to do with war — but his
heart is changed for peace." He counseled the Sioux to follow that "good
example" as one that would please not only the "Great Father" but also
the "Great Spirit." With peace, he told his listeners, "You will see your
children growing up around you and your wives smiling as you approach
from your day's hunt."

But the Sioux-Chippewa feud was too inveterate, fighting too inbred in
the Indian tradition of glory, to be cleared away by the words of even
so wise a man as Taliaferro. Nor was the military arm able to prevent
sporadic raids, scalpings, and fierce little Indian wars. The tactics of the
natives, according to Marcus Lee Hansen, the historian of Fort Snelling,
were to lurk "in the bushes to waylay their enemies on the woodland
paths," to hide "on the river banks to intercept hostile canoes," and to
pretend peace and even enjoy hospitality "in order to have an opportunity for treachery." Taliaferro and Colonel Snelling could take action
after an episode of violence, but penalties did not stop the feud. And
native ferocity all too often was inflamed by liquor supplied by traders,
a practice Taliaferro tried hard to abolish. Peace between the ancient
enemies was as evanescent as the smoke curling from the pipes they
used to pledge it.

An episode of 1827 illustrates the nature of the Indian problem. A
Chippewa delegation visited the fort, and the colonel allowed the Indians
to put up their lodges nearby. Taliaferro, who had been away when they
arrived, returned and many Sioux swarmed to the fort to welcome him,
with hopes of receiving presents. The agent preached peace to both Sioux
and Chippewa but informed the Chippewa that his authority no longer
extended over them, since they were now under the agency at Sault Ste.
Marie, a transfer of 1827 that he had opposed. All was placid, and some
of the Sioux visited a lodge of the Chippewa. There was a feast that
included roast dog. The braves puffed the pipe of peace. In the evening
goodbyes were said and the Sioux left. As they departed, they turned,
raised their guns, and fired a murderous volley into the Chippewa crowding the lodge.

This bloody event was followed by a melodramatic demonstration of
frontier justice. The murders (two of the Chippewa were killed) were an
affront to the flag of the supposedly protective fort as well as treachery

127

to the Chippewa. Colonel Snelling, acting for the government, took decisive action the next day, when several hundred Sioux appeared before the walls. Two companies of soldiers marched out; the Sioux ran away, but several were captured, including two of the murdering party. Two others were voluntarily surrendered later by the Sioux. Snelling handed the guilty Indians to the Chippewa for punishment; and the method employed was that of running the gauntlet. In each of two scenes of execution, two Sioux culprits were given a thirty-yard start on a dash to nearby woods and safety, where other Sioux were waiting. Signals were shouted, the desperate men ran for their lives, but they were shot down, their scalps torn off, their bodies mutilated and tossed into the river. Justice was barbaric and swift. Taliaferro felt that the lesson administered under the arm of the fort and his own office might prevent future eruptions — but later events proved him oversanguine.

Meanwhile the agent attended to a multitude of duties. Soon after his arrival he gathered up British flags, medals, and gorgets (crescent-shaped ornaments, usually of silver) from the Indians, symbols of their allegiance to the British. In 1824 he escorted a party of Sioux and Chippewa, also some Menominees, to Washington to meet the "Great White Father" (President John Quincy Adams), and to agree, along with other tribes, to hold a conference the next year at Prairie du Chien to work out peace guarantees for the Northwest. That conclave, a brilliant one, took place in 1825, and Taliaferro performed the difficult task of taking 385 Sioux and Chippewa to Fort Crawford without the bloody accompaniment of murder. A vast council was held, Commissioners Cass and Clark were present, Schoolcraft also — and pledges of peace were given. Of special Minnesota interest was an agreement on a boundary line between the Sioux and the Chippewa. This line ran down southeasterly from the Red River (at Goose Creek) to the Chippewa (below present Eau Claire, Wisconsin). The frontier, as it turned out, was more important in demarcations of later land cessions than as a line the Sioux and Chippewa were not to cross except on peaceful errands. So little did the Indians understand such a boundary that they tore up stakes when the whites tried to mark the line ten years later. Marauding excursions were not given up.

Another council and treaty marked the year 1830, this one also at Prairie du Chien. On this occasion a tract of land on the Minnesota side of Lake Pepin was signed away, in effect, to traders who had intermarried with the Sioux. The "Half-Breed Tract" was really in the nature of a reservation, but, thanks to the influence of Taliaferro, Presidents Jackson and Van Buren declined to issue individual patents. A land grab was thwarted at least temporarily.

More important were land-cession treaties negotiated in 1837, toward the end of the Taliaferro regime. One of these was handled by Wisconsin's governor, Henry Dodge, at Fort Snelling with the Chippewa; the other by the secretary of war, Joel R. Poinsett, at Washington with representatives of the Sioux under the guidance of Taliaferro. These treaties opened to white settlement the rich lands between the Mississippi and the St. Croix with a considerable thrust northward, and the boundary line of 1825 played an important role. The Chippewa cession was to the north of the line, the Sioux south. Permanent annuities were promised the Sioux; twenty-year annuities to the Chippewa; and there were collateral provisions to cover traders' debts, grants to half-breeds, and allocations for medical aid and instruction in farming and other occupations for the Indians. Most important was the implied invitation of the cession to pioneers — lumbermen and farmers — a harbinger of the approaching westward movement.

Few problems caused Taliaferro deeper concern than that of liquor in the fur trade. For much more than a century liquor had been poured into the Indian country. In a single year the North West and XY companies had sent more than 21,000 gallons to their western agents. The Indians, supplied by the French, English, and Americans, craved "firewater." They bartered their best furs for it. They resented trade without it. For Taliaferro, a southerner bred to genial living, opposition to liquor implied no puritanical stand. To him it was a matter of enforcement of a federal law prohibiting the introduction of "ardent spirits" into the Indian country "under any pretext." He himself, somewhat inconsistently, made friendly gifts of liquor to Indian chiefs, but he was firm in his conviction that "not one drop" should be used in the Indian trade.

Taliaferro knew much about the dire effects of whisky on the natives. In his diary he describes typical incidents. One records that a trader sold liquor for furs to an Indian who then invited a friend to share his throat-burning treasure. The friend imbibed, got drunk, and repaid the courtesy of his host by smashing a tomahawk into his brain. This murder, said Taliaferro, was "one of many hundred such occurrences." Individual murder was bad enough, but Indian warfare was worse. And liquor was a torch to tribal feuds. It also caused revolting spectacles. One scene of Indian intoxication caused Colonel Snelling to describe it as "the most degraded picture of human nature I ever witnessed."

Under Taliaferro and the successive commanders of the fort, boats coming up river were searched for liquor. From one vessel eighteen barrels were confiscated. But smuggling was incessant. Independent traders evaded regulations and laws. The traders of the American Fur Company, which took a nominal stand against the use of liquor in their trade, brought it in "by land and water," according to Taliaferro. The company's officials were so angry at Taliaferro for his whisky seizures that Robert Stuart in 1827 urged that charges of unfriendliness to the agents of the company be preferred against him. Ramsay Crooks presented the complaints to the superintendent for Indian affairs in the Mississippi country, who declared himself willing to arrange a hearing. Taliaferro, instead of retreating, launched a spirited attack on the traders, particularly on Joseph Rolette; the fur company officials withdrew their charges; and no hearing was held. Similarly Colonel Snelling came into sharp conflict with Astor, who complained to the secretary of war. The secretary instructed the superintendent of Indian affairs to release in bond any liquors confiscated under the liquor law by the irate colonel.

In 1836 Taliaferro averred that he had driven whisky out of the country. He had not done so, though federal law had strengthened his hand.

Taliaferro had a sincere concern for the welfare of the Indians. When the evil scourge of smallpox visited them, as in 1832, he secured the aid of Fort Snelling's surgeon in a campaign of vaccination. Not a few times, when bands of Sioux were starving, he drew on governmental supplies and even his own personal funds to help them. But his ideas went beyond crises. He was interested in a plan for civilizing the Indians.

Congress in the year Fort Snelling was founded made its first appropriation for Indian education ($10,000); and in 1822 the preacher and geographer Jedidiah Morse published a report to the secretary of war in which he recommended the establishment of "Education Families" in the Indian country — farms conducted as practical illustrations for the redmen. Morse even included the Fort Snelling area and Sandy Lake among the bases he suggested. Convinced of the abilities of the natives, he went so far as to recommend an American college, endowed by proceeds from public lands, for Indian youths. Taliaferro, in the heart of the Sioux country, believed that through farming the Indians might adjust themselves to changes that seemed inevitable. Toward the end of the 1820s he won the cooperation of Cloudman, chief of the Lake Calhoun band, and supplied him with plows, hoes, and other implements. He founded at Lake Calhoun an Indian farming community with a log village as its nucleus and named it "Eatonville" in honor of the secretary of war. It began humbly, but by 1833 numbered 125 persons and harvested between 800 and 1000 bushels of corn.

Few realized what a rough road the American Indian was facing in the world of white men. At the time, traders were suspicious, even hostile. The redmen had little interest, and progress was slow. But when the missionaries came, Taliaferro hailed them as allies in the work — in fact, to him their mission was primarily one of civilizing the Indians. And Indian treaties usually included allocations of money for farming aid, medical service, and other spurs to the work of civilizing the country's wards.

It is ironical that Taliaferro's final year as agent, 1839, was darkened by the worst outbreak of intertribal fighting in the two decades of his service. Raids, killings, scalpings had taken place intermittently, but in 1838 a train of events led to an Indian war. Hole-in-the-Day, Chippewa chief from the Gull River country, casually massacred some stray Sioux, mainly women and children, in April. Later, in August, he had the temerity to visit Fort Snelling with a few followers, was ambushed not far from the fort, and one of his party was killed. The Sioux delivered up to Taliaferro the two braves who had done the killing, and they were turned over to the fort commander, now Major Joseph Plympton. He in turn had the Sioux themselves punish the murderers. They did so, not by forcing them to run the gauntlet, but by flogging them unmercifully and cutting their hair short, a mortal disgrace in Indian eyes.

These events were a prelude to killing and scalping on a grand scale the next year. About nine hundred Chippewa, some from the St. Croix region, some from Mille Lacs, came to the fort in the hope of collecting annuities under their treaty of 1837; and nearly twelve hundred Sioux, who also expected to receive annuities, assembled. There were intertribal races, lacrosse games, and the traditional ceremony of smoking the peace pipe. But a couple of relatives of the Chippewa who had been murdered in 1838 ambushed a Sioux hunter and scalped him.

As the news spread, Sioux bands gathered in force to take revenge.

The upshot was a war hunt for the Chippewa, who had departed for their homes, one group by way of Lake St. Croix, the other by the Mississippi and Rum rivers. The Sioux timed their attacks craftily, catching the St. Croix contingent while they were asleep after a night of heavy drinking, and ambushing the Mille Lacs Chippewa after many of their warriors had left camp on a hunt. Twenty-one Chippewa were killed in the St. Croix attack, and seventy, chiefly women and children, on the Rum River, near present Anoka.

The Calhoun villages of the Sioux were scenes of barbaric rejoicing, although they had themselves lost seventeen braves. Scalps were flaunted on high poles, death chants sung, and scalp dances went on for a month. The very scene of Taliaferro's hopefully planned "Eatonville" was turned into a nightmare of savagery. Little wonder that the gentleman from Virginia departed late that year from the Minnesota country in a mood of discouragement. He was frustrated in his humane endeavor to civilize the Indians; and he was discouraged by his conflicts with traders who evaded the laws and undermined his influence. He was even disconsolate about the department in Washington under which he served, because it had split his domain and often delayed its shipments of needed goods. Yet he had the satisfaction of knowing that his commission as Indian agent had been renewed five times. Lawrence Taliaferro ranks as an honest, able, and conscientious official of the government at a frontier outpost, and yet in the perspective of history it must be added that, for reasons beyond his control, the sum total of his achievements as Indian agent was negligible. His importance rests in part on his personal integrity in an era of low standards in Indian administration. In part it also rests on his role as a contemporary recorder of the scenes and events that he witnessed during two early decades of Minnesota history.

Minnesota, fortunate in leadership under military and civilian authority, was enlivened by exploration and darkened by tribal animosity. But the basic character of the 1820s and 1830s was fashioned by the exigencies of business. The fur trade was in a new era. The scene was one of transition. It was one of traders and trading posts, of an advancing monopoly by the American Fur Company, ruthless exploitation, then decline. John Jacob Astor was in the ascendant. Tightening his organization in 1817, he chose a remarkable man as his business manager. This was Ramsay Crooks, a Highlander who had emigrated to Montreal with his mother in

1803 and later had a rich experience in the fur trade, including association with Astor in the Far West. Crooks was an organizational genius, alert to every facet of the fur business, in many respects the guiding force in the policies of the great company long before Astor sold out. He took a lively interest in the Minnesota trade, visited the region, and knew its problems and personalities.

The Scottish tradition survived in Crooks and others, but Gallic names are not uncommon in the American trade of the Minnesota country. Many French-Canadians were active — some, for a time, in competition with the American Fur Company. Thus Joseph Renville, French-Sioux in antecedents, a soldier on the British side in the War of 1812 and later famed for his trading at Lac qui Parle, set up with two associates an independent company in 1822, duly licensed by Taliaferro under the legal name of Tilton and Company (known also as the Columbia Fur Company), which did business from Lake Michigan to the Missouri. It lasted only five years. In 1827 the American Fur Company took it over and brought Renville himself into its fold by extending credit to him through Joseph Rolette, its agent at Prairie du Chien. The next year Renville, who lived like "an African chief," built a house at Lac qui Parle that was acclaimed for its hospitality and the linguistic prowess of its host.

Louis Provençalle, Canadian-born, an old voyageur who like Renville served on the British side in the War of 1812, appears at several places in the 1820s but is especially associated with Traverse des Sioux from as early as 1823. Shrewd and experienced, he affiliated with the American Fur Company, receiving his trading licenses from Taliaferro. One of his minor distinctions is that he kept books with a curious system of hieroglyphs, or pictographs, of his own devising. Jean Baptiste Faribault, picturesque French-Canadian trader, had been driven off Pike Island by floods and established himself in 1826 at Mendota, though he usually wintered at Little Rapids, some thirty-five miles away. He was a man of tough fiber. On one occasion in 1833 he was stabbed dangerously by an enraged Sioux, but he survived; and his life story runs from 1774 to 1860. His son Alexander, born at Prairie du Chien, was licensed to trade in the Minnesota River area as early as 1822 and by 1828 had a post on the Cannon River, where the city of Faribault now stands.

The fame of Henry Hastings Sibley, who in 1834 took charge of the post at Mendota and became the regional lord of the American Fur Company's empire, has tended to obscure the fact that Minnesota in the

1820s was dotted with fur-trading posts. They numbered, in all, more than forty, and most of them were controlled by the great company. Not a few were in the north and west — from Grand Portage, Grand Marais, and Fond du Lac to Sandy, Cass, Mille Lacs, and Red lakes as far as Warroad and Pembina. Others stretched from Pike Island and Mendota to Traverse des Sioux, the Cannon River, Lac qui Parle, Big Stone Lake, and Lake Traverse. Their business was considerable. In a single year on the Cannon River Faribault gathered up 50 buffalo robes, 130 martens, 1100 minks, 663 raccoons, 25 lynx, 5 foxes, 2050 pounds of deerskins, 125 of beaver skins, and 39,080 muskrats. Taliaferro had authority to issue fur-trade licenses, and no one could trade in his area without being duly licensed and bonded. Police power went with the authority, for under licenses traders were prohibited from using liquor in their business. In 1826 Taliaferro issued 25 licenses; in 1827, 11; in 1830, 13; in 1831, 14 — evidence of the extent of trading activity in that period.

A detailed study of the Minnesota fur trade from 1815 to the coming of Sibley in 1834 would open up a chapter in history not yet written. And it might reveal Alexis Bailly, in charge of the Mendota post from the early 1820s to 1834, save for a stay in New York from 1831–32, as a more important figure than he has seemed to be in the shadow of Sibley, who replaced him. Bailly, of a noted French family, son of a famous trader, and married to a daughter of Jean Baptiste Faribault, was a man of enterprise who as early as 1821 drove a herd of cattle to sell to the settlers on the Red River. His trade in the 1820s was extensive, but he clashed with Taliaferro, who on one occasion had soldiers confiscate two barrels of whisky from his Mendota establishment.

In 1834 Taliaferro took away Bailly's license because of "imprudence and folly" — chiefly violations of the liquor regulations. This action opened the way for a young man from Michigan to play an unusually long and significant role in Minnesota history.

The coming of Henry Hastings Sibley synchronized with a new organization of the American Fur Company. The charter held by Astor expired in 1833. Shrewdly aware of the fact that the fur business had seen its best days, he retired from this field and turned to investments in New York real estate. Ramsay Crooks in 1834 was made president of the reorganized company. The old name was retained. The central office was in New York, as before, and major establishments were at

Mackinac, Detroit, Prairie du Chien, La Pointe, Sault Ste. Marie, with many lesser stations. Close relations were maintained with the western-oriented firm of Pratte, Chouteau, and Company of St. Louis. Sibley worked with two noted traders at Prairie du Chien, Hercules L. Dousman and Joseph Rolette, and all three were under Crooks' vigilant supervision. Sibley was assigned to the "Sioux Outfit," with headquarters at Mendota. His trading interests extended from Lake Pepin to Little Falls, northwest to Pembina, through the Minnesota Valley, and westward to the rivers flowing to the Missouri. The trade employing the Lake Superior route and exploiting the northern area was organized in a Fond du Lac department known as the "Northern Outfit."

Sibley's assignment was a responsible one for a man of twenty-three years, but he was already well qualified by character and experience. He had been born in Detroit of New England stock. His father, Solomon Sibley, was chief justice of the Supreme Court of Michigan from 1824 to 1836, and his mother Sarah, a pioneer lady of ability and charm, was a granddaughter of Commodore Abraham Whipple of Revolutionary fame. Sibley attended an academy in Detroit, was tutored in Latin and Greek for two years and studied law, but his interests were in hunting, adventure, and business — an "active and stirring life." So at eighteen he broke away from home, went to Sault Ste. Marie, then to Mackinac as a clerk under Robert Stuart for the American Fur Company. He saw the infant city of Chicago in 1829 — a stockade and a half dozen houses — and Milwaukee, where the only house was that of Solomon Juneau, trader and the city's founder. Lithe, muscular, decisive, he tasted some of the hazards of western life. Once, when he was on Lake Michigan with nine voyageurs, his canoe struck a submerged rock. He stuffed his overcoat into a jagged hole and coolly ordered his canoemen to pull for shore, which they did successfully.

In 1834 Sibley crossed Lake Michigan from Mackinac to Green Bay, followed the old French route of the Fox and Wisconsin rivers to Prairie du Chien, then with Alexis Bailly and some other companions made his way northward on horse, stopping at Wabasha to feast on honey and venison with a French trader named Augustin Rocque. On October 28 he arrived at St. Peter's. He viewed the stone walls and towers of Fort Snelling and came to the tiny village of Mendota with its crude log huts, in one of which, Bailly's, he lived for some time. Thus began the Minnesota career of a man destined to supervise an empire of furs, help to

135

create Minnesota Territory and fashion Minnesota's constitution, serve as the first governor of the North Star state, command an army in an Indian war, and win renown as citizen and recorder of early Minnesota.

Sibley took up where Bailly had left off. The Sioux Outfit, drawing on the posts and resources that Bailly and others had developed, did a business worth some $60,000 in the year after Sibley's advent. Beavers, the coin of earlier trade, were a small part of this trade, but there were 389,388 muskrats (worth $44,702.08), the major crop. And there were 1027 otters ($4135); 1139 buffalo robes ($4156); 3243 deerskins ($972); 225 beavers ($900); and 609 fishers ($913.50). Minks were not expensive, 2330 netting only $698.40; and 2011 coons brought in $603.30. Sibley also handled in that year's business 462 martens, 100 bears (and 24 bear coverings for packs), 63 bear cubs, 34 wolves, 205 foxes, 12 badgers, 80 swan skins, 3 rabbits, 3 wildcats, and 2588 kittens. If the figures seem small by modern standards, they were big business in 1835. And profits were generous. The business was carried on by barter. A blanket worth $3.25 (or a tin kettle valued at $2.50) meant sixty muskrat skins, worth $12.00. A looking glass (4 cents) traded for 4 muskrats (80 cents).

The fur business functioned, in accordance with long practice, on credit. Goods were advanced to the Indian hunters who in the spring would deliver their furs and pelts to square their accounts. This credit system depended for its success on the season's catch of furs, which might vary from year to year, and it also hinged upon the reliability of the Indians in making available each year to the traders who had extended the credit whatever furs had been gathered. As time went on, many traders had extensive credits on their books which had not been met by the products of the annual hunts. It was this accumulation of credits that led the traders to seek compensation for their claims whenever land-cession treaties were negotiated. They asked the government to set aside certain sums of money from the totals awarded the Indians for lands in order to make good what the Indians owed them.

The returns from the fur trade in the 1830s were impressive, but, as Astor had divined, the American Fur Company was facing a decline. Its dividends were fairly high both in 1836 and in 1837, but only three years after Sibley appeared on the scene, the Panic of 1837 took place, marking the beginning of the end of the domain Astor and Crooks had created.

Sibley was not content to sit at the Mendota center, managing, receiving furs, and corresponding with Crooks in New York and others. In 1835 he mounted his horse and set out to visit the posts of his empire and to meet with hunters and trappers. At Traverse des Sioux he called on Provençalle, who recorded one transaction by drawing a wolf and a blanket (product and price paid). At Lake Traverse he met Joseph R. Brown, drummer boy at Fort Snelling in 1819, a versatile man who figures in history as soldier, trader, lumberman, editor, politician, and inventor. He also met with the Faribaults, Renville, Joseph Laframboise, and others; and inspected, at Lake Traverse, a trader's stockade, with its blockhouses and portholes, and a gate with an aperture through which untamed Indians could pass in their buffalo robes. These were a few of the many traders of the time in Minnesota. Others included William Alexander Aitkin, Scottish in birth, a man of experience who had charge of the Fond du Lac department and was associated at various times with posts at Vermilion Lake, Pembina, and Sandy Lake. William and Allan Morrison were familiar figures in the north country, at Leech, Red, and Sandy lakes, and William, who was at Rainy Lake in 1823, was the trader who claimed to have discovered Lake Itasca (Elk Lake) long before Schoolcraft's journey of 1832.

An amazing character in the fur trade was Martin McLeod of Montreal, who joined a bizarre filibustering expedition across northern Minnesota in 1836. Its leader was James Dickson, who posed as "The Liberator." He recruited some straggling followers for a private "army" and hoped to set up an Indian kingdom in far-off California. The cold and half-starved army and its commander's fantastic dreams collapsed miserably at the Red River settlements. McLeod, who found solace in reading Byron, Shakespeare, and the classics, made his way to Fort Snelling and later traded in Minnesota at Lac qui Parle, and especially at Traverse des Sioux in the 1840s. Still later he appeared as the sponsor of the basic common-school law of Minnesota.

A famed trader of Sibley's regime in the 1840s was Norman W. Kittson, Canadian-born, first with headquarters at Big Stone Lake, then at Pembina (south of the Canadian border) where he offered a sharp challenge to the Hudson's Bay Company.

Mendota, with the shielding walls of Fort Snelling nearby, needed no stockade. But Sibley built a stone warehouse there and also in 1835 a stone mansion, now preserved as a museum — historic not merely because it is one of the oldest private dwellings of the Northwest, but also because it was a friendly spot where both whites and Indians found genial sanctuary. It was distinguished by a library that boasted books of Hallam, Prescott, Froissart, Thiers, and Sparks; a "piano forte"; and the accouterments of a man of catholic interests. Here, over the years, he received guests with urbane courtesy and warm hospitality — scientists, soldiers, travelers. Sibley in his letters to the American Fur Company ranges over many problems and subjects. He deals with the Indians, the control of liquor, land cessions, seeds for his gardens, relations with Taliaferro (whom he regarded as "inimical" to the traders), and the fur trade in its declining period.

Sibley was a skilled hunter who kept records of his game. In one three-year period — in an age before restrictive game laws — he shot no fewer than 1798 ducks. He often joined the Sioux in their annual expeditions for skins and meat. From October 1841 until March of 1842 he accompanied a Sioux expedition that bagged more than 2000 deer, 50 to 60 elk, many bears, some buffaloes, and even a few panthers. But the interest of his hunting runs beyond his exploits — he was a writer who contributed to the literature of the frontier West. He wrote numerous articles and essays under pseudonyms (among them "Walker-in-the-Pines" and "Hal — a Dacotah") that were published in such contemporary magazines as the *Spirit of the Times.* Hunting in woods and on the prairies, Indian customs, tribal warfare, and character sketches were his favorite themes. Many years after his early adventures he took down the book-length story of the life and adventures of Jack Frazer, a famed Scotch-Sioux hunter and warrior better known as "Iron Face." And late in life Sibley wrote many reminiscent articles and also his *Unfinished Autobiography*, a narrative dealing with the earlier portion of his life. An observer who pictured things as he saw them, Sibley was a dependable recorder of scenes and characters of the primitive West. His sincerity of interest encompassed the French-Canadian voyageurs, important in the American period as they had been in earlier times. Again and again he described their ways and character. They were "merry, good-natured, and obedient" and they "were unrivalled as canoe, and boat, men, extremely skilful" in navigating lakes and streams. He pays unaffected tribute to their "honesty and fidelity."

The American Fur Company was a pioneer of big business, complex and far-reaching. Its activities, even in the Minnesota region, had facets beyond the area of Sibley's authority. There was, for instance, a flourishing business in the fisheries of Lake Superior in the 1830s, inspired by Crooks. The company studied the potentialities of the lake and established stations at Isle Royale, Grand Portage, Fond du Lac, and other places. At Grand Portage a half-breed named Pierre Coté packed several hundreds of barrels of whitefish and trout in a season. The large fishing depot for the lake, however, was at La Pointe, where the noted Danish merchant and physician Charles W. W. Borup managed the business from 1838 (Borup had traded at Rainy Lake as early as 1830). The company built and used several schooners, including the appropriately named *John Jacob Astor* and *Ramsay Crooks*. The total fish yield went as high as 4000 to 5000 barrels a year in the late 1840s.

The fisheries, however, were only one of many enterprises of the company. It was a dealer in land; it raised produce; did business in maple sugar and cranberries; sold merchandise; mined copper and lead; carried mail; and served as a banker and manufacturer. It even issued a paper currency of its own — "Beaver Money." It handled complicated problems of transportation in an era of slow travel and prodigious distances from source to market. It dealt with English and continental makers of blankets, with the Leipzig fairs, and with merchants in far countries. Whatever its diversification, the main business of the company was furs. As big business, it faced a constant problem in competition. This was somewhat eased in the north country of Lake Superior by a compact (1833) under which the Hudson's Bay Company paid an annual stipend for the privilege of operating the boundary trade. It was less easy for the company to stay the inroads of ambitious rivals such as the Ewings of Fort Wayne or of independents on ceded lands.

The company was shaken by the Panic of 1837 and Ramsay Crooks urgently called for economy and "prudent management." "We have been living in profusion for a few years back," he wrote to one of his western agents; "money was as plenty as the sand on the sea shore, but that abundance has given place to a frightful scarcity." Other forces than the panic contributed to the decline of the company, however, and to its receivership in 1842. The turn of fashion played a part. Taste had gone to silks rather than the long-favored beaver hats. The South American nutria, with fur not unlike that of the beaver, won popularity to the disadvantage of American sales. The vitally important European market declined. The British Army abandoned its traditional beaver headgear

(1842); and troubles in the Far East closed Chinese ports. Meanwhile change was stirring in the West. The land cessions of 1837, carrying grants to the Indians, slackened native effort — and trapping was no longer so productive as it once had been. Independent traders, filtering into the ceded lands, smuggled in whisky as liquid bait and snared much trade. Crooks himself, after the receivership, continued in the fur business — in fact retaining the company name — and in other enterprises until his death in 1859.

Sibley, dwelling in manorial fashion in his stone house at Mendota — especially after he married Sarah Jane Steele, a sister of the noted pioneer Franklin Steele, in 1843 — also persisted in the trade, working in part with the Pierre Chouteau interests in St. Louis. Wilderness life for him was a schooling for public service. It toughened his mettle as a pioneer founder in many fields. He had acumen, cool judgment, a sharp sense for business, and these were coupled with the urbanity of a well-read country gentleman. His experience in the Mendota fur barony deepened his feeling for past and future. He was a self-trained historian who grew with the times and whose eyes looked to the future commonwealth.

The fur trade, in a new era, would never regain its primacy as *the* industry of the region, but the fading of the American Fur Company did not mean any sudden cessation of the fur business. The garnering and marketing of furs continued with Mendota as a nucleus, and when St. Paul developed, the trade was transferred to that city, where it was important for many decades. Lumbering and farming were not far away. Trade is a major factor in frontier history, and it was nourished by products, marketing, enterprise, and the changing character and needs of society. Skins and furs had been the basis of the commerce that tied Minnesota to the world. But a time for change had come in the 1840s.

The "Basilica" of St. Paul in 1852, from an oil by R. O. Sweeney

★

Preachers, Word Hunters, Teachers

SOME moderns think of missionaries as people narrowly circumscribed in their interests, but the records of early Minnesota do not sustain such a view. With few exceptions the missionaries were men of generous interests and liberal education. They were curious and observant, versatile, practical, and buoyed by their faith. Some who were unlearned trained themselves in what can only be called scholarship. And the men did not stand alone. Their wives were "wilderness Marthas" — women who took part in the missionary work and adapted themselves to primitive living conditions with courage and poise.

The missionaries were not only preachers. They were also farmers, teachers, recorders of Indian life, writers, scholars, linguists, compilers of dictionaries, and frontier travelers. Inveterate writers — of letters, diaries, reports, speeches, and books — they did more than record their own experiences. They created a firsthand and valuable documentation of Indian ways and traditions and of the Indian country. They transmuted spoken to written languages. And if they won few converts to the Christian religion, yet they worked with devotion, and their services pioneered many of the churches whose future spires had been envisioned by Carver in the eighteenth century.

The Minnesota missions were focused upon the Chippewa and Sioux peoples. Some missionaries made their way independently to the Indian country, relying on their own resources. Much missionary endeavor was sponsored, however, by societies, boards, and other organizations at home and abroad. These included the American Board of Commissioners for Foreign Missions (with headquarters in Boston and representing the program of the Congregational, Presbyterian, and Dutch Reformed churches); the American Missionary Association; the Catholic Leopoldine Society of Vienna; the French-centered Society for the Propagation of the Faith; the Evangelical Mission Society of Lausanne, Switzerland; a zealous group at Oberlin, Ohio; the Wesleyans; and yet others.

The early nineteenth century swirled with religious and humanitarian movements concerned with Christianizing natives and improving their lot not alone in the Indian wilderness but also in many other corners of the world. Emissaries from New England, Bibles in hand, were especially active, and their Minnesota efforts coincided with ventures in other Indian areas, in Hawaii, and elsewhere among peoples whose heritage did not include the cross. In America, mission societies received aid through the Education Fund of the government, which gave money for the support of schools for Indian children. The period was one of denominational schooling. The mission societies gladly accepted subventions for enterprises in which their schools were leagued with religious objectives. Education was fundamental to Christianization, and the two went hand in hand in the Minnesota Indian missions.

Winning the natives to faith in the white man's religion and to an understanding of its teachings was no easy task. The common words of Christianity meant little or nothing to Sioux and Chippewa. They recognized a Great Spirit, but they had gods for diverse needs and occasions. Now they were exhorted not only to abjure their own deities, but to worship one God and only one. Their gods harmonized with the natural world they knew. Their forms of worship came out of an immemorial past. The Indians were puzzled by a history reaching thousands of moons back to peoples, lands, and ideas completely alien to them. They took note of the circumstance, strange to them, that Christians were divided — Congregationalists, Presbyterians, Methodists, Catholics, and others. They could not be blind to a disparity between the missionaries and certain of the traders. Some traders referred to the white man's God in tones that contrasted shockingly with the reverent accents of the missionaries. Both were white men — why the difference? The traders wanted furs and used liquor to get them. The missionaries asked nothing for themselves, and to most of them the use of firewater was sin. The white man's conception of sin was in itself difficult to comprehend. All the redmen were, in their way, religious; some white men were, others were not. The missionaries had to explain why. And they also had to learn Chippewa and Sioux in order to transmit the teachings of the Bible. The native languages were essential tools for effective preaching and teaching.

The schools and missions for the Chippewa were encouraged by traders of the American Fur Company who took an interest in the schooling of mixed-blood children. Indian marriages, conforming to the custom of the times, were common among the traders, and there were numerous children. Ramsay Crooks, Robert Stuart, Lyman M. Warren, and William A. Aitkin had a humane interest in starting schools for such youngsters. Warren, an intelligent trader and a devout Presbyterian stationed at La Pointe, was among the first to invite teachers. And in 1830–31 Frederick Ayer of Massachusetts conducted a school at that place. Eager for reinforcements, in 1832 he welcomed another New Englander, Sherman Hall, a graduate of Dartmouth and Andover Theological Seminary, to Madeline Island to launch a mission station there. Hall later made a Chippewa translation of the New Testament. This well-educated New Englander did not spend all his time translating or preaching. In one of his letters he wrote: "I have been obliged the past winter and spring to put my hand into the wash tub, to handle the mop and broom, to cook my food and wash my dishes."

Ayer in 1833 moved on to Sandy Lake on invitation from Aitkin, the trader there. How quickly this young Presbyterian grappled with the language problem is illustrated by his preparation of a Chippewa spelling book that he got into print the very year of his arrival. Backed by the American Board, Ayer centered his work from 1836 at Pokegama Lake (in present Pine County) where, in the late 1830s, an attempt was made to develop a missionary and school center allied with a program of agricultural teaching for the Chippewa; a farmer sent out by the Indian bureau gave instruction through demonstration.

William T. Boutwell, who had shared with Schoolcraft the sight of Itasca in 1832, returned to Minnesota as a missionary in 1833. This time he had with him Edmund F. Ely, another New Englander eager to convert Indians. Boutwell was a Congregationalist and, like Hall, a graduate of Dartmouth and Andover. He had already studied the Chippewa lan-

145

guage at Mackinac and the Sault. With Ely he journeyed from La Pointe to Sandy Lake and then pushed on to Leech Lake. Ely stayed on at Sandy Lake, starting instruction to the Indians though, as he wrote in his diary, "my lips can utter very few words intelligible to my scholars." He dug into the study of Chippewa, and in his teaching cut blocks of letters for his pupils to help them to learn "Syllables and words." He taught, led the Indians in singing, occasionally attended a voyageur dance, visited Leech Lake by dog train, and in 1834 joined a brigade to Fond du Lac, where he promptly started another school, served as a lay doctor, and compiled spelling, reading, and hymn books. In 1839 he gave up that mission and joined hands with others at Pokegama.

Boutwell first lived in a wigwam at Leech Lake and took his meals "sitting flat upon the ground." Like nearly all the missionaries, he kept a diary, and in it he records typical scenes, such as a cabin thronged with Indians "stretched and sprawling their whole length" on the floor. He often lived on a miserable diet of "mush and salt." Once he took a hard trip on snowshoes, forty miles in eleven hours. And he performed a marriage for two Catholics unable to get a license and expecting later to be wedded by a priest. He married Hester Crooks, the talented and well-schooled mixed-blood daughter of the famous American Fur Company magnate. Their wedding feast, at Fond du Lac, was one of tea and doughnuts, their honeymoon a journey up the St. Louis River, over the Savanna portage "through mud and water half-leg deep," and across wild country to the lake shore where Boutwell built for his wife a mud-walled cabin with deerskin windows.

The experiment of a consolidated mission center at Pokegama Lake came to grief in the 1840s to the accompaniment of war whoops and bloodshed. The Chippewa-Sioux feud broke out again in 1841 and 1842, with fierce raids, attacks, and counterattacks. The Chippewa understandably feared that Pokegama was dangerously exposed to assaults by war parties and this fear caused a dispersion of the natives. Lacking Indians to teach and convert, the missionaries abandoned the center in 1847.

The missionaries did not neglect the Sioux. Two ministers, Jedediah Stevens and Alvan Coe, made an exploratory trip to the region in 1829 for the American Board, studying possible locations for mission stations and schools.

Meanwhile, two Connecticut Yankees, the brothers Samuel W. and

Gideon H. Pond, laymen who had been converted in a New England revival, arrived at Fort Snelling in the spring of 1834. They were men of elementary schooling who came on their own, without support from any board or church. They were resourceful and gifted, and they rank as major figures in the history of Minnesota missions, especially as "word hunters" with linguistic talents, and as recorders of Indian culture. They were both in their twenties, six-footers, sturdy and strong, and the Indians dubbed them "Red Eagle" and "Grizzly Bear." Though independent initially, they soon were taken under the wing of the American Board and both were ordained as ministers. But their place in history is as self-taught scholars of language and as men who wrote about Indian customs with acute observation and impressive objectivity.

They began humbly. The commandant at Fort Snelling, Major John Bliss, urged Samuel Pond to go to the nearby Sioux village of Kaposia to teach the chief, Big Thunder, how to handle a plow. Samuel drove a yoke of oxen to the village and spent a week giving practical lessons, his own farm experience in New England coming to his aid. Gideon similarly was pressed into service at Lake Calhoun. Influenced by Major Taliaferro, then sponsoring the agricultural community at that lake, the brothers established a mission station there, on its southeast side. The agent hoped that they would concentrate on teaching the Sioux to cultivate their mother earth, but they had spiritual and linguistic objectives. Even before they arrived at Fort Snelling they had begun their study of the Sioux language, and they continued so assiduously that in a year's time they were able to talk with the Indians in Sioux. Samuel, commenting on a hunting party that he once joined, wrote, "The language was the game I went to hunt, and I was as eager in the pursuit of that as the Indians were in pursuit of deer." By 1839 he had a dictionary collection of three thousand Sioux words and had worked up a manuscript grammar. He and his brother adapted the English alphabet for use in reducing the native language to written form.

The American Board, meanwhile, strengthened its work with the Sioux. In 1834 it sent out Dr. Thomas S. Williamson, a Presbyterian minister who had been trained both in medicine and in theology, to survey Minnesota as a field for schools and missions. He interviewed fur traders, traveled from Fort Snelling to Lake Traverse, and concluded that the board should assign missionaries to the Sioux without delay. He urged the establishment of a boarding school near Fort Snelling as a "strong fortress" in the strategy for Christianizing the Sioux; and he asked not only for preachers and teachers, but also for farmers. Among places he suggested for stations were Wabasha Prairie, Lake Calhoun, Lac qui Parle, and Lake Traverse.

In the spring of 1835, as a sequel, Dr. Williamson himself and Jedediah Stevens, both with their wives, arrived in Minnesota, together with a lay teacher of farming, Alexander G. Huggins. The Ponds helped Stevens to build a mission house on Lake Harriet, while the doctor and the farmer, on the recommendation of Renville and Taliaferro, went to the former's post at Lac qui Parle. All was not sweetness and light, however, in the relationships of the missionaries. Stevens, conscious of clerical authority, treated the laymen as manual laborers and took title-page credit for a Sioux spelling book that Samuel Pond compiled for publication in 1836. Gideon escaped by joining Dr. Williamson at Lac qui Parle, and Samuel went east for theological studies and formal ordination. Stevens launched a double school at Lake Harriet for mixed-blood children and for Sioux children (with his niece as the teacher); but in 1839 he was transferred by the well-advised American Board to the Sioux band of Chief Wabasha. Samuel Pond went back to the Harriet station as an appointee of the board, but his return just about coincided with the Sioux-Chippewa massacres of 1839, which led to the abandonment of both the Calhoun village and the Harriet mission.

A major goal for the missionaries to the Sioux was the translation of the Bible. This became a cooperative venture, centered at Lac qui Parle, and the translating was done in unusual fashion. Gideon Pond by 1836 was already at home in Sioux; Dr. Williamson had worked diligently at the language; and Joseph Renville, who knew the Sioux language, was adept in French. As a consequence, beginning with the New Testament, a French Bible was used as the base. Renville, hearing the French read, translated it orally into Sioux, and Pond (later also a new recruit, Stephen R. Riggs) put the translations down in black and white. A Swiss missionary, Daniel Gavin, joined the circle for one winter and contributed his understanding of French, though his expertness was not pleasing to the proud Renville. Several of the Gospels were in this way turned into Sioux.

Riggs, who joined the group in 1837, was a man of college and theological education who first tutored with Samuel Pond, learned the language, and went forward in a long career, compiling texts, translating books of the Old Testament, and ultimately, from the Greek, the entire New Testament. He edited a vast *Grammar and Dictionary of the Dakota Language*, published in 1852. Riggs was able and dynamic and a tremendous worker, but the pioneering studies of the Pond brothers were basic to his *Grammar and Dictionary*.

The contributions of missionaries as writers, editors, and scholars are important in any perspective on the mission story. The Ponds in 1839 brought out a Dakota translation of the *History of St. Joseph*, from Genesis; Gideon worked with Riggs on a first *Dakota Reading Book*; Samuel did a second reading book (1842) and two years later a *Dakota Catechism*. Gideon edited a monthly newspaper or illustrated journal, the *Dakota Friend*, in the 1850s, much of it written in Sioux and having as its purpose the promotion of friendly understanding between white and red men. The Ponds finally settled down as missionaries and ministers in the Minnesota Valley (Gideon at Oak Grove, Samuel at Chief Shakopee's village). They were frustrated in their efforts to convert the Sioux — "lawless, reckless sons of Belial," Samuel bitterly called the Shakopee band — but they never lost their interest in the redman, his ways, and his speech. And their linguistic interests were so extensive that, in addition to the Dakota language, they acquired Hebrew, Greek, Latin, and French, and Samuel also learned German.

Samuel wrote an informing general account of the Sioux in his "The Dakotas or Sioux in Minnesota as They Were in 1834"; and he also recorded Indian legends in verse and wrote an extensive narrative of his experiences and those of his brother. Gideon was the author of a study of "Dakota Superstition." Riggs, who lived until the early 1880s, had an overwhelming production, including, in addition to many translations and his studies of grammar, a fascinating autobiographical work (*Mary and I*, 1880), and a series of "Dakota Portraits." The latter were sketches, with vivid detail, of Sleepy Eyes, Iron Cloud, Thunder Face, Lowing Buffalo, and other outstanding Sioux Indians. Riggs removed to Traverse des Sioux in 1843 but returned to Lac qui Parle three years later, and in the 1850s was active in the short-lived "Hazlewood Republic," an Indian state within a state. Riggs and the Pond brothers, like the missionaries generally, were voluminous writers of letters, and much of their documentation is preserved in manuscripts that have not found their way into print.

Gavin, the Swiss Protestant who took part in the translating adventure at Lac qui Parle, came to Minnesota in 1836 with a co-worker, Samuel Dentan, supported by the Evangelical Mission Society of Lausanne, Switzerland. At Red Wing they built for themselves an "Alpine hut," started a school, cooperated with the Ponds and others, married American wives, and carried on mission work for some years. The mission was launched with high hopes, but it had its up and downs. In 1847 the Dentans transferred to Kaposia, the Gavins having earlier left for New York; and their pioneering work was continued by the American Board which sent two Americans, Joseph Hancock and John Aiton, to Red Wing on the banks of the Mississippi, a village that became one of Minnesota's important cities.

The Methodists were also active in Minnesota missionary work. A frontier preacher, Alfred Brunson, Pennsylvanian by origin, had moved westward and was established at Prairie du Chien when, in 1837, he explored possibilities for a mission in Minnesota. His choice of a location fell upon Kaposia. There, with several assistants for teaching and farming, he opened a school for the Sioux and sought to teach them English. Neither the school nor the mission lasted long, however. Little Crow was surly and antagonistic, and the mission was not effectively conducted. In 1841 its work was transferred across the Mississippi to Red Rock, later famed as a Methodist camp-meeting center.

Meanwhile another Methodist, Samuel Spates, was sent to Minnesota in 1839; and in subsequent years he served at various places among the Chippewa. Farther to the west, a revival of missionary work among the Chippewa got under way in the 1840s, after the breakup of the centralized station at Pokegama Lake. The devoted Ayer was once more on the scene, this time at Red Lake, and Ely was there also. On their urgent solicitations, the American Board encouraged a group of dedicated and cultured Christians from Oberlin, Ohio — the "Oberlin Band" — to go to the north country, as emissaries of the American Missionary Association. Their number included Dr. and Mrs. William Lewis, the Alonzo Barnards, and others, with mission stations at Leech, Red, and Cass lakes.

Concurrently Canadian and English Wesleyans had taken a missionary interest in the Indians still farther north — those along the international waterway. The English-born James Evans in the late 1830s acquainted himself with the north shore and the interior country. Though he himself pushed on to the Canadian Northwest, he first set up a mission on the Rainy River that was active in the 1840s and 1850s and included among its workers a native preacher of wide fame, Peter Jacobs. Evans, known as "The Apostle of the North," devised a syllabic "alphabet" that enabled him to reduce the unwritten Cree language to written form.

The Catholics had missionary traditions with roots in the French period, and they had by no means abandoned their interest. Through the generation after the War of 1812 their contributions extended from the Superior country to the Red River; to the developing areas in the vicinity of Fort Snelling, notably the emerging capital city of St. Paul; and to yet other places. Considering the later strength of the Catholic church in St. Paul, it is curious that missionary beginnings in that region were as late as they were. Although a plan was under consideration by the bishop of Louisiana in the early 1820s for a Catholic mission station at the junction of the Mississippi and the Minnesota rivers, its realization was long deferred.

The Roman Catholic missionary activities in the Red River colony, and more particularly at the Pembina settlement, are of no little Minnesota interest. The Catholic bishop of Quebec, Joseph Octave Plessis, in 1818 responded favorably to recommendations and petitions for a mission in the Selkirk area, his own interest the warmer because such an effort, in his view, might strengthen the move toward official British recognition of the Catholic Church in the domain of an expanding Canada. The effort to establish a mission had the support of Lord Selkirk and of governmental officials, and as early as 1816 Bishop Plessis had authorized a preliminary investigation of the western field by Pierre Tabeau, a priest. Two years later, in 1818, Fathers Joseph N. Provencher and Severe J. N. Dumoulin were sent out to the Red River settlements; and Father Dumoulin soon concentrated his efforts at Pembina. In this nomadic "settlement" of some three hundred persons he tackled the Chippewa language, started a school, and laid plans for a chapel and mission house. Now and then he journeyed to Rainy Lake where another Catholic mission had been established.

Dumoulin remained five years at Pembina, and at the end of that period the mission was abandoned for some years. As Major Long ascertained in 1823, the settlement was on the American side of the boundary. But many other problems confronted Dumoulin and his associates — the death of Selkirk and less cordial relations with the Hudson's Bay Company, the nomadic character of the settlers themselves, grasshopper plagues, floods, and difficult seasons of food scarcity. Indian alarms and the "detestable liquor" peddled by traders added to missionary frustration. A new chapter in the story opened in 1831, when Father George Anthony Belcourt began a long period of service at Pembina. He made the frontier mission a center for activities ranging both eastward and westward, and he affiliated with the American Catholics.

A trio of Slovenian priests, from Carniola (then an Austrian crownland, now in Yugoslavia), figure prominently in the Catholic missionary activities of the Lake Superior region in the 1830s, 1840s, and later. These were Fathers Frederic Baraga, Francis Pierz (Franz Pireç), and Otto Skolla. Baraga was a talented churchman who had studied law in Vienna and theology at the Seminary of Laibach, had been drawn across the Atlantic by zeal for missionary work among the Indians, and appeared at Arbre Croche (now Harbor Springs, Michigan) in 1831. He was a linguist who commanded a half dozen languages before he arrived in America and, like the Pond brothers and other missionaries, he studied intensively the language of the natives among whom he worked. In 1832, little more than a year after he came to the United States, he published a Chippewa catechism and book of prayers; and by 1850 he produced a *Theoretical and Practical Grammar of Chippewa*. Three years later he issued a Chippewa dictionary. His linguistic learning was impressive, but it was his zeal that made him a great missionary leader.

In 1835 Baraga established a mission at La Pointe, the strategic fur-trading center and also a Protestant missionary and school center. He pushed his way onward to Fond du Lac the same year, and in the next twenty years he was there time and again, preaching, baptizing, and performing other religious services. His interest also extended to historic Grand Portage, which he visited for the first time in 1837. For nearly a decade Baraga worked out from La Pointe, and thereafter from L'Anse (Keweenaw Bay), but meanwhile he had journeyed back to Austria to interest the Leopoldine Society in providing funds for Indian missions and to find new recruits among his countrymen for missionary labors. Both Pierz and Skolla were influenced by him. In fact, Baraga as early as 1830 tried to interest Pierz in going to America, but five years passed before the latter yielded to the persuasion of Baraga's eloquent letters. After several missionary experiences, he was asked by Baraga to go to Grand Portage, open a mission station there, and also a substation farther north, at Fort William. Thus began a long career in which Pierz, with support from the Leopoldine Society and the Bavarian Ludwig Society, founded and served missions not only on the north Superior shore but also at Crow Wing, Mille Lacs, Sandy Lake, and Red Lake. His services extended into the later history of Minnesota. He is remembered and honored for his role in founding Catholic churches in many Minnesota parishes and helping to induce the Benedictines in the 1850s to make central Minnesota a focus for their educational and religious activities.

All this was veiled by the future when Pierz set up a mission at Grand Portage in 1838, with an improvised chapel of cedar bark and deerskin and a school of seventy-five pupils. A few years later, in 1842, he gave his attention to another site — the mouth of the Pigeon River, where he built a church. In the mid-1840s Skolla renewed missionary work at Grand Portage, and various other priests carried forward activities along the north shore at Pigeon River, Grand Portage, and Fond du Lac. The tireless Baraga, long the general superintendent of the missions, was again at Grand Portage for a visit as late as 1855, two years before he was made bishop of Sault Ste. Marie.

The missionaries in this enterprise made many junctions with pioneer settlement. Mission stations were nuclei for settlers. The missionaries, as the Sioux were constricted by land cessions in the 1850s, founded churches and became pastors for white settlers. The strategic reasons for locating Fort Snelling at the junction of the two great rivers of Minnesota operated to make this region one of special interest for pioneers when the westward movement began to pour streams of people to the virgin lands that lay open. Here was the head of steamboat navigation on the Mississippi. The Falls of St. Anthony offered power for mills. Mendota was a trading center. The frontier fort meant protection from Indian turbulence. And the land treaties of 1837 were an invitation extended to people of diverse interests to exploit the domain between the St. Croix and the Mississippi.

Minnesota lands were not legally open to settlers until after the Sioux and Chippewa treaties of 1837 were ratified. But squatters, indifferent to legalities, clustered about Mendota and the fort in the 1820s and 1830s, occupying lands and building cabins. Not a few were French-speaking voyageurs, who had been drawn to the region by the fur trade. In the 1820s many disheartened settlers from the Selkirk colony on the Red River — chiefly immigrants recruited from Switzerland — sought sanctuary near Fort Snelling. Some five families arrived as early as 1821, twelve or thirteen more in 1823, and no fewer than 243 persons migrated as a group in 1826, journeying from Pembina with Red River oxcarts and accompanying herds of cattle. By the fall of 1827, Taliaferro estimated that 330 Red River colonists had appeared at the fort. For most of these people the fort was only a pause in a search for lands that took them down river to Wisconsin, Iowa, Illinois, and Missouri. Some stayed on, however, including the family of Barbara Ann Shadecker, who later wrote a reminiscent narrative of the emigration from Switzerland and her own experiences in the friendly society of the fort.

The officers of the fort were complaisant for some years about the squatters — French-Canadian, Swiss, and others — and Colonel Snelling in the 1820s was helpful to the emigrants from Pembina. But in the 1830s, particularly after the land cessions of 1837 which drew to the left bank of the river "independent traders" whose chief stock in trade was whisky, the commandant found it expedient to remove the squatters from the area of the Snelling reservation. Another factor was that of the fort's timber supply, which it was feared farming might endanger. Military surveys were made of the fort area in 1837 and 1839. After repeated warnings, the squatters in 1840 were ejected and their cabins leveled. They moved a short distance down river into the area of the future capital of Minnesota. Much local lore relates to Pierre Parrant, a French-Canadian remembered by the nickname of "Pig's Eye." After the treaties he claimed land near Fountain Cave, now a part of St. Paul, but a survey showed that it was within the reservation. "Pig's Eye" continued his whisky-selling in the heart of what is now downtown St. Paul.

The beginnings of the capital city and the rise of Roman Catholicism are associated with the settlers who squatted on the military reservation and then moved to the river front of infant St. Paul. Minnesota west of the river in 1839 was a part of Iowa Territory and it fell within the Catholic diocese of Dubuque, whose bishop, Mathias Loras, was interested in missionary work among the Sioux and the mixed population of the Fort Snelling–Mendota area. Before this interest caused the bishop to visit the region, he had been in France and there had enlisted the aid of two priests, Fathers Joseph Cretin and Anthony Pelamourgues, as well as a number of "subdeacons," including Lucian Galtier and Augustin Ravoux, both of whom qualified for priesthood in 1840.

In 1839 Bishop Loras and Father Pelamourgues journeyed up "along the superb Mississippi and the beautiful Lake Pepin" and on to "St. Peter's," as the settlement around the junction of the Minnesota and the Mississippi was still called. They spent about two weeks in the community, and from their records we know that they counted no fewer than 185 Catholics, nearly all of whom spoke either French or Sioux. The bishop baptized many, confirmed others, married some couples, and received not a few as communicants; and his records have preserved the names of most of them. Nearly all these frontier Catholics were French in origin. As Father M. M. Hoffman, who explored records in the cathedral archives at Dubuque, writes, "Stately patronymics of old France stand out in the bishop's peculiar writing on the time-colored pages: Jean Baptiste Latourelle, Olivier Rossico, Louis Brunelle, Amable Morin; and the names of some of the women are redolent of the fleur-de-lis and cathedral incense: Julie Ducharme, Genevieve Cardinal, Josephine Beaulieu, Isabel Madelaine." Several were children of French fathers and Indian mothers. A few names, such as Graham and Quinn, were Gaelic.

The spiritual needs of these people and the bishop's concern for the Sioux Indians caused him to promise to send north a French-speaking clergyman. The next year (1840) he dispatched two priests, Fathers Galtier and Ravoux, the former to the Mendota region, the latter to work at various places, including Traverse des Sioux, Little Rock, and Lac qui Parle. Ravoux, a man of energy and zeal, studied Sioux and before long issued, in Sioux, a booklet entitled *The Path to the House of God.*

Father Galtier, a man still under thirty, busied himself with his clerical duties in the vicinity of Mendota, living for some time with the interpreter for the Indian agency, Scott Campbell. There, as he said later, he had "a separate room for my own use, and made of it a kitchen, a parlor and a chapel." He built an altar "out of some boards," concealing it with drapery when it was not in religious use.

After studying the needs of the community, following the removal of settlers from the fort's reservation, Galtier secured a site for a chapel, a garden, and a graveyard on the river bluff road, near the steamboat landing athwart later St. Paul. Here in 1841 he built a humble log church, "so poor," he said, "that it would well remind one of the stable at Bethlehem." On November 1 he "blessed the new *basilica,* and dedicated it to 'St. Paul, the apostle of nations.'" Thus designated, the church gave its name to the settlement, in accordance with Galtier's own wish, and it has been retained through all the years by the city of St. Paul. Galtier's Minnesota career was brief, for after three years he returned to Iowa, went back to France, came again to America, and died in 1866 at Prairie du Chien. In the capital, which today boasts an impressive cathedral, the pioneer priest and the primitive chapel that he likened to the stable of Christ's birth are remembered in historic honor. Father Ravoux took over and served the Catholic interests of the community until Bishop Joseph Cretin, who had spent a decade among the Winnebago, arrived at the territorial capital in 1851 to take charge of the newly created see of St. Paul.

Meanwhile the village abutting the landing was growing. Steamboat traffic, intermittent in the years after the *Virginia* made the maiden voyage up the Mississippi in 1823, was increasing, and in 1847 a regular line was in operation. Americans began to play a part in the business life of the trading village. Henry Jackson, a Virginian, established a store in St. Paul in 1842 and became a prominent merchant, as did Louis Robert, a Missourian of French background, who arrived two years later.

As transportation developed, mail service improved, and a St. Paul post office was opened in 1846, its equipment consisting of a board box with sixteen apertures for letters. The village was surveyed and platted the next year, with names such as Jackson, Sibley, Forbes, Lambert, Brunson, Larpenteur, and Guerin among the proprietors. The legalization of claims was forwarded when, in 1848, a land office was established at nearby St. Croix Falls. The Red River trails from Pembina were traversed by increasing brigades of oxcarts hauling furs to St. Paul and carrying supplies back to the distant settlement. The "Fashionable Tour" up river from places as far as New Orleans, St. Louis, and Pittsburgh attracted tourists from the South and East — couples, small parties, even groups of hundreds. Panoramists portrayed to America and the world the wonders of the river and its valley. One of the notable artists was Henry Lewis, who in 1848 toured the river from St. Louis to Fort Snelling and the next year began to exhibit a vast painted panorama — an unrolling canvas twelve hundred yards long and twelve feet high. People enjoyed moving pictures long before the day of the cinema, and to them the picturesque lands and waters of the West were of great interest.

The marks of change included the exploitation of the trees of the St. Croix Valley and the power of the Falls of St. Anthony. The lumber industry was alert to opportunities opened by the treaties of 1837. They heralded a new development in logging, and lumbermen were on the scene without delay. A sawmill was built at Marine-on-the-St. Croix as early as 1839, and not long thereafter the lumber city of Stillwater was founded. Meanwhile on the east side of the Mississippi at the Falls of St. Anthony, a village deriving its name from the falls was emerging. Here Franklin Steele, a frontier entrepreneur, set up claims, built a dam in 1847 and a sawmill the next year, utilizing logs floated down from the Rum River region. Lumbering was on the rise; and the platting of St. Anthony in 1849 was an early step toward the metropolis of the coming state.

The day of the missionaries merged with that of the founders of cities and builders of farms. Before the 1840s came to an end, the rumblings of population growth and of ambitions to create a new American Territory were audible on the Minnesota frontier. America was in a spasm of growth. From 1800 to 1850 its population leaped from something over five millions to twenty-three millions, and a westward surge was under way. By mid-century people were bursting into lands ceded by the natives in the Upper Mississippi Valley. States were being carved, one after another, out of the old Northwest Territory, and pioneers were already advancing beyond the Mississippi.

In the face of circumstances, missionary efforts faltered especially after the removals of Indians from their ancestral lands. But soldiers of the cross of a new generation appeared on the scene to grapple with problems in a new era. For Minnesota these included men of unusual dedication and force, such as the Episcopalians James Lloyd Breck and Henry B. Whipple. But the era of the pioneering missionaries, with its difficulties, heartbreak, and achievement, had run its course. A new day was at hand. Pioneers would build a modern commonwealth. Its prologue had been spoken and acted by explorers, traders, map makers, soldiers, writers, word hunters, and men driven by zeal for the Christianization of the redmen.

Treaty of Traverse des Sioux, from an oil by Francis Millet

"The Green Tree of Empire"

THE creation of Minnesota Territory was marked by ambition, hope, anomalies, and audacity. Its history ran from 1846 to 1849, and the organized territory preceded rather than followed a mushrooming of population. Even by the summer of 1849, when territorial status had been achieved, fewer than 4000 people (counting mixed-bloods but not the native Indian contingent) lived within the limits of what became the state of Minnesota. By a generous count, St. Paul had 910 residents, Stillwater 609, St. Anthony 248. When the federal census of 1850 was taken, Minnesota Territory (including Pembina and straggling settlements as far distant as the Missouri) had only 6077 persons.

Not impressive numbers, but the hope of multitudes to come motivated the drive for territorial status. That drive also took into account the advancing frontiers of statehood, particularly the birth of Iowa and Wisconsin as states in 1846 and 1848. If Minnesotans lacked numbers, they betrayed no lack of will. They insisted on having civil government for themselves; and through Indian land cessions they expected to open the gates for an inflow of settlers. They were as impatient as they were ingenious in their efforts to advance the time when they would have a capital, a governor, a legislature of their own choosing, laws of their own making, and the boom they anticipated.

Some uncertainties with respect to the boundaries of Minnesota were erased when Iowa became a state. In the Iowa constitutional convention,

159

covetous eyes were cast northward. Two projected northern boundary lines were among those given consideration — one slicing through Minnesota to the approximate location of present Brainerd, the other running along the Minnesota River to its junction with the Mississippi. A delegate pointed to the Falls of St. Anthony as a place of the future. "The water power there is incalculable," he said. "It will run machinery of every description and before many years it will be one of the most important spots in the western country." But Minneapolis and its mills of the future were saved for Minnesota by a congressional committee under Stephen A. Douglas which fixed the northern boundary of Iowa at 43° 30′.

Meanwhile Wisconsin was feeling the birth pangs of statehood. It is a curious fact that as early as 1846 the Wisconsin delegate in Congress introduced a bill to organize Minnesota Territory. Among the names suggested were "Minasota," then "Itasca," and then, before the bill died in the Senate in 1847, "Minnesota." A second effort in Congress to authorize a "Minnesota Territory," sponsored by Senator Douglas in 1848, also fell short of final action. The generating source for these abortive moves may well have been Joseph R. Brown, who lived on Lake St. Croix, was justice of peace for St. Croix County (in Wisconsin), and had served in the Wisconsin legislature. Versatile and resourceful, Brown had had a long frontier career, beginning with his service as a drummer at Fort Snelling. He knew that Wisconsin would soon achieve statehood, and he was an exuberant worker for Minnesota Territory.

When Wisconsin was delivered as a state in 1848, new zest was given to the drive of Minnesotans for an organized territory. Like Iowans, the framers of the Wisconsin constitution were not blind to the resources of the Minnesota country. One proposal favored a western boundary from the mouth of the St. Louis River to the point at which the Rum joins the Mississippi — a plan that would have made St. Paul and an adjacent area a part of the Badger state. In the outcome, however, the line was drawn from the St. Louis River to the St. Croix and then along its winding course to the Mississippi. And this boundary, which left unorganized that part of the original Wisconsin Territory lying between the St. Croix and the Mississippi, led to decisive political action by nascent Minnesotans.

After preliminary discussions, eighteen men signed a call for a convention to be held at Stillwater on August 26, 1848. Describing themselves as "citizens of Minnesota Territory," they invited the people in the various settlements to send delegates who, with "unity of action," would take measures to forward territorial organization. The convention was held, and resolutions were adopted with signatures by sixty-one delegates representing areas both east and west of the Mississippi. It is significant of the changing complexion of Minnesota leadership that the signers included such names as Brown, Sibley, Moss, Jackson, Lambert, Taylor, Norris, Wilkinson, Larpenteur, Robert, Holcombe, Banfield, Ford, Morgan, Simpson, Rondo, Guerin, Phalen, Godfrey, and Orange Walker. Brown himself was a central figure. The memorials, sent to Congress and to President Polk, voiced the sentiment of people on both sides of the river — unorganized parts of the former territories of Iowa and Wisconsin. They called for legislation to organize the "Territory of Minnesota" and bewailed the unhappy plight of citizens "virtually disfranchised," lacking officers, and depending for security only on "mutual good understanding." They went beyond pleas and chose Henry Hastings Sibley to go to Washington as their unofficial "delegate," there to act as their spokesman for early action.

The assumptions underlying the Stillwater Convention were that neither Iowa Territory nor Wisconsin Territory had any existence, that the Minnesota country was unorganized, and that the federal government as a matter of justice and of meeting the needs of people on the frontier should create a new territory to be called "Minnesota." But some ingenious soul now came up with the idea that the Territory of Wisconsin was still in existence and that it consisted of the part of the territory that had been left out of the state of Wisconsin! No hint of such a concept had been voiced in the Stillwater Convention. Whoever was behind it, the idea was activated by John Catlin, who had been secretary of Wisconsin Territory. If the territory still existed, it obviously must have a governor — but the former governor, Henry Dodge, had been elected senator. So Catlin assumed that he himself was acting governor. In this capacity, he saw no reason why he should not call an election to choose a new delegate from the territory to Congress. He went up to Stillwater and issued a call for such an election to be held October 30; and it was held, Sibley winning over Henry M. Rice (fur trader against fur trader). Catlin gave Sibley official certification of his election and then disappeared from the Minnesota scene. The plan was audacious. Sibley, who lived at Mendota in what had been Iowa Territory, set out for Washington to be the "delegate" of the "Territory of Wisconsin," though

Wisconsin had become a state. Would Congress honor his credentials and give him a seat as delegate? Sibley himself confessed that he embarked on his strange mission with "doubt" and "distress of mind."

To Sibley's astonishment, he was given a seat in the House as delegate from Wisconsin Territory. He made a remarkable speech (December 22, 1848) to the House Committee on Elections, and his own dignity and impressive appearance lent force to his reasoning. It was unthinkable, he argued, that his region should be cast off as a no man's land. With a side thrust at California, he asked who were the people of the area for which he spoke? "They have not been attracted thither by the glitter of inexhaustible gold mines, but with the same spirit which has actuated all our pioneers of civilization. They have gone there to labor with the axe, the anvil, and the plough." In a soaring peroration, he asked the House to establish the principle, as a "landmark in all coming time, that citizens of this mighty Republic, upon whom the rights and immunities of a civil government have been once bestowed by an act of Congress, shall not be deprived of these without fault or agency of their own." Sibley's triumph was personal, for the House, though accepting him, rejected a motion to provide salaries for the supposed officers of the "Territory of Wisconsin." In a word, the House took the position, as one member put it, that "there was no Territory of Wisconsin." The truth is that the Minnesota country lacked territorial organization until Minnesota Territory was created in 1849. The dismembered Territory of Wisconsin was a "benign fiction." Meanwhile, Sibley had "benign" status as delegate and proceeded, with the cooperation of his friendly rival Rice, to work for the objective that the Stillwater Convention had formulated.

It was fortunate that Sibley found himself in a strategic position. Only a few days after he took his seat (an obscure congressman from Illinois named Lincoln voted for accepting him), the Minnesota bill was introduced in the Senate by Douglas, with the proposed capital now designated as St. Paul (at Sibley's urging) instead of Mendota, which had been proposed earlier. With the support of Douglas the bill went through, but it had rough going in the House, the Whig majority of which wanted to postpone the implementation of the act until after President Taylor's inauguration. Such a delay the Senate would not tolerate. The bill was in danger of being "put to sleep," as one historian has it. Then Sibley proved himself a good bargainer by getting House approval without a delaying proviso. And so the measure passed on March 3, 1849, was given presidential approval, and became law at once. Yet it was too late for the Minnesota appointments to be made by the outgoing Democratic President Polk. Zachary Taylor, Whig and onetime commandant at Fort Snelling, took office two days after the Minnesota bill was signed, and he appointed the first territorial governor of Minnesota.

Under the act Minnesota's boundaries — south, east, and north — were identical with the present lines, but the territory on its western side stretched out to the Missouri and White Earth rivers. Territorial officers (governor, secretary, Supreme Court justices, marshal, and attorney) were to be appointed by the President with the usual safeguard of the advice and consent of the Senate. The legislature was to be elective, with an upper council and a house of representatives. All laws were to be submitted to Congress and were to be valid unless they were expressly rejected. The governor, with large authority, was to be appointed for a four-year term. As an expedient, the laws of the Territory of Wisconsin were applied to the new territory. Thus the governmental framework for Minnesota from 1849 to 1858 was constructed.

"Thank the Lord," a Minnesota pioneer is said to have exclaimed when he heard the news of Minnesota Territory, "we live in the United States again." When Sibley returned to the landing of St. Paul in April, the town greeted him en masse and gave him "three hearty cheers." Meanwhile President Taylor was reaping the spoils of office; and the new territory meant political awards to Whigs. To the good fortune of Minnesota, after successively offering the Minnesota governorship to a Missourian, a Hoosier, and a New Jerseyite, he tendered it to a young Whig politician, who accepted it as a recess appointment that was confirmed by the Senate early in January 1850. This native Pennsylvanian was Alexander Ramsey, then thirty-four years old. He had studied at Lafayette College, practiced law, served two terms in Congress, and as chairman of the Pennsylvania Whig state central committee had worked for the success of President Taylor. He qualified for political preferment. A biographer of the governor, reviewing his early career, describes him as "social, cool, cautious, and given to practical business." These qualities, plus a maturing political sagacity, a readiness to accept responsibility, an intelligence that appraised the potentialities of the frontier community, a gift for incisive phrase, and a generous span of cultural interests that left imprints on Minnesota institutions and life, marked the man in a long and distinguished career embracing the governorship of

163

both territory and state and service as a United States senator for a dozen years and as secretary of war (1879–81).

Legend has it that some of Ramsey's friends in the East wondered if, going to Minnesota, he would take the route by way of the Isthmus or sail around the Horn. Not less puzzled was Mrs. Ramsey, who exclaimed, "Minnesota! Where upon earth is it? In Denmark?" Ramsey arrived at St. Paul by Mississippi steamboat on May 27, 1849, with his young wife, accepted the hospitality of Sibley at Mendota, and went there from the St. Paul landing by birchbark canoe. After returning in the same fashion to the capital city, where a house had been made ready for the family, the youthful governor sprang into action. He proclaimed the admission of the territory, set up judicial and legislative districts, and called for an election on August 1, 1849, of a legislature (nine councilors and eighteen representatives), also of a territorial delegate to Congress (for which Sibley won all the votes, 682). Everything went according to schedule, and on September 3 the legislature met, not in a domed capitol but in a hotel not far from the wharf.

Here, after prayers by a young Presbyterian divine (Edward D. Neill), Ramsey presented his first message as governor on the next day. He spoke in a village which on his arrival had only a "dozen framed houses, not all completed, and some eight or ten small log buildings with bark roofs," but he had a vision of thousands of immigrants coming. He urged memorials to Congress for action to take over the Sioux Indian country. Its wide-spreading acres would mean "new inducements for the enterprise of our countrymen." Ramsey had in mind the "destinies of Minnesota," and he predicted that the lands would be "peopled with a rapidity exceeding anything in the history of western colonization." So speaking, he voiced the views of expanding America: the Indian must go, the white man's westward march was inexorable.

Ramsey also had a sense of history and he asked the territory to preserve its contemporary newspapers — every single issue — as "day-books of history." To him the news in the "fleeting registers of the day" would be "rich mines for the historian" of the future. He urged economy, good mail service, better roads, curbs on wild land speculation, restrictions on the Indian liquor traffic, and the building of a military road to the Missouri River. An interesting admonition to the legislators was that they should "guard equally" the "rights of labor and the rights of property, without running into ultraisms on either hand."

164

There were only a few houses and cabins in St. Paul when Ramsey appeared on the scene in the spring of 1849, but the village grew rapidly during the summer. "The whole town is on the stir," exclaimed a St. Paul editor. "Stores, hotels, houses, are projected and built in a few days. California is forgotten, and the whole town is rife with the exciting spirit of advancement." An Ohio visitor in July of the same year overestimated the population at 1200 and said that two-thirds of its houses had sprung up in 1849. He fancied that Aladdin had been there with "his wonderful lamp." He noted two hotels, commission houses, stores, bowling saloons, billiard rooms, a school, a Catholic church, four ministers, three printing establishments. He also described St. Anthony and Stillwater as thriving villages. Lumber and the Indian trade were the "main business of the country." Somewhat cryptic, but perhaps a spontaneous testimonial to the zeal of the people, was his concluding comment: "We have more little great men here than any place I ever saw."

The pioneer legislature, and its successors through the nine years of the territory, passed laws and adopted resolutions with prodigality. They partitioned off counties (originally nine); set up courts; passed a basic common-school law; incorporated the Minnesota Historical Society (October 20, 1849); and took an interest in roads, ferries, and dams. By 1851 the legislators had even chartered the University of Minnesota and fashioned from the earlier laws of Wisconsin Territory a revised code for Minnesota. A double need was paramount. This was for people — and for public lands on which they could stake out farms and towns. Growth, development, and "boom" were in the air, but the future hinged upon acquiring for legal settlement what Ramsey described as the "extensive, rich and salubrious region" beyond the Mississippi. The expected boom that would, it was hoped, lead to statehood could not materialize until and unless the Indians were prevailed upon to sign away their lands (beyond what they had ceded in 1837). For the territory, for its legislature, and for Governor Ramsey, land was a major goal.

Transactions could not be hurried through in a day or a month. Sibley in Washington had already been hard at work to set the machinery of negotiation in motion. He failed to get a congressional appropriation for a Sioux treaty, but he prevailed on the commissioner of Indian affairs to take action (with the approval of the secretary of the interior). Even before the first territorial legislature convened, Governor Ramsey and

John Chambers, former governor of Iowa, were named treaty commissioners with a mandate to secure the entire sweep of Sioux lands (at two to two and one-half cents an acre). Through Sibley, Ramsey invited the Sioux chiefs to meet at Mendota with him and Chambers in October, but few appeared. No treaty could be negotiated, and all that was accomplished was an arrangement with the Lake Pepin half-breeds to buy up their claims to the 1830 tract. But this arrangement was not ratified by the Senate.

The big break on the Sioux lands did not come until the territory was two years old. Few events in the history of Minnesota have attracted more historical interest than the Indian treaties negotiated in 1851. There were, for strategic reasons, two Sioux treaties — one at Traverse des Sioux with the Sisseton and Wahpeton (the upper Sioux), the other at Mendota with the Wahpekute and Mdewakanton (the lower Sioux). For the whites, the stakes were enormous — close to twenty-four million acres of land, which meant expansion, a burgeoning population, frontier dreams come true. For the Sioux tribes, the treaties meant abandonment of hereditary lands, a bowing to white power, reservations along the Minnesota River, temporary gifts, a trust fund, and cash payments which in large part would be diverted to satisfy debts to the traders.

The central objective of the American negotiations was agreement on land cessions that would take legal effect when the Senate ratified the treaties. Much unofficial maneuvering, however, revolved about the claims of the fur traders representing tabulations of older and more recent advances of trade goods to the Indians on credit. The traders were zealous for treaties, but their mundane interest lay in garnering from the Sioux as much as they could on debts. These, they alleged, amounted to a total not far from a half million dollars. Among the traders themselves there were rivalries, especially between the interests represented by Sibley (the old American Fur Company and the St. Louis Chouteau group) and by spokesmen of the Ewing concern in Indiana. Sibley, rich in experience and now delegate in Congress, effected what he called a "concert of action" among the traders for whom he was the spokesman. They were so powerful and confident in their relations with the Indians that, Sibley frankly said, no treaty could be negotiated "without our claims being first secured." The rivalry showed itself in anxiety about the choice of treaty commissioners. One certainly would be Governor Ramsey — by virtue of his prestige as governor and also the fact that, ex officio, he was superintendent of Indian relations. The Ewings wanted as a second commissioner one who would be friendly to their interests, and they nearly succeeded in their plans. That they were frustrated was mainly due to Sibley's influence in Washington. At the end, Ramsey and Luke Lea, commissioner of Indian affairs at Washington, were chosen.

Traverse des Sioux was movement, excitement, noise, color, smells, and display when officials, traders, chiefs, and hundreds of tribesmen crowded the trading center in the summer of 1851. The treaty grounds witnessed a riot of feasting, dancing, drum-thumping, racing, games of lacrosse, back-scene maneuvers by traders, and a liberal flow of liquor. Primary to the occasion were solemn councils held in what has been described as an "ample bough house." The chief figures among the white men were the commissioners, and accompanying them was the commission's secretary, Dr. Thomas Foster. Ramsey and Lea delivered speeches setting forth the purposes of the government in its effort to acquire the Indian lands and their intention, as representatives of the President, to deal fairly with the Sioux.

Fur traders present included Sibley, who was highly regarded by the natives. There were also such leaders as the experienced Hercules L. Dousman of Prairie du Chien, the poetry-loving Martin McLeod, the man of diverse talents Joseph R. Brown, the veteran Alexis Bailly, and — spokesman for the Ewings — Richard Chute. James Madison Goodhue, epigrammatic frontier editor, "covered" the treaty negotiations; and a talented artist from Baltimore, Frank B. Mayer, made drawings of such figures as Ramsey and Little Crow and later did a sketch in oil of the treaty council. Annoying delays took place, one caused by a doubting Sioux chief, whose reluctance led to a threat of stopping the issuance of rations and of an immediate departure by the commissioners. "What logic, what argument, what conviction there is in a beef steak!" exclaimed the sharp-tongued Goodhue.

On July 23, 1851, the drafted treaty was approved by thirty-five chiefs and headmen after its terms had been read aloud in English and, by Stephen R. Riggs, in Dakota. By it the Sioux nations gave up their lands lying east of the Red River, Lake Traverse, and the Big Sioux River and south of the boundary line of 1825. The commissioners assumed that the cession made a total of thirty-five million acres, but a modern computation places it as about twenty-four million — some nineteen million to Minnesota, about three million to Iowa, and more than 1,750,000

167

acres to South Dakota. Whatever the precise acreage, the pioneers were correct in thinking of it as an empire. The Sioux were to retain for a reservation a slice of land ten miles wide on each side of the Minnesota River from Lake Traverse to the Yellow Medicine River. The price to be paid the upper bands was $1,665,000, of which most ($1,360,000) would be set up as a trust fund, with the understanding that of the annual interest ($68,000) the sum of $40,000 would be cash, the remainder to be allocated to education and civilization funds and some goods and supplies. The future cash allocations were eyed with sharp acquisitive interest by the traders. The balance of the total price agreed upon was to go to the chiefs to "enable them to comply with their present just engagements" (this meant the traders' debts) and to meet the costs involved in the removal of the Indians to their reservation.

All this seemed plain enough, but the traders maneuvered the chiefs into approving another document (the "traders' paper") in which the Sioux pledged payments of debts to the traders (and allocations to the half-breeds). Somewhat later, since the total amount available was far from the grand total of the alleged debts, the traders worked out an apportionment of their claims and scaled their demands to the moneys in sight. The story is tangled, but no modern reader of the contemporary records can escape the impression that there was an admixture of knavery and deception. The chiefs almost certainly did not know what they approved in the second paper which, guided by "Joe" Brown and without explanations, they signed on the top of a convenient barrel.

So the council at Traverse des Sioux came to an end, and the commissioners repaired to Mendota to treat with the lower Sioux. The treaty signed there, on August 5, 1851, by eight chiefs and fifty-eight headmen was similar to that of Traverse des Sioux, but with a provision for a reservation on the Minnesota River from the Yellow Medicine to the Little Rock River. The interest of the fur traders similarly came in for attention in an engagement whereby the lower Sioux pledged themselves to pay traders' debts to the tune of $90,000. Much bickering took place then and later, however. An agent of the Ewings — a certain Madison Sweetser — made strenuous efforts to bring about a cancellation of the traders' agreements, exploiting the charges of the chiefs of the upper Sioux that they had been tricked into approving the "traders' paper" at Traverse des Sioux. Controversy, delay, and a long investigation followed.

The treaties themselves were not ratified by the Senate until June 23,

1852, and then only with certain amendments. One removed the provisions for reservations along the Minnesota River and vested in the President the authority to select suitable sites. The necessity of securing Sioux acceptance of the amendments led to new negotiations which were put in the hands of Henry M. Rice. For $10,000 and "necessary and proper expenses" he agreed to get the needed signatures of the upper and lower Sioux chiefs, and he was successful. Ramsey was accorded power of attorney to disburse what was called the "hand money" — to chiefs and through them to representatives of the traders (a total of $410,000 went to the latter). Later, Sweetser preferred charges of fraud against Governor Ramsey, and there was a governmental investigation. Not until 1854, after Ramsey's governorship had ended, did the case come to an end. The Senate Committee on Indian Affairs, after hearings and reviews, found Governor Ramsey "free from blame," his conduct "highly commendable and meritorious," and its report was approved by the Senate.

The traders were determined to get, by fair means or foul, as big a slice of the treaty money as they could. Historians do not doubt that their books showed unpaid debts owing them by individual tribesmen — Sibley is convincing on this point — though it seems likely that the totals were exaggerated. Fur-gathering had slackened and Indian hunters were in arrears under the credit system. Meanwhile the fur traders found their companies increasingly reluctant to advance trade goods to them. They pressed their claims with calculated purpose, knowing that Indian treaty precedents were on their side — and knowing also that the commissioners, as the treaty terms clearly disclosed, were friendly to their demands.

The charges and the investigation were focused on the moneys channeled to the traders' pockets. This much-discussed matter tended to minimize public concern over the larger transition confronting many thousands of Sioux, their relinquishment of millions of acres for a few cents an acre in negotiations of a kind they imperfectly understood, in which the denial of rations (beefsteak) at the treaty grounds was a lever to bring about acquiescence.

Much of the Indian problem of America and its long maladministration stood revealed at Traverse des Sioux and Mendota. Irresistible forces were at work: "manifest destiny," the American westward movement, the pioneer determination to open lands for settlement, the belief that the Indian must make way for the white man, and the mercenary manipulation of unsophisticated natives. Inevitably there was a legacy of smoldering Indian resentment that would one day flame into war. An interpreter said of the treaties of 1851, evidently without ironical intent, "They were as fair as any Indian treaties." But it remained for an Episcopalian bishop, Henry B. Whipple, some years later to excoriate the American system of Indian treaty-making. His words were these: "We treat as an independent nation a people whom we will not permit to exercise one single element of that sovereign power which is necessary to a nation's existence. . . . The treaty is usually conceived and executed in fraud. The ostensible parties to the treaty are the government of the United States and the Indians; the *real* parties are the Indian agents, traders, and politicians." There can be no doubt that Whipple spoke the truth.

The jubilant frame of mind of the frontiersmen was illustrated in the Minnesota seal, which pictures the Indian galloping toward the setting sun. A pioneer versifier apostrophized the gallop in these lines:

> Give way, give way, young warrior,
> Thou and thy steed give way —
> Rest not, though lingers on the hills
> The red sun's parting ray.
> The rocky bluff and prairie land
> The white man claims them now,
> The symbols of his course are here,
> The rifle, axe, and plough.

The tremendous fact to the white man was that the "Suland" was opened. To him the event heralded an American commonwealth. His mood was elation, and he betrayed little or no concern for the original occupants of hunting grounds that soon would feel the biting edge of the plow.

Governor Ramsey was pleased over the organization of the territory, evidences of growth, and particularly the acquisition of the Sioux lands; and his pleasure was phrased in his final message to the legislature in 1853. Surveying developments since 1849, he noted the "elements of a mighty change" and the advance of "civilization with its hundred arms." He paid tribute to man's "impetuous originality of action." The "reality of growth and progress" in Minnesota could be paralleled, he thought, only by the "fabled magic of the eastern tale that renewed a palace in a single night." He interpreted the rapid changes he had witnessed as "this shorter probation between the bud and the green tree of empire." Temporarily he retired from political office when the new national adminstration, under President Franklin Pierce, appointed Willis A. Gorman, a Kentucky Democrat, as governor of Minnesota Territory. Gorman, who had been an officer in the Mexican War and later a Kentucky congressman, received appointment on May 13, 1853, and served until 1857.

The drive for Indian lands by no means ended with the cession of the "Suland." There were still the vast Chippewa areas from the Lake Superior country and the northern pine lands to the Red River Valley (north of the Indian boundary of 1825). The ink was scarcely dry on the Traverse des Sioux and Mendota treaties when, in 1851, Governor Ramsey set out for Pembina with an escort of dragoons and with a frontier scout, Pierre Bottineau, as his guide on the Red River trails — the old oxcart route. With Dr. Foster as secretary and Hugh Tyler as "special agent," he proposed to negotiate a treaty with the Pembina and Red Lake Chippewa bands for the cession of the Red River country. Undoubtedly a factor in this early effort was the desire of the Pembina settlers for clear land titles. Ramsey had little difficulty in achieving a treaty for a cession of some five million acres (at a price under five cents an acre), but it was scrapped by the United States Senate in the heat of debates on the Traverse des Sioux and Mendota treaties. As a footnote to this abortive Pembina treaty, a Pennsylvanian, J. W. Bond, who had come to Minnesota in 1849, accompanied Ramsey's party and in 1853 published a detailed and vivid diary of the journey as part of a book on *Minnesota and Its Resources*.

The Chippewa, who in 1837 had ceded their lands between the Mississippi and the St. Croix, had agreed in 1847 to yield a further slice of land west of the Mississippi (between the Watab and Crow Wing rivers). This was for the desolate Winnebago Indians, an offshoot of the Siouan people who had once held all of southern Wisconsin. Under treaties many of the Winnebago had been herded out of Wisconsin into Iowa and then were pushed into Minnesota onto the lands given up by the Chippewa, their particular site having been chosen for them by Rice. They were discontented, and after much straggling found temporary sanctuary in a new reservation set aside for them on the Blue Earth River under an arrangement made in 1855. Soon, as a result of the pressure of settlers, they had to surrender half of the two hundred thousand acres allocated to them. And after the Sioux War, frightened by the antagonism of the

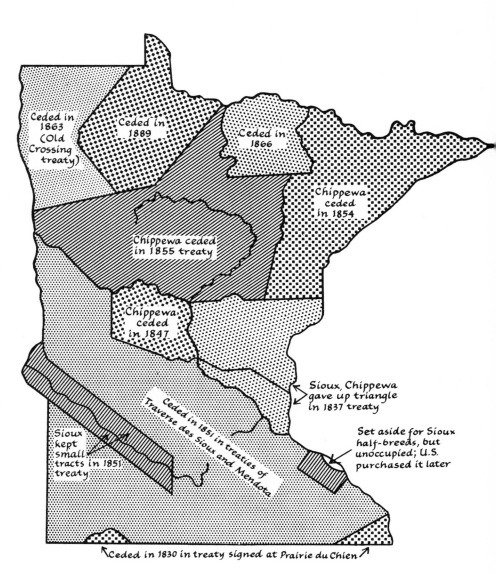

The land cessions by the Indians in Minnesota (adapted from
Poatgieter and Dunn's *Gopher Reader*)

whites, they willingly accepted transfer to the Upper Missouri. Their story is another chapter in the dismal history of American Indian removals — one of unhappiness and frustration.

The coveted prizes to be wrested from the Chippewa were in the north country, the area of minerals and pine, and — toward the northwest — the rich agricultural lands that Ramsey had already tried to acquire. Lumbermen were not unaware of the timbered paradise of the North, but the red earth of the iron range, though an earlier treaty had carried a hint of mineral riches, was yet to be discovered. In any event, Minnesota did not have long to wait before treaties nailed down most of the Chippewa lands. Treaties were negotiated in 1854 and 1855 for the north shore and the future iron country and for the deep timber lands. Not until 1863, however — a dozen years after Ramsey's premature effort — was the Red River country ceded (by the Chippewa of Red Lake and Pembina). The treaties of 1854 and 1855 reserved lands for Indian occupancy at certain cherished Chippewa spots, including Sandy, Mille Lacs, Cass, Leech, and other lakes over which the Chippewa themselves had won control only a century or so before. The treaties also provided annuities to the Chippewa, coverage of Indian debts to the traders, allocation of lands to mixed-bloods, and assurance of pre-emptive land rights for teachers, missionaries, and other whites who inhabited the region.

When Ramsey in 1853 let his fancy play with the metaphor of the "probation" from bud to the "green tree of empire," the full impact of the Minnesota boom of the 1850s had not yet been felt. That came in the fast-paced years from 1854 through 1857. But even from 1850 to 1852, the population more than tripled and was estimated at 20,000. Estimates ran to 40,000 by 1855 and 100,000 by 1856; and the official count in the pre-state census of 1857 was 150,037 (the census authorities later revised the total to 150,092). The seven-year period witnessed a population jump of 2485 per cent.

The magnet was land, which could be translated into people, farms, towns, lumbering, business, industry. But the fact of cessions did not at once open the Indian domains to settlement. Public lands had to be surveyed, land offices established, and public sales announced under presidential authority. Under the pre-emption act of 1841, actual settlers who had established claims could legalize their ownership by appearing at an appropriate office at a fixed time and paying the official price (a minimum of $1.25 an acre). The flaw in this liberal plan, from the point of view of settlers, was that it applied only to surveyed land; and from 1849 on, Minnesotans, led by Ramsey, made every effort to persuade Congress to extend the pre-emption privilege to unsurveyed lands. "The tide of emigration is always in advance of surveys and land sales authorized by the government," wrote a St. Paul editor. The squatters are the "true pioneers," and their acts should be "legalized and the benefits resulting from their hardy enterprise more firmly secured to them." To Ramsey the pioneers were the "rank and file" of the "army of peaceful progress."

The governor voiced the frontier doctrine that the squatter deserved first rights of purchase, whether public lands were surveyed or not. Western pressure prevailed (and it was applied with political skill by Henry M. Rice). In 1854 Congress extended for Minnesota the pre-emption privilege to unsurveyed tracts of public land. Undoubtedly this action gave impetus to the rush for lands in 1854–57. By 1855 there were six land offices in Minnesota (Minneapolis, Stillwater, Winona, Red Wing, Sauk Rapids, and Brownsville) and two years later there were eight. Actual sales of public lands for the four years from 1854 to 1857 inclusive totaled 5,250,119 acres, with their peak in 1856 (more than two and a quarter million acres). If to grumbling pioneers the surveys seemed slow, it remains true that in the decade 1850–60 about twenty million acres in Minnesota were in fact surveyed.

But settlers paid little heed to legal niceties. They moved into the ceded Sioux lands without delay to stake claims for farms (and townsites), and lumbermen sent crews into forested areas without waiting for surveys or titles. And pioneers turned to cooperative means to protect themselves against the competition of speculators. As early as 1848, when lands in the St. Paul area were offered for sale at St. Croix Falls, squatters were led to the land office by Sibley, who had been entrusted to act as their bidder at the public auction. Surrounded by friends and neighbors armed with "huge bludgeons," Sibley made the bids without interference by speculators, who (if they were there) had more concern for their heads than for their pocketbooks.

In the 1850s claim associations were formed. Extralegal in character, they yet were organized with constitutions, bylaws, and officers. "Club law" wore the seemly aspect of rules-of-order and parliamentary behavior. The historian of these frontier clubs has found records of at least nine claim associations — four in the Twin City area, others at Wabasha Prairie, Rollingstone, and Brownsville, and in Nicollet and Benton counties. The claim associations "left little imprint on our institutional life," writes the historian, but they reflected the "pioneer's resourcefulness in meeting conditions for which there was no existing formula." A view in larger perspective might interpret the associations as one of many revealing illustrations of the pioneer readiness to meet problems through voluntary cooperation — a trait that did leave its marks on American society and needs to be remembered alongside the "rugged individualism" of the frontier.

The folk who made up the onrushing thousands in the 1850s were recruited from varied sources, but the native American element constituted a majority. The clearest broad view is afforded at the end of the decade by the census of 1860. This enumeration showed a total Minnesota population of 172,023, and of these the native-born numbered 113,295. New York and other middle states furnished 30,075; the Middle West and West, 24,640; and New England, 18,822. The Yankee element lent special character and color to the Minnesota institutions and folkways of the decade, and here it should be remembered that many of the New Yorkers (of whom there were more than 21,000) came of families only a step or two removed from their original New England focus; and others — from Pennsylvania, Ohio, Indiana, Michigan, and Illinois — were similarly of New England background and tradition. Especially marked in such centers as St. Anthony (and Minneapolis) and Stillwater, but also widely dispersed in Minnesota, the tough-fibered people directly or by stages out of New England made basic contributions in this foundation era. They built farms, started towns, opened business places, invested money, speculated, pioneered professions, launched newspapers, schools, and churches, engaged in politics and government, and left the imprints of their leadership on numerous institutions.

Minnesota was not yet as cosmopolitan in its national origins as it became in the later days of immigration, but even in 1860 the foreign-born (numbering 58,728) made up 29.2 per cent of the total. Germans numbered 18,400; Irish, 12,831; Norwegians, 8425; those from British America, 8023; Swedes, 3178. Immigrants from Switzerland totaled 1085 and from Wales, 422.

The speculator who impinged upon the rights of farmers by jumping claims was detested in the territory, but town promoters and builders breathed the very air of speculation and gambled on the future. It was not speculation itself that was frowned upon by pioneer society — it was speculation that robbed the settler of the fruits of his initiative and enterprise. Land speculation was given a sharp push by the prevalence of Indian scrip and especially American military land warrants. Congress passed a sheaf of military bounty laws after the Mexican War, and land warrants to veterans who had no intention themselves of claiming land were bought cheaply, often by speculators, who then employed them in payment for tracts of their selection.

The pioneers dreamed of great cities at the head of steamboat navigation on "the river"; around the Falls of St. Anthony; and in the valley of St. Croix; and every trading mart looked to future growth. The mania for laying out towns went to such extremes that a witty legislator on one occasion offered a resolution to reserve a third of the region for farmers; and the promoters of the 1850s platted villages and cities with lots enough for more than eight times the population of Minnesota in 1860. Frenzied townsite speculation was the order of the day. Evidence shows that many alleged towns existed only on paper and in dreams. One plat pictured a mythical railroad station on a mythical railroad in a nonexistent town. Many of the towns were real, even though some became "ghost towns."

An unusual promoter was the English-born artist Edwin Whitefield, who made his way west in 1856 when the boom was nearing its height. With John H. Stevens and others he organized the Kandiyohi Town Site Company, which selected a site in the county of that name. Its boosters hoped that their town might become the capital of Minnesota. Under the later statehood act ten acres of land for the state "seat of government" were in fact set aside in that county, and several abortive legislative moves were made in the 1860s and early 1870s to shift the capital from St. Paul to the Sioux-named county northwest of the Twin Cities. One proposal, in 1869, actually passed both houses of the legislature but was vetoed by a wise governor. This was long after the Panic of 1857 had blasted Whitefield's hopes of a booming town. The artist did lithographs and water colors of Minnesota scenes, promoted Glencoe and other sites, took a beauty lover's interest in the state's lakes and rivers, and wrote several illustrated articles about the state for eastern magazines. As spirited with the pen as he was skilled as an artist, he found the frontier region blessed with "space enough for hundreds of thousands, if not millions of emigrants." Minnesota to him was a summer haven and resort for the unhappy people "from the consumptive East and the fever-stricken South." Though most of his townsites did not turn into towns, Whitefield nevertheless left a legacy of superb drawings and water colors depicting Minnesota in its frontier era.

Enthusiasts of the 1850s predicted that Nininger, Ignatius Donnelly's dream city near Hastings, would blossom into the New York of the West. The Nininger townsite was divided into 3800 lots; advertisements promised a great hotel, a ferryboat, a library; prices mounted; and Nininger had some five hundred inhabitants before its boom collided with the Panic of 1857 and its hopes collapsed like a punctured balloon.

Underlying town-building and speculation was a conviction that the decade was one of beginnings for a great state — that farms, industry, and commerce would indeed support cities and an expanding population, and that values inevitably would move upward. More than four hundred Minnesota towns, villages, and cities were tabulated in the 1860 census, but only eleven reported populations above a thousand. The capital city of St. Paul had 10,401; St. Anthony, 3258 (and its rising neighbor, Minneapolis, on the west side of the river, 2564); Winona, 2464; and Stillwater, 2380. Other cities having more than a thousand were Mankato, Faribault, Rochester, Chatfield, Red Wing, and Shakopee. Duluth, destined to be the third ranking city of Minnesota, made only a faint bow, with 80 residents. The figures are small, but it is clear that many of the Minnesota cities of future importance had roots in the territorial period.

The towns that aspired to be cities included Minneapolis, the future metropolis of Minnesota. St. Anthony, on the east side of the river, had early harbored the hope of becoming the city of the future — but the west side was equally endowed with water power and it boasted wide-spreading acres and a filigree of picturesque lakes. Thus it was a tempting morsel of townsite. And no one was more acquisitively sensitive to its potentialities than Franklin Steele. After beginning his service as Fort Snelling sutler (he ran a supply store), he had claimed land alongside the Falls of St. Anthony, made good his claim, purchased other claims, and then, with capital furnished by eastern businessmen, built a dam at the falls. He built it with firm will despite discouraging difficulties, and it was the start of the lumber industry at the falls. Steele was an investor and promoter who was never reluctant to seek eastern capital to forward his enterprises, and in 1849 he turned to a Boston financier for support, selling half his holdings for $20,000 (and four years later buying the half back again). He was a frontier businessman with an eye to urban development and real-estate speculation. His calculating judgment led him in 1849 to suggest to John H. Stevens, his clerk, that it might be good business to get a permit from the War Department to stake a claim on the west bank, above the falls, on lands then a part of the military reservation. Stevens got his permit and forthwith built a house on his claim, pledging in return free ferry service across the river (a concession to military needs). His house, begun in 1849 and occupied in 1850, was removed in later times to Minnehaha Park where it still stands as a historic shrine.

Minneapolis (its devised Sioux-Greek name dating from 1852) began to expand, with the Stevens claim as a focus. Squatters filtered into the area of the later city; and in 1855 a big advance was made. A splendid suspension bridge was flung across the Mississippi, the first of bridges to span the Father of Waters (another enterprise of Steele, this time in association with Henry T. Welles, a lumberman from Connecticut). The squatters were on reserved lands, but they hoped (as did all squatters) that their occupancy would be honored, and they even dared to look forward to pre-emption rights. Their daring was rewarded, for such rights were granted them in 1855 by special act of Congress – and within three months nearly twenty thousand acres were entered for title. Streets, buildings, stores, and community activities took form and shape. A promising future seemed open to Minneapolis, as indeed it was open, but hopes and dreams were dampened by the Panic of 1857.

Hard on the heels of the early growth of Minneapolis came a curious transaction. Few people had any prevision of the Panic, and still fewer, if any, anticipated civil war and Indian outbreak around the corner of the decade. Everything was going smoothly. The territory was on the verge of statehood, buying and selling floated high on rising prices. And Indian war, what with treaties and reservations, seemed altogether remote. Suddenly and without public notice, Fort Snelling and its remaining reserved lands were sold by the War Department. The sale, after a series of crafty maneuvers (of such a character that they later provoked a congressional investigation), was made by the government to none other than Franklin Steele. And it was made, not after a public auction, but through what Dr. Folwell described as a "clandestine contract with an

178

individual citizen." Fort Snelling was privately held from 1858, when the sale took effect, until 1861, when Ramsey, then governor of the state, commandeered the post at a moment of national crisis.

The sale was authorized by John B. Floyd, secretary of war, whose action was later stigmatized as a "grave fault" by a congressional committee. Its legal setting was a rider in an army appropriation bill of 1857 which (extending an earlier act) empowered the secretary to sell military sites "which are or may become useless for military purposes." That this rider was specifically aimed at Fort Snelling is certain, for its inclusion was engineered by Henry M. Rice who, soon after the act was signed, recommended the sale to the secretary. Precisely where and by whom the move was initiated seems not wholly clear, but Steele himself as early as 1856 had offered to buy the reservation, meeting with a refusal by Jefferson Davis, then secretary of war. In the spring of 1857 a Virginian and two New York politicians were leagued in a scheme to purchase the reservation, and Steele associated himself with them to the extent of a one-third interest. The sale was privately closed with Steele for $90,000, Steele himself furnishing $10,000 of the first installment, his associates the balance. The withdrawal of the fort's garrison did not take place until 1858, but meanwhile the Panic of 1857 had struck. Steele and his friends could make no further payments. And in 1861 the picture was changed by the opening of the Civil War.

These dismal happenings had a melancholy aftermath. The sale was not revoked, though it was branded fraudulent by the investigating committee. Franklin Steele owned Fort Snelling, and in 1868 he presented a rental bill for $162,000 to the federal government! This was for the use of his fort through the war years and after. True enough, he still owed $60,000 on the original purchase, but this he offered to write off against a comparable portion of the rent. His rental price was $2000 a month, for eighty-one months (and the records disclose no deductions for those many months during which Minnesota boys were trained for service — in many instances death — on southern battlefields). The case was not closed until 1871, and Steele emerged with much of the reservation nailed down as his property. He came out with more than six thousand acres of the Fort Snelling lands as defined in 1852, a valuable area of the future metropolis and its suburbs. The government retained the fort and a little more than fifteen hundred acres. One emphatic national note was sounded in the 1860s with respect to the historic fort.

This was the voice of General William T. Sherman, who visited the post in 1866. Fort Snelling, he said to the War Department, "should be held by the United States forever."

Minnesota's rise in the 1850s synchronized not alone with land maneuvers and a speculative mania that had its shameful aspects, but also with the play of various expansive forces in American life, including transportation. Once slow and cumbersome, it was undergoing a revolution, improved by canals, steamboats on the Great Lakes, roads and railroads, and fleets of vessels on the Mississippi River. By 1854 it became possible to travel all the way from New York to Rock Island, Illinois, by railroad, with transfers to steamboats headed for St. Paul. Steamboat arrivals at St. Paul, in excess of 100 in 1855, rose to nearly 300 two years later, and to more than 1000 in 1858. Intending settlers poured onto the wharves at St. Paul. One packet company alone brought in more than 30,000 people in the summer of 1855, most of whom could find no inns where they could sleep in the capital city before they made their way to villages and farmlands. Settlement customarily was a matter of individual and family action, but not a few groups of people banded together in colonization plans, migrating as communities, hunting — often after advance agents had been sent out in their behalf — for lands favorable to farming and to the building of towns of their own.

Newspapers "boomed" the territory with optimistic zeal. Travelers explored highways and byways and flooded the papers with letters and articles describing lands and lakes and resources. There was no little fear of the Indians, but gradually they were assembled on reservations (the President having endorsed for a five-year period the reservation agreements blocked out in the treaties of 1851), and the military established a series of forts, in addition to Fort Snelling, which offered seemingly adequate protection. These were Ripley (1849), Ridgely (1853), and Abercrombie (1857), strategically placed on the Mississippi, Minnesota, and Red rivers for possible emergencies. As early as 1849 a post on the Red River had been planned and an expedition of dragoons journeyed as far as Pembina by the Red River trail (via Sauk Rapids). Commanded by Major Samuel Woods of Fort Snelling, with Captain John Pope (of later Civil War fame) as topographical engineer, the expedition selected a site for the fort at the head of navigation on the Red River.

Every effort was made to reach the minds of easterners and immigrants with Minnesota propaganda. In 1853 the territorial legislature authorized a special exhibit at the Crystal Palace world's fair held in New York, and the enterprising William G. Le Duc went there with grains (from the Cottage Grove area), furs, wild rice, a birchbark canoe, photographs, and even a live buffalo (the fair officials refused space for this unusual "exhibit" and it wound up in a sideshow). The farm products won favorable editorial notice from Horace Greeley in the *New York Tribune*, and Le Duc fondly (though mistakenly) believed that this endorsement started the tide of immigration to Minnesota. More systematic were the efforts of a "commissioner of emigration," authorized in 1855, who went to New York to urge newly arrived immigrants to choose Minnesota as their destination. He distributed pamphlets packed with information about the territory and inserted Minnesota advertisements in several European newspapers.

The mood of Minnesotans was one of an all-out welcome alike to native Americans and to the throngs of newcomers arriving at Castle Garden. Their spirit was that of the American ballad which urged people to "come from every nation, come from every way":

> We have room for all creation, and our banner is unfurled,
> With a general invitation to the people of the world.

These and other aspects of the mid-century scene suggest that diverse ideas and forces conspired to swell the tide of settlement in the turbulently growing Minnesota Territory. Nine years after Governor Ramsey arrived at the frontier hamlet of St. Paul — and only five years after he made his optimistic allusion to "the green tree of empire" — Minnesota was to be ushered in as the thirty-second state of the Union.

St. Paul in 1851, from a water color by Jean Baptiste Wengler

Brave New Pioneer World

THE pioneers of the 1850s were young, optimistic, and hardworking. In building their "brave new world," they were kept busy — breaking land, starting farms, putting up cabins or frame houses, building roads, launching towns, opening schools, initiating business and professional practice. Fashioning the economic, social, and political life of a commonwealth in the making was a job for supple minds and strong muscles.

Minnesota pioneering by no means comes to a stop in the 1850s. As Minnesota was gradually filled in to the west and north, various regions experienced "pioneer periods." They were not all alike. Change characterized the development of later frontiers, notably the Red River Valley and the iron-mining country, but not a few earlier patterns were paralleled in these areas. Whatever the differences from decade to decade, appraisal of the society of the 1850s is fundamental to the interpretation of Minnesota. No period in the history of the region has attracted more research and writing, and the explanation — apart from a familiar interest in beginnings — lies in the fact that the 1850s generated forces and had reverberations felt and sounded through the sweep of state history from that time to the present.

Among the institutions that gave direction to the early community, few were more immediately influential or had longer aftereffects than the frontier press. It has been said that American newspaper editors were

183

in the vanguard of the westward movement, "setting up their presses and issuing their sheets before the forests had been cleared or the sod turned." This generalization comes very near the truth when applied to Minnesota, for James Madison Goodhue, a New England-born journalist pushing north from Wisconsin, reached St. Paul with his printing press before the territorial officers got there. On April 28, 1849, he turned out — on a hand press — the initial issue of the *Minnesota Pioneer,* the first of eighty-nine newspapers established in Minnesota during its territorial period.

Goodhue's paper typified the frontier press. It carried news of America and the world to the people. It promoted settlement with vigor; served business through advertisements; and was in some measure a literary medium in a day when books and magazines were not too easy to come by. It assumed leadership in social, cultural, and political affairs — and it exemplified "personal journalism." Goodhue, a graduate of Amherst College and sensitive to contemporary currents in journalism, was a pungent writer, skilled and daring in the use of rhetorical devices to enforce and dramatize his views. He was a flaming optimist, a prophet, an articulate preacher of progress. The unpretentious village to which he came was, to him, more glamorous than the Seven Cities of Cibola. He glorified Minnesota with its wide, blooming hills and plains, its "lands as fertile as the banks of the Nile," its forests of ancient pines, its lakes of crystal water, its "fresh, bracing climate." California, then in its gold delirium, was to Goodhue a place of "lingering, living death," whereas Minnesota spelled health and life. He foresaw the redmen "fading, vanishing, dissolving away," and for the future he pictured thousands of farms and cottages, waving wheat fields, and "jungles of rustling maize." He asked for bridges, railroads, better roads, wide city streets, fire protection, a town clock, improved mail service, the telegraph, and good schools. The steamboat wharf, he said, was a bad school where children were graduated with diplomas from the devil. He traveled "on horseback and by stagecoach, carriage, and steamboat, over rough trails, across fields, and up and down the rivers" — everywhere gathering news and descriptive material about Minnesota. He sent his paper east and south to recruit settlers.

Goodhue's writing had spice and wit. Bad government, he said, was "infamy on stilts." Boring speeches were "as long as the ears of the human donkeys that get up and bray them." He summed up the career of a dishonest public official by saying, "He stole into the Territory, he stole in the Territory, and he stole out of the Territory." He made room for hoaxes and jokes, and one of the latter anticipated a quip of Mark Twain's. A St. Paul man disappeared, was reported to have been drowned, then turned up alive. The "report of his death," wrote Goodhue, was "greatly exaggerated." On one occasion, after a scathing editorial, Goodhue was attacked and stabbed twice, while he enlivened the affair by shooting his assailant. He died in 1853, and the parson-historian Dr. Edward D. Neill described him as "the individual above all others who had promoted the general welfare of Minnesota."

But Goodhue's *Minnesota Pioneer*, always colorful and interesting, was, after all, only one of the many papers that reached the territorial people. Among others there were the *Sauk Rapids Frontiersman*, the *Red Wing Republican*, the *Wasioja Gazette*, the *Hokah Chief*, and the *Winona Argus*. If Goodhue was in some respects the James Gordon Bennett of the West, other good journalists were on the scene also, including the gentlemanly Earle S. Goodrich of St. Paul; the picturesque sailor and Arctic explorer Sam K. Whiting of Winona; the fiery antislavery crusader and feminist Jane Grey Swisshelm, editor of the *St. Cloud Visiter*; Ignatius Donnelly, whose career as the "stormy petrel of Minnesota politics" began with the editorship of the *Emigrant Aid Journal*, the organ of the mushroom city of Nininger; and Joseph A. Wheelock of St. Paul, editor and statistician, often described as the "dean of Minnesota journalists." These and others, along with Goodhue, founded the newspaper press of Minnesota, urban and rural. They promoted the interests of the pioneer commonwealth with acumen and zeal. Apart from meeting the needs of their decade, the frontier papers, whose preservation Governor Ramsey forwarded, are a mine of firsthand information for historians seeking to make that vanished decade come alive again.

Newspapers were "day-books of history," as Ramsey said, but the builders of Minnesota were not content to collect only these contemporary recordings of their life. The Minnesota Historical Society that they founded in 1849 took root, and from the first it had a broad program. "History in a land of yesterday!" exclaimed Alexander Ramsey, its first president, anticipating the surprise with which a society of history in a region that had just been made a territory would be greeted. But (in an address in 1851) he spoke of the footprints of early travelers, the "ancient explorer's pencil," the "myths and traditions" of the aboriginal races, and the struggles of white pioneers, all worthy of historical record and a cooperative collecting of sources. He did not forget that such an institution meant enhancement of Minnesota prestige in the East — a cultural move more important than "the golden sands of California." If history is "philosophy teaching by example," he said, historical societies are "the retorts in which the elements of that philosophy are collected and combined." The society got under way, issued *Annals* year after year, began to collect records, and laid the foundations of an institution that has continued to the present and has won rank among the leading historical societies of America. Its secretary from 1851 to 1862 was Dr. Edward D. Neill, the scholar-minister who by 1858 produced the first major *History of Minnesota*, a work of such basic value that, after five editions to 1883, it still stands as a contribution of scholarly value.

The foundations of Minnesota's school system were laid in the 1850s — evidence of the stalwart pioneer belief in education throughout its range from common schools to college and university. Land and the means of subsistence were essential, but not in themselves the end of the rainbow. Native-born and immigrants alike had dreams of opportunity for their children, and education was regarded as the road to their realization. The faith of the people explains the law of 1849 which provided that the common schools were to be open "to all persons between the ages of four and twenty-one years, free." The act authorized the forming of school districts, of which, by 1858, there were seventy-two. Three years later Minnesota counted 466 schools, and of these 235 were log-built.

School terms were short, in many instances three months of the year or less; reading, writing, arithmetic, and geography were the usual subjects; and it was difficult to find teachers (average salaries in the early 1860s were $13 a month for women, $21 for men!). Sometimes farmers would take jobs as teachers for the winter months, and the usual rule for other teachers was to "board around." Beginnings were slow, and schoolrooms often were primitive (the attic of a log cabin in one instance), but frontiersmen were engaging in what a modern educator has called "one of the boldest social experiments ever undertaken by any people" — universal education. Fortunately for Minnesota, Neill in 1851 accepted the position of territorial superintendent of the common schools, and he made his influence felt in the pioneer efforts to provide schooling for all.

Even before 1849 schools were started under private auspices — as in

St. Paul, Stillwater, and St. Anthony. As early as 1847 Harriet Bishop of Vermont was sent out by the New England National Popular Education Society, an organization interested in supplying women teachers to frontier schools. She transformed a log-cabin blacksmith's shop in St. Paul into a schoolhouse and taught children of Indian, Swiss, French, English, and American parentage. In 1857 she published a book entitled *Floral Home*, in which she told the firsthand story of her experiences on the Minnesota frontier.

The problem of recruiting competent teachers convinced the people of the territory that they must have special schools for the training of teachers. The first Minnesota state legislature responded to this need by authorizing the establishment of three normal schools (at five-year intervals), as a consequence of which the first of them, at Winona, opened its doors in 1860. Public high schools did not appear during the territorial period, but at least thirty communities chartered academies or seminaries. Many of these — especially those projected in 1856 and 1857 — existed only in dreams and on paper. Their role falls into the history of "town booming" rather than of education. But a few academies did function, and some institutions of higher learning (such as Hamline University and the University of Minnesota) conducted preparatory schools which paralleled the efforts of the academies. Some academies survived or were metamorphosed into colleges, but the academy movement in America (with Franklin's Philadelphia academy of 1749 as a prototype) began to lose its hold after 1850 (when the country actually had more than six thousand academies). Academies were not greatly significant in Minnesota Territory, but they made contributions to pioneer education and served as bridges to educational institutions and ideas of a later day.

Minnesota leaders were greatly interested in the early steps taken by Michigan, Wisconsin, and Iowa to establish public universities. There was a westward movement of higher education and it is an integral part of American frontier history, too often relegated to footnotes. Ramsey and Sibley, giants in the territorial earth, played creative roles in the founding of the University of Minnesota. Early in 1851 Governor Ramsey recommended to the territorial legislature that it memorialize Congress for a grant of 100,000 acres of public land to endow a university for Minnesota, and such a memorial was duly dispatched. But Sibley, in Washington, was a jump ahead. He had already acted to get a congressional bill for a university land grant. He had been influenced by William G. Le Duc, earliest known advocate of the University of Minnesota, who circulated petitions for a "well sustained" university — and who cherished the hope that the institution would be placed at Fort Snelling, converting "the school for the soldier into the school for the civilian." On February 9, 1851, Congress passed a bill granting two townships of land for a university in Minnesota — not indeed the 100,000 acres Ramsey had hoped for, but still a substantial amount (46,080 acres).

Meanwhile the territorial legislature drafted a charter for the university. A committee headed by John W. North, a Yankee with an "astonishing flair for cultural, legal, and economic pioneering," wrote a report recommending an act to incorporate the University of Minnesota, an "institution of learning which shall afford to the youth of the Territory an opportunity of obtaining a liberal, scientific and classical education." The committee pointed out that the very "character and destiny" of the infant commonwealth depended upon its pioneer children, for they would be "the citizens and rulers of the future." It recalled the advance of Harvard and Yale, small in infancy, great in growth and achievement; and it argued that the "New England of the West" needed its own institution of learning, however humble its beginnings might be. The charter was passed and signed by the governor (February 25, 1851).

The government of the university was vested in a board of regents elected by the legislature. Five departments were envisaged: science, literature, and the arts; law; medicine; agriculture; and the theory and practice of elementary instruction. Proceeds from the federal land grants were to be lodged in "a perpetual fund to be called the 'University Fund.'" The location was to be "at or near the falls of St. Anthony." Six years later the charter was given enduring validity by the state constitution and it remains to this day the basic document of the University of Minnesota. But the real university had a long gestation. A preparatory department, it is true, opened in the autumn of 1851 and was conducted for some years, and a huge building was erected in 1857 (the Panic year); but the university traveled a tortuous course before it initiated college work in 1869. Nevertheless the University of Minnesota is rooted in territorial times, the institutional offspring of frontier leaders who had no parochial vision of public higher education.

Foundations, meanwhile, were being laid for the private colleges of Minnesota. Pioneering this domain was Hamline University, a Methodist institution founded in 1854. It was established at Red Wing after spirited bidding by St. Paul, Faribault, and other communities; and it was named for Bishop Leonidas Hamline, who made a donation for its endowment. Like the university, Hamline was coeducational. Its planned studies included four departments: classical, preparatory, scientific, and "Ladies' Graduating." Necessarily the college had to provide a pre-college curriculum, but it functioned as an actual college, with a four-year course, and its first graduates were awarded their diplomas in 1859. Through most of the Red Wing period its president was Jabez Brooks, a classicist who later served as professor of Greek in the University of Minnesota. Virtually all of Hamline's men students enlisted in the Civil War, and the college had troubles in the 1860s before it disbanded in 1869, to be reestablished at St. Paul in 1880. Hamline was the only Minnesota college that actually offered college instruction in the 1850s. Some other collegiate institutions of later days had their roots in the territorial period, however, including Macalester College in St. Paul, which was related to pioneering schools of 1853 and 1855, brain children of Neill; and St. John's University at Collegeville, inspired from the St. John's Seminary established in 1856 by the Benedictines.

Few problems in the 1850s occasioned greater interest and concern than that of improving transportation, especially as settlement worked out from friendly river banks, river forks, and power-producing falls. Faster and better means of getting from place to place were vital to growth, opening farms, building towns, developing industry and markets, providing effective mail service, and indeed knitting the fabric of society and government. Improved channels of travel offered cheering therapy for the pangs of isolation and loneliness — a spur to the feeling of "belonging" to an organized community. The pioneers understandably hailed every advance from the era of canoes, pirogues, rafts, and oxcarts to steamboats, roads, and railroads.

Steamboating on the Upper Mississippi, as has been noted, expanded greatly in the 1850s, but the river was ice-locked for at least five months of the year, a situation that caused lament and concern. Excitement reached a high pitch in the spring when the ice of Lake Pepin broke up, usually in April, and the boats that had congregated just below the lake (at Read's Landing) raced for St. Paul. Whatever the time of day or night, St. Paulites made for the levee to cheer the first arrival — and the boat would come in with band playing and flags flying. In 1857 no fewer than twenty-two steamboats, with fifteen hundred passengers aboard, waited at Read's Landing until late in April before the icy tyranny of Lake Pepin gave way. Then a spirited race was on between the *Galena* and the *War Eagle* — a run won with a fifteen-minute margin by the *Galena* because a crew member of its competitor fell overboard and a stop was made to rescue him. The town was out at two o'clock in the morning to welcome the winner, and as days went by more than 4000 tons of freight were unloaded at the levee. Regular packet lines brought in thousands of people and contributed to the booming of St. Paul as the head of steamboat navigation.

Steamboating on the winding and shallow Minnesota River offered difficulties, but in 1850 three boats — the *Anthony Wayne, Nominee,* and *Yankee* — staged excursions on the river to prove that it was in fact navigable. The Indian treaties of 1851, which gave special impetus to settlement in the Minnesota Valley, opened a gala period in Minnesota River steamboating. Its big development came in the late 1850s, when such towns as Mankato, St. Peter, Henderson, Chaska, and Shakopee were thriving, and after Fort Ridgely had been established. Steamboat arrivals at St. Paul from the Minnesota River were 109 in 1855, and in the next three years, 207, 292, and 394. By 1857 vast quantities of freight were being transported to the river towns. This traffic challenged the interest of a famed riverman, William F. Davidson, magnate of the Mississippi, who put several vessels on the Minnesota, including the *Frank Steele*, reputed to be "one of the finest." At times the water of the Minnesota was so low that navigation became virtually impossible, but the joking master of the *Equator* advertised a boat that would require only "a heavy dew to enable her to run."

The author of *Walden*, Henry David Thoreau, was a passenger on the *Frank Steele* in 1861 from St. Paul to the Redwood Indian agency far up the river. In his *Familiar Letters* he describes the crookedness of the stream. The boat, he said, "was steadily turning this way or that," and in the entire trip there was not a single straight stretch of water as long as a mile. Often the boat ran aground, and frequently passengers would step ashore and walk to the next bend, where they would once more board the craft. Thoreau found merit in the many turns of the Minnesota River. "Ditch it straight," he wrote, "and it would not only be very swift, but would soon run out."

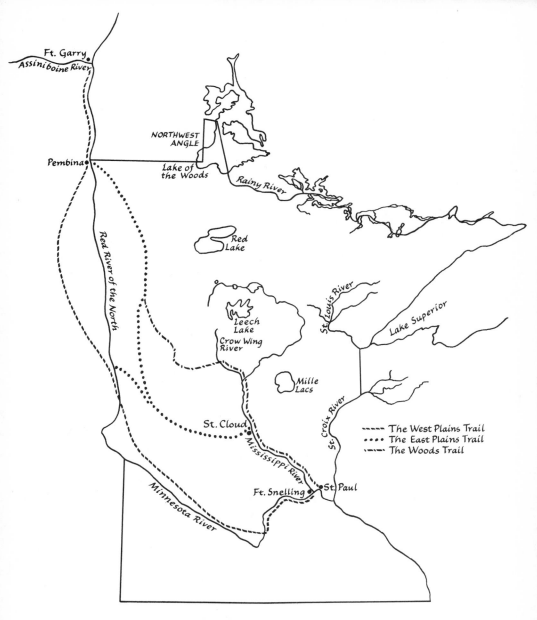

Early trails from Fort Garry and Pembina to Fort Snelling and St. Paul (adapted from Grace Lee Nute's "The Red River Trails," *Minnesota History*, September 1925)

Some effort was made to set in motion steamboat navigation on the Mississippi above the Falls of St. Anthony, and in 1850 the *Governor Ramsey* (Captain John Rollins) began to make trips between St. Anthony and St. Cloud. As settlement moved westward, steamboats carried passengers and goods up river and wheat on return. Meanwhile the large-wheeled, creaking Red River carts in summer and dog sleds in winter traversed trails between St. Paul and Pembina (and beyond to Fort Garry). This was a thriving business for many years and there are records of some five to six hundred carts a year in the late 1850s, southward-bound with buffalo tongues, robes, and pemmican, and northward with supplies of many kinds (including liquor) for the Red River colony.

Interest in this western fringe led to the development of steamboat traffic on the Red River, an even more slithery stream than the Minnesota. Spurred by the chance of a contract to transport goods to the Hudson's Bay Company, the St. Paul Chamber of Commerce in 1858 offered a prize of a thousand dollars to anyone who would put a steamboat on the Red River. This opportunity appealed to Anson Northup, ingenious Yankee in St. Anthony, who ran a steamboat up the Mississippi to Crow Wing, dismantled it, hauled it across country in winter with thirty-four ox teams, reassembled it on the Red River (at a townsite opposite the mouth of the Cheyenne), and started merrily down river to Fort Garry. His boat was named the *Anson Northup*, and was the first of several steamboats on a western river so crooked that, one pilot said, navigating it, he met himself coming back.

Steamboats on western waters were splendid and encouraging, but the paramount need was for roads. In part this was met by the federal government, which authorized several important Minnesota roads in the 1850s. These territorial highways bore a relationship to frontier defense, but Minnesotans wanted them for wagons and buggies. How can the public lands be sold "if the immigrant cannot reach them"? Sibley asked this question of Congress and won a favorable answer. One military road ran into the heart of the Minnesota Valley — Mendota to Mankato, then on to the Big Sioux — and others were built from St. Paul north to Superior, south to Iowa, and west to Crow Wing. A pioneer overland road, antedating the territory, ran from St. Paul to Wisconsin and Illinois via Stillwater. Meanwhile the territory, acting through ready authorizations by its legislature, developed a network of roads in southern Minnesota, especially in the second half of the decade, and stagecoach lines used the highways to carry passengers and mail, with stations at the various towns that were springing up. Large numbers of settlers, however, did not enjoy the comforts (rough as they were) of stagecoaches. They knew the jolting conveyances of wagons, covered or uncovered. A surveyor in 1854 noted one day a train of thirty "immigrant wagons, filled with Norwegians" headed for Mankato and other towns. Occasionally, he said, as many as two hundred wagons were seen "on the road at one time." Frequently the immigrants drove large herds of cattle with them. They were on the way to farms — not to the centers of speculation.

A cherished pioneer dream was for railroads. Hopes received a dramatic impetus when the railroad reached Rock Island on February 22, 1854 — a momentous event, for it united the Atlantic Coast and the Mississippi by rail. This occasioned a great excursion of some twelve hundred invited guests to Rock Island and up the Mississippi to St. Paul and the Falls of St. Anthony. Seven steamboats were filled by a gala party, which included former President Fillmore, the historian George Bancroft, Professor Benjamin Silliman of Yale, many other distinguished persons — and also a host of journalists led by Samuel Bowles, Thurlow Weed, and Charles A. Dana. At the territorial capitol Sibley welcomed this group, and Fillmore and Bancroft spoke, the latter hailing the future "North Star of the Union," destined to shine "in unquenchable luster." The irrepressible Neill delivered a sermon on "Railroads in the Higher and Religious Aspects," arguing that railroads were antidotes to bigotry and that a Pacific road would be "a voice in the wilderness." Important to Minnesotans was the appearance of numerous articles in the newspapers of the country telling of the excursion, praising the region, and extolling the "Fashionable Tour." And still more important was the reality of railroads that were being extended northward. East Dubuque was reached in 1855, Prairie du Chien two years later, and La Crosse (from Milwaukee) in 1858.

Neill's sermon on railroads in their "higher aspects" echoed the interest of Minnesotans in a northern transcontinental railroad. Such a road was not to be achieved for many years, but a Pacific railroad survey, made in 1853 under the leadership of Isaac I. Stevens, evidenced governmental planning for it. The survey traced a route from St. Paul to Puget Sound, Stevens leading a group from St. Paul westward, Captain George B. McClellan heading a detachment eastward from Fort Vancouver, the two ultimately meeting in Idaho. The Stevens expedition was big and spectacular. It included a military escort, astronomers, engineers, a topographer, a meteorologist, a surgeon and naturalist, and two artists, one of them the distinguished John McStanley. Guided by the frontier scout Pierre Bottineau, it followed the Red River trail on its first lap. The expedition itself and a magnificent report that recorded it impressed Minnesotans with the belief that, however big the job might be, a Minnesota-based railroad to the Pacific Coast would one day be built. They conceived it to be important in its mundane aspects as well as in that higher sphere envisaged by the frontier preacher.

Actual railroad building in Minnesota came after statehood, in the early 1860s, but plans for railroads were tumbled about in profusion in the territorial period. They took form in efforts to get land grants from Congress for railroads — precedent having been established by a liberal grant of 1850 to the Illinois Central Railroad — and to charter railroads by acts of the territorial legislature. A revelation of railroad dreams and the pioneer temper is afforded by the territorial record of railroads chartered. They began as early as 1853, with a charter for the "St. Paul and St. Anthony Railroad." Five charters were granted that year, one in 1854, two in 1855, seven in 1856, and twelve in 1857 — in all, charters for twenty-seven railroad companies. Their names reflect expansive hopes, as illustrated by the "Louisiana and Western," the "Lake Superior, Puget Sound and Pacific," the "Minnesota and Northwestern," the "Mississippi and Missouri," the "Northern Pacific," the "Nininger, St. Peter and Western," the "Minnesota and Pacific," and the "Nebraska and Lake Superior."

Memorials to Congress seeking federal aid were successful, but the federal lands granted were not to go, said the Congress, to any railroad already "constituted or organized." The Minnesota and Northwestern (to run from Lake Superior to the Iowa border and south to Dubuque, Iowa) was, however, pledged by its charter (in 1854) such federal land grants as were allocated to Minnesota. By some skullduggery the wording of the congressional act was changed, after the bill was passed, to "constituted and organized" — the Minnesota and Northwestern was constituted, but not yet organized. The records make it clear that the transaction was enmeshed in speculation by people in the East and in Minnesota who foresaw rapid advances in land prices along the route of the proposed road. The word substitution was found out, however, and Congress repealed the act only a month after it had been passed. A tedious history followed: the repeal was challenged and not until 1862 did the Supreme Court uphold the congressional negation of the act.

In 1857, however, Congress passed a new railroad land grant, and the legislature then granted lands to four companies: the Minnesota and Pacific, the Transit (for a line from Winona to the Big Sioux by way of St. Peter), the Root River and Southern (for two roads, one from La Crescent to Rochester, the other from St. Paul and St. Anthony to Mankato and to Iowa), and the Minneapolis and Cedar Valley. These represented bright hopes closely related to statehood plans — but the Panic of 1857 and the financial difficulties of the companies prevented their realization.

Thus the railroad problem was thrown over to the emerging state. Minnesota Territory achieved no real railroads, though it had the exhilaration of dreaming and planning them. When the first railroad in Minnesota ran a train, its line was that of the first charter proposal of 1853 — from St. Paul to its sister city of St. Anthony, ten miles away. Roads to the Pacific and other far places would come, but their time was not yet.

Some writers have intimated that the people of the 1850s were mainly speculators, not real settlers, but by 1859 there were nearly 18,000 farms (all in the area of the future state) with well over a half million acres of improved land (and a grand total of more than 2,700,000 acres). Farms had multiplied since the 1840s, when the pioneers of agriculture were chiefly in the Newport, Afton, and Cottage Grove areas of Washington County (south of St. Paul). Early efforts necessarily were concentrated on subsistence farming, but some produce was sold, and the main crops were corn, oats, and potatoes. Yet even in the 1840s farmers were growing wheat, barley, and a variety of vegetables. Through the 1850s farmers worked hard to build cabins, clear and break land, plant early crops (moving toward wheat as the decade advanced), put up needed rail fencing, tend to cattle and chickens, and buy such tools and implements as were essential. Speculation might indeed be in the air — and farmers were aware of rises in land values — but, as their diaries and letters make clear, they were industrious.

Apart from the specific jobs they tackled, farmers had to adjust themselves to winter blizzards, summer fires, and the isolation of areas ill supplied with roads and markets. Farms meant families, and the farmer's wife had her full share of work, making soap and candles, churning but-

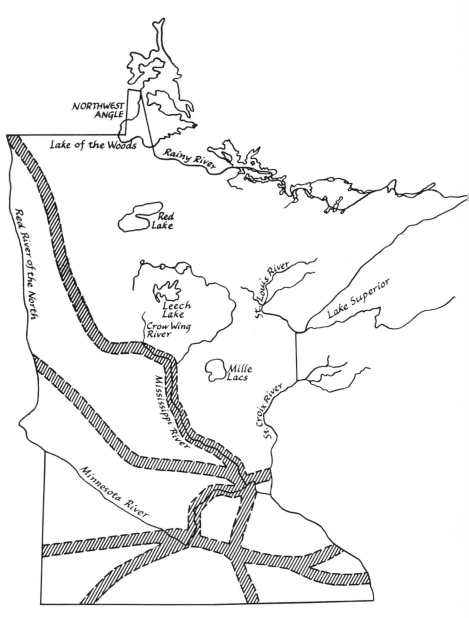

Railroad plans in 1857–62 (adapted from Folwell's
History of Minnesota)

ter, weaving blankets (if she had a loom and knew the art), mending
clothes, supplying her table, bearing and caring for her children, often
pitching in with her husband on outdoor jobs. Like the missionary wife,
she was a kind of "wilderness Martha," a dependable contributor to the
economy as well as the social amenities of the pioneer world. In sickness and childbirth she had to depend much upon herself and her neighbors. Doctors often were too far away to be called in an emergency;
here and there midwives, usually self-trained, were available; but many
times recourse was had to friendly wives in the neighborhood.

Children had both work and play, and their life was not so forlorn as
a later generation might suppose. According to Dr. Rodney C. Loehr,
"Child life was harsher than it is today; there was always plenty of work
to do, and children took their place in the fields at an early age. Yet
they were not without amusements. At school recess they played 'ante
ante over,' two old cats with yarn balls made from old stocking ravelings
wrapped around cotton, and such games as crack-the-whip, fox and
geese, and pom-pom-pullaway. Picnics were held in the summer, and in
the winter sleigh rides or spelling contests with neighboring schools provided excitement."

Minnesota families faced serious problems of health. Doctors were
scarce, hospitals few; and people depended much on their own resources
and those of their neighborhood. Doctor books were "as dear to emigrants as the family Bible." The records of the time reflect an enormous
and anxious interest in the climate. Much of the writing by Minnesotans
was defensive, promoted by the feeling that regions competing for settlers
"misrepresented" the climate of Minnesota. But there was also a widespread and sincere faith in climate as a giver and restorer of health.
Great claims were made in this respect for the air of Minnesota; and
many people came to the region with the hope that its climate would
in fact overcome tuberculosis or other ills. In the light of later knowledge,
there was a wide divergence between fact and fancy in the early accounts
of Minnesota's climate and its relationship to health. Even Sibley, usually restrained in his claims, described Minnesota in 1850 as a land
"where sickness has no dwelling place." Sibley was mistaken. The truth
is that sickness was a common dweller in the pioneer homes. There were
epidemics of measles, typhoid fever, diphtheria, mumps, scarlet fever,
even smallpox (though the protective value of vaccination was well
known). Tuberculosis was widespread, and its prevalence was doubtless

augmented by the many health-seeking "consumptives" who sought haven in Minnesota. The common cold and pneumonia were prevalent. And even the dread cholera was brought in on Mississippi steamboats coming up from regions to the south.

Medical practice was rugged — horse-and-buggy calls by doctors in summer, sleigh trips in winter, hand-carried cases supplied with quinine, aloes, calomel, and other drugs, also surgical instruments including the lancet. The newspapers were filled with patent-medicine advertisements for "anti-bilious, cathartic, vegetable, and ague pills," syrups, bitters, pitch, liniments, "pain extractors," Indian panacea, and balms for the ladies. Various kinds of quacks and charlatans were on the scene. But there were also doctors of competence and training, such men as John J. Dewey of St. Paul (who also ran a drugstore), John H. Murphy of St. Anthony, and an English-born country physician named William Worrall Mayo. Dr. Mayo was a health-seeker who "fled from the malarial hell of the Wabash Valley in Indiana" in 1854, first established himself in St. Paul and later in the Minnesota Valley town of Le Sueur. Before the elder Mayo arrived in Minnesota, the Minnesota Medical Society had been organized (1853), when there were only about twenty doctors in the territory. In St. Paul a notable advance was made when St. Joseph's Hospital was founded (it was opened in 1854), with Mother Seraphine and other devoted Sisters of the Order of St. Joseph of Carondelet in charge. Even before their hospital opened, they nursed cholera patients in the old chapel of St. Paul.

Many invalids who came to Minnesota to breathe its air and win health went back home again; others soon died; yet others did gain in health and strength. Meanwhile epidemics took their toll, especially among infants and children. Sickness did indeed have a "dwelling place" in Minnesota. The later advance of knowledge (inspired by Pasteur and Koch) and a growing skepticism among physicians with respect to the merits of climatotherapy opened the way to a new era in the fight against disease. Medical practice in the 1850s (as viewed many decades later) left much to be desired, but in this field, as in many others, the period was one of pioneering and of institutional founding. It witnessed the struggles of people against diseases whose causes were unknown. And it also saw foundations laid for the practice of medicine in a state that would one day establish leadership in that practice and in broad fields of medical science and education.

The pioneer houses — domestic scenes both of sickness and of vigor and strength — represent stages in settlement and a changing economy. The wagons that carried families over rough roads and trails were only temporary homes. Then came log cabins, dugouts, and sod houses, later frame, brick, or stone houses. The cabins might have earthen or split-log floors, fireplaces or stoves, a few small windows. Home-made furniture often served family needs. "Puncheon tables and benches," writes Eva-dene Burris, "were made like the floors, of split logs, with legs fastened into the rounded sides. A one-legged bedstead was sometimes fitted into a corner of the room. Two sides of such a bed would be fastened to the walls. The mattresses rested on cords or wooden slats. Trundle beds and cradles which could slide under the bigger bed during the daytime were often used in crowded homes."

Food was simple but usually ample. The housewife took comfortable advantage of her surroundings. Ducks, venison, passenger pigeons, fish from nearby lakes or streams, sometimes wild rice, corn, potatoes, home-baked bread, and a variety of vegetables helped to supply the hungry mouths she fed. The St. Paul market in 1850 — though rural housewives could not make more than rare use of it — offered buffalo tongues at $5 a dozen; at a later date venison was listed at 12½ cents a pound; even pemmican, brought down in Red River carts, could be bought (10 cents a pound). Families living away from river towns "would bring in sugar, flour, spices, lard, cheese, molasses and dried fruits for the entire season." Hans Mattson, Swedish pioneer in Goodhue County, once walked from Red Wing to his cabin, a distance of fourteen miles, with a smoked ham, thirty pounds of flour, a gallon of molasses, and some coffee, salt, and sugar, all strapped into a pack and carried on his shoulder — an example of endurance matching the feats of voyageurs on early portages.

People did not ordinarily go hungry, and there are records of gala meals. Thus the frontier scout Pierre Bottineau gave a breakfast in 1853 at St. Anthony at which he served two roast pigs, beefsteak, and eggs; and one dinner at Traverse des Sioux in 1851 offered boiled ham, beef, elk, duck, swan, and buffalo meat (served with a sauce from the prairie turnip). Some items were lacking, and a disconsolate Yankee is recorded as saying, "I'm homesick to get back to Massachusetts and have a meal of good salt cod." But a St. Paul woman wrote in 1853, "Then we have a cellar, filled with potatoes, cabbage, turnips, beans, molasses, onions, eight turkeys, three barrels of flour, 20 pounds of sperm candle, four of chicken, 50 dozen tallow candle for the kitchen, seven pound sage, 10 pound dried pumpkin, two bags buckwheat, ten dozen eggs, 30 pounds butter."

Even a quick look at Minnesota farming makes it clear that by the end of the 1850s the new state was becoming fundamentally agricultural. Logging and milling were important industries, but farming was coming into a stage of big production. Crops in 1859 ran to millions of bushels — corn leading, with 2,900,000 bushels; then wheat, with 2,186,000; and oats, with 2,176,000. In relation both to agriculture and to the frontier habit of voluntary organization, it is significant that the 1850s witnessed the beginnings of agricultural societies. One was formed as early as 1852 in Benton County, with a farmer named Oliver H. Kelley, much later the primary organizer of the Granger movement, as the leader. That year a similar society was started in Ramsey County, and in 1854 the Hennepin County society held the first agricultural fair in Minnesota. This was an approach to a territorial fair in 1855 and the first of the famed Minnesota state fairs in 1859. The fairs were centrally concerned with exhibiting the products of Minnesota farms and counteracting reports that the climate of Minnesota would not sustain a profitable agriculture. There was much concern over charges that Minnesota was "hyperborean" and that, because of the severity of the winters, agriculture, including fruit-growing, faced insuperable difficulties. The fairs were aimed at exhibiting actual products of the Minnesota soil, but then, as later, they offered varied attractions. In 1859 Cassius Clay, Kentucky politician, delivered a two-hour speech; "Flying Dutchman" trotted a mile in 4:11; and there was an exhibition of fire-engine companies.

Cultural variety was by no means lacking in the territorial society, though it was perhaps more marked in later decades. When the traveling Swedish novelist Fredrika Bremer viewed Minnesota in 1849, she burst into ecstatic prophecy: "What a glorious new Scandinavia might not Minnesota become!" For the Swedes there were "clear, romantic lakes"; the Norwegians would find rapid rivers; and the Danes could claim friendly pasturage for their "flocks and herds." Probably the Scandinavians came less for the lakes, streams, and meadows (though they loved them) than because the westward movement made Minnesota a jumping-off place at the time; but they came. The Swedes found the St. Croix Valley delectable — Marine by 1850, Chisago Lake soon thereafter; and they also were drawn to Goodhue, Nicollet, and other counties. Their communities bore the color of Swedish customs, language, song, church backgrounds, and industry. In 1850 a Norwegian colonizer, C. L. Clausen in Wisconsin, wrote Governor Ramsey that many Norwegians — farmers and mechanics — were looking for public lands. He himself explored the area in the summer, and in the following years thousands of his countrymen poured into the southern counties (Houston and Fillmore particularly) and into many other sections, including Goodhue County, where, a pioneer minister wrote in 1859, "Never have I preached to such large audiences as here in Goodhue." These were beginnings of settlements as colored on the Norwegian side as was the colony in the valley of the St. Croix on the Swedish side. The Danes fulfilled the Bremer prophecy at a later time.

New Ulm was German in speech and custom. Here under the leadership of William Pfaender, a German Land Association was incorporated in 1857 and a Turner Hall was built, a center for community interests, meetings, speeches, plays, music, gymnastics. By 1860 there were 653 people in the enclosing township, and they were "almost all Germans and their American-born children." Nininger, as has been indicated, typified frontier mushroom cities. The townsite was boomed with a gay enthusiasm matched only by the exaggeration of its promoters. Dominating Nininger lore is a colorful personality — that of the versatile Ignatius Donnelly. Zumbrota was organized in 1856 by the Strafford Western Emigration Society and functioned under rules drawn to guarantee a Puritan community. The Excelsior Pioneer Association sponsored a colony on the shores of Lake Minnetonka, and its distinction is horticultural. To it in the early 1850s came a man from Ohio, Peter Gideon, carrying with him apple seeds and seedlings, peach seeds, even small plum, cherry, and pear trees. He made the Minnetonka region a pioneer experiment station to prove that apples could be grown in the grim Minnesota country — and his proof was conclusive. In the St. Cloud region Old World influences reaching back to Monte Cassino and the Bavarian Metten made themselves felt when Benedictine priests (influenced by the devout missionary Father Pierz) opened St. John's Seminary. The next year Benedictine Sisters founded the convent of St. Benedict. An important German Catholic community, already under way, expanded in the St. Cloud area.

Rollingstone in Winona County was promoted by the New York Western Farm and Village Association, a planned community with a central square, New England fashion, and a newspaper of its own. It suffered a frustrating fate because of unwise land selection for the nearly four hundred easterners who pinned on it their hopes for Utopia. In the late 1850s Czech immigrants in McLeod County (at Silver Lake) laid the foundations for what a writer has described as a "New-World Bohemia." Welshmen drawn from states to the eastward found haven in the Minnesota Valley (Blue Earth County) for the cultivation of farms (and for singing and for cherishing homeland traditions). At Chatfield in southern Minnesota New Englanders built a culturally interesting community in what a historian has termed the "Chosen Valley." There native Americans in due time welcomed a dozen nationalities, including Irish, Czechs, and Norwegians, to join them in fashioning their settlement. In the mid-fifties the singing Hutchinsons, Yankee entertainers, founded the town that bears their name — an idealistic colony that endorsed equal rights for women, planned a religious center to be called "Humanity's Church," and put a ban on liquor and gambling. The Hutchinsons attempted to demonstrate a theme they expounded in song around the country:

> We'll cross the prairies as of old
> The Pilgrims crossed the sea,
> And make the West, as they the East,
> The Homestead of the Free!

The ebullience of westward migrants, it may be noted, is reflected in not a few ballads, one of which is a verse narrative of a Buckeye who set out to find the "land of milk and honey," boarded a steamboat at Galena, landed at Winona, then went "a-rambling" through Minnesota. His interests were not limited to mere matters of land, and he made some interesting discoveries:

> The Gopher girls are cunning,
> The Gopher girls are shy,
> I'll marry me a Gopher girl
> Or a bachelor I'll die.
> I'll wear a stand-up collar,
> Support a handsome wife,
> And live in Minnesota
> The balance of my life.

Though St. Paul, St. Anthony, and Minneapolis were not settled as "colonies," they were under pronounced New England influences and

202

they were deeply conscious of the fact. Goodhue, in St. Paul, saw Minnesota as the "New England of the West." It would supply the "moral wants" of the region as, in his opinion, New England had "supplied the old States with their education, their laws, and their religion." In 1856 a New England Society of the Northwest was organized, and the next year it held a gala festival in Minneapolis (at the Cataract Hotel on December 22). The occasion was a commemoration of the landing of the Pilgrims. Toasts went on until three in the morning, one speaker voicing the hope that "New England industry, New England enterprise, and New England thrift shall build here a glorious superstructure of education and Gospel truth."

In many ways frontier life was hard, especially on lonely farms. Difficulties engendered by distance and limited means of transportation distilled a sense of isolation, particularly during long and cold winters. It remains true, however, that the disconsolate feeling of being "far away" was lightened by amenities, diversions, and cultural interests. There were many "bridges facing east." These were in part economic — eastern investments in pioneer industry and interrelations between eastern business houses and banks and similar institutions in the West. There was much reading of eastern newspapers and in fact the *New York Tribune* in 1856 had nearly three thousand subscribers in Minnesota, more than any territorial newspaper. Home-seekers swarmed into Minnesota every summer, but there were also thousands of travelers who took advantage of the "Fashionable Tour" — people from the South and East. On the educational and religious fronts, organizations functioned as intersectional cultural bridges, such as the National Education Society and the American Home Missionary Society.

Nearly every considerable frontier town had a lyceum, some had library associations, St. Paul even a YMCA, where essays, lectures, and debates were heard. The Masons and Odd Fellows were on the scene early, in St. Paul in the very year the territory was organized. The pioneers liked the theater, supported some home-talent dramatic associations, and welcomed visiting actors. Charlotte Crampton starred in a Shakespeare play in St. Paul in 1854; the next year Sallie St. Claire played *Camille*; and in 1857 *Uncle Tom's Cabin* was performed in St. Anthony by a visiting company.

Music was popular. The Fort Snelling military band played at many functions. Now and then famous artists visited the frontier. The violinist

Ole Bull and thirteen-year-old Adelina Patti gave a joint concert in 1856. The Hutchinsons, Bakers, and other troupes, with their repertories of songs, were received with enthusiasm. St. Paul even formed an opera company of its own shortly after territorial days and in one season produced such operas as Rossini's *Cinderella*, Donizetti's *Elixir of Love*, Balfe's *Bohemian Girl*, and Verdi's *Il Trovatore*. St. Paul had three bookstores in 1856, and not a few of the leading pioneers had shelves of classics, histories, and biographies.

The German Turners gave frequent exhibitions of their gymnastic skills. The rise of organized sports was still to come, but the pioneers had games of their own. Baseball is generally regarded as a phenomenon of the period after the Civil War, but one town pioneered the game in Minnesota in the 1850s. This was Nininger, which organized a baseball club in 1857, its players using an open field for practice and ready to challenge the "whole West." A circus visited Minnesota as early as 1850, with a "splendid company of equestrians, gymnasts, acrobats, pantomimists, comedians, olympiads, and Herculeans." If such entertainments emphasized the lighter side, there was a Territorial Bible Society in St. Anthony in 1851; and there were church fairs, such as one in St. Paul in 1850 when the public was "respectfully invited to attend the fair by candle-light." Alongside temperance societies, there was a "liquorary association" that advertised nightly discussions of "Oysters, Sardines, Pigs feet &c." There were general stores, banks, hardware shops (one in St. Anthony was run by John S. Pillsbury, later miller and governor of Minnesota), bakeries, and "Daguerreans." Every larger town had a lively group of doctors and lawyers, journalists, bankers, merchants, ministers, many of whom had been trained in colleges or professional offices in the East or abroad. They cultivated the use of bridges eastward through correspondence and occasional trips.

In some ways frontier Minnesota was — to recall the wondering exclamation of Shakespeare's Miranda — a "brave new world," yet it was not so new as some pioneers believed. In folkways, practices, and institutions, they bore with them the worlds they sprang from. Frontier society was not only a migration of bodies — it was also a transit of culture. Illustrations leap out from education, the press, the distinctive "colonies," cultural institutions, religion, amusements, and social ways. Some further examples may illuminate a few general trends.

The special techniques of lumbering (to which further attention will be given) were transfers from Maine, a state that left many imprints especially on Stillwater and Minneapolis. New England piety and puritanism, as has been intimated, hover over the pioneer commonwealth, and "blue laws" were on the books though not rigorously enforced. The first territorial legislature placed a Sunday ban on work and on such diversions, "to the disturbance of the community," as hunting, shooting, and sport, with a fine of $3 for violating the law. More serious was desecration of the Sabbath by profane conduct, punishable by a fine of $10. With a sense for the fitness of things, fines thus collected went to the relief of the poor. Minnesotans later were forbidden by law to be present "at any dancing" or at public shows on Sunday. An early law was aimed at gambling, especially roulette and faro, but evidence indicates that it was not taken too seriously. Many pioneers liked gambling.

If the frontier communities had their Puritan elements, they also had rough and rowdy people. Street fights were common, and murder and lynchings were by no means unknown. A state historian, writing of "Wild and Woolly Minnesota," tells of robberies, sluggings, stabbings, and the disappearance of men known to have been carrying gold for investment in land. The river traffic undoubtedly contributed to the influx of ruffians and added to the troubles of such towns as Stillwater, St. Paul, St. Anthony, and Minneapolis. But not all the violations of law and order were attributable to that influx. As Walter Trenerry points out in his *Murder in Minnesota,* the settlers of the 1850s "praised the majesty of the law but often ignored it."

Nearly every city and town had its dives; red-light districts were common; and squabbles often erupted into shootings. Stillwater in 1858 was the scene of a riot that caused the mayor to call out the "City Light Guards," who made a bayonet charge on a mob. In St. Anthony in the years 1856–58 conditions were so bad that citizens, after the manner of western mining towns, took things into their own hands. They organized a vigilance committee, cleaned out one notorious resort, and on one occasion mustered some six hundred men who marched to a district of saloons and disorderly houses, ordered the proprietors and inmates out, and then dumped into the street the furniture of the establishments. Murder is not a phenomenon restricted to frontier communities, but it reared its ugly head on several occasions in pioneer Minnesota. Two murders were followed by lynchings and one ended in the legal hanging of a woman, with a vast crowd of spectators viewing the drop.

The conditions that caused crime and disorder to flourish in the booming years of the 1850s (and in towns of later frontiers) were a stern reminder to good citizens that their organized society had to develop an effective police system with courts to uphold the laws. And there can be no doubt that the pioneers were fully cognizant of the dangers inherent in an uncontrolled liquor business.

The seriousness of the liquor problem was accentuated by the proximity of Indians; and the national temperance movement had reached out early to the territory. In 1849 a lodge of the Sons of Temperance was organized in Minnesota. The first territorial legislature prohibited the sale or gift of liquor to the Indians and set up a license system; and in 1852 Minnesota passed a "Maine Law" — another transfer from East to West — which forbade the manufacture or sale of intoxicating liquors (save for "medicinal purposes"). Voting down a facetious amendment to impose the death penalty for the violation of this law (a typical note of frontier humor), the legislators submitted the act to a referendum, and it was supported by a vote of 853 to 662. In a test case, however, the territorial supreme court gravely held that the legislature had delegated its power. Since Congress had given it no authority to do so, the statute obviously was invalid. Later attempts to pass a Maine Law in the territory were unavailing — and the not unpopular social institution known as the saloon flourished — but in 1855 a St. Anthony newspaper printed a resolution (from Illinois) that read: "Resolved, that we young ladies . . . pledge ourselves not to keep company or join in the sacred bonds of matrimony with any young gentleman who is not in favor of the Maine liquor law, or some other prohibitory law." The records do not say what influence (if any) warnings of such sedate tenor had on the pioneer youth.

The transit of culture — and of tradition and faith — was implicit in the planting of churches on the frontier, in cities, villages, and country districts. They rank among the earliest of Minnesota institutions and they reflect the religious backgrounds of the people. Many church groups, organizations, and synods took an interest in the spiritual state of the frontiersmen. An example is afforded by the American Home Missionary Society, and its archives (in Chicago) are rich in letters from pioneer ministers in Minnesota. Thus Elias Clark, Congregational minister in Rochester, reports on December 1, 1857, that he began his labors there the preceding August. Rochester, with about a thousand inhabitants, had Congregational, Methodist, and Baptist churches, all organized that summer. In St. Paul, St. Anthony, and Minneapolis there were no fewer than thirty churches by 1859, half of them in St. Paul. From humble beginnings, the Catholics had developed strength, and in 1859 Father Thomas L. Grace was consecrated bishop of St. Paul. The great leader of Minnesota Catholicism, John Ireland, had been brought to St. Paul in 1852 as a boy of fourteen, but for nearly a decade he studied in France and he did not become a priest until his return in 1861. Another great churchman, Henry B. Whipple, was consecrated Episcopal bishop of Minnesota in 1859 and soon won, by his courage and forthrightness on Indian problems, the sobriquet of "Straight Tongue." The Swedish Lutherans, led and inspired by Eric Norelius, organized churches in the St. Croix Valley and elsewhere in the 1850s, as did their more numerous Norwegian brethren in Goodhue and other counties of the southeast. Quakers were on the Minneapolis scene in the mid-fifties and built a meeting house in 1860. Jews in St. Paul had a congregation as early as 1856. But the most flourishing denominations, along with the Catholics, were Methodists, Presbyterians, Baptists, Episcopalians, and Congregationalists. Wherever they went, the pioneer settlers of Minnesota carried with them a religious heritage out of the long past, and, with their piety and zeal, they kept it alive.

Puritanism had its bright sides, as research has disclosed in studies of colonial New England. The pioneers of Minnesota greatly enjoyed holidays, social calls, banquets, and balls. At the suggestion of a group of New England clergymen, Governor Ramsey set aside December 26, 1850, as the first Thanksgiving Day in Minnesota. He enumerated such blessings as crops and freedom from blasts, hurricanes, droughts, and epidemic diseases; and he invited thanksgiving "in the public temple of religion, by the fireside and family altar, on the prairie and in the forest." In St. Paul bells were rung at sunrise and sunset; Dr. Neill at a church service compared the "infancy of our favored Territory with that of the Puritan colonies." In the evening gala dancing took place in a hall equipped with "transparencies, paintings, pictures, and chandeliers in a style of superb elegance." Christmas, too, was celebrated in traditional ways — balls, carols, ladies' fairs, the giving of presents, amateur shows, sleighrides, and great feasts. A St. Paul Christmas menu of 1851 included "chicken, ham, turkey, lobster, oysters, sardines, buffalo tongues, pastries, jellies, pecans, and ice cream." New Year's in the urban society meant rounds of calls from ten in the morning to four in the afternoon; Governor Ramsey reported that "upwards of one hundred called on us" on January 1, 1851. There were lectures, sermons, balls, newspaper carrier greetings, and other characteristic ways of noting the advent of a new year. As time went on the Germans and Scandinavians and other nationalities added their own customs; and the Christmas tree, rare though not unknown in the early years, became universal. The Fourth of July was a day for community celebrations — parades, cheers, the reading of the Declaration of Independence, speeches on George Washington and other persons and subjects recalling the era of Independence, drums, firecrackers, fireworks, cannons, games, dances, excursions.

Pioneer optimism suffered a violent jolt in 1857. The boom had been at high tide in 1856 and 1857. Business expanded, speculation was rampant, the currency of the time was of the wildcat variety issued by banks in distant states, and prices of land and property went skyward. Businessmen sought to enlarge their capital and draw on credit as far as they could, and the pioneer banks of Minnesota were pushed to the extreme for loans. By 1857 there were some thirty banks in the territory, including the firm of Borup and Oakes in St. Paul and also the banking business of the Maine-born Parker Paine which formed the main root of the later First National Bank of St. Paul. Speculation in Minnesota was bad enough, but the troubles that beset the territory in the summer and autumn of 1857 were not the fruit of that speculative fever alone. The Panic of 1857 was national — and it was signaled by the bankruptcy of the Ohio Life Insurance and Trust Company, which closed its doors on August 24, 1857. Because of interrelations with eastern banks and increasing money stringency, Minnesota's banks were soon in serious difficulty. The banks in St. Paul suspended specie payments in October, and later that month the firm of Borup and Oakes collapsed. Only a few banks survived, among them that of the shrewd and careful Parker Paine. The real-estate boom was deflated, and a pioneer reported that business lots in Minneapolis worth as much as $3000 in the spring of 1857 could not be sold for a tenth of that sum in the fall. Business companies failed; many people left the territory; merchants could not dispose of their stocks or meet their debts. Minnesota, on the eve of statehood, found itself in an economic chaos that offered no easy way out. Time, planning, new banking controls, and the tempering of the speculative mania were urgently needed. Hard times and trying ordeals faced those who remained to deal with frontier problems. The burst of speculation left in its wake a sobered people whose optimism was temporarily shaken. The roots of optimism were deep and substantial, however: a new country, land (even if values declined), youth, the stimulus of beginnings, the belief in progress. Painful rebuilding lay ahead, but these elements did not vanish from the scene.

The pioneer community was unspecialized. Farmers, housewives, professional men in the towns had to be versatile, depending much upon themselves. Premiums went to the jack-of-all-trades. A St. Anthony dentist was also a jeweler and gunsmith. The frontier doctor was a general practitioner who often doubled as a druggist. The lawyer could turn from law to real estate or business. The minister sometimes was a farmer; farmers might occasionally teach school. Nearly everybody was ready to participate in politics.

Self-dependence spurred individualism, but an appraisal of frontier society bears out Frederick Jackson Turner's emphasis on the "power of the pioneers to join together for a common end without the intervention of governmental institutions." He cites house-raisings, husking bees, claim associations, and other activities, all of them a part of the Minnesota pioneer world. Turner speaks of the "habit of community life," characteristic of the Yankee stock, but the habit was also present in other elements. He takes note of the "motion and change" — and consequent restlessness — that went along with American mobility. The mobility was not merely a matter of moving from place to place, but also of change in economic and social status, basic to the belief in progress. Society was not quite so classless as some writers, emphasizing frontier democracy, have assumed. Like sought like, and in the urban centers one notes evidences of an emerging aristocracy of wealth and social distinction. But generally the spirit of the frontier was that of measuring men by what they did. Speculative excesses at times revealed ragged ethics, but it remains true that an aggressively pragmatic society had its idealistic sides. Cultural loss there may have been, as Turner insists, but a review of Minnesota life in the 1850s shows much cultural transfer and an eagerness to cultivate things of mind and spirit.

"We debouch upon a newer mightier world, varied world," sang Walt Whitman in his song of the pioneers, and he touched truth; but he missed reality when he also said, "All the past we leave behind." The past went west with the pioneers. With them also went faith in the future and in democratic opportunity, and the faith gave color to frontier society and left its marks on succeeding generations.

The first state capitol in St. Paul, 1857

A State Is Born

DURING the generating 1850s political lines were drawn in Minnesota. Alignments were marked out and traditions engendered. The frontier was no island separated from the political mainland. Every tolling national bell was heard in the Upper Mississippi Valley. In Minnesota villages and on farms only recently the hunting grounds of Sioux and Chippewa, American issues stirred debate and stimulated emotion. Bridges faced east and faced west. National problems were western problems. Western interests echoed in Washington; western papers reflected national crises; and eastern papers printed news from the frontier.

This stirring and eventful decade saw the birth of Minnesota as the thirty-second state. Its parturition was delayed by sectionalism and made painful by local political turmoil. Preceding and accompanying the birth were national forces and regional issues that gave direction to Minnesota's future.

Admonished by southerners to speak only on questions pertaining to Minnesota Territory, Henry H. Sibley replied that the territory was a part of the United States. It was concerned with the full range of national law-making, and he would speak as he pleased on national issues. This was good democratic sense, but from the beginning he thought of himself, not as a partisan, but as the territory's spokesman, above party lines. "I am known as neither Whig nor Democrat," he wrote early in 1849. In Minnesota's early territorial years Democrats and Whigs worked in "a loose alliance, or truce." The territorial government from 1849 to 1853 was Whig, thereafter Democratic; and the majority of the old-line settlers of St. Paul, Stillwater, and St. Anthony were friendly to the Democratic party. But there is no doubt that Minnesota leadership recognized the importance of a solid front, at least in Washington, to promote the territory's interests. In the home precincts, however, the rumblings of rival ambitions and clashes were audible.

As early as 1849 Henry M. Rice took the lead in effecting a Democratic party organization. A convention was called, a platform adopted, and a central committee appointed, including Rice, Franklin Steele, and Joseph R. Brown. A warning was issued of "no confidence in the professions of those who raise the cry of political neutrality in this Territory." The next year witnessed an election for delegate to Congress, but no sharply defined political lines were drawn. One group held a "Territorial Convention" in what seems to have been an attempt at fusion of Democrats and Whigs, and it nominated the territorial marshal, Colonel A. M. Mitchell, a Whig candidate promoted by Rice. Its platform aimed a shot at Sibley when it denounced the American Fur Company as "a dangerous monopoly." Another group opposed Mitchell, praised Governor Ramsey, and nominated a person who, it was hoped, would stand "aloof and disconnected from all the local parties or factions." The man was David Olmsted, who later withdrew from the race. A Stillwater convention, Whiggish in its sympathies, asked for the choice of someone from the St. Croix Valley.

Sibley, aware of Rice's opposition, announced his willingness to accept re-election as the "People's or Territorial" candidate, though traditionally he was a "Democrat of the Jeffersonian school." Rice did not challenge Sibley directly in this election, but in the campaign — Sibley remained in Washington — his faction, supporting Mitchell, centered its criticism on the American Fur Company as a flank attack on Sibley.

Issues were neither national nor indeed territorial. They were personal, entangled in controversies between Rice and Sibley over fur-trade interests and Rice's role in relation to the Winnebago Indians. Old labels were pushed aside, and because of barbs at the American Fur Company, of which Sibley was the symbol, the contest was waged between "Fur" and "Anti-Fur." "Fur" won. Sibley was strongly supported by Goodhue in the *Minnesota Pioneer*, but his margin was thin, only 90 in a vote just above 1200. He continued as delegate, but he did not run for a second

214

re-election. In 1853 Rice, now the Democratic candidate, won easily and embarked on his political career, serving in Washington to forward Minnesota interests, including the cause of statehood (after a re-election in 1855).

Frontier personal factions were shaken in 1854 by national events, notably the Kansas-Nebraska Act and the rise of the Republican party. Those who believed that the Compromise of 1850 had ushered in an era of political placidity suffered a severe shock.

The enactment of a hard-biting Fugitive Slave Law, the admission of California as a free state, and the opening of the Texas cession (east of California) to slavery led President Pierce, when he took office in 1853, to voice the hope that "no sectional or fanatical excitement might again threaten the durability of our institutions or obscure the light of our prosperity." Sometimes there is irony in the juxtaposition of historical events. No hope could have been more vain than that of the ambivalent Pierce. Indeed, signs were not wanting, even before the Kansas-Nebraska Act, that a national storm was brewing. The Free-Soil party had made its bow in 1848, vowing that there should be "no more slave states and no more slave territory." Abolitionism was on the rise. In 1851–52 a Washington newspaper ran a serial by Harriet Beecher Stowe, and in 1852 it was published as a two-volume novel. This was the emotion-charged *Uncle Tom's Cabin*, to be read, and seen as a play, by millions in the next few years — a work of incalculable influence on the minds of people by its portrayal of the shame of slavery.

But when Senator Douglas upset the political applecart in 1854 with the repeal of the Missouri Compromise, which had stood for thirty-four years, the big change came. Zealous for a transcontinental railroad, with Chicago as a terminal, and deeply interested in western development, Douglas wanted Kansas and Nebraska *in* as territories. As to slavery (prohibited north of 36° 30′ by the Missouri Compromise save for Missouri itself), Douglas would let the people of the territories decide for themselves on the basis of "popular sovereignty." He did not care, as he later said, whether slavery was "voted up or down." The Kansas-Nebraska proposals became law, and the storm broke in the East, North, and West, including Minnesota Territory, where "political neutrality" gave way to party issues and conflict. Many people, unlike Douglas, did care.

The repercussions of the repeal were swift and far-reaching. They in-

215

cluded the dissolution of the Whig party, already staggered by its defeat in 1852; the turbulence of "bleeding Kansas"; efforts by northern states to vitiate the force of the Fugitive Slave Law; an anti-Nebraska appeal to "Independent Democrats"; and waves of indignation and mass meetings against Douglas. The most critical aftereffect was a realignment of political parties brought on by the question of the extension of slavery.

The birth of the Republican party was a major turning point. It occurred in 1854 in the Middle West, at Jackson, Michigan, and Ripon, Wisconsin, with gatherings of men of diverse political origins, including Whigs, Free-Soilers, dissatisfied Democrats, railroad promoters, many immigrants but also some Know-Nothings. The new party demanded the repeal of both the Kansas-Nebraska Act and the Fugitive Slave Law. At the same time it pledged united effort to solve the slavery problem.

Many Minnesota newspapers joined the chorus of denunciation of Douglas. "A gigantic fraud has been perpetrated," said the *St. Paul Daily Times* as early as May 9, 1854. "A solemn compact has been violated. Weep, angel of liberty, weep. Call out the people. Let the alarm bell be rung." The *Minnesota Pioneer* took no sharp stand, and it described the outburst of the *Times* as "a high piece of falutin." "Goodbye," said the *Times*, to all compromises — "goodbye to plighted faith — goodbye to treaties — stipulations — bargains — in fact everything decent — goodbye. Mr. Douglas wishes to be President — make way for him." As the Kansas troubles developed, the Minnesota press printed extensive and shocking reports about them, about "border ruffians," bloodshed, and the encroaching menace of slavery.

Minnesota narrowly missed being the founding center of the Republican party, for on July 4, 1854 — two days before the meeting in Jackson, Michigan — "friends of freedom," under the leadership of John W. North and a minister, Charles Gordon Ames, met in St. Anthony to create a new political party. They lost their chance for national fame. Instead of doing this, they merely appointed a committee. Its purpose was to arrange a meeting at a later time, and that time was delayed until 1855. An organization conference was held in March at which a formal platform was adopted. A territorial Republican convention was convened in St. Paul on July 25, 1855. But the press marshaled its force long before the party emerged — the *Minnesota Republican* was founded October 5, 1854, with Ames as editor.

The Republican platform, in March 1855, denounced the Kansas-

216

Nebraska Act as a "violation of the plighted faith of the South." It branded the Fugitive Slave Act as unconstitutional; upheld the principle of "the supremacy of Freedom and free institutions over our whole country"; and called for the "enactment and enforcement of a Prohibitory Liquor Law." The puritanism of frontier Minnesota found expression in this plank, which coupled liquor reform with the ending of slavery as twin goals of a crusade. Not so prominent in the platform, but a clue to a stand of increasing importance to Republicanism, was a demand for "Free land in limited quantities to actual settlers." Homestead legislation was important to the West and early moves were under foot to bring it about. The South was instrumental in defeating it in 1854, but eight years later it would triumph.

William R. Marshall of St. Paul — a later governor of the state — was one of the leaders of the Minnesota Republican cause, but Ramsey, former Whig, also affiliated with the new party. Sibley aligned himself with the Democratic party. Thus as political lines were drawn, two of the giants in territorial affairs moved into contending positions for high responsibility. As the parties squared away, the Germans, even though they were antislavery, tended to take the Democratic side, partly because of suspected anti-immigrant strains in the new party, and partly because of its stand for prohibition. The Scandinavians, as stanchly anti-liquor and antislavery as the New Englanders, went Republican.

Essential to an understanding of the forces affecting Minnesota's move toward statehood is the fact that this move synchronized with the streaming of population into the southeastern agricultural area. The Democrats were strong in the older commercial and industrial centers of St. Paul, Stillwater, and St. Anthony, but the people settling on the new lands — immigrants, easterners, and middle westerners — were against slavery and for free land to settlers. They tended, with a few exceptions, to sympathize with the new party that was taking form at the very time they appeared on the scene. Minnesota leaders before 1856 were lukewarm about any quick move for statehood, but then there was a change. This was related to the challenge of the Republicans, the increase in population and especially its anti-Democratic trend, and the crucial question whether the new state, when its boundaries were fixed, should be east-west or north-south.

A wide but narrow state, extending to the Missouri, might mean dominance for the southern counties. A state cut off on the west but ex-

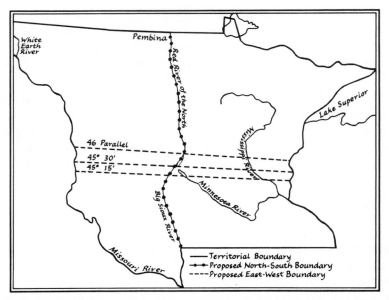

Proposed north-south and east-west boundaries for the new state
(adapted from William Anderson's "Minnesota Frames a
Constitution," *Minnesota History*, March 1958)

tending north to the Canadian border would assure lasting importance
to the St. Paul–St. Anthony center. And the pattern of railroads was
closely interrelated with the geographical question. The plans for a
northern railroad from Lake Superior to Dubuque had been shattered
in 1854, but other proposals and charters evidenced conflicting ideas and
sectional interests in railway strategy. From 1856 on, the pace of statehood agitation quickened. The Democrats, formerly cautious, now were
active, realizing that controls might slip away from them with the competition of newer political party strength.

The boundary issue was of major importance for the future. The state
would not encompass the entire territory. The area would be cut down;
and new states would be carved out of the segments omitted. A narrow-
chested Minnesota, its northern boundary cutting west on about the
forty-sixth parallel (relegating St. Paul to the northeastern corner),
obviously would have meant a farming state stretching to the Missouri
River. The forests of the north, the iron of the northeast, the headship
of the Great Lakes, and the diversified character of the north-south Min-

nesota as finally drawn would have been lost. The capital might have been moved. Winona, St. Peter, the Minnesota Valley, and points west would have been enhanced in importance, as leaders in the southern section fully understood. Modern Minnesotans are so accustomed to a north-south state — cut off on the west by the Red River and a boundary reaching down to the northwestern corner of Iowa — that the idea of a wide and narrow state seems like a fantasy.

Yet to some Minnesotans in the 1850s it was not a fantasy. It was a serious plan. In 1856 the territorial legislature incorporated the St. Peter Company, granting it "powers to engage in a large number of activities including mill construction, water power development, and real estate sales." Dr. Folwell was convinced that this seemingly innocent townsite promotion concealed "a plot of revolutionary proportions": namely, to change the capital of Minnesota from St. Paul to St. Peter. Specific proof of this is lacking, but collateral evidence suggests that the Minnesota historian was not indulging in a wild guess. For in 1857 the territorial legislature passed a bill providing for precisely such a removal. The St. Peter Company was to furnish not only the ground on which a new state capitol should be built but also a large sum of money toward building costs. That the legislature passed the bill proves that it was friendly to the east-west state (and perhaps to the speculation of the St. Peter Company). Moreover, the same legislature memorialized Congress to let the Minnesota people themselves determine the boundaries of the coming state — an almost despairing move, for no one could doubt that the boundary decision rested with Congress in its "enabling" legislation.

The removal bill, approved by the territorial legislature and certain to be signed by the sympathetic Democratic Governor Gorman, was a prelude to what has been termed "one of the most unscrupulous tricks in the history of politics in Minnesota." This was the planned disappearance of Joe Rolette, Pembina member of the Council and chairman of the committee on enrolled bills. With the enrolled bill in his possession, he went into a week of hiding (and poker with cronies) and did not turn up until the instant of Council adjournment at the end of its term. The bill came in too late. The governor did indeed sign a copy of it, and it is printed in the *Minnesota Laws* for 1857. But in a court case it was held invalid. Because of Rolette's trick it had not been properly passed. In all likelihood, the measure would not have stood up even if the picturesque Pembina councilman had not played his artful game. For the court ruled

219

that the legislature had used up its capital-locating power when it established St. Paul as the capital. So the scheme collapsed, a blow to east-west hopes. A half-comic sidelight on the story is that the optimistic St. Peter Company, before its hopes were finally quashed, actually built a capitol which later served as a county courthouse.

Even before Joe Rolette performed his histrionic antics to thwart legislative will, Henry M. Rice had taken decisive action in Washington. A Democratic delegate to a Democratic-controlled Congress, Rice favored a north-south state, but he understood the ambitions of southern Minnesota. Late in 1856 he initiated an enabling act. Congress, as he well knew, would fix the boundaries of the state, and in his bill he specified the western line so as to assure a north-south Minnesota. As a gesture to appease southern Minnesota, he also introduced his railroad land-grant bill, which provided potential grants for five railroads, one of them centered at Winona with a route to St. Peter and then west. The others had St. Paul and St. Anthony as a hub and safeguarded railroad mastery for the old centers.

The Winona–St. Peter proposal was a beguiling invitation to southern Minnesota to go along on the total plan for statehood and railroads. The two bills went through Congress virtually at the same time. The enabling act was approved on February 26, 1857, and the land-grant act on March 3. The enabling act won House approval by a vote of 97 to 75; and the Senate, after a violent and ranting speech by a Kentucky senator against the measure and a cool defense by Douglas, passed the bill 31 to 22, the negative votes all southern. The sharply expressed southern fear of increasing northern strength in the national councils was a warning of trouble to come when the question of admission should arise.

But the bills were law. They were a *fait accompli* by Rice even before Joe Rolette emerged from his hiding place. The scheme to transfer the capital from St. Paul to St. Peter has been interpreted as a "bold attempt" by "panic-stricken" leaders of the east-west forces "to save the wreck." They understood that if and when Rice's enabling act passed, their cause was lost. And so in fact it was.

The winning of statehood was and is still — as illustrated by Alaska and Hawaii a century after the advent of Minnesota — a complicated procedure, involving national and local political factors. The basic rules are simple, however. Assuming valid reasons for statehood, the territory must get enabling legislation from Congress. It then must adopt, in convention and by popular vote, a constitution. It must secure a basis for its representation in Congress through a federal census, and elect state officials, congressmen, and senators. These preliminary steps have validity only when Congress accepts the constitution and passes, with subsequent presidential approval, an act of admission.

The enabling act of 1857 for Minnesota is a fundamental document of state history. It delineated the geographical limits of the state. It called for the election of delegates to a constitutional convention and the assembling of such a body. It authorized, conditional upon popular ratification and congressional approval, the establishment of a state government. It specified a census; and it offered federal grants which, if accepted, would be honored as a national obligation if and when Minnesota became a state. These grants, in line with precedent, were of public lands, and their beneficent effects have been felt through more than a century. They included the allocation of two sections (16 and 36) in each township for schools; seventy-two sections for a state university; ten sections for aid in putting up state buildings; a batch of "salt springs" (not more than twelve), each with six sections of contiguous land for such use as the state legislature might determine; and five per cent of the proceeds from sales of public lands in Minnesota for public roads and internal improvements. The federal government thus offered a generous welcoming hand to the incipient state.

The stage was set for the next act in the drama, in some respects a melodrama, of Minnesota state-making. At the time (1857) the Republican party in Minnesota was two years old. The Whigs had collapsed, and contention for power was between Democrats and Republicans. The enabling act prescribed an election of delegates on June 1, 1857, and the assembling of the constitutional convention on July 13. President Buchanan replaced Governor Gorman by Samuel Medary, an Ohio journalist, and only a few days after his arrival at St. Paul (April 22), a special session of the legislature, which had been called by Gorman, convened. This session busied itself with railroad land grants, but also gave attention to details attendant upon the enabling act. The act had clearly and specifically authorized Minnesota to elect, for its constitutional convention, two delegates for each representative in a representative district — and this meant 78 delegates. But the frontier legislature chose to interpret this authorization in liberal spirit, and it sanctioned two delegates for each representative and also two for each councilor — in all, 108 instead of 78.

The election campaign for delegates revealed little public concern about the basic problems of statehood and their constitutional setting, but much about party politics and the control of the convention — and the subsequent choice of state officials. The election stirred national as well as local political interest, and the Republicans sent a corps of experienced stump speakers to the territory. Delegates were apportioned on an estimate of the population made in 1855, and the Minnesota Republicans felt themselves at a grave disadvantage, since the apportionment did not take into account the increases since 1855, which were largely Republican in complexion.

After the election, there were charges of fraud, contests, hot disagreements. Irregularity of the kind manifested before the election seemed to spawn irregularity. Though only 108 certificates of election were issued, 114 delegates turned up at the convention and they were all given seats.

Fifty-nine of the delegates were Republicans, fifty-five Democrats. Forty-four per cent of the Republican delegates were New Englanders, as contrasted with twenty-three per cent of the Democrats. Only eight per cent of the Republicans hailed from the Old Northwest, whereas twenty-three per cent of the Democrats came from that section. As to origins in the Middle States, there was no sharp difference — thirty-four per cent of the Democrats, thirty-one per cent of the Republicans. The foreign-born were about even — thirteen per cent of the Republicans, twelve per cent of the Democrats.

The Republicans had a clear majority of the delegates, but as the time for convening approached they were nervous and excited about the control of the convention, as indeed were the Democrats. At best the Republican margin was slim — four votes. The Democrats were a minority, but they were experienced in political tactics and they also held the territorial offices and therefore enjoyed status. The question was whether status and skillful maneuvering rather than a voting majority would prevail when the delegates assembled on July 13. As things turned out, the question was a real one.

The next scene was confusion and turbulence, a reflection of political emotions stirred to a high pitch. On Monday, July 13, the Republicans forgathered in the House chamber of the capitol awaiting the convention opening at noon. A few minutes before that hour the Democratic delegates came striding in. The territorial secretary, Democrat Charles L. Chase, stepped to the chamber platform, declared the convention in order, then took a motion to adjourn until the next day. Meanwhile John W. North for the Republicans was also on the platform. He too called the convention to order and amid the hubbub invited nominations for a temporary chairman. Chase put the adjournment motion; the Democrats then stalked out of the chamber; and they contended that the convention had duly and properly met and adjourned. This contention the Republicans rejected. They proceeded to choose a president and to organize the convention's business. After such an initial melodrama, one might have expected a cool-headed joint conference to bring about a united convention and put it on an even keel. But nothing of the sort happened. On the following day the Democratic delegates appeared at the chamber toward noon, found it occupied by the Republicans, then made their way to the Council chamber and began deliberations, with Henry H. Sibley presiding. With this prelude, Minnesota had two constitutional conventions, both functioning at the same time in the same building. They continued thus to meet for the entire convention period, though ultimately common sense led to a conference committee and agreement.

It seems clear that the Minnesota constitutional convention never once met as a whole body. It was bifurcated. Each group debated details and drafted a constitution. Each subsequently published a volume of *Debates and Proceedings*. At the end the Democrats inscribed their names on one copy of the agreed-upon constitution, the Republicans on another.

Both sides maintained a posture of political intransigency to the last moment. Somehow, out of the hurly-burly, the constitution of Minnesota was fashioned, and it has been sturdy enough to have lasted as the fundamental governmental framework of the state through all the decades since. The compromise was worked out by a joint committee, with five members from each convention, at the end of seven weeks of convention sessions. Both conventions adopted the committee's report on August 28, 1857. That night copyists turned out two complete handwritten manuscripts of the constitution — one on blue-tinted paper, the other on white — and it was these versions that the Republicans and Democrats signed separately. Many men took part in the copying and inevitably there were discrepancies in the two versions. Another curious irregularity — it is literally impossible even now for anybody to produce an absolutely precise text of the constitution. Substantially, however, the two copies are the same, with the differences so trifling that they have had no legal repercussions.

In viewing this constitutional drama, it should not be forgotten that nationally the time was one of turbulence, heated emotions, and a sharpening conflict of ideas. Kansas was "bleeding." Political parties in new alignment were preparing for battles to come. Crisis was in the air, and only a year later the Lincoln-Douglas debates in Illinois signaled the rise to national prominence of a great Republican and national leader. One can understand the state of high tension in Minnesota, but also appreciate the good sense that found a way out of dilemma by compromise. Whatever the emotion, Minnesota did not stage a civil war of its own. Convention leaders realized that to submit two constitutions to the people might not only stir up turmoil but also defeat or postpone statehood — and there is evidence that national party leaders counseled a compromise agreement.

The lasting quality of the constitution attests its rootage in the experience of older states. There was extensive borrowing, and "no very important innovations were proposed" in either of the two conventions. Another factor may have been the liberal amendment procedures (they were tightened forty years after Minnesota became a state).

The bill of rights included familiar guarantees such as jury trial, due process, freedom of conscience, and (echoing the Northwest Ordinance) the interdiction of slavery. "The liberty of the press," said one section, "shall forever remain inviolate, and all persons may freely speak, write and publish their sentiments on all subjects, being responsible for the abuse of such right." The north-south boundaries as set forth in the enabling act were confirmed, but the question of an east-west division was sharply debated, in the Republican convention in particular. Suffrage, especially for Negroes, drew lengthy discussion, but the decision was for "free white male" citizens, and immigrant declarants were also included (a provision negated in the 1890s). Negro suffrage was not countenanced until 1868. Woman suffrage was still far off in the future, and even modest steps in its direction would not be taken until the 1870s and 1890s. The usual three departments of government — executive, legislative, and judicial — were provided. A bicameral legislature was authorized, with no time limit prescribed on its sessions. An amendment in 1860 set sixty days as the limit; another in 1888 extended it to ninety;

and earlier, from 1877, sessions were prescribed as biennial. Two notable items on the educational front were the provision that funds from school lands "shall forever be preserved inviolate and undiminished"; and a constitutional validation of the university charter of 1851.

The political rivalry that split the constitutional convention was extended into the autumn, when approval or rejection of the constitution, the election of state officials, and the naming of representatives to Congress came up for decision. Statehood was devoutly wished for by virtually all the people, and the vote on October 13, 1857, was overwhelmingly in favor of adoption of the constitution (30,055 to 571). Such near unanimity seems surprising when one recalls the stormy convolutions in the making of the constitution, but the explanation is simple. Neither party wanted to incur the onus of voting down the constitution and delaying statehood, with all its expected advantages; and there was no separate ballot for the vote on the constitution. Each party printed its own ticket, placing at the top the words "for constitution," thereafter the list of candidates for the various offices. To vote against the constitution and for the candidates was an anomalous proceeding, and indeed it is surprising to note that as many as 571 actually did this. Professor William Anderson is correct when he states that "there was no separate clear-cut expression of approval or disapproval of the constitution." Historically one can merely say that the constitution was accepted by the voters.

The election of state officials involved political division and fight, as fierce in attack on both sides as it was close in outcome. "Party leaders," writes a student of this period, "assumed that a victory for either party in the first election might mean that party's control of state politics for some years to come. Nothing that might bring victory was left undone. Every candidate faced a barrage of vituperation from the opposition." Democrats and Republicans duly held party conventions, adopted platforms, and nominated candidates. The Democrats condemned the "unscrupulous attempt of the opposition" to control the recent constitutional convention; and the Republicans termed the refusal of the Democrats to "recognize the will of the majority" an example of "revolutionary conduct" without "a parallel in the history of our government" except in the "frauds and oppressions" in Kansas. The Democrats demanded withdrawal of the subject of slavery from Congress and endorsed nonintervention and popular sovereignty. The Republicans repudiated "Squatter Sovereignty" as "exemplified in the Kansas-Nebraska Bill," blasted slavery as a "social and moral evil," condemned the Dred Scott decision, and asked for the "consecration" of the public domain "in limited quantities, to the homes, the altars and the fires of free men, 'without money and without price.'" The Democrats nominated Sibley, the Republicans Ramsey — and the race was on between these two tested figures of frontier Minnesota. Sibley's chief assistant in the campaign was the veteran Joseph R. Brown, and Ramsey was aided by the spellbinding Donnelly.

As the returns of the election slowly became known, charges of fraud began to fill the air, and they were made from both sides. A canvassing board (consisting of two Democrats and one Republican) rejected 2128 votes for Ramsey and 1930 for Sibley under its adopted rules of procedure. Evidence was not lacking, however, that irregularities, which had dogged the statehood process, were present in this election of 1857. When the final figures were arrived at, Sibley led by the narrow margin of 240 votes in a grand total of 35,340. The Democrats carried not only the governorship but also the legislature and other state offices. The census of 1857, which revealed in its final and corrected figures a total population of 150,092, was in some respects as startling as the election. The canvassing board had thrown out votes from nonexistent communities — and now the census included faked population schedules for some of these places! The census takers were almost certainly trying to bolster "discounted election returns." With respect to totals, it must be added that the mythical inhabitants were not numerous enough to alter seriously the figure of some 150,000 people for Minnesota on the eve of statehood. But the totals were a grievous disappointment to Minnesotans, who had assumed, in their state planning, that the population would be in the neighborhood of 247,500. This was the basis on which the sanguine legislature had counted for Minnesota's claim to three seats in Congress. Three men were elected, but only two were given seats. This little problem was settled in the time-honored way of sportmanship when the three drew lots, and one dropped out.

A favorite saying of Lutherans in disputes on Biblical interpretation was "It stands written." The pioneer legislators of Minnesota may not have used that phrase, but they felt similarly about constitutional authority. It "stood written" in a section of the constitution called "Schedule" that the first session of the state legislature should convene on the first Wednesday of the next December after the adoption of the constitution.

Minnehaha Falls about 1868

Alexander Ramsey

Ignatius Donnelly

Early leaders in Minnesota politics, industry, and education

Henry H. Sibley

John S. Pillsbury

Floyd B. Olson

Luther Youngdahl

Two noted governors of the twentieth century

The Minnesota House of Representatives in session

The Minneapolis Symphony Orchestra in 1952

One of many art centers in Minnesota

This meant December 2, 1857 — and the "state legislature" duly met on that date. True enough, there was no state. Minnesota had not yet been admitted into the Union. But the adopted constitution said "commence" — and the legislators commenced. Thus the Minnesota frontiersmen, who had assumed a territory when there was no territory, proceeded now to act like a state when there was no state. Of the many irregularities attending the birth of Minnesota, the most irregular was the functioning of a "state legislature" more than five months before the state was born. One involuntarily thinks of the exclamation of Alice in Wonderland: "Curiouser and curiouser!" The legislators did not, of course, know that there would be a long delay in congressional action. Statehood to them seemed just around the corner, and it was assumed that things done a bit in advance would be validated as soon as Minnesota became truly a state (an assumption that turned out to be correct).

There was a small difficulty. Under the constitution all territorial officers were to exercise their offices until they were "superseded by the authority of the state." They could not be so superseded unless there was a state. Consequently the state officers elected in October could not take office until the state was admitted. Lacking state officers, how could a state legislature function? Who would convene it? Deliver messages? Sign bills, if any? The answer was simple. The legislature "recognized" the territorial governor (Medary). He returned the compliment, sent a message, and promised to "cooperate." The legislature went to work, though some Republican members were understandably doubtful about the validity of vetoes by an authentic territorial governor of acts passed by a dubious state legislature.

The big question was the election of the two United States senators to which Minnesota as a state would be entitled. Rice, the politically sophisticated state-maker, was an inevitable first choice, but the legislature sprang a surprise in electing a "dark horse" as its second choice. Passing over prominent Minnesotans, it chose James Shields, a recent arrival from Illinois, where he had also been a United States senator. He was a Democrat notorious for an absurd, abortive duel with Abraham Lincoln. He was an officeholder in Minnesota less than a year, served in the Civil War, migrated to California, and wound up as a senator from Missouri. His election as Minnesota senator was a typical dark-horse episode. Several well-established Democrats, including Brown, Steele, and Gorman, were separately strong enough to prevent any one of them from winning a majority vote from the legislature; and Sibley himself, who might have been the most logical candidate, had already been elected governor of the coming state.

The legislature, having chosen Minnesota's two first senators in joint session, was inactive for a time, hopefully waiting for Congress to terminate the ambiguity of its status. As time dragged on, the legislators grew bolder, passed more than a hundred acts, and even gave their assent to two amendments to the constitution — one authorizing the so-called "Five Million Loan," the other empowering the state officers to take office on May 1, 1858, whether Minnesota was admitted to the Union or not. Both were given popular approval, though the second (fortunately not implemented by action) came perilously close to being a new declaration of independence. An editor, commenting later on the amendments, said, "Our coat of state was altered a little even before it was put on for the first time." Meanwhile Medary, territorial governor, had left Minnesota, but his departure caused no difficulty about the signing of bills. The territorial secretary took on that assignment as acting governor.

The scene now shifts to Washington and the final delays in the admission of the thirty-second state. Minnesota adopted its constitution in October 1857. It was submitted to President Buchanan by Rice on January 6, 1858. The President sent it to the Senate on January 11, where it was referred to the Committee on Territories (Senator Douglas, chairman). The committee reported it out, with a bill of admission, on January 26. But Minnesota was not admitted until May 11, 1858. The delay, disappointing to impatient Minnesotans, resulted from the entanglement of Minnesota statehood with national politics, more especially with the blazing question of slavery and Kansas.

The civil war in Kansas and violent debates in Congress echoed throughout the country. Two days after President Buchanan's inauguration the Supreme Court had announced its decision in the Dred Scott case — the fateful pronouncement under Chief Justice Taney that a Negro was not a citizen, that the Missouri Compromise had been invalid, and that, in its effect (as Dr. George M. Stephenson puts it), "slavery had the right to go into all the territories." A battle royal ensued, with the Kansas question in the foreground — a battle in which Douglas broke with Buchanan over the proslavery Lecompton constitution and defended the Kansas squatters who insisted on an honest vote by the people on the slavery issue under the doctrine of popular sovereignty. Kansas was in turmoil and Congress heatedly debated the move by the President to usher Kansas in under the Lecompton constitution.

"If you admit Minnesota and exclude Kansas," shouted a southerner, "the spirit of our revolutionary forefathers is utterly extinct if the government can last for one short twelvemonth." Not until May 4 was the English Compromise passed, which put admission before the Kansas voters, who rejected the constitution by a tremendous majority, choosing to continue in territorial status rather than accept what they regarded as a fraudulent constitution.

The English Compromise opened the way to quick action. Not all the opposition to admission was southern in origin. The Republican John Sherman of Ohio in the House of Representatives described the Minnesota constitutional convention as "two mobs," charged violations of the enabling act and election frauds, and called for a new constitutional convention, but he was voted down. The bill for Minnesota's admission was passed on May 11, 1858, and signed by President Buchanan. The news reached Minnesota two days later; Governor Sibley and other officers were sworn in on May 24; and early in June the state legislature convened (or reconvened).

The happy news of Minnesota's admission was telegraphed to Prairie du Chien, then carried northward to St. Paul by a Mississippi steamboat; and newspapers in turn gave the story to the people. "We are a State of the Union," exclaimed the *Saint Paul Daily Minnesotian* (May 14, 1858). "No longer 'outside barbarians,' we are within the Chinese wall of the confederacy, and have donned our freedom suit." It predicted a half million Minnesota population in less than a decade and great advances "in wealth, manufactures, agriculture, the mechanic arts." There was rejoicing that the delay was ended, and there were notes of optimism despite the depression that followed the Panic of 1857. Statehood, it was believed, would bring better times, attract immigrants, invite capital, and open the way to prosperity. But the people did not soon forget the procrastination of Congress. Sibley in his first message to the legislature, referring to Minnesota, said that "it subserved the purposes of Congressional politicians to allow her to remain suspended for an indefinite period, like the fabled coffin of the false prophet, between the heavens and the earth." Some days before admission one newspaper (the *Red Wing Republican*) published a "Declaration of Independence of the State of Minnesota," reciting alleged wrongs and declaring that Congress had "rudely thrust in our way that monster Lecompton" whenever Minnesota grievances were mentioned. Another paper — its editor evidently delighting in unusual words — spoke of relief at escape from a local administration "of the epicene gender," from "a hermaphrodite conjuncation of State and Territory." Generally the public mood was pleasure that the "uncertainty and suspense" had been dispelled, and gladness for the "prestige of permanency and stability" afforded by statehood.

The travail of birth was over. "Minnesota enters the Union as the thirty-second state," said Sibley in his message to the legislature on June 3, 1858. "She extends a friendly hand to all her sisters, north and south, and gives them assurance that she joins their ranks — not to provoke sectional discord or to engender strife — not to enlist in a crusade against such of them as differ with her in the character of their domestic institutions — but to promote harmony and good will, and to lend her aid, on all occasions, in maintaining the integrity of the Union."

In nine years Minnesota created a territory and made a state. The drama — for drama it was — included foibles, errors, stratagems, impatience, quarrels, intransigence. There was "vanity, pride, and irresponsibility on the part of many actors in the play." The scenes reveal what Ramsey once described as man's "impetuous originality of action." The dramatis personae included sinners and saints, but they were all human beings. They were under the compulsion of interests. They were willing to compromise, though they did so reluctantly. They had a sense of the common good. No reader of the debates can escape the impression that they had shrewd ability. They were aware of American precedent and were not reluctant to borrow from the recorded experience of other states. Through all their deliberations there was manifest an underlying drive to add a new star to the flag.

The pioneers fashioned a constitution that has weathered change and the impact of novel needs through more than a century. They did their work amid the tumult of issues that divided the nation and soon exploded into civil war. Historians and citizens of later generations must view the founders of Minnesota in the setting of their time, their ambitions and hopes, their standards. And it may not be inapropos, as a measure, to recall the wise counsel in the Sermon on the Mount: "By their fruits ye shall know them."

The First Minnesota at Gettysburg, from an oil
by Rufus H. Zogbaum

★
Minnesota and the Civil War

MINNESOTA was only three years old as a state when the bombardment of Fort Sumter opened the Civil War. A little more than a year later it faced an uprising of the Sioux Indians on its home front. Two wars, coming hard on the heels of financial depression, made the 1860s a period of strain for Minnesotans and also of a nationalizing of their outlook. In their pioneering, they had turned to the nation for help — for enabling legislation, for land grants. Now, in a national emergency, they had to give as well as receive. Ordeal, with all its manifold demands, was a time of deepening maturity and of awareness of full partnership in national affairs.

Signs of transition were the rise of the Republican party and a political shift from Democratic predominance to a Republican hegemony. This hegemony began in 1859 and continued almost to the threshold of the twentieth century. Facing the second state election in 1859, the Minnesota Republicans were as confident that they could elect Ramsey governor as they were persuaded that only political chicanery had prevented him from winning the state election two years earlier. But they poured effort into the campaign. Sibley was not a candidate for the Democratic nomination, and Ramsey ran against George L. Becker, a prominent Democrat and lawyer of St. Paul. Ramsey and Ignatius Donnelly, the nominee for lieutenant governor, went up and down the state making political speeches, a teaming of frontier experience with Irish wit and eloquence. Both parties were aware of the voting importance of the foreign-born. Donnelly had published a series of letters to them; and alongside himself and Ramsey, the Republican ticket offered voters a German-born candidate for state treasurer. Among politicians brought into the state to campaign for the Republicans was Carl Schurz, who made a triumphant tour, speaking German when he faced German audiences. He was greeted with torchlight processions, serenades, mass meetings, and escorts — one procession had wagons and mounted men in a mile-long line. Among his German countrymen, Schurz wrote, "there was no end of handshaking and of assurances that now they would vote Republican."

The Republicans knew that the foreign-born made up about thirty per cent of the state's population in 1860 and that aliens could vote four months after applying for citizenship. Moreover, immigrants were attracted by the friendly attitude of the Republicans on the homestead question and were antagonized by Democratic reluctance to support free land for settlers. The Republicans, brushing away any taint of Know-Nothingism, adopted a platform assertion that they proscribed "no man on account of his religion or place of nativity"; and they were opposed to any abridgment of naturalization rights and to "discrimination between native and naturalized citizens." Not less concerned about immigrant votes, the Democrats accepted a similar plank in their platform and nominated a Luxemburg-born lawyer of New Ulm, Francis Baasen, for secretary of state — an office he already had held in the Sibley administration.

Schurz was not the only prominent Republican to campaign in Minnesota. Among others, Galusha A. Grow, original author of the Homestead Bill, joined him, emphasizing in his speeches land for the landless. He was critical of President Buchanan's proclamation of land sales in 1859, in effect an attempt to cancel the rights of pre-emptors to their land and improvements if they proved unable to buy the farms on which they had squatted. Grow himself had not only sponsored the Homestead Bill but in 1859 had advocated a ten-year postponement of public land sales as a measure to protect actual settlers.

The question of slavery was not forgotten. The Republicans denounced the "peculiar institution" as an evil, but their specific stand was against the extension of slavery, whereas the Democrats supported the doctrine of popular sovereignty — and some accepted the reasoning of the Dred Scott decision. To western minds, however, land policy was overwhelming in interest. One historian has even written that "whatever the causes elsewhere in the United States for the great political upheaval of 1860 and the election of Abraham Lincoln, the first Republican president, the decision in Minnesota turned upon distinctly local and western issues relating directly to the federal land policy, rather than upon such matters as Negro slavery."

The total vote in 1859 ran to nearly 39,000 and Ramsey won with a margin of 3753. The state legislature went Republican. William Windom and Cyrus Aldrich, Republicans, were sent to Congress; and the legislature, convening before Sibley's term as governor came to an end, chose the Republican Morton Wilkinson of Mankato as United States senator, an office he held through the Civil War years.

On January 2, 1860, Ramsey delivered his inaugural address. He gave some attention to the problem of slavery, advocating noninterference with the institution in states where it existed and nonextension of slavery into free territories, and he condemned "secession and disunion." But his address was largely directed to local problems. His gift for phrase, notable when he was territorial governor, again showed itself. He demanded the application of "the knife of retrenchment," after describing Minnesota's financial embarrassments, depreciation in property values, business stagnation, "onerous taxation," the "utter derangement of the currency," and other ways in which the young state had experienced "the uses of adversity." He called for economy. The legislature took him at his word, reducing his own salary (as he had recommended), from $2500 to $1500, almost halving the number of state legislators, and limiting legislative sessions to sixty days. The measures taken dropped the annual cost of Minnesota's state government from $149,500 to $95,000. The governor did not forget to voice the frontier desire for "free homes to actual settlers," a principle that he characterized as "wise in its humane policy, and beneficent in its undoubted effects." And he spoke for a Pacific railroad, expressing the hope that a route running westward from Minnesota would not be beaten by "mere sectional jealousies."

The Republican success in Minnesota in 1859 was a prelude to the presidential election of 1860. Trends in national politics were reflected in the frontier state, although its concern about land legislation overshadowed the slavery issue. Yet it was the sectional dispute that gave birth to the Republican party and also divided the Democratic party nationally. The Democratic disruption was noted in Minnesota, but the major wing followed Douglas and popular sovereignty and only a few Minnesotans supported John C. Breckinridge of Kentucky, who represented "federal protection of slavery in the territories." Actually there were four political parties in the national field: Republicans; Douglas Democrats; Breckinridge Democrats; and the Constitutional Union group, headed by John Bell of Kentucky, representing former Whigs and Know-Nothings.

In Minnesota the contest was between Lincoln and Douglas, however. Breckinridge did indeed have the adherence of Senator Rice and some other Minnesota Democrats, but the rank and file would not accept a pro-southern slant. Sibley stood with Douglas. Minnesota Republicans were friendly to Governor William H. Seward of New York, but when he lost the nomination, they gave sturdy support to Abraham Lincoln. Nationally as well as locally, the Republicans tried to capture the "foreign vote," and one eminent historian of later times attributed the election of Lincoln to the immigrant vote in the Northwest. Lincoln himself did not make speeches in the campaign, but Governor Seward and Charles Francis Adams, who later became Lincoln's minister to England, appeared in Minnesota on his behalf.

Seward delivered a notable address in St. Paul on September 18 on the political power of the West. "We look to you of the Northwest," he said, "to finally decide whether this is to be a land of slavery or of freedom. The people of the Northwest are to be the arbiters of its destiny." He interpreted the West as a harmonizer of races, a region where the immigrants and their children became American citizens. The governor was prophetic in his passages on the westward push of American power; and his address, in its friendly compliments, was designed to win votes for Lincoln not only in Minnesota but in the entire Northwest. Before he left there were dinners, tours, and torchlight processions of "Wideawakes," Republican marching clubs (whose members wore capes and glazed hats). In the election, held on November 6, Lincoln carried Minnesota with a vote of 22,069, while Douglas polled 11,920, and Breckinridge 748. Minnesota contributed four electoral votes to the total of 180 that sent Lincoln to the White House.

There was little abolitionism in the state. The Republicans, though hostile to the extension of slavery, did not propose to interfere with it in the southern states. Some light on prevalent attitudes is shed by a melodramatic incident in the summer of 1860. A Mississippi slave owner, on a vacation in Minnesota, was stopping at the popular Winslow House in St. Anthony, accompanied by his wife and a Negro servant named Eliza Winston. At some time in the past, she had been promised her freedom, but the promise had not been kept. In St. Anthony, with aid from an abolitionist, she petitioned for and secured a writ of habeas corpus on the grounds that she was "restrained of her liberty." Her case was heard in court, was not contested by her master, and she was freed. But sentiment in this northern state was so strongly anti-abolitionist that a mob proposed to take Eliza back to her "kind and generous master" and then to tar-and-feather the abolitionist who had befriended her. The proposed action was frustrated by several circumstances; the servant retained her freedom and was helped by the Underground Railroad to find haven in Canada.

Popular sentiment was colored by alarm among hotel owners over losing southern patronage if visitors were denied the privilege of bringing servants with them. Even before the St. Anthony incident a bill was introduced in the legislature (but not passed) to allow slave owners to keep slaves with them for a limited period in Minnesota. But the significance of the incident of Eliza Winston did not have to do primarily with her freedom. All agreed that she was entitled to it. The question was whether she herself took the initiative in the action. Or was she merely an instrument of abolitionists looking for a test case? The truth is that neither Republicans nor Democrats wanted to be charged with abolitionism.

Nevertheless, Minnesota had some uncompromising crusaders against slavery. Most outspoken was Jane Grey Swisshelm, editor of the *St. Cloud Visiter*. She had come to Minnesota from Pittsburgh in 1857 as a journalist already well known in Pennsylvania, and she had lived for some years in Kentucky. She wrote in vitriolic style, attacked slavery in her newspaper, and lectured on "Slavery as I Have Seen It in a Slave State" and on "Women and Politics." Her writing antagonized a prominent St. Cloud citizen, and the quarrel stirred so much ferment that a vigilance committee invaded her establishment and broke up her printing press. At a mass meeting friends came to her aid, promising funds for a new press. The feud reached such a stage that, as a means of avoiding a libel suit, she publicly promised to print no more attacks in the *St. Cloud Visi-*

ter. But her paper appeared on time the next week. She had changed its curiously spelled name to the *St. Cloud Democrat*. She had kept her promise and would not be intimidated, even though her opponents burned her in effigy, as in fact they did. That she had much influence on public opinion is open to doubt, but she richly earned the descriptive title of "Crusader and Feminist," given her by her biographer. Another abolitionist was Orville Brown, a New Yorker who with an associate bought a Faribault newspaper and named it the *Central Republican*. His writings on slavery and the Civil War made him known as the "Faribault Fire-eater."

Frontier concern over disunion deepened in the winter of 1860–61. Governor Ramsey in his message of January 9, 1861, after reviewing events in the South, said, "We are a young State, not very numerous or powerful, but we are for the Union as it is, and the Constitution as it is."

On the very day of Ramsey's message, the *Star of the West*, an unarmed merchantman that had been sent with aid for Major Robert Anderson at Fort Sumter, was fired on in Charleston Harbor by South Carolina batteries, and it was turned back. This episode induced a St. Paul newspaper to declare that war "is already upon us." On January 22, Governor Ramsey signed a legislative joint resolution offering aid in men and money to the President to preserve the Union. War was not far away, but many people clung to the hope that something would "turn up to keep the Union together." As late as February 23 "Union-loving citizens," meeting in St. Paul, declared against coercion of the seceding states and resolved that "civil war is no remedy for any evil, but the sum of all evils."

Minnesota viewpoints voiced in the United States Senate were divided. Senator Rice supported the Crittenden Compromise, but actually would have gone further than that proposal, which aimed at re-establishing and extending the line of the Missouri Compromise. Rice would have accepted separation rather than civil war. "We are a family of brothers," he said, "and if we cannot live together in peace, in the name of God, let us agree as brothers to separate in peace."

In the same debate Wilkinson declared for the Union even at the price of war. If war came, he foresaw a "victorious American Army" fighting under the flag of the Union. Though Rice hoped for adoption of the Crittenden plan, he had an alternative proposal and presented it in a resolution. The dispute was on the extension of slavery into American territories. Very well, said Rice, eliminate all territories and create New Mexico, Kansas, and Nebraska as states. Enlarge California, Oregon, and Minnesota to absorb the remaining territorial areas. In a word, sweep the territorial slavery problem aside. But Rice's resolution had no impact on the Senate and it was buried. When war came, he gave valiant support to Lincoln.

All hope of compromise between North and South ended in April 1861. Beginning the preceding December, South Carolina had led a procession of seven states in secession. Little more than a month before Lincoln's inauguration, the southerners formed the Confederate States of America and chose a provisional president. When Lincoln spoke on March 4 he made it clear that the United States government would not countenance the dissolution of the Union. But the clash of arms did not come until April 12–13, when Fort Sumter was fired on after Lincoln had ordered an expedition to supply the fort with provisions. The southern assault and the surrender of Major Anderson ended all hope of peace. Lincoln called on the states for men. The Civil War began its bloody course.

Governor Ramsey chanced to be in Washington when the war broke out. His purpose was to obtain positions for friends who had aided in the past political campaign. He had little success on this errand, but the fact that he was there and was a man of action won for him a unique distinction. He learned about Fort Sumter on the evening of April 13 and the next morning hastened to the office of the secretary of war with Senator Wilkinson and Thomas J. Galbraith, a Republican "wheel horse," as Dr. Folwell calls him, who later was appointed Indian agent to the Sioux. Ramsey at once offered 1000 Minnesota men for federal service. Secretary Cameron, about to leave for the White House, requested the Minnesota governor to submit his proposal in writing. This he did, and Cameron took it to President Lincoln. This was the first state offer of troops for the northern armies of the Civil War.

The offer represented a patriotic hope, for Minnesota had virtually no active militia from which it could draw such troops. On paper the militia counted 26,000 able-bodied men between the ages of eighteen and forty-five, but according to the adjutant general, there were in actuality only 147 officers and 200 privates. And he had doubts that as many men as those who held commissions would have responded if called. But the governor believed his promise would be made good, and he was right. With his customary concern for financial matters, he specified that his offer was of men only — the federal government would be expected to provide funds for clothing, arming, and equipping the soldiers. Only at great sacrifice, he said, and through issuing bonds or treasury warrants, could the state possibly raise the needed money.

Ramsey's offer preceded the President's proclamation of April 15, calling for 75,000 men for three months of service. One regiment from Minnesota was included in the presidential call. Ramsey wired the Minnesota adjutant general to send out a proclamation in the name of the governor, but Donnelly, lieutenant governor, jumped into quick action and issued one of his own. He requested an infantry regiment of ten companies.

As the news of war and the appeals for troops reached the state, the people gave patriotic response. There was no question about Minnesota support. War meetings were called in various towns. Citizens voiced loyalty and pledged service. Recruiting offices were set up. Enlistments were encouraged, with preference given to members of the volunteer militia companies that supposedly had already been organized. Actually many of these had functioned mainly in a social or ceremonial sense; their meetings had been ill attended; and they had been most active in readying themselves for holiday celebrations. They were now given priority in the raising of the regiment, but only three of the eight companies preserved any semblance of their earlier organization. Five decided against joining, though some of their members enlisted singly. The Minnesota Pioneer Guards of St. Paul, the Stillwater Guards, and the St. Anthony Zouaves retained their earlier names though most of their members were fresh recruits. The other companies were largely made up of men without military training or experience. But whatever the difficulties, on April 30 Colonel Willis A. Gorman reported to Ramsey that the First Minnesota Infantry Volunteers, nine hundred strong, had been mustered into service at Fort Snelling. Six additional companies, in varying stages of organization, failed to get into the First, but later had the opportunity of serving in the Second Minnesota.

Regimental organization was effected with Gorman, the former territorial governor, as the commanding officer. He had seen service in the Mexican War, but the men chosen for lieutenant colonel and major — Stephen Miller of St. Cloud and William Dike of Faribault — were without military experience. Company officers were elected by the men but had to be confirmed by the governor; and noncommissioned officers were ordinarily selected by the company captains. Early in May, to the disappointment of the regiment, two companies were ordered to replace regular troops at each of the three Minnesota frontier forts. Another order was received to re-enlist as many of the three-month men as were willing to serve three years or for the length of the war, whichever proved the shorter. Some difficulties followed, for 350 short-term men refused to sign for the longer period. Additional recruits were found, and by June the regiment was full size, with more than a thousand officers and men.

Meanwhile the soldiers tasted life at Fort Snelling in a time of improvisation. Food was poor. The men, lacking regular uniforms, wore garbs of red shirts and dark pantaloons; and equipment was inferior. Inadequacies seemed due to the governor's stand that the state could not assume financial responsibility for regimental organization and to the fact that the federal government did not at once provide the necessary funds for expenses. But gradually matters were worked out. For its first two regiments the state incurred obligations of more than $100,000, most of which the federal government in due time paid or adjusted. Minnesota units raised after the first two regiments were almost entirely armed, uniformed, and equipped by the federal government.

Notwithstanding difficulties and the grave fact of war, there was an eager and gala air about the mobilization of force. Visitors flocked to Fort Snelling carrying gifts. Parades were held in nearby communities. Flags, swords, and horses were presented to the regiment. Winona women made gray fatigue uniforms for recruits from their community; St. Paul women equipped the regiment with havelocks, a kind of headgear that served as a sunshade; and some communities tried to provide for the care of soldier families. Later the government set up a plan of allotments under which, with state cooperation, a certain part of the soldier's pay could be regularly transmitted to his family or other relatives.

Daily drills went on at the fort in company, battalion, and regimental formations; and most of the officers were as little familiar with the fundamentals of drilling and maneuver as were the raw recruits. But they studied Hardee's *Tactics* and other manuals and tried out in practice what they learned. A soldier's diary records a day: "Morning gun was fired at 5½ o'clock. Drill for an hour. Breakfast. Recreation for half an

hour. Drill for five hours. Dinner. Recreation. Drill again until five
o'clock, when the boys were again 'let out to play.'" The soldiers were
eager to move on to Washington, and Rice in Washington maneuvered
to bring about the necessary order. When it came, it was carried by
Ramsey to the fort, and he records that Colonel Gorman was overjoyed
and his men "rushed around, hurrahing and hugging each other, as wild
as a crowd of school-boys at the announcement of a vacation." The regiment left Fort Snelling on June 22, proceeding down river on two steamboats. They stopped at St. Paul, where the regiment paraded through
crowded streets and then returned to the river boats. Some of the troops
disembarked at La Crosse, others at Prairie du Chien, to continue their
journey by rail to Washington.

The regiment did not have long to wait for its first taste of fighting.
It fought at Bull Run on July 21 and suffered heavier casualties in killed
and wounded than any other northern regiment engaged in the battle.
Its position was at the extreme right of the Union line and it was subjected to repeated attacks. In the first of these, enemy troops approached
within a few feet before they were identified as Confederates. Batteries
raked the Minnesota boys with grape and canister. Bull Run was a hard
ordeal, but the regiment performed well. It was one of the last to retreat
and did so in an orderly fashion that contrasted with the stampedes of
most of the northern units. One soldier of the First, when asked later
how he felt at Bull Run, said "I felt *fight* all over." Though he survived
the battle, he had a presentiment that he would not come out of the war
alive. His bones, he thought, would be left on "this cursed Southern soil."
But if he was killed, he said, it would be "in defense of the only flag worth
dying for."

There was depression in the First Minnesota after Bull Run. The battle
had ended in confusion, but the men had other reasons for discontent.
They had received no pay since they were mustered in. Many were critical of their colonel's conduct in the battle. And one soldier challenged
the legality of the muster at Fort Snelling by which the three-month men
were enlisted for three years. On the ground that new enlistments had
violated prescribed regulations, Edward Stevens, who contributed letters
to the *Stillwater Messenger* under the name of "Raisins," secured a writ
of habeas corpus and a trial was held under a justice of the Supreme
Court (James Wayne). If the contention of Stevens had been upheld, it
would have meant that six hundred other soldiers were being illegally

242

retained in the regiment. Moreover, there might have been departures from regulations in other states, and a precedent might then have opened the way to disruption of the Army at the very time when the North needed to build greater military strength. Edwin Stanton, soon to be secretary of war, was counsel for the government. Secretary Seward is recorded to have said in a conversation with Stanton that if a wrong decision were rendered, it would not be carried into execution. The nation, he said, "is greater than the dignity of the nation's court." But the decision, from his point of view, proved right. Stevens did not win release and in fact was lodged for a time in a Washington guardhouse for "mutinous conduct." Once the issue was settled, regimental discontent subsided.

During the course of the war Minnesota furnished some 24,000 men for service in the Union armies and in suppressing the Indian Outbreak. The majority were volunteers — men from all ranks of life. They included city and country folk, students from Hamline University in Red Wing, special groups recruited in varied communities, native-born and immigrants from Ireland, Germany, Norway, Sweden, and other countries. From first to last eleven regiments of infantry were raised in Minnesota, but there were also special artillery, cavalry, and sharpshooter units. The system of recruiting soldiers involved, first, calls from the President of the United States for volunteers, with quotas assigned to the several states. Governors passed the calls on to the people, and Minnesota's quotas reached a total of 25,000.

The war was still young when the War Department resorted to conscription, but its first move in this direction, in 1862, proved ineffective. If volunteering failed to supply the needed quota, the states were to apply the draft to their militia for nine-month service. The initiative was left largely to the states, and in the case of Minnesota, perhaps in part because the draft was ordered only a few days before the Sioux War began, it accounted for no soldiers, though volunteering was active. A national conscription law was passed in 1863. Again, reliance was placed upon volunteering, but the law was to be applied if the volunteering did not produce the needed numbers. This called for service by able-bodied citizens and aliens in the age range from eighteen to forty-five. It provided exemptions if individuals could find substitutes or made cash payments of $300. This payment idea proved highly unpopular and was abolished in the summer of 1864. Minnesota, because of the Sioux War, could not meet its quota in 1863. Thereafter conscription was applied, and by the end of the war well over a thousand drafted men or substitutes had been assigned to various Minnesota units. But the number was small compared with the total of soldier strength contributed by the state. As one surveys the demands of the war, with the miserable addition of Indian troubles, one cannot fail to do honor to the state for its outpouring of men, remembering that in 1860 Minnesota counted only 172,000 people in its total population.

Minnesota troops played a valiant part in the far-flung battles and campaigns of the Civil War. Among their notable and outstanding efforts were Corinth, Vicksburg, Gettysburg, Chickamauga, Chattanooga, Brice's Cross Roads, and Nashville, and, on the home front, clashes with the Sioux.

Battles, charges, heroism, victory — these are singled out by the historians of war. But the story of soldiers is more than a chronicle of dramatic or heroic moments. The men of Minnesota's Civil War regiments marched in mud, rain, floods, and blinding dust. They tramped in humid heat that left them exhausted. They suffered from sickness — diarrhea, malaria, and other debilitating diseases — that took tragic toll in lives. After battles they faced surgery without the pain-destroying agents of modern medicine, and they knew agony and tedium in field and regular hospitals. Food was important in their everyday regime, and mess beef and hardtack were not always to the taste of hungry men. The pangs of homesickness were universal, and soldiers looked for letters with pathetic eagerness. Much documentation of the war is to be found in their own letters in which they wrote of events and poured out their hearts to their people at home. On days when they were not facing enemy fire, they had picket duty, drills, and dress parades. These and many other aspects of the war experience — including games, songs, humor, and fun — form part of the record of men translated from civilian to military life. The men faced death and tasted glory, but they knew drudgery, fatigue, boredom, the loneliness of separation from people they knew and loved, and unfamiliarity of scenes and experiences that seemed a world away from the life they had left behind on farms and in villages where they had lived as boys.

But war of course meant battles. At Corinth (October 4, 1862) the

Fifth Minnesota, occupying a position on the right flank of Confederates who already had broken the main line of Union defense, struck hard in an action that proved a major factor in forcing the nearly victorious southerners to fall back. The regiment was then under Colonel Lucius F. Hubbard, who in a later period became governor of Minnesota. The chaplain was John Ireland, subsequently archbishop of St. Paul. Father Ireland's pride in the Fifth Minnesota's achievement at Corinth expressed itself in ecstatic words: "With what unanimity, with what rapidity, what visible coolness and unflinching courage, they poured volley after volley into the ranks of their opponents!" The commanding general, William S. Rosecrans, was quoted as saying that the Fifth "saved the day" at Corinth.

On May 22, 1863, the Fourth Minnesota took part in Grant's head-on assault against the defenses of Vicksburg and suffered severe casualties. Thereafter the regiment fought in the siege that led to the surrender of the key southern stronghold on the Fourth of July. On that Independence Day the regimental band of the Fourth Minnesota led the Union forces of Grant as they made their entry into Vicksburg. Minnesotans had a special interest in opening the Mississippi River to the Gulf of Mexico. They could pride themselves on helping to make it possible for President Lincoln to say, as he did in 1863, "The Father of Waters again goes unvexed to the sea."

The Second Minnesota stood with General Thomas at Chickamauga on September 19–20 and it was one of the last of Union regiments to leave the field. Its contribution, which claimed 150 casualties out of the fewer than 400 men who took part, helped earn for Thomas the sobriquet of "Rock of Chickamauga." Later, on November 25, the regiment took part in one of the most spectacular charges of the Civil War, that at Missionary Ridge. Fighting under Lieutenant Colonel Judson W. Bishop, it went up the Missionary Ridge heights, helped to rout Confederate defenders from advanced positions, and joined the wild advance of Union troops to the very top. Of 170 men engaged from the Second Minnesota, the toll in casualties was more than twenty per cent.

The charge of the First Minnesota at Gettysburg on July 2, 1863, was made at a critical point in one of the most dramatic battles of the Civil War. It marks the climax in the heroic story of the regiment, and has been celebrated in history, reminiscence, and poetry. The First had

245

been toughened, since its baptism of fire at Bull Run, by many field and battle experiences, including the Peninsular Campaign, Antietam, and Fredericksburg. Originally commanded by Gorman, the regiment at Gettysburg was under Colonel William Colvill, a Red Wing newspaper editor who had been a captain at the outset of the First Minnesota's career.

At a tense moment, at sunset, on July 2, the Gettysburg battle was raging. A force of the Confederate Wilcox brigade was advancing toward the Union lines, and the Third Corps under Sickles was being pushed back from Peach Orchard. General Winfield S. Hancock, riding up, gave a quick order: "Charge those lines." Contemporary and later accounts involve some contradictions as to details, but the fact is that the First Minnesota, under Colvill, and in conjunction with other troops of a New York regiment, struck forward with courage and determination. Although other troops accompanied the First in its advance, the First was the only one of the units that did not turn back. It pressed forward to the completion of its bloody assignment. Traditionally the number of Minnesota men in the charge was 262, and it is this number that figures in Mackinlay Kantor's verse:

> Two hundred and sixty-two, they leaped
> Like birds from the spotted bowlders,
> An Indian screech on their aching lips,
> Their rifles up at their shoulders.

The glory of the charge is not lessened by historical revision. This places the number in the eight Minnesota companies that made the charge as about 335, and it counts casualties at 37 killed and 121 wounded, rather than the traditional total of 215. For Minnesotans the charge marks the high point of the Civil War in valor, disciplined steadiness, and sacrifice. The regiment well earned the accolade given it by General Hancock: "There is no more gallant deed recorded in history." The Minnesota Gettysburg epic was not over with the charge on July 2. On the next day the remnants of the regiment, with two companies that had not taken part in the valiant charge, helped to halt the Confederate advance under Pickett and Pettigrew — a turning point in the tremendous battle and in fact in the Civil War.

The First Minnesota came home on February 15, 1864, the final stage of its journey having been made in sleighs on the ice of the Mississippi from Hastings to St. Paul. Public schools were dismissed in the city.

Some five thousand people thronged the lower levee as the troops arrived. The soldiers marched through crowded and beflagged streets in platoons twenty deep, carrying their battle flags. At the Athenaeum a reception was held, and speeches of welcome were given by Governor Miller, General Sibley, and others, honoring the regiment for its deeds and as the state's "first offering upon the altar of liberty." Colonel Colvill, wounded at Gettysburg, was unable to walk and was carried by fellow officers from the sleigh at the levee to a carriage for the procession through the town. Fifty-eight of the veterans of the First re-enlisted and helped to form the First Battalion of Minnesota Volunteer Infantry.

The Seventh, Ninth, and Tenth Minnesota regiments participated in the Indian wars of 1862 and 1863 and then went to the South. During and after the fray at Brice's Cross Roads in Mississippi on June 10, 1864, the Ninth Minnesota was responsible for covering the retreat of a Union force under the incompetent Samuel D. Sturgis. His troops had been routed by the cavalryman General Nathan B. Forrest, whose numbers were inferior to those of Sturgis. The Ninth Minnesota, having retained its organizational strength, gave vital services in preventing a total disaster — but it paid a heavy price. It lost 233 men and 6 officers as prisoners of war, and of these 119 died later in Confederate prisons, chiefly at the notorious Andersonville Prison. Alexander Wilkin, colonel of the Ninth, later was part of a Union force that beat Forrest at Tupelo, Mississippi. The Tenth and Seventh Minnesota regiments were also in this engagement, in which Wilkin, then commanding a brigade, was killed.

Minnesota troops — the Fifth, Seventh, Ninth, and Tenth regiments — played a part in the decisive battle of Nashville, December 15 and 16, 1864, when the Confederate Army of Tennessee, under General John B. Hood, was crushed. The four Minnesota regiments were in line on the second day waiting for the order to advance. When it came in the afternoon, the men "greeted it with a feeling of relief." The assault was a success, the enemy was scattered, but once more the Minnesota boys suffered severe losses, more than 300. Two future governors of Minnesota — Marshall and Hubbard — were officers in the battle. Just a week earlier the Eighth incurred severe casualties in helping to defeat another raid by the ubiquitous Forrest, this one at Murfreesboro. The two Minnesota regiments, the Second and Fourth, as well as a Minnesota battery of light artillery, were in Sherman's march to Savannah.

General Forrest, earlier in the war, figured in an episode that constitutes an unhappy exception to the record of Minnesota valor in confronting the enemy. Colonel Henry C. Lester on July 13, 1862, surrendered the Third Minnesota to General Forrest at Murfreesboro without having been seriously attacked and without making a fight.

The Confederates had struck at a small contingent of Michigan troops and forced their surrender. Lester formed a line of battle but did not go to the aid of the Ninth Michigan, a mile or two away. Nor did he send help to his own camp of teamsters, cooks, and convalescents when Forrest's raiders fell upon them. They resisted but were overwhelmed, and their tents and supplies were burned. The colonel opened negotiations for surrender and took a vote from his officers, most of whom declared themselves for fighting. After a couple of his officers had left, he took another, secret, ballot, and he decided to surrender. Colonel Lester and the officers who supported him were later dismissed from the service by President Lincoln. The captured enlisted men, who were later paroled, took a worthy part in the Sioux War. One of the officers who argued and voted against surrender was Captain Christopher C. Andrews. Not only did he want to fight, but he believed that the Third might have turned the tide against Forrest. He was sent to Libby Prison, later exchanged, and rose to be colonel, then brigadier general, and later took rank as a highly distinguished citizen. Hans Mattson, an officer who was absent when Lester surrendered, wrote of the dismay of the regiment over the "horrible affair." Several reasons have been suggested for the supine surrender, but the chief one seems to have been Lester's exaggerated idea of the strength of Forrest's troops. In cashiering the colonel, President Lincoln unquestionably took just action.

War, Indian massacres, disruption, alarms, and civilian exertion in national and state emergencies ran their course during the 1860s. But it is remarkable how vigorously the grass-roots life of the Minnesota community went forward despite all these crises. Politics did not adjourn, railroad tracks were laid, people raised crops, population grew, newspapers were published, men who did not go to war worked at their jobs, trade went on, babies were born, children went to school (more than 50,000 in 1865, with some 2000 teachers), and many other normal activities were sustained. Life moved along, even though in hundreds of homes parents dreaded, with every passing day, to read the lists of dead and wounded in far-away battles where their own sons were fighting. Many a wife carried on the work of family and farm while her husband was marching and fighting in distant campaigns.

Several trends characterize state politics during the war period. One was the dominance of the Republicans under Ramsey's leadership. A second was the emergence of newer leadership, some of it representing Civil War experience. A third was the prevalent mood of national concern, officially voiced by Governor Ramsey in his message of January 9, 1862, when he said that "all purely local objects of legislation sink into insignificance beneath the shadow of this stupendous national calamity."

Both Democrats and Republicans gave support to the war from its beginning to Appomattox. In that support (up to the issuance of the Emancipation Proclamation) the Democrats emphasized strongly, as the central aim of the war, the preservation of the Union, as in fact Lincoln himself did, whereas not a few Republicans envisaged the war as a fight for freeing the slaves as well. Some Republicans were impatient with the President because of his declaration, in his famous letter of 1862 to Horace Greeley, that his "paramount object" was "to save the Union." In state elections in the North a year earlier, attempts were made by Democrats and some Republicans to form Union parties, but this effort in Minnesota failed to achieve success. A People's Union party was formed, but Ramsey and his followers shied away from it, taking note of the fact that its chief proponent was the editor of the leading Democratic newspaper and suspecting that its purpose was the salvaging of the Democratic party, then in eclipse. What happened was that the candidates nominated by the Union party for governor and lieutenant governor (William Dike, Republican, and C. C. Andrews, Democrat) refused to run — and the party collapsed.

In the state election of 1861, the Republicans won decisively. Ramsey had a margin of twenty per cent over his Democratic opponent, and the legislature went overwhelmingly Republican. In the congressional election of 1862, Aldrich, who had hopes of winning the senatorship, did not run for re-election, and he was replaced by Ignatius Donnelly. This change was in part an outgrowth of rivalry between Aldrich and Ramsey for party control in the state and for management of political patronage. The other congressman re-elected was an able man destined later for national leadership — William Windom of Winona.

Ramsey was chosen by the legislature in January 1863 to be United States senator, replacing Senator Rice, but he continued as governor until the following summer. Then he was succeeded by Henry A. Swift of St. Peter, who had been chosen president of the state Senate after Donnelly withdrew as lieutenant governor and therefore inherited the governorship.

The fourth governor of the state was Stephen Miller. During the national campaign of 1860, supporting Lincoln, he engaged in a long series of debates with Andrews, a follower of Douglas. In the war Miller had a meteoric career, rising to brigadier general in less than three years. He won the governorship in 1863, took office in 1864, and served until after the war was over. The Republicans came through the war with their leadership of Minnesota sustained and strengthened.

In the crucial national election of 1864, the people of Minnesota registered their choice of Lincoln over General George B. McClellan by a margin of 7688 in a total vote of more than 42,000 (25,055 to 17,367). Minnesota Republicans exhibited some reluctance about supporting Andrew Johnson, War Democrat, as Lincoln's running mate; but his selection was no fluke. It was a considered action intended to attract the support of War Democrats who were disaffected by the Democratic national platform of 1864, which flatly denounced the war as a failure. In line with this action the Republicans even changed their name to the Union party. The Minnesota vote reflected to a certain extent the forebodings of people in a dark period of the Civil War. The greatness of Lincoln was not yet fully comprehended, but a majority of the Minnesota voters grasped the force of the President's almost unanswerable simile. The people, he said, "have concluded that it is best not to swap horses while crossing the river, and have further concluded that I am not so poor a horse that they might not make a botch of it in trying to swap." Majority views were expressed by a Minnesota newspaper which, when Lincoln was re-elected, ran the headline "God Be Praised" and gave thanks that the American people had escaped the greatest of calamities, "National Death and the suicide of free government."

Minnesota in 1862 had passed a law that provided that every soldier and sailor over twenty-one years of age who had been a resident of the state for four months and of an election district for ten days before his entry into the service was to be allowed to vote for the duration of the war. Election commissioners were sent to men in the field to collect ballots and return them to home districts. That the soldiers voted is well known. In 1863 their votes were tabulated as 4750 — 3200 of them from within the state's borders. How they voted is a matter of conjecture, though the probability is that the majority were Republican.

The activities of Minnesota men and women throughout the state were unceasing in support of the war. Ladies' Volunteer Aid societies were formed to prepare hospital supplies, furnish clothing for soldiers, make flags, and do other services. Benefit concerts were given to raise money. A Minnesota branch of the United States Sanitary Commission was established and early in 1865 it managed a "Sanitary Fair" in St. Paul to raise money for the aid of soldiers in military hospitals. Raffles, sales of food, a grand ball, and other features of the fair resulted in a total profit, after five days, of $13,496. Generous funds were raised by subscription for war purposes. As labor shortages occurred, women stepped into men's jobs, a development that gave impetus to movements for women's rights.

Indignation found vent against secession and the South, and emotions were stirred by the terrible costs of the war in life and suffering. It is a tribute to the people of Minnesota, however, that some state actions, taken in anger, were subjected to sober and critical review. An example is afforded by the "Rebellion Act" of 1862. This law, passed on Governor Ramsey's recommendation, denied access to Minnesota's courts by persons "engaged in aiding or abetting the rebellion." All citizens, residents, and inhabitants of the Confederate states were in fact, under the terms of the law, aiding or abetting the rebellion. The act was aimed at southerners who held Minnesota property. In due time a case was reviewed in the state supreme court and the law was held unconstitutional under both the state and the federal constitutions. Residents of the southern states were citizens who could not legally separate themselves from the Union. The act was a denial of the right of redress to American citizens in civil cases. The supreme court handed down its decision in the spring of 1863 at a critical period of the war with a reminder that, despite perilous times, "justice and constitutionalism" must have sanctuary in the newly created state. The court's decision has been described as providing "a model for analyzing emergency legislation passed in time of crisis." Walter N. Trenerry states that "it serves as a reminder that from the earliest days of statehood any person claiming to be wronged had the right to ask redress in a Minnesota court." The state, through its high court, kept its head on a question of legal right in a time of crisis.

Under the policies of the federal government, few Minnesota soldiers served throughout the entire war. If they did, few failed to get home for

251

an occasional furlough. But for those gone from 1861 to 1865 the Minnesota scene to which they returned was one of surprising change. Functioning railroads were still a dream when the Civil War began, but by 1862 a line between St. Paul and St. Anthony was opened for service (four trains each way daily, fare per trip sixty cents). Railroad construction proceeded slowly, but by the end of 1865 the state had 210 miles of track and was on its way to a network of railroads that would bind communities together in the next generation. If pioneer visions of a road from Minnesota to the Far West were far from realization, the ten-mile railroad from St. Paul to St. Anthony was an earnest of things to come. It bore the hopeful name of St. Paul and Pacific.

In the background of these beginnings is the intricate story of the "Five Million Loan." The Panic of 1857 and succeeding hard times had halted ambitious plans for a series of railroads. With a view to repairing the situation Minnesota in 1858 amended its constitution to legalize the loan of the state's credit in an issue of bonds "up to but not exceeding $5,000,000." The idea was to exchange state bonds for those of the railroads. The bonds would pay for building the railroads, the roads would stimulate land sales, the sales and income from operating roads would cover construction expenses, pay interest, and redeem the bonds.

It was a pretty scheme. A historian describes it as "a fair sample of frontier financial philosophy; the only trouble was that it did not succeed." Bonds to a total of $2,275,000 were backed by the state and sold — but sold below face value. The land-grant railroads were not able to proceed on the funds available, railroads did not emerge, lands did not sell, the roads defaulted — and Minnesota owned them. It had no intention of instituting state-owned and state-operated railroads, however, and it soon restored the property to the railroads. After technical complications, legislation in 1862 permitted four new railroad corporations, one of which was the St. Paul and Pacific, to start afresh; and all four contributed to the total of 210 miles by 1865. The question of the redemption of the bonds plagued the state for many years. Governor after governor urged redemption and legislatures squirmed. Repudiation would have been a stain on the good faith of Minnesota. It was not until 1881, under Governor John S. Pillsbury, that the bonds were substantially redeemed through an act entitled "Minnesota State Railroad Adjustment Bonds"; and in some details the Five Million Loan was not put to final rest until more than a half century after the loan amendment was adopted.

252

The returning soldier might have been surprised to see that the state's population had increased from 172,000 in 1860 to more than 250,000 five years later. Only five towns in 1860 had passed the 2000 mark, but by 1865 there were eleven. Farming, despite the disruption caused by the Sioux Uprising, had made notable progress. The Homestead Act, so avidly desired by the West, was signed by President Lincoln in 1862 and under its provisions settlers, in 9500 entries, took up a million and a quarter acres of public land in Minnesota from 1863 to 1865. The production of wheat, stimulated by new demands, labor-saving machinery, and mounting prices, leaped from four and a half million to nearly nine and a half million bushels in the five-year period. Thus Minnesota began to move into its era of specialized wheat farming. The price of wheat advanced from about fifty cents a bushel in 1861 to three times that amount in 1866. War demands for wool gave some impetus to sheep growing, but as war needs dropped, the industry declined. When the war cut off the supply of southern sugar many Minnesota farmers grew sorghum for syrup. In 1863 Minnesotans held another state fair at Fort Snelling, exhibiting cattle, vegetables, and grain.

During the war years the farther West, especially the mining regions, drew pioneers beyond the agricultural frontier. The federal government, alert to the value of specie, encouraged mining migration by furnishing armed escorts for expeditions across the plains, where Indian attacks were a menace. Thus in 1862, 1863, and 1864 Captain James L. Fisk escorted organized parties from Minnesota across Dakota to the mining frontiers of Montana and Idaho. The 1864 expedition on one occasion was surrounded by hostile Sioux and was only saved from disaster by United States troops. Minnesota also witnessed something of the migration to the Cariboo region of British Columbia. Many Canadians and Englishmen passed through St. Paul and over the Red River trails on their way to that distant area.

The pinched economic times, of which Ramsey complained in 1860, began to give way to a rising prosperity, but hard money was scarce during the war period. Greenbacks, fractional currency, and even postage stamps were the mediums of exchange. Federal legislation in 1863 and 1864, however, led to reforms in banking and a national banking system that lasted until the Federal Reserve System was set up in 1913.

Earlier banking in Minnesota had been marked by instability. Many banks were organized under a state banking act of 1858, but they were

253

short-lived. As elsewhere, they were empowered to issue circulating notes, in denominations from $100 to $500, which functioned as currency and were secured by public stocks deposited with the state auditor. Unfortunately, the depreciating railroad bonds were accepted as valid backing for state note issues; and "this change," as one historian notes, "sealed the fate of the early state banks in Minnesota." Under the state act no reserves had to be set up to cover deposits, loans, or discounts. A bank could legally lend all its deposits (though it could not charge interest in excess of fifteen per cent). By the end of 1861 only four state banks were operating in Minnesota. And the shortage of circulating notes was accentuated by the depreciation of Wisconsin and Illinois notes. In 1862 Ramsey declared that the dependence of banking on state stocks was "false in principle and ruinous in operation." He favored federal treasury notes backed by United States bonds.

No quick response followed the National Bank Act of 1863, but in December of that year the First National Bank of St. Paul was organized with a paid-in capital of $250,000. The requirements to which national banks had to adhere were stricter than those of the state banks. Gradually, more banks followed the lead of the First National of St. Paul and by 1866 the state boasted fifteen national banks with an aggregate capital of more than a million and a half dollars. One of the results of the Civil War was a national currency composed in part of greenbacks and in part of national bank notes.

Minnesota, stimulated by improved banking practices and by the advance of its agriculture, lumbering, and flour milling, gave increased attention to exports. Governor Miller in 1866 asserted that no less than seven million bushels of wheat from the crop of the preceding year had been exported. Trade and better finances inevitably strengthened the demand for improved transportation, especially railroads, and this demand explains railroad beginnings despite the fiasco of the Five Million Loan and in the face of war conditions. Of importance also was progress in communication. A telegraph line was completed to St. Paul in 1860, and on August 30 of that year the first telegram out of St. Paul was dispatched to Governor Seward of New York. From him came a prompt and challenging reply: "You have grappled New York — now lay hold on San Francisco." A line to the West Coast was not soon achieved, but throughout the war years the Minnesota newspapers kept the public currently abreast of national and foreign news.

Some glimpses of Minnesota conditions are afforded in the messages of the war governors. Thus Ramsey in 1861 called attention to the increasing number of criminals and devoted attention to the state prison at Stillwater. "There are cells provided for twenty-two convicts," he said. "Fifteen of them are occupied, and the balance may be before the next session of the Legislature." A year later he reported that the prison would have to be enlarged. In 1862 he looked forward to the emigration of thousands of veterans from East to West at the end of the war and he asserted that Minnesota was the only "new country" available for farming by "the American emigrant." His conception of the lands to the west was by no means flattering. "West of us, beyond the turbid Missouri," he said, "the boundless Buffalo plains stretch in sterile nakedness to the mountain border of the Pacific, and southward to the Mexican boundary."

Swift in 1864 took account of agriculture, "the interest most directly assailed by the war," but also "the first to enjoy its compensations." He believed that immigration had "more than repaired the thinned ranks of our husbandmen" and that new people plus farm machinery had "probably prevented diminution of the area under cultivation." In 1865 Governor Miller suggested that the time had come to light the state capitol with gas, and he recommended an appropriation for this purpose. He also advocated the sale of swamplands not only to aid railroads but also for funds to "provide a suitable home for the insane, idiotic, deaf, dumb and blind in our midst." Supporting the state normal school at Winona, he expressed the hope that Minnesota's schools and churches would "ever be found keeping pace with her advancing settlements."

Minnesota, like all the other states of the North, rejoiced in the triumphant ending of the Civil War. It joined the nation in sorrow when Lincoln was struck down. "Seldom," said a Minnesota newspaper, "has the grief of the people for the death of their ruler been more sincere; never, probably, more universal." The newspaper voiced the feelings of all Minnesotans: "Without doubt, in all this broad land, there lives not a man who, all things considered, can, in the estimation and confidence of the great body of the American people, fill today the place of Abraham Lincoln." Twice chosen with the support of Minnesota, Lincoln was hailed as the man who saved the Union, freed the slaves, and embodied the judgment and courage of the people in the nation's crisis.

The problems facing Minnesota as a consequence of the Civil War involved reconstruction and readjustment. As the voluntary units were disbanded, veterans took up civilian tasks again on farms and in towns. They were welcomed home, but often, especially for those who had been crippled or worn down by sickness, it was not easy and sometimes it was impossible to resume the life they had left behind when they enlisted. And Minnesota shared in the problems of the nation in postwar times. But the normal forces of growth, rooted in earlier years, were so pervasive even in the war period that the primary later problems of Minnesota were construction and expansion — adapting law, education, agriculture, professions, and government to a new day grown out of the old. But the Sioux War, catching Minnesota in the midst of national crisis, left in its wake overt problems of reconstruction — reoccupation of abandoned lands and adjustment after fighting, not hundreds of miles to the south, but in the heart of the state.

Attack on the Redwood agency, from a panorama by Anton Gág, Christian Heller, and Alexander Schwendinger

*

The Sioux Go on the Warpath

THE Sioux War caught Minnesota by surprise. During the early hot days of August 1862, people had no realization that before the month was over the state would be the scene of one of the worst Indian uprisings in American history.

Readers of the St. Paul newspapers just before the outbreak found no stories of impending trouble with the Sioux. They read about the battle of Cedar Mountain; events at New Orleans and Baton Rouge; troubles in Missouri; Garibaldi in Italy; Civil War meetings in St. Paul, Henderson, and other towns; and local subscriptions to the war fund. They saw items about a singing tour of the Hutchinson family, new books by Victor Hugo and Anthony Trollope, watermelons and eggplant available at the St. Paul market, and Dr. Hurd's toothache drops and neuralgia plaster. But not a word about danger from Indians until August 20, when murders in Meeker County were reported, though the next day one newspaper, referring to reports of slaughter, spoke of the "excited imaginations of the people on the frontier."

Closer to the Sioux reservation, the *St. Peter Tribune* did print a brief note on August 13 about "Indian Rumors." This was occasioned by the impatience of the redmen at the Upper Agency over delays in the issuing of annuity payments, including food. The St. Peter newspaper took note of the fact that many men had gone away to the Civil War, and suggested that it might be desirable for the state to send arms to the Minnesota Valley towns on the chance of a "sudden freak of the aborigines." If trouble came the women had "spirit and courage enough to insure protection" if only they were supplied with guns. The issues of the German *Neu Ulm Pionier* through August (up to the 16th, the last for some time) contain not the slightest hint of coming troubles that soon would necessitate a defense of the town against formidable Indian attacks.

There was no serious anticipation among the whites of an outbreak, and it seems probable that the Sioux had not formulated any resolution or plan for war. The outbreak was improvised. It was set off by an episode of passion — and this was as a lighted match flung on a trail of powder leading to a powder magazine.

On Sunday, August 17, four young devil-may-care Wahpetons attached to a Mdewakanton camp were returning from a deer hunt in the Big Woods. They happened to pass the farmstead of a settler in Meeker County. Their almost incredible names were Killing Ghost, Breaking Up, Runs against Something When Crawling, and Brown Wing; and the farmer, who was also postmaster and storekeeper for his Acton community, had the ultra-American name of Robinson Jones. The Indians, after a hotheaded challenge uttered by one of them, decided to kill Jones, went to his house, first requested liquor, were refused, then followed him to the neighboring house of one Howard Baker, where Mrs. Jones was visiting. There — like some echo of the treacherous Sioux attack on the Chippewa beneath the walls of Fort Snelling thirty-five years earlier — the Sioux hunters first engaged in a seemingly innocent target practice with the white men. The game was a ruse. The white men did not reload after firing at the target; the Sioux did so immediately, then took aim and shot down Baker, Jones and his wife, and a man named Webster, who chanced to be there on a search for land (his covered wagon standing nearby). The Indians rushed back to the first farm and shot a girl, while the wives of Baker and Webster and some children saved their lives by hiding. Then, with five murders done, the Sioux stole horses and sped to their village on the Minnesota River near the mouth of the Redwood, where they reported their violent deeds to the leader of their band, Red Middle Voice.

Events now moved at a quick pace. The Indians understood that the murders would not go unavenged, that annuities might be denied them, that trouble lay ahead. Red Middle Voice took the murderers to Chief Shakopee, and he in turn went on with them to the village of the influential Chief Little Crow.

THE SIOUX GO ON THE WARPATH

Many favored war against the whites, some were opposed. Little Crow had misgivings. In a tense council, when accused of cowardice, he made a reply that proved he had no illusions about the power of the United States. "The Whitemen," he said, "are like the locusts, when they fly so thick that the whole sky is a snowstorm. . . . Yes, they fight among themselves, but if you strike at one of them, they will all turn upon you and devour you and your women and little children, just as the locusts in their time fall on the trees and devour all the leaves in one day. You are fools. You will die like the rabbits when the hungry wolves hunt them in the hard moon." He foresaw the inevitable end. "Kill one, two, ten, and ten times ten will come to kill you." To the hotheads he said, "You are like dogs in the hot moon, when they run and snap at their own shadows. We are only little herds of buffaloes left scattered; the great herds that once covered the prairies are no more."

Little Crow was only one of several chiefs whose sober counsel was swept aside by hot-bloods. Not a few of the experienced Sioux leaders were against war, knowing that it would mean defeat and disaster. Many Sioux were friendly to the whites and took no part in the uprising. Once the war had begun the wiser chiefs were against indiscriminate murder. But they had no control over young fighters thirsty for blood and glory, savages who made no differentiation between young and old in their resolve to strike and kill.

Notwithstanding his prescient speech, Little Crow yielded to the hot-bloods and agreed on war. He pledged himself to lead the Sioux in their fight. The question is why he did this, in view of his belief that the cause was lost before action began. The answer hinges on the Indian concept of glory. Little Crow had lost prestige when the Sioux somewhat earlier had chosen another Indian (Traveling Hail) as "chief speaker" for the lower bands. Now, in crisis, the Indians turned again to Little Crow. He would prove he was no coward. In battle he might regain prestige, demonstrate his military skill, and lead his people, no matter how forlorn the hope.

And so, the night of the murders, the fateful decision was taken. The next morning the Sioux would launch a surprise attack on the Lower Sioux Agency, shoot the traders and "short-hairs" (Indians who had accepted civilization), capture supplies of goods, and open an all-out fight. There was no turning back. That night Indian women molded bullets, drums throbbed, guns were cleaned, and warriors got themselves arrayed for fighting. The next morning the Sioux War began with an assault on the unsuspecting folk at the Redwood Indian agency.

What brought on a bloody Indian war in the midst of the fiery national ordeal of the Civil War? A century has passed, and with its perspective one can dismiss anger-bred or short-term explanations, such as the "Red Devil" theory or the merely local and immediate circumstances that bulked large in the eyes of contemporaries. For those who regarded the redmen as murderous demons because they were Indians, Dr. Folwell offers the sobering reflection that more people were murdered in the New York draft riots of 1863 than were killed in the Minnesota Indian war. The Acton murders were not the cause of the Sioux War. They blew up the powder magazine — but the magazine was there, its train laid. It was a blast that could be detonated by an incident. The murders, as horrible as they were casual, were the incident.

Three major lines offer clues to the underlying forces that account for the explosion into war. One has been suggested by the progress of settlement: waves of immigration from abroad and from the East; the hunger of white men for land and the prodigal attitude of the nation toward tillers of the soil, which found climactical expression in the Homestead Law of 1862. There was a westward movement of people, yes, but also of railroads, farming, industry, and state-making. These were a tide that engulfed the natives.

Another major line, closely related to the westward march of people and power, was the Indian policy of the United States. No one in Minnesota understood more clearly than did the Episcopal Bishop Whipple the disastrous consequences of the American treaty system. It involved the pauperizing effects of annuities, the political appointment of Indian agents, the compressing of the natives into narrow reservations — their tribal relations shaken, their hunting grounds dissipated. As early as 1860 Whipple sent an analysis of the Indian situation to President Buchanan, and more than five months before the Sioux War, on March 6, 1862, he wrote in similar vein to President Lincoln. He called for honest Indian agents, reform in the treaty system, workable plans for law and order among the Indians, control of the miserable liquor situation, and a paternal relationship under which the Indians would be fairly treated as wards. And he urged efficient management of the federal program for advancing the civilization of the natives. He denounced the administration of Indian affairs and said to Lincoln that "as sure as there is a God much of the guilt lies at the Nation's door." The Indian trade, he wrote in a newspaper article, was "a nursery of fraud," robbing "a whole people of their patrimony to pay the debts of the shiftless and dishonest."

Dr. Folwell, reviewing causes sixty-two years after the event, was not less emphatic than the bishop who courageously made public his views before the Sioux War. "In the Indian country," said Dr. Folwell, "there was no jurisdiction, no tribunal, no punishment for crime, and the Indian had no idea of obtaining redress for the white man's crimes against him other than by the torch, the rifle, and the scalping knife." In Dr. Folwell's opinion, the traditional American Indian policy was "calculated to invite outbreaks of passion and revenge."

Wisdom after the event is easy, but one cannot help wondering why the Sioux War caught Minnesota and the nation by surprise, why the government had so little inkling of frontier dangers that it actually sold and abandoned Fort Snelling in the late 1850s, why people did not grasp the meaning of the recurrence of Indian wars from colonial times onward in the history of America. Even historians, writes one of them, "have spent too much time on the local aspects of the Sioux War of 1862 and have placed too little emphasis upon its national significance." The war cannot be understood save in a national setting. As Governor Ramsey said later, it was a "national war." And as a modern scholar put it, "Similar causes had produced similar conflicts over and over again as the pressure of population pushed the Indians farther and farther towards the setting sun."

A third line of causation was the character of the Sioux Indians. They were proud, warlike, uncivilized. Their traditions of glory centered in fighting. Individual honor was enhanced by scalps and counting coup (that is, striking an enemy). And their warlike clashes with the Chippewa ran back to the first invasions of the north country. The Sioux took pride in their prowess and skill, their mastery of raids, their talent for disguise, their ingenuity in using trees and hills and ravines to protect themselves, their knowledge of the ambuscade. It was Sitting Bull, the great Sioux chief of the wars on the plains, who said that one of the differences between Indians and white men as warriors was that the Indians wanted to live, whereas the whites wanted to die. His reasoning was that the white soldier would make a stand and defend a hill against attack, while the Indian cared nothing about a hill except as it served to defend him.

The nature of the Sioux and especially their traditional ideas of warfare form part of the background for understanding what contemporaries called murder. The Indians fought the kind of war they were trained to fight and knew best how to fight. Added to their native pride was an awareness of strength, and indeed of magnificence, when the Sioux assembled in large numbers in the vicinity of weakly manned frontier posts and trading villages. The astute Little Crow might warn them that the whites in their unseen total were like clouds of locusts, but hot-blooded, impetuous warriors were unconvinced by the evidence before their eyes. They were strong. They were fighters. They were confident they could overwhelm the defenses they saw on the edge of the frontier. And they were not ignorant of the fact that many young white men had gone away to fight for the Union in the Civil War.

Alongside such causes were circumstances that intensified antagonisms deeply rooted in the past. The Sioux, granted reservations on both sides of the Minnesota River by the treaties of 1851, felt insecure about the shoestring tract where they were placed in 1853. They had reason for their feeling. No permanency of occupation had been guaranteed them. The President was vested with authority to take up their reserved lands, with a compensation of a few cents an acre, and to remove them to some new area — presumably to the west. He did not choose to do so, but in 1858 representatives of the Sioux were led by the Indian agent, Joseph R. Brown, to Washington, where in two treaties they signed away the portion of the reserved tract lying north of the Minnesota — close to a million acres.

The Sioux were now restricted to the single shoestring south of the river. Once more there were delays in payment, and in the outcome the Indian tribes (though Congress in 1861 allocated $96,000 for the Lower Sioux and $170,880 for the Upper Sioux) got very little of the funds. These figures meant about thirty cents an acre, but nearly the entire amount for the Lower Sioux went to traders and the Upper Sioux received only little more than half of the moneys set aside for them. Another large slice of land was forever lost to them — and they had small compensation. They were squeezed into a narrow tract reaching out to the edge of the plains. That the treaties of 1858 fed the smoldering resentment of the Sioux is attested by the reports of the Indian agents.

A second circumstance was the degradation of the office of Indian agent. Under the spoils system, Brown, who had been appointed in 1857, was removed from office in 1861 with the advent of the new administration. After the cutting down of the earlier reservation, Brown had given attention to the treaty provisions designed to promote the transition of the Sioux to civilization. The essence of the plan was the allocation of an eighty-acre tract of farming land to every Indian who chose to be a farmer (the tracts went to heads of families and to single men past the age of twenty-one). By 1860 Brown reported that well over a hundred Indian families were living in houses, cultivating the soil, raising crops. This may have been a sound development, but the farmers — the short-hairs, as they were called — were a minority compared with the thousands of long-hair, blanket Indians; and there was bad blood between the short-hairs and the wild Sioux. This feeling of suspicion found expression in the decision of Little Crow's council to wage war both on whites and on short-hairs.

Meanwhile, the management of the agency fell into the hands of a politician recommended by Governor Ramsey, Thomas J. Galbraith. Unlike Brown, who had had long experience with the Sioux, he was unfamiliar with their problems. He was not unsympathetic with Brown's civilization plan but it failed to blossom under his management. The short-hairs, meanwhile, were harassed by the untamed Sioux of the open regions stretching out to the west.

A third inciting circumstance was the Spirit Lake Massacre of 1857. This was a miserable and bloody affair in which an outlawed and vile Sioux chief, Inkpaduta, of the Wahpekute band, wantonly slaughtered more than thirty white people in northern Iowa and southern Minnesota, carried off captives, and escaped into the Dakota country. Panic swept parts of Iowa and southern Minnesota, and efforts to capture and imprison the renegade failed. The government abjectly called on the Sioux themselves to catch the murderers and threatened to withhold annuity payments until they did. Little Crow, anxious to avoid such a penalty, put himself at the head of a band of Indians who tried to apprehend Inkpaduta, but he had no success. Annuities, however, were not withheld, and a murderous assault on white settlers went unavenged. This was so sharp a blow to the prestige of the United States that a well-known missionary, who knew the Indian mind, regarded it as the "primary cause" of the Sioux War. This view one may question, but certainly the Sioux were unimpressed by the power of the government in the face of insolence and murder.

The history of the immediate circumstances before the outbreak reveals aggravations that stirred Indian exasperation to an unendurable pitch. Both the lower and upper bands of Sioux were awaiting annuity payments — provisions and money — in June 1862. The crops of the preceding season had been meager and many Indians were near starvation. Galbraith did indeed give food through the winter months to some of the Sissetons, whose plight was desperate, but when June came the expected annuity aid from Washington was not forthcoming. As the delay was prolonged, Indian clamor increased. Toward mid-July some five thousand Sioux swarmed to the Yellow Medicine agency center. By that time Galbraith had his needed goods and provisions in the agency warehouse, but, according to past practice, he chose to withhold their distribution until the annuity money had been received from the government — and it had not come. The agency had an armed guard of approximately a hundred soldiers of the Fifth Minnesota regiment, under a lieutenant named Timothy J. Sheehan, sent from Fort Ridgely as a precaution during the period of annuity distribution. As days passed, the situation grew tense. On August 4 a force of Indians numbering at least five times the strength of Sheehan's troops surrounded his camp while other Sioux burst into the warehouse and hauled out flour. Sheehan aimed a howitzer at the warehouse door, then courageously made his way through the Indian mass to the building of the agent, and urged Galbraith to make a distribution of food. This he did. A few days later a council was held. The agency then gave out further goods and supplies and persuaded the Sioux to return to their villages, with the understanding that their money payments would be made in due time and after notification. It was this episode that occasioned the comment on "Indian Rumors" that appeared in a St. Peter newspaper a few days before the Sioux War.

Not quite so menacing in the marshaling of Indian strength, the situation at the Redwood agency nevertheless came near duplicating that at Yellow Medicine. It occasioned a bitter colloquy between Chief Little Crow, Galbraith, and the traders stationed at the agency. Galbraith refused to issue provisions in advance of the annuity money, and the traders would extend no further credit. About mid-August Little Crow, flanked by followers, asked for food for the hungry Indians. He could not understand why, since food supplies were present, his people should suffer the pangs of hunger. And he made a threat: "When men are hungry they help themselves." Galbraith called on the traders to answer, and one of them, Andrew J. Myrick, replied with an insolence that Little

Crow later declared was in part the cause of the war. "So far as I am concerned," said Myrick, "if they are hungry, let them eat grass." Myrick was one of the first white men killed when the outbreak began, and the Sioux stuffed his mouth with grass. "Myrick," they said, "is eating grass himself."

Meanwhile the money for the annuity distribution was further delayed. Congress was late in passing necessary appropriations, and the Treasury Department debated for a month whether to make the payments in gold or in greenbacks. Finally the decision was reached to send the money in gold, and the order went from Washington to New York on August 8. The greatest irony in the chronology of the Sioux War is that the gold for the insistently demanded annuity payments failed to reach St. Paul until August 16. Though it was dispatched to the Redwood agency, it got only as far as Fort Ridgely — on the fateful Monday of August 18. Murder had stalked the Acton countryside the day before, and on that Monday the Sioux went on the warpath. The annuities never reached their destination. The messengers carrying the gold stayed on at the fort during ensuing battles and they carried the gold back to St. Paul later.

One of the unanswered questions of history is whether or not the Sioux War would have been averted if the gold had reached Minnesota at an earlier date. Dr. Folwell seems to have believed that even a few hours might have made the difference and that, with this margin, "the Sioux Outbreak would have had no place in Minnesota history." There are many other ifs, however — *if* Brown had been continued as Indian agent; *if* food and goods had been distributed generously at the time of pressing Sioux need; *if* the President had used his authority to remove the Sioux from their reservation along the Minnesota River; *if* the government had rigorously kept its promises and enforced its laws; *if* the admonitions of Bishop Whipple had brought about reform in Indian policy . . . Such hypothetical ifs defy answer. One can only say that thus events transpired. Conjectures could be extended to embrace conceivable crises beyond a punctual handling of the annuities. Who can know what might have happened, if . . .? But there can be no doubt that the Sioux War came as the outcome of deep-lying basic causes and special and immediate circumstances — and they exploded on August 18, 1862.

The first objective was the Lower Agency. The Sioux, some two hundred painted warriors led by Little Crow, poured into the area. Traders

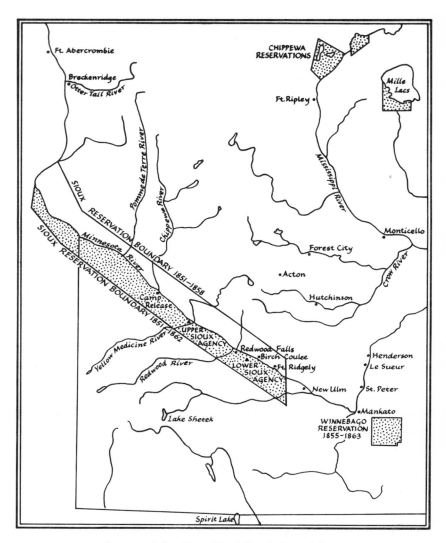

Scenes of the Sioux Uprising (adapted from
Folwell's *History of Minnesota*)

and clerks were shot down first, including the man who told the Indians
to eat grass — evidence of the focus of the resentment of the Sioux, and
of their eagerness to loot stores and burn buildings. The looting so absorbed the attention of the attackers that most of the white residents
(about fifty) managed to escape, were ferried over the river, and started
for Fort Ridgely, some fourteen miles to the southeast.

268

Legend attributes heroic aid by the ferryman whose dead body was later found near the ferry, but the identity of the hero and the precise circumstances of his heroism have not been conclusively established. Some of those who got across the river were later shot by pursuing Indians, including the famed fur trader Philander Prescott. As the fugitives made their way toward the fort they spread the alarm, and meanwhile Indians began to ravage the countryside, killing men and some women and children, taking others prisoners, burning barns, carrying off horses and cattle.

Fort Ridgely was alerted by a stream of horrified fugitives, and Captain John Marsh, occupying the fort with a company of the Fifth Minnesota, promptly left for the Redwood scene with a contingent of forty-six soldiers. Ignorant of Indian fighting, the captain marched his men to the Redwood Ferry, oblivious of the fact that the wily Sioux were hiding across the narrow river and that some of them had slipped across the stream above the ferry and concealed themselves. The result was quick disaster. The Indians opened fire. More than half of Marsh's men were killed. Others sought escape in the brush along the river. At a certain point the captain decided to cross the stream and head for Fort Ridgely on its south bank; but in midstream he was drowned. The Sioux did not pursue the survivors, most of whom made their way back to the fort. So the Indians won an easy triumph, confirming in their minds the idea that they could outwit and beat white soldiers.

Meanwhile war bands spread into nearby Brown and Nicollet counties, killing nearly a half hundred German farmers and numerous other settlers, some of them already in flight from their homes. The swiftly spreading alarms caused people to stream toward New Ulm and other centers where they hoped to find safety. Trouble also hovered over the Upper Agency, where a friendly and humane Indian, John Other Day, gathered the white people into a warehouse and later, while warriors were plundering stores, guided them across the Minnesota River and eventually to safety in the town of Hutchinson. Similarly the missionary families of Williamson and Riggs, living not far from the Upper Agency, were given warning and managed to escape, though not without peril and hardship.

The opening day of the war was one of surprise. It was a day of death to innocent people, flaming buildings, savage looting of property, horror, confusion, panic. The Sioux were elated, but their elation was premature.

269

Assaults on agencies, the stripping of stores, the killing of people on isolated farms or as they fled singly or in groups, even the ambuscade of a few armed men — these could not wrest control from the whites of a great valley or a state.

Disheartening as was the news for the people of Minnesota, August 18 was only the first day. Its gruesome happenings, as reports spread through valley and state, stirred people to quick measures of defense. Citizens in endangered towns organized, built barricades and stockades, and took other precautions. Lieutenant Thomas P. Gere at Fort Ridgely dispatched a mounted courier to Fort Snelling for reinforcements and to apprise Governor Ramsey of the Indian attack. Other reports, including one from Galbraith at St. Peter, reached the capital even before Gere's message arrived. Before the evening of the second day Ramsey hurried to Fort Snelling to confer with the officers there, and he secured the consent of Sibley to command a military expedition to the Minnesota Valley. By Wednesday it was under way by steamboat up the Minnesota River. The governor grasped the gravity of the situation, and on the 21st he addressed a proclamation to the state announcing the uprising and calling on the militia in areas adjoining the danger zone to organize and go to the aid of Sibley. The settlements, he promised, would "speedily be placed beyond danger."

Meanwhile Lieutenant Sheehan and his soldiers, who happened to be on their way to Fort Ripley, were recalled to Fort Ridgely and got there by strenuous marching about midday on Tuesday. Another armed contingent, assembled at St. Peter by Galbraith, reached the fort on the same day, along with refugees to the number of 250, some of whom volunteered at once for service. As a result the fort was manned by 180 men. They worked furiously to prepare for the anticipated Indian attack, at the same time hoping that Sibley's force would arrive with little delay.

Nearby New Ulm, crowded with refugees, was in imminent peril — and in fact was raided by a war party on the afternoon of the 19th. Messages to St. Peter secured the services of Judge Charles E. Flandrau of the state supreme court and formerly, for a brief period, Indian agent for the Sioux. Energetic and resourceful, the judge lost no time in recruiting volunteers. By about 10:00 P.M. of Tuesday he was at New Ulm with a corps of 125 men ready for service in defense of the city. Dr. Asa W. Daniels of St. Peter and Dr. William W. Mayo of Le Sueur were among these volunteers and later gave medical aid to wounded and sick people in New Ulm. That Tuesday there were scattered forays and killings in Renville and Brown counties and elsewhere. In one instance a group of twenty-five whites were shot after an Indian ruse. In another, near New Ulm, eleven whites were ambushed and killed.

The Indian leaders understood that they could have no real success unless they reduced Fort Ridgely, the military guardian of the valley. One of their number, Chief Big Eagle, later explained the Indian idea in these words: "We thought the fort was the door to the valley as far as to St. Paul, and that if we got through the door nothing could stop us this side of the Mississippi. But the defenders of the Fort were very brave and kept the door shut."

Keeping the door shut meant fighting off two Indian assaults on Fort Ridgely (August 20 and 22) and repelling a massed attack on the city of New Ulm (August 23). Fort Ridgely, lacking a palisade, was open to the very kind of attack the Sioux knew how to launch. Ravines led up to the fort, and the Indians made use of their natural protection. In the first assault they reached some buildings behind the barracks, but were held off by Sheehan and his men. Particularly effective in driving the Sioux back to their concealment in the ravines was cannon fire under the direction of Ordnance Sergeant John Jones of the regular Army, who had three pieces and had trained some "amateur artillerymen" in the business of handling them. The fort was still in grave danger, however, for supplies were low and water had to be sought from a nearby spring under cover of darkness. In the absence of palisades, wood and sacks of grain were piled up as protecting barriers. Jack Frazer, scout and hunter, served as a courier to carry an urgent message to Sibley at St. Peter and he got through in darkness and rain, cleverly eluding hostile pursuers.

Two days later, on Friday, the Sioux struck once more. Chief Big Eagle, who took part in the fight, described it many years later as a "grand affair." Little Crow, Mankato, "The Thief," and other chiefs were present. Big Eagle said that some eight hundred warriors were in the attacking party, though the actual number active in the fight probably was smaller. In any case, the Indians attacked in force, shooting and yelling, and the climax came with a rush from a ravine at the southwest. The men of the fort put up a good defense, and once more the doughty Sergeant Jones, discharging canister at the attackers as they were about to charge out from the protecting woods, turned the tide. The Sioux held back. "But for the cannon," said Big Eagle, "I think we would have taken the

271

fort," though he also asserted that the cannon "did not hurt many." A determined charge, with all its costs, probably would have taken the fort, but it was not made. The fort was not captured, then or later — and the failure meant that the cause of the Sioux was lost. Only three of the white defenders were killed and thirteen wounded. The surviving defenders were later awarded medals bearing the words, in Sioux, "They kept the door shut."

The day after the second assault at Ridgely the Sioux made a fierce attack on New Ulm, against which a preliminary raid had been thrust on the 19th. Under Flandrau the defending force at New Ulm had done all in its power to improve the barricades and to train men for the fight to come. It opened with a wild and screaming sortie by the Sioux that caused the defenders to retreat to their barricades, but defense then stiffened. The Sioux failed to press home their initial advantage. Some buildings were set on fire by the defenders to open an area that the attackers would have to cross under fire if they were to take the town. From another quarter the Sioux attacked again, setting buildings on fire, and charging at the barricades. This time the defenders met the charge with volleys and the Indians drew back. Though firing continued into the night, New Ulm was saved. Flandrau ordered buildings outside the barricades burned during the night, and it appears that, in all, by Indian action and white defense, 190 buildings of the town were destroyed by fire.

The "second battle of New Ulm" takes rank with the defense of Fort Ridgely as a turning point in the Sioux War. It was "no sham battle, no trivial affair." It was an all-out attack by hordes of Indians outnumbering the defenders, and the defense was resourceful and courageous. In casualties the battle was far most costly to the whites than the defense of the fort, for twenty-six "citizen soldiers" were killed and many wounded. Two days after the Indians withdrew, Flandrau decided to remove the entire population, which now included twelve hundred or more noncombatants, many of them women and children, to nearby Mankato. He accomplished this task while the Sioux themselves were making their way up the river toward the Upper Agency, their hopes of success at Ridgely and New Ulm frustrated. Actually, New Ulm was in no danger of another major assault — but this is wisdom after the event. Flandrau, later criticized for his abandonment of New Ulm, acted out of concern for the civilians under his care.

THE SIOUX GO ON THE WARPATH

The Sioux War was not over, but its early shocks had been sustained. There were attacks on other centers, including Henderson, Forest City, and Hutchinson. There were savage and murderous raids on lonely farms and on stray groups of settlers, with their families, as they sought protection in places where stockades had been built and where citizens were on guard against surprise attack. Meanwhile Sibley and his force made their way up the Minnesota River to St. Peter and then on to Fort Ridgely, but did not reach the fort until August 27, five days after the second attack on the fort and four days after the Sioux had been repulsed at New Ulm. With Sibley's arrival, the war entered its final phase. Governor Ramsey requested the militia to come to the support of Sibley, who soon had a force of some fourteen hundred men and effected an official organization, which included the Sixth Minnesota under Colonel William Crooks, a regiment of mounted volunteers under Colonel Samuel McPhail, and additional forces, among them some companies of the Seventh Minnesota.

Sibley did not march out to engage the Indians in pitched battle. His troops needed discipline and training. He tried to mold them into an effective fighting force while at the same time he struggled with the problem of getting supplies of guns, ammunition, food, and clothing. The importance for the whites of understanding the realities of Indian warfare was enforced by what is usually called the battle of Birch Coulee on September 2. A burial party under Major Joseph R. Brown was sent out to dispose of the bodies of slain civilians and of the soldiers in Captain Marsh's command. Some men were mounted, others were infantry. After the force had divided for various errands, it came together again and camped on a prairie near a coulee. The spot was exposed to ambuscade, notwithstanding Sibley's injunction to Brown to take every precaution to avoid surprise.

The Sioux meanwhile, after retreating to the region of the Upper Agency, had sent considerable numbers of warriors on expeditions to retrieve supplies left in their villages; to harass, if possible, wagons in the rear of Sibley's force; and to plunder settlements. Early on the morning of September 2, some two hundred Sioux, crawling through the coulee and wearing turbans of grass, opened fire on the camp. The surprise was complete and the camp was besieged for thirty hours, its defense in charge of Brown, who suffered a wound, and a Captain Hiram Grant. The soldiers sought protection behind dead horses — more than eighty

273

were killed by the Indians — and by digging in with spades, pocketknives, and sabers. The Indians made no overwhelming charge (the charge at heavy costs in lives was not a part of their military tradition) but in the end the whites were saved only by the arrival of Sibley's main force, which had been alerted by the sounds of distant firing but was slow in coming to the rescue.

As early as September 6, Governor Ramsey had sent a message to President Lincoln requesting federal assistance. "This is not our war; it is a national war," said the governor. On that date Major General John Pope was appointed commander of the Military Department of the Northwest. By the 17th he was in St. Paul issuing instructions to Sibley and sketching plans whereby the war could be pushed to a quick end. What he wanted was "a final stop to Indian troubles by exterminating or ruining all the Indians engaged in the late outbreak."

Though fierce forays and attacks continued in Meeker, Kandiyohi, and other counties, white strength now began to close in on the Sioux. On September 18 Sibley started his forces, now increased to more than 1600 men, on an advance toward the Upper Agency area. In that vicinity the Battle of Wood Lake was fought on September 23, a confused and random engagement. Little Crow had plans for another ambuscade, but it was frustrated by a foraging contingent of Third Minnesotans who unwittingly drew Indian fire and thus opened the battle. Sibley reported an attack by some three hundred warriors "whooping and yelling in their usual style and firing with great rapidity." But the white resistance was determined. Seasoned soldiers of the Third Minnesota, the "Renville Rangers," and companies of the Seventh Minnesota and several other regiments repulsed the howling attackers. The Sioux pulled back and, in effect, Sibley's campaign was over. Only seven of his soldiers were killed or mortally wounded, and some thirty-four less seriously wounded.

There can be little doubt that if Sibley had then advanced with determination against the retreating Indians, he could have delivered a crushing blow. This he did not do, but the Sioux understood that, having failed to defeat Sibley, their cause was lost. Substantially the Minnesota Indian war came to an end. Three days after Wood Lake, on September 26, it is true, there was an attack on Fort Abercrombie and a few days thereafter a skirmish, but these were minor episodes. Many of the Sioux fighters, including Little Crow, slipped away to the plains and there were no further head-on clashes.

Sibley was deeply concerned about the fate of the white prisoners of the Sioux. He had been in touch, through messages, with Little Crow ever since Birch Coulee, attempting to induce the Sioux chief to surrender; and the question of the prisoners had inevitably come up. "Return me the prisoners, under a flag of truce, and I will talk with you then like a man," Sibley had written Little Crow on September 8. But the calculating chief held the prisoners in the hope of obtaining a pledge of immunity for himself and his followers. Sibley feared that if he forced a final battle, the Indians might use the prisoners as a shield or massacre them. After Wood Lake, however, he learned that friendly Indians and half-breeds, including Wabasha and Taopi, had taken charge of the captive whites and were ready to release them. On September 26 Sibley entered the Indian camp where they were held. Captives to the number of 269 — 107 white people and 162 half-breeds — were put in his care amid scenes of rejoicing; and the place is known in Sioux War history as "Camp Release."

It would be difficult to exaggerate the intensity of the panic that swept Minnesota during the days of the Sioux Outbreak. If this panic shocks moderns, let them remember that the horror of Indian butchery was part of frontier and American lore, fed by a thousand tales, imprinted on the minds of young and old. Nobody wanted to be scalped — and fears saw stalking Indians at night in every tree, every shadow, tomahawks raised to strike, bloodcurdling yells a split second away. Many fled not only their farms or village homes but the state. Country people abandoned their farms and sought sanctuary in villages. Scores of communities hastily built stockades, some of logs, some with sod walls, which in time were organized into a veritable chain, with troops distributed for their protection. The established forts — Snelling, Ridgely, Ripley, and Abercrombie — were basic to the frontier defense. Abercrombie saw little action, but it was a stronghold on the western edge of the state, a restraining influence on the Sioux of the plains, and a depot for transportation, the guarding of wagon trains, and communication from Fort Snelling to the west via St. Cloud, Sauk Centre, and Alexandria. Ridgely was the door the Sioux could not open. Snelling was the rendezvous for raw troops; and Ripley was the wedge between Sioux and Chippewa.

The adjutant general's office did yeoman service in getting soldiers sent to many forts and stockades as well as to Sibley during the early days of the outbreak. Regiment after regiment was set in motion that spring and summer — from the Sixth Minnesota to the Eleventh — and enlistments from late May to September ran to nearly 4000. The federal government gave permission to use newly recruited troops to quell the uprising, but when Ramsey appealed to President Lincoln to postpone the Civil War draft because of the frontier crisis, the President said No. He had the Civil War on his hands. But he wired, "Attend to the Indians. If the draft cannot proceed of course it will not proceed. Necessity knows no law." The government understood that the Indian revolt had to be overcome.

Protective measures were taken immediately after the Sioux War began and they were continued and extended long after the main campaign ended and the Sioux who were not captured by Sibley scurried out to the Dakota plains. In the earlier stages of the outbreak dangers were immediate for the villages exposed to attack, and home guards and civilians took quick action to guard their communities. But even after the war had ended, occasional raiding parties of Sioux appeared in search of horses, food, even scalps. And the panic set in motion in the late summer of 1862 did not quickly subside. In fact, it spread far beyond the areas of danger, even as far south as Wisconsin communities in the vicinity of Milwaukee. If panic seems a fantasy on the part of people hundreds of miles away from the scenes of violence, it was no fantasy for the people in the valley of the Minnesota River and in areas of Minnesota reaching out to its western borders. Here fears were occasioned by danger, and communities took precautions to meet assaults by day or by night.

Much anxiety in Minnesota centered in the possible participation of the Chippewa and Winnebago in the war, but there is little evidence that these Indians did in fact take part. The Winnebago were unhappy and restless, however, and the Chippewa — particularly the Gull Lake band under Chief Hole-in-the-Day — were in a threatening mood.

If terror and panic are part of the story, courage and heroism also figure in the events of the outbreak. The Sioux War literature is filled with recountals of fortitude in the face of disaster. Among many, there is the story of Guri Endreson, who lived with her husband and five children not far from Willmar. A marauding party of Indians appeared at the farm, shot and killed her husband and one son, wounded another, and carried off two of her daughters as captives. Guri and one daughter somehow escaped, hid, returned the next day, and cared for the wounded boy who had been thought dead. She then went to a neighboring farm where two men were wounded and had sent their wives and children to a nearby settlement for aid. Guri bandaged the wounds of the men, placed them in a farm wagon, hitched oxen to the wagon, and drove thirty miles to Forest City, stopping and guarding the wagon in the night. Her two daughters escaped from the Indians and rejoined the family, but the wounded son died about a year later. Guri never thought of herself as a heroine. "God permitted it to happen thus," she wrote to her parents in Norway, "and I had to accept my heavy fate and thank Him for having spared my life and those of some of my dear children." Four years later she returned to her farm to take up its tasks. Today a monument stands over her grave, erected by the state of Minnesota "in memory of her heroic deeds."

Another memorable episode was the narrow escape of the wife and children of Joseph R. Brown who were living in a stone mansion — "Farther-and-Gay Castle" — some miles below the Upper Agency when the outbreak began. Two children, Samuel and Ellen, had gone to the agency on an errand on August 18, unaware of the fact that the war had begun that morning. Warned by friendly Indians that trouble was brewing, they returned home and reported what they had heard. The next morning the Browns and some of their neighbors hitched oxen to wagons and the party started out for Fort Ridgely. Suddenly, after a few miles, they were surrounded by hostile Sioux. Mrs. Brown, of French-Canadian, Sioux, and Scottish descent, was not intimidated, though she faced the ugly and vicious Cut Nose and other fierce warriors. She "stood up in the wagon, and, waving her shawl, she cried in a loud voice that she was a Sisseton, a relative of Waanatan, Scarlet Plume, Sweetcorn, Ah kee pah, and a friend of Standing Buffalo." She demanded protection from the Indians, who were brandishing bloodied tomahawks. One warrior then remembered that on a winter day Mrs. Brown had allowed him to warm himself in her house, and he thus had escaped freezing. He decided to give her protection. Others agreed, but they insisted that the men in the party should be killed. Mrs. Brown then said that if they were killed, the Upper Sioux, her friends, would take vengeance. Her courage prevailed. The white men were allowed to go, and the women and children were taken prisoners and conveyed to the camp of Little Crow himself, who gave them his protection. Their house meanwhile was set afire (its ruined walls are still standing in a small state park). Mrs. Brown and her children were among the captives given up to General Sibley at Camp Release.

Indian warfare, with little organized campaigning, no coordinated discipline, and many straggling and marauding bands looking for glory, killings, and plunder, traditionally has involved atrocities. Newspaper and later reports of the Sioux War tell of killing by tomahawks, knives, and guns; scalping; rape; disembowelment; beheading; cruel thrusts of spears into the bodies of dying victims. All this, in the white man's view, was murder and nothing else; and the reports inflamed people with hatred and rage and led to demands for vengeance. Some truth there was in the reports, but how much exaggeration no one can say. The most judicious historian of the Sioux War, Dr. Folwell, who studied the records critically long after the passions of the war period had subsided, said this: "The Indian . . . saw himself engaged in war, the most honorable of all pursuits, against men who, as he believed, had robbed him of his country and his freedom, had fooled and cheated him with pretensions of friendship, and who wished to force upon him an alien language and religion. He was making war on the white man in the same fashion in which he would have gone against the Chippewa or the Foxes. There were a few instances of mutilations of bodies, but they were by no means so numerous as the excited imaginations of refugees made them out. There were also isolated cases of tenderness and generosity to captives. The more reputable chiefs would gladly have restrained their warriors from indiscriminate slaughter, but that was impossible when there were hundreds of young braves to whom the eagle feather was the most precious thing in life; and that could be won by the murder of a baby as easily as by the killing of a foe in equal combat." The Sioux had no knightly tradition of war. They fought as they had since time immemorial. Their methods were stealth, ambuscade, concealment, surprise killings, raids, scalpings for the glory of eagle feathers, and unearthly yells to inspire fear. War to them was merciless, brutal, treacherous.

The close of hostilities was followed by statewide demands for vengeance. Sibley himself during the campaign had said he would sweep the Sioux "with the besom of death," and General Pope late in September advised him to treat the Indians "as maniacs or wild beasts." The newspapers of the state called for quick and extreme punishment. Meanwhile Camp Release was thronging with Sioux. Voluntary surrenders and captures of stray bands swelled the number of Indians in the camp until there were, by late October, some two thousand in all under Sibley's charge. All were concentrated before November at the Redwood agency.

Sibley by September 28 had set up a military commission of five officers to try the cases of Sioux warriors. Their final number was 392 and in the procedure much use was made of Dr. Riggs in gathering evidence from the released white prisoners and in identifying individuals. He served in a sense as a grand jury of one. At first Sibley intended on his own authority to hang prisoners sentenced to death, but as numbers mounted, and in close liaison with General Pope, he postponed executions. Finally it was realized that no hangings could take place until and unless they were authorized by the President of the United States. By November 5, after the trials of the 392 had been concluded, 307 were sentenced to death and 16 to imprisonment. Pope sent the names to the President, hoping for a quick confirmation of the sentences. This was not forthcoming, however, for the President instructed Pope to send him the full records of the trials and then set in motion a study of the cases preparatory to a final decision. He would not be rushed into action by the emotions of people on the frontier. He would not, as a noted historian has said, countenance "lynching, within the forms of martial law."

In the meantime the condemned prisoners were removed to South Bend, near Mankato, and the other Indians were concentrated at Fort Snelling after a long and miserable trip by wagon and foot from the agency, with jeering crowds in villages hurling objects at them as they passed. Everywhere cries of vengeance were heard. Newspapers ran indignant stories. Some of the Minnesota representatives in Congress declared that the Sioux had not conducted war, but only murder, rape, and robbery. Ramsey urged the President to approve the execution of all who had been found guilty by the tribunal. Unless Lincoln took such action, the road would be opened to private vengeance. "It would be wrong upon principle and policy," he wrote, for the President to refuse to sustain the executions. A Mankato newspaper declared that the condemned Indians would be finally executed "either by the order of the President, or by the will of the People, who make Presidents." And a St. Paul newspaper said that if the condemned were not given capital punishment, "the people will take the matter into their own hands, and do substantial justice."

Three important circumstances operated to bring about a radical revision of the Minnesota findings. One was the influence of Bishop Whipple, who understood as few did the underlying reasons for the outbreak and who had the courage to take a stand against the passionate thirst for vengeance. Accompanied by his cousin General Halleck, he had an interview with President Lincoln some time in the autumn of 1862, and the President commented on it in these striking words: "He came here the other day and talked with me about the rascality of this Indian business until I felt it down to my boots." A second circumstance was the fact that the commissioner of Indian affairs, William P. Dole, had no sympathy with wholesale and indiscriminate punishment for the Sioux warriors. The third circumstance was the balanced judgment and judicious character of Abraham Lincoln himself, who, once the trial records were in his hands, had them reviewed. He was unwilling to hang men condemned for having fought in the war, but he would approve the execution of those who had massacred defenseless civilians or had committed rape (of which only two instances were substantiated).

When Lincoln acted, he did so in an order personally written by him on December 6. He listed only 39 of the more than 300 Sioux who had been condemned to death. These he ordered Sibley to hang on December 19, a date soon thereafter postponed to the 26th. One of the 39 was reprieved, and thus when the day of mass hanging came, on December 26 at Mankato, with troops stationed around the common platform of execution on which the condemned Sioux were placed, and with great throngs of people watching, 38 Indians were plunged to their deaths at the same instant.

Many Sioux warriors made their way to the Dakota country, but many were also still in Minnesota, most of them huddled in camps near Fort Snelling. Universal sentiment in Minnesota demanded their expulsion. No one voiced this sentiment more furiously than Governor Ramsey, who in a message to the legislature on September 9, 1862, while the outbreak was in progress, declared, "The Sioux Indians of Minnesota must be exterminated or driven forever beyond the borders of the State." It was unthinkable to Minnesotans that they should be permitted to remain, and in February 1863 Congress abrogated its earlier treaties with the

Sioux. Annuities were cut off; the Sioux reservation and also that of the Winnebago were withdrawn and opened to settlers; and provision was made for sending the Minnesota Sioux out of the state. Once more the American policy of removal, which had long marked the westward movement, was set in motion. Different ideas and plans were offered, including the surprising one that the Sioux should be concentrated on Isle Royale in Lake Superior. In the end, however, they were removed, in the spring of 1863, to the Missouri Valley, not far from Fort Randall, as were the Winnebago. The convicts held at Mankato were transported to government barracks at Davenport, Iowa, and after some years pardoned and sent on to Nebraska. Relatively small numbers of friendly Sioux were gathered near the old Redwood agency, at Morton and also at Granite Falls and on Prairie Island in the Mississippi.

If the Sioux chapter in Minnesota history thus came very nearly to its end, the legacy of the war was long and painful. From the Minnesota point of view the expulsion of the Sioux was a major result, but nationally the war bred wars in a succession not finally quelled until nearly thirty years after Little Crow led his warriors to the Redwood agency. In 1863 Sibley pursued the hostile Sioux to the Missouri country. Campaigns under him and General Alfred Sully, a noted Indian fighter, opened a series of clashes that extended to the later 1860s and the 1870s and reached a tragic climax on the Little Bighorn River in 1876, when General George A. Custer and all his officers and troops (264 in number) were killed in a terrible Indian battle. The Sitting Bull War ended in 1877, but the redoubtable chief himself did not meet his death until 1890; and the Battle of Wounded Knee, in which some two hundred Sioux were killed, took place later that year.

War flamed in the West for a generation after the Sioux went on the warpath in the Minnesota Valley. Chief Little Crow, though he escaped to the plains after Wood Lake, did not survive to play a part in the later wars. In the summer of 1863, with a few followers, he entered Minnesota again. There was then a state bounty for Indian scalps, and a few miles from Hutchinson the tribal chief was killed by a settler named Nathan Lamson and his son. They had been hunting deer and shot the Indian as if he were a wild beast. For the slaughter Lamson later received an award of $500 from the state. Such incursions as that of Little Crow, involving several killings of whites, kept Minnesota pioneers in a state of alarm long after the major settlement of the Sioux War; and garrisons were posted at many frontier stockades to protect the countryside.

Some international problems were occasioned by the outbreak. The uprising caused annoyance to the British because many Sioux took refuge north of the boundary where they were most unwelcome. Little Crow himself visited the Red River settlements before his ill-fated reappearance in Minnesota and demanded food and ammunition (but received only food). The settlers asked for local cavalry protection, and the Council of Assiniboia requested troops from the Crown. The local patrols were not provided, and the British government took the position that the safety of Rupert's Land was not its responsibility. Meanwhile Secretary Seward extracted pledges from the British that arms would not be issued to Sioux refugees north of the boundary — pledges not too easy for the local people to live up to when roving bands of Sioux appeared, desperately in need of ammunition for their hunting. The situation became the more embarrassing for the British when in the fall of 1863 an American battalion under Major Edwin A. C. Hatch was stationed at the Red River, south of the boundary. This caused many more Sioux to scurry north of the line. By a plot involving collusion between the British and the Americans, two notorious Sioux leaders (Little Six and Medicine Bottle) were kidnaped, drugged into insensibility, and carried down to Major Hatch. This act had no diplomatic repercussions — and in 1865 the Indians were hanged at Pilot Knob near Fort Snelling. Major Hatch went so far as to request authority from the British Governor Dallas to cross the border in pursuit of Sioux refugees and was granted permission to do so, but he did not venture to use the authority, which had no sanction from Washington or London. The Sioux in British territory posed a problem that was not fully met until Canada, toward the end of the decade, bought Rupert's Land and the mounted police took over the business of protecting settlers.

The Sioux Uprising was a frontier and national calamity, a bloodspattered commentary on the failure of American Indian policy, a terrible ordeal for the people of Minnesota, a tragic final act in the drama of the Minnesota Sioux. The toll of white lives, if not so great as contemporaries thought, was nevertheless appalling. Not far from 500 white people were killed — a modern estimate is 486 (360 civilians and 126 soldiers). Many others were wounded, bereaved, scarred by suffering and by horrors experienced and witnessed. Large areas of land were abandoned; many people left the state, never to return; others, when they got back to their farms, found buildings burned and property looted. The growth of Minnesota's population was checked; economic loss was high; and costs for state and nation were heavy. And the border war came at a critical period of the Civil War, embarrassing the government, adding to the anxieties of the President, and imposing additional burdens on the people of the state.

The Sioux were driven beyond the borders of Minnesota, but the government, which had canceled treaties and annuities, was obliged to reestablish a system of aid to these people after removal — even during years when American troops were engaging in warfare on the plains against the hostile bands of Sitting Bull and Crazy Horse. The Indian problem was not solved, but its locale, as regards the Sioux, was transferred from the picturesque valley of the Minnesota to the farther West.

The Chippewa tribes, traditional enemies of the Sioux, had not joined in the war, and they remained in Minnesota. In 1863 the federal government secured the cession of the Red River Valley which Ramsey had attempted to bring about a dozen years earlier. Official objectives were peaceful relations and assurance of safe transportation of goods and people through the Indian country, but the underlying purpose was to open a vast area of fertile land to settlement. Ramsey was chosen as one of two commissioners to negotiate a new treaty. Sibley, returning from his expedition to the plains against the Sioux, furnished Ramsey with an escort of two companies of mounted men. At the Old Crossing of the Red Lake River, in September 1863, the commissioners met the chiefs and tribesmen of the Red Lake Chippewa and the half-breeds of the Pembina band.

Ramsey, the whites' chief spokesman, found the Chippewa reluctant to sign away their land. "The Indians to the east have sold their land and perished," wrote one chief to "Straight Tongue" (Bishop Whipple). "I want my people to live." A Chippewa orator said to Ramsey, "The Master of life has placed us here and gave the land to us for an inheritance." But the governor replied that white settlers would soon occupy and cultivate the land and that trade, steamboats, and even railroads would transform the whole region. Cash, annuities, and the distribution of food and goods finally won over the Indians, and the treaty was signed, a cession of some five million acres in a wide and deep tract on the Minnesota and Dakota sides of the Red River. Bishop Whipple, supporting an influential chief who refused to sign, later succeeded, with aid from Donnelly and others in Washington, in having the treaty amended to include more generous provision than had been made for educational, agricultural, and industrial assistance to the Chippewa bands; and a new agreement in 1864 replaced that of 1863. Though the treaties ceding the Red River Valley followed shortly after the Sioux War, they were not in any direct sense a consequence of the outbreak. In fact, commissioners had been sent out from Washington in 1862 to negotiate a treaty, but the plan had been interrupted by the Indian war. Thus in 1863 and 1864 it was carried through to completion — the closing of a quarter of a century of negotiations for Minnesota lands north and south of the dividing line between Sioux and Chippewa.

An emigrant train of the 1850s, from *Harper's Weekly*, September 13, 1886

Postwar Change

THE Civil War had a long aftermath in American life. But the dynamic forces of change in Minnesota from the war's end to the twentieth century were economic. This change was not so much a healing of scars as it was the building of Minnesota into its modern structure. The era witnessed extraordinary growth in population, the reduction of the land frontier, the building of railroads, a burst of agricultural production, the rise of the flour-milling industry, the golden age of lumbering, business and financial development, and the launching of the iron-ore industry. Not only expansion but educational and cultural change colored the period in a modernization that touched the lives of all the people.

On the political front Republican control was strengthened as the years went by through patronage within the state and at the federal level. In Minnesota rifts within the Republican party were more serious politically than Democratic rivalry. Third-party challenges, especially agrarian movements, were significant toward the end of the century. Not a few able men of integrity held public office, but the era exhibits signs of the public moral blight that infected the national scene in the wake of war. The Republican party understandably made capital of its patriotic leadership in the days of Lincoln, and its platforms were recurring reminders of the Civil War heritage.

On many issues the two major parties, despite rivalries for office, took similar positions. Both were concerned about economic progress, but their proposals reveal few major differences. One discerns, however, a Democratic leaning toward "strict construction," the states-rights conception of constitutional interpretation, whereas the Republicans stressed nationalizing concepts. During the war, in 1864, Ignatius Donnelly, then a Republican congressman, voiced this philosophy. "We who come from the far West," he said, "have not that deep and ingrained veneration for State power which is to be found among the inhabitants of some of the older States. . . . Our people move into a region and *make* the State. We feel ourselves to be offshoots of the nation. . . . We need erect no bulwark of State sovereignty behind which to shelter ourselves."

In practice no notable divergence showed itself between Minnesota's major parties on questions of local versus national control, and in time the Democrats allied themselves with third parties which advocated greater central control than did the Republicans. Traditionally, however, the Democrats were sympathetic with the doctrine of reserving to the states powers not specifically enumerated in the federal Constitution. In 1875 the state Democratic platform declared "That the national government is a government of limited and delegated powers, supreme within its own sphere; while the great bulk of the rights of the people must find their safeguard in the states and the people themselves."

Among political problems that enlisted the interest of Minnesotans was Negro suffrage. The state's Negro population rose from 250 in 1860 to 750 ten years later. Underlying the interest in suffrage was a concern for fairness paralleling the national movement for the Fifteenth Amendment; and the Negroes were recognized as industrious and law-abiding people, eager to establish themselves as good citizens. The Minnesota legislature acted on the suffrage question in 1865. An amendment to the state's constitution was put before the people to extend the vote to "adult males" (instead of only "free white males") — in effect, to give Negro men the right to vote. The measure was passed by the Republican legislature but was voted down by the people (14,651 to 12,135). As a candidate for governor in 1865 Marshall gave the cause sincere and vigorous support. In fact, he was elected on a platform favoring the extension of suffrage, whereas the Democrats opposed it, arguing that the immediate enfranchisement of "this enervated and ignorant race" might introduce "in our system an element of disaffection, danger and corruption." One of the curiosities of politics is that the voters sustained the candidate favoring suffrage for the Negroes, but voted down the reform he favored. This they did a second time in 1867, but Marshall stubbornly and valiantly insisted on the measure. In 1868 he triumphed; his amendment was adopted by a majority of more than 9000 votes. In his crusade he invoked Lord Byron:

> For freedom's battle, once begun . . .
> Though baffled oft, is ever won.

The Negroes in Minnesota jubilantly held a state convention of their own on January 1, 1869 — the anniversary of the Emancipation Proclamation — and listened to an address by Marshall in which he welcomed them to "liberty and equality before the law." The battle for Negro suffrage in the state was won two years before the Fifteenth Amendment to the United States Constitution was proclaimed, with its provision that the right to vote "shall not be denied or abridged by the United States or by any State on account of race, color, or previous condition of servitude."

Marshall, a native of Missouri, had pioneered in Minnesota in 1849, served as a regent of the infant university, and played a role in the founding of the Republican party. He had also served ably as an officer in the Civil War. When nominated by the Republicans in 1865 for governor, he faced as an opponent the popular Henry M. Rice. A chronicler of the campaign, telling of a debate between the two candidates, relates amusingly that each eulogized the other. When "Marshall had concluded, every one present felt like voting for Mr. Rice, and when Rice had concluded he had stemmed the torrent in favor of himself and turned it in the direction of Marshall." In 1867 Marshall was re-elected over the able jurist Charles E. Flandrau. The Republican platform of that year designated the party as one "of National limits, a National record and National purposes."

The political clash between President Johnson and the vindictive Thaddeus Stevens, spokesman for the harsh policy of treating the southern states as "conquered provinces," had repercussions in Minnesota. The state's senators then were Ramsey and Daniel S. Norton of Winona, both Republicans. Ramsey took his stand with the anti-Johnson forces, but Norton, who had won over Wilkinson in 1865, broke with the Republican majority on one issue after another. He was one of the nineteen senators who cast their votes against the conviction of President Johnson in his impeachment trial in 1868. Norton was vigorously condemned by the Minnesota legislature and was asked to resign, but he neither resigned nor made apology. He believed he was right in his view that the southerners should be dealt with, not as a subjugated people, but as citizens whose "destiny is linked with ours, for prosperity and happiness, for weal or woe." He died in office in 1870. The legislature, which had read him out of his party for his defiance of public opinion, now praised him as an "able and incorruptible" senator. His place in history is not unlike that of Bishop Whipple, who would not bow to heated popular passion in his appraisal of the problem of the Sioux Indians.

William Windom of Winona, who had served for a decade in Congress, was appointed in 1870 to the seat vacated by Norton's death. When the state legislature met in January 1871, it chose another Republican (O. P. Stearns) to fill out the remaining weeks of Norton's term and then elected Windom for the full senatorial term 1871–77. He held the senatorship for two terms save for a few months in 1881 when he was Garfield's secretary of the treasury. Later he was a member of President Harrison's Cabinet. In the Senate Windom won distinction as an advocate of railroad regulation. As early as 1874 he prepared an analytical report in which he recommended a bureau of commerce. In essential ideas, his proposed bureau was comparable with the Interstate Commerce Commission, established thirteen years later.

Meanwhile Donnelly, completing his third term as a Republican congressman in 1868, sought re-election. He had been "regular" in Congress and had aligned himself with the Radical Republicans on questions relating to the South. If he won a fourth term, he might loom as a contender for Ramsey's seat in the Senate, and this prospect brought about a split in the party — the regular Republicans led by Ramsey versus the insurgents led by Donnelly. There were rumors that Ramsey's choice would fall upon William D. Washburn, the miller, and this spawned a splattering feud between Donnelly and Washburn's brother, Elihu Washburne of Illinois, then a powerful figure in Congress. Newspaper attacks were exchanged and Donnelly delivered a fiery address in the House, shot through with invective, describing Washburne as a "bold, bad, empty, bellowing demagogue." Whether such ranting harmed or helped Donnelly is not clear, but W. D. Washburn chose not to run for Congress. Ramsey supported Christopher C. Andrews, now a Republican. Andrews and Donnelly split the Republican vote, with the result that a Democrat, Eugene Wilson, triumphed, though he polled 8000 fewer votes than his Republican opponents combined.

In the same election General Grant carried Minnesota for the presidency by a substantial majority over the Democratic Horatio Seymour. In Minnesota Republican control of the legislature assured the re-election of Ramsey early in 1869. Donnelly had withdrawn from the race and given his support to former Senator Wilkinson. These events are significant in the career of the volatile Donnelly as a "political maverick." He was a dissenter at heart who had hitherto been regular, but now found himself at odds with the leaders of his party.

Horace Austin was a New Englander who had settled in St. Peter in the 1850s, served as a volunteer in the Sioux War, and taken part in the second battle of New Ulm. He became a judge. Nominated for governor in 1869 by the Republicans, he won a close election over George L. Otis of St. Paul. A Temperance party, formed because the Democrats opposed prohibition and the Republicans by-passed the question, also ran a candidate for governor whose vote came close to the margin by which Austin won over Otis.

In a period of discontent over railroad practices, Governor Austin, with a sharp message of disapproval, vetoed a bill that provided for the distribution to seven railroad companies of a half million acres of lands allocated the state for internal improvements. The measure has been characterized by Minnesota's premier historian as a "land grab." Austin had favored a constitutional amendment putting to the people the question of the distribution of the lands for internal improvements. His veto was politically courageous, and with popular approval, he was easily elected for a second term. In the election of 1871 the Temperance party again offered a candidate for governor. He polled only a few votes, but his party came out for woman suffrage, the first stand by a Minnesota political party for such a reform, then regarded as radical.

The political picture of the 1870s reveals new issues that commanded far greater contemporary interest than woman suffrage or temperance. There was no lessening in popular demands for railroad expansion, but rural rumblings about railroad rates were not ignored by the legislature or the political parties.

A Minnesota pioneer farmer, Oliver H. Kelley, in 1867, with six associates, founded the National Grange, or the Patrons of Husbandry, a secret order of farmers. This was not a political party, but an organization to promote education in agriculture and to provide social and cultural opportunities for farmers, and their wives, through club meetings.

291

In 1868, working with Colonel Daniel A. Robertson of St. Paul, founder of the Minnesota Horticultural Society, Kelley established, at St. Paul, the North Star Grange. Influenced by Robertson, it included among its objectives the protection of its members against corporations and a plan for cooperative buying and selling. By 1869 a federation known as the Minnesota State Grange was formed. Before the end of that year Minnesota had 40 of the 49 local granges in the United States. Five years later the state had 538 granges.

The Grangers worked for reasonable railroad rates, opposed discriminations, and favored railroad regulation through state laws. The Republicans under Governor Austin gave serious attention to the railroad question in 1871. Freight and elevator charges as "practiced by some of our roads," said the governor, "are unjustifiable, extortionate and oppressive to the last degree." By state law maximum fares and rates were prescribed, and the office of railroad commissioner was established. Three years later a board of railroad commissioners was set up with power to establish a schedule of fares and rates. Both Republicans and Democrats in 1871 included in their platforms declarations supporting state control of railroads for the protection of the people.

The early regulatory legislation was hastily framed, and it did not last. The railroads flatly refused to comply with the laws. And in 1875, when the roads were in distress after the Panic of 1873, the last of the Granger acts was passed. Once again the state authorized a single commissioner, but it so restricted his authority that one historian, reviewing the story, comments that the official "had power to hold down a swivel chair."

The problem of public control was more complex than legislators at first realized. But it was the Granger legislation of the Middle West that established the principle that railroads and other corporations "clothed with public interest" are properly subject to public regulation. In 1876 the Supreme Court validated this principle in its decisions in *Munn v. Illinois* and other Granger cases, one of them a Minnesota dispute (*Winona and St. Peter Railroad Company v. Blake*). A constitutional way was opened for more carefully devised regulations than those provided in early laws.

The national political split of Republicans and Liberal Republicans in 1872 had relatively little repercussion in Minnesota. The Liberal Republican movement, led by such men as Carl Schurz, Charles Francis

Adams, and Horace Greeley, was a revolt of Republicans and independents against the Grant administration, with civil service reform and higher standards of public morality among the causes advocated. The Democratic party joined forces with the reformers. Donnelly and Wilkinson went along with the Liberal Republicans, as did the Minnesota Democrats, but the war-renowned Grant overwhelmed Greeley in the Minnesota vote. The Liberal Republican candidates for Congress — Minnesota now had three congressmen — were defeated.

It was 1873, rather than 1872, that was crucial in state politics. Once again there were factions in the Republican party. The split was between the older and more conservative group and younger men who challenged the "old guard." This campaign brought Cushman Kellogg Davis to the governorship for the term 1874–76. A New Yorker by birth, he was a graduate of the University of Michigan, served as a lieutenant in a Wisconsin regiment in the Civil War, and practiced law in St. Paul with former Governor Gorman. He had won a certain distinction by a lecture on "Modern Feudalism," an attack on railroads and other corporations, which he gave throughout the state. His Republican nomination for governor, supported strongly by anti-Ramsey men, was won over W. D. Washburn. Donnelly, meanwhile, had taken the lead in forming the People's Anti-Monopoly party, a political move backed by the Grangers, with a platform striking at monopolies, advocating state railroad controls, and denouncing postwar corruption in public life. That Davis triumphed seems to have been due to the fact that he was as earnestly for railroad regulation as were the Grangers.

The denunciation of postwar corruption was no haphazard episode. Nationally the postwar period witnessed laxity in public morality, as evidenced by the Credit Mobilier, the machinations of Boss Tweed and his ring in New York, and the "need of a complete housecleaning" in the country's civil service. Minnesota also exhibited signs of moral laxity in public office. A state treasurer, William Seeger, was charged with pocketing interest derived from state moneys lent to banks and business firms. A resolution to impeach him for embezzlement was introduced in the legislature in 1873. He resigned; the Senate ignored the resignation; and he then pleaded guilty and was removed from office.

Another case was that of a state auditor, Charles McIlrath, who was accused of having retained for himself funds from public timberland sales. In civil and criminal cases he was found not guilty. But a legislative committee, examining sales, found evidence of tree plunder on state lands. It declared that no Minnesota citizen, knowing the truth, could fail to feel "humiliated and indignant." There were yet other episodes that shook popular confidence in the integrity of public officials.

The Republican party in 1873, alluding to the Seeger affair, said that it presented "the first example of a great party, wise and just enough to correct its own errors and abuses." The legislature put to the people a constitutional amendment making it illegal for any state official to bank state moneys in his own name, and this was approved by the electorate in 1873.

With the administration of Davis, the Ramsey dynasty neared its end. Senator Ramsey was indeed nominated by his party's convention in 1875 for re-election by the legislature, but he failed to receive legislative endorsement. Nor did his Democratic–Anti-Monopolist opponent, the ubiquitous Donnelly; and a compromise candidate was chosen, Chief Justice Samuel J. R. McMillan, who went to the Senate for two terms. Ramsey, more than a quarter century after he came as governor of Minnesota Territory, was retired, but his political career was by no means over, for in 1879 he became secretary of war under President Hayes.

Public opinion in Minnesota was now ready for a businessman's administration of the state government, and this was assured by the election in 1875 of John S. Pillsbury of Minneapolis as governor. Davis had chosen not to run for re-election. For some years he devoted his talents to legal practice and to lecturing and writing, but in 1887 he was elected senator and he served in the United States Senate until his death in 1900.

Pillsbury, a pillar of Minnesota business and civic life and famed for his service to the University of Minnesota, was governor for three terms. He solved the long-postponed problem of the repudiated railroad bonds of the Five Million Loan. And he led Minnesota in various improvements in its official procedures. One of his reforms was the establishment of the office of public examiner. Pillsbury chose for this assignment Henry M. Knox, the cashier of the First National Bank of St. Paul. Knox's administration was vigorous, honest, and thorough, and the governor later said of the law creating the office, "No single act of legislation in this State has ever been productive of more good in purifying the public service." Pillsbury himself was a sterling example of integrity in his political and moral standards as the head of the state.

During both the Davis and Pillsbury administrations the farmers suffered from "grasshopper plagues" which had begun in 1873 and continued relentlessly through five summers. The grasshoppers came in vast clouds, destroyed vegetation wherever they landed, and caused millions of dollars of damage to wheat and other crops. Davis, Pillsbury, and the legislature made valiant efforts to help the afflicted farmers through appropriations for relief, offers of bounties for locusts caught by the bushel, and other measures. The governor in 1876 called a conference of midwestern governors to deal with the grasshopper invasions as a regional disaster that should be met cooperatively by the states involved. He even appointed a day for prayer, fasting, and humiliation, after delivering a so-called Grasshopper Message to the legislature in 1877. That summer, blessedly, the plague ended. The grasshoppers took flight and did not return in plague dimensions. Why or where they went was an unsolved mystery. But Minnesotans rejoiced, and the wheat crop in 1877 was excellent, a boon to the farmers — more than thirty million bushels.

While one political administration succeeded another, Minnesota grappled with the building of a state network of railroads. Railroads had a magical appeal for frontier people. They had depended, in earlier years, on oxcart, dog sled, buggies, wagons, stagecoaches, and steamboats. To them, the iron horse spelled increased speed, economy and efficiency, coursing arteries of trade, emancipation from primitive ways. After the Civil War the demand for railroads gained force as immigrants streamed in and as industry grew by leaps and bounds.

Pioneers of the 1850s had tripped on optimism. They had stumbled in the Panic of 1857. But the railroading concepts of their spokesmen were sound, even if, as one writer has suggested, they built their enterprises on rainbows. They worked out ideas for a railroad network which has been likened to "a large spider web with centers at the Twin Cities and Duluth." The web was spun by succeeding generations. If few understood that transportation is a process of persistent and continuous change, the pioneers realized that for the future beyond the 1850s railroads were essential to their progress. To them this was an article of faith.

As Minnesota entered its era of expansion, it was immeasurably aided by the completion, within a decade and a half, of its basic railroad system. By 1872, with fifteen railroad companies, the state had about 2000 miles of track laid and was on its way to the network which by the 1920s embraced more than 9000 miles.

The Minnesota and Pacific, renamed the St. Paul and Pacific, after running the first trains in Minnesota in 1862 between St. Paul and St. Anthony, struck westward and northwestward. It took two years for the road to creep to nearby Anoka and another two years to push on to St. Cloud. This was the line designed under the grants of 1857 to reach Pembina near the northwest corner of the state.

Meanwhile the road west to Breckenridge was under construction and it reached that city, on the border of Minnesota, by 1871. The Winona and St. Peter road (the renamed Transit road), pushing west, was beyond St. Peter by 1871 and continued to build to the Red River the next year. And the railroad heading almost straight south from the Twin Cities — the old Minneapolis and Cedar Valley line, renamed the Minnesota Central — reached the Iowa border by 1869.

Not infrequently railroad projects failed to materialize as planned, but somehow the roads got built in later years, though under different names. The Root River road designed under the land grants of 1857 was not built, but in 1864 its properties and grants were assigned to two companies. One was the Minnesota Valley Railroad, which built a line from the Twin Cities along the winding route of the Minnesota River as far as South Bend (near Mankato) and then southwest to the Iowa border. The second was the Southern Minnesota, which launched a railroad from La Crescent (below Winona) to Rochester and westward, across the state's southern counties.

The names of early railroads are unfamiliar to modern Minnesotans, but their routes can be identified with companies of later times. This is a reminder that the score or more of pioneering railroads were consolidated in the 1880s, and later, into a half dozen major roads which have served the state and its communities down to the present time. The key was not swollen ideas of greatness but land grants — subsidies from nation and state. These bulwarked private enterprise in its job of putting roads on a profit-making basis. The country wanted a system of transportation that met modern needs. It poured the equivalent of millions of dollars into the treasuries of railroads. This was not government in business, but a sharing of its resources with private enterprise that might strengthen state and nation.

A road connecting the Mississippi with Lake Superior had been in the dreams and plans of the pioneers. After the fiasco of the Minnesota and Northwestern, however, such a line was omitted from the land-grant schemes of 1857. The Minnesota territorial legislature had voted a grant of swampland that year to the Nebraska and Lake Superior Railroad. And this road, with its name changed in 1861 to the Lake Superior and Mississippi, became a reality. It was not opened for business until six years after the Civil War, but it was unquestionably an economic by-product of the war. War or no war, such a road would have come with time, for railroad connections between the Twin Cities and Lake Superior were imperative, but certainly the building of the road was hastened by the war. Spokesmen for the railroad emphasized transportation to the mineral areas of the Upper Peninsula and the need of outlets for wheat and lumber to the East, cheaper than those afforded by routes to Milwaukee and Chicago. Thus Ramsey in 1864 said, "We are the furthest inland state of the northwestern tier of states. Surely it is of importance to the Government to give us the readiest facilities of getting to market with that large surplus of wheat without compelling us to pass through Wisconsin and Illinois." Ramsey also argued for a lake line as needed for national defense. He and others who favored the road were not unaware, however, of advantages to the north country and especially to the growing lumber industry.

St. Paul, deeply interested in the Lake Superior and Mississippi Railroad, went so far as to grant a quarter of a million dollars to it through a municipal bond issue. Minneapolis men were not enthusiastic, since the terminus of the road would be their rival city. Wisconsin was skeptical of any federal grant to aid a railroad that might injure its own economic interests. Notwithstanding opposition, a Minnesota railroad land grant was passed by Congress in 1864 and received the approval of President Lincoln. The Minnesota state legislature in turn allocated the lands to the Lake Superior and Mississippi Railroad. Ignatius Donnelly, then in Congress, must have given aid to the cause, for in a letter he mentions that he had been presented with a substantial block of the railroad's stock in recognition of his services. Whatever the convolutions of the story, the company was given the lands. The railroad was built. And it opened for business in 1871. Of importance was the decision, determined by Minnesota interests, to run this road, not to a terminus on the Wisconsin side of Lake Superior bay, but to the Minnesota side. This meant that the great inland city of the majestic lake would be Duluth, destined to take rank as the third largest city of Minnesota.

The Minnesota railroad commissioner reported that two million bushels of wheat were shipped over the Lake Superior and Mississippi during its first year. Shippers using this route saved five cents a bushel in their freight charges. The railroad was leased to the Northern Pacific the year after it was opened.

If Minneapolis felt chagrin about the St. Paul terminus, it was offset when the milling interests, embarking on the Minneapolis and St. Louis Railroad, built a line from Minneapolis to White Bear in 1871, which there established Minneapolis connections with the road to Duluth. Actually the White Bear line was built under the name of the Minneapolis and Duluth Railroad, but it was an adjunct to the St. Louis road, which was planned to run southward to Albert Lea and then on to St. Louis. Perhaps there was rivalry, or "bitter jealousy"—as the historian of the Minneapolis and St. Louis Railroad suggests — between Minneapolis and St. Paul in the days of competitive railroad building, but it is well to be reminded that, as the Twin Cities grew into a metropolitan center, every railroad development meant interconnections between the two cities. They were jointly the heart of the railroad web.

Railroads were flung south, southwest, west, and northwest of the Twin Cities, and northeastward to the shores of Lake Superior. Not only was the Minnesota web formed, but railroad connections with Milwaukee and Chicago were achieved in the same era. Chicago and Milwaukee interests bought the Minnesota Central and constructed a connecting line north from McGregor, Iowa, in 1867. And in 1871 the Milwaukee and St. Paul was built from St. Paul to Winona, running southward along the picturesque Minnesota side of the Mississippi below Hastings. Shortly thereafter lines were opened to La Crescent and below, thus joining the road constructed from Milwaukee. The line became the Chicago, Milwaukee, and St. Paul. The frontier had rejoiced when the railroad reached Rock Island in 1854. Now, with connections open to Milwaukee and Chicago, it was possible to go the whole way from Minnesota to New York by train, and, perhaps more important, to have regular freight connections by rail between West and East. The frontier community was overjoyed.

A major railroad development in the encompassment of Minnesota was a line across the north-central part of the state, from Duluth to Moorhead on the Red River. This road was built as part of a national plan. As early as 1844 Asa Whitney had proposed a northern transcontinental road from Lake Michigan to Puget Sound. In the 1850s the idea of a railway to be thrown across the continent from Lake Superior to the Pacific evoked enthusiasm and no little planning in Minnesota Territory. But the impetus came in Civil War times — 1864 — when the Northern Pacific was chartered by Congress and given princely land grants. In Minnesota alone it got more than three million acres.

The building of the road from Duluth to the Pacific was undertaken by Jay Cooke, who had proved himself spectacularly successful in helping the United States to sell bonds for the support of the Civil War. Heading a great banking concern, Jay Cooke and Company, he worked out ambitious plans, but because of the weight of his investments he failed — and the failure was a precipitating cause of the Panic of 1873.

The Northern Pacific line through Minnesota was surveyed in 1870, and the road was built from Duluth to Moorhead by the fall of 1871. Its trains were running by 1872. The route was by way of Brainerd, and it contributed to the development of that frontier town. A telegraph operator, Frank Johnson, who went to Brainerd in 1871, wrote in his diary that the road by that time extended through Brainerd, but that trains were not yet operating. Brainerd he described as "Houses all rough boards or tents, about 100 houses altogether, half of them saloons or gambling houses."

In the saga of Minnesota no name has more golden luster than that of James J. Hill, leader of the Great Northern Railway, statesman of railroad expansion and finance, universally accorded the accolade of "Empire Builder." In view of his wide fame, it is startling to realize from the record of history that the basic railroad system of Minnesota had been envisioned and created before Hill emerged as a railroad man.

Not until 1878 did Hill, with Norman W. Kittson — the pioneer fur trader and Red River steamboat magnate — and with Donald Smith and George Stephen, Canadians renowned in the railroad and financial history of their own country, purchase the bonds of the old St. Paul and Pacific and lay the foundations of the Great Northern Railway.

Once Hill entered the railroad picture, his ability as an organizer and railroad executive, his vision of transportation in the economic life of state and country, his skill in meeting problems, and the sweep of his interest in agriculture, industry, and trade made him a true giant in the earth.

When in 1912 Hill withdrew as chairman of the board of the Great Northern Railway, he said, "Nearly forty years ago the thought of a possible railway enterprise in the Northwest began to occupy my mind. It was born of experience in Northwestern transportation problems that had occupied most of my early business life, of faith in the productive powers and material resources of this part of the country, and of railroad conditions at that time." Reviewing the story, he added, "Most men who have really lived have had, in some shape, their great adventure. This railway is mine."

The adventure was born of his pioneering experience. Hill had come out from Canada to St. Paul as early as 1856, when he was eighteen. He was born near Guelph, Ontario, in 1838. He had traveled in some of the eastern states before heading westward by way of Chicago and the Mississippi. His head buzzed with the idea of going to the Far West, perhaps to the Orient. St. Paul was a convenient jumping-off place, where he could join a brigade of Red River carts for Pembina and Fort Garry. Happily for Minnesota, the last brigade of the season had left before he arrived, and he settled down in St. Paul, took a job as a steamboat shipping clerk, soon made himself independent, acquired a warehouse, and went into the river freight business and later into fuel supply. After the Civil War his business expanded and he served as agent for the infant St. Paul and Pacific, built a new warehouse, and began to sell coal instead of wood as fuel for engines and stoves.

Hill's interest in transportation quickened when in the spring of 1870 he visited the Red River Valley. He went from St. Cloud by stagecoach, then by dog sled to Pembina. He saw the possibilities of transporting freight to the Red River, and then shipping it north by boat. His enterprise led to the building of a new steamboat for the river trade and to an association with Norman W. Kittson in a company to develop the trade. He went to the valley again and again and had the experience of making tea with snow, eating pemmican, and sleeping on the ground. These were commonplace happenings for pioneers, but interesting as part of the story of a chief agent in doing away with such primitive conditions of travel. Hill, after viewing the Red River Valley and interesting himself in overland trade from St. Cloud to Pembina and in the river business, began to consider the idea of managing a railroad, especially one that could exploit the trade of the rich lands he had come to know.

The Panic of 1873, and the failure of the St. Paul and Pacific and of Jay Cooke and Company and the Northern Pacific, opened the way for Hill and his associates to take over the road that Hill built into the Great

Northern. It had been badly managed fiscally and in its operations. In 1864 a reorganization had in effect created two companies, the one known as the First Division, the other as the St. Paul and Pacific. The land grants were increased in 1865 and New York financiers drew from moneyed interests in Holland funds secured by mortgages. The Dutch poured more than $13,000,000 into the enterprise, but when the Panic of 1873 struck, the railroad went into bankruptcy. Financial distress also fell upon the Northern Pacific, which, eager to strengthen its own system, had acquired nearly all the stock of the St. Paul and Pacific and the First Division and had influenced, through its prestige, the securing of the Dutch investments. But this attempt to combine the roads collapsed in the wash of the Panic.

These events were sure signals to James J. Hill that the time was at hand for a move to gain control of the St. Paul and Pacific. Railroad building was suffering from panic and foreclosures. About 350 miles of road had been constructed in 1872, but in 1873 the total of new railroad building was 7.5 miles. Little was done during the next three years — in 1874, 40 miles; 1875, 10; 1876, 29.5. It was not until 1877 that railroad building got back into stride. The time invited the skill of a master builder.

Hill's opportunity synchronized with plans of his Canadian associates, Smith and Stephen, who were interested in a road for profits and wanted to build a branch of the Canadian Pacific from Winnipeg to the border. This fitted into Hill's own purpose of pushing the American railroad to a point where the two would meet. It is a clue to the shared interests of the associates that when in 1878 they consummated the deal by which they became the owners of the St. Paul and Pacific, they incorporated the property as the St. Paul, Minneapolis and Manitoba Railroad Company.

The financial details in the acquisition of the road from the Dutch bondholders were intricate and involved, with legal repercussions. George Stephen, president of the Bank of Montreal, was a major figure in raising the funds required to buy the depreciated bonds. But working with him in the negotiations for the purchase were Hill, Smith, and Kittson. These four men, with a representative of the J. S. Kennedy Company of New York (which had acted for the Dutch bondholders), were the incorporators of the railroad when it took form under its new name. Hill had estimated that the road could be bought for half or less than half its real value, which he placed at some $15,000,000. The proceeds from the land grants, he believed, would cover the purchase costs.

The bargain as finally made with the Dutch investors was not far from the estimates Hill had formed. There had been successive issues of bonds from 1862 to 1871, and the buyers got large blocks of them at prices ranging far below their original par value. A biographer of Hill, referring to subsequent sales of lands in a total of more than $13,000,000 — far beyond the total price paid for the road — remarks that the Dutch investors "lacked faith." They may have done so, but Hill and his friends had no lack of faith. They staked everything they had, and their deal went through. The road, with only 657 miles of track, was taken over. Hill became its manager, soon its vice president, and then president through a long period (1882–1907). The net earnings in 1879 were in excess of a million dollars. By 1883 Hill himself was in control of the road which, seven years later, would be called the Great Northern. By 1887 the railroad had been pushed across Dakota to Great Falls, Montana — and in 1893 it was through to Seattle, 1816 miles from St. Paul.

In full compass the story of James J. Hill, with its ramifications in railroading, banking, lands, iron ore, agriculture, and education, runs across the generations and even beyond his own death in 1916 to the present day. But his career had its setting, as Hill never forgot, in the pioneer era. With this era he was identified from his arrival in St. Paul in the territorial period to the winning of control in the 1870s of the railroad he expanded in succeeding decades. That expansion was interrelated with the peopling of lands and with the economic growth of the empire stretching westward to the Pacific. He helped to build that domain and fairly earned his title of "Empire Builder."

In history's recall, the role of everyday people is often forgotten — the workers at the base of society, the grass-roots people. The railroad story is not all Jim Hill. It is not all land grants, charters, strategy, location, finance, investment, companies, leaders at central spots. Railroads were built by the work of men. The job was hard, sweat-producing, stubborn. Thousands of workmen made their contributions. Some were day laborers, some engineers and contractors, some inventors and manufacturers. Men were recruited from near sources of supply. A historian of immigration writes that the bulk of the American labor force in railroad building was provided by immigrants, notably the Irish, later the Scandinavians — a mobile force available before people found lodgment on farms or in cities.

The Scandinavians were active in the Minnesota railroad story because their flooding of the region coincided with the extension of the iron horse.

Their quest was for land, but they took jobs as they found them. The railroad managers had no concern about origins. They recruited labor from the immigrant army, lumber camps, floating workers in the cities, and farm hands. They asked for muscle, strength, willingness to work. They offered jobs. They wanted "tie placers," whom they equipped with heavy picks. They wanted track layers, scraper gangs, bridge builders, men to work pile drivers, engineers to run their trains, handy laborers to set and string telegraph poles. Directing many people were engineers, such as the contractor D. C. Shepard of St. Paul, who took big jobs one after another.

As workmen for the Northern Pacific made their way across the state, they slept in bunks on boarding cars. Like the lumberjacks, they were great eaters, and the roads provided "cook cars" supplied with food and run by cooks who made up in volume what their fare lacked in culinary distinction.

The roads also had supply trains — freight cars loaded with ties, rails, gravel, and other materials for day-by-day work. There were even "pay cars," usually sent out once a month with cash for earned wages — money that frequently disappeared when the laborers got into villages. The work was tough, and sometimes discontented men quit. Stewart Holbrook tells of an occasion, early in Hill's career, when he was driving his labor force "at a furious rate." When many workers quit, Hill "wired his man-catchers in Minneapolis, St. Paul, and Chicago to ship him more men, fares prepaid, with a thug at each door to prevent skipping before reaching the job at the end of steel."

If the ground was level and weather conditions were favorable, crews made surprising progress. A mile a day was excellent, but a diary-writing worker in 1872 on the Northern Pacific, somewhere between Brainerd and Moorhead, wrote one day, "Laying tracks at the rate of two miles a day." In the autumn snows came and progress slowed down. Snow plows were brought up, men wielded shovels, ears and noses were frozen. Wages were good — the diarist records $2.00 a day in the summer of 1871 and, later in the year, a drop to $1.75.

In the background of railroads were manufacturers of freight and passenger cars and of the tools and machines needed for construction. American ingenuity went into the making of trains, but there was also the job of transporting them to the West. In early days this was not simple. The first Minnesota engine — the *William Crooks*, named for the chief engineer

303

of the St. Paul and Pacific — was built in Paterson, New Jersey, sent by rail to La Crosse, Wisconsin, then hauled up the Mississippi by the steamboat *Alhambra* in September 1861. At St. Paul it was eased ashore on heavy planks from a barge and placed in a shed that served as its berth until 1862, when, with tracks built to the shed, it made its pioneer run to St. Anthony.

The early engines, with their balloon smokestacks, were wood-burners, though Hill, as has been noted, took an interest in substituting coal for wood. As railroading developed, many of the engines for the Minnesota roads were supplied by the Baldwin Locomotive Works of Philadelphia.

The prosperity of railroads, as of the state, hinged on people. They opened lands, built towns, forwarded trade, and strengthened the economy. Railroads eased the conveyance of immigrants, gave jobs, sold land, conveyed goods to trading centers, carried products to markets, and helped people to keep in touch with the world they had left behind.

Minnesota continued to welcome natives and foreigners. As in the case of the territory, the state made efforts to attract settlers and laborers to Minnesota as to a Land of Canaan. And the railroads, notably the Northern Pacific, embarked on programs of colonization. Donnelly, who voiced opinions on just about everything, expressed the western viewpoint when he said in Congress in 1864, "With nearly a billion acres of unsettled lands on one side of the Atlantic and with many millions of poor and oppressed people on the other, let us organize the exodus which must come and build if necessary a bridge of gold across the chasm that divides them that the chosen races of mankind may occupy the chosen lands of the world."

Bridges of gold were chimerical, but in Donnelly's home state a Board of Immigration was established in 1867, and Hans Mattson, Swedish-born immigrant who knew pioneering at first hand and had functioned as a land agent for the St. Paul and Pacific, was its secretary. The board sent out advertising pamphlets in Norwegian, Swedish, German, and Welsh, as well as in English. It dispatched agents to the East and to European countries. It cooperated with railroads in efforts to get cheap fares for immigrants and their families; and it built immigrant-receiving houses for their temporary accommodation.

Mattson himself went to Sweden in 1868 to recruit immigrants. In his autobiography he tells of the sensation he created among the common people. "Wherever it was known that I would pass," he wrote, "people flocked from their houses to the roads and streets in order to catch a glimpse of the returned traveler." He was a modern Marco Polo returning from fabulous lands beyond known horizons, and he never ceased to describe his chosen state as a land of milk and honey. While in Sweden he organized two shiploads of emigrants to accompany him to that land. In 1871, by that time an emigrant agent of the Northern Pacific, Mattson again went to his native land to search for prospective immigrants, and he returned in 1873 with another contingent. Agents representing the state were sent also to Milwaukee and Chicago to give aid to emigrants, and one was delegated to give them protection and advice when they reached St. Paul.

Another example of Minnesota "promotion" is illustrated in the story of Paul Hjelm-Hansen. He was a Norwegian journalist employed by the state in 1869 as a publicist of the glories of the Red River Valley. He visited the valley, wrote newspaper letters about it for publication in Norway and America, hoping that his countrymen would stream to its lands. In his first letter he said, "I have made a journey, a real American pioneer trip, into the wilderness, with oxen and a farm wagon. I have spent the nights in the open wagon with a buffalo hide as a mattress, a hundred-pound flour sack as a pillow, and, like Fritchof's Vikings, the blue sky as a tent." Western Minnesota, he believed, would become "one of the richest and most beautiful regions in America," and thousands of Norwegians endorsed his findings by settling there.

The state was sensitive to the competition of other middle western states for immigrants, and this led to even more defensive and exaggerated claims for the therapeutic benefits of the Minnesota climate than had been made in the 1850s. One writer said, "If fever and ague occur in Minnesota, the germ was imported; if consumption claims its victim, the cause is to be sought elsewhere than in our climate." Mattson wrote in 1867, "Thousands of invalids from the eastern and southern states make their way to this state and become well again through no other means than breathing the fresh air." A volume was brought out on the Minnesota climate by one writer in 1871, with two chapters on consumption and one on hints for invalids. The claims overlooked the actuality of sickness, of which there was much in pioneer Minnesota, but the climate was an article of faith to all who tried to induce people, healthy or ill, to join the land-seekers.

Health certificates were not required by the railroads when they sold their lands. They subsidized agents, gave financial aid to the state program, organized land departments, arranged for through tickets from Europe to Minnesota, cut fares from New York, sold their lands at two or three to ten dollars an acre, and offered rebates for the job of land-breaking. And they built immigrant-receiving houses at such centers as Duluth, Brainerd, and Willmar. The Northern Pacific, from an early date, ran a bureau of emigration and issued pamphlets and maps. The road took a special interest in promoting "immigration by colonies, so that neighbors in Fatherland may be neighbors in the New West." It sponsored a New England colony of former Civil War soldiers in Becker County between 1870 and 1872. Glyndon in Clay County was developed by a commercial company under contract with the Northern Pacific; and colonists from England were encouraged to settle at several places in western Minnesota. German "Forty-Eighters" promoted Minnesota interests in Germany in the 1860s and 1870s, notably Eduard Pelz, who represented first the St. Paul and Pacific and later the Northern Pacific. He wrote pamphlets and articles and even published a little magazine in 1872 called the *Pathfinder*, in which he gave special attention to Minnesota. Albert Wolf, sent by the Minnesota emigration board to Bremen in 1869, wrote that he and Pelz were engaged in a "humanistic and public-minded effort *to concentrate German emigration* to Minnesota."

An English colony was established in Martin County in 1873, near Fairmont, by a persuasive land agent with railroad backing. Younger sons and country gentlemen were brought out to create a "bean center" in the West. Plants were grown and then devoured by grasshoppers. A second crop was destroyed by frost. For four years one dismal failure succeeded another. The stubborn English did not give up; but they turned to American neighbors for practical advice. A Yankee remarked that the English had money but no experience — the Yankees had experience but no money. In a few years, he reported, the Yankees had both the money and the experience. But the English were debonair and colorful. They held fox hunts, had a boat club, organized racing, football, and cross-country riding. The colony failed, but left a legacy of interesting lore.

The Yankee, German, Norwegian, Swedish, Irish, Czech, Welsh, and other settlements and "colonies" that took root in the 1850s expanded in numbers and deepened in their special character in the decades after the Civil War. Meanwhile, waves of migration as part of the postwar

306

immigration to America contributed to an ever-increasing cosmopolitanism in the state's population. The state census of 1865 revealed a Minnesota population of 250,000 — and the federal census of 1900, 1,751,394. In thirty-five years the population leaped to seven times its size at the close of the Civil War. Minnesota in 1880 had a total population of 780,773, and of these the foreign-born comprised 267,676, roughly, thirty per cent. More revealing of the complexion of the people is the fact that by 1880 seventy-one per cent of the total "represented European blood of the first and second generations."

The most numerous single foreign element in the state in 1880 was the German-born, who contributed 66,592 to the total. The Scandinavians, taken as a related group, numbered 107,768. Of these 62,521 were Norwegians, 39,176 Swedes, and 6071 Danes. There was a considerable English-speaking contingent of foreign-born. The Irish made up 25,942, the English 8495, Scots 2964, and Welsh 1103, while there also were no fewer than 29,631 from British America. The diversification of cultural patterns becomes the more notable when it is added that there were 7759 Bohemians, 2828 Swiss, 2218 Poles, 2272 Russian-born, and 1351 French. And a further evidence of variety was the presence of 2300 native redmen and of a Negro population which had doubled since 1870, numbering 1564 by 1880. This variety, increased by many other nationalities in later decades (and never forgetting the native-born Americans from the East and the Middle West, and by 1880 nearly 300,000 Minnesotans by birth), underlies the conclusion of a writer on Minnesota expansion: "Each nationality, bearing with it its own special heritage, has woven strands in the web of Minnesota's cultural life, helping to make a rich fabric of unique design."

It is a commentary on the youth of the commonwealth that not one of its fourteen governors from the beginning of statehood to the twentieth century was a native of Minnesota. Its leadership reflected pioneer migrations, with some anticipation of the Scandinavian strain that would be notable in later politics. Of the first fourteen governors, three were born in New York, three in Pennsylvania, two in New Hampshire, and one each in Connecticut, Ohio, Michigan, Missouri, Norway, and Sweden.

The Germans lent sturdiness to Minnesota farming and business, and to the state's cultural and religious strength. They were not all of like mind in their church affiliations. There were Lutherans, Catholics, Methodists, Reformed, also freethinkers, reflecting the varied backgrounds

307

and stirrings of their native Germany. Like many other immigrant groups, they sought neighborhoods where people spoke their language and shared their traditions. This trend explained the increasing German strength in the St. Cloud area, where Catholicism and educational institutions bred leadership and cultural unity — and also in Brown County, where the heirs of the revolutionary Forty-Eighters imprinted the stamp of their ideas, the Turners held sway, and New Ulm functioned as an independent core.

The Germans were hard-working, systematic farmers who sought out the rich river valleys, notably the Mississippi and the Minnesota. They built flourishing farms. But they spread into many parts of Minnesota, far from these favored valleys. They also went to towns and cities where their skill in trades made itself felt. From early days they were repelled by the Puritanism of New Englanders, and this sentiment, here as in other states, tended to draw many of them away from the Republican party, which in its earlier years was influenced by temperance sympathies. The Germans in the cities were skilled in trades, and not a few of them, including Theodore Hamm, a native of Baden who came to St. Paul as early as 1856, pioneered the Minnesota brewing industry. The Germans, as farmers, craftsmen, bankers, and business managers, made efficient progress, their traits exhibiting themselves in organizations such as the Turners, in music, a "language press" of their own, schools of their devising, and a way of life that grew out of their heritage but was modified by middle western mores.

The Irish-born and the American-born Irish have been "a witty, brawny, colorful, and dynamic population stock" in the making of Minnesota. They sought lands here in the 1850s and 1860s, and by 1870 there were almost 22,000 people of Irish birth in the state. The numbers of Irish-born never became a flood comparable to that of the Germans and Scandinavians. By 1890 there were only some 28,000. The story of the Irish reveals the leadership of the vigorous and imaginative Catholic prelate John Ireland. "The largest and most successful Catholic colonization program ever undertaken in the United States," writes James P. Shannon, "was that sponsored by Bishop John Ireland in Minnesota between 1876 and 1881."

In the 1860s both Bishop Thomas L. Grace and Father Ireland were active in a Minnesota Irish Emigration Society, but the early organization was dwarfed in scale by the Catholic Colonization Bureau of Minnesota. It was started in 1876 by Bishop Ireland, working in close collaboration with Dillon O'Brien, a gifted writer and the editor of the Catholic weekly called the *Northwestern Chronicle*. Bishop Ireland's concept of colonization involved the cooperation of church, railroads, and incoming settlers who would occupy railroad lands selected in advance. All in all, Bishop Ireland arranged contracts with five different railroads for 369,000 acres. He sponsored some nine or ten settlements; and he also gave assistance and advice to a colonization effort undertaken by John Sweetman of Dublin, a landowner who took a deep interest in the emigration of people from County Meath and in the early 1880s built an Irish colony on 10,000 acres of land in Murray County, at Currie.

The Irish settlements were rural, in western and southwestern Minnesota — from Graceville, Clontarf, and De Graff, north of the Minnesota River, to Minneota, Ghent, Currie, Avoca, Iona, Fulda, and Adrian, south of the river, in the southwestern corner of the state. Each community had its church and priest. The settlements were Irish in their major aspects, but other nationalities were also present, including Belgians, French, and others. Because some settlements, notably Sweetman's colony at Currie and a small colony of Irish from Connemara at Graceville, had little success, there has been some tendency in historical writings to ascribe failure generally to the Irish agricultural ventures. Father Shannon points out, however, that Bishop Ireland's efforts were concentrated on bringing in Irish-Americans from the East, who, as he puts it, had been "conditioned" by the processes of emigration and training in American ways, and who did not come, as did Sweetman's emigrants, without background in American labor and farming.

The Irish from the East were for the most part small farmers, miners, shopkeepers, laborers. Many were already emancipated from the abject poverty of newly arrived immigrants. The Irish-Americans, by and large, were successful on the land and many thriving settlements in western Minnesota still retain the genial characteristics that spring from the Irish heritage. In Minnesota, as in the United States generally, the Irish for many reasons, including the imperative necessity of taking jobs without delay after arrival, stayed on in cities. Many of the Minnesota Irish settled in larger cities, notably St. Paul, where their gifts for political, professional, and social leadership have left deep marks.

The Scandinavians, especially the Norwegians and Swedes, had initiated trends in their settlements of the 1850s. These blossomed in the

309

three next decades. The earlier migrations were by wagon and boat. Naturally the Norwegians, coming in individual family groups from Iowa and Wisconsin and also from Illinois, worked into the attractive lands of the southeastern sections of the state. As their numbers increased, they pushed north and northwest, and spread into the Big Woods area. They found the Red River Valley immensely to their liking when, in post-Civil War days, settlement moved into that region of rich soil and crops of wheat.

By 1890 half of the Norwegian population of Minnesota was in the western counties, but there was no one route or boundary for the spread of Norwegians. The people from Norway flourished in Goodhue County. They liked the bend of the Minnesota River (Nicollet and Sibley counties). They streamed into Minneapolis. By the time the Red River Valley was opened, railroads served incoming immigrants, and waves of emigrants direct from the old country joined those from older states. In earlier years, the Norwegians shied away from prairie lands, preferring wooded areas of a kind they were familiar with in Wisconsin and in their homeland. Gradually the prejudice was overcome and they moved toward the southwest and out onto the Dakota plains. Many were farmers, but there were also fishermen who went to the north shore, lumberjacks who made for the pine woods, and workers and trades people who found haven in cities and towns. But the great magnet was land, not only as an economic base but also because traditionally land ownership meant, in their minds, dignity and stability.

The Swedes also sought lands widely, but they favored the older centers in Washington and Chisago counties, the fertile, lake-studded region between the St. Croix and the Mississippi. Like the Norwegians they knew farming, loved the land, sought out communities where their neighbors spoke their language and shared their religious interests. Their story as a chapter in immigrant history is humble, but perspective has revealed it as a saga embodying deep human interest.

Norwegians and Swedes usually built separate settlements, even in counties such as Goodhue; and the Danes, whose numbers were much smaller (there were only some 14,000 people of Danish birth in Minnesota by 1890), also developed their own settlements or colonies. They chose Steele and Freeborn counties, with Clark's Grove as a center, and also Lincoln County to the west, with Tyler as a focus.

The numbers of Scandinavians, recruited from internal migrations from other states of the Middle West and from the rising tide of Scandinavian immigration after the Civil War, went well past 200,000 by 1890. The concentration of the Scandinavians in the richest farming areas of Minnesota and in urban centers gave a certain Scandinavian flavor to the state. This was accentuated by the retention of the languages, Norwegian, Swedish, and Danish; and by the pioneer churches, notably Lutheran but also Baptist, Methodist, and of other denominations. The Lutheran churches did not, like the Catholics, sponsor great colonization projects, but their missionaries and preachers, some trained in the home countries and some in religious schools of the Middle West, were never far behind the rims of settlement. Newspapers in Norwegian and Swedish were early on the scene. Schools and colleges followed the churches; and a vigorous social and professional life developed in towns and cities. To the cities came not only Scandinavian workmen and tradesmen but also doctors, lawyers, engineers, educators, and artists, who gave professional character and leadership to the entire contingent. The Scandinavians were interested in education and in local self-government. Their political proclivities soon drew them into state politics; and their devotion to education resulted in such colleges as Augsburg, St. Olaf, Gustavus Adolphus, and Concordia.

Many other Old World nationalities helped to develop the state and to enliven its cosmopolitan character. A few Dutch pioneers came into Minnesota in the 1850s, in one of the southern counties, and after the Civil War many efforts were made to attract their countrymen to the state. In 1868 the Minnesota immigration office even issued a pamphlet in Dutch extolling the advantages of Minnesota for settlers. Notable colonization plans were undertaken in the 1880s and 1890s by an enterprising Dutch businessman, Theodore F. Koch. In 1884 he began to export Holstein cattle to this country from Holland. He came to the United States and soon was deeply interested in western lands. In association with men of capital in Holland and through many years as the head of a real-estate company of his own, he acquired hundreds of thousands of acres of Minnesota land and made energetic efforts to sell them to settlers. He encouraged Hollanders from nearby states and from the old country to buy his lands (bought by him from railroads and the state), and he founded several towns as nuclei for farming communities, including Clara City, Friesland, and Groningen. Though his great interest was in his Dutch Protestant countrymen, he also encouraged Danish and other settlements. Large numbers of Netherlanders did not come to Minnesota (the count of Holland-born people in the state in 1890 was under 2000), but they formed distinctive communities marked by skill and thrift.

The Czechs, 8000 strong by 1880, continued to build their settlements in the Silver Lake and New Prague regions, and they also found their way to farms in other counties and to the cities, especially St. Paul, where Antonin Jurka taught his native language and also German in the public schools for a generation. The Czechs were mainly Catholic, though some were Protestant; and all were devoted to the interest of the Sokols, athletic and social organizations of their own. The Slovaks followed the Czechs, and after 1880 they made up the largest proportion of emigrants from old Hungary to America. They sought work in the iron mines and also in the cities, and like the Czechs found social outlets in the Sokols.

The Poles numbered about 7500 by 1890. Their earlier trend was to farm lands, but as time went on their chief colonies were in the cities — St. Paul, Minneapolis, Duluth, and Winona especially. They have had newspapers in Polish since the 1880s; and their religious choice has been Roman Catholic. True to their national traditions, they have taken deep interest in music and other arts; and they have felt a sympathetic attachment to their kinsmen in Europe struggling gallantly for freedom and against oppression.

The Finns, whose contributions will be noted in connection with the iron-ore industry, were land-seekers, not just miners. Their story is part of the saga of western farming, in Otter Tail County and elsewhere. But these energetic people, who retained the lore of the *Kalevala* and pioneered cooperation, were notable in the labor that produced ore for the steel mills of the country.

Interesting and colorful settlements were made in various parts of the state by relatively small groups, as illustrated by the Russian-born German Mennonites, most of whom, coming in the 1870s, gave distinctive character to the rural area near Mountain Lake. The Icelanders similarly developed a thriving settlement near the village of Minneota. There are now about a thousand people of Icelandic origins living in the state. Important in the religious and business life of Minnesota have been the Jews, a part of the scene from the 1850s onward, first with a strong German core, merchants moving to the frontier from the eastern part of the United States. Later there were direct migrations of Jews from Russia, Poland, Rumania, Lithuania, and other lands.

One cannot view the varied strains in the population without underlining the contributions of these national elements, not only to agriculture, industry, trade, and the professions, but also to the folk arts and cultural life of the state. Dr. Carlton Qualey emphasizes "Choral singing, food preparation, richly idiomatic immigrant-American speech and writing, immigrant literature, immigrant newspapers and magazines, folk ballads and heroes, and the strong belief of all groups in the benefits of the American way of life." Much of this cultural heritage has been lost through the decades and by shifts from generation to generation, but Dr. Qualey believes, and rightly, that what has survived is recognized and appreciated. The patterns of the varied strains are reflected in institutions of many kinds, including churches, schools, and social and cultural activities and organizations.

From the era of the French to contemporary times Minnesota owes much of its distinctive character as a commonwealth to its cultural ties with the New and Old Worlds that brought vigor and talent to the task of building a modern state in what was once a wilderness.

Lumbering on the Rum River in Minnesota about 1863

★
With Ax and Saw

A POET says that "America is West," but a writer on forest history declares that "When explorers landed, America was trees."

America was both West and trees (and more). The two were wedded in the lumber industry, and their union is illustrated in the history of Minnesota. The armies of ax and saw were an American advance from east to west. Lumber, after furs, ranks as the second industry of Minnesota, and its story embraces the decades from the 1820s to the present. Its gala period is the era after the Civil War, synchronizing with that of wheat as a major crop and of flour milling as a major industry.

Lumber is a saga of primeval forests of white pine, of the westward advance of a great industry, of companies and owners and managers, land and finance, transportation by water and rail, mills, markets, and construction, of interrelations with other industries, of lumberjacks, camps, logging, and folklore. Its ramifications and its long development make its history one of infinite detail. But the detail is important only when viewed in relation to the broad outline of the industry.

Lumbering is no isolated phenomenon of Minnesota, though the industry became very important in and for this state. The industry had its roots on the Atlantic seaboard. Jamestown had a mill in 1625, and Berwick, Maine, operated one in 1631. Through two centuries, Maine was a leading lumber center, with many mills on the Penobscot River. Bangor was a lumber capital in the first part of the nineteenth century, and Maine contributed lumbering techniques and skilled lumbermen to the country in later times.

As forests were felled and milled, and as population surged across the continent, with its insistent need for billions of feet of lumber, the industry pushed into New York and Pennsylvania, then on to the rich treasures of trees in Michigan. Lumbering then penetrated the regions beyond the Great Lakes and Wisconsin and Minnesota came into their productive period. The sweep of the industry encompassed the northern coniferous forests from the Atlantic Coast to the very edge of the great prairies of America. After the pine forests of the north country had been denuded, the industry turned southward and to the fabulous woods of the Far West. The Minnesota record reflects an industrial storm that began lightly, grew in volume, reached a prodigious climax, and then moved on to virgin uncut areas, leaving behind a wasteland as a problem for succeeding generations.

Each area lumbered furnished materials not alone for its local needs but also for the speeding construction of a lustily growing country. It was regions like Minnesota, blessed with deep forests, that came to the aid of those less bountifully endowed with trees or even treeless. White pine was abundant in Minnesota and it was the basis of a gigantic industry, but even its rich resources were not enough. Through many decades great quantities of hardwood were taken from Minnesota's "Big Woods." The economic importance of this area, however, is often overlooked because of the majestic pine. The Big Woods did not create an industry of national proportions, but they supplied fuel for steamboats, fence posts, cooperage, building materials for houses in villages and on farms, firewood, lumber for building bridges, and much more. Still, the epic is that of white pine.

Not infrequently, thanks to convenient rivers on which to float logs, and before local towns furnished markets of importance, exports preceded home community use. This was well illustrated in the case of the pioneer Minnesota mills on the St. Croix River.

A long perspective reveals the ruthlessness of the harvesting of Minnesota's white pine. Forests were swept away by a generation that exploited the resources of nature as it found them and met needs as fast as forests, men, machines, and ingenuity permitted. Businessmen, in acquiring and stripping lands, followed the standards and practices of their time. Their approach is dramatized in Edna Ferber's novel of Wisconsin lumbering, *Come and Get It,* and the approach had a grave aftermath. "Nothing in Minnesota," said the state's planning board in the 1930s, made more clear "the necessity of sober middle age than the forests of the state." It pointed out that only about a third of the state was then in forests, that little virgin timber remained, and that much of the second growth was poorly started, whereas originally two-thirds of Minnesota's land area was covered with forests, chiefly commercial timber. With sober middle age came conservation, reforestation, state control, the application to tree resources of the science of forestry, and wisdom pragmatically absorbed by industry. As early as 1902 a pioneer in the science of forestry, Samuel B. Green, urged the "renewal of forest trees upon the land" and suggested practical ways in which "regeneration" could be brought about. Minnesota in its modern mood has accepted the challenge thus offered more than a half century ago.

Many lumbermen exemplified the conception underlying the fictional *Come and Get It.* But the phrase does not typify the whole lumber business. Some writers, portraying it, forget that hazards were many and that the industry has not spawned a perpetual "success story." Not a few men lost fortunes in lumber. Some were victimized by the vagaries of nature, such as the lack of spring waters on which to float a winter's cut. Others, facing unanticipated sags in prices, had to sell their logs at less than cost. Many mills disappeared. A historian of the mill towns in the Upper Mississippi Valley observes that one or more mills in each of these towns managed to survive "competition, panics and depression, price changes, disastrous floods and fires." But he implies that many did not survive. Those that did faced the need of amassing large capital, especially after the Civil War, to offset costs of construction, operation, and competition. Little wonder that the men who won out were described as a "rugged class."

It is necessary to understand not only the procedures of the lumbermen but also the attitudes of the earlier pioneer generation with respect to natural resources. The prodigal exploitation of the soil for wheat was contemporaneous with the tremendous expansion of the lumber business. In that era people could not conceive of the need for conservation. A few voices of caution were indeed raised, but generally people regarded the forests as so extensive that their depletion was not foreseeable. A Stillwater newspaper in 1855, speaking of the immense territory of the pine region, said, "There is no end to it, and it may never be exhausted." A

317

St. Paul newspaper described the pine country as "perhaps the most extensive in the world" and found "no ground to apprehend a want of logs." A traveler, noting that lumbermen were cutting trees on unsurveyed lands, believed they were "doing a great service," rescuing forests from fire and making timber available for human use. A missionary in the 1860s, observing the operations of a lumber camp, welcomed lumber for houses and declared that moral and spiritual blessings were "in some sense dependent upon the abundance and cheapness of pine." Concepts of reforestation, controlled use, and state intervention to lessen devastation by fire were presented and discussed in the generation after the Civil War, while the lumber industry was growing in magnitude. But it was a later generation that awakened to a realization that essentially the same timber yield could have been harvested from the Minnesota forests in such fashion as to have averted their depletion.

The legacy of problems left by the industry has caused some writers to undervalue the importance of Minnesota lumber in its own time both for the state itself and for the country and the world. It is true, as Samuel T. Dana says in his study of *Minnesota Lands*, that the forests were among "the most potent factors" in the economic life of the state during the last half of the nineteenth century. "They provided," he writes, "a cheap and ample supply of raw material that was essential for the construction of homes, factories, and other buildings; and they offered welcome opportunity for the useful employment of labor and capital." Agnes Larson, in her studies of the white pine industry, presents a picture of the uses made of billions of feet of lumber taken from the woods. The forests of Minnesota, she writes, entered into the very life of the nation: "Much of the lumber went on to St. Louis to help make it a city and to help develop the surrounding country. Indeed, lumber followed immigration. Eventually everything from shipmasts to matches was made from this king of the Minnesota forest. In time white pine was sent in the form of barrels to the West Indies to bring back molasses. To Brazil it went to bring back sugar. The markets of Europe and the markets of the East of our own country used Minnesota white pine."

Minneapolis and St. Paul, the smaller towns of Minnesota, Omaha, Kansas City, Des Moines, Topeka, and many other cities were. largely built of lumber taken from the wooded lands of Minnesota. Long rafts were floated down the Mississippi, and when railroads reached out toward the West, they supplied lumber for building in the Dakota and

318

Yellowstone regions. In a single year, 1882, Minneapolis and St. Paul alone made use of about three hundred million board feet of lumber (a board foot was a foot wide, a foot long, an inch thick). The industry supplied lumber at a time when state and nation were growing furiously, when buildings were being erected by the millions, when even the fast-growing railroads found it difficult to supply freight cars in sufficient numbers to transport the immense quantities of lumber ordered in many parts of the United States.

In other respects lumber played important roles in the economic development of Minnesota. It was influential, through its capital, in financing the flour industry, in giving impetus to railroad building, in spurring employment, and in forwarding manufactures. As in the case of the flour mills, lumber was also important to Minnesota banking and finance. The industry is significant, too, because of its leadership from Maine, Michigan, Illinois, and other parts of the country; the lumberjacks who in the "golden age" numbered many thousands; the ingenuity of men in meeting the problems of getting logs to mills; and the human lore that colors its saga.

Lumbering prospered because of a coalition of circumstances. Timber of high quality and in abundance was available. Markets down along the Mississippi were ready. Rivers furnished arteries of transportation and trade. Funds and leadership from the East moved in, and American experience in logging techniques was transferred to a new setting for the industry. Such factors set in motion the lumber industry in the white pine forests of the Minnesota country. Especially important in the pre-railroad era and even later were the water highways, not only the great river itself, but also the St. Croix, Rum, and lesser streams on which logs could be floated by stages to mills and then put to their myriad uses.

When the Indian treaties of 1837 opened the pine lands in the triangle between the St. Croix and the Mississippi (as far north as the upper edge of Mille Lacs), the way was cleared for the coming of the lumbermen in force. The consequence was the rise of Minnesota lumbering as a major industry from the late 1830s to 1860. Enterprising lumbermen from Illinois, notably Orange Walker and L. S. Judd, were on the St. Croix before the ceded lands had been surveyed, and they built a sawmill in 1839 at Marine, naming the place for Marine, Illinois. These men and others formed the Marine Lumber Company, which continued to produce lumber through many decades, and their mill, save for the sawmill built

319

by Fort Snelling soldiers at the Falls of St. Anthony in the 1820s, ranks as the pioneer mill of Minnesota. But beginnings at Stillwater were not far behind, for Mainites were on the scene there. One was John McKusick of Stillwater, Maine, who in 1844 with others formed the Stillwater Lumber Company and began milling. In 1854 Samuel Hersey and Isaac Staples, also from Maine, built a steam-power plant at Stillwater which soon had five circular saws, a gang saw, and other machinery that set standards in the West for productive capacity and efficiency. The Hersey-Staples company four years later had title to 34,000 acres in the valley. Yet other companies operated in Stillwater, including one sponsored from St. Louis which sent its entire product to the Missouri metropolis for markets in the Southwest.

The spurt of the industry made Stillwater the logging center of Minnesota. It was called "Queen of the St. Croix," and "it was expected to become the metropolis of the Middle West." The St. Croix lumbermen united in 1851 to build a great boom, placing one first across from Osceola, Wisconsin, later moving it a few miles above Stillwater. Here, in a gigantic water bowl, millions of logs were identified and sorted, rafts were made up, the logs sent to nearby mills or floated out to the Mississippi and southward. Three and a half billion feet of logs went through the boom up to 1874.

But other centers were developing in the 1850s, notably at the Falls of St. Anthony and at the river town of Winona. Water power at the Falls of St. Anthony (as has been noted) induced Franklin Steele to build a sawmill there in 1848, using logs from the Rum River country. Eastern capital was secured, first from Caleb Cushing and Robert Rantoul of Massachusetts, later from others. By 1856 there were no fewer than eight mills there — the boom period before the Panic of 1857 — and they were producing twelve million feet a year.

The Maine influence, notable at the Falls of St. Anthony, illustrates the national leadership in lumber methods and management that long experience had given the New England state. Steele in the 1840s engaged the services of Daniel Stanchfield, a lumber-wise man trained on the Penobscot who explored the pine resources of the forests north along the Rum River to the Mille Lacs region. Paddling up the Rum River in 1847, he stopped many times and climbed tall trees to survey the scene on the last fifty miles before he got to Mille Lacs. Everywhere he saw pine, "as far as the eye could reach," billions of feet by his reckoning, much more than anticipated. "Seventy mills in seventy years," he said, "couldn't exhaust the white pine I have seen on the Rum River."

Other Maine people prominent in the industry included Caleb Dorr, C. C. and William D. Washburn, Dorilus Morrison, and the De Laittres and Boveys. A fascinating narrative by Joseph A. De Laittre recalls a proud lumberjack who was asked where he came from. "He hitched up his pants and took another chaw of tobacco and said, 'I'm from the Penobscot, B'God.'" So large was the exodus of Mainites from their native haunts that a Maine congressman in 1852 declared that "the stalwart sons" of his state were "marching away by the scores and hundreds to the piny woods of the Northwest." He added that the state or territory that received the "largest accession of them" would be most fortunate — a judgment with which Minnesotans would concur. New England states other than Maine likewise made notable contributions in such men as Joel Bassett, the Pillsburys, Eastmans, and Welleses — names familiar in Minneapolis and the state through several generations.

Winona was not a gateway to forests of white pine, but it was a strategic point on the Mississippi, adjacent to rich farming lands opened to settlement after the Sioux relinquished their claims. It was a point of assembly for logs floated down the Mississippi and also down its Wisconsin tributary, the Chippewa River; and it was a focus of lumber manufacture to supply the needs of communities and farms north and west. To Winona in 1852 came a Pennsylvanian, John C. Laird, who in 1855, with two brothers, established a wholesale and retail lumber business that a few years later was expanded into Laird, Norton, and Company, when two cousins (James L. and Matthew G. Norton) joined hands with the Lairds. At first distributors of lumber sawed elsewhere, the Lairds and Nortons had their own mill by 1857, one of ten mills built in Winona in the course of its history, including that of two brothers, Earle S. and Addison B. Youmans from New York, opened in 1857.

By 1860, therefore, there were three lumber centers in the state. These were Stillwater and Marine, St. Anthony Falls, and Winona; and their relative importance at the time is indicated by census figures of 1860 tabulating the value of lumber produced in the three respective counties. Washington County was at the top, with a value of $419,650; Hennepin next, with $212,400; and Winona County stood at $97,050. The figures are modest when compared with those of later years, but the total ran close to three quarters of a million dollars, and this, in the setting of the time and place, was very big business. Governor Ramsey in his message of January 2, 1860, reported the export in 1859 of thirty-three million feet of sawed lumber and seventy-one million logs. The next year he estimated the exportable surplus of Minnesota lumber products (for 1860) at $629,000.

The pine lands of the St. Croix triangle — the rich and beautiful delta — were alluring to lumber-hungry men, as were the deep forests of the north country in later years. These men acquired thousands of acres of pine-laden lands that erupted lumber to state and country and yielded wealth to their owners and managers. One cannot depict the lumber era without looking at the ways in which these men secured cutting rights. They were able and knowledgeable about the value of virgin timber, and they understood the financial methods countenanced by the laws and practices of their time. Lumbermen functioned under public laws for land acquisition "fashioned," as Lucile Kane writes, "for the settler rather than for an industry utilizing trees as its raw material." In buying the pine lands of the St. Croix country, the lumbermen, in accordance with prevailing customs, used military land warrants and cash. The warrants, which they bought at discounts, were really a currency that could be applied to the purchase of public lands. Thousands of veterans, after the War with Mexico, held such warrants, but they lived in other parts of the country and few of them had any intention of taking personal advantage of land allocations and moving west. Not more than one in five hundred former soldiers who qualified for such military bonus lands used the warrant for himself. "Assignable" papers were therefore bought by people who had money and knew where opportunities were promising. In the 1850s many of these were speculators and lumbermen on the frontiers, including those who knew the fragrance and splendor — and potential profits — of the Minnesota pine woods.

Land warrants and other kinds of scrip were bought in large quantities through banks and special dealers in such papers. That there was an abundance of the warrants may be inferred from the fact that by 1860 the United States had issued them for the amazing total of sixty-eight million acres. Generally they were purchased for well under the minimum price of public land under pre-emption ($1.25 per acre). Horace Greeley of the *New York Tribune* once said that many of these rights to land were transferred by veterans for as little as ten cents an acre. Most of

322

the veterans with governmental paper in their pockets wanted money and had little if any idea of its value in exchange for pine lands in the remote West. How extensively the land warrants were used in the St. Croix delta is illustrated by the record of purchases in one year alone, 1850, when nearly 34,000 acres were bought by warrants and less than 4000 acres by cash. Many of the leading lumbermen acquired extensive personal holdings, notably Dorilus Morrison, who bought big acreages both for cash and for warrants and assured his mill at the Falls of St. Anthony of a timber supply for decades. Hersey and Staples took some 40,000 acres of pine land in the St. Croix region by land warrants, but also added still more acreage by cash purchases at the public minimum price of $1.25. In 1854, when both the Territory of Minnesota and the lumber business were booming, the Stillwater land office disposed of about 425,000 acres, of which nearly 362,000 were paid for by land warrants. Later, after the passage of the Morrill Act of 1862, agricultural college scrip was extensively used. This scrip was made available to states, such as New York, that lacked within their own borders a sufficient amount of public land to meet their grants under the college act, and the states sold the scrip to raise funds for educational purposes. Earlier, Indian scrip was also employed in land purchases by timbermen.

After the Homestead Law was passed in 1862, much pine land, when ownership had been authenticated, went to lumber companies. It is often assumed that homesteading meant a minimum of five years of individual occupancy of the land, but under the law, six months after entering claims at a land office individuals could in fact acquire the land by meeting the minimum price, for which warrants, scrip, or cash could be used. The records make it clear that much unsurveyed land was cut over by lumbermen. Lands were also "re-located" on the basis of scrip already used for other areas, after the pine had been removed from the earlier pieces. The normal method of acquisition, it must fairly be said, was purchase for cash or through the use of legally validated military land warrants and sundry kinds of scrip.

In viewing the practices of the time, one must take note of the official "stumpage system," which reveals the state's benevolent attitude toward the industry. As early as 1863 Minnesota's legislature gave authority to the state land commissioner — an office held ex officio by the state auditor — to issue permits for cutting timber on school land if, in his view, this would promote the interests of the school fund. Commercial wood users — and the lumbermen were the pioneers — coveted pine. For pine they acquired lands. Once they took the trees, they had little or no use for the land, the ownership of which meant taxes — though a time came, in the later day of pulp and paper, when second-growth land had value. In any event, state policy opened a channel whereby lumbermen could get timber without buying the land on which it grew. The state philosophy was to aid private industry to undertake jobs that would contribute to the economy of Minnesota and of the United States — a frame of mind akin to that which supported land grants for building railroads.

Unhappily, serious abuses crept into the stumpage system. No permits were to be granted save at public auction and after due notice, but the devious device of adjourned sales eliminated competition; trespass was common as in the larger history of lumbering; and officials allowed cutting before estimates or bids were made, with judgments taken later on values. The McIlrath case in the 1870s, as mentioned earlier, provoked a public investigation, and in 1877 the law was changed. Thereafter pine could be sold only when it seemed clear that the standing timber was in peril of fire or other forms of destruction.

Hazards seemed plentiful, for the volume of permits increased year after year — and hazards were in truth plentiful, as the story of Christopher C. Andrews and the beginnings of conservation will reveal. But once again abuses in the administration of the law called for reform; a more stringent law was passed in 1885; and further changes came in the 1890s. Investigations disclosed lax methods of appraising the amount of timber on given tracts. One case involved a state estimator who reported 357,000 feet when actually the timber on the school land in question measured seven million feet. In the period 1864–1906, the state sold stumpage rights for a total of more than five million dollars. Dr. Folwell writes that the "number of millions of dollars lost to the state, especially to her school and university funds, by a vicious forest policy and unconscionable depredations will never be computed." During these years the public began to realize that the white pine was not inexhaustible and that posterity would pay toll for its depletion; and some leaders in the lumber industry began to grasp the fact that a new day of conservation and reforestation was coming.

After the Civil War the lumber industry took on gigantic dimensions as it supplied the needs of state and nation. Inevitably there were shifts in the relative importance of producing centers. Time wrought changes in the sources of timber, particularly as railroads and lake shipping spurred logging in the north and northeast. New centers, notably Duluth, rose to high importance in the lumber story. Stillwater continued its dominance in the St. Croix region, sent 225 log rafts down river in 1869, and had nine mills in busy operation by 1874. The St. Croix Valley persisted bountifully as a source of white pine. It did not reach its peak until 1895, when it produced 373,000,000 feet of lumber. But Minneapolis, with advantages as a railroad center and resources of power and capital, achieved lumber leadership long before the St. Croix Valley reached its high productive point. By 1869 there were fifteen sawmills at or near the Falls of St. Anthony. The Minneapolis lumber business leaped far beyond that of Stillwater as expansion continued in the 1870s and 1880s. By 1890 Minneapolis, cutting close to a half billion feet, was the premier lumber market not only of Minnesota but of the world.

The figures of lumber production go to such fabulous totals that they almost defy translation into understandable terms, but Agnes Larson, taking the Minnesota production of 193,000,000 feet in 1876, pictures in specific terms what such millions meant. The product — lumber, shingles, laths, and other materials — would have packed 24,000 freight cars, provided buildings for twenty-nine towns each with a population of a thousand people, and if put lengthwise in one-foot boards would have extended one and a half times around the earth. Multiply these figures by ten and one approximates the actuality of Minnesota's peak production in 1905 of about two billion feet. If such pictures can be comprehended, one may then recall that in 1882 nearly all the lumber produced in Minneapolis went into building in the Twin Cities, 300,000,000 feet or so. The picture is made the more vivid when it is remembered that Minnesota in 1880 had 234 sawmills, with a capital of about $7,000,000. Ten years later, though the number of mills had increased only to 317, the capital had advanced to more than $28,000,000.

Many laymen think of lumber solely as sawed boards for houses and other buildings, but as the mills developed, they turned out not only such boards, but laths, shingles, materials for sashes and doors, wood for wagons and carriages, and barrels for shipping flour and pork. And they processed cuttings for a variety of other human uses. Among these uses were railroad freight cars, once made almost entirely of wood, and even automobiles of early vintage. Residual materials furnished fuel for power; and sawdust, as people of an older generation may recall (with a touch of nostalgia), often carpeted the floors of butcher shops and other establishments. As one considers the manifold uses of wood, one is reminded of Professor Samuel B. Green's confident assertion, made more than a half century ago, that it is "the most useful of all natural products, excepting only food."

With the spread of railroads, notably the Lake Superior and Mississippi, the gradual decline of the St. Louis market, and the passing of the apex of Michigan lumbering after 1880, Duluth became an important lumber center. It grew into a major city on the basis of lumber plus its advantageous location for connections with markets such as Chicago, Cleveland, and the great cities of the East. In the same year, 1882, that Minneapolis produced more than 300,000,000 feet of lumber, Duluth had a production of 83,000,000. It built elevators and lumber warehouses and enlarged its docks for the lumber-carrying trade. More than that, Duluth and the white-pine resources of its hinterland were magnets attracting Michigan lumbermen who looked to new regions as the pine resources of their own state dwindled. At the same time Minneapolis drew experienced Michigan men with capital. They included the New York-born Thomas H. Shevlin, who established himself in Minneapolis in 1886, and Henry C. Akeley, who arrived a year later and soon organized his own company, with a capital of a half million dollars. Shevlin and S. C. Hall, his father-in-law, organized a company that grew tremendously, with a huge mill in Minneapolis. E. L. Carpenter, coming from Iowa, joined forces with Shevlin after Hall's death; and in 1888 their company alone produced more than 43,000,000 feet of lumber.

Different streams of talent and experience converged upon Minnesota. The historian of the industry observes that whereas the people from Maine were the basic builders of the lumber industry of Minnesota, the Michigan contingent gave the business the momentum that carried Minneapolis to its top level as the primary white-pine market. But there were other lines of influence also. Thomas B. Walker was an Ohioan who appeared in Minnesota as early as 1862, began to buy pine lands in the 1860s, and gradually built a lumber empire. His interests looked to the northwest, with Crookston as a central point. He formed the Red River Lumber Company, which in the single year of 1889 produced no less than 45,000,000 feet of lumber. Nor should one overlook the influences emanating from Wisconsin, with its Wausau group (including the Wintons) and powerful lumber forces in the Chippewa Valley. As Minnesota approached its "golden age" of lumbering, it was influenced more and more by the ability of leaders to effect concentration of owner-ship and syndication of lumber-milling on a big scale.

In this setting Frederick Weyerhaeuser, working into the Minnesota region, not from Maine or Michigan but from Rock Island, Illinois, had an impact that left deep marks not alone on Minnesota lumbering but on the industry in its expansion to the Pacific Coast. He was born at Niedersaulheim in the Rhine Valley in 1834, emigrated to America in 1852, and worked his way forward from one humble job to another. In 1860, with a brother-in-law (Frederick C. A. Denkmann), he bought the Rock Island sawmill where he had gained experience in counting, loading, and selling lumber. Soon there were two mills under their con-trol in the Rock Island Lumber and Manufacturing Company. Then Weyerhaeuser moved northward, interested himself in the Chippewa River area and also formed with associates the Mississippi River Logging Company (chartered early in 1871). This company took over the so-called Beef Slough boom, a project that led to a pooling of interests in the Chippewa Logging Company, an enterprise in which Weyerhaeuser's skill was a paramount factor. What was at stake, in conflict with Eau Claire lumbermen, was the logging of the Chippewa River country, the use of the river, and mastery of a great boom for handling the logs.

The Weyerhaeuser lumber story started in Illinois, but the records make it clear that Wisconsin timber lands played a decisive role in the emerging business of Frederick Weyerhaeuser. As his field of operations grew, he demonstrated in working with other down-river groups a talent for organization. By 1887 he had establishments at five places in Wis-consin in addition to Rock Island, and he had even pushed into the St. Louis River region of Minnesota. His purchases included large tracts of the Cornell University pine lands. Further expansion came when in 1890 he and the lumber groups cooperating with him bought land-grant holdings from the Northern Pacific — and this was but an early step to-ward still greater pine lands in the north country. Weyerhaeuser fol-lowed the direction of his enterprise and made St. Paul the headquarters of his business. Stumpage rights were acquired from the St. Paul and Duluth Railroad, and the lands of the St. Anthony Lumber Company were bought in 1893. The Mississippi River Lumber Company emerged,

327

with Weyerhaeuser at its head, and it was followed by other organizations, including the Pine Tree Company at Little Falls, the Northern Lumber Company at Cloquet, even a paper manufacturing company, also at Cloquet. The climax was the Weyerhaeuser Timber Company, a timber-holding concern that reached out to the Pacific Coast.

Such a recital of a few landmarks does not, of course, go to the heart of the success achieved by Weyerhaeuser. The records reveal him as a man of rare "foresight and judgment in planning and policy." He had unusual skill in appraising ability and character. His leadership, according to family lore, was based on "intelligent courage," and it must be added that he was an extremely hard worker and consistently ready to associate himself with other timbermen of experience and competence. It has been said that "the manufacturing side never appealed to him," and this is borne out by the concentration of his interest in timber-holding from his earlier ventures in northern Minnesota to the concern that became one of the largest owners of timber in America. Carried forward by men of the second, third, and fourth generations, the company has demonstrated enlightened leadership through the years since the elder Weyerhaeuser died in 1914. It has adapted itself to changes in the management of timber resources and in the American economy. The company has been a major mover in the development of American industrial forestry and has given support to research along many lines, even on the history of the industry itself.

With one powerful interest after another joining in the harvesting of the white pine, the industry ran its course — the long road from an infant Minnesota business of $57,800 in 1850 to a production in 1900 valued at more than $43,000,000. The decline after the high level in 1905 came fast. Great centers of lumber production were now in the north, at Virginia and Cloquet. The machine age, with steam power mechanizing operations at all levels, hastened the end. The lumber industry reached its heights at the very time the steel industry, with stimulus from Minnesota iron ore and from new techniques in steel-making, was creating the steel age. Steel emerged in a thousand-and-one uses earlier pre-empted by wood and iron. Thus the forces of transition in the lumber industry were related not only to shifts in sources of lumber supply but also to a new era in the technology of the modern world.

Lumber has no value unless it is distributed to the places where it is needed and put to use. Alongside the industry there developed "line yards" for retailing lumber. These were centrally owned and managed, sometimes by lumber manufacturers, but more often, as the business grew in volume, by specialized and independent concerns. Prices of lumber had their ups and downs in relation to shifts in the national economy, and there was sharp competition in wholesale and retail selling. That the line yards became very important is evidenced by the fact that at one time in the early 1900s no fewer than fifty such companies were located in and managed from Minneapolis. The importance of this metropolis as a lumber-distributing center in fact outlasted its dominance of lumber production.

The lumber product of Minnesota slumped by 1914 to about half its volume in 1905, and it dropped to about a fifth just after World War I. Mill after mill terminated its processing of white pine — in Minneapolis, Stillwater, Winona, Duluth, even Virginia, which before the war had the largest mill for white pine in the country. The great companies pushed their business to the west, though not a few retained their old centers as a base. Yet other lumbermen — a new breed of entrepreneurs — turned to paper-making and an industry that meant a new era in forest products. This era developed in part as a result of chemical discoveries that led to the manufacture of paper from wood pulp instead of rags or straw. Coupled with new processes was the invention of cylinder machines and other techniques that facilitated paper manufacture. Underlying the changes was an insatiable American demand for newsprint; paper for books, magazines, and typing; and materials for packing boxes, cups, milk containers, towels, and literally thousands of other purposes. It is said that the United States uses more paper than all the other countries of the world combined. Technology and resources cleared the path for a host of paper-making companies, many of them of great importance in Minnesota industrial history, including such concerns as Minnesota and Ontario, Northwest Paper, and the Blandin interests at Grand Rapids. Meanwhile, pioneers of transition were preaching forest fire control and reforestation. Public action, spurred by disasters, took form in law and administration, and a new era opened in the forest-related industries. This harmonized with the development of a new Minnesota philosophy with respect to the multiple use of forest resources.

The history of the lumber industry is much more than an account of finance, management, and leadership. It also must deal with people whose names are forgotten, but whose labor and skills were essential. It was chiefly such people who transferred techniques from older regions to the pine woods of Minnesota and introduced special tools and contrivances in the work of the woods. The rafting of the lumber is a colorful part of the record; and thousands of lumberjacks contributed strength, dexterity, and human color. Lumbering reveals an astonishing technological revolution, from manpower to ox-power and horses, to locomotives and caterpillar tractors — the use of bigger and better machines and the application of modernized techniques to a changing industry. There was a special vocabulary of logging; the songs and ballads and folklore of the lumberjacks have been gathered up and studied; and the ways of lumberjack life have been recounted in reminiscence and in historical studies. Lumbering is like a pageant that has passed by but is vivid in recollection. It constitutes, with its triumphs and tragedies, a significant part of the state and national experience.

Lumber camps, logging techniques, and strong-muscled lumberjacks figure in all the successive stages of the white pine industry, but there were many changes. In the early period, Maine ideas and management were predominant, camps were primitive, and the chopper was at the top of the heap. French-Canadians and Scotch and English loggers, migrating from the eastern woods of Canada, played a role in the industry. As bigger camps were developed, lumber workers came from New York, Pennsylvania, the Scandinavian countries, and other sources. The crosscut robbed the lordly chopper of his eminence. In the modern stages of white pine, camps were mechanized. Invention kept abreast of the industry — or the industry of invention. One writer says that the camps became veritable hotels, with "steam heat, hot and cold water, bathrooms, and electric lights." In all periods, however, work in the woods tested youth, strength, endurance, and capacity to meet hardship through winters of extreme cold. The regime was one that strained the strength of even the toughest men. They were men of fiber and will; and the stereotype of the lumberjack stumbling along skid road does injustice to the sturdiness of the bearded workers who cleared the forests.

The early camps and many of the early tools were transfers from Maine: the "shanty," with a roof hole for the escape of smoke; the bean hole with its bed of coals; tea as a favorite beverage (the Norwegians and Swedes of a later day took coffee); the go-devil, a crude sled used to haul a tree down to a spot near the river; and the "peavey" — a long sharp-pointed pole used in manipulating logs. The cant hook, on the other hand, was Canadian, an instrument for rolling logs that were cut before being transported to the riverside; and it was this practice that led to log roads, the use of teams, and the piling up of big loads that could not be carried on the primitive go-devil. The early St. Croix shanties of the Maine style were single-room, all-purpose buildings for cooking, eating, sleeping, drying wet clothes, or sitting on the "deacon's seat," a bench which in some shanties ran the length of the room. A visitor to the St. Croix pineries in 1855 described a camp of some twenty-five or thirty workers in which the men sprawled along the floor to sleep and a "blanket was spread from one end of the row of bodies to the other."

A writer has described some of the specializations of work in the Lake Superior country for the period from the 1870s on to the 1890s. There were timber cruisers, whose job was to spot the areas to be cut — to find a site for the camp and to determine the best routes for tote roads and suitable water routes for bringing the logs out. Choppers, swampers, and barkers had each their allotted work — cutting trees, stripping branches, and slashing off bark from one side of the tree so that it would slide easily. When crosscut saws were used, the logs were measured out and cut at once; and they were carefully labeled with a company mark. Using a heavy stamp hammer, a lumberjack would drive a raised pattern into each end of every log and also make an imprint on the bark. The result was a durable identification similar to the cattle brands of the western plains. Crosses, letters, figures (as of a snowshoe), and other curious marks appeared. It is an astonishing fact that some twenty thousand different log brands are on record in Minnesota's state archives.

As camps were enlarged, there were not a few buildings, including a wanigan, or store; the bunkhouse, which might house as many as eighty men; and the cookhouse, where cook and cookee (an assistant) prepared gargantuan meals on a great cook stove — the inevitable pork and beans, flapjacks, molasses, biscuits, meat and potatoes when available, and other foods that hungry, hard-working men devoured in silence. Evenings until nine, when lights were put out and men went to the rows of bunks to sleep, might be spent in pipe-smoking, chewing tobacco or snuff, storytelling, singing, sometimes stag dances with fiddles and accordions supplying the music. After tough work from dawn to dark, even the strongest men were tired and they tumbled into their bunks at the specified time. Since each hung three or four pairs of soggy socks on wire lines, the atmosphere often was very ill-smelling.

Mainites, New Yorkers, Pennsylvanians, French-Canadians, Norwegians, Swedes, Irish, Scotsmen, Germans, and men of other nationalities were among the thousands of lumberjacks who made for the woods. A great many Canadians came to the lumber camps, but from 1870 to 1890 Scandinavians were in the majority. The hardy Finns, long trained to life in a wood economy, were active in the later periods. Not a few boys took jobs in mills and at lumber camps.

Lumbering meant an open life of rigorous work, and by and large the men who chose it were young and hardy. But the camps did not escape illness, and in the early 1880s smallpox ravaged the workers, especially in the Grand Rapids area. Life in the woods offered many hazards. Often there were accidents, broken legs, cuts, men crushed under heavy loads of logs or by falling trees. Wages were paid in accordance with standards of the time; and there were gradations in levels, from foremen, cooks, teamsters, choppers, swampers, and sawyers to "ordinary hands." The foremen, at the top, might receive as much as a hundred dollars a month, sometimes more; and other wages ran often in a range from about seventy dollars to twenty dollars. Apart from the money, the lumber workers of course received meals and bunks as a part of their compensation.

As a rule no liquor was permitted in the camps, but when the men, after a season in the woods, got their pay and wandered into towns and cities, they sometimes made up for the drouth of the camps and spent their cash in a hurry. Just as the cowboy has been turned into a mythical figure by romantic writers and the movies, however, so this aspect of lumberjack life has been overdrawn, according to recorded interviews with men of the woods. There were hell-raising times along the skid roads, and bartenders and prostitutes unquestionably took a toll of the lumberjacks, but it would be misleading to characterize such episodes as normal or typical of lumberjack experience. Not a few of the lumberjacks came down from the woods not to carouse, but to take jobs in Minneapolis sawmills after their winter's work.

Much work in logging called for deftness acquired through practice — not only in the woods but also on the rivers and in the management of booms. Lumberjacks knew how to "ride" the logs, control their spinning, and perform deeds where death by drowning or crushing was the penalty for a mistake. When log jams occurred, they had to be broken, and skilled "river pigs" would search out key logs for release. Sometimes dynamite had to be used to overcome a particularly big or difficult jam.

Rafting logs was in itself a specialized business and one of high importance. Oarsmen propelled many rafts in pioneer days; sails were used also; but from the 1850s sternwheel steamboats, under contract, more and more towed the rafts on their journeys down river. Rafting companies sprang up and some of them carried on what was in effect big business, a collateral offshoot of lumbering, actually a part of the industry though the companies usually were independent. One company was that of the Van Sant family, which came up river by stages from St. Louis and made Winona its base of operations in the 1880s. Samuel R. Van Sant reported that one contract alone, with the Musser Lumber Company, involved towing charges over a thirty-five-year period to a grand total of a million dollars. It was this Van Sant — he and his father pioneered modern rafting and had a fleet of towboats — who later went into politics and served as governor of Minnesota for two terms.

Around lumbermen and lumberjacks there is an aura of folklore. The lumberjacks were singing men, and in 1926 a volume of *Ballads and Songs of the Shanty-Boy* appeared. The shanty-boy was the lumberjack, and the collection is derived from Minnesota, Wisconsin, and Michigan in the period from 1870 to 1890. Its compiler believed that when the age of steel and great machines transformed lumbering, singing fell away. The ballads bear the marks especially of the Irish, though some have a French-Canadian or Scottish flavor. Some of the titles are "Ye Noble Big Pine Tree," "The Festive Lumber-Jack," "The Crow Wing Drive," "The Merry Shanty Boys," "Ole from Norway," "Jim Whalen," "The Three McFarlands," and "Bung Yer Eye." Their lilt and spirit may be suggested by "The Crow Wing Drive":

> Says White Pine Tom to Arkansaw,
> "There's one more drive that I'd like to strike."
> Says Arkansaw, "What can it be?"
> "It's the Crow Wing River for the Old Pine Tree."

The shanty-boy often complained of his toilsome life; but he had zest for the woods:

> Blow high or low, no fear we know,
> To the woods we're bound to go,
> Our axes swing, the woods do ring
> With shanty men, heigho!

333

One ballad tells of a man wandering through the woods and coming to a meandering brook:

> On its banks and right before me
> Stood a pine in stately glory.
> The forest king he seemed to be
> He was a noble Big Pine Tree.

The lumberjack bent on adventure in the city figures in the ballads:

> He's a wild rip-snortin' devil ever' time he comes to town;
> He's a porky, he's a moose-cat, too busy to set down.

Jack Haggerty was a raftsman who wanted to marry the blacksmith's daughter but lost her and blamed the girl's mother for his tragedy. He offered melancholy advice:

> So come all you bold raftsmen with hearts stout and true,
> Don't depend on the women, you're beat if you do.
> For when you meet one with a dark chestnut curl,
> Oh, just remember Jack Haggerty and his Flat River girl.

A recently discovered St. Croix Valley verse from 1871 reports the sad story of "Old Joe," the cook, and an Indian who stole the beans he had baked:

> Joe on the chain-hook hung the pot,
> A bustin' coffee-maker —
> He pulled the beans, all smokin' hot,
> From their ground-oven baker.
> He flew and flung the biscuit round,
> To give them browner singeing,
> Turned — where he'd set the baked beans down,
> Gosh! There stood Lo, an Injun.

The singing men were also talking men, with hundreds of words devised for the life and work they knew, many of their terms picturesque. A cruiser was a timber wolf; the cook was a hashslinger; a preacher a sky-pilot; getting drunk was kegging up; tea was swamp water; doughnuts were cold shuts; the foreman was the kingpin; a cookshack was the chuck house; sweat was Swedish steam; and snuff was Swedish condition powder. These are but a few of the expressions that spiced the lumberjack's conversation.

No stories claiming color from lumber lore have had greater vogue in America than those about Paul Bunyan and Babe, the Blue Ox. They have been "publicized" in books for adults and children and interpreted, as Richard Dorson writes, in "art forms and pageants: sculpture, ballet, musical suite, lyric opera, folk drama, radio play, oil painting, lithography, wood carving, and even a glass mosaic mural." Paul Bunyan festivals have been held from coast to coast, with Minnesota taking the lead in such affairs, while newspapers and magazines across the country have made the lumber demigod a household name. Paul Bunyan has been presented as a myth, a folk tale, drawn from oral tradition in the lumber camps — an American story glorifying fabulous strength and incredible achievements. The stories have had wide circulation; and few people have questioned their authenticity as tales told and re-told from the deacon's seat in camp houses, with bewhiskered lumberjacks listening to them spellbound. But there is scarcely a shred of evidence that the lumberjacks were familiar with Paul Bunyan, told stories about him, or indeed had ever heard of him. Dr. Larson, in her years of research on the Minnesota lumber industry, found no records of Bunyan tales actually told in the camps. The collector of the nineteenth-century ballads and songs of the lumbermen found none celebrating the hero. The present author interviewed a lumberjack of rich experience in the 1920s, Wright T. Orcutt, who had written about lumberjacks and woods lore, and he had never heard a Bunyan story in the woods. And the Forest History Society in its far-ranging investigations of the sources for woods history has unearthed no evidence that Paul Bunyan was the subject of bunkhouse tales.

This does not mean that the lumberjacks were not storytellers. They were, and they had their own lore about men of prodigious strength and about fearsome beasts. As long ago as 1910 lumber tales were gathered up about the Hugag, a monster with jointless legs and corrugated ears; and the Hodag, a striped and checked animal with a spade extending from his nose. There were also the hard-faced Splinter Cat, which crashed open trees head-on in his search for honey and raccoons; and the frightful Agropelter (*Anthrocephalus craniofractens*), ape-faced, with arms like whiplashes, whose aim as he hurled dead branches at passing lumberjacks was so deadly that only one man is known to have survived an attack. This was Big Ole Kittleson on the Upper St. Croix — the limb thrown at him was shattered against his head. Big Ole even caught a glimpse of the beast as it leaped from tree to tree before vanishing in the woods. The Side-Hill Dodger was a curious animal. His legs on one side were shorter than those on the other, and he climbed a hill by going around it, one turn after another. If skeptical moderns question the presence of such beasts in the woods, they should consult William T. Cox's *Fearsome Creatures of the Lumberwoods*, which even includes drawings of the animals by an artist who is alleged to have met them "on tote road and trail." The book is solemnly dedicated to the "Concatenated Order of Hoo-Hoo."

The lumberjacks liked to tell tales of such animals in the bunkhouse. They admired the French-Canadians and others who were gifted in story-telling. But before about 1910 neither they nor the world, as far as present evidence goes, seemed to know about Paul Bunyan. In 1910 a newspaper writer in Detroit wrote a feature article about "The Round River Drive" and followed it with others; and about the same time someone in Oregon wrote about Paul and his ox. Then in 1914 the Red River Lumber Company brought out a Bunyan pamphlet, with cartoons; and drawings made by William B. Laughead became the trademark of the company. The stories spread like wildfire and spurred imitation and invention; books came out in the 1920s; newspapers invited tales in special columns; and as years went by a vast Paul Bunyan bibliography was built up. It is a curious episode. One is left with a suspicion that there may well have been a "slender trickle of oral tradition" behind the colossal total of story material created in a half century. But if trickle there was, it was not discerned in Minnesota by the most patient and scholarly student who has written on the state's white pine industry. Tentatively one is obliged to accept the judgment of Dr. Dorson, one of the leading folk-lorists of America, that Paul Bunyan is the "pseudo folk hero of twentieth century mass culture," a popular symbol of bigness and promotion seized upon and used in any and every cause.

The stories caught up in the 1920s tell of a fabulous giant of a lumber-jack who, when he tossed as an infant, "knocked down four square miles of standing timber." When grown, he required a water reservoir for icing his logging roads, scooped a hole that filled and now is Lake Superior. When he smoked, an assistant employed a shovel to keep his pipe filled. Babe, the Blue Ox, took on her amazing hue during the winter of the blue snow. She measured forty-two ax handles and a tobacco box between the eyes. The thousands of Minnesota lakes are her hoof marks. In Paul's cook shanty men got lost between potato bin and flour bin. Paul blew blasts on his dinner horn, but once he forgot to point it to the sky and ten acres of pine were blown down. These and scores of other tales are told, and every year adds new ones. Recent or old, they take rank as tall stories reflecting bigness in the continental sweep of the lumber saga. Paul Bunyan is the apotheosis of raw strength, size, and prowess.

An epilogue to the drama of Minnesota lumber is the record of generous contributions not only of money but also of interest and encouragement made by many of the families that derived their wealth — or much of it — from the industry. This record is imprinted on several private colleges in the state, the university, libraries, institutes devoted to the fine arts, a great symphony orchestra, and foundations that have forwarded many other cultural, social, and educational objectives. It is of interest, in this context, to note that the Forest History Society, with headquarters in St. Paul, was launched in 1946 to promote the collection and preservation of the historical records of the industry, not only in Minnesota but throughout the United States and Canada. Its activities, supported by leaders and companies in the forest-products industries, have been directed toward the cooperation of businessmen and scholars seeking to forward understanding of the history of one of the great industries of America.

The milling district of Minneapolis about 1908

✗ *Dual Domain*

WHEAT became a major crop in the 1850s and it maintained its priority for several decades. An economic historian of agriculture designates 1860–80 as the period of specialized wheat farming in Minnesota. This too precise dating — obviously influenced by decennial statistics — does not mean that wheat production did not increase after 1880, as acreage widened and population expanded. It implies rather that the two decades were a major era of wheat growing and that, from 1880 onward, diversification, already well under way, attracted more and more attention from the men of the soil. Though wheat was highly popular, the familiar tag of "King Wheat" suggests a domination that the facts do not fully sustain.

When the territory was young, the dominant land use was for oats, potatoes, corn, and vegetables — a self-sufficing agriculture. By 1860 wheat was taking a big lead. A visitor to Hastings on the Mississippi in 1859 saw "wheat everywhere; wheat on the levee; wagon loads of wheat pouring down to the levee; wheat in the streets; wheat in the sidewalks." And a minister wrote in 1862, "Minnesota or that part of it known as Cottage Grove has gone to wheat. Men work in wheat all day when it does not rain, lounge around talking about wheat when it is wet, dream about wheat at night and I fear go to meeting Sabbath Day to think about wheat."

Wheat may possibly have fascinated some farmers with its colors like

339

"liquid gold," a "marvel of yellow and green," running "before the wind's feet," as in Hamlin Garland's later songs of the Middle Border; but its mundane attraction was as a cash crop grown through the generous fertility of soil. Land was cheap and the earth was rich. The promise of prosperity seemed great; and not many gave serious thought to the depletion of the soil that would follow annual cropping. It is easy to take long views after the event; it was not easy when, as in 1860 and 1865, the average wheat yield in Minnesota exceeded twenty-two bushels an acre.

The wheat domain increased prodigiously after the 1850s. In excess of 2,000,000 bushels by 1860, the crop jumped to 18,866,000 bushels in 1870. In the next ten years it advanced to 34,601,000, and by 1890 it stood at 52,300,000 bushels. Lands under tillage were enlarged with every year and decade. The acreage of such lands in 1859 was 345,000; ten years later it was slightly above 1,500,000 acres; by 1880 there were 4,400,000; and in 1890 the tilled area reached 5,900,000. Light on the wheat story is afforded by the percentages of tilled land devoted to wheat at selected dates. In 1860 the wheat crop filled 54.4 per cent of the tilled area; the figures were 60.1 per cent in 1869; 68.98 per cent in 1878, the high point; then a drop to 45.89 per cent in 1889.

Such statistics have little meaning, however, unless they are interpreted in conjunction with other factors, including the growth of population. This growth in the thirty years after 1860 lifted the total population from less than 200,000 to more than 1,300,000. The country population in the same period rose from 122,530 to 708,114. These census totals for "country population," it should be added, exclude all incorporated places as contrasted with the usual statistics for "rural population," which include towns and villages of less than 2500 population and report a total of close to 870,000 by 1890. Whatever statistical base one elects to use, it is evident that Minnesota through this period was pre-eminently rural. Lumbering, flour milling, and other industries, including the early mining of iron ore, were of great economic significance in the generation after the Civil War, but farming, wheat-oriented for some years and then moving into diversification, was predominant. The economy, problems, and viewpoints of the farmers bulked large in the generation after the Civil War and in fact have done so through the course of Minnesota's life from pioneer days to the present.

Often in history interlocking forces clarify significant movements and changes — and this truth finds illustration in the Minnesota wheat era. The pouring of wheat in a flood of millions of bushels from the 1860s to the end of the century was no circumstance of chance. Nor was it the consequence of any single cause. The explanation for it is to be found in the mechanization of agriculture by invention, the upward trend of wheat prices during the Civil War, the availability of free or cheap land through the Homestead Act and the railroad land grants, the influx of many thousands of immigrants after the Civil War, and the spread of settlement to the Red River Valley. It is related to the achievement of a state network of railroads, the development of local and export marketing, the rise of flour milling, and the basic facts of virgin soil, large initial yields, and the drive for cash returns from a market crop. Farmers tried to meet as quickly as possible the costs of land, machinery, buildings, and living. All these and probably yet other circumstances contributed to the domain of wheat. Viewed in the large, agricultural changes to the early farmers of Minnesota were probably as exciting as were the automobile and airplane to later generations.

The shortage of men for work during the Civil War promoted the use of machinery. National records show that a quarter of a million reapers of different kinds were sold in the United States from 1860 to 1864. On its way out was the back-breaking hand labor of cutting the grain with cradles and of raking and tying it in bundles with cords of straw. Reapers began to be used in Minnesota while it was still a territory. They were introduced by the mid-fifties, perhaps as early as 1854. The McCormick reaper, early on the scene, soon faced competition from other machines. Horse-driven threshers seem to have appeared even before the reapers; and well-drilling machines, also available in the 1850s, were of immense aid to farmers who faced difficulty in getting water.

Plows and fanning mills were made in Minnesota in early years, but just about all other kinds of farm machinery were brought in from the East. "All grain cradles, horse rakes, forks, spades, shovels, straw cutters, and hoes," writes Dr. Merrill E. Jarchow, "were imported, and only about thirty of the thousand reapers sold in Minnesota in 1861 were manufactured there." Self-raking reapers began to be used in Minnesota in the early 1860s, and several varieties were in sharp competition — such as those named Esterley, Dorsey, McCormick, and Manny. Harvesters came on the market in 1864. The great companies commanded much of

341

the Minnesota market and cultivated it with busy agents, but gradually Minnesota manufacturers entered in competition, especially in making plows, of which many improved kinds were devised.

In the long story of mechanization one improvement followed another. An advance that made large contributions to the wheat industry was the steam thresher, introduced into Minnesota in the second half of the 1860s. The self-binder came in the 1870s as steam threshers gradually replaced horse-powered machines. Confidence in the use of inventions increased and the sales of farm machinery catapulted. For 1876, it was estimated that more than 5000 reapers were bought by Minnesota farmers, about 600 threshers, and 25,000 plows. Meanwhile manufacturing concerns such as the St. Paul Harvester Works (begun in 1872), the Minneapolis Harvester Works, and the Hubbard Harvester Company (also of Minneapolis) were busy making agricultural implements. An ambitious firm was the Seymour, Sabin Company of Stillwater, from 1875 manufacturers of a thresher known as the "Minnesota Chief." The exploitation of labor-saving devices Dr. Jarchow interrelates with the "easing of the farmer's toil, better farming, the displacement of horses and mules, the freeing of acres formerly devoted to forage crops, the relation of farmer and machine agent, improved machines," and yet other changes.

Through invention man's arms were mechanically extended and multiplied in a process destined to revolutionize not only agriculture but industry in its widest extent. Motor-driven tractors and "combines" were still far in the future. The horse was an important adjunct of the farm, though oxen were disappearing from the scene. The "horse population" of Minnesota increased from 874, as recorded in the census of 1850, to more than 257,000 by 1880. Yet engine-driven threshers, replacing the patient circular tramping power of horses, were a warning of a coming day when horses would become almost a rarity in the jobs of the farm.

The price of wheat rose from about fifty cents a bushel in 1861 to more than $1.50 in 1866. This advance reflected a mounting demand for wheat in a period of labor scarcity — a demand stimulated by the Civil War and the earlier disruption of the European grain markets as a result of the Crimean War. But rising prices were by no means an unmixed blessing to the farmers. The war period witnessed an inflation brought about in part by a depreciating paper currency. The costs of machinery and of commodities rose alongside vaulting prices for grain. Cash was

342

offered for harvested wheat — a prospect that tempted many farmers to incur heavy debts to enlarge their enterprises and thus take as full advantage as possible of markets open to them. The penalties came later when they had to pay their debts in a period of deflation. Price levels dropped below eighty cents a bushel by 1870, and average wheat yields slipped from more than 22 bushels per acre in both 1860 and 1865 to 12.28 in 1871, 9.61 in 1876, and 11.3 in 1879. Such gyrations in prices and reductions in yields per acre did not mean that the production of wheat was not mounting from year to year, but shifts in the farm economy were taking place.

Other forces, as well as the impetus that wheat raising received in the Civil War years, help to explain the increases of wheat crops during the decades from 1870 to 1890. Transportation and marketing were of primary importance. Once the grain was ready, there was the cumbersome job of hauling it to mill or primary market. River towns were strategic in the early development of wheat marketing, just as nearness to rivers, especially the Mississippi and the Minnesota, was basic to pioneer farming. Winona, Rochester, and Red Wing were early centers to which farmers went to unload and sell their wheat. The shipping period was in the fall, when the rivers were open and the farmers needed quick returns on their summer's work. St. Louis and Milwaukee were the big markets for wheat exported, with Milwaukee gradually outdistancing St. Louis and then yielding primacy to Chicago. The marketing picture was revolutionized by the spread of railroads, not only those connecting with the East but also the Minnesota network built in the decade and a half after the Civil War. Along the railroads, towns sprang up and elevators appeared. Farmers could then sell their grain at nearby points, where it could be stored and finally shipped out on the railroads — an emancipation from the earlier need of being near navigable rivers and of marketing before ice blocked river traffic.

Gradually the elevator and the railroad won supremacy over the transport of grains, and Minneapolis, with its milling development, became the central wheat market. Through most of the 1850s wheat was ungraded, but a step toward grading came in 1858, when the Chicago Board of Trade established a system of three grades, with price differentiations. The practice of grading soon became general. The declines in wheat prices, early absence of public supervision of grading, the lack of control of elevators throughout the state, costs of storage, the organization of wheat-buying "pools," and the problem of differential railroad rates were all of concern to farmers, whose dissatisfactions ultimately led to agitation for governmental intervention and to the establishment of the Railroad and Warehouse Commission in 1885. No small part of the Minnesota political story is interrelated with the problems of wheat. Agrarian political parties represent one aspect of the effort of farmers to extricate themselves from difficulties imposed upon them by the wheat era, but a more fundamental road of escape was scientific and economic. This was the road to a diversified agriculture that did not stand or fall by virtue of the success or failure of wheat or because of transient difficulties in marketing.

No analysis of wheat as a major crop can fail to take cognizance of the Homestead Act, the sales of railroad lands, and the swarming of a rural population across the state northwestward to the wheat-growing acres of the Red River Valley. As has been noted, even in the Civil War years, up to 1865, a million and a quarter acres of public lands were entered by more than nine thousand claimants; and the rush for homesteads went steadily forward through the next decades. Lands patented under the Homestead Act reached 255,648 acres in 1873 and a peak of more than 367,000 in 1885. Generally through the 1870s and 1880s the totals never fell below 200,000 acres a year.

Concurrently the railroads were making spirited efforts to market their lands, thus raising funds for the financing of their expansion and also developing sources of railroad business. Small down payments, with planned installments running over stated periods of years, usually between five and ten, were lures to settlers. The railroad land grants, approximately ten million acres, represented one-fifth of the Minnesota land area.

Free land under the Homestead Act, and inexpensive land bought in the areas of the railroad land grants, coincided in time with the extension of the roads to the Red River Valley and also with the pioneering of the western lands by Scandinavian and other immigrants. Much of that pioneering was carried on by farmers whose acres were modest compared with the extent of the bonanza farms. But these huge farms contributed to the fame of the Red River Valley, on both the Minnesota and the Dakota sides, as an incredibly rich wheat-producing area.

The bonanza farm was wheat growing on a grand scale, taking advantage of machinery in large quantities, cheap land, and virgin soil. By

1880 more than fourscore Red River Valley farms were each larger than a thousand acres and ten years later there were more than 300. Most of these farms were in Dakota, but an agricultural journal from 1879 reports thirty Minnesota farms in the size range from 2000 to 3000 acres. One man, John H. Camp, owned 33,000 acres in the Willmar region; and William F. Davidson, the river magnate, had 20,000 acres in Redwood County.

Best known of all the bonanza farmers was Oliver Dalrymple, a well-educated Pennsylvania lawyer who arrived in St. Paul in 1856. He engaged in land-office work and after the Civil War had sufficient funds to buy 2600 acres in the Cottage Grove region, which he managed in three farms (he named them Grant, Sheridan, and Sherman). In 1875, working under contract with a group of investors who exchanged depreciated Northern Pacific bonds for railroad lands, Dalrymple broke 1280 acres of land some miles west of the Red River and the next year had a harvest of 32,000 bushels of wheat. His average for all the land he cultivated was more than twenty-three bushels an acre. The Dalrymple holdings went to 100,000 acres, of which (by 1895) 65,000 were under cultivation. A series of bonanza farms comprising some 38,000 acres near Mayville, in which Dalrymple had an interest, employed 300 men and used 300 horses, 100 plows, 75 binders, 10 separators, 10 engines, and other kinds of machinery in proportion. These great farms were under the management of J. L. Grandin and two brothers, Pennsylvania businessmen. Red River Valley folklore tells of a worker who started out in the spring, plowing one furrow, got to the end in the fall, and harvested his way back.

A humble worker on Dalrymple's bonanza farm in 1887 was the later Nobel Prize winner Knut Hamsun. To him the prairie was "golden-green and endless as a sea." He drove one of ten mowing machines in harvest, working sixteen hours a day; men followed the machines to shock the wheat bundles. The scene was "wheat and grass, wheat and grass, as far as the eye could see." One may assume that the mounted and armed foreman had no idea that a humble workman of his crew would one day be more widely known throughout the world than the bonanza farms on which he worked.

The time came when the great farms were divided and the industry was diversified, but there can be no doubt that the Red River Valley — through its bonanzas and through the small farms that immigrants and others homesteaded or bought from the railroads — strengthened the wheat domain in its later period. The small farms were humble. The pioneers began with sod houses, few machines, and strong arms. Pioneering for them involved many difficulties, including that of plowing the tough prairie land. But the soil, once it was opened up, planted, and harvested, was rewarding. After early ordeals — and with lumber supplied from the railroad towns — primitive sod houses gave way to frame houses and improved living. Soon the farmers knew villages, stores, elevators, churches, the frontier clubs called saloons, the sound of railroad whistles, the crunch of passing caravans of wagons.

Farming in Minnesota in the 1860s and 1870s is not all a record of wheat. As prices shifted, as hard times followed the Panic of 1873, and as grasshoppers caused tremendous losses to farmers in the period 1873–77, wheat had its ups and downs. One historian of agriculture traces three "culminations" in wheat growing, each followed by a "reaction." Even by the end of the 1860s there were signs of soil exhaustion in some of the older wheat-growing areas, and by the early 1870s "conditions were ripe for a return to mixed farming." But new circumstances, such as the opening of lands to the west, the exploitation of great farms, and the development of flour milling, gave impetus to a prolongation of wheat specialization through another decade or more.

Important as wheat undoubtedly was, in 1880 Minnesota farms produced 23,000,000 bushels of oats, close to 15,000,000 of corn, more than 5,000,000 of potatoes, about 3,000,000 of barley, not to forget more than a half million gallons of sorghum syrup and more than 75,000 pounds of maple sugar. The Minnesota population of milch cows was 275,000 and would pass the half million mark by 1890. Such figures support the view of the geographer Hildegard B. Johnson that the concept of "King Wheat" is probably an oversimplification of the farming story — that wheat was by no means a "mono-crop." The forces of diversification gained impetus while wheat was still the mainstay of farming in the tilled areas of the state.

Many wheat-growing farmers went west in the 1870s and 1880s to start anew in the Red River Valley the kind of agriculture that had faltered in the regions where they had formerly lived. H. V. Arnold tells of the migration westward from southern Minnesota in 1880. "It was said by some," he writes, "that farmers must pay more attention to stock raising with improved breeds of both hogs and cattle. But there were hundreds of the small farmers who were unable to cope with the changed situation, since to adjust matters to the required new conditions would take several years." He meant that while wheat crops were good and prices high, farmers had expanded, bought machinery, incurred debts. They now had to choose between staying on where they were and making slow adjustments or going west for a new start. Many moved, including the Arnolds, who left Houston County for the Red River Valley. They loaded their goods into two farm wagons, bought five yoke of oxen, then made their slow way to the Red River Valley, where once again they entered upon the cycle of wheat raising.

William A. Marin was a boy in the Red River Valley, near Crookston, in 1880, and saw the passing caravans of farmers from southern Minnesota or Iowa or Wisconsin. Late in life he recalled the scenes: "We watched the schooners come up from the south, zigzagging up the tortuous trail like ships beating up against the wind. Slowly they drew nearer — sometimes one, sometimes five or six in a fleet. Out to the road we went to watch them pass. . . . Usually the woman was sitting at the front driving the team, and beside her or peeking out of the front opening were a flock of dirty, tousled, tow-headed children. Often she held a small baby in her arms. Behind followed a small herd of cattle or horses driven by the man and the boys on foot, for the rate of travel was a walk."

The caravan would stop, stories would be exchanged, and then the trek was resumed and the schooner slowly moved on, "very much like a real ship plowing its way over a trackless sea and then disappearing below the horizon." This picture from life is not unlike that in the opening pages of the novel of prairie pioneering *Giants in the Earth*. O. E. Rölvaag tells of the immigrant caravan of Per Hansa and Beret crossing southern Minnesota to Dakota over a "plain so wide that the rim of the heavens cut down on it around the entire horizon."

To present the drama of wheat without relating it to flour milling would be akin to playing *Hamlet* without Hamlet. Flour was a principal character; and the milling industry in turn entwined itself with the manufacturing, professional, and metropolitan sovereignty of Minneapolis — the "Mill City" — through a period that ran on into the twentieth century, far beyond the era of wheat specialization. In due course the industry expanded nationally and internationally. As in the story of wheat, flour involves a complex of reinforcing circumstances: cascades of wheat, invention, water power, advances in railroads and marketing, agricultural science, money and organization, and a leadership that was flexible in adjusting a growing industry to a technological revolution and to changes in the nation's economy.

The milling reputation of Minneapolis became world-wide, but the concentration of the industry in the city built around the Falls of St. Anthony did not occur until after wheat had been dominant for a decade. "None of the Minneapolis mills or millers," writes Dr. Charles B. Kuhlmann, "had more than a local reputation up to 1870." Many mills were established in the 1850s and 1860s in Minnesota towns as "custom operations," grinding wheat for tolls as a service to farmers in their localities and supplying local flour needs. By 1860 there were 85 mills in the state (63 powered by water, 22 by steam); and the product, nearly 255,000 barrels of flour, was valued at more than $1,310,000. During the next decade the number of mills increased to 216 (and gristmills brought the total of mills to 507). This was a long advance over the single gristmill established by Fort Snelling soldiers at the Falls of St. Anthony in 1822–23, which turned out flour that made "wretched, black, bitter tasting bread." And it was progress far beyond the mill built at the Falls of St. Anthony in 1849 and leased to Calvin A. Tuttle, who operated it until 1858.

Meanwhile mills were erected at Northfield, Faribault, Hastings, Dundas, New Ulm, and other localities. Most of these were small, though the Archibald Mill at Dundas occupied a three-story building and had four pairs of millstones. It is said that farmers, for quality milling, sometimes drove wheat as far as eighty miles to use the Archibald facilities. Most of the early mills were powered by water, but some relied on horses and a few used windmills of the Dutch type. One mill, "The Minnesota," a five-run enterprise at the Falls of St. Anthony, reported profits of $24,000 from its first year of operation (1854–55) after an investment of $16,000.

Transportation in the pre-railroad era offered serious difficulties, but it was evident by 1860 that flour meant an export business for Minnesota. The home market in that year was estimated at 172,000 barrels, but flour production exceeded this figure by 82,000 barrels, and most of the excess was sent to eastern markets, with profits that averaged a dollar a barrel. As wheat farming developed, mills became characteristic features of towns that boasted water power, but the decade of the 1860s revealed a tendency toward milling concentration. Thus Hennepin and Winona counties had fourteen and thirteen mills respectively by 1870, while Rice, Goodhue, Houston, Le Sueur, and Stearns counties had from six to eight each.

That St. Anthony and Minneapolis did not win primacy as a wheat market and milling center in the 1860s was in part because railroad connections with the expanding wheat areas were not yet available. Another reason was that settlement of the Red River Valley, whence would come floods of hard spring wheat for the city mills, had not yet reached its high stage. But the metropolitan center of the state had advantages which in time would give pre-eminence to its milling. One was the water power furnished by the shackled Falls of St. Anthony, at the heart of the city, with milling potentialities on both sides of the Mississippi. A second advantage was the lumber industry which stimulated a local market and seems to have provided funds that farseeing businessmen could channel into flour mills. And a third advantage was the developing railroads. They made the Twin Cities the hub of a network that would reach to nearly all parts of the state. In the three decades after the Civil War they would extend lines into the western areas beyond Minnesota in almost precise step with the westward advance of wheat growing.

It will be recalled that the all-important dam across the Mississippi had been completed in 1858 by Franklin Steele, who had sawmills on the St. Anthony side, and by the Minneapolis Mill Company, formed by Cadwallader C. Washburn who, a few years earlier, had bought water rights and eighty-nine acres of land on the west side. This event marked the entrance of the famed Washburn family into the industrial history of Minnesota. Cadwallader was one of five remarkable brothers, sons of Israel Washburn of Maine, who achieved the unusual eminence of contributing to the country "a Secretary of State, two ministers abroad, a senator, a major general, three authors, two governors, and four representatives in Congress." Cadwallader wedded his fortunes to Wisconsin, of which he became governor, but he had an acquisitive eye to the potentialities of milling on the Upper Mississippi. The beginnings in the 1850s led to the construction of a huge mill in Minneapolis after the Civil War. This was the "B Mill," with twelve pairs of millstones and six stories, built at a cost of $100,000. It had a difficult existence for some years, but it was the foundation of an expanding milling enterprise.

By 1870 the signs of milling strength at the Falls of St. Anthony were unmistakable. Thirteen mills represented investments of a half million dollars and produced flour valued at three times that amount. But the gigantic expansion that made Minneapolis the Mill City took place during the next two decades, when Minnesota's wheat production jumped from less than 20,000,000 to more than 52,000,000 bushels a year. If many forces account for the phenomenal increase in wheat and an explosive expansion in the value of the products of Minnesota mills — from $7,500,000 in 1870 to more than $60,000,000 in 1890 — there can be no doubt that technological advances in milling played roles of major importance. These constituted a manufacturing revolution which had impact not alone on the industry itself but on the larger economic history of Minnesota.

Milling processes before this revolution were simple. Three main steps were involved: (1) the separation of the wheat from the chaff; (2) the grinding of the cleaned wheat; and (3) the bolting — or sifting — of the ground wheat through a fine cloth that permitted passage of the flour but not of the husks or bran. It is true that Oliver Evans (1755–1819), an American inventive genius, had devised machinery in his early career to cut down the costs of flour manufacturing. His inventions, run by water power, included conveyors, elevators, and other devices, and he even dreamed of practicable ways of substituting steam for water power. But, all in all, his innovations applied to established procedures. They replaced manpower with machines — important in pioneering the concentration of the industry but not fundamental in changing age-old concepts of flour-making.

As millers moved west and north, however, they faced the difficult problem of handling spring wheat and they had to make basic changes. The husk of the kernel of spring wheat was brittle. When ground by the old low or flat grinding process (millstones close together and run rapidly) it crumbled into particles that could not be wholly removed from the flour by bolting. The consequence was a discolored or "specky" flour. In addition, the oily germ at the base of the kernel was crushed along with the remainder of the kernel. This crushing produced an unfavorable effect alike on color, baking quality, and the storage life of the flour. Even more important, the glutinous cells next to the husk were only partially ground and thus were frequently sifted away with the husks. Flour without these cells, or "middlings," was apt to be inferior and lacking in nutritious strength. Such special milling problems had not been acute with winter wheat, since it was easier to grind than the spring wheat — and it was preferred because its flour was whiter, stronger, less likely to spoil. It commanded higher prices per barrel than the spring-wheat flour. The problem of the western millers, in a word, was to devise a way of making flour from spring wheat that could compete with the best flour ground from winter wheat. Unless they could do so, their future was uncertain.

The answer was found in the "middlings purifier." This was a French invention taken over and adapted to the needs of American flour milling. Its introduction to Minnesota is attributed to two brothers named La Croix (Edmund and Nicholas), French-trained engineers employed by Alexander Faribault in the 1860s. Meanwhile George H. Christian, who had come to Minnesota in 1865 and was reputed to be the best milling operator in the state, was taken into the Washburn B Mill as manager and partner. Christian was a man of rare ability who promptly studied practices in the Gardner Mill at Hastings, the Archibald Mill at Dundas, and other establishments. He met Edmund La Croix in Minneapolis and learned about the crude purifier on which the La Croix brothers had worked. He then, in 1871, persuaded La Croix to build a middlings purifier for the B Mill, and in its several stages of development other men, including the head miller George T. Smith, contributed to the perfecting of the machine. It did the job. It "transformed spring wheat from a kind of Cinderella of the trade to heiress of its best tradition." It introduced a "patent" flour that was soon accepted as the best bread-making flour in the world. The purifier separated middlings by rising air currents or blasts which blew out the husks, leaving the middlings which then were reground with the flour. Flour thus made was of high grade, outranking the winter-wheat flour and producing twelve per cent more bread than its rival.

The profits from patent flour rose sharply. A few years later, in 1877, the Washburn B Mill was reported to have realized gains of $650,000 in a single year. Competition soon cut down the initial advantage that Christian's enterprise had won for the B Mill. The purifier could not be kept secret from the trade. George T. Smith transferred as head miller to C. A. Pillsbury and Company, which had been organized in 1874. John Sargent Pillsbury came to Minnesota from New Hampshire in

351

1855 and from backgrounds of hardware, lumber, and land went into milling. But it was his nephew Charles A. Pillsbury who organized the company that completed in 1883 the Pillsbury A Mill, the largest flour mill in the world.

The benefits of the middlings purifier were shared by all the mills in the St. Anthony area. It added two new steps — purification and regrinding of the middlings — to the traditional methods in flour manufacture. The "New Process," thus introduced, granulated rather than ground the wheat, and it thereby eliminated the crushing of the oily germ. It retained as much of the middlings as possible, and the millstones were set farther apart and run more slowly than previously.

By 1876 there were twenty mills clustered about the power-producing falls in Minneapolis, and their combined product ran to a million barrels of flour. Then, a frightful explosion and fire on May 2, 1878, seemed to spell disaster to Minneapolis milling. The Washburn A Mill, which had been built after the B Mill, was destroyed and five or six nearby mills collapsed from explosions or caught fire. Eighteen men were killed, and, as a historian of milling writes, "Nearly half the city's milling capacity had been destroyed at a stroke."

The imperious Washburn met disaster by rebuilding at once. He took measures to control the menace of flour dust by installing dust-collecting machines, since it was believed that the explosion had been caused by ignited dust. Washburn was a chieftain who turned calamity into triumph. He set plans into motion while the ruins of his plant were still smoking. In a year he restored capacity. By 1880 production had doubled, and two years later Minneapolis was acclaimed the leading flour-milling center in the United States.

A new technological development of importance came into use in the 1880s. This was the replacement of millstones by rolls, first of porcelain, later of chilled iron or steel. Like the middlings purifier, the roller-mill process was of European origin, primarily Hungarian, but it was adapted to American use. The process marked another advance, for its technique of "gradual reduction" made better flour in increased amounts from the wheat and at lowered costs. As in the case of the purifier, the roller-mill machinery became the common possession of all the mills though it was the enterprise of Cadwallader C. Washburn that turned the European idea into practical American use.

Invention, water power, and location had much to do with the expan-

352

sion of the Minneapolis mills. But other factors were of great importance, one of which was the application of large-scale production to the industry. Up to about 1880 the larger mills reaped no absolute advantage by virtue of their size save in volume of flour. Many smaller mills made relatively higher profits because they were built at spots where they could buy choice grades of wheat at low prices. Their costs of operation were lower. Since they bought wheat in local markets, they were not so quickly exposed to price fluctuations as were the great mills. They could prosper, as long as machinery was simple and cheap.

But the picture changed after 1880. The large mills could more easily find funds to finance investments as milling procedures became elaborate and expensive. They sought out and engaged the ablest managers and superintendents. If crops were poor in a given area, their purchasing range corrected the balance. They could afford, and their leadership encouraged, research and experimentation. They also had access to wider markets and embarked on modernized selling methods, employing advertising, salesmen, and bridges of popular education to users of their flour. The smaller firms tended to rely on the aid of commission houses. The large mills also, because of volume, secured more favorable freight rates from railroads.

As marketing reached overseas in the 1880s the big companies found it possible to fill orders promptly with flour of good quality. Alongside large-scale production, concentration of ownership developed. The number of mills did not increase appreciably after 1876; in fact there was a trend toward fewer independent operators. In 1876, twenty mills in Minneapolis were operated by seventeen different firms, whereas by 1890 four corporations controlled 87 per cent of the milling capacity of the city. There was no conscious effort by the millers to establish a monopoly, writes Kuhlmann, but the results represented "the logical working-out of the economic forces of the period."

Largest of the firms was C. A. Pillsbury and Company. The three Pillsbury mills by 1889 had a capacity in excess of 10,000 barrels of flour daily. Second largest was Washburn, Crosby and Company, with the redoubtable Cadwallader Washburn in the background, but with such resourceful men as George H. Christian in earlier years and then John Crosby and William H. Dunwoody as the active managers of mills and their products. These were leaders of unusual talents. Crosby, who came from Maine in 1877 to join the firm as a partner, was superbly efficient as a home manager. Dunwoody, a Philadelphian trained in milling, guided the growth of the company's export trade from almost nothing in 1877 to 100,000 barrels in 1878 — and 4,000,000 by 1895. The versatile William D. Washburn had been a partner, but was perhaps more actively interested in politics than in the business. He was dropped as a partner but in 1878 founded the Washburn Mill Company, and by the end of the next decade had two mills capable of producing 2800 barrels daily.

Increases in flour production, plus competition among companies, contributed to a decline in prices and profits in the 1880s. At the end of the decade a British syndicate purchased the Pillsbury mills and also those of William D. Washburn. A new firm, "Pillsbury-Washburn Flour Mills Company Ltd.," was organized in London in 1889. The British, with large funds to invest, were eager to buy the Minneapolis mills, partly because their products were invading the British market, partly because of the high reputation of Minneapolis flour for quality. They failed to get control of the Washburn-Crosby concern.

As movements toward combination matured, independents strengthened themselves for competition with their powerful rivals. Thus six mills combined in 1891 to form the Northwestern Consolidated Milling Company under the leadership of A. C. Loring, manager of the Galaxy Mill; two years earlier three other mills had formed the Minneapolis Flour Manufacturing Company.

Much of the leadership of Minneapolis milling came from New England and other sections of the East, but the Minneapolis industry was not an extension of established firms in the East. The eastern millers had heavy investments in their own plants, power, and machinery, and they faced grave difficulties in transferring their interests to the West. The Minneapolis mills, for the most part, were owned and controlled by Minneapolis men. An exception was Cadwallader Washburn who, however closely he was linked to business in Minnesota, continued to live in Wisconsin. Even after the purchase of the Pillsbury and W. D. Washburn mills by the British syndicate, much of the stock was owned by Minneapolis men, and the mills were under Minneapolis management. In 1924 an American corporation dominated by Minneapolis men absorbed the Pillsbury-Washburn firm under the name of the Pillsbury Flour Mills Company.

Adequate supplies of wheat were vital to the millers of Minneapolis. As early as 1860 supplies were in part brought in from other states.

Until the late 1870s the millers bought wheat as they needed it, whether from Minnesota or elsewhere. When supplies ran low, as in the spring, they faced competition from wheat buyers in Chicago and Milwaukee as well as from Minnesota rivals. In a move to meet the situation most of the Minneapolis millers formed a buying pool, the Minneapolis Millers' Association, incorporated in 1876 after informal cooperation for some years. The supplies obtained by the pool were distributed in proportion to the relative capacities of the mills. The power of the pool is said to have established "a practical monopoly in most of Minnesota." Farmers and their spokesmen alleged that they, as producers, were not receiving fair prices and that their wheat was being improperly graded. The millers answered that the prices they paid were higher than those offered in Chicago and Milwaukee, and that the operators of elevators, and not the millers, were responsible for the grading. Inevitably the controversy had political repercussions.

In the congressional campaign of 1878 W. D. Washburn defeated Ignatius Donnelly, spokesman for the farmers, but the farmers won their point later when a system of grading and inspection was established by state law in 1885. The millers meanwhile built elevators of their own, with storage capacities that enabled them to buy wheat in large quantities in the fall, at the time farmers were most eager to sell. The storage capacity of the elevators, only about 1,000,000 bushels up to 1879, rose to 12,500,000 bushels in 1887 and more than 27,000,000 in 1899. In 1881 the Minneapolis Chamber of Commerce became active as a grain market that represented commission houses and businessmen. The Millers' Association disbanded and thereafter bought wheat on the floor of the Grain Exchange.

The magnates of the milling business took a great and sustained interest in transportation, which was vital to their industry. After the days of the steamboats, they needed railroads to carry wheat to their bins and transport flour to markets. Railroad connections with Duluth were achieved in 1871, but the ice of Lake Superior blocked lake traffic with the East during the winter months. A route that eluded the thralldom of ice was provided by the Soo Line from Minneapolis to Sault Ste. Marie in 1887, and in the first year of its operation it freighted more than a million barrels of flour on the way to eastern markets. This service was appropriate, for the Soo Line was a millers' railroad, planned and financed by the makers of flour. So also was the Minneapolis and St. Louis, which provided facilities for the shipment of wheat from the farmers of southern Minnesota.

The railroad enterprises of the millers were an economic move toward independence, not merely from winter's icy grip on Great Lakes shipping, but also from the competition of the centers of Milwaukee and Chicago and the railroads serving those cities. The Chicago and Milwaukee line preferred wheat to flour for shipping, and it offered advantageous freight rates to wheat shippers who chose their route. But to the Minneapolis millers, such efforts were a diversion of wheat from their own mills to those of Wisconsin and Illinois — and they rebelled by creating railroads of their own.

The dual domain of wheat and flour flourished from the 1860s to the 1890s and longer. Twenty-four Minneapolis mills by 1890 were producing more than 7,000,000 barrels of flour annually. The farmers of the state in that year harvested more than 50,000,000 bushels of wheat. Production and manufacture went hand in hand. Minneapolis became the world leader in flour milling, and the milling empire developed its interrelations with finance, banking, business, and the general economy.

No review of Minnesota milling can fail to pay tribute to the galaxy of talent that the industry placed in responsible assignments. There were Washburns, Pillsburys, and Crosbys, names that glitter across the generations, and there were many others. One was the expert miller and "greatest merchandiser of his time," James S. Bell. Others included Frederick G. Atkinson, Charles C. Bovey, George Barnum, and Benjamin S. Bull. The tradition of leadership was carried into a later generation that included James Ford Bell, son of the master miller. He was a creative promoter of research, ingenious in applying new ideas not only to milling but more generally to industry and trade.

Leaders of imaginative skills are one side of the story. Their encouragement and interest also contributed in many ways to the social, educational, and cultural richness of the state. But any appraisal of contributions must also recognize the grass-roots folk who, through good years and bad, whether prices were high or low, cultivated the soil and raised the crops that traversed the road from field to factory to consumers. Trade is fundamental, but undergirding it is the job of production. The glamour of flour in national and world markets could not have been achieved if

356

farmers had not done their unglamorous job of sowing, cultivating, reaping, hauling.

And the smaller flour mills must not be forgotten. Some are now only picturesque ruins, but many communities still have excellent flour mills of their own, not a few boasting well-known brands of flour, including Hastings, New Ulm, Mankato, St. Cloud, and Red Wing. In the cities of St. Paul and Duluth there are flour mills with tested traditions. These and other mills have made contributions, small perhaps in proportion to the milling power of Minneapolis, yet qualitatively important in the saga of flour milling.

Flour production went forward to great volume in the twentieth century and by 1915–16 it reached the almost incredible total of 20,443,000 barrels. In the 1920s General Mills emerged as a reorganized outgrowth of the Washburn-Crosby enterprise. The empire of flour reached out to Buffalo, Kansas City, and other centers which in time surpassed the Mill City in production, but the "strategic base" remained at the Falls of St. Anthony.

The catchy slogans of the millers — "Pillsbury's Best" and "Eventually, Why Not Now?"—rolled across the country and became household words. And the serrated towers of mills and elevators that cluster about the falls Hennepin discovered in 1680 are a creative monument to farmers and millers who fashioned in their day the dual domain of wheat and flour.

The Missabe Mountain open pit mine

Red Earth, Iron Men, and Taconite

FEW chapters in the history of Minnesota offer dramas comparable with that of iron ore. It is one of dusty red earth, iron men, titans of finance, workers from the four corners of the earth, and laboratories where ideas were formulated and tried out. The state's iron ore and the industry to which it gave birth have such gigantic dimensions that it is surprising they have not spawned legends dwarfing even those of Paul Bunyan.

The Indians had their indigenous tales of a hero. He hunted wild animals with granite boulders torn by his hands from the ground. After many years, he went to sleep in the "contours of the earth." This giant of the North bore the name "Mesabi." The mining and transportation of the rich ore of the iron ranges, and the development of "beneficiation" processes for lower grade ores and of taconite concentrates, form the epic of his awakening in modern times — his rising from the hills where, through long generations, he had slept.

It is no easy task, and a futile one, to set bounds to this mineral drama. It has many scenes and a host of characters. Its action reaches out to nation and world, and it is not lacking in cosmic romance. The iron deposits go back into the recesses of geologic time. Minnesota, molded by the alchemy of ages, prehistoric oceans, and slow-working chemical changes, is heir to three great iron ranges — the Vermilion, Mesabi, and Cuyuna. Through long years after white men arrived on the western

359

scene, tantalizing rumors of mineral riches in the north country cropped up. The Industrial Revolution created an imperative demand for iron and steel, and the Bessemer and open-hearth processes for transforming pig iron into steel heralded a new era. Discovery and development came in the wake of invention and the need for raw materials. Iron men play their parts in the drama. They walk onto the stage and make their exits. Then giants in the financial earth advance to the center, and big business assumes control. Railroads, aided by receiving docks and cavernous ore-carrying vessels, help to carry the mineral fruits of the earth to eastern manufacturing centers where coal is abundant. Steel made from the iron is a major factor in a booming age of invention and construction. It contributes to America's power in war and in peace. Workers from many nations stream to the iron mines; "range cities" are founded and grow; taxation strengthens the economy of the state. When the years of the rich ores seem numbered, laboratory research opens the way to the profitable use of nearly illimitable supplies of taconite. These are some of the elements that enliven the iron drama — human, industrial, and scientific — as the submerged giant "Mesabi" shakes himself loose from the hills in the hinterland of Lake Superior.

Poets have said that necessity is the mother of invention and of the useful arts, but perhaps it also is the mother of discovery. Historians cannot help wondering why the use of Minnesota iron did not begin at an earlier time, for evidence indicates an awareness, long before mines were opened, of the mineral potentialities of the region beyond Lake Superior. Explorers in the eighteenth century were primarily interested in furs and the way west, but were not indifferent to minerals. La Vérendrye at Fort St. Charles in 1734 specifically queried visiting Indians about iron; they said they were familiar with it. But the iron they talked about seemed to be from regions lying west and northwest of Lake of the Woods. In 1807 John McLoughlin, at a trading post on Lake Vermilion, wrote, "The only mineral I have seen in the Country is Iron which though very common I never saw in any large quantity." The Chippewa treaty of 1826, negotiated at Fond du Lac, specified for Americans the right to search for and take minerals in the Chippewa domain. In the late 1840s the United States geologist David Dale Owen made extensive surveys in the north Minnesota country, and his report, published in 1852, has several references to iron ore, including mention of "thin

360

layers" discovered by Dr. J. G. Norwood, one of his associates, in a rocky ridge near Flint Lake (Gunflint Lake), at the eastern edge of the Mesabi Range.

Governor Ramsey took an active interest in the mineral region and his first message to the territorial legislature, in 1849, asked for a road to Lake Superior primarily to afford access to the assumed mineral riches. The Chippewa land cession of 1854 is commonly referred to as a "miners' treaty," though it seems probable that men were thinking of the possibility of copper deposits and gold, rather than of iron. But in 1860 Ramsey, by that time governor of the state, urged the development of close relations between the Superior country and other parts of the state and spoke of mineral lands of "magnificent extent." He referred to copper and iron ores "known to be of singular purity." Governor Swift in 1864 declared that the northeastern counties abounded in "precious ores," and that year two survey commissioners for the state reported that they had observed beds of iron in the region. And in 1865 Governor Miller dispatched Henry H. Eames on further exploration. He evidently was looking for minerals of greater market value than iron, but near Vermilion Lake, on ridges close by the mouth of a stream called "Two Rivers," he found iron ore "fifty to sixty feet in thickness." This was discovery, and yet nearly two decades were to go by before any iron ore was taken out to a lake port for shipment.

The so-called Vermilion Lake Gold Rush of 1865 and 1866 is a minor episode. It was touched off by a report of highly promising assays of samples of quartz said to have been taken from veins in slates near the northeastern lake. Reporters rushed to the area; companies were organized, including the Minnesota Gold Mining Company with Sibley as president and Governor Stephen Miller as secretary; and an expedition of some thirty-five men made their way to the "gold mines" in mid-winter. One reporter wrote that he saw a great deposit of iron ore and heard tales of rich gold veins. By May of 1866 some three hundred people were at the lake; mining operations were under way; and a little town was started. But the gold of the samples was not matched by finds in the field; and a decade and a half later a scientist made a re-examination of the region and flatly asserted that he could find no trace of gold.

The episode is puzzling, for no evidence seems to be available on the crucial question of where the quartz specimens came from that were assayed as having rich gold content. One wonders if the gold rush was a hoax, and if so, to what purpose? People were not blind to iron. It was glimpsed in the Vermilion area, and samples were carried away. Pieces of Minnesota hematite (a red, nonmagnetic ore) were exhibited at the Paris exposition in 1867, and in that year the Smithsonian Institution of Washington sent out at least a hundred boxes of cabinet specimens of hematite from Vermilion Lake to institutions such as academies.

The railroad promoter Jay Cooke was interested in mineral lands; and in 1869 Ramsey, who had consistently stressed the importance of mineral resources in the northeast, attempted to secure a federal land grant for a railroad connecting Lake Superior and Vermilion Lake. Donnelly, W. L. Banning, Jay Cooke, and others joined in efforts to get a bill passed, but it was not brought to a vote. Men did not doubt that iron awaited miners in the Vermilion area. In 1870 Banning urged Donnelly to work for an amendment to the railroad bill and added that, if it succeeded, "we can secure the iron formation in direction of Vermilion." These early plans soon collided with the Panic of 1873, and Dr. Nute writes that "the Mesabi Range was almost forgotten." Not entirely, however, as she makes clear, for an experienced explorer, Peter Mitchell, was engaged to search for ore-bearing lands. He had his base at Beaver Bay in the 1870s and tramped over the eastern Mesabi, spotting promising ore country in the vicinity of Birch Lake. A syndicate formed the Mesaba Iron Company, which was incorporated in 1882, with Alexander Ramsey as its president; and the company acquired nearly ten thousand acres of land, taking advantage of Mitchell's finds. Earlier — only a year after the Panic of 1873 — the Duluth and Iron Range Railroad had been chartered; and the next year the Minnesota legislature voted a grant to this road of ten sections of swampland for every mile of road built.

As evidence of iron ore in abundance mounted, plans took new form. A key figure in the transition was Massachusetts-born George C. Stone of Duluth, an enthusiastic promoter, who in 1875 informed two Pennsylvania millionaires, Charlemagne Tower and Samuel Munson, about the riches of ore in Minnesota and sought their financial support. They were interested, but as men of business they wanted confirmatory evidence and so they sent out an exploring party headed by a professor of chemistry who was also a mineralogist, Albert H. Chester of Hamilton College. It was his report that directed financial attention to the Vermilion Range rather than the Mesabi and that explains in part why the rich Mesabi was passed over in the earliest Minnesota mining of iron ore. Chester was guided by the knowledgeable George R. Stuntz of Duluth, who had pioneered in the Duluth area before that city was born, had observed iron ore at Vermilion as early as 1865, and knew portions of the Mesabi Range. The college professor looked at the lean eastern end of the Mesabi but not at the heart of that range (as yet undiscovered). He concluded that the big opportunity was the Vermilion Range, in the Archean formations. A second exploratory trip in 1880 renewed his faith in the great value of that range. Early conceptions of the Mesabi Range embraced only the region east of Mesaba, where the bands of magnetic rock were not considered wide enough to justify exploitation.

Newton H. Winchell, state geologist and professor of mineralogy and geology in the University of Minnesota, visited the iron country (in 1878), confirmed the validity of claims of great iron deposits at the Vermilion, and made the startling suggestion that the University of Minnesota should undertake the opening of iron mines. The time would come when university research would pioneer taconite, but the regents did not accept the scientist's idea that the institution should become "directly instrumental" in disturbing the sleeping giant of the ranges. It remained for private industry to take up the challenge, and it did so with forthright action. First, Tower got assurance that taxes would not frustrate his plans. Stone served as his agent in inducing the legislature in 1881 (Stone was a member) to pass a law establishing a tax of only a penny per ton of iron ore, half of the tax to go to the county, half to the state. The tax, obviously intended to guarantee virtual exemption from taxation at the outset, was a boon not only to Tower but also to the Mesaba and other iron-mining companies (and incidentally to copper companies). The measure was headed an "Act to encourage mining in this state."

Thus the way was opened for the organization of the Minnesota Iron Company, incorporated in 1882 by Tower, Stone, Stuntz, and others; and for the acquisition by this company of the rights granted the earlier Duluth and Iron Range Railroad which had built no tracks and therefore had not taken over the swamplands. Tower bought thousands of acres of land, and the town of Tower was established. The methods employed by Tower and indeed by all the iron-ore men — as by the lumbermen — were those countenanced by the practices of the time. It is true that as early as 1872 the United States had removed mineral lands from the class of public lands open to pre-emption and homesteading, but the law was amended in a later session of Congress with respect to the iron, copper, and coal lands in the Lake Superior country. Thus iron-ore lands were open to acquisition by any of the recognized procedures that applied to timber lands and were fundamentally based on the philosophy of public lands for settlers. Tower and his agents, notably Stone, went into a most vigorous campaign for the acquisition of the lands they wanted. Tower's "ethical principles and practical methods," writes the historian Allan Nevins, "were in part those of a very rough-and-tumble competitive era" — a statement that in general can be applied to virtually all the men who entered into the scramble for iron lands.

A governmental investigation in 1882 revealed widespread entries for pre-emption and homestead without visible occupation of the lands claimed. Much land was bought with scrip, but not a little seems to have been acquired in dealings with dummy entrymen under pre-emption and homestead. A local Duluth historian reports that Tower put up some $40,000 in cash for 17,000 acres. Actually by 1882 Tower had ownership of more than 20,000 acres, according to the author of *Iron Millionaire*, a biography of Tower, and the total enterprise had cost him something over a quarter million dollars. The lands were transferred to the Minnesota Iron Company.

The Soudan mine at Tower got under way and a mining boom was started. Miners came from Michigan, Cornishmen and Swedes predominating, to take work. The railroad, essential to the industry, was built from Tower to Two Harbors and the first ore was loaded and shipped to the lake port in 1884. On August 1, 1884, Tower's son sent this wire of high elation to his seventy-five-year-old father: "First ore train ten cars two hundred and twenty tons brought . . . to Two Harbors July thirty-first put into ore dock pockets Aug. first all in good order." Before the end of that year a total of 62,124 tons had been sent down, and the next year the tonnage rose to 225,000. By 1887 the volume was nearly at 400,000. Meanwhile, in 1886, ores had been discovered at Ely; the railroad reached that town in 1888; and the fabulous Chandler Mine produced in 1889 more than 300,000 tons of ore. Yet other mines were opened at Ely. And there was a proliferation of iron-mining companies. Indeed, the pace was so swift that Minnesota by 1890 had incorporated no fewer than 284 such companies.

364

These steps were impressive, but they were only a little advance toward the freeing of the entombed iron giant. Despite the flooding of money into land and companies, men had not yet learned that much of the body of the giant was lying on the surface or just beneath the surface in the Mesabi country — ore to the extent of hundreds of millions of tons. The red earth awaited exploitation by the fashioning of "terraced amphitheaters." But people thought of iron mines in the traditional sense of underground treasures — near-vertical deposits to be worked by means of burrowed shafts, not as pits scooped out by steam shovels. Iron on the surface seemed to be one of "nature's jokes," as Grace Lee Nute has suggested. If so, its humor, like its reality, long evaded serious attention.

The Mesabi had been grazed by iron hunters, but few realized that its range was a hundred miles or that at the heart of its forested lands and swamps were iron treasures open for the taking. Too open, in fact. Those who passed by failed to identify them for what they were. One expert, after the discoveries had been made, said ruefully, "I have kicked myself ever since that I did not put my hand in that ore, and then I would have known it was ore." Bred in the mining tradition, men could not easily shake loose an *idée fixe* — namely that the only sure clue to discovery was hard ore. The soft, powdery, earthy material to which the expert prospector did not put his hand was something the like of which had never been seen before. It was new; it was unprecedented. If the expert did not identify it, neither did steel plant operators appreciate its utility when it came to their attention. New finds, like new ideas, are often tardy of recognition and acceptance.

Discovery was bound to come with time. That it came when it did is the achievement of the Merritt brothers, the "Seven Iron Men." Their discovery was not one of pure chance, though superficially it may lend itself to such an interpretation. The Merritts, sons of Lewis H. Merritt, a Duluth pioneer of 1865, and led by Leonidas, chief of a clan of seven brothers, hunted for years in the Mesabi lands, combining timber cruising with their search for iron. Their father had impressed on them his conviction that there was iron in the Mesabi, and through nearly two decades they looked for it — not only the brothers but also three relatives. Others searched also, including James B. Geggie, David T. Adams, Frank Hibbing, and the Longyears, and their finds and observations strengthened the belief of many that somewhere in the Mesabi area exciting discoveries would be made.

The Merritts — especially Leonidas, tough, self-confident, enthusiastic, half poet, half prospector — were indefatigable, and the dramatic climax of their search came in 1890. Leonidas and a brother had returned to Duluth from the Mesabi, where in the Mountain Iron region they had already spent much money in drilling but had had little success. They were eager to recruit funds with which to push ahead with their search. Then on November 16, 1890, at the site of what came to be known as the Mountain Iron Mine — a few miles west of Virginia — the wheels of a heavy wagon cut down in the soil to a red, powdery substance. Captain J. A. Nichols, head of a test-pit crew, gathered up and brought into Duluth a fifty-pound pack of this red earth. On assay, it proved to be 64 per cent iron, soft hematite. A stirring account of this "turning point" in the long hunt is told in an unpublished narrative by two members of the Merritt family. The manuscript relates how Captain Nichols, his "words tumbling over each other," reported on "the day of dreams come true. . . . To all of us, it was a day of days, but to Lon, the natural leader of the Necondis, as he loved to call our Merritt clan, to Lon, whose goodly fortune had been all spent in this determined and hectic search for iron, to Lon, whose vision had by turn swept and driven us all along toward this hour, what must it have meant in the secret places of his generous heart!"

The Merritts had made a memorable beginning. The year after their discovery further finds widened the development. An uprooted tree exposed red earth. The place was some ten miles to the east of Virginia — the Biwabik Mine. Soon rich ores were found in the region to the south and west, where the thriving cities of Eveleth and Hibbing were to spring up. Leonidas and his clan tried at once to turn discovery into production. They understood that the mining technique fitting the circumstances was to strip away whatever covering of clay and gravel they found above the iron ore and then lift the metal, load it, and send it off to a Lake Superior port. Loading meant cars, a railroad, docks — the big job of transporting ore to Superior or Duluth for shipment to eastern mills. The discoveries posed the triple and intricate problems of railroads and docks, finances running into the millions, and the marketing of the mineral products that their enterprise had revealed for meeting the country's needs of iron and steel.

The control of Mesabi quickly slipped away from the Merritts, but they played an important role not only as discoverers but also in taking steps toward the organization of the industry. Paramount needs were mining equipment and labor, railroad tracks and cars. These they tackled without delay. They organized a railroad of their own in 1891 — the Duluth, Missabe, and Northern; but knowing that time and money would be required to complete such a road, they first built tracks to make a junction, some forty-five miles away, with the Duluth and Winnipeg Railroad. Notwithstanding its name, this road ran to the ore docks at Superior, Wisconsin. As early as 1892, on October 17, the first shipment from the Mountain Iron Mine was sent down — a load of 4245 tons. The next year a branch was run from the Duluth and Iron Range Railroad to Biwabik, and the tonnage jumped to more than 600,000. In 1893 eleven mines were active on the range. By 1896 there were twenty mines and their product came close to 3,000,000 tons; and in 1901, only a decade after the mining had begun, thirty mines on the Mesabi sent out more than 9,000,000 tons of ore.

Long before the first decade of Mesabi mining was completed, the Merritts had to relinquish their ownership of the business they so earnestly and even desperately tried to put on its feet. They set about the job of financing a railroad and ore docks and developing the mines without large capital and in the face of a severe panic that struck the country only three years after their discovery of the red earth. The Merritts expanded their holdings in 1890, obtaining as many as 141 leases, most of them on state lands under a law that authorized such transactions (in lots of 160 acres and with the proviso of a royalty of twenty-five cents to the state for each ton of ore mined). The Mountain Iron Company was capitalized at $2,000,000 and the Duluth, Missabe, and Northern had an authorized capital of $5,000,000. But these were funds on paper. The Merritts had difficulty in marketing their bonds and stocks, and their troubles deepened as they extended their operations and piled up debts in a time when the country was feeling the stringencies that reached a climax in 1893. They owned holdings of stock in a half dozen mining companies; to build their railroad they had issued $2,400,000 in stocks and bonds, though the line by 1893 had cost only $660,000. Late in 1892 they had debts of not less than $2,000,000, but Leonidas went confidently ahead with plans for railroad building, ore cars, docks, and other enterprises.

A New York promoter named Charles H. Wetmore had noted the loading of Mesabi ore onto a whaleback at Superior, an ore-carrying vessel invented by Alexander McDougall. Wetmore liked the Mesabi prospects and through him contacts were made with one of John D. Rockefeller's chief assistants, Frederick T. Gates, when the Merritts in 1893 were trying to market $1,600,000 of bonds for their railroad and dock-building needs. On the recommendation of Gates, Rockefeller bought one-fourth of these bonds. This set off a train of events that dislodged the Merritts. The panic came, and once more they were in need and turned to the man of millions.

The upshot was the formation in 1893 of the Lake Superior Consolidated Iron Mines Company. This was a holding company under the laws of New Jersey. To it the Merritts surrendered their share in five mining concerns plus their railroad and ore docks, while Rockefeller put in his holdings in a half dozen mining and iron companies, advanced a half million dollars for the railroad, and promised to buy all the iron shipped that year from Mountain Iron. Rockefeller took first mortgage bonds in the new company; the Merritts took stock and continued the Mesabi mining operations. They issued further amounts of stock, but the times were bad, investors held back, and the shares sold at a discount. In 1894, now desperate, the Merritts offered to sell 90,000 shares of their stock to Rockefeller at $10 a share. He accepted the offer, but gave them an option to buy back 55,000 shares within a year. One of the brothers requested renewals of the option. They were granted, and when the United States Steel Corporation was formed, he realized several million dollars.

The others, convinced that they had been ill treated, fought a legal battle which they lost. They did not continue their options, made a settlement, and withdrew certain charges they had made against Rockefeller. At the end, the Merritts lost control of the properties and were replaced by the American oil magnate. Success in the iron industry obviously hinged on large capital which could be drawn on to tide over crises and periods of lean or no income. The "shoestring operators went to the wall," among them the Merritts.

Many people know about the Merritts through Paul de Kruif's highly popular (but not wholly dependable) book *Seven Iron Men*, published in 1929. The author wrote with dramatic vividness; he felt free to present alleged day-by-day remarks, comments, and conversations by the principals. He appreciated the initiative and courage of the Merritts. He wove moving episodes into the epic and traced its gamut from early hope and success to failure. His book reflects the stamina and faith of the iron men, but it also reveals their inability to master problems piled up by panic, financial stringency, the magnitude of their enterprise, and the juggernaut of big business in its gala age. Though defeated, the Merritts — particularly Leonidas — occupy a significant place in American history as timber cruisers turned iron hunters. They spent themselves in their efforts to move the red earth to the iron and steel centers of the United States.

In the 1890s Minnesota iron mining went into high gear. Rockefeller bought company after company with ore lands and ore leases; and in 1895, when the Merritt option expired, he was the master of the Lake Superior Consolidated Iron Mines. As his holdings increased, the value of the stock rose, and his dominance was watched with concern by the manufacturers of steel, who feared that he would invade their domain after capturing immense sources of ore. But he entertained no such purpose. His interest was in ores and their transportation by rail and boat to the steel-making centers. Having entered the field, he put millions into organizing and expanding his iron empire. Meanwhile another industrialist appeared on the mining scene, a powerful figure who had won a fortune in farm machinery. This was Henry W. Oliver of Pittsburgh, and with his advent in 1892 a chain of circumstances brought Andrew Carnegie, the steel king, into the picture.

Oliver attended the Republican national convention in Minneapolis in 1892, but seemed more interested in talk about Mesabi than in presidential politics. He went to Duluth, visited Mountain Iron, met the Merritts, bought leases, and returned to Pennsylvania a convert to the Mesabi faith. Faith, for Oliver, was translated into works. A man of decision and vigor, once a messenger boy, later a soldier who fought at Gettysburg, he had risen to success as an ironmaster by his own abilities. He was a real-life counterpart to Horatio Alger. He soon became one of the most powerful and influential men in Minnesota mining. He organized the Oliver Iron Mining Company and secured agreement with the daring Henry Frick for the Carnegie Company to take half of the $1,000,000 stock in the new company and to advance a half million dollars as a mortgage loan. Carnegie, the dour laird, was pessimistic about this plunge, but he did not say no to Frick.

Oliver introduced giant steam shovels in the mining operations and these instruments in part accounted for prodigious increases in Mesabi production. Edmund J. Longyear — one of the most skilled and industrious explorers of the Mesabi Range, the man who used the first diamond drill there and for two decades did an amazing amount of test-pitting throughout the range — saw a pioneer steam shovel at work at Biwabik and wrote, with characteristic understatement, that it was "making quite a hole."

It was Oliver who evolved a plan set in motion in 1896 which marked a new step toward consolidation and cooperative arrangements in Minnesota iron-mining. It also gave evidence that Rockefeller had no intention of entering upon steel manufacture in competition with Carnegie and other leaders in the industry. An agreement was made under which the Carnegie and Oliver interests leased the Rockefeller mines — or most of them — for fifty years at twenty-five cents per ton for ore taken out. All the ores would be shipped on Rockefeller's railroad and on his ships and barges. "For the time being," as Nevins writes, "Carnegie kept out of transportation, and Rockefeller out of steel manufacture." Highly important in the picture was lake transportation of the ore. Alexander McDougall built no fewer than forty-six whalebacks in the ten years after 1888. But the Rockefeller organization in the 1890s constructed a fleet of steel ships and barges, starting with a dozen. By 1901, under aegis of the Bessemer Steamship Company, it had close to sixty ships. Earlier, when there were only twenty-eight, the fleet as a whole could convey well over 300,000 tons of ore in a single voyage. Lake transportation, like mining, was a tremendous business.

Iron mining offers some contrasts with the flour-milling industry. The flour manufacturers, with a few exceptions, were or became Minnesota men, but most of the giants of the mineral earth were industrialists and capitalists in the East. Notable examples were Tower, Munson, Rockefeller, and Carnegie. One exception was James J. Hill. He was a railroad builder, and it was interest in railroads that drew him toward the iron country. First, the Great Northern purchased the old Duluth and Winnipeg Railroad in 1897, when that road was dangling in receivership. Then Hill, out of his own pocket to the tune of $4,050,000, bought in 1899 a small lumbermen's railroad called the Duluth, Mississippi, and Northern, which ran past the Mahoning mine — with some 25,000 acres of land in the Mesabi region. This ore land was his own, but he chose to allocate it to the Great Northern stockholders. He then formed the Lake Superior Company, which bought additional land, handling its ownership (because of state restrictive laws) through subsidiary companies. In

1906, the land was placed under a concern called the Great Northern Iron Ore Properties, with sharing certificates issued to the stockholders in the Great Northern. Hill's sons, Louis W. and James N. and Walter, were active in these iron transactions. In less than twenty years the owners of Great Northern stock benefited to the extent of more than $50,000,000 in earnings based upon their certificates. Hill and his associates became owners of ore lands which he himself in 1907 thought were worth at least $600,000,000.

About the same time that Hill interested himself in the north country, two other figures in American finance came into the iron-ore picture through the medium of the Illinois (or Federal) Steel Company, a holding company headed by Elbert H. Gary and backed by the titan of American magnates of finance, J. Pierpont Morgan. This company, organized in 1898, absorbed the Duluth and Iron Range Railroad and the Minnesota Iron Company, and it had a large fleet of ore ships.

The industrial temper of the time favored mergers and consolidations, and to the master minds of iron and steel the time was ripe in 1901 for a new move. Behind it loomed the gigantic figure of J. Pierpont Morgan. Some lesser companies were still active in the ore regions, but the great holdings were concentrated in the Lake Superior Consolidated under Rockefeller's control; the Oliver Mining Company, the major part of it owned by Carnegie; the Federal Steel Company; and the Great Northern Railroad. The question was whether or not these and other related corporations could be brought together in a vast strategic concern. It was the imperial Morgan and his associates who achieved this colossus, though, for good reasons, it did not include Hill's empire. The first step had been taken through the Federal Steel Company. Three years later, in 1901, Carnegie's properties were purchased for a sum in excess of $500,000,000. All-important were the vast Mesabi holdings and ore carriers of Rockefeller, and these were next acquired — $80,000,000 for the Missabi mines and $8,500,000 for the fleet of the Bessemer concern. Thus the United States Steel Corporation came into being — an industrial cosmos of steel plants, mines, coal lands, blast furnaces, railroads, ore vessels, and yet other properties with an authorized capital of $1,404,000,000. For administrative and operative purposes the Oliver Mining Corporation was created to handle some of the major enterprises. Carnegie and Rockefeller bowed out of iron and steel as major participants but they were among the owners of extensive stocks in the giant corporation.

The steel corporation had nearly everything, but there was still the property controlled by the Hills, untouched by the merger. The Hills, father and sons, were railroad people, not miners. James J. Hill had no more intention of turning miner than Rockefeller had of becoming a steel manufacturer. Nevertheless the Hill interests had thousands of acres of land in the Mesabi area — more than 39,000 by 1907 — and the steel corporation was concerned about the future. How long would the rich deposits under its control last? What reserves were there? What hazard was there of competitors buying ore lands that would be vital to United States Steel? The answer was an agreement in 1907 with the Great Northern Ore Properties, and in it Hill drove a bargain. The corporation agreed to explore the Hill lands, ship ores from it in annually increasing amounts until a minimum of more than 8,000,000 tons a year was reached, pay eighty-five cents royalty per ton, and have the ore transported on the Great Northern line to Superior at eighty cents per ton. The royalty was to be increased annually until it reached $1.12 — far more than twice the customary royalty of the time. Hill's terms were described as an "inexorable demand," but they were accepted and in operation until 1914, when, under specified terms, the corporation withdrew from the lease. While it ran, the company removed more than 26,000,000 tons of ore and paid in more than $45,000,000. Thereafter the trustees of the Ore Properties marketed their products and leased ore on royalty bases, with continuing profits.

The Cuyuna Range, in Crow Wing County, southwest of the discoveries of earlier years, is a bed of ore differing from those of the Vermilion and Mesabi ranges because of its manganese content. The area is one of glacial and drift deposits, and the iron ore was not surface-exposed (though excavations ultimately made possible open-pit mining). Several persons in the 1870s and 1880s suspected iron, including one Henry Pajari who did test-pitting, and a Swedish settler who took note of the erratic behavior of a dip compass. In the 1890s a surveyor with a magnetic needle, Cuyler Adams, explored the area — the iron lay in a region extending from a spot in Morrison County to the vicinity of Aitkin. Adams concluded that down underneath the surface there was iron; he explored, drilled, and acquired lands; and in 1911 the Kennedy Mine, near the villages of Ironton and Crosby, was opened. He was right. There was iron, and in a half dozen years twenty-one mines were opened (by 1918, thirty-two).

In World War I American imports of manganese were cut down, and the Cuyuna ore was of strategic value to the country. More than nine-tenths of the nation's manganese, in fact, came from these Minnesota mines. Cuyuna was the third major iron-ore area in Minnesota. Its richness and grandeur did not compare with Mesabi, yet it was a major iron-ore range of the north country. Some people assume that its name is one of far antecedents, but the simple and endearing explanation is that "Cuyuna" is the first syllable of Cuyler's own name combined with the name of his dog Una.

From the 1880s to the early 1900s, the great Minnesota iron ranges had thus been discovered and opened, the three varying in character but all of them important in their uses. Mesabi was of course the undisputed giant of the trio in richness, extent, and productivity.

A late and surprising arrival in the iron saga, outside the area of the three ranges, is a series of ore deposits on farm lands in southern Minnesota. Near Spring Valley in Fillmore County, pits of iron ore have been found in sandy soil and under clay covering. As at Cuyuna, the presence of iron had been suspected long ago, but mining was not begun until the period of World War II. After a lull, operations were resumed in 1947 and have continued, with an astonishing total production to 1960 of 4,795,000 tons. The surface is stripped and the ore shoveled out from open pits, usually in pockets containing from 10,000 to 50,000 tons. The ore, containing from 37 per cent to about 48 per cent iron, is processed into concentrates; the yawning holes are refilled with earth; and the lucky farmers, with a leasing bonus of twenty-five cents per ton, can then replant their land with corn or other products.

A discerning writer, L. A. Rossman, has suggested that the story of minerals discloses a general pattern: first, discovery; then "the depletion of those minerals which are cheapest to mine and highest in value"; thereafter, "exhaustion and abandonment." Communities "founded in high hope often end in deep despair," but meanwhile people search for what is "rich and cheap." If that search is unavailing and the best minerals are gone, "men turn to that which has been poorer and with science and invention attack remaining metals, build plants, re-create communities, expand employment and rebuild an industry whose resources may have unlimited life." In some measure the Minnesota iron-ore industry conforms to this picture, but there was one notable exception. This was that the industry did not wait for depletion of the best ores before trying to solve the problem of profitable mining of the leaner ores. Their effort constitutes a tribute to the wisdom of the leaders of the industry, and it is a significant phase of the iron saga.

The rich Mesabi mines, it is true, were exploited in amounts of ore that stagger the imagination. The first decade of Minnesota iron mining produced more than 43,000,000 tons, a prodigious amount at the time; but the second decade (1901–10) witnessed a total of close to five times that amount – 208,600,000 tons. In the first half of the 1930s nearly two-thirds of all the iron taken from the earth in the United States came from this one state; and in one year during World War I, Minnesota sent out more than 46,000,000 tons. Inevitably World War II placed extraordinary demands on the mines for ores and in the first half of the 1940s they poured out more than 338,000,000 tons. In one year alone, 1942, shipments of Mesabi ore exceeded 70,000,000 tons. In the decade 1941–50, the volume of Minnesota-produced iron ore reached an amazing 643,500,000 tons. The 1950s had their ups and downs in production, but they saw some of the largest crops of iron in the history of the industry – 79,000,000 tons of ore in the year after the Korean war began (1951), 81,000,000 in 1953, and 70,000,000 in 1955. But the picture soon changed – a drop to about 49,000,000 tons in 1954, then some higher years, and then in 1958 and 1959 (even with the enlarging taconite production included) respectively 42,000,000 and 36,000,000 tons (a recession and a disastrous steel strike contributing to the decline). In 1960 there was again a rise (to 55,000,000 tons).

Looking at the full record, one finds that the total bulk of ore mined, up to and including 1960, goes to the fantastic figure of 2,484,854,372 tons! The repose of the iron giant had been disturbed, but with taconite in its early stage of development, the full emergence of "Mesabi" is still in the future. Such colossal totals are the more impressive when it is remembered that an overwhelming part of the mined ore came from the Mesabi mines – in no year did the total ores drawn from the Vermilion and Cuyuna ranges go beyond 5,000,000 tons.

As one contemplates such figures, the popular picture that comes to mind with reference to Mesabi is that of open-pit mines with ore of high content and of tremendous shovels loading the mineral onto trains to be carried off to docks and vessels. The actualities are not quite so simple, however. There was of course much such loading of "direct shipping ore" from open-pit mines, with steam shovels and steam-hauled trains of ore cars. In time diesel engines were used for the trains and revolving electric shovels replaced the earlier steam shovels. Both trucks and belt conveyors began to be used in the 1930s to move the ore — the trucks in pits too small for the operations of trains. One is not surprised that the industry made use of new and improved kinds of machines both for excavating and for moving tiie ore. The fact is, however, that "beneficiation" of the leaner ores has been carried on for more than a half a century. "Concentrates" from low-grade ores have been producing close to half the total tonnage of iron ore in recent years. Beneficiation means removal of silica from the ore by washing or other methods, and a great plant for this purpose (the Trout Lake Concentrator) was built by the Oliver Mining Company in the period 1907–10 (with the city of Coleraine developed at one end of the lake). Sizable shipments of ore concentrates were made as early as 1910; and the development of workable methods of beneficiation meant the mining of much iron-ore land in the western Mesabi. In 1957 concentrates accounted for about 31,000,000 tons of the total Minnesota ore production of 68,296,000 tons. About eighty beneficiation plants were then operating in the iron-range country.

The importance of this engineering achievement lies not only in totals but also in the circumstance that the production has, to the extent of its tonnage, prolonged the life of the richest open-pit ores, of which it was estimated in 1958 that only 456,000,000 tons remained. In the late 1950s the Oliver Iron Mining division of United States Steel, as a matter of fact, ceased to do direct shipping of ore from its Mesabi holdings. With the inauguration of new screening plants, all the ore now is processed, not only to eliminate silica but also to crush the ore into small pieces, screen it according to size, and modify its structure with various kinds of machines to meet the more precise demands of the blast furnaces. The newer processes make possible sintering (or melting or clinkering lumps of suitable size) before the ore goes to the furnaces; and the revolution in technical procedures is aiding the industry to meet the competition of rich ores from Canada and elsewhere.

United States imports of iron ore have increased greatly in recent years. As late as 1946 only a few million tons were imported, whereas in 1960 the total was nearly 35,000,000 and constituted close to a third of the total consumption of iron ore in this country. The chief sources were Venezuela and Canada, with lesser amounts coming from Chile, Peru, and Brazil. In a word, Minnesota no longers enjoys a monopoly of the ore supply for the steel mills. Competition is in a world commodity market, and the life of the iron industry in Minnesota is contingent on high success in handling low-grade ores.

An important consequence of the early interest in beneficiation was the establishment in 1911 of the Mines Experiment Station of the University of Minnesota for testing, demonstration, and training purposes. With state-appropriated funds, its facilities and research gave special attention to low-grade ores, working in cooperation with the operators of mines and manufacturers of mining equipment, also with the federal Bureau of Mines and the state itself, and helping to solve complex and difficult problems involved in the processes of beneficiation.

The men of iron were not all discoverers, organizers, magnates of steel and finance and railroads, and owners of underground treasures. There were surveyors who mapped the range lands; testers who drilled thousands of pits; engineers, railroad builders, and inventors of machinery. There were manufacturers and builders of docks and ships, and there were contractors who managed actual mining operations. Among the latter may be mentioned the five Butler brothers, sons of an Irish-born engineer (and brothers of Pierce Butler, who became a justice of the United States Supreme Court). The brothers (William, Walter, John, Cooley, and Emmett) gave attention especially to mining operations in the western Mesabi and the Cuyuna ranges, and by 1914 had eighteen mines under contract. They used modern equipment in shoveling and washing and transporting the ores. And in later years, especially under Emmett Butler, they employed a thousand or more men. Contractors, builders, and engineers, they created a Minnesota firm that has left its marks not only on the iron-ore industry but also on vast building operations, including Minnesota's state capitol.

Nor should one forget the crews needed to man trains, ships, trucks, and shovels, and the miners who went underground in the Vermilion area and into the open pits of Mesabi and Cuyuna. As people swarmed into the mining frontier, villages and cities sprang up — Virginia, Eveleth, Hibbing, Chisholm, Ely, Crosby-Ironton, and others. On Lake Superior,

Two Harbors, Duluth, and the Wisconsin city of Superior grew mightily as railroad and harbor towns serving as outlets for the millions of tons of ore brought by train to be loaded onto the fleets of ore-carrying vessels.

Thousands of workmen were brought in to do the mining jobs — trained miners from the Michigan country, including Cornishmen, Swedes, Norwegians, Irish, Finns, French-Canadians, Germans, Poles, Slovenes, Italians, and others. Most of them were of European immigrant strains of the first and second generations. They were vigorous, hard-working folk whose backgrounds gave color to the communities they built. The Cornishmen, known as "Cousinjacks," had backgrounds of experience in Michigan and in the tin mines of Cornwall. Among the Scandinavians, the Swedes predominated (and there also were many Finland Swedes). Most of the Canadians, including those of French ancestry, got to the iron mines via the lumber industry as in fact did people of many other nationalities.

A student of the people of the Mesabi Range points out that members of various nationality groups sent money and letters to people in the old countries and thus attracted their countrymen to emigrate. Many, especially of the Slavic groups, came from eastern and middle western cities, however. As time went on, southeastern Europeans tended to replace the Scandinavians in the mine work, though not a few of the latter stayed on as craftsmen and officials. Slovenes and Croats were numerous, and people from the Ukraine, Romania, Montenegro, and many other European lands arrived to find employment. Half the Mesabi population was foreign-born in 1900, and 20 per cent in 1940; and now immigrants and their children make up more than four-fifths of the total population.

The Minnesota Finns went to the mines, many to the lumber camps, and not a few onto farms, some in western counties. But it is especially as miners that they made their contribution to the state's economy, and Finnish names are common in the range towns. The Finns brought not only muscle and will for the hard jobs they tackled, but also the lore of their ancient fatherland and the politico-economic interest that manifested itself in consumers' cooperatives.

A singular aspect of range-town life was the blossoming of schools, community buildings, parks, splendid streets, and other public improvements built generously, not to say lavishly. They set standards far beyond those of most Minnesota cities at the time. These reflected at once a public desire for the best, a concern on the part of citizens for the education of their children, and the availability of taxes to provide funds without stint for public wants. County and local governments reaped large revenues from the ad valorem taxes — property taxes imposed on a rated assessment of 50 per cent of the "full and true value" of the iron properties held by private owners and companies — the valuation made by the State Department of Taxation and not by local assessors. So large were the revenues of the local iron-mining communities that the state legislature in the 1920s intervened to place per capita limitations on the annual amounts levied for general and school taxes.

The tax policy of Minnesota as expressed in the law of 1881 to encourage mining was later reversed. The early act, which placed a tax of a penny per ton of ore, was declared in 1896 to be unconstitutional and it was repealed a year later. Ad valorem taxes were regularly leveled thereafter. Through ensuing years intermittent efforts were made to alter the iron-ore tax system. These efforts reflected sentiment favoring the "natural heritage" principle with respect to irreplaceable natural resources — the principle that the iron companies should share with the commonwealth a larger portion of their profits, as derived from the Minnesota earth, than they then were paying in taxes. But it was difficult to find an acceptable formula outside the ad valorem taxes, and the "natural heritage" argument was countered by those who stressed the hazards of capital in mining, its contributions to labor and economic enterprise, and the view that the heritage philosophy might with equal logic be applied to granite, forests, agriculture, and manufactures on navigable waters. Tonnage taxes were advocated; valuations were placed on the iron properties to establish bases for ad valorem taxes; and two governors vetoed tonnage and royalty measures in 1909 and 1919.

A constitutional amendment in 1922 authorized an "occupation tax" on the value of iron ore mined or produced — a tax described as a "modified severance tax on income." The next year a royalty tax was added, in effect a tax on rent as royalties paid by operators to land owners. Straight royalties on ores taken from state-owned lands, paid under leases, go into the state's permanent trust funds and are allocated according to the sources of the lands in question, as, for instance, the permanent school fund or the permanent university fund. The permanent trust funds of Minnesota, which are in four categories (school, university, swampland, and internal improvement land) had attained by 1961 a total of more than $306,000,000, and of this some $256,000,000 had been derived from iron ore. Both the occupation and the royalty taxes were begun at a level of 6 per cent, but later additions, including a war bonus and surtaxes, elevated the percentage to 14.25. The moneys have gone to the state, with 50 per cent allocated to the General Revenue Fund; 40 per cent for the permanent trust funds for elementary and secondary public schools; and 10 per cent for the University of Minnesota. A constitutional amendment in 1956 authorized the direct apportionment of the school and university allocations for the current use of these institutions instead of placing them in the trust funds.

The great bulk of revenue derived from the ad valorem taxes has gone to the local governments: cities, villages, or towns; school districts; and counties. Distribution depends upon individual levies in the various subdivisions, within certain limits; figures may vary in different years. The division is approximately 40 per cent to school districts, 33 per cent to counties, 20 per cent to cities, villages, and towns, and 7 per cent to the state. For taconite and semitaconite, state law provides fixed percentages. A tabulation of moneys paid in ad valorem taxes from 1914 to 1959 reveals a grand total of more than $771,000,000. For the same period — including the ad valorem taxes, the occupation tax (from 1921), the royalty tax (from 1923), and the taconite tax (from 1949) — the totals of iron ore taxes paid reached $1,204,854,000.

The iron-ore story has ramifications so wide that they invite, not a chapter, but a series of volumes. These ramifications include the great ore docks at Duluth, Superior, and Two Harbors; and also the enormous locks, American and Canadian, of the Sault Sainte Marie Canal System, developed and improved through many decades and accommodating such heavy traffic that in sheer tonnage the Sault waterways have become the most important in the world. The tale of iron also includes modern ships, now numbering more than two hundred, some of which can carry up to 25,000 tons; ore trains that dump loads of 250 cars or more into a single vessel, with assortments and blendings of the ores handled according to carefully designed plans; the speed with which the loadings of ore (and unloadings of coal) are carried out; the building and development of a great steel mill at Duluth; the many companies engaged in the iron-ore business; the continuing emphasis on beneficiation, with new plants applying the fruits of research and invention; the intensive study by the

379

industry of ways in which to improve the changing business in which it is engaged; and the cooperative application of skills to the entire business.

Robert Libby, a mining official, describing the precision and timing of loading at the mines and of unloading at the docks, sums up by saying, "Geologists, mining engineers, plant foremen, chemists, trainmasters, dispatchers, ore graders and ore dock employees — all have contributed, working together to make and prepare this cargo for vessel shipment to the iron and steel making centers." The fundamental factor underlying the industry is the use of iron and steel by the nation, for railroads, automobiles, airplanes, buildings, agriculture, industry in myriad directions, the elaborate construction and devices employed in the handling of oil, water, and gas, bridges, plants, tunnels — the needs of America in peace and war in an intensifying steel and technological age. Rossman, noting that the "per capita consumption of steel in America" was "1500 pounds annually for each man, woman and child," went so far as to say that "everything that America uses is either made from steel or with it." In the national and world setting he regarded the Minnesota iron ores as "the greatest natural resource ever bestowed upon a commonwealth."

If iron ore constitutes a drama, a new actor, silent as to words but economically eloquent, has come on the stage. This is not an iron man or an eastern financier or a test-pitter, but an iron pellet, a concentrate that is less a mining than a manufactured product. It is taconite, which holds out the promise of prolonging Minnesota iron mining into an indefinite future. Another example of man's resourcefulness, it represents hardheaded research and pilot-plant experimentation applied to a complex problem. Its outcome is now being written in plants that are turning out iron pellets by the millions of tons.

Men since Peter Mitchell's explorations in the 1870s have known about taconite, mother rock extending a hundred miles from Grand Rapids to Birch Lake, near the now thriving town of Babbitt. It is the "original iron-bearing formation rock from which our high grade ores were derived by nature's slow method of concentration." One may think of taconite (a black, magnetic ore) as a wide sheet the length of the Mesabi Range, perhaps from 100 to 200 feet in thickness, sloping toward Lake Superior and possibly passing under the lake (a theory originally advanced by the Longyears). It is interesting to know that a modern project of the universities of Minnesota and Michigan contemplates the drilling of deep holes in the bottom of Lake Superior to ascertain the nature of its underlying rock formations. The very rich deposits of iron ore made ready for man by nature through eons of time have been likened to "raisins in a Christmas fruit cake," but great inroads have been made on such deposits, whereas the mother rock is in such abundance that, if it can be mined with success, it means a long future for Minnesota iron. Some estimates of the supply just of the magnetic taconite run as high as five billion tons.

In the very hard rock the magnetite is about one-third of the content, and it in turn consists of about three-fourths iron and one-fourth oxygen. The problem of extracting the taconite involved formidable difficulties — scientific, technical, and financial. An electrical engineer at the University of Minnesota, Edward W. Davis, became interested as early as 1913 in the magnetic taconites of the eastern Mesabi. He took samples to his laboratory, made tests, worked on the washing out of silica, got new equipment, and joined the staff of the University Experiment Station, for which he served as director through many years. As he developed his theories he worked in cooperation with others, testing knowledge at pilot plants in Duluth and at Babbitt. He was persistent, believed that human ingenuity could come up with a solution, and had an inborn unwillingness to accept defeat. In early years he labored with meager funds, but managed to try out washers, magnetic tube concentrators, separators, ball mills, spigot classifiers, filters, and other devices. As time went on support for his work increased and mining interests, convinced of the importance of beneficiation, were ready and willing to cooperate in what might prove a major advance, even if temporary failures should prove to be preludes to success.

Getting taconite out of the ground was a problem of incredible difficulty, and it was not solved until new drilling methods, utilizing liquid fuel, were devised. After drilling, there was the problem of blasting out the rock, then crushing it to a fine powder, and thereafter separating the iron from the other elements by magnetic means. And after all this, the powdered iron had to be run through "balling drums" and given hardening furnace treatment to make pellets or small lumps before the product could be shipped to blast furnaces.

Progress was slow, disappointments punctuating various stages, but by 1941 the prospect seemed sufficiently favorable to engage state attention to the problem of taxation. The mining companies would face costs running into hundreds of millions of dollars in building plants, installing machinery, constructing railroad lines from rock sources to processing plants, and even building new cities as manufacturing and shipping centers. The state exempted the taconite companies from the traditional ad valorem tax and instead established a fixed tax per ton on pellets actually shipped, though the taconite industry was required to pay occupation and royalty taxes at a reduced rate (12 per cent instead of the 13.65 per cent rate generally required of the ore industry).

Since that time notable strides have been taken toward the development of the taconite industry. Plants have been built and expanded at Silver Bay by the Reserve Mining Company and at Hoyt Lakes by the Erie Company at tremendous costs. The Reserve Company expended some $200,000,000 in launching its first plant and has entered upon a great extension at a cost of $120,000,000 more; and its capacity is being increased from 5,500,000 tons a year to 9,000,000. The Erie Company, building for a capacity of 7,500,000 tons, launched its plant in 1953 at a cost of $300,000,000. At Mountain Iron the Oliver concern about the same time built an experimental plant with a capacity of 1,000,000 tons. Many of the problems of mining and manufacturing pellets have been met, as is evidenced by shipments in 1960 — 4,891,000 tons by Reserve, 5,500,000 by Erie, and 800,000 tons by the experimental Oliver plant. Meanwhile the mining companies are building or have built immense plants for the nonmagnetic ore known as semitaconite and for highly advanced beneficiation projects — at such places as Nashwauk, Coleraine, Chisholm, Biwabik, Grand Rapids, and Ely. A state law of 1959 extended to semitaconite tax benefits similar to those accorded taconite.

Iron mining, after more than three-quarters of a century, is entering upon a new era in which the business will concentrate more and more on the lean ores, on taconite and semitaconite, seeking by every known means to extend the life of Minnesota iron mining. Not least interesting as an aspect of the newer trends is the springing up of new towns as illustrated by Silver Bay on Lake Superior, with industrial buildings, docks for shipping, residences, shopping centers, and all the appurtenances of a nascent metropolis created by iron and the inventiveness of man.

A generation ago people were alarmed about the future of the iron-ore industry. They foresaw the depletion of reserves and even dated it (to the mid-1960s). The future of taconite was dim. Beneficiation, though progressing, had not established itself so securely that much confidence was entertained as to its effects in prolonging the industry. But now the picture has changed. Iron ore, taking into account technological advances in recent decades, is a continuing industry of long potentiality. It is conceivable that down underneath the Mesabi, once its surface riches are gone, there are taconite reserves not yet measured, not yet understood. Man's ingenuity, in an age that has witnessed the unleashing of nuclear power, may find ways of further harassment of the iron-limbed underground giant.

As the state moved into the 1960s, more than three-quarters of a century after the first ore train puffed its way into Two Harbors, Minnesotans were giving thought to a future for iron that might run far beyond the span of years already embraced by the drama of ore. Much concern centered in the problems of growth and expansion in the American iron and steel industry, increasingly competing with newer non-steel materials; the pressures of competition from South America, Canada, and even Africa in producing iron ores of high grade; the effects of state taxation on the location of beneficiation and taconite plants; and the further application of technology to ores of every kind. Concern also extended to the role of changes in transportation, especially that of the St. Lawrence Seaway, which opens ocean-going traffic from Minnesota to the outer world but also brings ore-carrying traffic from that world to the steel-making centers. And no thought of the future could ignore the even more fundamental question of the future of America in a divided world.

Whatever the problems, hazards, and uncertainties, one thing was certain. The sleeping giant of Indian lore was incredibly greater in size than anybody realized when mining operations were launched in the wilderness country to the west of the lake to which fur hunters and the architects of empire had come in the seventeenth and eighteenth centuries.

A Minnesota state fair exhibit around the turn of the century

Land and Ideas in Transition

✶

TRANSFORMING forces in the use of natural resources marked the closing decades of the nineteenth century in Minnesota. Farmers, it is true, were still raising wheat in huge amounts, and industry was cutting away the white pine. But at the same time the farmers were turning to diversification. Some escaped to the West, but most stayed at home and found ways of adapting themselves to new conditions. Many, in desperation, turned from plows to politics, and a few reforms were achieved as a result of their demands. But law did not provide decisive answers. What ushered in a new age was not statutes. It was education, invention, organization, experiment, cooperation, conservation, and leadership, allied with science.

In the 1930s a historian praised the demonstration by Minnesota farmers of the power "to adjust themselves to the many changes that have confronted them from decade to decade." The praise was merited, but it missed the significant point that the farmers themselves, through grass-roots efforts, promoted the very changes that occasioned adjustment.

Another student of farming history blocked out three stages from the 1860s to the 1920s: wheat and small grains; livestock farming; and farming as a business, not just as a "mode of life." He gave specific dates, but they are not important, for the stages overlap. In fact they run concurrently and cannot be marked off in schoolbook fashion. They denote trends of importance, however, and must be kept in mind as one interprets the transition in the state's rural economy.

Politics did not adjourn while these trends were in motion. But the Minnesota political front in the 1880s and 1890s does not fully reflect the larger forces — agricultural, industrial, and educational — that gave direction to Minnesota's progress. Political campaigns were turbulent, however, and the Republican ascendancy faced storms, especially in the 1890s.

Following Governor Pillsbury's three terms (1876–82), Lucius F. Hubbard, versatile newspaper editor, Civil War general, merchant, and railroad executive, served as governor from 1882 to 1887. It was during his regime that the Railroad and Warehouse Commission was established (1885), and a law was passed for uniform grading and weighing of grain at terminal points. Arguing for regulation, Hubbard declared that corporations were "the servants and not the masters of the public." The powers of the new commission were enlarged in 1886, when it was accorded virtually full rate-making authority (a provision later held to be unconstitutional).

Other governors in the Republican sequence were Andrew R. McGill (1887–89), William R. Merriam (1889–93), Knute Nelson (1893–95), and David M. Clough (1895–99). McGill came from the "home of governors," St. Peter, and had served as a newspaper editor, as superintendent of schools in Nicollet County, and, for many years, as the state's insurance commissioner. He won the governorship over the notorious but popular political boss and ofttime mayor of Minneapolis, Dr. A. A. Ames, on the issue of high license fees for saloons. Ames was a municipal politician who favored a "wide open" city, and he was opposed to all sumptuary legislation. McGill, after taking office, successfully led a move for a high license act (1887) — saloon licenses were put at $1000 in cities of 10,000 or over. One of the chief crusaders against the saloon was the Catholic prelate Bishop Ireland; and the rather close election of McGill has been ascribed largely to his efforts. After achieving the legislation he favored, McGill was not rewarded by re-election. He was followed for two terms by a St. Paul banker, William R. Merriam, a native of New York who had served as a member and speaker of the state House of Representatives. Merriam, whose re-election in 1890 was won by a very close margin, was a businessman, sports lover, horseman, and agricultural enthusiast. His governorship was competent, but he grappled with few large issues as measured against the problems of the times. Dr. Folwell fairly records the Australian ballot system as the "most conspicuous act of legislation" passed under Governor Merriam.

In 1892 the first in a succession of governors of Scandinavian backgrounds appeared on the political scene. This was the Norwegian-born Knute Nelson — salty, gruff, independent, schooled politically by local and regional political battles. He was a man for whom the governership was a steppingstone to the United States Senate and a distinguished national career. His emergence cannot be understood, however, without appraising the agrarian crusade, which contributed to the 1880s and 1890s a less placid character than seems to be reflected in the gubernatorial administrations.

The Grange, as has been noted, lost ground in the period of hard times after the Panic of 1873, when railroad bankruptcies were frequent and various Granger laws were repealed. By 1880 there were only 4000 chapters nationally, as compared with 20,000 in 1874. But farmers had on their palates the taste of organization to advance their social and political interests. The Farmers' Alliance, launched at Chicago in 1880, spread widely in the West and South. Like the Grange, it emphasized educational, social, and economic purposes and activities. It held picnics and congresses; organized reading groups; sponsored newspapers; and experimented with cooperative elevators and marketing. Toward the end of 1881 Minnesota had some eighty local alliances and a state organization.

Meanwhile fiery national leaders emerged, including William A. Peffer and Mary Elizabeth Lease in Kansas — it was Mrs. Lease who urged farmers "to raise less corn and more hell." Inevitably Ignatius Donnelly in Minnesota came forward, and he was the most eloquent orator of the movement. Something of the spirit of the Alliance is echoed in songs and ballads, one of which included these lines:

> I cannot sing the old songs,
> My heart is full of woe;
> But I can howl calamity
> From Hell to Broken Bow.

Calamity howling arose from concrete complaints. The one-crop system, overexpansion in booming times, then hard times and low prices, and world-wide competition — all these contributed to the distress of farmers. But specific grievances were alleged impositions by warehouses and commission merchants; discriminations in railroad rates; and unregulated grading practices.

Governor Hubbard gave sympathy to the Alliance viewpoint and led the state to significant reforms, such as the Railroad and Warehouse Commission; and his action undoubtedly was influenced by the policy of the Farmers' Alliance of cooperating with one or the other of the major parties. In the perspective of Minnesota political history it is of interest also to note that in 1886 the Minnesota Alliance held a joint convention with the recently organized Knights of Labor and that a platform embodying the demands of both farmers and workingmen was adopted. A joint committee went before the older parties. The Republican party seated the committee members in its own convention and gave a friendly ear to their views. Only a few years later, however, the Farmers' Alliance (in 1889) took on the character of an independent party and elected thirty-three representatives to the Minnesota House of Representatives. This was advance notice of full third-party action in 1890, when the Alliance nominated the editor of *Farm, Stock and Home*, Sidney M. Owen, as its candidate for governor — passing by Donnelly, then the state Alliance lecturer.

In the ensuing campaign, Owen attacked the protective tariff, inequitable taxation, "overcapitalization," and special privilege. He polled more than 58,000 votes, but lost the election to Merriam. Governor Merriam faced a divided legislature, in which the Alliance people, working with the Democrats, held the balance of power.

The election of 1890 has been interpreted as a sign that "the period of unchallenged Republican supremacy had ended." Though Merriam won the victory, Democrats, Farmers' Alliance, and Prohibition candidates for governor together polled 152,781 votes to his 88,111. Underlying the change was agrarian disaffection, and its stronghold was in the western portion of the state, among Scandinavian, especially Norwegian, farmers. The year 1890 marked the emergence of third-party protest on a large scale in the traditionally conservative state.

A year before the election of 1890 Donnelly had entertained a hope of winning Republican support for legislative election to the United States Senate. The choice went instead to William D. Washburn, the milling magnate. In his bitter disappointment Donnelly wrote a doleful novel, *Caesar's Column*, in which he forecast the destruction of modern civilization. At its end he set up an isolated Utopia in Uganda, where his favorite social and political ideas were carried out. The Alliance platform of 1890, it may be noted, came out for the election of senators by popular vote instead of by the legislature!

The desire to accomplish nationally what the Alliance was doing in Minnesota and other states led in 1891 to the formation of the People's party at Cincinnati. Donnelly headed the Minnesota delegates and emerged as a national leader of Populism. Upon his return to the state he persuaded the Alliance to enter the new movement, and in 1892 the Minnesota Populists named an entire state ticket. This time Donnelly was chosen to run for governor, and a spectacular campaign followed. A Donnelly broadside read: "From Forge and Farm; from Shop and Counter; from Highways and Firesides come and hear the 'Great Commoner' on the mighty issues which are moving mankind to the ballot box in the great struggle for their rights." He spoke everywhere with vigor and in violent criticism of railroads and grain men; and he supported state-built terminal elevators and backed the national People's party.

But the scintillating agrarian orator faced Knute Nelson as the spokesman for the Republicans. Nelson was a politician experienced in the rough-and-tumble of political battles (as well as of Civil War battles). He had been schooled as a member of Congress. Hailing from Alexandria in the western part of the state, he was a farmer so implicitly trusted that many hoped he would align himself with the Alliance and the Populists. Nor, in looking for a candidate, did the somewhat alarmed Republican leaders of the time ignore the fact that Nelson had considerable support among Scandinavian voters — especially the Norwegians of western Minnesota, where rural discontent had been rumbling.

The election was no landslide. Nelson won against a split opposition, since the Democrats and Prohibitionists also had candidates in the field. Donnelly himself felt "overwhelmed and humiliated" by his defeat. Historians of a later day regard the political emergence of Knute Nelson as a phenomenon that probably would not have come about when it did had it not been for the agrarian movement.

As governor, Nelson gave his support to a measure, in 1893, to bring local elevators under state inspection. A law was passed for the building of a state elevator at Duluth — but this was later declared unconstitutional. Nelson even gave his approval to an act making the creation of pools and trusts illegal. In Nelson's view, the problems of the farmers demanded an adjustment of agriculture to the industrializing economy. Govern-

389

ment had a dual role. On the one hand, it must forward agriculture by education. On the other, it must ensure for the farmer "equal access to marketing and transportation facilities."

Sidney M. Owen, the Populist candidate who opposed Nelson in the election of 1894, did not differ much, if at all, from these views. Certainly he was sympathetic with the forwarding of education in the farmers' interest, but he embraced as well the demonetization of silver as a key solution of the farmer's problems, and Nelson would have no truck with the "silver heresy." The people gave decisive support to Nelson in re-electing him over Owen and George L. Becker, Democrat. But he did not serve out his second term. The legislature in January 1895 chose not to return Washburn to the Senate and instead elected the governor, who had barely embarked on his new term. He resigned, went to the Senate, and began a national career that ran on for twenty-eight years until it was closed by death in 1923. Whatever the shifting political currents at home, Nelson was re-elected by successive legislatures, and finally, in 1918, by popular vote. He became a Minnesota institution, highly regarded by his home state.

Amid political changes and while agrarian organizations ran their course, the farmers moved forward with diversification of their crops and economy. The factors contributing to change go beyond the soil exhaustion and declining wheat yields. Increases in land values are one explanation of the transition of wheat farmers in southeastern Minnesota to dairying, which meant larger profits than the one-crop system could yield as basic conditions changed. An authority on the history of the wheat market suggests that even the calamities that visited the wheat farmers — such as grasshoppers, rust, and blight — were a blessing in disguise. They helped to shake confidence in wheat as the primary answer to the problem of the profitable cultivation of the soil.

American history records a westward movement of wheat growing, as it does of settlement. Wheat was a banner crop for lands on frontiers. Even within a single state, with Minnesota as an example, diversification for obvious reasons did not proceed evenly or at the same time in varying sections. It began in the older areas, synchronizing with declines in wheat yields, expansion of population, and rises in the values of land, most of which had been homesteaded in earlier years or bought at low prices from the government, railroads, or land companies. Later, the actualities of change had to be faced by the farmers who had trekked to the Red River Valley to grow wheat as long as circumstances permitted.

Stages and variations mark the gradual shift of farming. But diversification became statewide through the sweep of a half century. This is disclosed by a view of Minnesota farm products at a few selected years, such as 1880, 1900, and 1930. Wheat totaled between 34,000,000 and 35,000,000 bushels in 1880, then rose to 95,000,000 bushels in 1900 and dropped to 19,000,000 in 1930. Oats and corn became major crops — oats advancing from 23,000,000 bushels in 1880 to 74,000,000 in 1900 and 126,000,000 in 1930. Corn advanced from 14,000,000 bushels in 1880 to 47,000,000 in 1900 and 104,000,000 in 1930. The half century saw a tremendous increase in improved farm lands in Minnesota — from 7,200,000 acres in 1880 to 30,900,000 in 1930; and it is shifts not only in production but also in land use that illuminate significant changes. By 1900, 43 per cent of Minnesota's crop land was still being farmed for wheat, whereas by 1930 the percentage had declined to 10.

In the half century barley increased from 2,000,000 bushels to 47,000,000; rye from 215,000 bushels to more than 6,500,000; potatoes from 5,000,000 bushels to 25,000,000; and alfalfa, for which no figures are available for 1880, from under 2000 tons in 1900 to 1,366,000 tons in 1930. Butter production was 19,000,000 pounds in 1880 and 82,000,000 in 1900; and, to go a half dozen years beyond 1930, the creamery butter produced in Minnesota in 1936 — more than 272,000,000 pounds — led all the butter-producing states of the country. The obliging census furnishes statistics even for eggs — more than 8,000,000 dozen in 1880, 43,000,000 in 1900, and above 107,000,000 in 1930. The trends thus illustrated may be tested further by moving forward to another date, 1954, and noting the allocation of Minnesota land to particular crops. One discovers that corn, oats, and hay accounted for nearly three-fourths of the harvested areas (respectively, 28, 25, and 20 per cent); soybeans, 10 per cent, barley 6, flaxseed 5, wheat 4, and rye and vegetables 1 each. How far wheat lagged behind is indicated by the fact that corn alone claimed crop lands of nearly eight times the acreage devoted to wheat.

State-federal statistics in 1957 showed Minnesota fifth in the nation in the value of its total production. It was among the first ten in eleven important crops (second in oats and sweet corn; third in flax, corn, and soybeans, introduced in 1934; fourth in hay and green peas; sixth in barley; eighth in rye and sugar beets; and ninth in potatoes — but it stood seventeenth in wheat). By 1960 the corn crop, despite the idling of a million or more acres under federal programs, exceeded 315,000,000 bushels.

Statistics offer clues. They do not, however, reveal the real story of the farmers and their leaders, of organizations, and of education as creative forces in the changing agricultural scene. No single prophet or apostle fully symbolizes the emerging age. James J. Hill took a persistent interest in agriculture and from an early time preached and on his lands practiced diversification. He took an interest in stock raising and dairying as well as in varied crops. The many-talented William G. Le Duc made agriculture a lifelong interest that won wide recognition when President Hayes appointed him commissioner of agriculture in the 1870s. Minnesota's history includes not only such men of large affairs and national reputation, but also men of experiment and ideas who were close to the soil, who were not content to settle for wheat as the only crop that promised agricultural well-being, and whose names are not so well known as those of Hill and Le Duc. The record of diversified farming is bigger than the efforts of a few individuals, but among its pioneers were Oren C. Gregg for dairying, Wendelin Grimm for alfalfa, and — in the related field of horticulture — such men as Peter M. Gideon and John S. Harris for apple growing. Lay experimenters were followed by men of scientific agriculture who, applying their knowledge to regional problems, went far beyond what individual farmers were able to achieve.

Here the University of Minnesota through its Agricultural Experiment Station, farmers' institutes, school and college of agriculture, and branches established in various sections — northwest, west and north central, and southern Minnesota — made contributions of inestimable value. Through the dedicated work of its teachers and scholars, the university gave notable service to farmers in the state and also throughout the nation.

Cattle raising and dairying were familiar practices in pioneer days. There are records of shipments of Minnesota cattle to eastern markets as early as the late 1850s. But it was in the 1870s and 1880s that these industries took on major importance. By 1880 the beef cattle "population" had gone to nearly 350,000; and a meat-packing concern had been established two years earlier in Minneapolis.

As the production of cattle, calves, hogs, and sheep increased, South

St. Paul (a few miles below St. Paul on the Mississippi) became an increasingly important livestock terminal. There the St. Paul Union Stockyards Company was established as early as 1887 — largely as the result of the business acumen of A. B. Stickney, president of the Chicago Great Western Railway. As the years went by packing plants were built in South St. Paul, with thousands of pens for incoming livestock, and the business grew to vast proportions.

While wheat was still the major crop, farmers experimented with cheese and butter factories. Owatonna was a center, and in 1875 George Woodward, an enterprising farmer in the Cottage Grove area, took the lead in organizing the Langdon Butter and Cheese Factory. This was a joint stock company, incorporated in 1876 and capitalized at $10,000. During its first season, operating on Woodward's farm and using St. Paul as a market, it produced 52,000 pounds of cheese and 300 of butter; and in 1879 its butter won the highest award of the Minnesota Dairymen's Association.

An unmistakable evidence of interest in diversified farming was the organization of this dairymen's association in 1878 as well as of the Minnesota Butter and Cheese Association in 1882. Minnesotans, asserted an advocate of dairying in 1882, were facing the "same necessity for a change in the methods of farming" that had "existed in some of the older and now more prosperous states."

By 1885 the state had a total of sixty-three creameries and forty-six cheese factories. They marked a significant beginning, particularly since they were well under way before the De Laval Cream Separator (invented in Sweden in 1878) and the Babcock test for butterfat content gave new impetus to the industry. As dairying moved forward in the 1890s, an observer described its progress as "the most remarkable feature in the recent development of the State of Minnesota." By 1900 the dairy products of Minnesota farms had increased in value to more than $16,000,000 and ten years later to more than $30,000,000. Cattle of all kinds numbered 1,871,000 in 1900 and 2,347,000 in 1910.

The gospel of dairying was spread across the state by a Vermonter who arrived in Minnesota in 1865, at the age of twenty — Oren Gregg of Lyon County. When wheat was rampant, he began to ask questions. "My grandfather," he said, "used the cow to turn the grass of the old Green Mountains into butter. Why could not I use the cow to turn the grass of the western prairie to butter?" With inborn shrewdness, he turned aside

393

from the custom of the farmers to have their cows freshen in spring and go dry through winter. Instead, he became a champion of winter dairying. One of his converts said, "You get more for the same amount of butter or cream, and you have the satisfaction of putting it on the market when dealers want it." When farmers asked Gregg whether to go in for beef or for dairying, he cast his reply in Biblical mold: "Choose ye this day whom ye will serve. If beef then serve him, and if dairy, then serve her." Gregg took pride in Minnesota's capture of honors for butter at a world industrial exposition in New Orleans in the mid-eighties. He preached diversification up and down Minnesota. For more than twenty years, after the University of Minnesota established a Farmers' Institute in 1885, he served as its resourceful superintendent.

Gregg had allies in spreading his gospel. The practical test devised by S. M. Babcock for measuring butterfat in milk came to his aid in the 1890s. Gradually the centrifugal cream separator became more widely used. The silo, though not yet a standard feature of farms, had made its appearance in the United States in the 1870s and was winning farmer approval. As a result of the new inventions that came into use in the 1890s, dairying was given a scientific base, and butter making, as one scholar puts it, was transferred from the farm to the factory.

Not least important among the newer ideas was refrigeration. A pioneer refrigerator railroad car carried beef from Chicago to New York as early as 1867; and mechanical refrigeration came into use in the 1890s. Pioneers, with their spring cellars and ice houses, were by no means ignorant of the uses of refrigeration. In 1860 several barges loaded with ice were sent down river to St. Louis. But modern refrigeration as a factor in diversification — and in many aspects of living — was a far cry from the primitive efforts of pioneers to cool their milk and butter.

Other allies in the movement testify to the interest of Minnesotans in diverse agricultural undertakings. Many non-wheat organizations took form in the so-called wheat era. They included a Minnesota Fruit Growers' Association in 1866 and a State Farmers' Club in 1868 (established to forward farmers' clubs in communities throughout the state). A state poultry association was formed as early as 1874; a stock breeders' association in 1877; and a wool growers' association in 1879.

A monthly agricultural magazine, the *Minnesota Farmer and Gardener*, was launched at St. Paul even before the Civil War — in 1860. Other early publications included the *Farmer's Union* in 1867; the *Minnesota Monthly* (a Granger publication) in 1869; and the *Independent Farmer and Fireside Companion* in 1879. These were, for the most part, short-lived magazines. But the *Farmer*, begun by Edward A. Webb at Fargo in 1882 and shifted to St. Paul in 1890, has appeared ever since. *Farm, Stock and Home* began in 1884, gave "notable pioneer service" to dairying, and continued until 1929, when it was merged with the *Farmer*. These magazines were pre-eminent, but it is worth noting that, from first to last, Minnesota had more than a hundred farm journals. They served the farmers on a wide front of information about agriculture, crops, machinery, new devices and ways.

Minnesota's Territorial Agricultural Society was reorganized and the State Agricultural Society was formed in 1860 to promote "agriculture, horticulture, manufactures, mechanics, and household arts." By the mid-1870s county agricultural societies were general and many of them held annual fairs. The state fairs, held in various places in earlier years, were established permanently in St. Paul in 1885. These fairs, like the specialized associations, gave much attention to diverse farming products and notably to dairying and beef cattle. The state fair of 1877 was a joint exhibition of the State Agricultural Society and the stock breeders' association, a significant recognition of farming interests.

As the fairs went forward year after year, their exhibitions reflected a widening sweep of interest. They blossomed into an institution of social as well as economic and educational significance. Phil Stong in his novel *State Fair*, and the movies, have celebrated the story of the American state fair in the national life. Ideas and practices were given tests of competition and scrutiny. A book on agricultural history declares that "no institution, perhaps, has exerted greater influence upon American rural life than the agricultural fair." It could be argued that agricultural colleges, with their experiment stations, have had a more fundamental influence, but the Minnesota State Fair has been a dynamic force in Minnesota agriculture, especially in the realm of diversification, through the long years of its existence.

The word "diversification" may not have been familiar to a German immigrant, Wendelin Grimm, who came to Minnesota in 1857 from Külsheim in the Duchy of Baden. But he ranks as a farmer-pioneer in the movement because of his persistent work with alfalfa. When he arrived in Minnesota he carried with him a twenty-pound bag of alfalfa seed. In 1858 and every season thereafter he planted alfalfa seed, replanting even after very severe winters when little of his crop had survived. It has been said that he did not understand the "practical or the scientific importance of his experiment in acclimatization." But he knew that what he called his "everlasting clover" was good feed for beef cattle. The year 1863 was one of slim corn crops in Minnesota. A curious neighbor, noting that Grimm's cattle were fat and sleek, asked him how he had managed to get corn for their feed. "Kein Körnschen," he said, "nur ewiger Klee" (not one kernel, only everlasting clover). He sold his precious alfalfa seed to neighbors, and they adopted his practice of growing the crop. By the late 1880s nearly half of all the alfalfa raised in Minnesota came from Grimm's home county (Carver).

The news of the "everlasting clover" spread. Another farmer, A. B. Lyman, experimented with it near Excelsior. He then reported results to the head of the university's Agricultural Experiment Station, Professor Willet M. Hays. Four years later the United States Department of Agriculture took cognizance of Grimm Alfalfa and an official said, "We have been searching the world for a variety of alfalfa that does just what this variety does."

Scientific experiments proved that the Grimm Alfalfa stood the cold winters far better than most other varieties. Scholars found a partial explanation in a Eurasian strain that made for hardiness, but they also regarded Grimm's long-continued work in acclimatizing the plant as a major contribution. The alfalfa product in Minnesota leaped from under 2000 tons in 1900 to more than 1,000,000 three decades later, and the crop spread to thousands of fields beyond Minnesota — in Canada and in northern areas of the United States. A Grimm Alfalfa seed producers' association was organized in North Dakota in 1916 and a similar association in Minnesota in 1924. Fittingly a bronze marker was erected on the Grimm farm in 1924 to honor the achievement of this farmer. One of the speakers who paid tribute to Grimm commented on society's debt to the patient men and women who in obscurity have "worked out great benefits to humanity." And another asserted that the contribution made by Grimm to the livestock industry was "as great as that of the breeders."

The cooperative movement gave impetus to agricultural diversification, and particularly to dairying. In this field, as in other areas, major advances came in the 1890s. Some experimentation in cooperation had been made as early as the 1860s in farmers' mutual insurance companies — two were incorporated in 1867 (one of them having been started two years earlier); and a law of 1875 gave official authorization for "township mutual insurance companies." The movement grew and by 1912 there were 154 companies which carried more than $300,000,000 of insurance.

The major cooperative movement, for producers and consumers, came long after the mutual insurance companies were begun. Early developments were in producers' cooperatives, and they centered in creameries. The inventions that contributed so strong an impulse to dairying as a business gave impetus to cooperatives. Both the Grangers and the Farmers' Alliance had attempted to forward cooperative enterprises, but other influences played roles, and one of these involved the Danish settlement at Clark's Grove.

The idea of farmers' cooperatives was not new in the United States. In the 1850s cooperative cheese and butter factories had been organized in New York State, and there are even eighteenth-century American precedents for the cooperative marketing of farm products. But in Minnesota a direct line of influence ran from Denmark to Clark's Grove. A Danish farmer, Hans Peter Jensen, visited his homeland in 1884 and took note of the amazing progress Denmark was making in its dairy industry. Through the Royal Agricultural Society, the Danes since the 1860s had studied methods of improving butter making. In the cream separator they perceived an invention that made both cooperation and expanded production practicable, and in 1882 they started their first cooperative creamery. Jensen visited it, found it running successfully, and liked its basic principles. They were simple: farmers as members delivered their milk to the dairy, and profits were shared on the basis of what each member contributed.

Jensen returned to Clark's Grove an enthusiast. Another member of his settlement went to Iowa to look at cooperative experiments in that state. The result was a meeting of Clark's Grove farmers at the local Danish Baptist Church, called for the purpose of starting a cooperative creamery. An investigating committee was chosen, and a constitution was framed, with eighty farmers enrolling as members.

Clark's Grove was one of four cooperative creameries started in Minnesota in 1889 and 1890 — others were in Dodge, Olmsted, and McLeod counties. Clark's Grove (in Freeborn County) does not have priority in time, but its influence was pervasive — and for a special reason — throughout the state. The creamery itself was hugely successful and in forty years produced 12,000,000 pounds of butter and paid its participating members $3,715,000.

The special reason for the influence of Clark's Grove was Professor Theophilus Haecker, often called the "Father of Dairying in Minnesota." This remarkable man was brought to Minnesota from Wisconsin in 1891 as a teacher of dairying. His assignment was the starting of a school of dairying in the University of Minnesota's College of Agriculture. For twenty-seven years he gave service as scholar, as research man, and as trainer of more than two thousand creamery operators. He was interested in every aspect of dairying, particularly nutrition, high-quality butter, and cooperatives. "To him," a scholar has written, "the dairy cow was the most wonderful animal in the world." To his students Haecker liked to say, "Treat the cow kindly, boys. Remember she is a lady — and a mother." As a preacher of cooperation, Haecker had widespread influence. He acquainted himself with the cooperative ideas and practices of the Danes at Clark's Grove. He prepared in 1894 a bulletin on "Organizing Co-operative Creameries." He spoke, traveled, wrote, and visited farmers. Everywhere he impressed people with the importance of cooperatives and of the application of scientific principles to dairying.

By 1898 Minnesota had 560 cooperative creameries. Twenty years later, when there were 1400 in the United States, 671, or 49 per cent, were in Minnesota. Haecker in 1913 described Clark's Grove as "the mecca where committees were sent to see what could be accomplished." The example of the Danish community, he said, "has been worth to Minnesota many millions of dollars."

As the cooperative business grew in volume, its leaders organized to handle cooperative marketing on the same principle. They did this first through the Minnesota Co-operative Dairies Association (1911) and a decade later through Land O'Lakes, Incorporated. The latter organization became the largest butter marketing concern in the world and by 1929 was handling more than 91,000,000 pounds of butter in a business that went beyond $52,000,000.

The philosophy of cooperation soon spread to other areas. Farmers in Minnesota began to build cooperative elevators in the 1890s and by 1921 had a total of 417 and processed 47,000,000 bushels of grain. For livestock, a Central Cooperative Commission Association was formed.

Potato marketing associations began in 1908, and a dozen years later the Minnesota Potato Exchange was formed. Other kinds of farmers' producer cooperatives were attempted; and official sanction came in 1923 when a Minnesota law was passed according cooperatives legal standing.

With the movement spreading, one is not surprised to find that its ideas were given application in consumers' cooperatives. The Grangers started cooperative stores, but had little success. The Clark's Grove community, encouraged by its success in the producers' field, experimented with several kinds of consumers' cooperative services. But much of the inspiration for consumers' cooperatives in Minnesota came from the Finns in the northeastern section in the second decade of the twentieth century. They were interested in organization, churches, temperance societies, and labor groups. Their cooperative interest was not unrelated to old-country beginnings, though a historian of the Finnish immigrants points out that few of the Finnish immigrants had had much experience with cooperatives before coming to America. The movement in Finland emerged "mainly after 1899 with the aid of government funds and with university-trained leadership."

The Minnesota movement was closely related to workingmen's organizations and interests. A Virginia Work People's Trading Company was started in 1909, and a Cloquet Cooperative Society, which became the largest in the country, in 1911. A half dozen years later a central exchange was launched, the Central Cooperative Wholesale, which by the mid-thirties had more than a hundred stores and associations affiliated with it, forty-six in Minnesota. By that time, including independent as well as affiliated societies, there were more than a hundred in the state and Minnesota led the nation.

As cooperative ideas took root, they reached out to insurance, telephones, farm supplies, credit unions (or consumer loan associations), and other enterprises. There was a steadily expanding retailing of dairy products. The movement also included oil, with the Midland Cooperative Wholesale entering the picture in 1926 (as the Minnesota Cooperative Oil Company). From the 1920s on, the Minnesota Farmers Union appeared on the scene, first through locals, then through regional cooperatives. It entered into terminal and wholesale markets. The Union grew enormously and, for the Minnesota region, took form in the Farmers Union Grain Terminal Association and the Farmers Union Central Exchange. The former has been described as "the nation's largest co-op marketing firm," and the latter as one of the country's "leading farm supply wholesale co-ops."

As one views the changing farm economy, it is not only diversification and cooperation that play prominent roles, but also education and a public dissemination of information on rural problems in diverse ways. In this context importance attaches to the Minnesota Farm Bureau Federation and the statewide activity of county agricultural agents, particularly after the passage in 1914 of the Smith-Lever Act, which made available federal support for "extension" programs and the county-agent movement. Nearly every county in the state in time formed a local farm bureau, and the extension program reached out to every part of Minnesota, with the county agents in touch with farmers in programs of concrete and invaluable informational service. An adjunct to this service has been the 4-H Movement (Head, Heart, Hands, and Health) for rural youth, and another has been an organization for young people in the state's public high schools — the Future Farmers of America. The 4-H Movement in Minnesota had an inspiring leader through many years in T. A. "Dad" Erickson of the University of Minnesota, whose life story, *My Sixty Years with Rural Youth*, is a classic of "extension" service.

Cooperation — but not in the technical "co-op" sense — marked the cultivation of fruit growing in Minnesota. This field affords further evidence of the sweep of diversified agricultural interests. Daniel A. Robertson, whose Granger activities have been mentioned and who served as the first professor of agriculture in the University of Minnesota, gave an address in 1867 in which he commented on the prevailing opinion that Minnesota was "too far North for the successful cultivation of apples, pears, cherries and improved varieties of plums." Neither he nor other orchardists of early Minnesota shared this opinion. From the 1850s onward there was incessant experiment with fruits, vineyards, and berries.

Farmers were not willing to accept a life without fruits. John S. Harris, an orchardist who developed "Sunnyside Farm" at La Crescent, planted apple trees the first year after his Minnesota arrival from Wisconsin in 1856. On a January day in 1860 he wrote in his diary that Minnesota would be a pleasant place indeed "if we had plenty of fruit." He voiced the faith of many when he added, "By the hand of enterprise and industry, this must be the garden of the great Northwest." For many years he devoted effort and experiment to fruit culture and became so expert that for a time he served as horticultural editor of *Farm, Stock and Home*. With Robertson and others, he helped to found in 1866 the Fruit Growers' Association, later known as the Minnesota State Horticultural Society. For sustained interest and influence through all the years since 1866, it would be difficult to find any organization devoted to the fruits of the soil which can match the constructive record of this society.

Much historical attention has been given, and deservedly, to the exploits of Peter M. Gideon. He was an Ohioan who settled in Minnesota in 1853 and won fame for his development of the Wealthy apple. But his outstanding achievement has obscured the fact that he was but one of many laymen who contributed to the early horticultural progress of the state. Harris himself almost singlehandedly and largely from his own products prepared an elaborate exhibit of apples, pears, grapes, and small fruits for the Rochester state fair in 1866. John Shaw from Maine grew an early orchard near Winona, beginning with apple seeds from his native state. So did Theodore Furber of Cottage Grove, and Edward H. S. Dartt experimented extensively with fruits on a farm near Owatonna. Wyman Eliot, a progressive settler from Maine, built an eighty-acre farm in the heart of what is now South Minneapolis. He was the first market gardener in Minneapolis and formed a garden and nursery company before turning to the real-estate exploitation of a farm enveloped by a fast-growing city. Andrew Peterson, a Swedish pioneer of the 1850s in Carver County, planted seedlings, grew vines, fruit trees, and raspberries, currants, and strawberries, and he recorded his doings in a remarkable diary covering the years from 1854 to 1898.

Robertson, editor, soldier, and orchardist, set up a kind of forum for state legislators on such questions as "Can Minnesota grow apples?" To support his own answer, he created a demonstration orchard in what is now the heart of residential St. Paul (the area abutting Summit and Snelling avenues). Many gifted and enthusiastic men were active in horticulture from the 1850s and 1860s onward. And it is in this setting that one must appraise the work of Peter M. Gideon.

Gideon was as much a pioneer of horticulture as Gregg was of dairying or Grimm of alfalfa. He had come from Ohio to the south shore of Lake Minnetonka in 1853 with thirty varieties of apple seedlings, pear, cherry, and plum trees, a peck of peach seeds, and a bushel of apple seeds. He encountered grave trouble as a consequence of severe winters, and after a decade nearly all his trees had been killed. His money reserve was reduced to eight dollars and he badly needed to buy a warm coat, but he preferred a coatless to an appleless state. So he used his money for apple seeds from Bangor, Maine, and patched together some old clothes to warm himself in winter.

In 1873 Gideon wrote that of the first eight to ten thousand trees set in his orchard, not forty remained. But he had some four thousand trees grown from seed, with about two hundred varieties. From his experimentation he had produced the Wealthy apple, which was publicly announced in the *Western Farmer* in 1869. It was a hybrid, its precise origins a matter of conjecture by scholars of later years. It was given wide distribution, in part through his own sale of trees and his writings, in part through the efforts of others, including Suel Foster, one of the founders of the Iowa Agricultural College. And it became one of the famous apples of the north country.

Gideon had a singular ability to attract public attention to fruit growing, and he never lacked confidence in his apple, a faith supported by its hardiness and success through nearly a century. He named the apple for his wife, Mrs. "Wealthy" Gideon. One may assume that Gideon shared the ecstasy of someone who said it was the best apple produced by man since Adam and Eve departed from the Garden of Eden.

Something akin to a pattern emerges in the "growth of the soil." Pioneers arrive, not a few self-educated and competent, with a bent for experiment. Beginnings are made in diverse products. General organizations are formed. Then men set up organizations devoted to their specialized interests. Lay efforts expand and achieve success. Scholars and teachers appear on the scene to test what has been done. They give leadership, and bring to bear on agriculture the forces of science coupled with controlled experimentation.

Just as farmers organize their efforts, education organizes its enterprise. After pioneer beginnings, the advance by the University of Minnesota came on this front when the Minnesota Agricultural Experiment Station was established in 1885. Two years later, Congress passed the Hatch Act, which provided federal aid for such agricultural experiment stations (beginning, for Minnesota, with $15,000 annually). As scientific men assumed leadership, lay interest and organizations rallied in support. The Minnesota State Horticultural Society counted more than ten thousand members in 1961. Affiliated with this central society were nearly five hundred garden clubs united in a state federation.

On the professional front the roles of such men as Willet M. Hays and Theophilus L. Haecker have already been mentioned. They were only two of many who have advanced agriculture from the 1880s and 1890s to the present.

The university and the state took a sharp interest in Gideon's enterprise in developing a private experimental farm. As early as 1878 the state, influenced by the Horticultural Society, passed a law for the encouragement of fruit culture. This measure authorized the university Board of Regents to purchase land near Minnetonka for an experimental farm. Such land was bought for fruit breeding, not far from the Gideon orchards; and he was appointed superintendent. His career of testing went forward, but not without minor storms because of his individual traits. He was a proponent of simplified spelling, an opponent of racing at the state fair, and a doughty controversialist on other issues. The man embraced curious idiosyncrasies, but no appraisal of his career can fail to recognize his ability to do the right thing with trees.

The station functioned from 1878 to 1889. The university established another experiment station — for fruits, forests, and ornamental trees — at Owatonna following a second legislative act, in 1887; and this was placed under the direction of another pioneering horticulturist, Edward H. S. Dartt, and it continued until 1925 — in its later years under Thomas E. Cashman.

The most significant forward step came in 1907, again with legislative sanction (backed by special appropriations), when the Excelsior Fruit Breeding Farm was authorized. This had the active support of the Horticultural Society but was largely the outcome of the ideas and planning of Samuel B. Green, the university's horticulturist and authority in forestry. The station, with its brilliant record of achievements, is a monument to Professor Green.

"Monument" is a misleading term, however. It suggests something finished, silent, static, whereas the station is active, creative, and continuing. By means of hybrids, testing for desirable fruit qualities, and research in many basic and applied ways, it looks ahead. The station got under way in 1908 under Charles Haralson, and another stage in its development came under William H. Alderman, chief of the university's division of horticulture, who took over as superintendent in 1923 and served for thirty years.

Development and testing are time-demanding. New varieties are not

403

introduced until and unless they have been found worthy. No detailed account can be presented of the more than sixty varieties of trees and small fruits released up to the late 1950s, but mention must be made of the Latham red raspberry, which is grown widely in this country and Canada; the Haralson apple (from 1922), a great favorite in Minnesota; the Red Lake currant (1933), which attained first place in the United States; and a newer apple variety, the Beacon, productive and hardy, introduced in 1936. There have also been long-continued researches on flowers, shrubs, and trees.

Among the interests of the Minnesota State Horticultural Society were trees — not just apple trees, but tree culture in general. This society took the lead in bringing about legislative acceptance in 1873 of a Tree Bounty Law. This was designed to encourage farmers in treeless areas to plant groves. A modest bounty was offered for tree planting up to ten acres — and in thirty-five years some sixty thousand acres of trees were the result.

Concurrently with the state action, the federal government adopted a Timber Culture Act, which promised the farmer a quarter section of land as a reward for planting and tending for a period of a decade forty acres of timber (the specified cultivation was later reduced to ten acres and eight years). The Horticultural Society did not relax its interest, and in 1876 it took the lead in organizing a Minnesota State Forestry Association, the first of its kind in the United States.

These events were portents of changes in ideas about forest lands. They occurred early in the era of lumbering on a gigantic scale. As in other "causes," that of forest conservation, or "regeneration" as Professor Green wrote, had an outstanding apostle. This was the happily named Christopher Columbus Andrews, prominent Minnesotan who was appointed United States minister to Sweden and Norway by President Grant in 1869 and served through both of the Grant terms.

As Andrews traveled about Sweden, he took note of a curious checkerboard pattern in the forests and learned that the Swedes were controlling their forest resources by restricting annual cutting to the annual forest growth. They were applying a formula for perpetual forests at the very time Minnesotans were cutting down the white pine with little thought of a pineless posterity. In 1872 Andrews detailed his observations of Swedish forestry to the secretary of state in an extensive report, and when he returned to this country in 1877 he was an out-and-out conservationist. As Denmark and Finland contributed to Minnesota co-operatives, so Sweden was helpful to Minnesota conservation.

Andrews made his views known, preached about the dangers of fire, and advocated in 1880 experiment stations for research in forestry. Two years later he wrote a paper on "The Necessity for a Forestry School in the United States." Forestry was taught in the University of Minnesota as early as 1889 by Professor Green, whose book *Forestry in Minnesota,* first published in 1898, was prepared for his students. The School of Forestry (in earlier years a "division" of forestry), offering a full course for the training of foresters, dates its beginning from 1903.

But progress was slow. Most people were complacent. No political party took a stand for conservation until 1892, when the Populist party advocated planned management of forests. It called for concerted efforts to prevent their destruction by fire. It favored state attention to water resources and checks to private exploitation of Minnesota's wealth of trees. But the Populists were a third party. Their warning went unheeded, as did the preaching of Andrews. Crisis brought about reform, and the crisis came in the summer of 1894. One of history's tragic ironies is that nine days before disaster struck Andrews gave a public address in the East on "The Prevention of Forest Fires."

The Minnesota summer had been dry. Forests about the village of Hinckley were like tinder. For many days smoke had warned of danger, and birds, with nature's wisdom, were flying south. Of a sudden, on September 1, disaster struck. A hurricane of fire swept from nearby forests into Hinckley and the town was destroyed. A train managed to get out with 276 men, women, and children. It crossed a bridge five minutes before the structure collapsed; and the train reached safety. Another, approaching Hinckley, stopped near the doomed village, and its frightened passengers scrambled into a nearby mud lake for succor. The state was infinitely shocked to learn that in the fierce forest fires of that summer of 1894, 413 persons were burned to death, 197 of them in Hinckley.

This was but one of many disastrous forest fires that have ravaged Minnesota and nearby Wisconsin. Chisholm, Baudette, Spooner, Moose Lake, and Cloquet are others. Often there are lags between the cautionary teachings of reformers and action taken after their warnings come true. Men and organizations had urged reform for close to a score of years But calamity scared Minnesota in 1895 into adopting a law designed to preserve the state's forests and to "suppress" forest and prairie fires.

This was a beginning, though it was late in coming. Andrews was appointed chief fire warden, and he continued to voice his matured philosophy of perpetual forests. Four years later a State Forestry Board was established. A devastating fire at Chisholm in 1908 led to the inauguration of a ranger service. In 1911, after yet other disasters, Minnesota authorized a state forester. The Forestry Board was discontinued in 1923 and the state forester was made commissioner of forestry and fire prevention. Later the forest service became a unit in the Department of Conservation.

Official action did not keep up with the imaginations of forward-looking men. Later times brought many steps of progress: tree nurseries, plans for reforestation, the state department, and the development of state parks and forests. This development had been initiated as early as 1891, when Itasca State Park and Pillsbury State Forest were established. As time went on, the problems of forestry, the "regeneration" of trees, soil erosion, and tree planting received more and more attention from the University of Minnesota, state officials, and the national government. The national concern took form, among other ways, in reserves for the future through such areas as the Chippewa and Superior-Quetico National forests. The university, through its forestry school under such leaders as Samuel B. Green, E. G. Cheyney, Henry Schmitz, and Frank Kaufert, and with outstanding teachers (including Professor J. H. Allison), gave service in training foresters, in research on scientific and practical problems in the management and uses of timber resources, in the technology of wood, and in the many values, practical and recreational, of trees.

The story is no purely local one. What happened in Minnesota was a part of an emerging science of forestry in America and an awakening of the people to potentialities in the nation's resources that could be realized through conservation, "regeneration," and the application of a basic understanding to which the pathway was training and research. On the national front such leaders as Theodore Roosevelt and Gifford Pinchot dramatized problems and possibilities to which the American people had not been alert. But it was men like Green whose ideas and initiative fostered forestry as a recognized science. Green understood the importance of natural laboratories. It was largely through his efforts (aided by the Weyerhaeuser lumber people) that a Forest Experiment Station — now designated as a Forestry Research Center — was established at Cloquet in 1909. About the same period — and again the fertile mind of Green was at work — a forestry station was developed at Lake Itasca for practical training of foresters. Here biological studies were also given sanctuary in later years.

A transition in the state's economy and in the thinking of people with respect to natural resources characterized Minnesota through the decades from the 1850s to the twentieth century. The transition embraces politics, the agrarian crusade, agricultural diversification, and the work of farmers. It includes organizations, the testing of products, and enlightenment by means of the printed word. Closely related to the changes were the activities of cooperatives, the extension of knowledge by research, and newer concepts of society's obligation to posterity. A frontier society attained maturity through leadership and adjustments to conditions that few foresaw when the lands were opened. Minnesota was no sleeping giant, no iron-limbed "Mesabi." It was a people's commonwealth, alert to problems, alert also to challenges in an era of revolutionizing technology.

The pillared entrance to Northrop Auditorium on the university campus

Education Moves Ahead

No historian, in the fashion of Turner's essay on the significance of the frontier, has interpreted education as a major force in the shaping of the nation. Yet few will dissent from the view that it has been far more significant as an American influence than the westward-moving frontier. There is need of a new Turner to formulate an interpretation comparable in importance with the "frontier hypothesis." More forces than one shaped the American destiny, but education in its unceasing impact through more than three centuries might furnish the framework for a new and major interpretation of the national experience.

Illustrations of the role of education leap out from the story of Minnesota. Building on foundations laid in pioneer times, the state erected a system of schooling from elementary and secondary levels to colleges and university that extended its influence to all the people. To native-born and immigrants alike, the schools were ladders for their children, with rungs leading to professional careers, to public service, and to cultural and social richness. The building of Minnesota needed hewers of wood and carriers of water; and the pioneers cheerfully undertook these humble tasks. But they had an innate belief in the idea of progress and in a society of democratic ways. For their children they wanted opportunities that compelling circumstances had denied to many of them. Their faith and purpose were translated into self-sacrificing support of public education, parochial schools, private colleges, state colleges, junior colleges, a great state university, and various special academies and related institutions.

The school system is often taken for granted because it is so widespread, visible, and everyday, but it is one of the outstanding achievements of the people and constitutes a chapter of high distinction in their history. The system grew and developed from pioneer times. It responded to needs, changed decade after decade, received new ideas with open mind, and constantly widened the base of its support. Agriculture, industry, the professions, institutions, cultural advance, and life in its varied activities today bear the marks of the popular faith in education for all the people to the limit of their potentialities and their earnestness of purpose.

The book-loving fur trader, Martin McLeod, who sponsored Minnesota's common school law in 1849 favored public support of high schools. But the concept of public secondary education made little headway in the 1850s. Private academies largely pre-empted the secondary field; and the infant colleges and the University of Minnesota established preparatory departments before they undertook college programs. In a few of Minnesota's special school districts slight beginnings were made when instruction was offered pupils beyond the common-school level. Such instruction was meager, however. A Minnesotan has described his experience as a pupil in a school at St. Peter in the early 1870s. The entire school, he wrote, was in the attic of an eight-room building, the grammar school on one side, the high school on the other. The high school had one teacher, some fifteen pupils, a term of fourteen weeks, with classes in Latin, mathematics, and a few "armchair sciences."

In 1860 an act authorized the St. Anthony board of education to establish a "central high school for instruction in the higher English branches." This was a recognition of a public obligation to provide education intermediate between the common school and the university. Progress was slow. St. Paul had no high school department in 1861, but Winona was authorized to open one, and the next year it had thirty-five pupils. By 1870 only seventeen communities recorded high school classes, and many of these were merely adjuncts to the graded elementary schools. Winona stepped into the lead with a four-year high school course, but most of the schools offered only three years or less. There were some signs of impending change, however. The Minnesota State Teachers'

Association had been established as early as 1860. In 1872 the state superintendent appointed a commission to develop a course plan for high schools. And in 1878 a state high school board came into being and the principle of state aid for high schools was established. These official actions, urged by the teachers' association and by President Folwell of the university, were foundational for public secondary schools in Minnesota. Later amendments to the laws added to their effectiveness. The key ideas were free tuition as contrasted with the tuition-charging private academies, financial aid by the state, and state inspection of high schools as a means of enforcing good standards.

That high schools developed slowly is understandable in the light of the times. Collegiate education in the young state was struggling to get a foothold. The normal schools, coping with problems of elementary training for teachers in the common schools, were as yet under no pressure to train high school teachers. The academies, already declining, functioned in part as "finishing schools," usually with English, scientific or practical, and classical courses. The early "College of St. Paul" (actually an academy) offered courses in such subjects as mechanics, civil engineering, geology, and chemistry, and took the position that "in a young country the demand is for practical men rather than complete scholars." In 1877 there were 117 Minnesota graduates of high schools, but educators have said that fewer than twenty of them were adequately prepared for college entrance.

In the 1890s courses of high school study were drawn up based less on the earlier concept of a terminal "people's college" than on preparation for university or college studies. Three courses were provided: scientific, classical, and literary; and such subjects as physics, geometry, algebra, and English were required in all three.

The later development of high schools across many decades is one of tremendous growth spurred by state aid, the advancing population, and recognition of the importance of education beyond the elementary level. Coupled with growth were special factors. One was the development of normal schools. Between 1860 and 1913 six were established — at Winona, Mankato, St. Cloud, Moorhead, Duluth, and Bemidji. Thus through a half century a statewide system was built for the training of teachers, first for the elementary schools, later for high schools. By 1921 these schools were designated as state teachers' colleges, with four-year courses and the authority to confer bachelors' degrees. In 1957 they became state colleges, with the exception of Duluth, which had already been made an organic part of the University of Minnesota. These institutions grew with the years, expanding their programs, and contributing streams of trained teachers for the schools of Minnesota. They raised their standards in accordance with times, needs, and rising state requirements for the granting of teachers' certificates.

A second factor was a series of far-reaching changes in the high school curriculum. These were not the result of some dated master plan, but came about, decade after decade, as conditions and new ideas influenced the public services of education. If the high schools moved a long way from orientation to classical college entrance requirements, it is also true that colleges and the university modified their traditional courses and policies, with many new offerings and departures from older traditions. As the high schools developed — even by 1905 there were no fewer than 174 state-aided high schools, with some 20,000 students enrolled — the curriculum expanded to include vocational training, agriculture, art, physical education, home economics, business, and other subjects close to the realities of practical living.

An extraordinary experiment was under way. This was nothing less than universal education through elementary and secondary levels, and its goal came very near realization by the end of the first century of statehood. Pioneer schooling had been conducted for only a few months during the year. In time the nine-month year was standardized both for elementary and for high schools. The original schools in rural and village communities were little units serving their neighborhoods, but after some modest experiments in district consolidations, the state in 1911 authorized consolidated school districts with special state aid as an encouragement. This action ushered in a revolution in public education. School planners, architects, and citizens collaborated on buildings, facilities, faculties, and modern means of transportation to enable cooperating communities to keep in step with American education in an era of progress. The "little red schoolhouse," cherished in American folklore, became obsolete. It could not meet the demands of the modern era.

Standards for the education of teachers, originally negligible, rose year by year. By 1913 the bachelor's degree was fixed as a minimum requirement for high school teachers. It took a long sweep of time for the requirements for teachers in public elementary schools to be elevated to four years of education beyond high school, but this standard was reached by 1961. Many changes took place in school organization, and a notable development was the inauguration of junior high schools after 1915. Impetus to practical education came through special aids to vocational training and to secondary work in agriculture, home economics, and other fields. State aid was enlarged gradually for both elementary and high schools, and the state income tax, beginning in 1933, was allocated to school support. Before this, in 1929, authority to determine standards for certifying teachers was completely vested in the State Board of Education. This board extended its earlier policy of demanding special professional education among the prerequisites for sanction to teach in the public schools.

These were some of the developments that characterized the state movement for public education. With growth came changes in concepts and purposes and also in teaching standards. Public-school teaching won recognition as a profession alongside specialization in scores of other fields. Not infrequently there were differences of opinion with respect to standards for the training of teachers, but these manifested the interest of the people in good education for their children. The university, state colleges, and many of the private colleges gave serious curricular thought to programs of study for prospective teachers which included professional courses and apprenticeship in classroom experience alongside their training in mathematics, history, chemistry, or other particular fields of knowledge.

Clashes of views bred a tradition both of controversy and of public concern. But through the decades public support deepened, and as enrollments increased, the schools were modernized. There was a concerted effort by earnest teachers, administrators, school boards, and legislators, and by influential organizations. The latter included not only the State Department of Education and the Minnesota Education Association, but also the grass-roots parent-teacher associations. They were organized on a statewide basis in 1922 after local clubs under various names had paved the way. Citizens in every community lent their efforts to improving public education. The schools, as they rightly insisted, were their schools, serving their children.

Alongside the public schools, a system of parochial education took shape. In Lutheran circles there was spirited controversy about public education. Some of the clergy regarded the common school as heathen,

413

but it also had defenders. Some Lutheran parochial schools were founded, but by and large the Scandinavians accepted and supported the public schools. An outstanding Norwegian church and educational leader, Georg Sverdrup of Augsburg Seminary in Minneapolis, vigorously defended the public schools in the 1870s. "Our children," he wrote, "must grow into the language and history of this country." The common school, in his view, was not heathen, but a "civic" school. "Heathen," he said, was a bad word used to frighten people. He found no reason why Christians should not send their children to the public schools. Unless they did, these future citizens would not be able to play their part in American life. If the state took over the religious schools, the result would be a dead church; if the church set up civic schools, the outcome would be priestly rule. There was a place for summer parochial teaching, but he urged his followers to give wholehearted support to the public schools. The immigrant press and the people generally supported such views. Other church groups of different denominations planted schools uniting religious and secular instruction, and some of these, including the Pillsbury, Shattuck, and Breck schools, achieved excellent standards.

The Catholic church, consistently with its traditions, built a far-reaching system of parochial schools at both elementary and secondary levels. This system extended throughout the state but was especially strong in the metropolitan centers. The extent of the system may be indicated by noting that by 1961 there were about four hundred Catholic parochial schools in Minnesota and that they gave instruction to well over a hundred thousand children. They kept abreast of the rise in educational standards, had staffs of trained teachers, maintained excellent facilities, and coveted high standing.

The state also had some private schools, especially in the larger cities, which gave special consideration to the adequate preparation of children for entrance into colleges of the classical tradition.

Minnesota higher education, after pioneer beginnings in the 1850s, had wide range and represented varying interests and approaches. Though separate institutions were planned and nurtured without any over-all direction or strategy, it remains true that a veritable system, characterized by diversity in ways and functions, was created. It includes private colleges, the state university, state colleges, public junior colleges, and theological seminaries. If viewed as a system, Minnesota's higher education embraces not only the more than thirty institutions offering collegiate instruction, but also educational societies, public and private libraries, museums of art and history and science, musical organizations, and other institutions and enterprises that have enriched the resources available to students.

A distinguished educator, exploring higher education in Minnesota, finds its "taproot" to be "faith in education as a means of social progress." This faith underlies not only higher education but also elementary and secondary education, public and private. Another root has been Christian idealism, and it is significant that every one of the state's fifteen private colleges of 1960 had been founded under religious auspices, Protestant or Catholic. The belief in liberal education, influenced by Harvard, Yale, and other universities founded in colonial times, has been a force of great importance in the growth of Minnesota higher education, allied with the religious motivations of the private colleges, and also significant in public higher education from its very beginnings.

In appraising the advances in the state's system of higher education, one must also take into account the increasing emphasis upon college work as basic to service and careers in a variety of professional fields and to education beyond undergraduate levels. On the public side the land-grant idea, with its emphasis on agriculture and mechanic arts, has played a creative role in the development of the university, especially in its advanced studies, researches, and the various kinds of specialized training essential to the needs of a changing American society.

Such underlying forces help to account for the founding and growth of the institutions that constitute Minnesota's system of higher education. There have also been motives of a somewhat more mundane character, such as the boosting proclivities of communities, the rivalries of various denominations, and a spirit of regional competition with older states. A Minnesota newspaper as early as 1849 expressed this competitive feeling when it declared that "not a single youth of either sex should be permitted to leave the territory to acquire an education for want of an institution at home."

Private colleges, among the "institutions at home," afford further illustrations of the "transit of culture" which has left deep marks in Minnesota's history. The backgrounds of these colleges were basically eastern and European. As one recalls sponsorship by Methodists, Presbyterians, Congregationalists, Baptists, Lutherans, and Catholics, one remembers

415

not only streams of migration from New England and other parts of the United States, but also spiritual heritages derived from Wesley, Calvin, Knox, Luther, St. Benedict, and other leaders of Old World Christianity. However varied the Christian traditions thus exemplified, the colleges, with their emphasis on liberal education, also embodied heritages reaching back to Plato, the classics, humane studies of earlier ages, and the English concepts of the centrality of the humanities. Geographically the private colleges link Minnesota institutions with Palestine, Greece, Italy, France and Germany, Norway and Sweden, England, Scotland, and other lands. In some instances, including such colleges as Augsburg, Gustavus Adolphus, St. Olaf, St. John's, Concordia at Moorhead, and Bethel, Minnesota developments are interrelated with the nineteenth-century immigration to America of people, faiths, and ideas.

The private colleges started humbly. They depended on churches and private gifts to meet expenses at their beginning. Often they pushed forward with plans and buildings without assurance, other than faith, that costs could be surmounted. Virtually all the colleges began as preparatory schools and maintained these as departments until their college divisions were established and the secondary schools of the state made it less necessary than it had been in early days for them to handle the preparatory work themselves. Thus Hamline University continued its preparatory department after its re-establishment at St. Paul in 1880 and did not terminate it until 1912. Carleton was authorized as "Northfield College" as early as 1866, had a preparatory department functioning by 1870, and took the name of Carleton College after a gift of $50,000 made by a Massachusetts friend of the school's president. But it continued its academy until 1907. Augsburg, transferred to Minneapolis from Wisconsin in 1872, opened its college two years later, but continued its preparatory school until 1933. Macalester College backgrounds reveal a long and brave struggle to develop a good preparatory school before, in 1885, the college itself emerged. St. Olaf began as "St. Olaf's School," founded in 1874 by a Lutheran pastor, Bernt J. Muus. The first college class was graduated in 1890, a year after the official name of the institution had become "St. Olaf College." These illustrations typify the efforts of the early colleges to train pre-college students as a base for their collegiate work and they also evidence the relatively slow and conservative approach made to genuine college programs.

The private colleges have had dedicated leadership in their struggling pioneer years and also in the time of later growth and adjustment as standards were raised, enrollments increased, and staffs of well-trained teachers secured.

The record of every college reveals men who made large contributions in successive periods, facing problems that taxed their resourcefulness and courage. The Canadian-born George H. Bridgman served as president of Hamline University from 1883 to 1912 and did much to transform an institution of humble beginnings into a good college. His central purpose was to select a strong faculty and to foster, not a narrow spirit of denominationalism, but one of tolerance and genuine catholicity. The reins of Hamline leadership passed from hand to hand as the years went by, and in recent times the college has made notable strides under the historian Paul H. Giddens.

Dr. Edward D. Neill, the founding father of Macalester College, was pre-eminently a scholar, and he stamped the college with his own standards of scholarship as essential to liberal education. Among his successors were James Wallace, classical scholar, and in a later time Charles J. Turck, crusader for freedom in the forwarding of liberal education, and Dr. Harvey M. Rice, president for the modern era of the college. Carleton College had firm leadership from its two long-term presidents, James Woodward Strong and Donald C. Cowling, who, with only a half dozen years between their terms, led the college from 1870 to 1945 in a growth that established its national renown. The gains they achieved were consolidated and advanced in recent years under the leadership of Laurence M. Gould. A new president, John W. Nason, took office in 1962. Declaring his faith in liberal education, he said, "If civilization is to survive in this perilous century, it will be because enough people can see the issues in the perspective of human history and human destiny."

Augsburg College in its pioneering era enjoyed the intellectual stimulus of such men as Georg Sverdrup and Sven Oftedal, both trained in theology in Norway. The traditions they set in Christian aims and classical education were carried forward and developed by their successors, George Sverdrup, Jr., and Bernhard Christenson. The eminent Swedish-American preacher and educator Eric Norelius played an originating role in the backgrounds of Gustavus Adolphus College; and in late years the college has enjoyed able leadership under Dr. Edgar Carlson. Among the Catholics, John Ireland, with his flaming devotion to education, had a similar role in the founding of St. Thomas College and St. Thomas Aquinas Seminary. A long-time president of St. Olaf College was John Kildahl, an educational statesman, and his successors include Lars W. Boe, who guided the college with sprightly vigor in its "growing-up" years; and Clemens M. Granskou, leader for nearly two decades of vigorous growth. Concordia College, a sentinel of higher education on the western rim of the state, grew into a good arts college under successive leaders of purpose and vision.

These men are among those who poured talent and vision into the building of liberal-arts colleges in the state. Their task and that of their devoted faculties was not easy. The road upward was steep. But they looked beyond temporary discouragements, envisioning a long future. Their monuments are the vital and expanded colleges of the present generation.

Some of the liberal-arts colleges of Minnesota were coeducational from the start, notably Hamline University, which opened its doors to men and women from its founding in 1854. A few of the Protestant institutions that started as colleges for men eventually became coeducational. An example is Augsburg, which remained a men's college until 1921. All eight of the Protestant colleges that were functioning in 1960 were coeducational.

By 1960 there were seven Catholic colleges in the state. Four of these — St. Benedict, St. Catherine, St. Scholastica, and St. Teresa — were women's colleges. St. Catherine's (in St. Paul) grew out of the early endeavors of the Sisters of Carondelet. Like the Protestant institutions, its early stage was an academy. And like other colleges, the institution, noted for its emphasis on scholarship, enjoyed leadership of rare quality in the formative years, notably that of Mother Seraphine Ireland, a sister of Archbishop Ireland. The College of St. Benedict, developed by the Sisters of that Order, similarly began with an academy and emerged in 1915 with a full collegiate program. It is located at St. Joseph. St. Teresa, at Winona, was founded by Sisters of St. Francis and graduated its first college class of lay students in 1914. The College of St. Scholastica in Duluth, a daughter institution of the College of St. Benedict, developed from an academy into a college in 1932.

The men's colleges under Catholic auspices included St. John's University, in the St. Cloud area. Site of a famed abbey, it was rooted in early

The South St. Paul stockyards, about 1915

An early cooperative, the creamery at Claremont

View of the Mississippi River near Maiden Rock, from a
water color by Edwin Whitefield

Red River carts loaded with furs on the trail
from Pembina to St. Paul

The first airplane flight over Minneapolis, on January 12, 1913

A 1914 forerunner of the Greyhound Bus Company (from *Beginnings of the Bus Industry* by Mrs. A. G. Anderson)

One of the research balloons developed by Minnesota industrial concerns

Minnesota history. St. Thomas, located in St. Paul, the largest of the Catholic men's colleges, has had outstanding leaders in such presidents as Fathers Vincent Flynn, versed in literature, and James P. Shannon, Yale-educated historian. A relatively late comer was St. Mary's, founded in 1913 at Winona and offering full college work since 1925.

Of the fifteen private colleges, including Protestant and Catholic, six were in the Twin Cities, five in southern and southeastern Minnesota, two in the central part of the state, one on the western border, and one in the northeast.

Whatever their origins, these colleges emphasized liberal education. They have been characterized by a progressive widening of curriculum. Physical sciences and social sciences began in due time to play large roles in their work. Classical studies dwindled, and place was found for physical education, home economics, nursing, music, art. Studies arranged into majors took account of the trend toward specialization in American education.

Liberal education was fundamental, but thought was given to weighting courses in the direction of professional and graduate studies. With expansion came enlarged campuses, arrays of modern buildings for classrooms, libraries, laboratories, dormitories, gymnasiums, athletic fields, auditoriums. Endowment funds were built up with the million as a unit; libraries were enriched; and by the late 1950s the total number of private-college students in any given year went to fifteen thousand or more and faculties reached a combined total of a thousand or more. Regional and national recognition and accreditation testified to faculties and facilities adequate to the increasing needs of the colleges.

Denominational interest and control continued in many institutions, but a tendency developed toward the secularization of education in some of the private colleges. There was also a leaguing of interest not only among the private colleges but throughout the entire system of higher education. This cooperative concern meant no retreat from the aspirations of the individual colleges, but an acceptance of the idea of "strength in diversity" and a recognition of educational aims commonly shared. Higher education was recognized as a partnership of obligation to the youth of Minnesota, and this embraced all the colleges. Cooperation also implied awareness of the fact that, however important college education may have been in earlier years, its importance would increase as the curtain unrolled on the future. The colleges, cognizant of their responsibilities, were supported by their own constituencies, by the state's citizens, and by private foundations concerned with the advancement of American education.

Through a century the University of Minnesota has been central to the state's educational history and in innumerable ways to the life of the Minnesota people. Its functioning as a public agency of higher education, however, came long after its charter of 1851. In fact, eighteen years of frustration and travail — years in which panic, Civil War, and Indian outbreak had their dire effects — preceded its opening for college work in 1869.

With the abandonment of the preparatory school, the university's cavernous building, "Old Main," stood empty for many years, and university debts mounted despite the land grants of 1851 and the confident anticipation that under the statehood act the institution would receive an additional two townships of land. This in fact it did, but not until after confirmatory action by Congress in 1870. Nor indeed did the Morrill Act of 1862, with its promised donation of still further lands in support of instruction in agriculture and the mechanic arts, set the university into motion. The land-grant college act meant 120,000 acres for the university, but at the outset it seemed possible, even likely, that the grant would channel to an institution at Glencoe unconnected with the university.

The university was reorganized in 1860, but progress in untangling its fiscal difficulties did not come until the hard-driving and large-minded John S. Pillsbury became a regent in 1863. A believer in the idea of a true state university, he was determined not to let "the institution sink under debts and unpaid mortgages." In 1864 he secured a reorganization that put the affairs of the university in the hands of three regents, including himself. Vigorous action followed. University bonds were bought up at discounts and nearly all the debts were paid. Pillsbury and his associates astutely saved most of the federal land grant of 1851, and in three years they rescued the university from threatened bankruptcy.

In 1867 the preparatory school again opened its doors. "Old Main" was renovated after having served as a veritable barn. The legislature assigned the Morrill Act lands to the university, thus opening the way for an agricultural college as a part of a central state university. A new organization act was passed in 1868, providing for nine regents, including the governor and state superintendent of public instruction and seven gubernatorial appointees. The three-man board had done its work, and Pillsbury had won the accolade later given him as "Father of the University." In terminating their heroic efforts, Pillsbury and his colleagues urged that the university should forthwith begin to function as a real university.

Getting started was a matter of having a president, a faculty, students — and a college curriculum. For president the regents found the man, William Watts Folwell. Born on a farm near Romulus, New York, he was a scholar and soldier who had served in the Army of the Potomac as an officer of engineers, a versatile man of thirty-six with a restless prophetic imagination. After graduating from Hobart College in 1857, he had made the European grand tour, visited Germany, Greece, Italy, Switzerland, and then hurried home for the Civil War. Afterwards he engaged in business and held a professorship at Kenyon College in Ohio.

Folwell arrived in Minnesota just before the university opened in 1869. He came to St. Anthony, was bundled into a two-seated surrey with his wife and children and driven to a temporary abode. He found a university faculty of nine, a freshman class of thirteen, and a preparatory department numbering more than 200. He interested himself in every aspect of the infant university. It must have more land for an experimental farm. It must build a library. It must take scientific and literary journals. These were items quickly noted, but when, on December 22, Folwell gave his inaugural address, he spoke as a prophet. He presented one of the major state papers of American educational history and challenged the state as it had not been challenged before in the educational field.

Fittingly Pillsbury presided at the inauguration, held on December 22, 1869, in Old Main. Folwell there set forth a breath-taking conception of a state university — a federation of schools with a faculty of teachers and investigators. He stressed both science and the humanities, a university open to all "worthy comers," an institution that would become the "head and crown" of the school system. He asked for a museum, a department of public health, a state geological survey, a program for training experts in legislation and administration, a great library, an observatory, and faculty research. The institution, he said, was "not merely from the people, but for the people." Its future support would demand millions of dollars. He planted ideas as "the hopeful toil of the sower." The address

421

was a modern charter of university services and concepts, far in advance of its time. His spirit, as a later president said, "was possessed with the future, not as a dream or mirage, but as a realizable reality."

One of Folwell's ideas was that of junior colleges which would function in high schools and academies until students were "somewhere near the end of the sophomore year." He later developed his proposal into what he called the "Minnesota Plan," and it was adopted by the regents in 1870. A well-known historian has described it as "the first public proposal of its kind in America." The trouble was that at that period well-developed high schools were few. The junior college idea was so far ahead of its time in fact that it existed only on paper. The regents themselves soon withdrew their support of the plan. Folwell in his mellow years described it as a "premature romance." It was not until 1915 that the first Minnesota public junior college was established — at Rochester, forty-six years after Folwell had spoken. Today there are eleven such institutions in the state — community colleges serving needs close to the home areas of their students. Five of the colleges are in the iron-range country, a sixth is at nearby Brainerd, and five more are in southern and western Minnesota. Their activities are a blooming, however late, of the Folwellian romance. If his role was chiefly prophetic with respect to junior colleges, he took practical steps to improve the secondary schools, notably by his support of state aid to high schools in 1878.

Like the private colleges, the University of Minnesota has had leaders of dedication and varied skills adapted to the changing needs of institutional growth. Folwell himself, however fertile in ideas, was a prophet, not an administrator. He served as president from 1869 to 1884, when he resigned on request. Much of what the university became was envisaged by him, but in his period Minnesota was not ripe for the modernized higher education he wanted. Neither regents nor faculty betrayed any enthusiasm for his proposals. He worked with a small student body, most of the students having enrolled in the preparatory division. The first graduating class, in 1873, consisted of two students. His curricular efforts included physics and history, and both of these were eliminated by regent action in 1879.

Apart from Folwell's vision of what the university might be in the future, two achievements in his time were noteworthy. One was the sale of farm land adjacent to the Minneapolis campus and the purchase of the lands that became the nucleus of the College of Agriculture. The other was the creation of a faculty that included some teachers of high quality, including John F. Downey in mathematics and Maria Sanford in English. The latter was a Connecticut Yankee of salty personality, an inspired teacher, and an eloquent speaker. For a long generation she influenced students and reached out to the people of state and country with her patriotic fervor. Today she is one of the two Minnesotans honored in Statuary Hall in Washington.

A new stage in university history came during the administration of Cyrus Northrop as president (1884–1911). Schooled by experience as a teacher of rhetoric and literature at Yale, he was urbane, wise, witty, kindly, and patriarchal. Neither a theorist nor a crusader, Northrop was a man of accommodation and peace. Humane in his interests, he was a master of mellow and persuasive oratory. He endeared himself to the people, won support from every group, and as the years went by became the most beloved of all Minnesotans.

During the Northrop regime Minnesota moved into the "federation of schools" which Folwell had advocated for a true university. The move was step-by-step, a seemingly casual sequence. The arts college, which had mainly constituted the university under Folwell, was enlarged and strengthened. Gradually, over the years, the university established colleges or schools of law, medicine (amalgamating several non-state schools), agriculture, engineering, mines, pharmacy, dentistry, and education. Graduate work was begun in modest fashion before 1880; the first Ph.D. was awarded in 1888, and a Graduate School was established in 1905. Late in the Northrop years a School of Nursing was begun (1909), the first collegiate school of its kind in the world. All these divisions began modestly, but they provided a framework for expansion through a long future.

Enrollments, small in early years, grew into thousands (3900 by 1905). Research developed, much of it interrelated with service to the state, especially after the Hatch Act of 1887. State support mounted through Northrop's persuasion and in consequence of an increasing public recognition of the importance of the university to the state and its people. Funds for many new buildings were secured. The agricultural division continued as an integral part of the university, though some effort was made in the 1880s to bring about a divorce — a move defeated by forceful arguments offered by Northrop and by Pillsbury.

The organization of new schools, the erection of buildings, and the

423

suave leadership of Northrop were important, but it was a faculty of distinction that gave character to the rising institution. The roll of teachers, not a few of whom were genuine investigators, is long. The faculties numbered 140 by 1905. A few names will serve to suggest the quality of the steadily enlarging staff. The university in Northrop's time had such outstanding men as David F. Swenson in philosophy; Willis M. West, Frank M. Anderson, and Albert B. White in history; Oscar Firkins and Joseph W. Beach in English; Frederick Klaeber in philology; Henry F. Nachtrieb and Charles P. Sigerfoos in zoology; Conway MacMillan in botany; Thomas S. Roberts, known later for his remarkable studies of birds; Alfred Owre in dentistry; Frederick Wulling in pharmacy; W. R. Appleby in mines and metallurgy; and Willet M. Hays, Samuel Green, and T. L. Haecker in agricultural fields. Alongside such scholars were teachers like Richard Burton whose verve and histrionic skills made them immensely popular. And others of an older generation, including the strong-minded Maria Sanford and the glowing Greek professor, John Corrin Hutchinson, added to the excitement of learning for neophytes. These and other distinguished teachers did much to lift the university from infancy to maturity. Northrop did not have the acumen of a Folwell as an originator of ideas and as a prophet, but he had an eye for character.

A great university was in the making. When the benevolent Cyrus Northrop withdrew from the academic scene in 1911, the time had come for what a later president called "a second founding of the university." This came with the advent of George Edgar Vincent, sociologist from the University of Chicago, executive of extraordinary vigor, witty and solid speaker whose ideas were voiced with gatling-gun rapidity and crystal clarity. He was an academic house-cleaner, and his educational affinity was with Folwell. An apostle of education for a new era, this dynamic leader in six turbulent years transformed the university and set it on its way to the achievement of national and international pre-eminence.

Vincent had a genius for choosing lieutenants of large views, action, and courage. The Law School was reorganized under Dean William R. Vance and its faculty rebuilt. The reshaping of the College of Medicine was nothing less than revolutionary. Working for a full-time staff of medical teachers and research men, the president in 1913 called for the resignations of all the members of the medical faculty. Then, with a dean of modern outlook in Elias P. Lyon, the school was overhauled. The

Graduate School had a new birth under Guy Stanton Ford as dean (1913). His skill in finding scholars and teachers of high quality enriched the entire university and made the Graduate School a center for teaching and research that soon won national and international recognition. He joined Vincent and the Doctors Mayo in a move to make the medical resources of the Mayo Clinic a part of the Graduate School, with emphasis on specialized training beyond the M.D. The result, after spirited public controversy, was the Mayo Foundation for Medical Education and Research.

The College of Science, Literature, and the Arts blossomed under the leadership of an imaginative scientist, John B. Johnston. The division of education was metamorphosed into a genuine college under the vigorous Lotus D. Coffman, whose insistence on studies of university problems led to the Bureau of Cooperative Research (later the Bureau of Institutional Research). The Extension Division developed as an important partner in the scheme of university education, with Richard Price at its head. And the teaching and researches of the faculty of the College of Agriculture and the Experiment Station came into a new era under Albert F. Woods, with many investigators of original mind.

The university vibrated with change, reform, reorganization, unification, and fresh talents. It was the work of many gifted men, but at its heart was the gay and ebullient spirit of Vincent, builder and modernizer, whose goal was a university of excellence for twentieth-century advance.

The dynamic Vincent, with most of his reforms accomplished, pranced off to New York in 1917 to take over the presidency of the Rockefeller Foundation. Turbulence did not end, however, for World War I greatly altered campus life. Many students went to war and faculty members joined them, not a few in specialized war services in Washington. The university was disrupted, but the administration of Marion Leroy Burton (1917–20) was a breathing spell after the exciting and revolutionary years of Vincent — an "uneasy interregnum," as the historian of the university terms it. Burton was aligned in temperament and purpose with the easygoing Northrop tradition — not with that of Folwell, the idea-driven seer, or Vincent, the scintillating reorganizer. Apart from war problems and limitations on academic freedom that he lacked the courage to oppose, he is remembered for helping to launch the School of Business Administration and for his concern about the university's expansion and campus planning.

In the decades that followed the regimes of the first four presidents,

425

the University of Minnesota expanded enormously in its physical facilities. Its enrollments reflected changing tides in population growth and in public appreciation of the importance of higher education. There were ups and downs as depression succeeded prosperity, as war interrupted education, and as crises of many kinds occurred. But the trend was toward increasing enrollments, and by the beginnings of the 1960s the university (in its fall quarter) passed the 30,000 mark. Faculties were enlarged, research increased in volume and significance, and many new programs added to the complexity of the curriculum and to its challenges to students of differing objectives. The tradition of high leadership — in tune with changing standards and demands — was deepened by the presidencies of Lotus D. Coffman (1920–38), Guy Stanton Ford (1938–41), Walter C. Coffey (1941–45), James Lewis Morrill (1945–60), and O. Meredith Wilson, who, as the ninth president, succeeded Dr. Morrill in 1960.

Coffman was an experienced and decisive schoolman. He became known in the state and nation as a perceptive interpreter of the state university, a defender of freedom in teaching and research, and a builder who found no clash between bigness and quality. With growth came new conceptions not only of buildings and expanded campus, but also of programs and courses. Organization, already well set, developed along new lines. University College, reaching across the boundaries of other colleges, was created to meet the needs of students who did not fit into the established college programs. A research-oriented Institute of Child Welfare took shape. For students who could not look forward to a conventional four-year course, the General College was established in 1932 as a terminal two-year school. A novel experiment that won permanent status within the university framework was the Center for Continuation Study (1936), an instrument for adult education for people in need of bridging the gaps between past training and the advances since made in their respective fields. A University Press, inspired by Dean Ford, began its productive career.

With the university's proliferation, Coffman welded the institution into a unity, counteracted tendencies toward fragmentation, and defended the university's independence, with a significant triumph in the Supreme Court's decision in the Chase case (1928). He gave support to scientific testing and to systematic studies of university problems and needs, and he defended the university's size as an inevitable growth demanded and needed by the people. His interest in the intellectual and social development of students is remembered and honored in the Coffman Memorial Union.

Dr. Ford's short presidency climaxed a career of distinctive university service as professor of history, dean of the Graduate School, and co-pilot with presidents through a quarter of a century. No less a defender of academic freedom than Coffman, he took the lead even before he was president in righting an injustice done to a member of the faculty at a moment of hysteria during World War I. And he gave form to an eloquent affirmation of university ideals engraved over Northrop Auditorium:

Founded in the faith that men are ennobled by understanding
Dedicated to the advancement of learning and the search for truth
Devoted to the instruction of youth and the welfare of the state

His presidency, coming shortly before his retirement, tided the university through the close of the depressing 1930s and the anxious time just before the storm of World War II burst.

Another short-term president guided the university through the period of World War II when, once more, the institution was disrupted by war and urgent national needs and demands. This was Walter C. Coffey, the administrator of the university's Department of Agriculture. He kept the academic ship steady, through four years of crisis. Despite difficulties, he never ceased to expound the general role of the university. To him the institution was "interwoven with the fabric of life in Minnesota." "There is scarcely a family," he said, "with whom it has not had an instructional contact; the results of its research have made life better and more secure in rural and metropolitan areas alike; its services, whether in providing medical care for the sick, in helping the farmer with his problems, or in aiding industry and the professions, ramify through the entire population."

When James L. Morrill took over the presidency in 1945, the university had been forged into the "head and crown" of the state's school system — the future status coveted by Folwell three quarters of a century earlier.

The decade and a half of the eighth president witnessed a succession of new problems and of enormous expansion. Experienced in educational administration, President Morrill led the university with a statesmanship sensitive to the times and their exigencies. He was alert to new needs, unafraid of experiment, and a convincing interpreter of the land-grant college philosophy. His ideas, framed in his humane way for the mid-twentieth century, were in many respects akin to Folwell's concept of a state university from the people and for the people.

The postwar years were marked by crises and unprecedented developments. A surge of veterans, with governmental aid, streamed into the university. Research, supported by the state and by industry and the federal government, took on new and enlarged dimensions. By legislative action the State Teachers' College at Duluth was absorbed as a branch of the university, and in a decade it grew to impressive heights. A College of Veterinary Medicine came into being on the St. Paul campus. A liberal arts college branch was instituted at Morris. Vast new buildings were erected and put to use, including a towering medical center. And the university, looking ahead to the 1960s and 1970s, worked out plans for an extended campus on the west bank of the Mississippi.

Every college in the far-flung institution responded to the president's insistence on scholarship of high caliber, on integrity in teaching, research, and public service. The campus was the scene of self-study. Agriculture grappled with intricate problems of research, as did Medicine and the scientific and professional schools. Large emphasis was placed on high standards both in teaching and in research in the areas of the liberal arts. The Graduate School drew thousands of students for advanced work and widened the university's reputation throughout the world. The university library grew into one of the basic research libraries of the country. Its collections neared the two-million mark, and it attained special excellence in many fields, such as trade, commerce, exploration, and South Asia.

Radio, television, agricultural schools and experiment stations, a wide-ranging extension division, bureaus, institutes, a productive University Press, a University Theater, a World Affairs Center, a program of concerts and lectures, a plan for the continuing education of women — these and scores of other enterprises of the university reached out to the people. All Minnesota became the university campus. Legislatures reviewed university needs in the light of the president's presentations and gave increasing support. Folwell's prophecy that the million would be the unit of costs had long since been realized. Economic ups and downs occurred and legislatures took them into account. By and large, however, the state and its people understood what the university meant in its services to their progress and well-being.

Amid recurring crises Dr. Morrill preached freedom, opportunity, and a flexibility that made room for change. He practiced the "art of the possible." His aims, as he himself said, embraced "the philosophical and the practical as scholarship and science and society are able to perceive and conceive these aims." He and his colleagues interpreted the university as one of the many institutions, public and private, serving the people in the realm of higher education. In this spirit he forwarded cooperation among all the colleges, as he did in his working relationships with faculty members, administrative associates, and students, and he promoted understanding among the public of the problems, needs, and values of education in a changing world.

Minnesota entered the 1960s as one of the leading universities of America. Its graduates and postgraduates by the thousands went out to professional service and attainment. Its faculties, augmented by its new streams of talent, taught undergraduate, professional, and graduate students, and made research contributions of amazing variety and recognized importance. Teaching and research touched virtually every field, basic and applied, from agriculture to mining; from medicine to literature and classics; biology to history; economics to chemistry, physics, and engineering; education to art and music.

President O. Meredith Wilson, in his inaugural address in 1961, interpreted the basic aims of the institution. "The genius of a university," he said, "is satisfied when professors and students are gathered together in one community engaged in a joint enterprise — perpetuating the wisdom of the ages, increasing the community of men capable of intellectual inquiry, and together expanding the frontiers of truth."

Through more than eleven decades the Minnesota people fashioned a school system. By virtue of its growth, quality, services, leadership, and popular support, it won distinction. Viewed as a whole, the system was characterized by diversity, strength, and a general level of excellence. The schools, serving succeeding generations, always thought of themselves as "ongoing." This they were. They dealt with problems and needs of their own time, but, by the very nature of education, they had to look ahead constantly.

School problems are never solved once and for all, and the modern state is not unaware of deficiencies, unmet needs, and the imperatives of a mushrooming population. Challenges are many. There are shortages of classrooms and facilities. Many promising students unfortunately fail to finish high school or drop out of college or university with inadequate preparation for work and careers. As standards for the teaching profession have increased, salaries have tended to lag behind the levels that are merited by high training and experience. Not all school boards are enlightened, and occasionally obscurantism raises its head to the detriment of educational advance. The Russian menace has accentuated the need for science at every level of education, but many urge the importance of the social sciences and humanities. Much thought has been devoted to the curriculum and to new methods of study, and it has been projected in a period of controversy and emotion with respect to the role of the schools. The problems of financial support are pressing, with needs and costs running a never-ending race.

Whatever the problems and difficulties of the Minnesota school system, however, it is a living legacy from the past — a past of ideas, purpose, sacrifice, and service. The people have been steadfast in their devotion to universal education and in their support of its steadily mounting costs, even though at any given time the job is unfinished and ongoing.

The Doctors Mayo, from a memorial at Rochester, Minnesota

PHOTO BY JOHN SZARKOWSKI

✶
Toward Social Maturity

W HEN John Lind, blunt-spoken teacher, lawyer, and politician, took office as governor of Minnesota in 1899, he spoke for a state modernizing its outlook.

The Swedish-born Lind won the governorship a half century after Minnesota's birth as a territory. He served across the borderline between the nineteenth and the twentieth centuries. His experience had embraced three terms in Congress as a Republican, but intellectually and by temperament he was an independent. Cutting loose from old ties, he called himself a "political orphan." In 1896, the year of Bryan's first candidacy for President, Lind ran for governor with the triple endorsement of Democrats, Silver Republicans, and Populists. That election he lost to the stanch Republican, David M. Clough, who had succeeded Knute Nelson. In 1898, after service in the Spanish-American War, Lind tried again. Once more he ran as a fusion candidate. And this time he won — the first election since pre-Civil War times in which a Republican had failed to capture the governorship of Minnesota.

Lind, saluted as "Honest John" by the people, did not carry out large reforms as governor. He faced skeptical Republican majorities in both houses of the legislature. But in his inaugural address he offered the people a memorable "inventory of Minnesota life and problems at the turn of the century."

He looked at the state's progress, urged reforms in taxation, called for improvement in the care of the mentally ill and retarded, advocated

433

support for education, agriculture, and forestry, and voiced approval of direct democratic controls of state government by the people. Lind predicted for the twentieth century a state population of ten millions — a prophecy that time thus far is not sustaining. But he sounded a caution to those who might think the state should rest its claim to greatness on material achievements. "The greatness of the state," he declared, "does not consist alone in the material wealth within its boundaries, nor in the number of its population." Instead, he pointed to just laws, enlightened public interest, and a fair sharing of the state's wealth by its people.

John Lind was a one-term governor. When he ran for re-election in 1900, he was narrowly defeated by a genial, experienced, and popular riverman, the Republican Samuel R. Van Sant, last of Civil War veterans to hold the Minnesota governorship. However short his term of service, Lind symbolized transition in viewpoint as the state stood on the threshold of the new century. It was no fortuitous circumstance that he devoted attention to correctional, charitable, and penal institutions and to related social problems. Significant beginnings had been made in frontier days; social needs of modern character had been foreshadowed; and some forward steps had been taken. But Lind, Van Sant, later governors, and successive legislatures had to look in new spirit at modern problems. They understood the need of reorganization and coordination of effort. They realized that they were dealing with a state shifting from an agricultural to an industrialized stage.

As early as 1851 Minnesota recognized its obligation to provide a penitentiary. But official concern for unfortunate people — the poor, sick, and mentally retarded — expressed itself only in gradual and haphazard steps taken as one situation after another forced action. Mental troubles, inherited ills, delinquency, and the bite of poverty were part of the pioneer age, as of later times. But there was no early awareness of the need for social planning and coordination of effort in dealing with social problems, and the medical and social sciences had a long way to go in the understanding of such matters. Many people were reluctant to turn aside from the traditional efforts by families, churches, and volunteer services and sacrifices to cope with mounting social ills.

These efforts were not enough. The complexity of problems whose solution went beyond local care brought one state institution after another into being. Organized society faced and had to deal with perplexing actualities. A school for the indigent deaf and dumb was launched by the state at Faribault in 1863, and provision was shortly made at the same place for the blind. In early years there were makeshift arrangements for the mentally abnormal, but in 1866 Minnesota found it necessary to open a hospital, at St. Peter, for the insane. The next year an institution for errant youth was started in St. Paul which, after some years, was transferred to Red Wing. As population increased, the numbers of mentally afflicted also increased. Additional hospitals for the insane were begun at Rochester and Fergus Falls in 1879 and 1890. These were not enough, and still others, at Hastings, Anoka, Willmar, and Moose Lake were opened later (between 1900 and 1938).

Meanwhile, in 1889, a "reformatory" for younger men was started at St. Cloud, to be followed in another generation by a school for delinquent girls at Sauk Centre (1911) and a reformatory for women at Shakopee (1920); a modernized state penitentiary at Stillwater opened in 1912, sixty-one years after the institution was founded. In 1879, a sanctuary and school for retarded children — the feeble-minded — was added to the assignments of the hard-pressed institution at Faribault. This marked constructive beginnings of state effort to aid such young unfortunates. At first the training of these children was merely an adjunct to the earlier school, but in 1881 the legislature authorized a permanent school and a building at Faribault. Minnesota secured for the institution a superintendent of rare competence, Dr. A. C. Rogers, whose skill made it one of the best institutions of its kind in the country.

At a midway point in this diversification of state institutions, Minnesota realized that something more was needed than casual steps or specific hospitals or schools for special groups or classes of unfortunate persons.

The state was not unaware that people in other parts of the country were coping with similar problems. It took note of moves toward coordination of public effort in Massachusetts and other states. The upshot was that in 1883 Minnesota, on the recommendation of Governor Hubbard, set up a central State Board of Corrections and Charities. It was not given much authority, but it was charged with the responsibility of investigating "the whole system of public charities and correctional institutions of the state." It was authorized to examine the conditions and management of "prisons, jails, infirmaries, public hospitals, and asylums," and to make recommendations for improvement and advancement.

Time and need seem to produce dedicated leaders in nearly every field of human advance, and the area of social betterment is no exception. Hastings Hornell Hart, a social-minded minister in Worthington, was appointed secretary of the new Board of Corrections and Charities. Undeterred by his lack of authority, he gave dedicated service and careful thought to the assignment for a decade and a half. His contributions were so many and worthy that Dr. Folwell has fittingly named him Minnesota's "Apostle of Charities."

Hart reported miserable, even horrifying, conditions in county jails and poorhouses. He emphasized the need of uniform accounting in the correctional and charitable institutions. He recommended many reforms, and legislatures heeded his advice. A parole system was inaugurated in the state penitentiary. The St. Cloud reformatory was started. Red Wing instituted schooling as a means of youth rehabilitation. Laws improved conditions in county jails. A state public school was established at Owatonna. There, through the years, thousands of dependent and neglected children of tender years were given training and then sent out to homes where, it was hoped, they could live normal lives. Hart investigated the mental hospitals, and his findings led to reforms in supervision, care, and physical surroundings.

In lectures and reports, Hart educated the public on responsibility for standards in society's care of its victims of misfortune. Not the least of his contributions was the initiation, in the 1890s, of a series of annual conferences, modeled on the already established national conferences on charities and corrections. He brought together officials and other citizens from all parts of the state to consider Minnesota's institutions and problems of social amelioration. The precedent he thus established is the background of annual social work conferences that have been continued to the present time. They have been projected into an age when social work has become a profession in which men and women are highly trained, theoretically and practically, for specialized social services.

Governor Lind in 1899 favored a strengthening of the existing state board. Each separate institution had its own board of trustees. The state board was supervisory to the extent of investigating and recommending reforms. But authority and fiscal controls were not centralized. Lind suggested that vesting authority in the state board would mean an administration, as he put it, "free from local influences and politics." It might mean improvements in the total system. He balanced arguments and was cautious about offering final conclusions as to what precisely should be done. His very caution may account for the fact that the legislature did nothing.

But Lind's successor, Governor Van Sant, an advocate of fiscal reform, recommended that the Board of Corrections and Charities should be abolished. In its place he proposed a new and salaried State Board of Control. It should be charged with responsibility for "the management and control of the charitable reformatory and penal institutions of the state." The legislature accepted Van Sant's views, and with only a few exceptions the separate boards of trustees for individual institutions were swept away.

Both Lind and Van Sant took into account patterns of administration adopted in other states, notably Wisconsin and Iowa. They wanted Minnesota to be in step with national progress. Their primary purpose was economy, not a new and broad social advance. With time, however, central authority contributed not only to economical procedures, but also to a rise in institutional standards.

Innumerable advances have characterized later public administration in the areas of penal institutions and the care of the mentally ill or deficient. They evidence a wholehearted acceptance by society of responsibilities to individuals suffering from social circumstances beyond their control. Revealing of new attitudes were moves to assist the poor and the aged. Humanitarian influences were forwarded by national leaders, including the humane-minded Theodore Roosevelt. In Minnesota mothers' pensions were authorized as early as 1913. The blight of depression in later years, beginning in 1929, opened a wide path to old-age assistance. As problems deepened and unemployment and hunger stalked the land, state and nation worked hand in hand, and in 1935 social and economic concern resulted in the Social Security Act.

While state and federal intervention went forward, the tradition of voluntary cooperation in meeting common problems did not lose its vitality. Governmental aid and action had their place and were important, but the people, outside official action, formed voluntary groups and organizations to strengthen institutions and activities designed to ameliorate oppressive conditions of living in cities large and small. Voluntary association, voluntary giving — these were typical of Minnesota, as they were of communities throughout the nation.

Representative of the modern mood have been community chest campaigns which in recent times have been organized into comprehensive United Fund campaigns. Annually these efforts raise money for a wide array of local and national causes. They include the YMCA and the YWCA, girl and boy scouts, campfire girls, neighborhood houses, and family social services. They aid organizations fighting particular diseases, such as diabetes, arthritis, cerebral palsy, polio, and cystic fibrosis. They support moves to cope with problems of mental health, retarded children, and rehabilitation. And their support reaches areas and groups struck by disaster.

In all this the social historian discerns a civic-minded society that lends a steadying hand to the efforts of men to promote health and a rewarding community life. No law or edict compels people to give, but they pour hundreds of thousands of dollars each year into humane causes that deserve and enlist their interest. It is a continuing interest. Underlying it is the hope of men for a world in which affliction and unhappiness will be lessened. It is an ironical circumstance that not a few foreign observers, swallowing the fallacy of a "dollar-mad America," have failed to note the willingness of Americans, rich and poor, to share their goods with people less fortunate than themselves. Citizens contribute to causes that translate dollars into health, recreation, human balance, and richness in family and community living.

A Department of Public Welfare replaced the old Board of Control in the late 1930s, and in 1959 a State Department of Corrections took over various functions and institutions formerly administered by the greatly expanded Department of Public Welfare. An agency that helped to promote coordination, training, and research was the Minnesota Corrections Association (begun in 1933 as the Minnesota Probation and Parole Association).

In all the counties of the state local welfare boards function in liaison with the Department of Public Welfare. Mental hospitals, mental clinics, health services for mentally ill children, institutions for the mentally retarded, community health centers, aid to the disabled and to the deaf and blind, plus old-age assistance and other forms of public help suggest the ever-widening scope of public responsibility on the social front. Before the separate Department of Corrections was established, the Department of Public Welfare reported (in 1958) that it operated twenty-one institutions, had more than 19,000 patients and inmates, and through its services affected more than 140,000 Minnesotans every month.

Significant phases of the modernizing of Minnesota public action, through the years, have included the development of a juvenile court system (from 1905), the abolition of capital punishment (1911), the opening of a colony for epileptics (1925), the establishment of a Youth Conservation Commission for offenders under the age of twenty-one (1947), and numerous counseling services set in motion for both adults and children. In state and in community and private social activities, the profession of social workers played important roles in specialized services.

Social agencies took account of shifting conditions of population, urbanizing trends, problems of congestion, the ups and downs of economic conditions, and advances in social theory. In its detail, the development of social amelioration has countless ramifications. A summary outline, however, emphasizes the care and vigor with which Minnesota implemented, publicly and privately, a philosophy with respect to those who cannot meet their fundamental needs. The pattern is one of leadership, transfers from the experience of other states, a professionalizing of humane services, and a rising civic conscience.

Closely related to society's pragmatic efforts to apply modern ideas to social problems were advances in public health, medical education, medical practice, and hospitals.

As in other fields, beginnings were small, then came prophetic leadership, and the traditional American talent for organization made its contribution. Progress across the years was so notable that Minnesota won national and international pre-eminence. Today, to many people the world over, the very name "Minnesota" brings to mind doctors, clinics, hospitals, medical research, and leadership in the crusade for good health. Minnesota has become a mecca for the sick and afflicted in body and mind.

In public health, the pioneer was a richly experienced Civil War surgeon who settled in Red Wing in 1866 and there began medical practice. He was Dr. Charles N. Hewitt, a thirty-one-year-old graduate of Hobart College and the Albany Medical College. He was a physician of ideas and of furious energy, a fighter against filth (of which he knew much from his grisly surgical work in the Army of the Potomac). He was an enemy of bad sanitation and of diseases which he believed modern man could master. He had not been long in Minnesota before he was convinced that the state must officially join the fight against disease.

439

Massachusetts had established a state board of health in 1869. California and Virginia had followed suit, but such boards were untried in the Middle West.

Dr. Hewitt pioneered this kind of board for Minnesota. He wrote the draft of a law and used his influence to get it adopted by the legislature in 1872. It was approved, and he became the executive officer of the board. This position he held for a quarter of a century. The man had tremendous drive. He launched a magazine called *Public Health.* In 1873 he was invited to accept a nonresident professorship in public health in the university, a decade before its College of Medicine got under way. Dr. Hewitt accepted and some years later was made professor of preventive medicine in the university's newly organized College of Medicine.

Dr. Hewitt preached and worked for good sanitation. He sponsored laws for quarantine against smallpox, diphtheria, and other diseases. He promoted vaccination and ran a vaccine station near his home base at Red Wing. He advocated a law (1885) requiring villages, boroughs, and cities to establish local boards of health. And he crusaded against the adulteration of foods long before Upton Sinclair wrote the frightening novel called *The Jungle* or Harvey W. Wiley stirred the public conscience to do something about reform in food controls or President Theodore Roosevelt sponsored, in 1906, the national Pure Food and Drug Act.

Dr. Hewitt's leadership left marks in legislation and in the local enforcement of health regulations. He stimulated public appreciation of the importance of public health. A few years after his regime, the movement to protect the public even took into account diseases in livestock. In 1903 the Livestock Sanitary Board was established to combat tuberculosis and other diseases in cattle.

The State Board of Health has continued its work through nearly a century. Its responsibilities grew tremendously as a state agency for enforcing regulations demanded by changing times and problems. The modern board deals with environmental sanitation. It has extensive laboratory services. It sponsors programs to control and prevent disease. It cooperates with local health administrations and it offers many special services, such as those for maternal and child health. It extends state aid and counsel in the field of hospital planning and construction under the federal Hill-Burton Act. And it also licenses nursing homes and uses its influence to promote improved standards in their administration.

Dr. Hewitt was a medical organizer. He was an exhorter and evangelist. But he did not stand alone. In many towns and cities health officers and doctors valiantly fought disease. They met head-on the horrors of smallpox, typhoid, and other epidemics. They worked for pure milk and foods; and they did what they could to improve sanitation. They supported vaccination, helped to establish hospitals, and in not a few instances pioneered new modes in medicine and surgery.

Dr. Justus Ohage in St. Paul was a resourceful and progressive leader, as was Dr. Arthur J. Gillette, whose concern centered in crippled children. So earnest was Dr. Gillette that in the 1890s he offered his services free if the state would furnish funds for the care of indigent crippled and deformed children. The state took him at his word and set up a modest appropriation for him in 1897. Fourteen years later his pioneering efforts were crowned by the establishment in St. Paul of the Gillette State Hospital for Crippled Children, the first institution of its kind in the United States.

Others enlisted in the grim fight against tuberculosis. A state that has largely won its war against the killing white scourge owes a lasting debt to Dr. H. Longstreet Taylor of St. Paul. He secured support for a hospital for consumptives, and in 1907 established a state sanatorium, Ahgwah-ching, near Leech Lake. A sanatorium in itself was good, but this was not enough to satisfy Dr. Taylor. He helped to start an Association for the Prevention of Tuberculosis, and this blossomed into the Minnesota Public Health Association. Moreover, what the state did at Leech Lake was echoed, within modest limits, in more than a dozen county sanatoriums throughout the state. People understood that tuberculosis was an insidious and wicked enemy. But they rightly believed that care and vigilance could allay its ravages.

As ideas developed, men fighting disease put more and more emphasis on prevention, with early testing, vaccination, and inoculation. They enlisted the aid of schools, health centers, and a public that was beginning to understand that diseases could be checked through science and devoted effort.

The State Board of Health had creative support in its work from men of laboratory skill, such as Dr. Louis B. Wilson; from leaders in medicine and surgery, such as the Mayo brothers; and from medical educators, such as Frank F. Wesbrook, professor and later dean of the university's medical college. After Dr. Hewitt's pioneering service, the board continued to enjoy resourceful leadership under Drs. Henry M. Bracken,

441

Albert J. Chesley, and Robert N. Barr. It expanded its work in campaigns for pure water and against one disease after another. It kept abreast of scientific advances in the areas pertinent to its activities; and its success ranked Minnesota among the leading states of America in the realm of public health.

Meanwhile the medical profession recruited new forces, doctors trained at the Rush Medical College in Chicago, at Michigan, and elsewhere. Hospitals, after pioneering by the Sisters of St. Joseph in the 1850s, increased as the health needs of the people increased. Medical organization, launched as early as 1853 by the Minnesota Medical Society, took new forms. Publications, including the *Northwestern Lancet*, were initiated. And, step by step, medical education was organized.

St. Joseph's Hospital in St. Paul did heroic service from the days of its modest beginnings through large growth in later years. In 1857 St. Luke's Hospital in St. Paul was founded, and in the 1870s and 1880s Bethesda Hospital and the public Ancker Hospital appeared. In Minneapolis the pioneer doctor A. E. Ames opened a "free dispensary" in 1871. In the same year an Episcopal minister, David B. Knickerbacker, started a "Cottage Hospital" which grew into the St. Barnabas Hospital. Northwestern Hospital, a "retreat for sick women and children," began in 1882; and the General Hospital and St. Mary's in 1887. Earlier, in 1881, the Minnesota College Hospital began, housed first in the old Winslow House on the St. Anthony side of Minneapolis, but later absorbed by the medical school of the university. What happened in the Twin Cities reflected modern trends that found vigorous expression also in Rochester, Stillwater, Duluth, Winona, and other cities.

It was one thing to establish hospitals, another to supply them with trained nurses. The hospitals themselves, one after another, established training schools. Recognition of nursing as a profession developed slowly, and, as has been noted, the university's School of Nursing, begun in 1909, was the first university school of its kind. To its founder, Dr. Richard O. Beard, nursing was one of society's important "life-serving and life-saving callings."

One cannot measure human service alone by numbers, but the purpose of the Minnesota people in their search for health is suggested by the growth of a remarkable hospital system. In Fort Snelling days Minnesota had one fifteen-bed hospital. By 1961 the state had as many as 160 general and special hospitals and infirmaries, and more than 500 nursing homes, boarding care homes and units, maternity homes, and convalescent care units. These institutions, in all, had more than 40,000 beds. In the earliest pioneer days there were no trained nurses in Minnesota. By 1961 there were more than 17,000.

Synchronizing with hospital expansion, medical education took initial form and soon made strides, first in independent medical schools in St. Paul and Minneapolis, and from the 1880s through the medical college of the University of Minnesota. As early as its charter in 1851, the university had envisaged a college of medicine, but its reality was long deferred. A small medical faculty was instituted under Folwell in 1883, headed by Dr. Hewitt. The driving force behind this move was Dr. Perry H. Millard, a graduate of the Rush Medical College. He realized that it was all-important to bring together in one state school the several institutions already functioning. In 1888 the St. Paul Medical College and the Minnesota College Hospital in Minneapolis relinquished their charters and were merged into the university's department of medicine. So also was the Minnesota College of Homeopathic Medicine. Some years later the Minneapolis College of Physicians and Surgeons, after a period under the banner of Hamline University, also was drawn into the university system. A unified and centralized medical school got under way, and its growth in research and student training, in hospital and laboratory facilities, in graduate specialization, and its numerous advances in the science of medicine are a major chapter of history not alone for Minnesota, but for the nation.

The course of dentistry in some respects parallels that of medicine. In early pioneer days anybody who could extract a tooth was a dentist, but standards were professionalized in the generation after the Civil War. City and state dental societies were formed in the 1880s. The Minnesota College Hospital introduced dental training. Alongside a state board of medical examiners, a similar board of dental examiners began to function; and the University of Minnesota, when it unified and improved the teaching of medicine, also embarked on a program in dentistry. Standards were modernized and elevated especially during the regime of Alfred Owre, dean of the dental school for more than two decades after 1905, a leader of versatile skill and prophetic vision.

Perhaps no Minnesota achievement has echoed more resonantly throughout the world than that of the "Doctors Mayo" — father and two sons. It begins with William Worrall Mayo, English-born physician who

443

came to Minnesota in the 1850s. He saw Indian war at first hand when he sewed up wounds at New Ulm in 1862, and in after years he made Rochester his base of action. A country doctor who kept himself *au courant* with medical advances in Europe and America, he won fame for his surgical skill. When a tornado struck his town in 1883, he ministered to the many injured and leagued himself with the Sisters of St. Francis, who built and developed what became one of the great hospitals of Minnesota, St. Marys. This was also the start of the world-famed Mayo Clinic. Its success was due not only to the originating energy of the elder Dr. Mayo, but also to the genius of his two sons, William James and Charles Horace Mayo, who earned their medical degrees in the 1880s and joined their father in his widening practice.

The Mayo story reveals extraordinary leadership and a partnership between hospital and clinic, both alert to new advances. The Mayo brothers, skilled and daring in surgery, never ceased their education in medical science at home and abroad. They grew to the stature of world-renowned statesmen in medical science and practice. They sought out men of high ability to work with them, established a clinical laboratory and museum, encouraged research and publication, and supported St. Marys and other hospitals. They attracted patients first by the hundreds, then by the thousands, from all parts of America and the world. Even by the early 1920s more than 23,000 patients crowded into the little Minnesota town yearly to reap benefits from its specialized talent, and in later decades the numbers seeking services from the many-branched clinic went beyond 100,000 a year. It is not so much numbers, however, as quality that is the key to the distinction of this country town metamorphosed into a world medical center. As specialization advanced, the clinic attracted experts of national and world reputation in virtually every field. And many of its leaders were developed within the clinic itself through its never-ending emphasis on learning and the fruits of experience.

No aspect of the greatness of the Mayo brothers is more impressive than their action in seeking an educational liaison with the University of Minnesota. By the second decade of the twentieth century it was clear that Rochester offered unusual opportunities for post-M.D. training in clinical specialties and in research. The Mayo brothers were not content with a highly successful clinic and practice. They chose to align themselves with education and research for a long future. Dr. "Will," in particular, was a scientist and planner of unusual vision, but the brothers functioned as a dynamic team. If Dr. "Will" often was the spokesman, his favorite phrase was "My brother and I."

The result of long planning was the creation in 1915 of the Mayo Foundation, affiliated with the Graduate School of the University of Minnesota. This move the Mayo brothers initiated and supported with a magnificent endowment. The university received it with the active interest and stalwart support of President Vincent and Dean Ford, notwithstanding stubborn opposition from within the ranks of the medical profession of the time.

Through the succeeding years graduate training in medicine has flourished both at Minneapolis and at Rochester in a productive educational and research partnership. Both centers are famed for specialized expertness, resources in talents and funds, and their contributions in scores of fields to basic knowledge and practical application. The unity that Millard brought about in the metropolitan area has been widened to embrace the richness of medical science that three doctors named Mayo created in an obscure Minnesota town named Rochester.

An Emersonian aphorism was that a "broad, hard-beaten" road would be built to any man who could make better chairs or knives or church organs than anybody else. The Mayos and their associates, and their colleagues on the Minneapolis campus of the university — the men who built interrelated medical centers — were productive in wide-ranging research. It would be difficult to measure their many contributions to scientific knowledge and to the well-being of the thousands who sought their aid in diagnosis, surgery, treatment, and care. By their work, they attested the wisdom of the American philosopher. Not chairs or knives or organs, but medical training, research, and scientific leadership, and the application of all three to the ills of human beings — these they contributed to man's age-old quest for health. And it is no exaggeration to say that the world has beaten a road to their doors.

The crusade for health knows no end. Old problems are met, new ones arise. Knowledge increases in specialties and specialties proliferate. New methods, new drugs, new approaches, new understanding cut down the mortality from traditional diseases, but changing conditions always add new problems.

The medical achievements of past decades seem almost incredible, and honors are shared by many. Trained physicians have played constructive roles. Research scholars in basic and applied medicine have pushed back the frontiers of knowledge. Pharmaceutical science has stockpiled the arsenal of weapons with which to fight disease. Hospitals and nurses have made vital contributions. Health agencies have served the public welfare. Nation, state, and community have showered grants on individuals and institutions to aid research, diagnosis, and medical care. Public-spirited citizens have given gifts for innumerable purposes. Health education has promoted public understanding. And medical science the world over has shared the fruits of its always advancing knowledge.

In this setting, a few Minnesota facts and figures take on special significance. The death rate for infants under one year of age was 70 per thousand in Minnesota in 1915; 47 by 1934; and between 21 and 22 in 1960.

Diphtheria was a fearful scourge in pioneer days, especially in the 1880s when epidemics ravaged whole communities. As late as 1910 this disease killed 566 Minnesota people, but it accounted for only three deaths in 1960.

Each year, even now, there are many cases of measles, but, whereas this sickness caused 282 deaths in 1923, only five were reported in 1960.

Scarlet fever, once a remorseless killer, claimed no Minnesota lives from 1955 to 1960. Typhoid fever disappeared from the ranks of mortal diseases in the 1950s. Smallpox, which hit Indian communities in early times and many pioneer communities, has become a rarity, not only in Minnesota, but throughout the nation. Even tuberculosis, one of the most dreaded of human ills, retreated from an appalling 2157 Minnesota deaths in 1920 to only 88 in 1960.

The modern world knows full well the story of poliomyelitis, with its unhappy aftermath of crippled bodies. The Minnesota record reveals ups and downs, with very bad years in 1921, 1925, 1946, and 1952. But deaths from this insidious enemy dwindled from more than two hundred in two of the years mentioned above to only six in 1960.

Not so encouraging is the record in relation to syphilis. Theoretically the battle against this disease, fought with all the resources of modern medicine, could be won. Campaigns were launched in the 1920s and

446

1930s and the outlook seemed encouraging. But in 1960 the state reported 220 cases and 27 deaths. Syphilis had not yet been defeated in Minnesota, and its incidence was also rising nationally.

The several gains thus far mentioned omit reference to innumerable diseases that have been curtailed. Remarkable advances in surgery are also an important part of the record of achievement, especially in heart surgery at the University of Minnesota Hospitals, where Dr. C. Walton Lillehei and his associates have won world-wide renown; and in the stubborn fight against cancer, in which Dr. Owen Wangensteen has been a great leader. Gains there have been, but alongside them have appeared newer problems, particularly those associated with the "aging" of the population in Minnesota and generally in the United States. A notable fact about American life in the period 1900–60 is that life expectancy has advanced by a total of twenty-two years. The American average in 1900 was just a little better than 47 years. By 1960 it was 69.4. Through the years the average life expectancy for women has stood higher than for men — the statistical sources do not tell us why. In any event, the figures for 1960 were 67.2 years for males, 73.7 years for females.

Minnesota has stood high in the life expectancy of its people. In recent years it has ranked third among the states of the Union, its figure well above the national average. In fact, about 1950 the life expectancy of men in Minnesota (68.02 years) was already above the national average as noted for 1960. Whatever the explanations may be for divergences between national and state averages, the rise in longevity in nation and state reflects concurrent advances in medical science and in standards of living.

Though many killing diseases of former years were brought under control, generations advancing into the older years faced in appalling force the onslaughts of cancer, heart disease, and other ills to which the aged seem especially susceptible. In 1940 Minnesota had 3766 deaths from cancer, but in 1960 the number advanced to 5312. And heart disease in 1960 took nearly 12,000 lives, ranking as the number one killer in this state.

A significant social change has taken place in the population of the state, as of the nation. Frontier Minnesota was not only a young society, but a society of young people. In modern Minnesota people are growing old. The trend, discernible for more than a half a century, is continuing.

447

It is common, even normal, for people to pass the Biblical three-score years and ten. Society is concerned not only about the physical problems of "aging," but also about its social, economic, occupational, and humane aspects. A science of "gerontology" — the term was unfamiliar until recent years — is challenging medical and social experts.

Meanwhile, both for old and young, disease is not the only hazard of modern life. In Minnesota accidental deaths reached a total of 1762 in 1960. Of these, 777 were occasioned by motor-vehicle accidents; 409 by accidental falls; the rest by a variety of causes. Cars, highways, streets, sidewalks, and stairways are hazards comparable in lethal consequences with epidemics in a less mobile era.

The rise of cities played a major role in the modernization of Minnesota. Inevitably it contributed to the social and medical problems with which the state had to deal, but it has to be interpreted in a much broader context. A noted historian says that the state's economic history reached a climax in the building of a great metropolitan community — the Twin Cities — as the heart of a vast "metropolitan area."

Minneapolis and St. Paul became a twin metropolis not only in their concentration of trade, business, industry, and finance, but also as a cultural, social, educational, and creative center. Other towns blossomed into important cities, with varied specializations of function, but the center of urbanization was the metropolis around the Falls of St. Anthony, the head of navigation on the Mississippi, and the junction of the great river and its tributary, the Minnesota.

The setting of this movement is not local or regional. What happened was related to the advancing industrialization of the United States. In Jefferson's day American democracy, as George M. Stephenson points out, represented a "yearning" for an agrarian society rooted in frontier soil. The yearning had been realized, but the 1880s and 1890s were a time of fundamental change. The traditional rural America was giving way to an urban and industrial America; and the change is reflected in Minnesota, where hamlets in the course of a few decades grew into cities counting thousands of inhabitants. The factory was becoming nearly as familiar a landmark of the state's economic life as the barn.

The transition was brought about by people, by will and work, by ambitions and dreams — not by statistics. Yet a few figures may suggest

448

some of the larger outlines of Minnesota's urbanization. St. Paul at its pioneering outset was a minor river village. By 1860, after statehood, it numbered some 10,000 people. Twenty years later its population was about 41,000. It advanced to 163,000 by 1900, 271,000 by 1930, and by 1960 it was a city of 313,411.

In early years, St. Anthony and Minneapolis were separate towns, scowling (and sometimes smiling) at each other across the Mississippi. But they united in 1872 and by 1880 numbered 46,000 people. To their not hidden satisfaction they had already outdistanced St. Paul. With steady strides Minneapolis advanced to 202,000 by 1900 and 464,000 by 1930 — but by 1960 the figure, surprisingly, was only 482,872.

Such figures obviously are clues, but they do not reflect the realistic picture of Minnesota's metropolitan center. In Minneapolis and St. Paul, as in many great cities throughout the country, municipal growth jumped beyond city boundaries. Suburban villages reached out in all directions, administratively independent, but still a part of an expanded metropolis. The grand total population of the Twin Cities and their suburban filaments — the "metropolitan statistical area" — in 1960 was 1,482,030. But even these figures do not fully illuminate Minnesota's urban growth. Taking into account all the cities and towns of the state, the total urban population in 1960 was 2,122,566, as compared with a rural population of 1,291,298.

Minnesotans, traditionally accustomed to thinking of the state as rural and agricultural, were compelled to realize that the commonwealth, with all its triumphs and its developing problems, was a sharing partner in the urbanization and industrialization of the United States. In the total 1960 state population of 3,413,864, close to two-thirds of the Minnesota people were urban. Even more revealing is the fact that the Twin City metropolitan area accounted for more than 40 per cent of the entire population of the state.

St. Paul had many early advantages in the race for urban supremacy, such as priority in time, the steamboat trade, the territory's pioneer commerce, the earliest banking, and the political capital. It was not without rivals in towns along the Mississippi and Minnesota rivers, but it soon outdistanced them in the volume of its commerce. As early as 1872 it boasted ninety-two jobbing firms, and its business went beyond a million dollars in each of a variety of products, including boots and shoes, dry goods, groceries, hardware, wool, iron, and hides. Its wholesale business

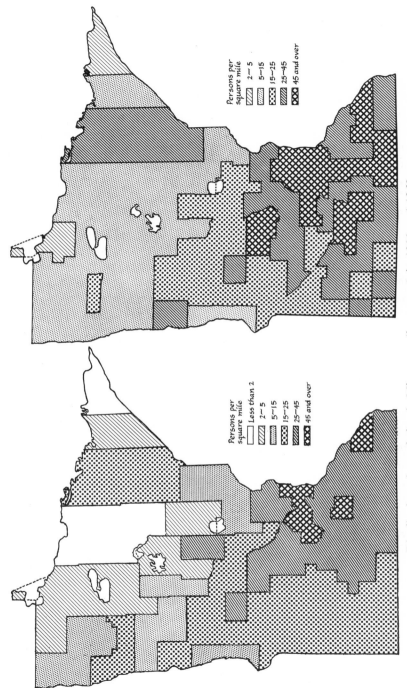

Distribution of population in Minnesota (by county) in 1900 and 1960

Persons per
square mile
2—5
5—15
15—25
25—45
45 and over

Persons per
square mile
Less than 2
2—5
5—15
15—25
25—45
45 and over

by 1881 reached $46,000,000. Such figures testify to a thriving commercial city, but St. Paul also had a variety of manufactures, including boots and shoes, packing, farm implements, and beer and liquor.

Minneapolis, blessed with great water power, gave early promise of becoming a manufacturing center. Lumber, flour milling, and the industries that developed alongside milling contributed to the power of the city. With its rise as a major grain market, it also became a powerful financial center. Railroads were vital to both cities, but with its proliferating industry Minneapolis more than rivaled St. Paul.

Both cities faced urban competition from St. Louis, Milwaukee, Chicago, and other fast-growing metropolises, but as they gained in population, trade, and industry they took on the character of a metropolitan center in their own right. Large areas to the west were dependent on them. Finance, after early dominance by St. Paul, developed even more intensively in Minneapolis, but large banks were built in both cities. Localities which earlier had turned eastward for financial aid and leadership shifted to the Twin Cities. In 1914 Minneapolis became the home of the Federal Reserve Bank. Two years later the federal farm loan system was centered in St. Paul, and a few years later the Federal Intermediate Credit Bank also.

Comparisons of the two immediately adjacent cities stress St. Paul as commercial and Minneapolis as manufacturing, but St. Paul developed manufactures, and Minneapolis competed in commerce. No city of enterprise and high ambition restricts itself to one or a very few lines. As the decades spun out, Minneapolis became the larger city by a very wide margin. But the Twin Cities, with specializations and some discernible social and cultural differences, constituted a metropolitan community. They shared advantages. They joined forces in common endeavors. They were politically and governmentally separated, but physically, and in many respects economically, they were a single, functioning urban center.

There was sharp rivalry between St. Paul and Minneapolis, as was true of many other closely adjacent communities throughout the state. County-seat "wars" are a part of Minnesota history and of the state's folklore.

The rivalry of the Twin Cities did not lead to pitched battles. But the United States census of 1890 provoked emotion and extravagant charges. As first reported the returns gave Minneapolis a population total of 182,967 and St. Paul, 142,581. St. Paul was crestfallen to have dropped

451

so far behind its rival. It soon became evident, however, that the Minneapolis census had been padded. Families, in the official count, were swollen by children and boarders who, on later investigation, proved to be nonexistent. Many houses were fictitious, and not a few employees were counted both in the shops where they worked and also in their homes.

St. Paul was indignant. Its newspapers had a field day, and they nicknamed Minneapolis the "Pad City." Unhappily for St. Paul, however, it turned out that its own census was by no means above suspicion. The Union Depot, for instance, had a "population" of 275. A dime museum housed an enormous family. And more than ninety persons seemingly lived in the building of a St. Paul newspaper. As these reports came out, Minneapolis in turn was indignant. The federal government could not ignore the intercity feud, and a new count was taken. It revealed the sad fact that Minneapolis had exaggerated its population by 18,000 and St. Paul by 9000.

A farcical court case followed. A St. Paul citizen was charged with overstating the number of residents at the Union Depot. He was put on trial before a St. Paul jury — and promptly acquitted. The rivalry between the two cities did not wholly disappear in later years, but in recent times it has worn a genial aspect, not untinged by humor and by an interweaving of cherished folklore.

Lumber, railroads, grain, iron ore, and a geographical position of strategic value spurred the growth of the metropolis at the tip of Lake Superior. Duluth got under way slowly, but vaulted in population from about 33,000 in 1890 to 101,000 in 1930. It grew into a great shipping center, with its outpouring of ore and grain and its imports of coal and other commodities. Manufacturing and diversified wholesaling added immense impetus to its growth. Like the Twin Cities, Duluth on the Minnesota side and Superior in Wisconsin were immediate neighbors. Together, by 1960, they formed a metropolitan area of more than 276,000 people (Duluth contributing 106,884). Duluth took and maintained its rank as the third largest city of Minnesota and with the opening of the St. Lawrence Waterway, it became a world port.

Urban development marked many other areas of the state, though city populations were modest in comparison with Minneapolis, St. Paul, and Duluth. Certain thriving cities are distinguished for special industries, such as St. Cloud for its granite, Austin and South St. Paul for meat-packing industries, Red Wing for its potteries, and International Falls for paper-making. Others, including Crookston, Albert Lea, Mankato, and Fergus Falls, are commercial cities which also have varied industries. Rochester is distinguished as a medical center. Northfield is the home of Carleton and St. Olaf colleges. St. Peter is the site of Gustavus Adolphus College (and the home of governors). Moorhead is the city both of Concordia College and a state college; and Mankato is an educational center and a flour-milling town. These and many other cities contribute variety to the state scene.

Municipal government and the tangled problems of cities — regulation, control, recreation, safety and protection, and periodic abuses of public trust — led to cooperative efforts to improve conditions. In the 1890s the Twin Cities and Duluth joined the National Municipal League, which looked for solutions of municipal problems. A pioneering municipal organization in the state was the Municipal and Commercial League of Minnesota, started in 1903. It concerned itself with charters, transportation, parks and playgrounds, sanitation, and other problems. In 1903 the League of Minnesota Municipalities was formed, a cooperative venture of municipal officials and university specialists in administrative, legislative, long-term planning, and educational actions designed to strengthen city government. This organization has continued to the present. It has had influence not only in the inner circles of city officials but also in the spread of public enlightenment in the realm of municipal government and affairs.

Urbanization and industry spurred another modernizing trend in Minnesota. This was the rise of labor. Organizations were concerned with improving conditions of work, shortening the workday, raising wages, emphasizing the dignity of labor, and promoting state intervention in behalf of workers.

Open lands in the 1850s, coupled with the newness of the country, the absence of organized industry, and vague lines between labor and capital, account for the slowness with which unions and other labor organizations got started. Only two Minnesota unions are known to have been launched in the 1850s, and they were in the technical field of typography. Further moves were made in the 1860s and early 1870s in several trades, but their influence was limited and just about erased by the Panic of 1873.

In the 1870s and 1880s, however, labor — not unaware of the Granger movement and the Farmers' Alliance — turned to larger plans than specific unions. The Knights of Labor began as a secret society in Philadelphia. After a few years it came under the leadership of Terence V. Powderly, a clever organizer and orator, and by the middle 1880s it had some 700,000 members nationally. It promoted unionism, took an interest in cooperatives, and worked for recognition of labor by industry and the public. By 1883 Minnesota had its own state organization of Knights, and two years later it sponsored the first Labor Day in this state (September 7, 1885), an institution that became permanent. Laborers were asked to leave their benches and shops to "swell the great army of peace and production."

The outstanding achievement of the Knights of Labor, however, was its advocacy of a State Board of Labor Statistics. Such a board was authorized by a Republican legislature in 1887, after active support by the Knights of Labor working hand in hand with the Farmers' Alliance.

Labor envisaged potential gains through organization, but it employed the strike as a weapon. There were few strikes in the early period, but a historian of the labor movement reports that from 1881 to 1900 there were, in all, 383 Minnesota strikes, affecting some 70,000 workers in several hundreds of industries. A notable outburst was that of 1889 against the street railways in the Twin Cities. Workmen had been reduced two cents an hour in wages, and met the reduction by going on strike. On one occasion a crowd estimated at ten thousand overturned streetcars and destroyed track. The company replied by demanding that its employees sign contracts (popularly called "yellow dog" contracts) pledging themselves not to join a labor organization. In the end the company retreated from this stand, and thus recognized trade unionism, though the laborers did not get back their two cents.

The Knights declined in prestige in the late 1880s, but worked for better working hours, improved conditions in factories, and the arbitration of disputes. They also demanded the abolition of child labor. Meanwhile an Eight Hour League was formed (1889), a bridge to the establishment in 1890 of the Minnesota State Federation of Labor. This marked a new stage in state labor history. The Knights and the League did not immediately disintegrate, but the state federation grew tremendously and by the mid-1890s achieved primacy in the labor arena. The labor movement gained momentum and by 1914 the state had more than four hundred labor organizations, which were spread through more than fifty cities.

Just as the cause of corrections and charities had an outstanding and prophetic leader, so LeGrand Powers is known as Minnesota's "Apostle of Labor." In its first few years the State Board of Labor Statistics made relatively modest progress. Powers, a clergyman, held the office from 1891 to 1899 and proved a vigorous commissioner. He secured an enlargement of the board's powers in 1893 and it was renamed the Bureau of Labor. He forwarded the adoption in 1895 of a child labor law, promoted improved conditions in factories, studied industrial accidents and deaths, and even recommended a plan of workmen insurance. This proposal was twenty years ahead of his day, for it was not until 1913 that the first Workmen's Compensation Act was passed in the state of Minnesota.

Meanwhile the state federation worked to forward improved working conditions in factories, the eight-hour day, minimum wage laws, postal savings banks, workmen's compensation, and other reforms. It increased in power as labor organizations multiplied. Its policies were nonpolitical, but its proposed reforms involved legislative acceptance. It therefore took a lively interest in the policies of the political parties. As was true in other Minnesota "causes," labor was articulate not only through organization but also through a vociferous press of its own in the three urban strongholds of the state — Minneapolis, St. Paul, and Duluth.

State concern with labor deepened as legislation achieved nearly all the reforms originally proposed on its behalf. State administration expanded. By 1921 the Industrial Commission of Minnesota replaced the earlier state organization. Through succeeding years laws have been multiplied. Under the commission a many-branched Labor and Industry Department functions in workmen's compensation problems, accident prevention, employment agencies, problems relating to women and children, boiler inspection work and steamfitting standards, and other divisions. Here as in other areas the state government has taken on new functions. Under its wing are supervisory and administrative duties designed to give protection to labor, to encourage standardization of working conditions, and also to permit aid to industry.

As Minnesota grappled with changing ways and problems in its state affairs, it was not cut off from the mainland of American public questions.

National economic, political, and social forces affected the state. Minnesota, facing state problems, scrutinized patterns and precedents in other parts of the land. When panic and hard times descended on the country, Minnesota shared in their depressing effects and in the crises of need and adjustment. The state responded to the excitements and emotions of presidential campaigns. The people felt the spell of Bryan's soaring oratory in 1896 and 1900, but at the polls they gave majorities to William McKinley, and in 1904 they accorded overwhelming support to Theodore Roosevelt.

In 1898, as the Spanish-American War was approaching, Minnesota harbored opposing points of view. Archbishop Ireland had no sympathy for the sensational Hearst-inspired newspapers that fomented war. He believed that a settlement could be achieved through mediation, and he worked for peace with all his ability and energy. Senator Cushman K. Davis, chairman of the Senate Committee on Foreign Relations, favored force in settling the perplexing Cuban problem. When war began, despite the heroic efforts of the archbishop, Minnesota responded in a spirit of patriotism in line with its Civil War traditions.

Governor Clough took the lead in mobilizing men and support for Minnesota's war contribution. Of four regiments raised for service, three went to camps in the South, where they were decimated by illness, especially typhoid fever. The Thirteenth Minnesota, under Charles McCormick Reeve, saw action in the Philippines. When that regiment returned home, it was acclaimed by the state, with President McKinley joining Minnesota in a welcome and review of the troops. It is a melancholy commentary on the war that, although only four Minnesotans were killed in action, eighty died of disease and many more suffered from its debilitating effects.

On the local political scene, Van Sant's governorship extended over two terms (1901–5). Notable was his success in creating the State Board of Control. He also sharply opposed the Northern Securities Company. The famous case involving this company was the culmination of a battle of railroad magnates and financiers — James J. Hill and J. Pierpont Morgan on one side, Edward H. Harriman and allied financial interests on the other. After preliminaries, a working settlement was reached through the organization of the Northern Securities Company as a holding company effecting a merger of the Great Northern, the Northern Pacific, and the Chicago, Burlington, and Quincy roads. In this company

Hill and Morgan had majority control. The court drama opened in Minnesota, where a suit for the dissolution of the merger was prosecuted. President Theodore Roosevelt took action under the Sherman Anti-Trust Act, and in 1904 the Supreme Court by a vote of five to four upheld the government's contention that the Northern Securities Company was in illegal restraint of trade. As a result, the company was obliged to dissolve.

Van Sant was a competent and friendly, if not distinguished, governor who, after Lind, led the state into the swirl of the twentieth century. It was in 1901, during the Van Sant administration, that Minnesota adopted a direct primary law after a preliminary direct primary authorization of 1899, applied only to Hennepin County.

Few men in Minnesota history can compare in glamour with the state's sixteenth governor, John A. Johnson. As a Democrat, he was three times elected governor in the traditionally Republican state. His gubernatorial service is less associated with legislation or political reforms than with a personality that endeared him to the people. The first native-born Minnesotan to be elected governor, he was born in St. Peter of humble parentage. His mother was a washerwoman, his father an unfortunate victim of drink.

Johnson helped his mother in her chores, took one humble job after another, was a clerk, a pharmacist, a debater, a newspaper editor. He won election to the state Senate and developed remarkable skill as a speaker. Nominated for governor, he was publicly confronted by the story of his parents' misery and poverty. A reporter asked him what he had to say. He replied, "Nothing. It is true." He later told of his background in his own way, without pathos or apology. The people rose generously to his support. He ran in a presidential year (1904) in which Theodore Roosevelt carried the state by a majority of 161,000 — but Johnson, Democrat, won by about 8000.

Johnson drew to himself the love of the people. He was elected again in 1906 by a huge majority, and a third time in 1908 — another presidential year, in which William H. Taft carried Minnesota by a majority of 86,000. The man's sympathy with the people, his rise in a tradition dear to Americans from early times, his simplicity, and his oratory marked him for honors. He brought about some tax reforms, despite the fact that he worked with a legislature politically opposed to him. He effected an insurance code, established a state banking department, gave larger powers to the old Bureau of Labor, and approved a law for cities to operate

457

public utilities. When the legislature passed a tonnage tax on iron ore, he vetoed it.

Although Johnson's administrative and legislative achievements were by no means outstanding, he nevertheless became a national figure. His ingratiating presence won every audience he faced, and by 1908 he was boomed for the presidency. He was presented for the Democratic nomination in that year. Then tragedy struck. He was taken ill, and his career was cut short by death in 1909.

The ifs of history are lost in the mists. It is conceivable that, had John A. Johnson lived, he might have won the presidency in the election of 1912, which instead put Woodrow Wilson into the White House. Though he missed the top prize of American politics, he left a legacy of character. He is remembered as a man of compassion, human sympathy, and like-mindedness with the people. A statue of John A. Johnson, built from funds contributed by a hundred thousand Minnesotans, young and old, stands in front of the state capitol, flanked by a monument honoring Knute Nelson.

As Minnesota worked its way into the twentieth century, it wore the unmistakable marks of growth and prosperity, and in its attitudes toward modern problems it had advanced toward social maturity. It had changed dramatically from the territory of the pioneering 1850s. The thinly populated but empire-visioned frontier of a half century in the past had grown into a state of 1,750,000 people.

Railroads had built tracks in nearly every direction from the Twin Cities. Farming was still very important. Diversification had invaded the rural scene, though wheat was still a dominant crop. But cities and urban industry were challenging the rural economy. Towns had sprung up and a "metropolitan center" was extending its orbit of influence into state and region.

"Mesabi," the mineral giant, was stirring, and iron ore was being shipped eastward in millions of tons. Yet the business race was still led by flour and lumber. These two industries claimed about 46 per cent of Minnesota's invested industrial capital at the beginning of the new century.

Conservation, with its concern for posterity, was making headway. State institutions, generous benevolence, and civic organizations were focused on social ills. Public health, hospitals, medicine, and research were striking down diseases that had run wild in earlier times. Education was expanding and adapting its ways to new opportunities, needs, and demands. Cultural activities, the press, and the social life of the people betrayed a spirit of confidence.

In the perspective of history one can understand the optimism of the Minnesota people as they measured their progress. If they had little realization of what lay ahead, they yet were conscious of achievement, of maturity, of things done through years of trial. This meant strength for meeting the storms of coming years. Time has no stop. Problems of peace, war, the machine age, and depression faced the state. Oncoming years would mean new dilemmas, new decisions, new ordeals, new sacrifices. But the state, like the nation, had reserves of courage, toughened by traditions.

Traffic at Nicollet and Sixth in Minneapolis, 1905

★
Peace, Turbulence, and War

OLD ideas jostled with new as people welcomed in the twentieth century. If they rejoiced at the wonders of the developing machine age, they also were increasingly aware of its problems and dangers. It was a time of enterprise, invention, and industrial concentration, but it was also one of "trust busting," extensions of public control, and a regression from old-time faith in *laissez faire*.

Minnesota shared in the novelty and excitement of the interests that stirred the country. There was an outburst of national and world fairs — Pan-American (1901, at which President McKinley was shot), St. Louis (1904), and Lewis and Clark (1905). People sang "Meet Me in St. Louis, Louis" and "In the Good Old Summertime." Best sellers in 1904 included *Rebecca of Sunnybrook Farm*, *Beverly of Graustark*, and Churchill's *The Crossing*. Popular on the stage was *Raffles*, but on a sophisticated level Arnold Daly was playing Shaw's *Candida* and Minnie Maddern Fiske was interpreting Ibsen's *Hedda Gabler*. Thousands read the adventures of Sherlock Holmes. Fad after fad swept the country, including jujitsu and Charles Wagner's "Simple Life." Theodore Roosevelt lent his support to simplified spelling, but enlisted less sympathy on the spelling front than he did with his doctrine of the "strenuous life."

Campaigns against deleterious patent medicines and adulterated foods made headway. Lincoln Steffens, Ida Tarbell, and others led a "muckraking" campaign merciless in its exposure of contemporary evils. This was brought home to Minnesotans, for Steffens branded Minneapolis as

461

one of the "worst governed" cities of the country. Popular magazines multiplied, taking advantage of wood pulp, photography, and sensationalism. Journalism was in a spirited cartoon phase, and one of the most adept artists of the time was "Bart" of the *Minneapolis Journal*. The Hearst press, fattened by the Spanish-American War, now flourished on an anti-trust crusade. News streamed out of Theodore Roosevelt's exciting Washington: an anthracite coal strike, the "taking" of Panama, the sending of the American fleet around the world, race suicide, conservation, and "nature fakers." "Mr. Dooley" (Finley Peter Dunne) made homely and humorous comment on passing events, and his popularity was expressed in the song "Oh, Mr. Dooley, I Love You Truly." He was a forerunner of the lariat-swinging Will Rogers.

These were among the surface manifestations of American ebullience during what a popular historian has termed "the good years." More basic, however, was the rapidly advancing mobility of the people.

The pattern of Minnesota's railroad system had been worked out by 1900, though the next few decades saw "feeder lines" thrust into areas and resources not yet exploited by main lines and earlier railroad interlacings. The Great Lakes floated ever larger fleets of ships in ice-free months for the transport of iron ore, lumber, grain, coal, and other products.

The larger cities, as they spread out from their hubs in the days of carriages and wagons, developed streetcar systems. St. Paul delighted its citizens in 1872 by instituting a streetcar drawn by a single horse. Soon teams were used. Streetcar companies were chartered in the Twin Cities, and also in Duluth. Horses did faithful service, but people wanted an efficiency beyond their tramping power. Steam engines were tried, but by the 1890s horsepower and steam gave way to electric-powered streetcars. These became standard in many Minnesota cities and contributed to the business and pleasure of multitudes. Probably many urban dwellers would have been incredulous if anybody had then predicted that in time trolley cars — a triumph in their day — would disappear from their avenues. The electric railways bound together such cities as Minneapolis and St. Paul, sprawling out onto lands that only a few years earlier had been placid farms. The city cars got people to their work, facilitated their shopping, and took them out to parks and playgrounds and lakes — even to such glamorous resort lakes as Minnetonka and White Bear.

462

Streetcars and trains were helpful, but legs also were propelling powers. The bicycle was known in America as early as the 1860s. It did not become a fad and sport, however, until the 1870s and 1880s. As clever manufacturers improved machines, the vogue of the bicycle became universal. The two-wheeled contraption was good for business uses and it contributed to sport and to the pleasure of excursions. It was no easy task to pump a bicycle over bad roads in hilly country. Cyclists naturally asked the logical question: why should not the state and its communities provide good roads? Thus the invention gave impetus to the movement for improvement in the construction and maintenance of highways. Some of the larger cities were quick to build bicycle runways alongside their principal avenues. Meanwhile cycling grew steadily in popularity. To the delight of the romantic, the "bicycle built for two" — the phrase is from a song of the time — was not uncommon. By 1882 Minnesota had a branch of the League of American Wheelmen, and it soon established a magazine called the *Minnesota Wheelman.*

The revolutionary flights in an airplane by two brothers named Wright at a place called Kitty Hawk, North Carolina, on December 17, 1903, did not seem to attract much contemporary American notice. But in the 1890s and early 1900s the public was becoming aware of a curious coughing, ill-smelling vehicle called the "horseless carriage."

One of the puzzles of American technological history is that this country lagged behind the Europeans in developing the automobile. Germans evolved the "four-cycle internal combustion hydrocarbon motor" as early as 1876. In the mid-eighties the first motorcycle was made by the German Gottlieb Daimler; and a year later an automobile powered by a gasoline engine was devised by Karl Benz. The French were prompt in applying the new engineering knowledge, but Americans failed to swing into action until the early 1890s when two brothers named Duryea, Henry Ford, Elwood Haynes, R. E. Olds, and others went to work. They more than made up for the lag, however, by their energy and their inventiveness.

The history of the American motor industry reveals the 1890s as an experimental period, but progress thereafter was fast and furious. In 1900 a dozen companies turned out 4000 cars. Ten years later the production was 181,000 cars, and there were sixty-nine companies. Cars soon appeared in Minnesota. Minneapolis had about a dozen automobiles in 1902, and in that year Tom Shevlin, son of the lumber magnate,

463

violated the established Minneapolis speed limit of ten miles per hour and was arrested.

Experiments in propelling cars were made with electricity, steam, and gasoline, but by 1900 races had indicated that gasoline seemed to be the most effective force. The American ambition for speed was not slow in showing itself. In 1902 two Minneapolis men drove from Minneapolis to Monticello, forty-two miles, in 2 hours and 12 minutes — "actual running time," as a newspaper reported. In the same year three men achieved the tremendous triumph of driving from Chicago to Minneapolis in six days. The first trip by car across the entire country was made in 1903 — in a Packard car — and the time was a breath-taking sixty-one days.

As automobiles reflected the advancing ideas of American inventors and competing companies, they changed styles. They gained power and changed from clumsy-looking imitations of carriages to sleek, purring, streamlined, modern, powerful vehicles in their own unimitative right. The early open cars, in which women wrapped cordons of veils around their gigantic hats and their faces to protect themselves from wind and dust, were followed by successively improved cars. As time went on, the new models were enclosed, heated in winter, cooled in summer, and provided with increasing speed as powerful engines replaced those of early days (the car that made the run from Minneapolis to Monticello in 1902 had an 8½ horsepower engine).

The automobile was a monster new on Minnesota streets and roads. It was a curiosity, a contrivance for the rich, a blatant educator of the nerves of horses, a noisy phenomenon that nobody quite knew how to control. Minnesota, for instance, waited until 1908 before passing a license law. In 1909, 7000 automobiles and 4000 motorcycles were licensed. Cars contributed to the pressures in the state for good roads, but, as we have seen, public interest in improving the rough roads of earlier times was present before the advent of the automobile. A convention called to forward the cause of good roads in 1893 listened to a speaker who said, "A perfect highway is a thing of beauty and a joy forever. It blesses every home by which it passes." As early as 1898 a constitutional amendment paved the way for a highway commission and a state tax to help Minnesota road building.

Even with this authorization, there were delays, and the Minnesota Highway Commission was not set in motion until 1905. In 1906 a "State

Road and Bridge Fund" amendment to the constitution was adopted under which the income from the internal improvement land fund was authorized for the construction and improvement of public highways and bridges, and the legislature was empowered to levy, for the same purposes, an annual tax of one-fourth of a mill on property in the state. A legal squabble followed with respect to the balloting for the amendment, but it was upheld after court action. The state tax was increased in 1913 to one mill on the dollar under a new constitutional amendment, but progress in road building was slow until World War I and later. A highway department with a single commissioner at its head was authorized in 1917, and three years later the state approved the "Babcock Amendment," which launched the modern system of state trunk highways.

There can be no doubt that the automobile was a spur to the "Good Roads" movement, which was officially blessed in 1913 by the inauguration of a Minnesota "Good Roads Day" (the third Tuesday in June). It may be of interest to leap across decades and take note of the increase in the number of motor vehicles in the state: in 1921, about 333,000; 744,000 by 1930; by 1937, 677,000 passenger cars, 112,000 trucks, and 26,000 trailers. In 1960, the count of all kinds of motor vehicles registered in Minnesota reached the astonishing total of 1,758,619. Of this total, more than 1,275,000 were passenger cars.

No longer a plaything of the rich but a mobile and readily available servant of the whole population, the automobile became a commonplace of state travel. It served city and country and an amazing variety of purposes. It was an adjunct of the "moving American," with uncountable influences on the life of the people.

If Americans lagged in grasping the revolutionary potentialities of the automobile in its early stages, they were resourceful in perfecting cars and producing them in fantastic quantities. And they were quick to realize that gas-driven cars, built as passenger buses, opened the way to a novel form of public transportation.

In the bus field, Minnesota was a pioneer. Philosophers have written about historical causation, but often they have overlooked the casual circumstances that can set off trains of consequence. For instance, mining operations in 1914 occasioned the removal of a Minnesota town from one site to another. The town happened to be Hibbing, and a couple of enterprising young men, Carl Eric Wickman and Andrew G. Anderson, made use of an open car to convey passengers from the old Hibbing to

465

the new. This seemed to them a beginning for a money-making business. They put in an order for a bus — believed to be the first built in the United States — and meanwhile they tinkered with a grocery truck, equipping it with seats and windows.

These beginnings were humble — as humble as any in the pioneer era — but out of their efforts emerged, first, the Mesaba Transportation Company, then the Northland Transportation Company, finally the Greyhound Corporation. The latter became one of the greatest bus companies of the nation, spreading from Hibbing to state, then Middle West, then country.

As with the railroads, bus transportation saw multiplying companies, thereafter consolidation — not monopoly, but a corporation with operating lines over the length and breadth of the United States. Unlike many chronicles of American corporations, this one reveals the originators remaining with the business as it grew to gigantic dimensions. They directed its strategy. The story is one of initiative and individual success, but its larger significance lies in the fact that buses supplied the country with an alternative to the railroad in moving people from place to place. How fast the system grew may be indicated by the fact that the bus lines in 1927 transported 15,000,000 persons in Minnesota over routes having a sweep of 16,000 miles.

Yet other changes in transportation attracted attention, though their great repercussions would not come until after World War I. The early experiments of the Wright brothers and other pioneers of the airplane demonstrated convincingly that a new era was approaching. As early as 1911, Minneapolis witnessed the start of the first American long-distance airmail flight. Meanwhile traffic on the Mississippi River, once crucial to the economy of Minnesota, had all but disappeared. Its rejuvenation awaited some realizable plan for raising the water level of the river from St. Louis to the Twin Cities.

Like transportation, politics, nationally and locally, bore marks of change in the decade before World War I. Progressive forces were encouraged by the dynamic Theodore Roosevelt, but his successor, President Taft, provoked insurgency when he supported and defended the high Payne-Aldrich Tariff Act (1909). Both Senator Nelson and his associate in the Senate, Moses E. Clapp, voted against the bill, as did every Minnesota representative save one, James A. Tawney of Winona.

Among the opponents of the measure was Charles A. Lindbergh of Little Falls, father of the famed flyer of later times. President Taft himself visited the state in 1909 and defended the tariff as the best ever passed by a Republican Congress, but his stand won few if any Minnesota converts. When in 1912 Theodore Roosevelt broke with Taft and led the "Bull Moose" party — the Progressive party — in the presidential election, Minnesota gave its support to Roosevelt over both Taft and Woodrow Wilson. The split in Republican ranks assured the national victory of Wilson, exponent of the "New Freedom" and champion of liberal forces in the Democratic party.

On the home front Adolph O. Eberhart, Swedish-born Republican, succeeded John A. Johnson as governor in 1909. He was elected to the office in 1910, and once again in 1912. He had been educated at Gustavus Adolphus College — the fourth of Minnesota's sixteen governors up to his time who was college-trained. He was experienced and skilled as a politician and adjusted himself adeptly to the moves in the progressive swing that came in 1912. The state legislature in 1913 reflected this turn, and not a few reforms were adopted. These included mothers' pensions, workmen's compensation, preference primaries for both national and state offices, and the elimination of partisan political designation for state legislative candidates. Constitutional amendments to set up machinery for the initiative and referendum and for the "recall" of public officials won legislative approval, but did not receive the necessary votes by the electorate. When Governor Eberhart differed with the majority in the legislature, he did not hesitate to exercise the veto, as in the instance of a measure to place telephone companies under the Railroad and Warehouse Commission.

The seventeenth governor of Minnesota was a Democrat, Winfield S. Hammond, a schoolman, a graduate of Dartmouth College, and a courtly politician seasoned by four terms in Congress. He was a man of broad interests and favored reforms, including woman suffrage — a cause that had been brilliantly championed in Minneapolis by Mrs. Andreas Ueland. Governor Hammond's career was cut short by his sudden death less than a year after his inauguration, and his place was taken by the Republican lieutenant governor, J. A. A. Burnquist, a graduate of Carleton College and the University of Minnesota Law School, who was elected in 1916 and 1918.

Minnesota in 1912 had given its approval to the Sixteenth and Seventeenth amendments to the federal Constitution (the income tax and direct election of United States senators). No senatorial election following the Seventeenth Amendment was held in Minnesota until 1916, when Moses E. Clapp, who had served in the Senate since 1901, faced the test of re-election. The major contest was for the Republican nomination, a three-cornered race of more than local significance. The state by 1916 was deeply conscious of the increasing impact of the European war on American policies. Two of the candidates for nomination were Senator Clapp and Congressman Charles A. Lindbergh, both of whom had voted in Congress against measures which, in their judgment, seemed to be veering the United States toward possible participation in the war. The third candidate was Frank B. Kellogg, who had won fame in the Northern Securities case and was an advocate of action looking to American defense in the face of international danger. Kellogg won the nomination and in the election carried the state by a substantial majority over his Democratic opponent. In the same election President Wilson lost the state's electoral votes to Charles E. Hughes by a scant margin.

World War I was a darkening shadow. Its encroachments menaced the maintenance of the American policy of neutrality instituted at the beginning of the war. And in the same period a political-economic storm was brewing in North Dakota — a storm destined to have many and violent repercussions in Minnesota. This was the rise of the Nonpartisan League under the leadership of a facile speaker and organizer, Arthur C. Townley, a Minnesotan who had become a farmer in North Dakota.

The agrarian movements of the past had not been forgotten, and from the early 1900s the American Society of Equity, devoted to the idea of cooperatives, was an intermediate organization that had considerable appeal for farmers. The Nonpartisan League, launched in North Dakota in 1915, functioned, not as a political party, but as a move to dominate state governments by electing people to office — whatever their party — who stood for the League's program. This program, as the historian of agrarian movements, Dr. John D. Hicks, writes, was essentially an experiment in state socialism. The grievances were largely centered on marketing by grain farmers.

The North Dakota platform called for state ownership of terminal elevators, flour mills, packing houses, and cold-storage plants; state inspection of grain and grain dockage; exemption of farm improvements from taxation; state hail insurance (on an acreage tax basis); and rural banks operated at cost. The League had success in North Dakota, won thousands of members, and soon made headway in electing sympathizers to state offices and the legislature. It was able to write much of its program into law. It soon spread into Minnesota, where a state organization was started, and by 1918 the League backed a Republican candidate for governor of Minnesota. But by this time America was in the swirl of World War I, and the efforts of the League collided with the emotions of a people absorbed by the war and its urgent problems.

The coming of World War I shocked the people of the "good years." The new century had seemed to many to hold out a realizable hope of peace. Modern invention in many of its phases appeared to be knitting the world into closer and more friendly communication. Many organized movements for peace were in progress. These included peace conferences at The Hague, a World Peace Foundation, the Carnegie Endowment for International Peace, the establishment of a National Peace Council (in 1911), and various treaties negotiated by the United States in the early Wilson years to advance the peaceful accommodation of quarrels between nations.

As the war clouds thickened in Europe, American agitation for peace intensified. A Minnesota Peace Society was launched in 1913 and quickly expanded in membership. Other organizations, including a Woman's Peace party, joined in the crusade. In the very year of 1914 when the European world exploded into war, the Minnesota State Fair took as its theme "Peace and Plenty," employing the slogan that "Flour barrels are better than gun barrels."

But the war in Europe was an inescapable fact. Its issues, despite the President's call for neutrality, were of concern to millions of Americans. The country, as is now seen with after-wisdom, was facing an era when European wars were likely, if not certain, to broaden into world wars. America was a world power. It could not hold itself in isolation from the decisive forces of the age. The dream of peace was in every human heart. But the United States faced the ugly reality of a war on which the fate of the Old World hung and in which modern devices of destruction reached out into the seas, into the air, and impinged on American security.

Amid American efforts for neutrality and peace, newspapers carried daily stories of the conflict raging in western Europe. Propaganda for the

Allies and for Germany flooded the country although much American opinion took form as a result of events and without regard to the efforts of propagandists. A train of events gave rise to American moves for military preparation. Even Cyrus Northrop, head of the Minnesota Peace Society, lent his name as honorary president in 1915 to a branch of the National Security League, with the simple assertion that "We should prepare against war." Border troubles with Mexico, in which four Minnesota National Guard regiments were called out, heightened the sense of perils which the country had to be ready to meet. The early Minnesota sentiment for neutrality in the war was dramatically underlined in 1916 when every Minnesota congressman and one of its two senators supported a resolution warning American citizens not to take passage on armed merchant ships of the Allies. In the national election of 1916, President Wilson waged his campaign under the slogan "He kept us out of war."

One overt action after another by Germany stirred American public opinion. Diplomatic relations with Germany were ended on February 3, 1917. The drastic turn came when the Kaiser's government blatantly adopted a policy of unrestricted submarine war. In the tightening crisis support greatly increased for the President, who now was urging the vital importance of national preparedness. St. Paul started a Patriotic League and Minneapolis a Loyalty League. The peace movement lost momentum, although there still was much distress about America's possible entry into the war and protesting mass meetings were held. But the march of events was inexorable, and on April 2, 1917, President Wilson gave his war address to Congress with its demand that the world must be made "safe for democracy."

The years of peace, whether good or not, came to an end. Minnesota, notwithstanding the fact that four of its congressmen voted against the war resolution of April 6, joined the nation with a demonstration of zeal and devotion that accorded with patriotic traditions reaching back through the decades to pioneer times.

The home front in World War I offers a remarkable picture of a people mobilized for war. It was "everybody's war," as the Minnesota Commission of Public Safety said. This commission, established by legislative authority in April 1917, consisted of the governor, attorney-general, and five appointed members. It was given near-dictatorial authority. For

470

protection, defense, and war support, it was in fact empowered to do anything not in conflict with the state and federal constitutions.

The commission flooded the state with informational bulletins, news, and reports. Some of its most effective material was supplied by the national Committee on Public Information, in which Dean Guy Stanton Ford played an important and wise role. The commission authorized a Home Guard to replace the National Guard, which went into federal service. It commissioned some six hundred peace officers clothed with the powers of constables. It was believed that their watchfulness throughout the state would have "a deterrent effect upon evil-minded persons plotting crime or destruction of property."

The commission barred strikes and lockouts. It forbade moves to extend unionization of labor. It required the registration of all aliens. It regulated the liquor traffic, and it issued a "work or fight" order. The commission extended its concern to the schools. It referred to the state superintendent of public instruction the question whether the teaching of German should be discontinued in the public schools. Later, after a study by a committee of schoolmen, it published a "black list" of German books which should not be used in German instruction. It noted that in many parochial schools instruction was given in languages other than English, and on this ground it asserted that ten thousand children were being brought up "as aliens and foreigners." The commission adopted a resolution requiring English to be used as the "exclusive medium of instruction" in all the schools of the state. The commission also took action against minorities suspected of pro-Germanism, putting bans on meetings of people or organizations believed to be still favoring the idea of peace.

Through local councils the commission spread its organization to all parts of the state. Meanwhile twenty thousand women were organized for war work in Minnesota communities. They pitched into the war bond campaigns, of which there were five — four Liberty Loans and a final Victory Loan. They and thousands of other women performed innumerable additional services. "Four-minute men" by the hundreds spoke at every kind of meeting to aid the bond campaigns, the total war effort, and a succession of "drives" for soldier aid and other causes. In the bond campaigns, Minnesotans subscribed a total of approximately $450,000,000. National calls, one after another, were met with energy and alacrity. Wheat and other grains were grown in prodigious crops. Iron-ore production was pushed to the limit and reached close to 90,000,000 tons for the war years of 1917 and 1918. This was a productive achievement of critical importance in meeting the needs of the nation at war.

Organization, at which Americans are traditionally adept, played a big role in home-front activities and it took many forms. There were a council of defense, a state committee on food production and conservation (alongside a federal food administrator for Minnesota), and a state fuel administration, in addition to the powerful Commission of Public Safety. The National Protective League, a "sort of private detective organization," searched for "slackers."

Seven important welfare organizations were given official status in their far-ranging efforts to be of service to the military in American training camps and overseas. These were the YMCA, the YWCA, the National Catholic War Council (in which the activities of the Knights of Columbus were highly important), the Jewish Welfare Board, the Salvation Army, the War Camp Community Service, and the American Library Association. In these organizations thousands of Minnesotans gave voluntary, devoted, and patriotic service.

The Red Cross, with units active throughout the state, had nearly a half million hard-working and eager members. A book crusade took the form, first, of money raising, then of collecting books to send off to camps. Nearly 140,000 volumes were gathered up in Minnesota as part of a national campaign that reached a total of more than 3,000,000 volumes. Clubs and spirited campaigns of many kinds reached into the schools. Boy scouts, girl scouts, and other youth organizations did enthusiastic work. And the people joined in observing "days" set aside to conserve resources for national needs. There were wheatless, meatless, and gasless days, and even "daylight saving." If not a few Minnesotans looked with some skepticism on daylight saving, they accepted it cheerfully as a war need, but opposed its continuation in later years.

Posters, slogans, buttons, badges, meetings, parades, newspaper publicity and support for war causes, the activities of churches, clubs, lodges, theaters, business, and industry — these were among the spurs to a united effort to put Minnesota strength behind the war for victory. "Fight with food," said one poster. "Save on sugar," said another. "Eat onions to finish the fiendish Hun," urged a third. Days of abstinence were reported to have saved 36,000,000 pounds of sugar in 1918 and — in restaurants, hotels, and clubs — more than 5,000,000 pounds of meat.

The Commission of Public Safety was aware of the prewar divergence in Minnesota opinion. It harbored suspicion and concern about possible tangles and obstructions in a state of varied national strains, with numerous ties of tradition and relationship. It devoted sessions to suspected disloyalty, alleged pro-Germanism, potential dissent, and possible efforts to evade the draft.

The commission did not prevent Senator La Follette of Wisconsin from speaking at a meeting of the Nonpartisan League in September 1917, but in the storm of criticism that followed his address, it recommended his expulsion from the United States Senate. The chairman of the commission wanted to unseat the mayor of Minneapolis, who had opposed America's entrance into the war. In the state election of 1918 the commission and many citizens hurled charges of disloyalty and pro-Germanism at the candidate who opposed Governor Burnquist for the Republican nomination. The commission was functioning legally under the wide powers given it by the legislature, but dissent within the commission led to the withdrawal of John Lind, whose integrity and patriotism were beyond question.

The emotions of World War I are now viewed with the perspective of more than four decades, and one conclusion is abundantly clear. The Minnesota people, 70 per cent of whom were immigrants and the children of immigrants, with few exceptions, gave wholehearted, generous, willing, loyal, eager, and patriotic support to the state's effort and to American success in the war. They were Americans whose sons were fighting at the front. Their loyalty, their blood, their money, their devotion were enlisted.

It cannot be doubted that the commission tried to mobilize the energies of the Minnesota people. Neither can it be doubted that the state learned a lesson from its experiment in wartime with a local form of dictatorship. When America entered World War II, directed against the arrogant dictatorships of Hitler and others, Minnesota did not again adopt the device of an official commission clothed with dictatorial powers. Nor was there a repetition of the detectival Protective League.

Minnesotans gave patriotic and all-out service in the armed forces of the United States. Because of the national dispersion of troops among varied branches of service, it is difficult to trace the operations of Minnesota contingents in identifiable units, as was possible in the numbered series of Minnesota regiments in the Civil War.

Some years after World War I, Colonel J. E. Nelson of the adjutant general's office presented a broad picture of what the Minnesota troops had accomplished in the war. They were "represented in every important engagement," he said, but were so intermingled with troops from other parts of the nation that only a review of all the American forces engaged in the war could reveal the full history of the achievements of the Minnesotans. Some figures, however, offered a wide conspectus of Minnesota's contribution. More than 126,000 Minnesota men and women saw service of one kind or another in World War I. Among them were 104,000 in the army, 12,000 in the navy, 2900 in the marine corps, more than 700 nurses, and others in special services. Of all the Minnesota troops, "3480 marched away never to return" — killed in action or dead from wounds, illness, or other causes. Nearly 5000 were wounded.

The pace of state action was swift after war was declared. The First Minnesota Infantry was in fact back in federal service even before the beginning of the war. The Naval Militia departed from Duluth for Philadelphia only two days after the war declaration. Speedy efforts filled out the four National Guard regiments. The infantrymen were sent first to Camp Cody in New Mexico. The field artillery went to Camp Mills in New York to be made a part of the 42nd Division, a composite of National Guard soldiers from many parts of the country.

From first to last during the war period some 40,000 Minnesota men enlisted in the several branches of the armed forces. Special contingents went into the Engineering Service, and one is not surprised to learn, in the light of Minnesota history, that the state made important contributions of trained men to forestry and railroad regiments. Various special units were also formed — a hospital unit by the University of Minnesota, an ambulance unit by Hamline University.

Volunteering in Minnesota was spirited, but the basic recruitment policy of the nation was the Selective Service. It was first applied to men 21 to 30 years old, and in 1918 it was extended to the age bracket of 18 to 45. In the drafts, more than a half million Minnesotans were registered. From them about 75,000 entered the service. Draft boards functioned throughout the state.

Even these numbers and activities do not fill out the picture of state mobilization and training. Fort Snelling — nearly a century after it was founded as a frontier sentinel — was again a military scene, functioning now as an officers' training center for more than 2500 men from Minnesota and neighboring states. Thousands of mechanics, radio and telegraph workers, bakers, and men for other trades were given specialized training at the Dunwoody Institute in Minneapolis. St. Paul trained ten thousand mechanics for air services in a special school. In the colleges and the state university, Student Army Training Corps were organized at the beginning of the academic year 1918–19. Thus, while far-reaching civilian efforts were being set in motion throughout the state, Minnesota was a stern and exciting scene of volunteering, Selective Service, the preparation of men for technical duties important in the country's effort, and departures day after day of men on national calls, national assignments, national duties.

Minnesota men were in the thick of the war after the American armies arrived in France to join their hard-fighting allies. Saint-Mihiel, the Argonne, Château-Thierry, Belleau Wood, Vaux — these and other names figure in the record of action, courage, and sacrifice by men from Minnesota. If many units or men cannot be followed in the maze of the nation's fighting forces, one group did maintain its identity as a part of the famous Rainbow Division. This was the 151st Field Artillery under Colonel George E. Leach of Minneapolis. Trained and ready, it had its baptism of fire in Lorraine, went on to the Champagne sector, played a heroic part at Château-Thierry, and was active in pushing back the German armies in the fierce Meuse-Argonne fighting. Colonel Leach and his soldiers were near Sedan when the war ended on November 11, 1918.

The 151st Field Artillery emerged with a distinguished record, as did the division of which it was a part. The 151st was such a cohesive and unified force throughout the war that its detailed story could be told in a volume published some years later.

Minnesota effort, military and civilian, had been bent, from April 6, 1917, to November 11, 1918, on winning the war. The announced victory was the signal for a release of tension and celebration such as the state had never before experienced. Business houses closed on Armistice Day, streets of cities and towns were scenes of parades, bells clanged, horns blew, surging people shouted their joy, and churches held services of thanksgiving. The long strain was broken. Happiness reigned, but there was sadness, too. Many families had lost sons, brothers, husbands, fathers. Yet others, awaiting the return of veterans, would welcome home men hurt in combat, handicapped for their re-entry into civilian life and work.

Many soldiers came back singly or in small groups, detached from the units in which they served. They were usually met by families and friends or by voluntary organizations, without fanfare. But the 151st, after marching into Germany, where it was stationed for a few quiet months on the Rhine, returned as a unit to Minnesota in the spring of 1919.

The regiment was welcomed at the state's capital on May 8 with another unrestrained outburst of joy, an arch of triumph, parades, the cheers (and tears) of fellow Minnesotans. The homecoming symbolized more than the return of the battle-scarred 151st, even with its heroic record. To thousands, the regiment symbolized the sacrifices of all Minnesota men and women who had served the country in its ordeal of fighting, courage, and suffering.

Homecoming was good, but much of the jubilation in Minnesota, as elsewhere in the nation, reflected the faith of the people that a durable peace had been won. They believed that the goal of a world made safe for democracy had been achieved. The war was "over, over there," and peace was at hand.

Few realized how rough the path of peace would be as the world moved onward into the twentieth century. The dominant thought was that "it must not happen again." One world war was enough! The League of Nations came into being, and many pinned their hopes to it. Few, if any, had any inkling that in a little more than two decades another and even more destructive world war would follow.

Free elections in wartime test a democracy. President Lincoln recognized this in his comment on the election of 1864. It demonstrated, he said, that a "people's government can sustain a national election in the midst of a great civil war."

The year 1918 was not civil war, but it was a year of war. Emotions were heated, people were excited, and anything that looked like opposition to prevailing trends was viewed in Minnesota with suspicion, anger, and alarm.

As World War I neared its climax, Minnesota staged a state election. The campaign was bitter. The Nonpartisan League championed farmer demands. It challenged the administration of Governor Burnquist and gave its support to Lindbergh, who in the primaries sought to capture the Republican nomination from the war governor. The League was charged not only with socialism, but also with pro-Germanism and hostility to the national war effort. Meetings were disrupted. The houses of some League sympathizers were smeared with yellow paint. Lindbergh himself was subjected to insult, scorn, and abuse. Some League advocates, including Townley, were placed under arrest. The Supreme Court set aside one charge, but another, three years after the war ended, brought jail sentences for Townley and one of his associates.

Lindbergh faced many hostile audiences with courage. In the primary election he polled a surprising 50,000 votes, but he lost by a wide margin to Burnquist. In the later election the governor defeated a candidate endorsed jointly by the League and the State Federation of Labor. This man, David H. Evans, ran under the banner of the "Farmer-Labor party," the first appearance of this name in a Minnesota election. The governor ran well ahead of Evans, but in the total vote, which included a Democrat and two minor parties, he stood behind the combined votes of his opponents.

Burnquist held office as governor to the end of the war and beyond. Political protest was obviously making an impact, but the Republican party, experienced in administration, led the state through the war years and through the entire postwar decade, with its maze of problems.

The farmer-labor political liaison continued. But in the postwar election of 1920 a new Republican candidate, J. A. O. Preus, defeated by a decisive majority a rising Farmer-Labor candidate, Dr. Henrik Shipstead, a Minnesota dentist with political aspirations. The farmers and laborers convened separately, but they agreed on a common candidate to represent what they viewed as their common cause.

Preus, trained as insurance commissioner and state auditor and also as a former secretary of Senator Nelson, served as governor from 1921 to 1925. Scion of a distinguished Norwegian Lutheran clerical family, he had been educated at Luther College and the University of Minnesota. He was an able, well-informed, hard-hitting politician.

Preus was governor in a period when two new amendments to the federal Constitution were in force, both of which had significant repercussions across state and nation. These were the Eighteenth Amendment, approved in 1919, which through the Volstead Law inaugurated national prohibition; and the Nineteenth Amendment, validating woman suffrage in the nation and state (1920). In Minnesota women soon began to play active parts in state and national politics. The League of Women Voters was organized in 1920. A woman was made a member of the State Board of Control in 1921 (Blanche LaDu). Another was nominated in the primaries of 1922 for the United States Senate. Four served in the Minnesota House of Representatives in 1923; and a few years later a Minnesota woman was elected to the state Senate. The dreams of the crusader Mrs. Andreas Ueland were being realized, though it must be added that in later years relatively few women have won election to the state legislature.

Governor Preus took quick account of rural problems by declaring that the "overshadowing issue" centered in the marketing of farm products. He encouraged cooperative marketing, and it was during his administration that the cooperatives were granted legal status under Minnesota law (1923). Preus also attempted to work out a solution of the problem of iron-ore taxation. He proposed measures to use the Babcock Amendment to the constitution as the basis for an effective working plan to build trunk highways for Minnesota.

Despite Governor Preus's vigorous efforts to forward the farmers' cause, the Farmer-Labor party in 1922 gave dramatic notice of the new state political trend. Senator Kellogg's term came to an end, and in 1922 he was defeated for re-election by Dr. Shipstead. Decisive as this turn was, it was less startling to the people of the state than the special election of 1923, which followed the death of Senator Knute Nelson. The popular Governor Preus entered the contest for the Senate seat against a "dirt farmer," Magnus Johnson of Meeker County. He lost. Thus Minnesota's two senators in 1923 were both Farmer-Laborites — a situation that soon changed when, in 1924, Johnson in turn was beaten by a Republican candidate, Thomas D. Schall.

The Farmer-Labor strength was threatening the Republican control of the state. But the emergence of Theodore Christianson as governor in 1925 (after defeating Floyd B. Olson of Minneapolis in the state election of 1924) signaled a continuation of Republican dominance. Christianson, a graduate of the University of Minnesota, an editor, an experienced legislator, and persuasive speaker, was re-elected twice, winning over Magnus Johnson in 1926 and over Ernest Lundeen in 1928. Thus he served as governor from 1925 to 1931.

Christianson was remarkably successful as the chief executive. He served the state through years of economic troubles and turbulence occasioned not alone by the difficulties of enforcing prohibition but also by the economic and social turmoil of the decade following the war. His

478

administration was noted for its businesslike reorganization in the state government, particularly the inauguration in 1925 of the Commission of Administration and Finance (which came to be called the "Big Three"). He gave impetus to the state's highway development, to the public fight against liquor banditry, to the furtherance of public health, and to other causes important to the state.

It was during the Christianson administration that the "Chase case" confirmed the power of the Board of Regents to govern the University of Minnesota under the authorization of Article VIII of the state constitution. The newly formed Commission of Administration and Finance, attempting to promote state economy through control of expenditures, challenged an item approved for payment by the university. This resulted in a test case that went first to a district court and then to the supreme court of the state. It took its name from the state auditor, Ray P. Chase, who declined to give his approval to a minor invoice submitted by the university. The university's case was presented by Dean Everett Fraser of the Law School, who argued forcefully against political control of the institution and for its government under a disinterested Board of Regents. The case came to a head in 1928. The supreme court held that the people had placed in the regents the "whole power to govern the university," that no part of that power "could be put elsewhere but by the people." As the historian of the university has indicated, the outcome sustained the position that the university was not to be one of political powers, but of the people. Political dependence, as Fraser made clear, might mean a yielding of policy to bigoted minorities. It might open the way to mediocrity for an institution whose service and greatness depended upon freedom from partisan control.

Through the decade Minnesota remained steadfast to its national Republican traditions. It gave its electoral votes to the ill-fated Warren G. Harding in 1920, to Calvin Coolidge in 1924, and to Herbert Hoover in 1928. It was in this period that Kellogg served in high diplomatic posts — first as a delegate to the Conference of American States in Chile in 1923, then as United States ambassador to Great Britain, and from 1925 to 1929 as secretary of state under President Coolidge. The next year he was awarded the Nobel Peace Prize as a recognition particularly of his role in the negotiation of the Briand-Kellogg Pact of 1928.

Once only, from 1860 to 1932, did Minnesota break loose from its traditional stand on the national front. The single exception was a Progressive Republican, Theodore Roosevelt, in 1912, chosen in preference to a conservative Republican and a liberal Democrat.

Descriptive tags now and then gain currency and receive popular acceptance through the influence of story writers who dramatize the superficialities of an age. Thus the 1920s are interpreted in fiction as the "jazz age" and as the era of the "flapper."

Actually the 1920s were a decade of hard work by people on farms and in industry. The time was one of advancing education, of soldiers getting back to jobs, mergers and consolidations in banking, expanding mobility, invigorating outdoor recreation, economic hardships for many (and speculation for many others), progress in broadcasting, cultural growth, and normal churchgoing. It was a period of decent living for thousands of people who neither defied the law by drinking themselves into a stupor nor indulged in wild orgies that lent themselves to fictional exploitation.

This does not mean that there were not changes in social mores. There were indeed, and they included a new spirit of candor, retreat from mid-Victorianism, and an increasing sophistication. But whatever the readjustments, most people after the war lived normally, reared children, supported schools, took part in clubs and organizations, and gave voluntary aid to community undertakings. They shared with good sense in many of the diversions of the changing years.

Fundamentally the 1920s were an age of advancing industrialization, of further progress in communication and transportation, of social and cultural advance, and of political revaluations. Fads and fashions swept the country, it is true — and the decade moved toward a new panic and depression. But few farmers, workers, educators, businessmen, and professional men dashed off to the Riviera for relief or escape. They did not dodge responsibility for work that had to be done.

Living, after the pressures of war, was, for most people, a sober business. It was not an abandonment of standards, not a retreat from realities. Every age has its excrescences, including the 1920s — but the social periphery is not the center of human endeavor and action.

Notwithstanding soaring levels of stocks in Wall Street, financial reverses marked the 1920s in Minnesota and the Middle West. From 1921 to 1929 as many as 320 state and 58 national banks in Minnesota were obliged to close their doors, and many depositors lost their savings. In 1921 there were 1160 state banks in Minnesota. Ten years later there were 675. In the same period the number of national banks dropped from 341 to 244. Minnesota did not stand alone in its fiscal misery. It was one of seven western grain states that suffered nearly half of all the bank failures in the United States from 1921 to 1929. These figures do not reflect the full story, however. Although 582 state and national banks passed out of the Minnesota picture in the course of a decade, bank deposits increased. Branch banks were established, and consolidations took place, though many banks were left out.

Minnesota farm crops were valued at $506,000,000 in 1919. Ten years later, despite big increases in acreage, the values sank to $310,000,000. The depression that came in the early 1920s subsided, and business boomed through most of the remaining years of the decade. But farmers had no easy time, and they turned, as they had so often done in the past, to politics. They supported a "farm bloc" in Congress, secured a federal farm board, put faith in "farm plans," and hoped, forlornly, that freighting would be re-established on the Mississippi and that a St. Lawrence–Great Lakes waterway would soon be achieved.

Farm mortgages mounted and foreclosures were many. Meanwhile milk production increased and the cooperative movement forged ahead — developments that attested the value of diversification and somewhat alleviated the economic burdens of the farmers. Their troubles may suggest some of the backgrounds for the growing strength of the farmer-laborer coalition at the end of the decade.

Events in the 1920s indicated that prohibition did not seem to represent the "settled conviction of society." The state, under Governor Preus, passed an enforcement code in 1921. Federal enforcement personnel included Andrew Volstead — the Minnesota congressman whose name was tagged on the federal prohibition act of 1919 — as a legal adviser. A border patrol tried to cut down the smuggling of liquor into the state. There can be no question as to the prevalence of drinking in violation of federal and state laws. Arrests for drunkenness in Minneapolis rose from 2546 in 1920 to 7294 five years later. Federal agents raided stills and confiscated large quantities of liquor, but it continued to be sold illicitly.

Minnesota was plagued, as were many other American communities, notably Chicago and New York, by underworld rings, rackets, and crime. By the end of the decade it was evident that the Eighteenth Amendment did not have behind it the support of the majority of the nation, despite the

481

long-continued crusade of Americans against the saloon and its evils. Prohibition was pragmatically adjudged a failure. Late in 1933 the amendment was repealed by the adoption of the Twenty-First Amendment.

Minnesota did not escape the sultriness of intolerance which, in varying degrees, settled on the country after World War I. The Ku Klux Klan, anti-radical, anti-Catholic, and anti-foreign, was present in the state. Minneapolis is reported to have had ten klans in 1923, and there was even a Klan publication in Minnesota. The state knew the shame of burning crosses. By and large, however, Minnesota good sense did not bow to the furtive intimidations of intolerance. The Klan was anathema to most Minnesotans.

An instance of sane state balance is afforded by the fundamentalist controversy which came to a climax in 1927. Fundamentalism had an eloquent Minnesota defender, as did anti-fundamentalism or "modernism." The episode would not be worthy of notice save for the fact that in 1927 a bill was introduced in the legislature to prohibit the teaching of evolution in "all the public schools, colleges, state teachers colleges, and the University of Minnesota."

Leading citizens of various faiths opposed this limitation on the freedom of learning. Minnesota wanted no such blight on its name as the Scopes trial of Tennessee, where Bryan wrangled with Clarence Darrow. The Minnesota legislators "indefinitely postponed" consideration of the anti-evolution bill, and this was a death sentence to the measure.

Like other decades, the 1920s were colored by shifts and absurdities in popular taste. New fads, such as mah-jongg and miniature golf, enlisted devotees. Ankles came out of hiding. By 1925 the skirts of girls and women reached only to their knees. The traditional ban on smoking among women was being lifted. Popular songs of the day — such as "Ramona," "St. Louis Blues," and "Brother Can You Spare a Dime?" — echoed across the state.

Broadway moved to Main Street, by way of Hollywood. At the opening of the decade Minneapolis saw Griffith's *The Greatest Question*. On the silent screen were such stars as Constance Talmadge, Elsie Ferguson, Pauline Frederick, and Mary Pickford (playing in *Pollyanna*). At the end, pictures were revolutionized by sound, and Minnesotans saw and listened to Greta Garbo in *Anna Christie*, George Arliss in *Disraeli*, and Dennis King in *The Vagabond King*. Minneapolis by 1930 had forty-eight motion-picture theaters.

482

The radio brought the world into the sitting rooms of homes. In the early 1920s crystal sets and earphones were the regular radio equipment. A station known as "The Call of the North" (WLAG) opened in 1922. The next year there were twelve broadcasting stations in Minnesota. WLAG was taken over by the Washburn-Crosby company in 1924 and became WCCO. That year the university inaugurated a course in radio engineering. By 1930 there were nearly 300,000 radios in the state. Speeches, plays, music, and advertising were beginning to flood the air waves. Meanwhile authors were trying to interpret the age. Their books, to be noted later, depicting Main Street and the "jazz age," occasioned fierce and emotional debates. A reminder of pioneer traditions came through the writing of the immigrant novelist O. E. Rölvaag. But the most un-jazzlike manifestation of Minnesota thought during the decade was Dr. Folwell's four-volume *History of Minnesota* (1922–30), a sober and mature review of the state's past.

John Lind's prediction of a colossal state population by the end of the century received no statistical support in the 1920s. The population increase was only half that of the preceding decade. But if the rate of population growth faltered, urbanization surged forward. The movement of people from farm to town did not stop. Meanwhile the skylines of Minneapolis and St. Paul rose higher and higher, with such structures as the Foshay and Rand towers in Minneapolis and the First National Bank in St. Paul — also the beginnings of a new and modernistic court-house in the capital city.

Advances in transportation left as deep marks on the 1920s as any other factor. The state and the Middle West took an increasing interest in the prospect that the Mississippi River might be opened for barge conveyance of heavy goods. The Panama Canal tied East and West together in shipping, but the Middle West seemed to be at a disadvantage. For certain goods, shipping costs from the Missouri country to the eastern seaboard were higher than costs from California via the Panama Canal. Commerce, it was believed, would be stimulated by river traffic between Minnesota and the Gulf — if only the river in its upper reaches, from St. Louis north, could be deepened and kept to a standard depth level.

Attempts to control the river levels were made between 1884 and 1912 by United States engineers who built dams at a half dozen northern lakes at a cost of $2,000,000. The purpose was to create reservoirs that could be drawn on in the period of slack water. This was achieved, but the project stirred opposition from loggers and also from northern communities that blamed the system when floods came (even though overflowing reservoirs had held back enormous quantities of water). Others, noting that the released reservoirs added to the water power of Minneapolis, were critical. Nevertheless, the reservoirs proved effective, and gradually opposition dwindled.

In a later era, however, it was realized that a colossal engineering plan was needed — one that would make the northern reservoirs obsolete. The objective was an assured nine-foot channel, and businessmen interested in freight traffic took the initiative in forwarding it. In Minneapolis the Upper Mississippi Barge Line Company was started in 1925. In 1927 the Inland Waterways Corporation (under the War Department) sanctioned a fleet of towboats and barges for the Upper Mississippi. A "Minneapolis-to-Gulf" day was celebrated that year. Three barges carrying sugar reached Minnesota from St. Louis. This event symbolized the purpose of the business interests, but unfavorable river conditions would bar any large development unless the problem of slack-water navigation could be fully solved. Congress intervened in 1930 by authorizing a nine-foot channel. Engineers found that twenty-seven locks and dams would have to be built to attain it — and the costs would run to $150,000,000!

Minneapolis and St. Paul built docks and terminals. In 1933 the nine-foot-channel project was included within the scope of the Federal Works Program. That year the "Lakes to Gulf" waterway was opened, and Chicago became a part of the river barge traffic. Locks and dams on the great river were constructed with energy and dispatch, and by the late 1930s the northern river route was functioning. The achievement was a tribute to the skill of engineers, to forward-looking men of business, and to the alerted concern of the federal government.

Meanwhile, advances were made in road-building. Governor Burnquist gave earnest attention to the state's highway system in 1919. To him it meant better rural life, the forwarding of consolidated schools, and advances in marketing. The Babcock Amendment to the state constitution projected seventy major highways. A bond issue was authorized. Car licenses, at first nominal, were increased. At the middle of the decade a gasoline tax was instituted. By 1930 more than 1400 miles of road had been paved, and nearly as many had been given bituminous treatment. These developments were supported by a succession of governors. Supervision was under the man for whom the road amendment was named, a veritable "apostle of roads," Charles M. Babcock. Inevitably the improvement of Minnesota's roads gave impetus to the automobile age, to passenger cars, buses, and trucks, as well as to old-fashioned conveyances.

Concurrently, advances in airplane construction were spectacular and presaged the coming of passenger airlines. The Wold-Chamberlain Airport was opened on the edge of Minneapolis in 1923, and five years later it became a municipal airport. St. Paul had its Holman Memorial Airport ready for operation in 1927, and that year witnessed the first passenger plane flight from St. Paul to Chicago.

The year 1927 was memorable for another, impressive, and dramatic reason. It was in that year that a young Minnesotan, Charles A. Lindbergh, electrified the world by flying (May 20–21) a solo, nonstop flight across the Atlantic, from New York to Paris.

This epochal flight, completed in a little over 33½ hours, was a symbol of man's conquest of the air. To the millions who waited in prayerful anxiety for the safe completion of the flight, it was more than a brave and spectacular individual achievement. It marked for the world the decisive inauguration of the modern air age. The young airman was applauded everywhere, returned to the United States, and was showered with deserved honors. On a tour of the country, he visited Minnesota and received a glad and unprecedented ovation from his home community. His state took deep pride in what he had done. It also gave him admiration for his poised and modest bearing in receiving the plaudits of his countrymen and people the world over.

Hiawatha and Minnehaha by Jacob Fjelde

The Advancing Arts

A WRITER on Florence in Renaissance times speaks of the "impulse to beauty" which helped to give the Italian city the luster of undying fame. Main Street is not Florence, but the age-old impulse has not been wanting among Minnesota people. Many of them have painted, carved, composed, written, performed, collected, designed buildings, and cultivated human and natural lore.

In the early periods, people built cabins, houses, churches, and public buildings simply and quickly, with an eye to immediate use. In succeeding decades, though much building was haphazard, architecture began to take its place as a recognized profession.

With urban growth and advances in mobility, the Minnesota scene was dotted with parks — city, state, and federal. Cities widened some of their streets, and as specialization increased, municipal planning took advantage of expert counsel.

The interest in esthetic goals and cultural understanding found expression in galleries and museums, orchestras and singing, dramatic entertainment, libraries, schools, churches, and private collecting.

If, as some writers have suggested, pioneering entailed cultural loss, the migrating folk carried with them traditions and crafts, faiths, and song. To most people, on the frontier as elsewhere, life seemed insupportable if it did not make room for the nontangible values that surmount crops and dollars.

487

Voyageurs and lumberjacks, as has been noted, sang chansons and ballads. Pioneers cherished folk songs and made up narrative ballads of their own. Familiar hymns were sung in churches, which also gave a place to organs, quartets, and choirs.

Traveling troupes of singers — notably the Hutchinsons and the Andrews family — gave delight to audiences that crowded concert halls to hear them perform. The Andrewses were an opera company that frequently presented *Carmen* and *Faust*. Bands and orchestras enlivened the pioneer musical scene. Some artists of high renown ventured out to the frontier; and in the decades after the Civil War, many famous singers, pianists, and violinists appeared in Minnesota concerts. Germans, Scandinavians, Welshmen, and people of other nationalities rich in song traditions organized societies and held musical festivals. From early years onward, teachers of music were present. Clubs of music lovers emerged in the 1880s, 1890s, and 1900s. Now and then great talent appeared, including that of a Minneapolis singer of the 1890s, Olive Fremstad, who vaulted into fame as an operatic star in the 1900s.

Modern Minnesota is noted for a symphony orchestra, *a cappella* choirs, and good schools of music, but these did not suddenly spring into existence. Interest, organization, talent, and work provided their artistic and historical setting.

A St. Paul orchestra, started in the early 1860s and active for more than two decades, included in its programs Haydn and Beethoven symphonies. George Seibert, its director, also led a band of local distinction. In Minneapolis Frank Danz conducted a good orchestra, and in the 1880s his son, Frank Danz, Jr., succeeded him. These St. Paul and Minneapolis orchestras offered music of quality, and their efforts were encouraged by occasional concerts given by visiting orchestras from the East.

While these developments were taking place, German and Scandinavian singing societies were active in stimulating musical interest. In the 1870s, for instance, three Scandinavian singing clubs were started — the Scandinavian Music Corps, Scandia, and the Scandinavian Singing Society. Swedish singers formed the Orpheus Singing Society in the late 1880s, and in 1891 a song festival of the United Scandinavian Singers of America was held in Minneapolis.

In St. Paul, Minneapolis, and Duluth, women organized societies or clubs to sponsor good music. St. Paul led the way, after informal efforts in the 1870s, by launching in 1882 the Ladies' Musicale, which some years later (1891) adopted as its name the Schubert Club and which has been a creative influence through all the decades since that time.

Minneapolis was the scene of the Thursday Musical, begun in 1892. It was similarly zealous in opening opportunity for local talent and in inviting to Minnesota some of the noted musicians of the world. The clubs in the Twin Cities were matched in Duluth by that city's Matinee Musicale, organized in 1900. It would be difficult to measure the influence of these dedicated and well-directed organizations and of societies of like sort in stimulating informed musical appreciation in Minnesota.

Orchestras needed places where they could rehearse and perform, and they were constantly on the move. In Minneapolis an Academy of Music — less glamorous in reality than its name — was tried. Local orchestras played at a Turner Hall, Harmonia Hall, occasionally at the Grand Opera House (opened in 1883), later at the Metropolitan Opera House (1894), famed in the theatrical history of Minneapolis. Through home talent and visiting orchestras, singers, pianists, and violinists, the people of the town heard excellent music. The time was nearing for local initiative to launch a symphony orchestra of high quality.

It must not be forgotten that music advanced on many fronts in the 1890s. One was musical education. A highly gifted English-born Swedish musician, Gustavus Johnson, came to Minnesota in 1880 and later founded the Johnson School of Music, Oratory, and Dramatic Art. Another good school was the Northwestern Conservatory of Music, which later turned into the MacPhail School of Music and Dramatic Art. This was the special domain of William MacPhail, a member of the Danz orchestra, an excellent violinist, and through many years the director of the Apollo Club. The music schools instructed youngsters, held recitals, nurtured talent, and made long-lasting contributions to musical taste. In the 1890s two important singing clubs were formed. These were the Apollo and the Philharmonic clubs, the one a men's club, and the other a mixed chorus. They were eager, ambitious, competitive. Both had backgrounds in earlier organizations; and both sang their way into the musical history of Minneapolis and the state.

An event of singular importance was the arrival in Minnesota of the German-born and German-trained Emil Oberhoffer — violinist, organist, pianist, conductor, and composer. He and his wife came to Minnesota with a roving Gilbert and Sullivan troupe and were stranded. Oberhoffer took one humble job after another, playing in restaurants and elsewhere in the early 1890s. He became a church organist in St. Paul and was befriended and encouraged by the St. Paul Schubert Club, for which he gave recitals and talks. He went to Minneapolis as an organist and choir director, was chosen to head the Apollo Club in 1896, and four years later transferred his talents to the rival Philharmonic Club.

Oberhoffer was dedicated to his art, ambitious, and gifted. He understood that the Philharmonic Club without a symphony orchestra was incomplete. He wanted nothing less than a full-fledged permanent symphony orchestra. For this, as John K. Sherman has written, "he began to talk, to plead, to persuade." One of his most persuasive arguments was what he himself was doing artistically with the Philharmonic Club. But the truth is that other interacting forces helped to bring the Minneapolis Symphony Orchestra into being. One of the most potent was the rich background of Minneapolis musical interest. Finally, Oberhoffer enlisted financial backing from Minneapolis citizens who cared about music and to whom a great orchestra seemed a crowning glory for the city.

The Oberhoffer dream turned into a reality. The Minneapolis Symphony Orchestra was organized, recruiting its talent in part from the players trained by Frank Danz. On November 5, 1903 — with Oberhoffer at his fastidious best — the orchestra gave its first concert. It played in the vast Exposition Building (where the Republicans had held their national convention in 1892). The governing board of the orchestra could have engaged a singer at a modest price, but instead it chose a great operatic star of the day, Marcella Sembrich (at the then stupendous fee of $1800). If the first concert proved a somewhat less finished performance than the orchestra attained in its concerts of later years, it was by no means an inauspicious start.

Through threescore years, the Minneapolis Symphony Orchestra has maintained rank as one of the great orchestras of America. Its growth and success were sustained by widening public approval and by gifts from sincere friends of music. Especially notable was the support of E. L. Carpenter of Minneapolis through many years. A man of business, he was at heart a musician who wanted the very best and poured enthusiasm and funds into the enterprise.

For a quarter of a century (1905–30), the concerts of the Minneapolis Symphony Orchestra were given in the Minneapolis Auditorium. Since that time the orchestra's home has been Northrop Auditorium on the university campus. The move was fortunate for its identification of the orchestra with the university, a musical center, and also because the location was readily accessible to music lovers in both of the Twin Cities. As the years went by, the orchestra became an all-state institution, enjoying patronage and gifts not only from the Twin Cities but from people in communities throughout the state.

In addition to its weekly symphonic programs each season, the orchestra has presented popular concerts and special programs for children; and it performs on tour in many cities of the United States. Oberhoffer led it for nearly two decades, years of increasing fame for the orchestra. Since his time it has enjoyed a succession of gifted conductors in Henri Verbrugghen, Eugene Ormandy, Dimitri Mitropoulos, Antal Dorati, and — in its latest phase — Stanislaw Skrowaczewski.

The Minneapolis Symphony Orchestra, as its historian has said, is "Minnesota's outstanding contribution to the world of music." Other Minnesota cities have nurtured good orchestras for longer or shorter periods, including Duluth, St. Paul, Hibbing, Rochester, and St. Cloud. Schools and colleges, and the University of Minnesota, have supported orchestras of their own, not to mention bands, glee clubs, and choruses.

The year that saw the launching of the Minneapolis Symphony Orchestra also witnessed the arrival at St. Olaf College of F. Melius Christiansen to head its then infant department of music. This Norwegian-born genius had been a student at Augsburg College. He went to Germany to study music in the 1890s, returned, and served as organist in a Minneapolis church. In 1903 he began teaching at St. Olaf College.

Director, composer, violinist, and arranger, Christiansen first developed a superb band and then gave his primary attention to a choir in a Northfield church. This developed into the famous St. Olaf Choir (1912). Year after year, he trained it to tonal nicety in the *a cappella* singing of chorales, with subtle gradations in volume and with artistry in every fine detail. Christiansen, a leonine personality, was a "master of music." His choir through the years of his leadership toured America and Europe, winning triumph after triumph.

Song without accompaniment soon gained immense vogue regionally and nationally. The St. Olaf Choir spread its influence by virtue of its standards through five decades and it is still active. Two sons of Christiansen, Olaf and Paul, have attained a distinction almost equaling that of their father as directors at St. Olaf and Concordia colleges. Augsburg,

Hamline, Gustavus Adolphus, other colleges, the University of Minnesota, various private groups, Norwegian and Swedish singing societies, and yet other clubs have contributed to the total Minnesota singing achievement.

Minnesota music progressed in diverse ways. World-famed artists appeared with the Minneapolis Symphony Orchestra. Mrs. Carlyle Scott, a gallant supporter of music in just about every form, launched a series of university artists' courses. Chamber music had zealous adherents. Opera was occasionally presented by traveling companies, and finally the Metropolitan Opera Company began an annual spring series, with the university's auditorium normally crowded for every performance.

St. Paul led in Minnesota civic opera, with home talent supporting singers invited to play leading roles. The steadfast Schubert Club had much to do with the encouragement of local opera.

Minnesota musicians tried their hands at composition, including Oberhoffer, Christiansen, and other conductors. The state has not produced a composer of world renown, but it has had writers of good music — of songs; of chorales, to which Paul Christiansen and Leland Sateren made memorable contributions; and of quartets, concertos, symphonies, and other forms, in which such composers as Ross L. Finney, Paul Fetler, and Earl George have won distinction. Its schools — notably the University of Minnesota and the MacPhail music schools — have done educational service of good quality. In appraisal and criticism, Professor Donald N. Ferguson of the University of Minnesota has set standards of sensitive and sophisticated musical analysis and interpretation.

Painting, sculpture, and other arts were not unrelated to Minnesota's exuberant interest in music. Painters like Rindisbacher, Catlin, Eastman, Lewis, Mayer, Whitefield, and Johnson, enamored of western scenes, recorded them in early years. People in some frontier homes made sketches. At their looms, in wood carving, and in other ways they wove elements of inherited folk art into their daily lives.

Now and then a competent artist sought out Minnesota as a field for creative work. Peter Clausen, a Dane, highly trained in Denmark and Sweden, came to Minnesota in the 1860s, painted skillfully for churches, did portraits, murals, fresco pieces, even a panorama; and he was esteemed as the most gifted scenic painter for theaters in the Northwest.

Jacob Fjelde, Norwegian-born sculptor, came to Minnesota in the late 1880s and was creatively active until he died in 1896. His works included the romantic monument to Hiawatha and Minnehaha above the Falls of Minnehaha, the statues of Ole Bull in Minneapolis and of Ibsen in St. Paul, the monument at Gettysburg to the heroic First Minnesota, and the figures on the atrium of Burton Hall at the University of Minnesota. His art has won few plaudits from modernists, but he was a sculptor of skill whose products evoke pleasure and admiration among thousands of onlookers who are not repelled by naturalistic and artistically wrought sculpture. Fjelde's son Paul followed in the footsteps of his father and won high standing as a sculptor. One of the tragedies in Minnesota art history is that Homer D. Martin, a distinguished American landscape painter whose works are now treasured in American art collections, died in poverty, nearly blind, in St. Paul in 1897, little regarded by his contemporaries, and virtually unknown to Minnesotans.

American life cannot be interpreted without reference to organization. Many people in early days were devoted to arts of one kind or another. Now and then a semiprofessional enthusiast appeared on the scene. One was a Minneapolis teacher, Theodore J. Richardson, who for thirteen years from 1880 taught drawing in the Minneapolis schools. He was a charter member of a new organization, the Society of Fine Arts, established in Minneapolis in 1883, with the far-seeing President Folwell of the university as one of its promoters. Three years after the founding of the Arts Society, it enlisted the instructional aid of a well-trained artist, Douglas Volk, as the head of its art school — and this proved a significant step forward in Minnesota art history.

The school was comparable in its consequences (and within its field) to the founding of the symphony orchestra or the Northfield choir. In it many good artists received their basic training. They included Alexis J. Fournier, Adolf Dehn, Wanda Gág, Gilbert Fletcher, and John Flannagan, to mention only a few of many students. Paul Manship, sculptor, studied at the St. Paul School of Fine Arts but also took night classes at the Minneapolis school and then went east and to Europe for advanced training. His creative imagination is recorded in the New York Rockefeller Center, but some Minnesotans will recall with affection his Indian hunter and dog in a miniature St. Paul park.

A dynamic force in Minneapolis art was introduced by the arrival of the German-born Robert Koehler in 1893, and his appointment the next year as the director of the school of fine arts. He led the way to the establishment in 1911 of the Minneapolis Institute of Fine Arts as an outgrowth of the Society of Fine Arts. In many ways he stimulated widespread appreciation of art in Minnesota, utilizing, among other institutions, the Minnesota State Art Society. This was started in 1903, with legislative support, and it devoted its energies to forwarding appreciation of art in farm and town homes, in industry, and in fact everywhere.

As in the experience of other middle western states, Minnesota has seen many gifted artists depart for the East or elsewhere. These have included Wanda Gág, printmaker and illustrator of books for children; Dewey Albinson, gifted painter of North Shore scenes; Adolf Dehn, water colorist.

The passing years, however, have witnessed increasing home patronage of local artists. Museums, galleries, and the state fair have been generous in exhibiting their work. Increasing numbers of Minnesota houses have original paintings hung on their walls. Planners and architects in various Minnesota cities have engaged local artists for murals and sculpture.

John Rood, a versatile university sculptor and author, fashioned a memorable gate for Hamline University, a monumental symbolic interpretation of books and learning for the Minneapolis Public Library, and many other works of distinction.

The paintings of Cameron Booth are widely known. Josephine Lutz Rollins has done a series of water colors of Minnesota historic houses. Several university artists, including Bernard Arnest, Malcolm Myers, Kyle Morris, and Walter Quirt, have won plaudits for their exhibits. Photography as an art has also made noteworthy contributions, especially through the work of Allen Downs and Jerome Liebling. John Szarkowski, in *The Face of Minnesota*, offered an arresting photographic interpretation of contemporary Minnesota scenes.

If young painters and sculptors do not rush off to New York and other art centers as avidly as once they did, the explanation is then in some degree an enlarging home market for art. This may not be unconnected with the fact that hundreds of amateurs (of all ages) have turned to painting and sculpture and other forms of art as an avocation. It may be conjectured that they have been somewhat influenced by the publicized examples of Winston Churchill, President Eisenhower, "Grandma Moses," and other illustrious figures.

Another influence is that of the collections of high-quality art in the state — at the Minneapolis Institute of Fine Arts, the Walker Art Center, the St. Paul Gallery and School of Art, the University Gallery, the Tweed Gallery in Duluth, and other institutions. Many collectors have been generous in presenting or willing their treasures to museums, thus making them the common possessions of the people. A pervasive influence — perhaps fundamental — is also the widespread teaching of art in the schools and colleges of the state, including the handicrafts and "art education."

Art is integral to living — not a fad or frill, not an esoteric accomplishment, not a rich man's hobby. The philosophy of "art on Main Street" was persuasively voiced by Laurence E. Schmeckebier, onetime chairman of the university's department of art, and it is winning grass-roots endorsement. Farmers, businessmen, doctors, lawyers, and many more are finding art rewarding in its many fields. Long after Dr. Schmeckebier expressed his views in speeches and writings, the manager of a gas station in northeastern Minnesota engaged none other than Frank Lloyd Wright to plan his establishment. The result was a uniting of utility with the artistic designs of a daring modern architect.

A noteworthy illustration of private collecting channeled to an institution in order to share treasures with the people is found in the benefactions of Thomas B. Walker of Minneapolis. This businessman was as avid an art collector as he was shrewd in his business as a lumberman. He stirred public appreciation of art to such an extent that the venerable historian Dr. Folwell named him "Minnesota's Apostle of Art."

From the 1870s onward, Walker collected paintings and other art objects. He added gallery after gallery to his house until there were fifteen in all. In the 1890s his enterprise became so extensive that he felt obliged to employ a curator for his collection. Through many years he invited the public to visit his house and galleries. When he reached the age of eighty-five, he formed the Walker Foundation and a new building was put up to house his collection. From these beginnings, the well-known Walker Art Center developed (in 1940). It has since carried forward a collecting and educational program, encouraged regional artists, recognized values in contemporary art, and reached out to the community and state, to people of every age, lay and professional folk alike.

Repositories of art in Minnesota are not limited to the Twin Cities and Duluth. Rochester, for instance, has a flourishing and interesting center that serves a community alert to the inspiriting values of art in modern life. Under able direction, it is an example of what smaller communities can do in forwarding artistic interest.

In the 1850s and later the Greek revival in architecture found expression in private dwellings and public buildings. In large towns and small, during the post-Civil War period, much of the architecture that did not follow very simple styles or log-cabin techniques represented what Professor Schmeckebier calls "Victorian eclecticism." Builders, turning to available handbooks and guides, borrowed ideas from any and all sources. The result was a motley of standards. In architecture, as in many other fields, specialization did not appear in early times. The pioneer academic institution offering specialized training in architecture (the Massachusetts Institute of Technology) did not start its program until 1868.

As years glided into decades, architects modified the Minnesota scene. Like the country at large, the state was influenced by the Chicago World's Fair in 1893. The eclecticism of earlier years was succeeded by what has been called a "Beaux-Arts" era. Using less pretentious labels, Dr. Schmeckebier designates four periods of Minnesota architecture — the Pioneer, Mansion, Metropolitan, and Functional. In studying a small town (Red Wing), he found all these periods illustrated in the "community's cultural development."

Among illustrious Minnesota architects in the decades after the Civil War were LeRoy S. Buffington and Cass Gilbert. Both left their marks on the building history of the state. Buffington, coming from Cincinnati in 1871, after training and experience in engineering and architecture, opened a Minneapolis office in 1874, and in the 1880s designed one great building after another, including the Pillsbury A Mill, the West Hotel, several university buildings, and some private residences. He is perhaps most famed for his skyscraper patent in 1888, which was an ingeniously planned device for "a braced skeleton of metal with masonry veneer supported on shelves fastened to the skeleton of each story." This invention, given publicity as an architectural scheme that would make possible buildings as high as twenty-eight stories, won for him the accolade of "Father of the Skyscraper." His plans for such a building in Minneapolis did not materialize, but a writer in the 1930s said that the public interest in his conception of a twenty-eight-story building did much to advance the dissemination of knowledge "of this form of construction in the architectural world." Buffington went on to design many buildings, including a number of capitols in other states.

Cass Gilbert, an Ohioan like Buffington, won a spirited competition for the design of the new Minnesota state capitol. It was built in the late

1890s and early 1900s and opened in 1905 — a domed structure in the "Renaissance tradition." Sculpture by Daniel French, murals by John La Farge and Kenyon Cox, and panels by Francis D. Millet, Edwin Blashfield, and Howard Pyle added distinction to its interior. Gilbert elaborated plans for the future expansion of the University of Minnesota and for an impressive capitol approach in St. Paul. Later he won fame for his design of skyscrapers, notably New York's Woolworth Building, at the time (1913) the tallest building in the world. He was acclaimed for many other structures, including the white, glistening Supreme Court building in Washington.

Gilbert won honors nationally and internationally. He was unquestionably one of Minnesota's foremost architects. Some modern architectural critics, however, have not sustained the praise given him by his own contemporaries and have described much of his work as "pretentious." Newer design has turned away from dependence upon tradition and launched experiments uniting originality with adaptation to functional utility and simplicity.

Many Minnesota banks, churches, public buildings, and private dwellings bear the marks of the modern architectural craft, with its novel and arresting ideas. The profession of architecture has been bulwarked by the School of Architecture in the University of Minnesota, where Professor Roy Jones and his successors have combined rigid training with freedom from traditional restraints and a liberal concern for architecture as a servant of the changing needs of a new age. And many colleges in the state have adopted daring, ultramodern, and forward-looking building programs.

Architecture is no provincial field. Modern construction, gradually changing the aspects of Minnesota cities — their suburbs, and even smaller towns and the rural scene — represents in part the ideas of architecture as a universal art. Thus Frank Lloyd Wright designed a number of unusual Minnesota houses; and the Saarinens (Eliel and Eero) fashioned a Minneapolis church of original quality. Some churches of various denominations have built houses of worship in styles of daring individuality. Examples of novel interest are St. Peter's Lutheran Church in Edina; Mount Zion Temple in St. Paul; and an exquisite chapel at St. John's in Collegeville.

Architectural firms, such as those of Clarence H. Johnson and the Ellerbe Company of St. Paul, took over the designing of numerous large

497

buildings. Small companies, even single architects, played no unimportant role, however, in the shift from traditional to modernistic architectural concepts in building.

Single-floor houses, prefabricated houses, urban and suburban "developments," and massive apartment buildings (some involving individual or family ownership of separate apartments) — all these contributed to the altered architectural geography of modern Minnesota. To the eyes of many laymen, as they viewed the "developments" with their hundreds of ranch-type structures, the eclecticism of the Victorian age seemed to have been replaced by a depressing uniformity of modern style. Possibly this mechanized architecture augurs new departures in the future.

History does not unfold that future. From generation to generation styles, ideas, fashions, tastes, and the adaptation of building to needs and demands have brought about architectural change. Living professions do not stand still, and architecture is such a profession. Tradition has its place, but new ways, new mobility, urban congestion, the ingenuity of man, new building materials, and modern standards of family living — all these point to further changes in the future that could be as revolutionary as the shift from Victorian eclecticism to mid-twentieth-century functionalism.

Landscape architecture has an honored place in the domain of the arts, and in this field, as in so many others, pioneer planners were a generation ahead of their own times.

A nineteenth-century landscape architect, Horace W. S. Cleveland, a gifted son of New England, came to St. Paul as early as 1872 and presented to its city council a plan of imaginative vision. He wanted parks at Lakes Como and Phalen — still far out from the residential centers of St. Paul. He asked for a lookout over the Mississippi River. He advocated a high and commanding hill for state buildings — an idea not turned into reality for more than thirty years. He recommended great radiating avenues, a splendid interurban street between St. Paul and Minneapolis, and generous boulevards along the river flowing through both cities. Cleveland correctly foresaw a growth in future years that would make the Twin Cities physically one. He scorned "artificial decorations," but had a concern for a permanent "heritage of beauty."

The St. Paul of his time was lethargic. The city did indeed acquire Como Park in 1873, notwithstanding the opposition of an alderman who was blind to the longer future. He branded the park as a recreation spot for the rich alone — those only who could reach it with their carriages. Minneapolis was no less lethargic. In 1864 it declined an offer of about twenty acres in what is now a part of its solidly packed southtown, but was then out in the country. Similarly it refused a chance to buy all of Nicollet Island, above the Falls of St. Anthony. And in the 1870s it declined an opportunity to purchase at a modest price a large tract around one of the most beloved lakes of its later history — Lake Harriet. Cleveland made a report and then left Minnesota. But he returned in the 1880s to work with a man named Charles M. Loring.

Loring, a native of Maine, became president of the newly created Minneapolis board of park commissioners in 1883 and quickly took one vigorous step after another. The temper of the times had changed. He was fortunate in securing the expert Cleveland as a principal aid and adviser. In a matter of two years the city purchased ten pieces of land for park purposes. Other forward steps included the acquisition of the area bordering Minnehaha Falls (1887); and the designing and construction of a scenic parkway linking the falls and the Minneapolis lakes. Most important was an arrangement with St. Paul whereby lands on both sides of the river, from the university to Fort Snelling, were secured for park and driveway purposes.

The day of cars was still in the future — and super-highways were not dreamed of — but Loring did not rest content with parks and the preservation of the charming banks of the river. His thought was of a beautiful city. This to him meant not only parks and playgrounds, the river and its picturesque gorge, but also trees — a veritable city of trees. He launched a movement for extensive planting to shade city streets and to add natural beauty to travel-ways.

Dr. Folwell designates Loring as the "Apostle of Parks and Playgrounds." He deserved honor, but the apostleship should be shared with Horace W. S. Cleveland, by far the more original mind. Both men were planners to whom the Twin Cities can look back with profound gratitude. By the 1930s Minneapolis had nearly 150 parks; St. Paul had more than a hundred; and the park movement had spread to many other cities of the state. Much progress centered in the nurturing of "beauty in nature." This was a cherished doctrine for Cleveland, who spoke contemptuously of those who "washed the face" of nature, who "combed her hair and put her in stays."

499

What Minnesota cities did in their park programs was more than matched by an all-Minnesota and federal program for parks and forests. The state and federal government participated in movements to provide recreational areas, preserve wild life, retain some of the virgin white and Norway pine, and take other steps to conserve soil, water, forests, natural wealth, and primeval beauty. Since Itasca State Park was established in 1891 and Pillsbury State Forest in 1899, great areas have been set aside by the federal government in the Chippewa and Superior-Quetico reserves. Minnesota by 1962 had taken over more than a hundred thousand acres for forty-six state parks (not all of them as yet fully developed), twelve "monument areas" or state historic sites, and fourteen waysides and recreation areas. In addition there were two "national monuments" — Pipestone and Grand Portage.

Prophets sometimes fail to win honor not only in their own countries (and their own houses), but in their own generations. Neither the designers of buildings nor the artists of landscapes in Minnesota won any great honor or quick and easy triumphs in their day.

In the perspective of history, however, the arts in this middle western state were effectively served by Cleveland and Loring, the Fjeldes, Buffington, Cass Gilbert, and the many men and women who conceived life to be barren without the lift of music. Some of the creative artists of past times have not escaped acrid criticism by authorities of a later and more sophisticated age. But the architects, painters, sculptors, and musicians of an earlier day were genuine builders of Minnesota. They contributed to the advancing arts; they helped to conserve the state's heritage of beauty; and they merit honor in the country (and the Minnesota cultural house) to which they gave without stint their talents and energies.

Theatergoers at St. Paul's Metropolitan Opera House in 1906

The Theater and the Book World

BEFORE the advent of movies, radio, and television, no form of popular entertainment excelled the theater in Minnesota public interest and favor. The decades after the Civil War witnessed a succession of theaters in the Twin Cities, and by the mid-1880s nearly a half hundred Minnesota towns had theaters or halls where touring companies could perform. Plays were in fact so popular that a circuit was established from the Twin Cities and lower river towns to the western border of the state.

For music, plays, and lectures, Minneapolis through four decades had at least eight or ten theaters and halls. They wore such names as Harmonia, Harrison's, Pence, the Academy of Music, Theatre Comique, the Grand Opera House (later called the Lyceum), and two "People's" theaters, one known in subsequent years as the Bijou, the other as the Metropolitan Opera House. St. Paul also had many playhouses through the years. A German theater was functioning in the capital city as early as 1857, and the Germans built an Athenaeum two years later. St. Paul's Opera House opened in 1867. Other theaters had their day, but the St. Paul Metropolitan in later years fulfilled a role similar to that of its twin Metropolitan in Minneapolis.

For no small part of the gala theatrical period from the 1860s to the early 1890s, the Pence Opera House in Minneapolis, which has been described as the "Playhouse for Pioneers," was a major theater. It opened brilliantly in 1867, with Governor Marshall and Senator Ramsey present. Later it presented Ole Bull, master violinist, and Laura Keene in *The*

Rivals and *Our American Cousin.* The second of these was the play that Abraham Lincoln was watching on the fateful evening of April 14, 1865. *Richard III* and other plays of Shakespeare were produced at the Pence. Several stock companies used the theater in the 1870s and 1880s. Later the house faced severe competition, first from the Academy of Music, next from the Grand Opera House.

The forerunner of the Lyceum opened in 1887 with *Julius Caesar,* starring the famous tragedian Edwin Booth and Lawrence Barrett. The Metropolitan Opera House took its place in the Minneapolis theatrical picture in 1894 and for many years thereafter captured the bookings of the best plays. Meanwhile melodrama had its noisy heyday at the Bijou, and burlesque was also popular.

Hundreds of plays were presented in the theaters of Minnesota. They included many of Shakespeare's, *Uncle Tom's Cabin, Rip Van Winkle* (with the inimitable Joseph Jefferson), *The School for Scandal, Camille, Ten Nights in a Bar Room, Under the Gaslight,* and *In Old Kentucky.* Minstrel shows were a part of the theatrical fare, as were the operettas of Gilbert and Sullivan. In later days Ibsen, Shaw, Pinero (especially *The Second Mrs. Tanqueray*), Oscar Wilde, and James M. Barrie were represented, not to forget George M. Cohan's exuberant musical comedies. Minnesota produced a few professional players who won wide fame, notably Blanche Yurka, a talented Czech-American artist.

The Scandinavians in Minneapolis, like the Germans in St. Paul and New Ulm, were fond of plays. They staged many in the original Norwegian or Swedish. A curiosity in the history of the drama is the fact that Ibsen's *Ghosts* had its first performance in the world in the United States. It was played in 1882 by a Dano-Norwegian company in Chicago, Minneapolis, and other cities.

The late nineteenth century and early twentieth were a thriving theatrical period. The movies had not yet challenged the sovereignty of the legitimate play, but far-reaching changes were under way. Vaudeville was on the rise, with country-wide circuits, and its vogue shook the dominance of drama and melodrama. In an intermediate period several Minnesota cities harbored excellent stock companies. In Minneapolis, for instance, Dick Ferris in the early 1900s and later A. G. "Buzz" Bainbridge produced effectively many of the best current plays with their companies. The Twin City Metropolitan theaters meanwhile attracted brilliant stars, including Edward H. Sothern and Julia Marlowe, Robert

Mantell, Sarah Bernhardt, Mrs. Patrick Campbell, the Barrymores (Ethel and Lionel), Otis Skinner, Maude Adams, and others.

Bainbridge's company presented plays by Barrie, Ibsen, Shaw, Andreyev, Benavente, O'Neill, and Sudermann, among others. It had a versatile actress in Marie Gale, but from time to time Bainbridge engaged eminent players from the East as special stars, including Blanche Ring, Edith Taliaferro, and Martha Hedman. Appreciation of Bainbridge was by no means limited to applause in the theater. It went so far that the citizens of Minneapolis elected him mayor of their town!

Some wise person once said that drama is "the book of the people." Efforts to keep the book open were persistent and gallant. But motion pictures arrived; times changed; and in 1937 the old Metropolitan theaters in Minneapolis and St. Paul were torn down.

Other theaters fortunately if somewhat inadequately were available for stage plays, and many Broadway shows came to town. Hollywood's invasion of Main Street was intensified, however, and as the cinema became universal, the leadership in drama passed into the hands of eager amateurs.

The University of Minnesota, colleges, community theaters, summer theaters, and "little theaters" in the larger cities and their suburbs produced many plays, old and new. They developed a competence comparable with the best in the professional past. Experimenting with innovations and guided by able directors, they helped to maintain stage drama notwithstanding the competition of hundreds of movie houses. Especially noteworthy was the University Theater under a succession of professionally minded directors. In recent years, Frank M. Whiting's imaginative achievements in scores of plays marked a renaissance in drama for the people. The teaching of dramatic art in the university and the various colleges, as well as in several special schools, added to the restoration of the legitimate theater.

This revitalization of acting on the home front has resulted in recent years in a concerted move, with the support of Sir Tyrone Guthrie, to create in Minneapolis a repertory theater dedicated to the best in dramatic art. Minnesotans are unwilling to let the legitimate theater, with its great traditions, sink into a state of innocuous desuetude.

Intimately related to the theater (and to music) is the ballet. Its popularity, encouraged by visits of famous ballet groups, is a relatively recent development. St. Paul, after World War I, had an enterprising

505

leader in Marie Rothfuss. Later, Minneapolis was the scene of artistic dancing promoted by the gifted Gertrude Lippincott, who formed a modern dance center in the 1930s. In the 1940s Mr. and Mrs. Lorand Andahazy, experienced in the Ballet Russe of Monte Carlo, came to Minnesota, developed a school of their own in the Twin Cities, and formed a ballet company of exquisite artistry (Ballet Borealis). These and related activities have proved an inspiration to the dance and have enhanced the quality of pageants, St. Paul's civic opera, and various college, university, and community performances.

From ancient to modern times the flourishing of the arts and of culture has been interrelated with books and reading, with private and public libraries.

Books were a boon to Minnesota in its frontier days — in the fur-trading era and in the pioneer settlements, as has been related. Central in influence was the Minnesota Historical Society as a collecting, publishing, and educational institution from its inception in 1849. The day of the public library was not yet at hand in frontier times, but people who cared for books formed library subscription clubs, or joint-stock associations, of the kind that Benjamin Franklin sponsored in the eighteenth century.

The Minneapolis Athenaeum had a building of its own by 1866 and a few years later received heartening support from a book-loving dentist, Dr. Kirby Spencer. To it he left the entire income of his real-estate properties (worth $200,000 by 1890). The Athenaeum prospered. It became the largest of the Minnesota subscription libraries. And its success contributed materially to the fortunes of the Minneapolis Public Library (1885), when the Athenaeum collections were placed with the new public institution (though the earlier organization retained its corporate identity).

The subscription libraries, often initiated by informal groups of women or by literary clubs or businessmen, spread rapidly. By 1879 there were at least two dozen in the state, forerunners of public libraries. Book collections of churches, academies, colleges, and clubs of various sorts ran into several hundreds. Not all the subscription libraries were financed by the sale of stocks or shares, though this financing method was followed in the Twin Cities and Duluth. Some were supported by membership fees or popular subscriptions or through proceeds from lectures and special entertainments (including basket socials and oyster dinners).

506

Public concern for libraries opened the way to a new stage in Minnesota library history in 1879. The legislature passed an act authorizing local communities to finance public libraries by levying local taxes. This was a revolutionary change.

Women's clubs took a lively interest in spurring action to start public libraries in their communities. Such clubs, which played a significant role in the state's musical development, were active in many ways in promoting cultural and civic advance. Libraries were important, but they represented only one among the various cultural and political goals for which the women's clubs worked. By 1894 the club movement had become general. A Minnesota Federation of Women's Clubs was established, and a notable leader, Margaret J. Evans of Carleton College, served as its first president. The clubs and the federation have been alert and active ever since.

Public libraries were founded in many cities and towns. Gradually the library associations disappeared, though some continued into the twentieth century. The state entered the field officially in 1899 by establishing a State Library Commission, and concurrently, with the women's clubs exerting decisive influence, a state traveling library system was set in motion as a way of reaching out to villages and rural areas where no public library was available.

Meanwhile the large cities — St. Paul, Minneapolis, and Duluth — joined the public library movement. The St. Paul Library Association transferred its book collection to the city in 1882, and in 1883 the St. Paul Public Library opened.

In 1889 a new public library building was built in Minneapolis, the Athenaeum books at that time far outnumbering those of the public library. By 1962 the Athenaeum holdings were close to 100,000 items — about a tenth of the total Minneapolis Public Library. Duluth formed its public library in 1890 after a fire destroyed the library collection of the city's enterprising Ladies Library Association.

Emphasis on the development of tax support should not obscure the fact that private benefaction contributed much to the enrichment of libraries in the state. Andrew Carnegie, as part of his unexampled largess in aiding more than 2800 libraries, made princely gifts to Duluth, Mankato, and other Minnesota cities. Winona, Rochester, Owatonna, Sleepy Eye, and other cities received generous gifts or bequests that enabled them to build and develop their public libraries.

Thus, step by step, the movement forged ahead. St. Paul and Minneapolis, as the cities grew tremendously and demands for books catapulted, built up impressive libraries. St. Paul's central building was adjoined by the splendid James J. Hill Reference Library. Minneapolis, after more than seventy years in its old building, moved (1961) into a library building in the heart of its "loop," representing high and modern standards in book accommodation and service. In these, and in other cities, branches were established, mobile book units were sent out, and library services of varied kinds reached out to every element in the population.

Research and special libraries added momentum to the movement. The University of Minnesota won rank as a leading research library. Every college in the state, and hundreds of other schools, gathered up books to meet their instructional needs. The Minnesota Historical Society did not rest on early laurels. It continuously built its collections and attained distinction in national and regional history. Specialties of various kinds developed. The state nurtured a law library, and the Mayo Clinic at Rochester and local medical societies, notably in Hennepin and Ramsey counties, built libraries in their fields of special interest.

Supplementing formal libraries were many special institutions. These included the university's Museum of Natural History; St. Paul's remarkable Science Museum; the active American Swedish Institute in Minneapolis; local historical societies in the eighty-seven counties of the state; and other organizations. Nor must one forget the efforts of private collectors. They were many. Their devotion is symbolized by James Ford Bell of Minneapolis, whose treasures of literature in commerce and trade grace a special collection named in his honor at the University of Minnesota.

No one can appraise fully the long-term values of libraries, books, book-collecting, and museums in the cultural history of Minnesota. The problem is the more baffling when one recalls the proliferation of magazines, the continuing influence of the schools, the stimulating role of the theater, and the opening of nearly all homes to radio and television. One conclusion is certain, however. Books, art, drama, history, the recorded fruits of man's mind — these were woven into the intellectual and educational experience of the Minnesota people from log-cabin days to the present.

Minnesota has been described as a "writing state." Evidence supports this description, but the distinction is not unique. Every state, every region, in greater or less degree, has had its historians, novelists, poets, essayists, nature writers. Whatever the Minnesota ranking may be in the American picture, it has had writers from early times to the present, including some who have enlarged the mainstream of the nation's literature.

Explorers pictured Minnesota and the middle western country, from Radisson and Carver to the Alexander Henrys, Pike, Schoolcraft, Beltrami, Nicollet, and a host of others. They were recorders of scenes and events. Their diaries and narratives are of historical interest, and they illuminate backgrounds. But these authors cannot be described as creative figures in the "writing state." They came, saw, recorded, and left.

Many pioneer authors are a part of the writing story, however. It will be recalled that William J. Snelling, at an early time, presented scenes of realism in describing the Indian life he saw at first hand. Mary Eastman wrote out Sioux legends with poetic feeling. Sibley left a prodigious and dependable fund of historical and biographical writing. Harriet E. Bishop pictured Minnesota romantically as her *Floral Home.* Edward D. Neill was a historian of scholarly merit. Many others left behind them informing autobiographical works. Charlotte Van Cleve recalled old Fort Snelling. The Pond brothers were so assiduous that they left almost no part of their experiences and observations unrecorded. Bishop Whipple surveyed the sweep of his brave career. Hans Mattson, pioneer and soldier, told his own fascinating emigrant story. Charles E. Flandrau, versatile jurist, spun tales of the frontier with humor and salty characterization. Christopher C. Andrews, soldier and conservationist, wrote memorable *Recollections* of his career.

These are only a few of many frontier authors. They typify the open-eyed awareness by pioneers of the historical interest of their experiences, coupled with an urge to chronicle the epic with which their lives were identified.

Minnesota fiction was of slow bloom. A few writers, however, made early bows. One was a clever Irish-Catholic editor, Dillon O'Brien, who wrote four novels, one of them (*Daly's of Dalystown*) published in St. Paul as early as 1866. Edward Eggleston is famous nationally for his *Hoosier Schoolmaster* (1871) and his historical work, especially *The Transit of Civilization* (1901). But he lived in Minnesota in the 1850s and 1860s as a Bible agent and a preacher. Out of his experience, especially his observation of the unrestrained speculative boom before the

Panic of 1857, he wrote a novel. It was *The Mystery of Metropolisville*, which took book form in 1873. If not quite so memorable as his master-piece, this Minnesota tale is precise in its observation. It echoes frontier speech and contains humorous portrayals of curious frontier characters.

Most versatile of Minnesota's nineteenth-century writers was Ignatius Donnelly, whose literary career more than matches his achievements in politics.

As a novelist, Donnelly wrote *Caesar's Column* (1890), *Dr. Huguet* (1891), *The Golden Bottle* (1892). His fiction has won no high place in literature, but it constitutes social commentary of interest. In *Caesar's Column* he pictured the wiping out of civilization by destructive forces (from air and ground) let loose by class struggle. He wrote in a period of utopian literature (Bellamy's *Looking Backward* appeared in 1888). At the end of his novel he permitted a saved remnant of society to live in a state (in Africa) exemplifying his own cherished reforms. *Dr. Huguet* came out nearly seven decades before "integration" became a vital issue in American social and political thought and action. In his story Don-nelly transposes the mind and personality of an educated southerner into the body of a Negro. This highly melodramatic tale was a bitter assault on "the hates of races and the contentions of castes." His third novel was a sharp partisan criticism of monopoly.

Donnelly's fiction was only a part of his production. His *Atlantis* (1882), inspired by Plato's account of a fabled civilization engulfed by the Atlantic Ocean, won countless readers (through some fifty editions). *Ragnarok* (1883) rejected, with Donnellian nonchalance, the proved fact of glacial invasions. Instead it told of a comet striking the earth several times in a far past and by its action spreading gravels and soils on the surface of the globe. Most controversial of all Donnelly's books was a mountainous volume called *The Great Cryptogram*. In this he em-ployed an alleged and complex cipher in Shakespeare's plays. In the book and in public lectures and debates, he contended that the author was Francis Bacon, not Shakespeare.

Donnelly and Thorstein Veblen may seem a world apart. The one was a writer of fantasies, the other a philosophic-economic thinker. The one was Irish, the other Norwegian, the one a politician, the other a trained scholar who seemed to look at his times with the unearthly objectivity of some visitor from Mars.

Both were moved by agrarian protest. Both were middle western. Both

510

were frustrated in their careers. Both were critics of the society in which they lived. Their writings voiced a deeply felt dissidence. Veblen was more penetrating, fundamental, and acidulous in criticism than Donnelly. His analyses were presented with masked irony, while Donnelly pitched headlong into what he regarded as contemporary evils in American life.

Few writers of Minnesota backgrounds, outside the realm of fiction, have won wider fame than Veblen. He was born in Wisconsin, brought to Minnesota as a boy, sent to Carleton College, and later won a Ph.D. after studies at Johns Hopkins and Yale. This strange genius — from his *Theory of the Leisure Class* (1899) through eleven ponderous books — played the role of a "mocking Prometheus" in America and the world. He wrote about fundamental problems. He scorned pecuniary standards in modern life and institutions. Business, to him, was money-making, predatory and wasteful — industry was fruitful, productive. His polysyllabic and ironical style provoked ridicule, but he was an original phrase-maker. From his pages come such oft-quoted tags as "conspicuous consumption," "conspicuous leisure," "pecuniary emulation," "honorific expenditure," "collusive sobriety," and "business sabotage."

Veblen's fame as a diagnostician of society's ills has lasted. But leisure is no longer restricted to a narrow, moneyed, and elite class. Veblen did not envision leisure in a later age of heightened living standards and of a prolongation of man's span in a new era of medicine, health, and approved retirement from the workaday world.

If a diagnostician, Veblen prescribed no remedies. He offered no programs. He was analyst, satirist, moralist, a dissenting voice on industrialism, war, and pecuniary standards. Though his concept of leisure did not reach out to modern times, he offered some predictions that came true. Thus he foresaw and foretold World War I and the depression of the 1930s. His analyses were invariably negative — more ruthless than those of the novelists and poets who wrote about wastelands and barrenness in American culture.

Minnesota experimented in early years with literary and semiliterary magazines, but none compared in quality with the *Bellman*, founded in 1906 by William C. Edgar of Minneapolis. For thirteen years he applied high standards in this periodical, encouraged regional writers, and attracted contributions from some of the best authors of the English-speaking world.

511

A Minnesota poet of more than parochial distinction was Arthur Upson, whose life came to a tragic close in 1909. Two volumes of his poetry were brought out in that year by his admiring colleague on the University of Minnesota faculty Richard Burton, who characterized him as an "aristocrat in verse." Familiar to Minnesotans is Upson's contribution of the second and poetic stanza of the university hymn "Minnesota, Hail to Thee."

Another author of the period was the St. Paul-born essayist Charles M. Flandrau. He wrote with art and humor about student life at Harvard, travels in Mexico, books, and a variety of experiences. He had a nicety of phrase for anything that caught his interest, and he hated cant in any form. Characteristic are the titles of two of his books: *Prejudices* and *Loquacities*. By the savor of his informal pieces, Flandrau made a genuine contribution to Minnesota writing, though he has long been neglected by the reading public.

Significant in the second decade of the century was the reorganization of the Minnesota Historical Society and the launching of its quarterly magazine (1915), now known as *Minnesota History*, by Solon J. Buck, historian of the agrarian crusade. For nearly a half century this magazine has been a vehicle for selected essays and documents dealing with state and regional history. In the same decade that saw the birth of this magazine, William Watts Folwell, pioneer university president, old in years but with exuberance and originality, was at work on his broad-gauged story of the state.

National attention has been focused upon certain novelists who reached their peaks in the 1920s. Two of them, however, were very busy writing in the preceding decade. One was a professor at St. Olaf College, O. E. Rölvaag, whose first published novel appeared in 1912, written, as were all his later books, in Norwegian. The second was a restless, gifted, curious, and individualistic son of Sauk Centre, Minnesota, Sinclair Lewis. He produced five unimpressive novels (and a story for boys) before *Main Street* brought him national and international fame.

The 1920s glitter in Minnesota's literary history. These were the years of the major work of Lewis — *Main Street* (1920), *Babbitt* (1922), *Arrowsmith* (1925), *Elmer Gantry* (1927), and *Dodsworth* (1929). Gopher Prairie, the Kennicotts, Babbitt, Dr. Arrowsmith — these and other names from his fiction became known everywhere.

Lewis at once scolded and loved the society and culture that he described with sharp and ruthless observation of its foibles. He faltered in his later novels, but his work of the 1920s was a major achievement, marking a transition in American writing. He exhibited an uncanny talent for reproducing Main Street talk. And he portrayed "types" that occasionally, though not too often, seemed to take on flesh and blood. Lewis voiced an American self-criticism that betokened American maturity. He was translated throughout the world and at the end of the decade won the Nobel Prize for literature, the first of American writers thus honored.

The precocious F. Scott Fitzgerald, native of St. Paul, leaped into fame the same year that saw publication of *Main Street*. Fitzgerald's first novel, *This Side of Paradise*, came out in 1920. By 1925 he had six books to his credit, including *The Beautiful and the Damned*, a play, *The Great Gatsby*, and two collections of short stories, one called *Flappers and Philosophers*, the other *Tales of the Jazz Age*.

Fitzgerald gave vogue to such labels as "jazz age" and "flappers." What he wrote, early and late, he distilled largely from his own experiences. He fictionized his craving for wealth and social standing, his unending struggle with debts (despite high earnings), and his unhappy personal problems. In his stories he portrays frailties, despair, disaster, emotional bankruptcy, the impact of purposeless living on human lives. His descriptions of extravagance remind one of Veblen's "conspicuous consumption."

Critics point to a wide disparity between Fitzgerald's best work and his worst, a disparity that he was fully aware of. But some of his novels and a few of his short stories exhibit human insight and good craftsmanship. Though in 1934 he published one of his most probing novels (*Tender Is the Night*), he had been almost forgotten when he died in 1940. His final, maturely conceived, but unfinished novel, *The Last Tycoon,* came out after his death.

Late years have witnessed a renewal of interest in Fitzgerald. His books have been reprinted in enormous editions, and he has been the subject of at least two biographies. His work, two decades after his death, is viewed without any shadowing of its merits by his own foibles and frustrations. Critics concede his lack of depth and his superficialities, but at his best he dealt with what has been called "the serious complexity of society." In utilizing his personal experience and emotions, he presented the kind of "self-revelation that reveals humanity." Such an uninhibited revelation read in a later age of disillusionment reminiscent of the postwar 1920s may in part explain the interest of a new generation in Fitzgerald.

The phenomenal years at the beginning of the 1920s also witnessed the appearance (in 1920 and 1921) of two of Rölvaag's novels in their original Norwegian version. These were the books that came out in English, a decade or more later, as *Pure Gold* and *The Boat of Longing*. The Norwegian-American novelist is best known, however, for *Giants in the Earth*, first published in two parts in Norway in 1924 and 1925 and brought together in a splendid English version in 1927.

Giants in the Earth was described by Vernon Louis Parrington (in his *Main Currents in American Thought*) as a "great and beautiful" book. To him it suggested the "wealth of human potentialities" in immigrant life. A review in a national magazine characterized it as the "fullest, finest, and most powerful novel that has been written about pioneer life in America." Its theme was big. Its interpretations were subtle in their understanding of the spiritual costs of pioneering. Its writing was vibrant and its people came alive. Some readers, however, forget that it was one of a trilogy that included *Peder Victorious* and *Their Fathers' God*. And the trilogy in turn was a part of a production that included a luminous study of the immigrant in city life (*The Boat of Longing*), and other stories.

Rölvaag's masterpiece is powerful, but the significance of his work as a whole is its fundamental interpretation of immigrant transition, of which prairie pioneering represents only one phase. Novelists in Norway and Sweden have written about the immigrant theme, but none has equaled the universality of meaning imparted to character and experience that gives to Rölvaag's novels their permanent importance. He ranks as a giant in Minnesota's literary earth. In part inspired by the imagination of Rölvaag, immigrants and their descendants took new cognizance of their part in the making of America. One among many results was the organization in Minnesota of a national Norwegian-American Historical Association in 1925. It has since brought out more than forty volumes of historical studies, essays, and documents.

The triple galaxy of Lewis, Fitzgerald, and Rölvaag by no means fills out the story of Minnesota's surge of creative writing in the 1920s.

Margaret Culkin Banning's interesting first novel, *This Marrying*, appeared in the portentous literary year of 1920. By 1930 this productive Duluth author had a shelf of ten novels. Then and in later works she took a deep interest in the contemporary scene, in people, in manners and ideas. She drew on her observation of people and life in her own city and in her extensive travels in America and abroad for character, setting, and action.

Another writer making her bow in the 1920s was Martha Ostenso, whose backgrounds were Norwegian. She began with a volume of verse (1924) and then, in quick succession, wrote *Wild Geese* (1925), a story of farm life, and four more novels by 1930. In the 1940s she produced *O River, Remember!* — a poignant narrative of life in the Red River Valley through the span of three generations.

Yet another novelist of the period was Maud Hart Lovelace, a native of Mankato, who published *Black Angels* in 1926 and three years later *Early Candlelight*, a charming romantic novel depicting the era of Henry H. Sibley and old Mendota. With her husband, Delos Lovelace, she went on in the 1930s to write two historical novels, *One Stayed at Welcome* and *Gentlemen from England*, both the products of painstaking study of pioneer times in southern Minnesota.

William J. McNally, a graduate of the University of Minnesota, is remembered chiefly for a novel exploiting nostalgic historical backgrounds, *The House of Vanished Splendor*, published in 1932. But he wrote a story called *The Barb* in 1923 and also produced several plays in the 1920s (the first of them in the germinal year at the beginning of the decade). A highly accomplished writer of St. Paul backgrounds is Grace Flandrau. She is noted for her novels *Being Respectable* (1923) and *Indeed This Flesh* (1934). Both are sensitive social analyses of the milieu with which she was thoroughly familiar and which she portrayed with discernment and literary skill.

During the 1920s, and in the years since, scholars of the University of Minnesota and in the many colleges of the state have poured out books on history, criticism, politics, and sociology, and on many other subjects. It should not be forgotten that Dr. Folwell's *History of Minnesota* added distinction to the decade. Viewing the period as a whole, one wonders at the uncritical popular acceptance of descriptive phrases that touched little more than its periphery and failed to reflect its creative, original, and fundamental character.

Significant of the literary interests of the time, the University of Minnesota Press took its rise in the 1920s. In all the years since that time, it has encouraged scholarship and creative writing in a wide array of fields.

These have included the backgrounds and problems of state, nation, and world, and the domain of literature has not been omitted. In 1928, to give an illustration, the Press brought out a volume of delicately wrought one-act plays by Oscar Firkins, literary critic and author of basic works on some of America's great writers. A colleague of Firkins, equally distinguished as a critic, was Joseph Warren Beach. Through his long career he published many memorable books, including one in the 1920s — a critical and challenging view of *The Outlook for American Prose*; and he was a poet of unusual quality.

The creative spurt of the 1920s did not just happen. It had antecedents, and its explanation probably involves the interplay of many circumstances and forces. One unquestionably was the fact that Minnesota had come of age. Many minds betrayed curiosity about its history and its problems and mores — as well as those of nation and world. Another factor was that the war was over. Energies were released, and writing was one manifestation of ferment in the arts.

Many people made contributions, though few won wide acclaim. Distinction, however, was not always measured by popularity or royalties. Some writers who achieved wide recognition were quite unknown to laymen. An illustration is Elmer Edgar Stoll, a Shakespearean scholar of major rank. Another is Frances Densmore of Red Wing, whose writings were read by few, but who was a recognized American authority on Indian customs, music, and lore.

The writing of the 1920s gave impetus to authorship in the decades that followed. Many authors continued their productive work through later years; some, including Rölvaag, barely outlived the decade. New writers who were getting their bearings in the 1920s made contributions in later years. The outpouring of books grew in volume during the depression, in the decade of World War II, and throughout the 1950s. The sheer numbers of authors — and the variety of their books — merit a listing far beyond the limits of any quick survey. A few illustrations may be offered here, however, which will at least point to trends in Minnesota's literary advance.

Notable work was done in the fields of history and biography. Grace Lee Nute, after exploring original sources far and wide, told the story of *The Voyageur* in an artistically conceived book (1931). In later years she traversed, with scholarly and literary skill, *The Voyageur's Highway*; wrote a history of Lake Superior; and, with unexcelled knowledge of the French period, produced a joint biography of Radisson and Groseilliers.

Philip D. Jordan, historian, folklorist, and writer, traced out the story of *The People's Health* — the absorbing recountal of Minnesota's public-health movement. This was but one of his many books. He has written extensively about American history and folklore, including a dramatic narrative about the singing troupe of the Hutchinsons. George Malcolm Stephenson, university teacher of history, made major contributions to the history of immigration (especially from Sweden). He wrote a scholarly biography of John Lind, a two-volume history of the United States, and other books.

Many university scholars have written books of interest and importance. They include A. L. Burt, historian of Canada and of the British Empire, and Herbert Heaton, economic historian. William Anderson has done fundamental work on local and federal government and on political ideas. Ernest S. Osgood has written a classic work entitled *The Day of the Cattleman*. A. C. Krey, medievalist, took an interest in regional history, as did Edgar B. Wesley, authority on education, who wrote a model history of a local community (Owatonna). Among many others, mention may be made of Alice Tyler, social historian; Werner Levi, a political scientist who has written important works in the field of international relations and problems; Ralph Brown, historical geographer; David Willson, biographer of James I of England; John B. Wolf, authority on French history; Harold C. Deutsch, expert on Germany and contemporary problems; and Harold S. Quigley, authoritative writer on politics and government in the Far East.

Bertha L. Heilbron of the Minnesota Historical Society devoted special attention to frontier artists, including Henry Lewis, the panoramist. She has also written an interesting pictorial history of Minnesota, interweaving story and pictures. Paul Giddens of Hamline University has depicted the rise of the American oil industry; and James P. Shannon of St. Thomas College has related the story of Irish colonization in Minnesota.

These — and scores of other scholars — are still only a part of the writing picture. Much has been done in the art of biography. Best known of all Minnesota books in this field is the masterly biography of *The Doctors Mayo* by Helen Clapesattle, a book that has won world-wide fame. Among other Minnesotans who have attracted the attention of biographers may be mentioned James M. Goodhue, Edward D. Neill,

Governors Lind, Johnson, Olson, and Youngdahl, Ignatius Donnelly, Bishop Whipple and Archbishop Ireland, Cyrus Northrop, Maria Sanford, Georg Sverdrup, James J. Hill, Wanda Gág, F. Melius Christiansen, and the literary quartet of Lewis, Fitzgerald, Rölvaag, and Veblen.

The Minnesota biographical shelf may seem to be bulging, but many important biographies remain to be written. Autobiography, popular among nostalgic pioneers, seems to have been less alluring in later times than it once was. It is possible that many autobiographies, though written, have not yet found their way into print. The artist Wanda Gág published her diaries in a candid book entitled *Growing Pains*; and a Norwegian-American lawyer of Minneapolis, Andreas Ueland, brought out a witty, ironical, and urbane life story in his *Recollections of an Immigrant.*

The versatile James Gray has written plays, novels, literary criticism, and histories, notably the centennial history of the University of Minnesota. John K. Sherman, literary and musical critic, has told the story of the Minneapolis Symphony Orchestra in his interesting *Music and Maestros.*

Other writers have described Minnesota's nature in summer and winter. Thus Florence and Francis Jaques, the one a writer, the other an artist, have collaborated in such memorable books as *Canoe Country* and *Snowshoe Country*. In *The Singing Wilderness* and other books, Sigurd F. Olson has interpreted the primitive beauties of the northern stretches of streams and lakes and woods. Walter O'Meara and J. Arnold Bolz are among others who have written interestingly about the north country. Dr. Thomas S. Roberts is the author of a masterly two-volume work on *The Birds of Minnesota.*

If Minnesota fiction in later years has not matched that of the giants of the 1920s, it has had many practitioners who have made contributions to the writing tradition of the state.

Herbert Krause, a native of Fergus Falls, knows western Minnesota, and in such novels as *Wind without Rain* and *The Thresher* he has written realistically about the region's rural backgrounds. Frederick Manfred, an Iowa-born writer, had a tumultuous production of novels in the 1940s and 1950s. Like Krause, he probed rural hopes and disenchantment in his novel *This Is the Year*. Max Shulman, Thomas Heggen, and Norman Katkov all came out of the University of Minnesota to achieve prominence as young writers in the 1940s. Shulman, beginning with *Barefoot Boy with Cheek* (1943), has produced a succession of novels

518

marked by his own brand of satiric humor. Before Thomas Heggen died at the age of twenty-nine, he wrote a poignantly comic tale about World War II, *Mister Roberts* (1946), which became a best seller and was made into a long-running play and later a motion picture. Katkov has written both fiction and nonfiction. His first novel, *Eagle at My Eyes*, was published in 1948.

Some Minnesota authors have written successfully for children. Carol R. Brink won national recognition for her captivating *Caddie Woodlawn*, and has written many other books. Outside the juvenile field, she wrote *Harps in the Wind*, the story of the singing Hutchinsons, and an interpretation of *The Twin Cities*. Borghild Dahl, with Minneapolis and Minnetonka backgrounds, has written engaging Norwegian-American stories for children, including *A Minnetonka Summer* and *Homecoming*.

The University of Minnesota and the various colleges have had on their faculties novelists, critics, poets, and other writers. Some have come, stayed for a few years, and then left — their Minnesota experience an interlude. Examples are Robert Penn Warren, famed novelist, and William Van O'Connor, brilliant literary critic. Others have come with national literary reputations already built in other parts of the country. An example is Allen Tate, distinguished poet and critic. Such men, by their writing and teaching, have added to the state's fame and have influenced younger talents.

When Minnesota in 1958 looked back on a century of statehood, a bibliography appeared which listed some seven hundred Minnesota authors, with the titles of many of their books. Two editions of a work containing autobiographical sketches by many Minnesota authors have been published in the past two decades, and several anthologies of Minnesota verse have found their way into print.

A volume or two would be needed to do justice to the men and women who have made contributions to Minnesota literary history. Even a quick survey makes it clear, however, that writing constitutes an important chapter in the cultural story of the state. It is an unfinished chapter, for every year witnesses new writers, new themes, new books.

A ski tournament at Red Wing in the 1930s

Depression, Readjustment, and War

IT was no temporary Wall Street squall that struck Minnesota
and the country in 1929. It was a convulsive and protracted deflation of
values. The depression that followed went swirling with ups and downs
through much of a decade.

Minnesotans, as in earlier economic reversals, were reluctant to believe
that a crisis in the New York financial district could signal hard times
for the commonwealth of the Middle West. Wall Street was far away.
Conditions at home seemed hopeful. And newspapers printed optimistic
stories during the first few days after the debacle in stock prices. The day
after the catastrophic crash on October 29, 1929, a Minneapolis newspaper published an article with these headings: LEADERS FIND BUSINESS
GOOD IN NORTHWEST. GENERAL SITUATION FUNDAMENTALLY SOUND,
BANKERS AND OTHERS REPORT. FARMERS ARE OPTIMISTIC. LIVESTOCK IN-
DUSTRY SATISFACTORY. MORE EMPLOYMENT THAN A YEAR AGO. This was
brave, but it was a case of whistling in the dark.

Suddenly an inflated Minneapolis company went bankrupt, with close
to $20,000,000 of debts (the head of the organization was sent to prison
in 1934). This was the beginning of a succession of financial reverses
in Minnesota. The depression swept remorselessly across the country.
The Wall Street crash introduced a contraction which, by the spring of
1933, had reduced the values of American stocks to a figure below one-
fifth of their level in the gala opening days of October 1929.

Minnesota had experienced bank failures and acute agricultural distress in the 1920s, but these bore little comparison with the slump after 1929. The "great depression" affected not banks and farmers alone, but the gamut of the economy of state and nation. The country was paying the price for the vast and swift expansion of its industry and agriculture, the spread of credit, the inflation of capital surpluses, the very efficiency of new machines, and the absence of stabilizing governmental controls. Stock prices had been working upward since 1924, and speculation, uncontrolled, had been rampant. Troubles were deepened by tariff policies that impinged upon America's foreign trade. Interrelated with these factors was a world situation accented by national debts and uneasiness in international relations. Turbulent forces were loose in Europe, the Far East, South America — in fact, in the broad sweep of the contemporary world. World War II, it is true, was a decade off in the future, but signs of unrest were visible, though many failed to read their meaning.

Against such backgrounds, Minnesota shared with the country the burdens of adjustments to a major turn in the American economy.

As Minnesota entered the depression, Theodore Christianson was in his third term as governor. He had been re-elected a second time by a tremendous vote in 1928 — the same election that witnessed the decisive victory of Herbert Hoover over Alfred Smith for the presidency. Governor Christianson was at the height of his popularity. As he neared the end of six years of a very successful administration, he chose to step aside. He would not run for a fourth term.

Floyd B. Olson, the Hennepin County attorney, had made a challenging run for the governorship in 1924, but in that campaign he took what his biographer calls an "ambiguous stand" on the Communist issue. In a word, he did not reject Communist support. This contributed to his defeat and it also led, in 1925, to the breakup of the Farmer-Labor Federation. That organization was replaced by the Farmer-Labor Association, with a constitution that endorsed the old Nonpartisan League demands but specifically denied membership in the association to Communists. Olson, busy with his duties as county attorney, was inactive in the state election of 1926. In 1928, after some hesitation, he chose to decline the Farmer-Labor nomination for governor, which went instead to Ernest Lundeen, who was overwhelmed by Christianson.

In 1930 Olson entered, once more, the race for the state's highest office. It was a depression year, without doubt an auspicious time for a party of protest. But the biographer of Olson presents evidence to show that he had made up his mind to enter the contest before the collapse of the stock market — an event he did not foresee.

In the 1930 campaign Olson turned aside from the ideas on state socialism of the Nonpartisan League as echoed in 1925 by the Farmer-Labor Association. He chose instead to emphasize the fundamentals of "good government." He favored an old-age pension law. He spoke for more effective conservation of natural resources. He assailed monopoly, but avoided radical proposals. He urged measures to help farmers and laborers in difficulties accentuated by the depression. In general, he advocated moderate policies as the state faced its problems, and he invited widespread public support.

The Olson of 1930 — campaigning after the Wall Street crash but before the advent of the New Deal — offers something of a contrast with the Olson of later elections and of Minnesota popular tradition. His appeal, though backed by the Farmer-Labor party, was in essence unpartisan. In the election he won by a landslide (a majority of better than 180,000) over the experienced state auditor Ray P. Chase, a personable and very popular politician, but scarcely a match for the persuasive Olson as a candidate. The depression was inevitably a factor in the outcome of the election, as Olson later admitted.

When Floyd B. Olson took office in January 1931, he did so as the first Farmer-Labor governor of Minnesota. Born of Norwegian-Swedish parentage in north Minneapolis (in 1891), he had had rough and hardening experiences as an itinerant laborer who sampled many kinds of jobs. He had put in a year at the university, studied law in a night school, and was admitted to the bar in 1915. He was chosen county attorney for Hennepin County in 1920, elected to the office in 1922, and re-elected in 1926. He soon became known as a formidable trial lawyer and also as a very skillful public speaker and debater. He was adept in political maneuver, plain-spoken, unafraid of the rough and tumble of controversy, a leader of natural force. By virtue of his backgrounds and his experience as a worker, he thought of himself as very close to the rank and file of the electorate.

Governor Olson followed a rather moderate policy during his first term. Foreshadowed by his campaign, this was reinforced by the failure of his party to win a legislative majority. He presented no comprehensive attack on the problems of the depression, but asked for a unified state program of conservation, expansion of the state highways, old-age pensions, prohibition of injunctions in labor disputes, and various other measures that were not greatly controversial. The legislature approved a conservation commission and a bond issue for highways, but it held back on the pensions and the barring of injunctions. The governor vetoed several measures, including one for reapportioning congressional districts.

The economic crisis seemed to many to be essentially a national problem, and the state looked to Washington for action. Meanwhile, however, unemployment increased alarmingly in Minnesota. Its severity was underlined in the fall of 1932, when 70 per cent of the Minnesota iron-range workers were jobless. Farm prices dropped. Wheat production sank to low levels. The income of dairy farmers fell in 1931 to a fourth of its level before the slump. A Farm Holiday movement took form in Iowa, made inroads in Minnesota, and induced some farm strikes. Relief costs were draining the finances of many counties. In the cities people without jobs multiplied, and many families were hungry. Farmers wanted a moratorium on mortgages, a stable floor for the prices of their products, and legal ways of refinancing farm loans, with reductions in their interest rates. Such aid they sought from the federal government.

Hard times, inability to get work, and the hungry mouths of children breed popular impatience. People wanted alleviation, action, reform. They hoped for a reversal of the downward trend. In the 1920s many had sung an absurd song entitled "Yes, We Have No Bananas" — now they sang it, if at all, with an ironical tone. Governor Olson was urban, not a farmer, but he headed a Farmer-Labor movement, and now he began to understand the "farmer side" of his own party. A spokesman for the underprivileged, he knew that speeches would give no food to the 137,000 families in Minnesota that could not get through the winter of 1931–32 without help. He appointed a committee under a Minneapolis leader, F. T. Heffelfinger, to gather up clothing and funds to aid needy families via their community relief agencies. This was extragovernmental emergency action, humane and helpful — necessary but less than fundamental. As the state and national elections of 1932 neared, the voters understood that America was in crisis. The dimensions of the depression, they realized, were too big for dependence alone on state or local action. President Hoover, though deeply concerned about the depression, was reluctant to embark upon direct aid for the needy, and instead favored the extension of credit to undergird sound business. But

524

pressures induced him to make funds available for relief, and these, for Minnesota, were handled, on behalf of destitute families, by the State Board of Control.

There was no adjournment of state politics in the 1930s, and as the political pot boiled, Olson moved toward an informal alliance with Franklin D. Roosevelt, the rising leader of the Democrats. He met the New York governor in 1931 and found himself in sympathy with his views. In the spring of 1932 Roosevelt visited Minnesota for a Jefferson Day address, and afterward he had a warm and friendly conference with the Minnesota governor. The two discovered that they spoke much the same political language.

As election time neared, Olson made no overt effort to unite Farmer-Laborites and Democrats, but he did not hide his friendly feeling for Roosevelt and the emerging New Deal. In the campaign of 1932 the Minnesota Democrats presented a candidate for governor, John E. Regan, who polled a large vote. Olson easily won the governorship, however, over both Regan and the Republican candidate, Earle Brown. By a much greater margin Roosevelt was approved by Minnesota voters over President Hoover — the first time in Minnesota history that a Democrat had ever carried the state for President.

Some historians write that the financial turn in 1929 was not technically a "panic." Perhaps it was not, but the nation and state moved toward real panic in 1933. The period up to the inauguration of President Roosevelt was one of increasing bank failures, foreclosures, dwindling savings, unemployment, crises in the financing of the state's schools, distress, tension, and protest. Olson was sensitive to the mood of desperation, and when the legislature met, he called for reform after reform. As the New Deal took shape after March 1933 when the Roosevelt administration took office, federal action was fast and furious.

The measures taken by state and nation to fight the depression were so many and varied that any detailed description of them would run beyond the bounds of this narrative. A few items may be noted, however — first on the state level.

The governor did not succeed in inaugurating state unemployment insurance, but a state income tax became law (1933), with its proceeds to be given to school support. By executive authorization the governor called a temporary halt to mortgage sales late in February 1933, an action to which the state legislature later gave somewhat reluctant sanction in law. In efforts to rescue the banks, the governor called on a highly regarded Minneapolis banker, John N. Peyton, who set in motion several thoughtfully considered moves to avert disaster. On an occasion when Governor Olson was out of the state, the acting governor proclaimed a bank holiday, a move that Olson disliked, though he acquiesced in it on his return. It proved to be merely a prelude to the national bank holiday soon thereafter proclaimed for the nation by the President.

In Minnesota the system of old-age pensions finally got under way in 1933. Injunctions in labor disputes were banned. "Yellow-dog contracts" were prohibited. Among other legislative actions was the creation, from tax-delinquent lands, of some thirteen state forests. Legal measures were also taken to protect conservation in the forest country of the north, supplementing the federal Shipstead-Nolan Act of 1930, which banned the lease of lands in the Superior National Forest to private users.

Under the impact of the depression, the state began to move into reforms that probably could not have been passed in earlier years. The Farmer-Labor governor, aligning himself more and more with the New Deal, embraced policies far more aggressive than those he had supported a year or two earlier. The gravity of the problems of the 1930s, as Olson's biographer has said, tilted "the axis of public opinion." The state accepted actions formerly regarded as radical, though not without acrimonious controversy in the legislature.

In the state, as in the nation, relief costs mounted tremendously as the depression continued. In Minnesota alone, they were above $9,000,000 in 1933 and more than $33,000,000 the next year. The New Deal was in stride, and the federal government absorbed 85 per cent of the state burden.

The depression was calamity enough, but grasshopper plagues and drouth added to the distress of farmers. Governmental intervention took many forms. Farmers who lacked feed for cattle and seeds for crops were legally enabled to borrow money. Resettlement plans were worked out for afflicted areas. Cooperatives in trouble could get needed loans. Banking was subjected to reforms. The air was full of plans for planning, and Minnesota was one of many states in which planning commissions were established.

Federal administrations were set in motion for many purposes. They included (to mention only a few) the N.R.A. (National Recovery Administration) in 1933 and its successor, a year later, the N.I.R.A. (National Industrial Recovery Administration). An early emergency act was the creation, also in 1933, of the Civilian Conservation Corps, popularly known as the CCC. Its purpose was to give employment, in reforestation camps, to young men out of jobs. Thousands were put to work under army leadership in tree planting, road work, and other assignments, with enlistments for one year. Many Minnesota youths were enrolled. President Roosevelt concerned himself with the "security of the men, women, and children" of America "against certain hazards and vicissitudes"; and in 1935 the Social Security Administration was begun (benefit payments starting in 1938). An Agricultural Adjustment Act passed in 1933, under which the government attempted crop controls, was declared unconstitutional by the Supreme Court and was replaced in 1936 by a soil conservation program and in 1938 by a new Agricultural Adjustment Act. Early in the New Deal federal legislation gave attention to controls and restrictions to offset evils in the handling of stocks. The result was a Federal Securities Act in 1933, supplemented the next year by the Securities Exchange Act.

Enormous funds were poured into work relief in successive organizations, beginning with the Federal Emergency Relief Administration (1933) and continued in the Works Progress Administration and other agencies. The big problem for the nation was an estimated 15,000,000 people without jobs. Funds were allocated for public buildings, improvements, and special projects in a bewildering array to provide work relief and to contribute to better times. In conservation alone, the Minnesota commissioner reported in 1936 that under various emergency relief projects, including the CCC, 45,000 enrollees had been given work in this state and also 5000 supervisory and technical persons — with an expenditure of more than $55,000,000 since the inception of the work in the spring of 1933. This was only a part of vast relief enterprises in which nation and state cooperated — buildings, highways, libraries, hospitals, playgrounds, archival surveys, a writers' project, and creative work by artists.

While these and other activities went forward, Minnesota confronted one crisis after another. Governor Olson intervened where he thought it necessary. One instance was a severe truck strike in Minneapolis in 1934, where the governor invoked martial law. His intervention is regarded as having promoted union recognition by employers.

The governor faced difficulties in his own party, in part brought on by his uninhibited assertions of radicalism. The party in 1934 adopted a very radical platform. It went so far as to demand state operation of public utilities, mines, banks, transportation, even factories. The governor, in his interpretations, softened these demands, and his state committee, in view of violent public reverberations, amended and interpreted the platform to such an extent that the original declaration was changed "beyond recognition."

Notwithstanding such complications, Olson carried the election of 1934 over his Republican opponent, Martin A. Nelson, and the Democratic John E. Regan. The vote marked a turn, however. Rural support dwindled, and the governor found his chief strength in the urban areas. The final period of Olson's administration was turbulent — a virtual deadlock with the legislature, further strikes, and intraparty squabbles.

Through the years the governor had gained considerable national stature. He was spoken of as a contender for national honors — possibly as a third-party candidate for the presidency. He himself, however, supported Roosevelt and favored his re-election in 1936. He had no intention of running against Roosevelt.

Meanwhile Senator Thomas D. Schall, Republican, died in 1935 after an automobile accident in Washington, and his death set in motion a series of political changes. Elmer A. Benson, bank commissioner, was appointed to fill out Schall's term. But he held the senatorial office only from late December 1935 to early November 1936. It had been expected that Olson himself would run for the Senate; and Benson was nominated for governor by the Farmer-Labor party. His selection appears to have been pushed by party politicians in part because of the prestige of his brief senatorship. The choice left a trail of intraparty dissension, for Hjalmar Petersen, the lieutenant governor, had seemed to be the "heir apparent" for the governorship, and he resented the action of his party's convention. He in fact had broken with Olson who, he believed, had implied support for him and then failed to deliver it. All this augured troubles for the Farmer-Labor party. In 1936, however — the election in which Roosevelt to the chant of "Happy Days Are Here Again" carried Minnesota by a tremendous majority — Benson won the office of governor.

As events turned out, Olson did not appear in the election of 1936 as a candidate for the Senate. Instead tragedy closed his career during the preceding summer. His years as governor had been made physically painful for him because of ill health, though courage enabled him to meet the demands of his office. Late in 1935, he was operated on at the Mayo Clinic, and it was discovered (though not at the time revealed to the public) that he had incurable cancer. He tried to carry on his governorship and his candidacy for the Senate, but in the summer he underwent another operation, and on August 22, 1936, he died.

The grief of the Minnesota people was deep and sincere, not unlike that evoked by the death of the beloved John A. Johnson. More than a quarter of a century has passed. There is still divided opinion among the people as to Olson's place in Minnesota history. His biographer, Dr. George Mayer, pictures him as a "crusader for social justice," and many will agree with this judgment. Olson was governor in a time of anxiety, tension, and readjustment, of difficulty and controversy. His views in the economic crisis of his times tended to move along with those of President Roosevelt. He liked to think of himself as a "radical." In historical appraisal, however, he seems to have been an opportunist, a characterization he himself cheerfully accepted. In his own opportunistic way, he tried to advance the welfare of the people he served.

Hjalmar Petersen took over as governor for the remainder of Olson's term, and Ernest Lundeen won the seat in the United States Senate (against former Governor Christianson). Benson served for two years as governor. Changes in the shifting 1930s influenced the political temper of the people. The depression was stubborn, but great effort and huge funds had been expended to improve conditions both nationally and in the state. The results were visible. The Farmer-Labor party found itself in difficulty. After the death of Governor Olson, according to a Farmer-Labor spokesman (Karl F. Rolvaag), "forces of internal confusion, disorganization and collapse," coupled with left-wing infiltration, led to a crumbling of the party organization that Olson had fostered and led.

The story of the 1930s is by no means one only of economic tension and political controversy. There was certainly an undercurrent of disquiet as people faced problems and readjustments. But forces in normal life, even though interrupted by hard times, proceeded in many and various ways. People seemed to respond to the President's challenge to put aside fear and to meet problems with hope and courage. Apart from measures taken to cope with specific ills in nation and state, many institutions and activities provided an easing of anxiety and not a few salutary safety valves.

The churches of every denomination — Protestant, Catholic, Jewish — were active through the years. Their memberships increased, and to their adherents went, Sunday after Sunday, the age-old messages of faith and hope. They were a bulwark to the thousands who joined in religious worship and in the many church-directed activities.

Schools, public and private, and the colleges and university functioned across the decade with astonishing vitality, notwithstanding financial troubles. College faculties took reductions both in salaries and in numbers; and many families lacked sufficient funds to meet the costs of college educations for their children. Both governmental employment aid and institutional scholarships and loans came to the rescue of some of them. Despite difficulties, there was no calamitous break in the continuity of Minnesota education, though it had no easy time.

Viewing the broader social scene, one notes evidence of many forms of relief from tension. The theaters and movies, for instance, afforded diversion and entertainment. The decade witnessed memorable film plays, including *Cavalcade, Little Women, It Happened One Night, Mutiny on the Bounty,* the fantasies of Walt Disney (*Snow White* in 1938), *Goodbye, Mr. Chips, Lost Horizon,* and others.

Popularly read books included *Anthony Adverse, The Good Earth, Northwest Passage, Gone with the Wind,* and (late in the decade) *The Grapes of Wrath.* Many who could not buy books for themselves crowded into the libraries. If the majority of the widely read books represented escape into life and adventures of the past, it is also true that works of serious contemporary import appeared; among them were such volumes as Hornell Hart's *Recent Social Trends* and Thurman Arnold's *Folklore of Capitalism.*

One of the safety valves of American society is humor. It found outlets in "depression anecdotes," and also in songs, the latter including the half-serious defiance voiced in "Who's Afraid of the Big Bad Wolf?" But one of the most salutary contributions to social morale — and health — was the vogue of recreation, sport, and the outdoor life for the increasing urban population. The five-day week largely supplanted the old five-and-a-half-day week, and the longer weekends invited outings and allowed time for the games Americans so much liked to play. The enjoyment of the open air, and of games, summer and winter, had been forwarded through a long period, however, antedating the troubles of the 1930s.

Many factors popularized and democratized sports. They included cars, bicycles, and good roads. Invention played its role, as illustrated, for instance, in the game of basketball which an ingenious YMCA instructor in Massachusetts, James Naismith, devised in 1891. Through the years, it won enormous popularity. The schools in their emphasis on physical education trained young America in games, exercise, sport. The organization of associations and leagues, with elaborate rules, added momentum to the movement.

Baseball, football, and basketball won universal favor — from sandlots to amateur and professional teams and in schools and colleges. Wherever particular sports emerged, the American talent for organization was utilized to the full. This was no sudden or recent manifestation of American ingenuity. It harks back to the second half of the nineteenth century. The basic period of the "rise of sport" in the United States has been defined by a distinguished historian as running from 1876 to 1894 — from the inception of the first major American baseball league to the first golf tournament held in the United States. Sport thus offers a refreshing departure from the traditional dating of American history by presidential administrations!

A Minneapolis Baseball Association was organized in the 1870s. Minneapolis entered the Western League in 1882 and later, from 1902, played in the American Association. The Millers of Minneapolis and the Saints of St. Paul enjoyed fierce rivalries and stirred baseball interest in every corner (and corner lot) in the state. Perhaps the social importance of baseball lies less in the professional sphere than in the fact that youngsters everywhere learned to play the game. On the professional side a new phase came long after the disturbed 1930s. In 1961 Minneapolis and St. Paul took over the Washington club of the American League, sponsored the Minnesota Twins, used a new Metropolitan Stadium, and achieved the coveted status of "big league."

Football, originally only an amateur sport, also knew the discipline and stimulus of organization. The University of Minnesota played its first intercollegiate football game in 1882 (against Hamline). The Western Conference was formed in 1896 and later the Big Ten emerged. University football teams played season after season, produced gridiron heroes, and had coaches of national fame, including the redoubtable Dr.

Henry L. Williams, inventor of the "Minnesota shift" and famed for his crafty football strategy from the time of his appearance as the Minnesota coach in 1900. It is noteworthy that in the depression decade Minnesota teams won conference championships time and again and a series of national championships (under the tutelage of Coach Bernie Bierman). Stocks might be low, wages down, unemployment up — but Saturday after Saturday crowds of forty to sixty thousand spectators jammed the university's stadium to witness the exploits of the teams. Football too became a domain of professionals, who drew their stars from the college amateur ranks. Both college and professional football reached out to an immense public as radio and later television carried the games, play by play, into thousands of homes.

Golf, once thought of as only a rich man's hobby (played at private country clubs), expanded into a popular sport. Public as well as private courses were built. The Twin Cities toward the end of the 1930s had close to forty golf courses — and people of all ages (capable of swinging a club) flocked to the links. In the following years nearly all Minnesota towns of some size, and many small communities, built golf courses. Local, state, and national tournaments were held on Minnesota courses. A year after the stock-market crash the popular hero of America was Bobby Jones of Georgia, who achieved the "grand slam" in 1930 by winning the British and American open and amateur championships (the American Amateur on a Minneapolis course).

Minnesota, with its lakes, rivers, and north country, was a vacation land, alluring to Minnesotans themselves and to people throughout the country. Promoters of the tourist traffic were not lethargic in exploiting its attractions, just as Goodhue and others in pioneer years had been lyrical in their praise. The potentialities of a domain of thousands of lakes were irresistible to many, and as early as 1916 the Ten Thousand Lakes Association of Minnesota was formed. It was not enough to celebrate the general glamour of Minnesota, and in 1933 a Minnesota Arrowhead Association was launched to draw public notice to the beauties of the northeast. From the early 1930s the state itself conducted a Tourist Bureau which in later years expanded into a department of business development, with frank recognition of the fact that tourism meant dollars and cents to the state and was a business.

Minnesota summer residents, and tourists from other states, found recreation and natural beauty in numberless places throughout Minnesota. Especially favored were the north Superior shores, with their vistas of waters of the great lake; the river and valley of the St. Croix; Lake Pepin on the Mississippi; Minnetonka with its bays and islands and inlets; White Bear Lake; and the almost bewildering number of lakes to the west and north, up to the international waters. All this meant no sudden effusion of vacation enthusiasm, but the tourist rush took on larger dimensions than it had had in the past. Fishing was popular as a sport (and for many in troubled times or good as a source of food supply). Many hundreds of thousands of Minnesota people went to the lakes in summer (and many in winter to fish through the ice). Tourist fishermen joined them during the depression when the number of nonresident fishing licenses rose from some 37,000 in 1933 to more than 80,000 in 1939. These figures are modest indeed compared with those of later years, for in 1960 there were more than 300,000 nonresident fishing licenses, and fishing Minnesotans numbered half of the state's population.

Winter and summer sports were given impetus by municipal action. St. Paul had built an ice palace as early as 1886. In 1916, after the lapse of decades, it resumed its snow-and-ice carnivals. Minneapolis, not to be outdone, inaugurated summer "aquatennials" in 1940. Skiing, skating, and tobogganing gained great vogue in the state, as did sailing, motorboating, and other water diversions. Skiing, with high contrivances for speedy runs and jumps, was greatly prized. As early as 1883 Norwegian enthusiasts had organized a skiing club at Red Wing. Other organizations and tournaments — and the Minnesota snow! — added to the vogue of the sport.

The tourist industry took rank as an important enterprise. Its Minnesota dimensions are suggested by an estimate of close to $140,000,000 of income in 1939. A couple of decades later the trade had gone well past $300,000,000 a year (in volume the fourth ranking industry of Minnesota). This meant resorts, lakes crowded with cabins, large summer camps, motor courts, puffing motorboats, swimming, water skiing, sailing, exhibitions and special events of diverse kinds. For many it meant also the ripple of lakes, the wailing of loons, the wash of waters where voyageurs once paddled their canoes, the stillness of nature when skies were clear on summer evenings or on mornings when the lakes of the North were wilderness mirrors.

City and state parks offered spots for excursions on free days and vacation periods for many thousands of people, and camping was highly

533

popular. The state fair continued its annual expositions. The fair grounds were patronized year after year not only for agricultural and industrial exhibits, but also for races. Horse races dominated the scenes in early days, automobile races later. It was on the race track of the state fair that Dan Patch, the most famous and most loved horse in Minnesota history, paced a mile in 1:56 in 1906 — a world's record.

Bowling, hockey, and many other games attracted thousands of players. Special competitions included a national corn-husking championship in 1934, won by a Minnesota farmer and witnessed by an outdoor audience of more than 75,000; also a log-rolling championship a few years later. Boxing was liked by Minnesotans in early days. The great John L. Sullivan fought in Minneapolis in 1887, and Bob Fitzimmons boxed in the same city in 1891. In the summer of that year he was training for a fight in St. Paul, when public opposition reached such emotional heights that Governor Merriam — himself an ardent sportsman — ordered the forthcoming match canceled. The fighters protested that there was no Minnesota law prohibiting boxing, but the governor retorted that there was no law permitting it. He ordered state militia to surround the arena where the fight was to be held, and it was called off. The state legislature took action in 1892. Boxing was prohibited by law in Minnesota from that date until 1915 (though a chronicler of sports reports that there were many surreptitious fights arranged in private gymnasiums). Since the legalization of boxing in the state in 1915 and the establishment of a Minnesota Athletic Commission, the sport has flourished. Minnesota has contributed not a few boxers of finished skill. Notable were Mike Gibbons, the St. Paul "Phantom," and Tommy Gibbons, who lasted fifteen rounds against the world's heavyweight champion Jack Dempsey at Shelby, Montana, in 1923. (Gibbons for many years later served as sheriff of Ramsey County.)

The love of play even gave rise to many fads. An instance is miniature golf, originated in the South in 1929–30. Soon thereafter it was copied in thousands of American communities, including cities and towns in Minnesota.

Sports and recreation eased the stress of life in the 1930s, but their role is larger than their special contribution in a period of anxiety. They contributed to balanced living in the modern, industrializing state. In their diverse forms, they took advantage of increasing leisure and of the interplay of town and country in the era of modern transportation. In a broad sense sport has contributed to the poise and well-being of Minnesotans from pioneer days to the present. The contribution was enlarged as population increased, as urban life with its industry and business became more marked, and as sport itself and recreation were made the object of organization and of civic and state exploitation.

Another aspect of the 1930s was the repeal of the Eighteenth Amendment. The era of prohibition, with its miserable problems of enforcement of the Volstead Act and of illicit trade by rumrunners and bootleggers, by racketeers and speakeasies, had run its course. A modification of the federal law as to beer — changing from one-half of 1 per cent to over 3.2 per cent the legal definition of an intoxicating beverage — had been passed by Congress in March 1933. Earlier, in February (while Hoover was still in office), Congress sent to the states, for action by state conventions rather than by legislatures, a proposal for the repeal of the Eighteenth Amendment. This was rushed through. By early December 1933, thirty-six states, including Minnesota, had given their approval, and the Twenty-First Amendment went into effect. Governor Olson, anticipating the repeal, called the Minnesota legislature into special session for December 5. He had also appointed a committee of citizens to recommend suitable methods of liquor control for the state.

The governor submitted his committee's report, but he kept aloof from any special plan except that he made it clear that he was for retention of local option and against the return of the traditional saloon. The session was stormy. Various proposals were presented, including one for a state dispensary system. Fighting "hard liquor" were both those who, despite the unhappy history of the Volstead Law, were committed by principle to prohibition, and also the interests especially devoted to the sale of beer. The ensuing problems became so snarled that the legislature was on the point of adjourning without action when Olson announced that, if it did, he would forthwith call another special session. And so a law was passed early in 1934. The state dispensary idea was rejected. The bill adopted and signed was described by the governor as a "good compromise." Local option was protected. Sunday closing was prescribed. The saloon as such was not exactly reinstated, but cocktail bars, or "lounges," took its place; restaurants properly licensed could dispense liquors with meals; and the sale of liquors by regularly licensed dealers was made legal (save as counties might choose to retain "dry" com-

535

munities). Thus Minnesota joined the nation in its stand against writing "sumptuary legislation into the fundamental law of the land."

The death of Floyd B. Olson and the term of Governor Benson (1937–39) were turning points in Minnesota political history. The succeeding period, 1939–55, has been characterized by a political scientist as a time of "resurgent Republicanism." This description is accurate. In the period indicated Minnesota had an unbroken succession of four Republican governors — Harold E. Stassen (1939–43), Edward J. Thye (1943–47), Luther W. Youngdahl (1947–51), and C. Elmer Anderson (1951–55).

The Benson regime was wracked by deterioration in the Farmer-Labor organization and by public distrust. The governor faced a legislative deadlock in 1937, and a special session had to be called. Legislation passed included authorization of county welfare boards; establishment of a state geographic board; elimination of state levies on homesteads; and an act requiring employers to carry compensation insurance. But as the months went by, it became clear that the governor was losing the confidence of the majority of the people, within and outside the ranks of his own party. The time was nearing for a drastic change.

The change that came was directed and inspired by a brilliant young politician who, as early as 1934, while Olson was governor, took the lead in a re-formation of the state Republican party through a crusading Young Republican League. Harold E. Stassen, then in his twenties, was a lawyer in South St. Paul and a graduate of the University of Minnesota in arts and law. He was a native-born Minnesotan who had signal qualities of leadership and an infectious belief that a reconstituted Republican party could wrest control from the Farmer-Laborites. He had a flair for politics and was a persuasive and effective speaker. Even before he was elected governor, he had had the experience of sitting as a delegate to a national political convention (that of the Republicans in 1936). The Young Republican League, under his leadership, took hold, drew to itself adherents, young and old, who saw in his program hope not only of Republican victory but — as the Farmer-Labor party lost ground under Benson — a swing away from his "leftist" tendencies without a turning aside from progressive and humanitarian reforms. Stassen's advocacy of "enlightened capitalism" was a bid to Republicans and independents who previously had supported the Farmer-Labor party.

536

By 1938 he was ready for, and won, the Republican nomination for governor. He launched a sharp challenge to the Benson administration in the ensuing campaign. He made his run on state civil service reform, anticommunism, proposals to improve relations between labor and management, and reorganization of the state government. He wanted to find ways of economy and to strike at corruption wherever it might be found. In the election he overwhelmed Benson by a margin of more than 291,000 votes. Not yet thirty-two years old, he took office on January 3, 1939.

In his inaugural address the new governor declared that "one of the first and most important problems" of the time was "to raise the standards of public service and to improve the morale of state government." He called for a civil service law for state employees. State departments had grown like Topsy, he said, and he favored consolidations where they could appropriately be effected, including a department of social security and public welfare. He recommended the abolition of the so-called "Big Three," with revisions in administrative controls. He strongly urged the passage of a labor-relations act. And he asked for adequate aid to people in need of public assistance, a program for youth, legislation to "curb the small loan sharks," and other reforms.

Stassen's leadership, coupled with the fact that the landslide of 1938 gave him majorities in both houses of the legislature, had the remarkable result that every one of his proposals was carried into law. A drastic reorganization act was passed. A civil service system for state employees was instituted. Other achievements were a labor relations act, an anti-loan-shark law, and improvements in social security benefits. A commissioner of administration was authorized and also the office of a single tax commissioner. The state debt was reduced considerably during the Stassen term; and losses in wages from strikes dropped. All this gained solidity of public support for the governor and his administration.

An opinion poll in 1939 indicated that four-fifths of the voters who were asked to respond gave their approval to the governor's program. This did not mean, however, that there was a lack of criticism both within and outside his own party. His political rise was in part the result of a challenge by youthful Republicans to the conservative "old guard," some of whose members referred to him as a "boy scout"; and Professor G. Theodore Mitau, in his book on Minnesota politics, writes that "Farmer-Laborites scoffed at Stassen's claim to kinship with midwestern liberalism and progressivism." Critics alleged favoritism by the governor to public utilities and the iron-ore corporations, and there was a sharp attack on the administration for its dismissal of large numbers of Farmer-Labor appointees to public office in the summer before the new civil service reform went into operation.

The state still leaned heavily on the federal government for alleviation of unemployment. In 1940, the WPA organization in Minnesota gave work to more than 40,000 persons at a cost in excess of $44,000,000 — evidence of the stubborn pull of the depression.

Meanwhile Stassen won political recognition and fame nationally. As the state and national elections of 1940 approached, Minnesota and the nation were in the shadow of World War II. The governor demonstrated his anti-isolationist principles when in 1940, after the death of Senator Lundeen, he appointed Joseph A. Ball, a pronounced internationalist, to the unexpired term. In that year Stassen had the distinction of delivering the keynote address at the Republican National Convention which nominated Wendell L. Willkie to run for President against Roosevelt. The governor spoke for a "strong America." "Blackouts of dictators," he said, "take the place of lighthouses of free men." He called for advance on what he called the "fronts" of national preparedness, fifth-column defense, domestic economic welfare, and governmental effectiveness and integrity. He was floor manager for the Willkie candidacy and supported him vigorously for the presidency. In the election of 1940, Stassen, now contending against Hjalmar Petersen, the Farmer-Labor candidate, was continued as governor by a margin of close to 200,000 votes, while Roosevelt in Minnesota led Willkie by somewhat less than 50,000. Senator Shipstead by this time had turned his back on the Farmer-Labor party — he now ran for re-election as a Republican and won by a large majority.

Stassen, with continuing support from the legislature, strengthened Minnesota's work for child welfare and enlarged the Gillette State Hospital; he liberalized old-age assistance, took measures to make good rural credit losses, and improved the labor conciliation law. The central idea of this law was a "cooling off" period in labor squabbles. Ten days before a strike or lockout could be started, a state conciliator had to be notified. His job was to bring about agreement and settlement. If he failed, and if the public interest was involved, he then reported to the governor, who named a fact-finding committee which had a thirty-day period in which to explore the issues and make its findings. What this meant was delay, investigation, and recommendation before action was taken that might lead to public loss and suffering. It signified also that the labor movement, from its beginnings in the 1880s and 1890s, had gained cohesive strength. By 1939 the 134,000 trade union members in Minnesota represented 24.8 per cent of the nonagricultural working force of the state (and by 1953 the figures went to 328,000 and 38.1 per cent).

State and nation are inextricably intertwined, in peace as in war. As one tries to interpret the world wars of the twentieth century — in their backgrounds, events, and aftereffects — the story becomes essentially one. What happened to America happened to the part of America called Minnesota. The events of the 1930s and 1940s, with World War II as their bloody climax, are part and parcel of this history, though it is possible here to sketch only some of the larger backgrounds. Minnesota minds were charged with the grave and changing news of world happenings. They might seem far away to many, yet when the war came, more than 300,000 Minnesota men and women took part in it, and more than 6000 gave up their lives. Minnesota resources were drawn upon to the uttermost.

No more than in the years of early trade and the clash of seemingly distant empires could the fortunes of Minnesota be isolated from the world. Not long after the Nazi dictator gained control of Germany in 1933, the shadow over Europe darkened, with the buildup of Hitler's armed strength, the Nazi persecution of the Jews, threats and moves of aggrandizement, a mounting belligerency, and a commitment to policies founded on force. It was not only the European world, however, that endangered the maintenance of peace. In the Far East the militarists of Japan gained power and in 1937 they struck at China.

The isolationist hope of neutrality was written into American law in acts of 1935, 1936, and 1937; but the country was sensitive to the menace of Hitler and Roosevelt's famous "quarantine speech" in Chicago in 1936 voiced the concern of millions. Efforts were made to promote a world conference on disarmament and cooperation in the economic sphere. These failed, and the United States was obliged to give serious attention to a readying of the country for defense. Among other things, this took the fortunate form of congressional authorization in 1938 tc build twenty-four new battleships.

Meanwhile Hitler, emboldened by easy triumphs, provoked crisis after crisis, including that over Czechoslovakia in 1938, followed by the Munich agreement and Chamberlain's assurance of "Peace in our time." American defense spending increased toward the end of a decade which, far from assuring peace, brought instead the Russo-German pact, the German and Russian military assault on Poland, and the determination of Britain and France to fight in defense of their treaty obligations. The European tragedy, soon to become a world tragedy, came to its climax in September 1939.

Americans realized the grave import of President Roosevelt's words: "When peace has been broken anywhere, the peace of all countries is in danger." The sense of danger to the free world led to the repeal of the arms embargo in November 1939. And that sense was intensified when, in the spring of 1940, Germany struck down Denmark and Norway and overran the Low Countries. These moves were a prelude to the conquest of France, leaving Britain alone to challenge the tyrant and to defend freedom in the European world. These happenings, in broad terms, were the setting for the American Selective Service Act, which went into effect in September 1940. Early in that month also, the United States came to the aid of Britain with destroyers in an arrangement that made bases available to this country. It was in this atmosphere that the American elections of 1940 were held, in which Roosevelt was returned for a third term as President (449 electoral votes to 82 for Wendell Willkie), and in which Stassen won his second term as governor of Minnesota.

Spurring military preparedness, President Roosevelt now pictured America as the "arsenal of democracy." Britain alone stood up against Hitler's forces under Churchill, who called for valor but offered nothing "but blood, toil, tears, and sweat." The United States, sympathetic to the British cause, gave aid on a large scale. Lend-lease went into effect on March 11, 1941. In June, Germany, frustrated in its hope of conquering England by invasion, struck at Russia. Roosevelt met Winston Churchill in August of that year. This was the portentous Atlantic Conference (the occasion for the enunciation of the "Four Freedoms"); and in September Japan joined the Axis.

These and other events furnish clues to the backgrounds of the "date that will live in infamy" — the assault by Japan on Pearl Harbor, December 7, 1941. On December 8 Congress, on the President's recommendation, declared that, by Japan's act, a state of war existed between Japan and the United States. Three days later Germany and Italy declared war on the United States.

A united country rose to the challenge of all-out participation in World War II. Minnesota played its part along with all the other states. The dream of peace, cherished before and after 1917, was shattered less than a quarter of a century after the soldiers came home from the shell-torn battlefields of World War I.

The Minnesota people were united as they entered World War II. The reports coming by every medium of communication left no doubt in their minds as to the world danger from the rampant tyrannies abroad. Governor Stassen, some eleven months before America found itself at war, said in his second inaugural address (January 8, 1941), referring to the happenings in Europe, "Bullets, and dive bombers and destruction, have taken the place of ballots, and deliberation and progress." Aware that the United States might be drawn into the "horrible hammering of war," he called on a united people to do their full share in building national defense and to support the President of the United States. He did not neglect to voice his interests in housing at home, in the problems of dependent children, and in other social and economic matters, but his paramount thought was for the nation in the crisis that was now confronting it.

In the 1920s and 1930s Minnesota had taken military steps that proved fortunate in the light of after events. Soon after World War I, the Minnesota National Guard had been re-established, with support from the federal government under the National Defense Act of 1920. During the next few years it was increased in strength to more than five thousand officers and men. An aero squadron was begun. The naval air reserve was formed; and several other defense moves were made. The National Guard was available for emergencies at home — disaster rescue operations, the enforcement of martial law if declared (as it was in 1934), and other duties. The state in 1931 furnished funds for the building of a new Camp Ripley in the area of the pre-Civil War Fort Ripley, and summer encampments of guardsmen were instituted there in 1933.

The Selective Service Act of September 1940 was a warning of determined national preparedness. Men between twenty-one and thirty-five registered with local draft boards, and in the United States 1,200,000 troops were put in training and a reserve of 800,000 provided. The term was for only one year, but in 1941 the President called for an eighteen-month extension and the proposal narrowly won approval in Congress.

Various special units in Minnesota were called up in 1940–41, and in February 1941 the National Guard, by that time recruited to a strength of more than eight thousand, was activated. When the Japanese blow fell upon Pearl Harbor, the country had an armed and trained force of 1,600,000 men, and Minnesota from the first shared in the nation's defense.

The story of Minnesota men and women in the armed forces is one of heroic service in the Army, Navy, Air Corps, Marine Corps, Coast Guard, and many special units, including a tank battalion, medical and hospital services, WAACs and WAVEs, even a division in the military railway service (under Brigadier General Carl R. Gray). It takes one to virtually every area and campaign: Pearl Harbor, the Pacific and its hard-fought island landings, the Aleutians, New Guinea, the Philippines, the North Atlantic, North Africa, Sicily and Italy, the Normandy invasion, France, and Germany.

Virginia B. Kunz writes that a Minnesota naval reserve division, serving on the destroyer *U.S.S. Ward*, fired the first United States shot of the war. The *Ward* detected a submarine at the Pearl Harbor channel entrance and from a four-inch gun the Minnesotans made a direct hit on the submarine's conning tower. Another heroic story is that of the tank battalion from Brainerd, under Colonel Ernest B. Miller, which was in the Philippines when the war opened. It was at once engaged in severe fighting, with terrible casualties. It covered the American withdrawals to Bataan and helped to defend Bataan during the succeeding siege. Minnesota National Guard units were sent early to the Aleutians in coast artillery service. The 151st Field Artillery, rich in military history, saw violent action in Africa, at Salerno, Anzio, and elsewhere in the fierce Italian campaign.

On seas and in lands the world over, Minnesotans played their parts in campaign after campaign, fighting alongside comrades from other states and America's allies. State identity was submerged to a great extent in the American units, but wherever they served, Minnesotans paid costs in dead and wounded, in hardships and suffering, in the years of their lives. Because of the dispersion of troops throughout the changing fronts of the war, their record is written into the total effort which brought on the collapse of the Italian, German, and Japanese armed might. No brief

542

summary can do justice to the individual achievements in action on almost innumerable fronts — achievements which ultimately carried the war to its conclusion.

Statistics do not reveal the story save as one remembers that the state sent 304,100 men to the war and that every individual played his or her part in the total effort. Mrs. Kunz reports numbers: "209,500 in the army and army air corps; 79,300 in the navy; 11,800 in the marine corps and 3,500 in the coast guard." She also records the deaths of 4399 Minnesotans of the Army and its Air Corps "in combat or of wounds" and of 1444 in the Navy, Marine Corps, and Coast Guard. The over-all toll was increased by more than 400 who died in prison camps and more than half a hundred listed as missing. These figures do not take into account the many who carried scars into civilian life on their return. Nearly two decades have gone by since the guns were stilled in World War II, but many Minnesotans still bear the marks of their wartime service and sacrifice.

The Minnesota people at home, as men went away to war, gave every possible support to the national drive for victory.

The state was not less resolute than it had been in World War I, but the "high-tension mobilization of public opinion" that marked the earlier war was absent. Some salutary lessons had been learned. There was no authoritarian commission of public safety, generated in suspicion and distrust, and there was no detectival protective league. Governor Stassen favored placing powers in the constituted executive branch of the state government, not in a special commission with indefinite powers; and the state had no wish to repeat the experiences of World War I in striking at supposed pro-Germanism.

This does not mean that the native flair for organization did not find characteristic expression. Minnesota had a Defense Council, with a state defense coordinator (Ernest L. Oelrich). It had a state War Finance Committee. It had also a State Postwar Council, concerned with planning. It had even a state committee on the conserving of Minnesota's cultural resources. This group tackled a survey to determine what irreplaceable or peculiarly valuable cultural and scientific treasures were exposed to danger. The precautionary move was not inspired by public knowledge of atomic bombs, still in the future, but it bespoke awareness of danger from air attack.

Minnesota organizations pitched in to forward the sale of government war bonds and to assist in anything else that needed citizen aid. The women of Minnesota organized into Victory Aides, operating with civilian block workers. They effected in 1942 the first campaign made from house to house to solicit pledges. A woman was selected as vice-chairman of the Minnesota War Finance Committee and she also served as director of Minnesota "woman-power in promoting the War Bond program." These activities were only a part of the contributions made by Minnesota women in their communities — in schools, in national programs, in response to every call for service. The Red Cross was prepared for war work from the first, with its home nursing, canteen service, accident prevention efforts, and aid in other fields. The United Service Organizations (U.S.O.) represented a pooling of training, experience, and aid wherever feasible to men in service, and some support from community funds was channeled into U.S.O.

Stassen campaigned again for governor in 1942, once more against Hjalmar Petersen, and he was triumphantly re-elected (this time with Edward J. Thye as his running mate). In opening his third term, he called for "complete victory." With the National Guard in the service of the nation, he announced the organizing, uniforming, and equipping of a Minnesota defense force.

Everywhere throughout the state, he said, people had volunteered for whatever services they could perform, and their numbers, he reported (in his inaugural address of January 6, 1943), had then reached 143,000. He asked the legislature for funds to give aid to fighting men on their return from the war. He projected plans for postwar reconstruction — highways, public buildings, and housing. That the iron-ore industry had come to the aid of the nation in its crisis was indicated by the governor's report that during the recent season a total of 92,000,000 tons had been sent out.

Stassen's interpretation of the meaning of world events was disclosed by his remark: "It is clear that the walls of isolation are gone forever." A month before the legislature adjourned in 1943, the governor announced that he was resigning from his office to enter war service. He did this on April 27, went into training in the Navy, and during the war was a flag officer under Admiral W. F. Halsey. His departure was in effect a farewell to the Minnesota political scene. After the war he did not return as an active participant in state politics, though his role in national political affairs had echoes in the state. Before he left Minnesota

544

he delivered an address (January 7, 1943) in which he advocated a "definite united nations government," leaving no doubt as to his commitment to postwar international control aimed at preventing the recurrence of wars. Thye took over as governor, and in 1944 was elected to the office by a huge vote. In the national election of 1944, which returned Roosevelt for a fourth term, the President carried Minnesota over Governor Thomas E. Dewey by a margin of 62,448.

During the war years Minnesota farmers produced record crops; the iron mines surpassed all previous levels of production; and thousands of people in villages and cities grew "war gardens." Many scraped up pennies and dollars to buy defense stamps (sold in denominations as low as ten cents) and war bonds. At the end of the war an official report of the seven war loans, the final Victory Loan, and "in-between buying," revealed a grand Minnesota sale of more than $2,844,000,000. The sales of "E Bonds" reached a total beyond $824,000,000. School children chipped in by turning their pennies into defense stamps. In its total sales of bonds, Minnesota attained 168 per cent of the quotas assigned to the state. The watchwords of the time were saving, conservation, production, help to the country in its effort. As needs tightened, rationing was imposed to offset shortages in gasoline, tires, meat, sugar, and other items. Such restrictions were cheerfully accepted by the people. They were mild indeed compared with the ordeals of the youth of the state who were at the war fronts.

An extraordinary chapter in the history of World War II is that of the American miracle of production. It has been characterized as a "joint effort by managers of industry, engineers, technicians, scientists, laborers of all categories of skill, and farmers." To the list must be added the government, which poured millions of dollars into technological development and production. There was an exuberant, but purposeful, release of energy after the sagging years of the depression. Airplane manufacture offers an illustration. The President was criticized as a visionary when in 1940 — a year in which the United States made six thousand planes — he challenged industry to produce fifty thousand a year. To many the figure seemed fantastic, yet American industrial plants manufactured some 96,000 airplanes in 1944.

Minnesota shared in the fashioning of the American productive "miracle." Physicists, doctors, chemists, engineers, and other scientists, as well as scholars in diverse nonscientific fields, worked in laboratories, libraries, Washington agencies, and special research centers on problems relevant to success in the war effort.

Far-flung medical resources were mobilized. The education of nurses was accelerated; and vocational training, essential to meeting the need for technicians, was speeded in public schools and in special institutions such as the Dunwoody Institute of Minneapolis. Even before America entered the war, Dr. Alfred O. C. Nier of the University of Minnesota was the first man in the world (1940) to separate the isotope of uranium. Professor I. M. Kolthoff, also of the university, an analytical chemist, contributed to the development of synthetic rubber (as well as to basic chemical research). Studies of starvation by Dr. Ancel Keys, an authority on nutrition, led to the development of the K ration, used in the war for emergency situations. Physicians and surgeons found new techniques, including Dr. Owen Wangensteen's suctional siphonage treatment for severe intestinal obstructions (the Wangensteen tube). The device saved or prolonged many thousands of lives and its use became so common that war nurses working in a ward for cases of abdominal surgery are said to have called their domain "Wangensteen's Alley." Dr. Cecil Watson gave special service in coping with hepatitis both in Europe and in the Pacific area. Dr. William R. Lovelace of the Mayo Clinic, a surgeon who specialized in aviation medicine, devised a "human centrifuge" for testing airplane pilots under conditions of whirling stress.

The federal government developed vast ordnance plants in Minnesota at New Brighton and Rosemount. Numerous industrial firms, backed by governmental contracts, played important roles in the joint effort. Not only did their varied products help to win the war, but they gave impetus to postwar manufacturing based on technological research. This impetus in turn, in the later era of world conflict between democracy and communism, had reverberations of significance with respect to the schools and the education of scientists.

Minnesota illustrations in the area of war productivity are so many as to defy a comprehensive listing. Some items may be mentioned, however, to indicate at once the spread and magnitude of the state's industrial effort.

The Minneapolis-Honeywell Company helped to perfect airplane controls and to develop the proximity bomb. The Northern Pump Company manufactured gun mounts — notably navy twin gun mounts — and much other war equipment. Minneapolis Moline produced artillery shells, and

546

the Crown Iron Works (also of Minneapolis) built portable bridges, pontoons, and related war-use materials. The Minnesota Onan Corporation of Minneapolis manufactured electric power plants, generators, and other specialized electrical equipment.

Duluth was a natural center for ship-building, and construction companies in that city turned out oil tankers, submarine chasers, and coast guard cutters. But Duluth was not alone in the building of ocean-going vessels. At Savage tankers and barges were made, then sent out on the Minnesota River and on down the Mississippi.

The Minnesota Mining and Manufacturing Company of St. Paul turned out tapes in vast quantities for scores of uses, including strips as window protection in buildings situated in areas exposed to bombings. Tapes were also used on ships, airplanes, and jeeps; reflective sheeting was made for highway signs, even for paddles on life rafts; and sheeting of non-slip quality was made for wings of airplanes and other purposes. Much of the firm's work was along its usual lines, rather than specialized war machinery, but the major resources of the company were made available for war purposes.

The St. Paul branch of the International Harvester Company made aircraft guns and spare parts. The Andersen Corporation at Bayport, utilizing wood products from International Falls, turned out prefabricated insulated hutments for army air corps bases. And the Owatonna Tool Company achieved a tremendous production of tools for the war.

The Northwestern Aeronautical Corporation (St. Paul) made gliders and jettison fuel tanks for long-distance plane flights. General Mills of Minneapolis not only manufactured flour and other food products in prodigious quantities, but, under such industrial leaders as Harry Bullis and James Ford Bell, went into extensive mechanical work. The company turned out gun sights and even "jitterbug torpedoes" that could chase shifting targets, swerving as enemy targets dodged, sometimes doing the figure 8 in torpedo maneuvering. Like many companies, General Mills thought of itself as a "corporate citizen" serving the country "for the duration."

WPA construction workers improved strategic airports. Trained men in civilian capacities were willing to tackle just about any kind of assignment. Hundreds of Minnesotans were dispatched to Greenland to help build air bases. Even such illustrations by no means complete the picture of Minnesota's part in producing the varied materials essential to effective participation in a war of world magnitude. The Munsingwear Company in Minneapolis, for instance, produced great quantities of underwear for men in the armed forces; and the North Star Woolen Mills made blankets for both Army and Navy.

Fighting men on the ground, in the air, and in ships at sea were the front line of the war effort, but even a fragmentary survey from a single state demonstrates how fully the American people stood behind them. Productive might in factory, on farms, and in every area of the home fronts gave the fighters tools, materials, resources, devoted and undeviating support. Thus the joint effort was one both of people at work in the home states and of soldiers, sailors, and others who helped to bear the brunt of head-on attack and defense. The home aid contributed to national strength, morale, and the will to win.

The ordeal of World War II, coming on the heels of a decade of depression, ended in 1945. Allied might crumbled the power and pretensions of the dictators. In Minnesota the men and women who served the country in its armed forces came home. They came home less to bands and parades, as in previous wars, than to thankful hearts, the joyous welcome of families, friends, and neighborhoods, the state's appreciation of what they had done, bonus legislation as material thanks, and a federal G.I. act that came to the aid of those who chose to continue their education. The welcome was glad and sincere, but, as after earlier wars, Minnesota homes were shadowed by hurts in bodies or minds or both sustained by young people in their experiences in far places; and in many families there was lasting sorrow over the losses of young lives.

Every war is followed by the hopes and prayers of people that such human disasters can and will be averted in the future. This was true in a special sense after World War II, for the science and engineering skills that did so much to help America and its allies win the war brought upon mankind the horrors of nuclear weapons.

Even before atomic bombs were dropped on Hiroshima and Nagasaki, men of good will planned for a world order that might ensure peace. The thinking rose above partisan divisions. Thus Wendell Willkie in 1943 published his book called *One World*, in which he pleaded with eloquence and wisdom for international cooperation and an end to isolationism. The great charter conference of the United Nations was held

548

in San Francisco in 1945. The voice of President Roosevelt having been stilled by death, his successor, President Truman, spoke the sense of universal humanity when, in his address to the conference, he said, "If we do not want to die together in war, we must learn to live together in peace." Harold E. Stassen, still a young man, was a member of the American delegation to the San Francisco conference, working to bring about the kind of world organization he himself had advocated before he entered the Navy.

A taconite processing plant at Silver Bay

✶ *Changing Modern Scenes*

EVERY period in the state's past has been marked by political undulations, economic and social change, the rise of new leadership and the withdrawal of old, new problems and new ways of tackling old problems, and the interweaving of tradition with novel ideas as past has merged with present. Things occur in their time and place; and as Carlyle once said "Today is not yesterday," though today flows out of yesterday. Needs, causes, human concerns, and talents are architects of change. Shakespeare understood some of the variants of change when he wrote:

That we would do,
We should do when we would; for this "would" changes
And hath abatements and delays . . .

To many observers, the era from World War II to the early 1960s was one in which the tempo of change seemed to be accelerated by invention, especially electronics, and by the responsibilities of America as the leader of the democratic world. In other ways, however, changes that had been foreshadowed in the past or were well under way took mature shape. A lengthened perspective — a generation or two — may reveal significant tendencies only dimly perceived now if seen at all.

The recent political scene has been one of shifts in state and nation (and world). Industry and business in Minnesota evidenced lusty growth, and they were inevitably influenced by the newer technology and by national imperatives. Industrialization and urbanization moved steadily forward. Agricultural diversification reached full bloom, and the tradi-

551

tional divergence between town and country lessened. Life in country, town, and city clung stubbornly to tradition and tested institutions. But the social, cultural, and educational scene was never static. It was modified year after year by growth, new problems, the faiths and foibles of the postwar generation, and the anxieties of Americans in a divided world — notwithstanding "abatements and delays." Invention seemed endless and fabulous in its production of new devices. They ranged in their utility from kitchen magic to airspace travel. Machines brought the world to home firesides, and streamlined trains, jet planes, and scores of other wonders stretched farm and city yards to embrace state and country and world.

Governor Thye, in his inaugural address (1945), emphasized the need of continuing the wholehearted cooperation that marked the state's war support. He spoke of postwar planning, the development of material resources, humane reforms, and continuing support of education. He drew attention to the recent establishment of a Minnesota Inter-Racial Commission for advancing unity among the people — a state action prophetic of the national move for desegregation in the 1950s.

When Thye was chosen to run for the United States Senate in 1946, a new figure in Minnesota Republican politics at the gubernatorial level appeared in the person of Luther W. Youngdahl. He was a graduate of Gustavus Adolphus College, trained in the law, and experienced as a district judge and as an associate justice of the state's supreme court. One of a large and gifted Swedish-American Lutheran family of Minneapolis, Youngdahl was an incisive speaker, vigorous, and possessed of an impelling fervor for social betterment. His biographer describes him as an exemplar of the "Christian in Politics." Elected governor in 1946, 1948, and 1950 by large popular majorities, he won the sympathy and approval of the Minnesota electorate as a crusader for moral, social, and humanitarian advances.

As Youngdahl began his governorship, he was aware of the danger of a slump in the "disillusioning aftermath of war." He therefore urged a "bolstering of our moral and spiritual resources" and struck out at the evils of greed and bigotry and of war itself. He wanted no moral letdown of a kind all too familiar in the history of after-war periods in the American past. He translated his social principles into advocacy of improved care for the mentally ill, welfare services, aid to the blind, support of education, decent housing for the underprivileged, public health advances, law enforcement, the curbing of gambling, and strict control, under the law, of the liquor traffic. With unceasing energy he sought public support for the reforms that he urged upon the legislature, and in his efforts he had signal success.

A Youth Conservation Commission was authorized in 1947. This commission, now administratively within the Department of Corrections, functions, as Youngdahl intended it should, as an agency to prevent or lessen crime among younger people. Persons under twenty-one years of age who are guilty of felonies or gross misdemeanors are now committed to the commission for whatever sentences the law imposes; and the commission may also give probationary care to children certified by juvenile courts to be delinquent. It operates nine centers, schools, and camps. The year 1947 also witnessed an effort by the governor to make slot machines illegal in the state. The annual "take" of such machines was said to be $4,000,000, and some five thousand persons each paid a federal tax of $100 on their machines. A law enforcement committee was set up by the governor to make recommendations, with a prominent Minneapolis citizen, Bradshaw Mintener, at its head. Notwithstanding bitter opposition, including that of some of the owners of summer resorts, the measure won legislative approval; and Youngdahl promptly called on law officers for rigorous enforcement of the law.

He secured a strengthening of the laws controlling liquor sales, and in his second term he requested and was given authority to invest liquor control officers with the power of arrest. He also secured an act authorizing aid to local units of government for public low-rent housing. The school district system was reorganized in 1947. Appraising mental health problems, Youngdahl proposed the recruitment of a "psychiatric corps"; and in 1949 an important Mental Health Act was passed. On the administrative side the governor brought about, through consolidation, a state department of business research and development; and he also sponsored a legislative research committee which gathers up material and information needed in relation to proposed legislation.

Old-age assistance, he believed, should be based, not on some arbitrary maximum, but on actual needs. The governor opened the National Guard to colored people, and he favored, though he did not secure, a fair employment practices law which, he said, would be a "devastating blow to the armor of the forces of darkness."

A soldiers' bonus, approved by popular referendum, was carried into effect, and in 1951 Youngdahl announced that payments had been virtually completed. The bonus was paid to approximately 291,000 veterans, and the total of the payments was in the vicinity of $85,000,000. It should be added that in 1943 a state department of veterans affairs had been established and it has continued to function for Korean as well as World War veterans, offering many forms of state aid and benefits as well as cooperation in relation to federal benefits.

The Korean troubles ran their bloody course from 1950 to 1953. The United Nations recognized South Korea as the Korean government and intervened after President Truman ordered an American delaying action when North Korea struck at its southern neighbor. The assault by the Chinese Communists precipitated a major war effort by the United Nations, and the United States supplied the chief fighting forces. Before the armistice came in the summer of 1953, more than 25,000 American men had been killed. Once again Minnesota was involved; its National Guard was called out and guardsmen and drafted troops from the state were sent to the fronts in the Far East. The magnitude of Minnesota's part is indicated by the fact that more than 86,000 Minnesota men served in the Korean war; and 890 were killed in action in Korea. The world, as Governor Youngdahl said in 1951, once more found itself "in turmoil and crisis." The struggle was between "two totally opposed philosophies of life" and was destined to go on as a cold war long after the Korean crisis ended.

The recommendations made by Governor Youngdahl in state affairs reveal the zeal with which he applied his own dictum that politics is the "machinery by which society makes its moral decisions." A commentator on the Youngdahl era suggested that some people suspected partisan politics "in the garb of moral righteousness"; that others were alarmed at the cost of the programs of social amelioration; and that yet others believed that administrative and other reforms had been less emphasized than they should have been.

Whatever the criticisms, human relations and the conservation of human resources were at the heart of the governor's philosophy, as the record shows — but he was also concerned about highways, business development, soil conservation, agriculture, aeronautics, and other aspects of the state's economic progress.

He was also interested in the state's history. In 1949, in his second inaugural address, he took account of Minnesota's Territorial Centennial. In his judgment, it marked a "luminous place" along the state's path. He hailed laborers, tillers of the soil, merchants and businessmen, leaders of industry, professional men, homemakers, teachers, political and religious leaders, and builders of communities. All were "builders of Minnesota."

In the summer of 1951 Governor Youngdahl was appointed by President Truman as a federal district judge in Washington, and he promptly accepted the appointment. There was much speculation at the time about the reasons for the governor's withdrawal, with fifteen months of his term yet before him. He himself ascribed his action to the "emotional and physical strain" of the office and made it clear that in any event he would not have campaigned for a fourth term. His friendly biographer, however, ventures to suggest some "behind-the-scenes political developments" that added to the difficulties of the position. One seems to have been a move to persuade Youngdahl to head a state campaign for Stassen for President, and the biographer indicates that the governor did not choose to play such a role. Another suggested reason was that his social program did not marshal enthusiasm and support from traditional Republicans.

There can be no doubt historically that the governor's strength with the Minnesota people transcended party lines. An observer, sensing this, remarked after Youngdahl's decision to resign that "Republicans can go back to being Republicans and Democrats to voting for Democrats." Whatever the precise reasons for the decision — and the historian must have respect for the governor's own explanation — he had been consistent in his principles and actions as a humanitarian. He held fast to his commitment to advance the welfare of the people.

The governorship was taken over by C. Elmer Anderson of Brainerd, who had served as lieutenant governor under Stassen, Thye, and Youngdahl. He completed the term; and in 1952 he was triumphantly elected governor in his own right. Like Youngdahl he endorsed social and humanitarian causes: mental health, youth conservation, penal reforms, and law enforcement. He evidenced awareness of modern changes by suggesting as an area for legislative action the increasingly complex problems of metropolitan areas. If his inaugural message in 1953 did not seem to take into account basic and far-reaching changes in the state's industry, he did urge, in general terms, the removal of obstacles to the recruiting of "new enterprise" that could utilize Minnesota's skilled labor.

Mid-century meant appraisal, review, and stock-taking. The Territorial Centennial in 1949 and the anniversary celebration of statehood in 1958 stimulated historical interest in records, sites, organization, and activities of many kinds. Many Minnesotans, like Governor Youngdahl, were thinking about the meaning of the past as well as about the state's prospects for the future. A century is no little segment of time, even though it can be spanned by a single hard-fibered life. To most Minnesotans, aware of the ways in which the state had come into maturity, ten decades seemed a long time — and in the context of the state's history they were right. Some, however, pictured Minnesota as still "plagued with the growing pains of youth." This phrase was used in 1949 by President Gould of Carleton College in an address embodying a world perspective and focused upon the state of "today and tomorrow." Sensing the indivisible relationships of past, present, and future, Dr. Gould recalled some pungent lines of T. S. Eliot:

> Time present and time past
> Are both perhaps present in time future,
> And time future contained in time past.

"Time present and time past" were reflected in the growth of Minnesota's population. By 1950 the state was a little short of three millions and it would advance in the next decade to almost three and a half millions. Absolute figures of population, however, do not illuminate the true interplay of forces of change. Much has been said in this work about the urbanizing of Minnesota through a long period of years. The trend is described statistically by Lowry Nelson in a study of *The Minnesota Community*. He points out that, whereas in the 1860s less than 10 per cent of the state's population was urban, by 1950 the percentage had mounted to more than 50. Even this does not reveal the actualities of the change, for he adds, "From 1860 to 1880 more than 50 per cent of all gainfully employed workers were engaged in agriculture, compared with 30 per cent in 1940, and 22 per cent in 1950." In weighing such figures, one must remember that, with unceasing mechanization, the numbers of workers by no means reflected the magnitude of agricultural production. It is startling to know that at the present time, only 8 per cent of the American population work on the soil. But the farm production meets the needs of the other 92 per cent, with an appalling surplus as a result of science, research, and machines. The present-day nation is in a "crisis of abundance," with its subsidized storage bins piled high with sur-

556

pluses — all this while the burgeoning competitor of America, the Soviet Union, needs (as Minnesota did nearly a century ago) half of its population to grow the foods required by the other half.

Inevitably, however, the rural-urban shift does find reflection in the relative positions, in the Minnesota economy, of agriculture, manufacturing, mining, and forest products at the mid-twentieth century. The significant change comes just about at 1950, but for comparative purposes one may look at the years 1948 and 1958. For it was in this period that manufacturing in its total value surpassed the estimated "cash farm receipts" of the state. In 1948, farming led, with a total of $1,332,213,000, as compared with $1,022,000,000 for manufactures; but ten years later, manufacturing reached a total of $2,050,000,000 and agriculture stood at about $1,467,750,000. Such figures suggest a transition of importance, but as always statistics are perilous. Here one must recall that no small part of the manufacturing total was derived from food processing and manufacture of other products based upon the fruits of the Minnesota soil. The state today has more than a thousand food-processing plants, and it is estimated that about 25 per cent of the manufacturing employment in Minnesota is in this area. Obviously, any interpretation seeking, through comparative figures, to minimize the importance of agriculture to the state's economy would fly in the face of the facts.

The figures for mining were ahead of those for forest products in both years of the decade under consideration (mining $227,000,000 in 1948 and $396,000,000 a decade later; and forest products $136,000,000 in 1948 and $197,000,000 in 1958). It is interesting to observe, once more, that the tourist trade, granting difficulties in measuring its dollar value with precision, reached a total that was well beyond $300,000,000 by 1958.

One among many factors in the industrial and business development of the state was the impetus given by World War II to technological manufactures, implemented by research in science and engineering. More and more industries, following the examples set by such concerns as General Mills, Minneapolis-Honeywell, Minnesota Mining and Manufacturing, Remington Rand, and International Business Machines, gave high priority to research as a foundation for their specialization and expansion. Their own research divisions, the University of Minnesota and other colleges and universities of the Middle West, the public vocational schools

557

(with those of St. Paul and Minneapolis setting very high standards), and private electronic trade schools or industrial institutes (such as Dunwoody in Minneapolis) stimulated further research and trained skilled workers and engineers for the tasks of industries undreamed of in pioneer days. Such installations as an atomic power plant (at Elk River), a great linear accelerator at the University of Minnesota (under the direction of Dr. John H. Williams, a noted physicist and former director of the research division of the Atomic Energy Commission), and a DeGraaff generator, also at the university, represent research and experimentation of a kind not envisaged a generation ago.

Evidence of the growth of the electronics industry is the fact that by 1960 the state numbered 117 establishments in this field and in related engineering and scientific areas. Estimates of sales of products went beyond $600,000,000. Much of the industry centered in Minneapolis and St. Paul, but a dozen or more of the producing companies were in other cities of the state. Scores of thousands of persons were employed in the manufacture of electronic equipment and devices and electronic components, and in engineering and research enterprises.

So relatively recent are these and related manufacturing fields that even a random mention of the varied products involved reads like an inventory of a new and modern era. It includes tape recorders, electronic circuits, hearing aids, electrical brake equipment, motor control centers, systems for electronic digital computers, radar indicators, high altitude balloons and the intricate instrumentation used with them. It also encompasses conveyor systems, amplifiers, audiometers, biomedical instruments, precision switches, stamp vending machines, radios and television sets and the equipment associated with them. It includes shipboard missile launching devices, airport runway arresting devices, copying machines, modernized telephone equipment, transformers, telemetering code drums, micro-equipment, thermostats, magnetic components, miniature lights (as for computers), electronic input measuring devices, industrial control systems (as for water or for petroleum piping), gyroscopes, and electronic flash guns. The Jupiter C rocket, the Bellanca airplane, balloon stratospheric research (with the noted Dr. Jean Piccard of the university as an active participant), wind-tunnel aeronautical studies at Rosemount, and other spectacular developments are a part of the technological saga of modern Minnesota. In the electronic area alone, Minnesota has attained a fourth-ranking position among the states of the Union. The

558

industry, with heavy governmental support, has been a dynamic force propelling forward Minnesota's scientific modernization.

Emphasis upon electronic and related industries is needed for an understanding of newer trends in Minnesota industry, but it must not blind one to the industrial and business activities of Minnesota outside this field.

Minneapolis alone by the end of the 1950s had 1400 manufacturing plants. Taking backgrounds into view, one would expect to find flour milling, cereals, and feeds of high importance, as in fact they are. The city's grain exchange ranks, and has ranked for many decades, as the primary cash grain market of the country. The great milling companies, as has been made clear, are no longer local. General Mills, the Pillsbury Company, and International Milling have branches throughout the country, but they are still centrally located in Minneapolis and have industrial strength here. In their production and research they are vital links with the past of the Mill City.

The Twin Cities rank fourth in printing and publishing in the United States. Minneapolis products, in addition to electronic equipment and devices, include clothing, farm implements, paint, boats, heavy machinery, brewing, bags and paper boxes, seeds, and linseed oil and cakes. Manufacturing, in the city built near the power-producing Falls of St. Anthony, is highly developed, but there is also a far-reaching wholesale and retail business involving thousands of products and millions of dollars.

St. Paul, jobbing center from pioneer days, retains strength in wholesaling. Its magnitude is indicated by estimates of annual sales to a total of $800,000,000. Yet, even as the earlier jobbing declined, so the larger future of the wholesale business is not fully certain, for direct selling by manufacturers to retailers, spurred on by modern transportation, seems with every passing year to be gaining momentum.

In St. Paul, not a few special enterprises add distinctive character to the city's productive efforts. Built up through many years, the West Publishing Company ranks as the largest law-book concern in the United States; the H. B. Fuller Company, a manufacturer of adhesives, has built subsidiary plants in a dozen or more cities of the country; and St. Paul makes vast quantities of calendars.

The state's largest cities are the focus for great banks (national and state), vast insurance companies (including five of the largest in the country), savings and loan associations, and numerous business and industrial specialties, including the graphic arts. They also serve as state and regional centers for large mercantile firms, some of them founded in early days, including the Dayton, Donaldson, and Young-Quinlan companies in Minneapolis and the Emporium, the Golden Rule, and other concerns in St. Paul. Like the banks, with their branches, many of the large mercantile enterprises have expanded into the suburbs and outlying cities, and there has been a trend toward the merging of Minneapolis and St. Paul concerns.

For Minnesota — as for the United States — a feature of recent business expansion has been the building of shopping centers away from crowded "loop" areas in large cities. They serve not only thriving suburbs but also large segments of the city populations, and the same tendency has expressed itself in scores of smaller cities and towns. The shopping centers are modernized "main streets" — villages of shops, many of them subsidiaries of downtown companies. Their designs include parking areas or plazas to accommodate customers from far and near. Cars, good roads, and clusters of residential "developments" are the lifeblood of such centers. How extensive the movement has become is indicated by the fact that in 1962 the Twin City metropolitan area had thirty-three centers, one of them (Southdale) with as many as sixty-five stores clustered together, five others with more than thirty each, and more than a score in the range of ten to thirty. They wear such names as Miracle Mile, Knollwood Plaza, Richfield Hub, Sun Ray, Highland Center, Sibley Plaza, and Southdale.

The business and industrial concentration in the Twin Cities did not "just happen." Like many other basic changes in Minnesota life, it reflected a congeries of factors rooted in the past. One significant factor was the system of trunk-line railroads (as many as ten) which made the two cities a transportation hub not alone for the state itself but also for a wide-stretching domain in the Middle West. This domain is perhaps best represented by the regional sweep of the Ninth Federal Reserve banking district, though Twin City business is by no means limited to that fiscal area.

The Mississippi barge traffic, though in certain respects yet in its developmental stages, has attained impressive totals of tonnage. In 1961 the freight received in St. Paul and Minneapolis reached almost 3,500,000 tons (St. Paul having 2,886,000 tons in this figure). The barge traffic is in heavy goods — principally coal, burner oils, and gasoline. Outgoing barge freight, primarily grain, totaled more than 900,000 tons (St. Paul again leading with better than 692,000 tons). Thus the traffic centering in the Twin Cities (and not including the lower river towns or the Minnesota River ports) attained in a single year approximately 4,400,000 tons. The nine-foot channel, built by army engineers, obviously gave great impetus to a new era in river traffic. The potential docking facilities above the Falls of St. Anthony have not been exploited, but new locks will extend the barge traffic to that area.

The highways of the state have been improved decade after decade and there are more than 100,000 miles of surfaced roads. Great freeways are appearing, and car traffic has increased enormously. From the business point of view, special mention must be made of the armies of trucks which traverse the state and engage in interstate traffic. The state's business and research department reports that the Twin Cities rank as the third largest trucking center in the United States. More than a hundred common-truck carriers use Minneapolis and St. Paul as a hub.

Meanwhile transportation by air has increased prodigiously. Some eight airlines (one of them a freight line) serve the Twin Cities, with the Wold-Chamberlain International Airport as the central point of arrival and departure. The expansion of air traffic for the state as a whole finds illustration in the fact that in communities throughout Minnesota there are nearly 500 airports and landing fields.

The power of the Twin Cities and the urban center of which they are the heart has concentrated fiscal, industrial, and business leadership in the state's metropolis. Any survey of the economic picture revealed by modern Minnesota, however, must take into account the variety of specializations that mark communities throughout the state.

Duluth in its modern phase has made good the promise of its development as a port, a lumber center, and an iron-ore shipping area. With its more than 100,000 inhabitants, the city has become the second port of the United States in the volume of its tonnage, yielding priority only to New York. With the completion of the St. Lawrence Seaway in 1959, Duluth blossomed into a world port, the commercial significance of which cannot yet be fully measured. The city was prepared for huge volumes of shipping with its maze of iron-ore docks, coal docks, and freight wharves. But Duluth lost no time in adding to its facilities. A vast Public Marine Terminal was constructed (1959); and in 1961 a $20,000,000 interstate bridge, rising 120 feet above the harbor and connecting Duluth and Superior, was dedicated with official ceremony.

Duluth has more than a score of grain elevators and is a busy manufacturing center, with steel and iron, farm machinery, telephonic equipment, and other industrial products. It is also a busy commercial center, with more than 250 wholesale firms; good railroad facilities; and two airlines that serve its needs.

Specialized industrial activities have marked the growth and development of many other cities and sections of the state. Thus St. Cloud is noted for its granite quarrying, especially its monumental granite. Its production largely accounts for the fact that Minnesota ranks third among the states in granite quarrying. Austin, South St. Paul, Albert Lea, and Winona have great meat-packing establishments, all with varied products, including (as an instance) the Hormel Company's "Spam," developed from early pioneering work at Austin in canning pork. The lively interest of Minnesota manufacturers in research was exemplified by the late Jay Hormel. Not content with the ingenious applied researches of his own plant, he took the lead in setting in motion an institute of fundamental research affiliated with the University of Minnesota and staffed by highly trained scientists — and the work of the institute has won international fame.

Resources, ideas, and human ingenuity help to explain the diversity of Minnesota's industry in the smaller cities of the state. A panoramic view reveals interesting variations. Red Wing on the Mississippi is a center for the manufacture of pottery. Mankato has been called the state's "soybean capital." Le Sueur, situated at the heart of lands rich in peas and corn, has developed a $50,000,000 canning industry that produces a total of close to 2,000,000 cans of processed foods annually and has earned for its chief business the proud title of "Green Giant." Worthington is a "turkey capital"; Chaska and the Red River Valley towns of Crookston, Moorhead, and East Grand Forks are sugar-beet centers; Benson is a grass-seed mart; and the little village of Braham produces a considerable amount of the country's potato-harvesting equipment. International Falls is strong in pulpwood and paper manufacture. The range towns are necessarily iron-ore communities; and the glistening new village of Silver Bay is a taconite port. Montevideo, Windom, and Winona process (from flax) the raw materials for cigarette papers; and Winona has a traditional industry in liniments and medicines. Albert Lea turns out heaters and ventilator fans; Owatonna has a national reputation for its rings, medals, and other ornaments for school graduates the country over, and that city also cans pumpkins in large quantities. Mankato and Kasota are noted for their limestone; and Fairmont specializes in railroad work cars and their engines.

These illustrations by no means make up a comprehensive listing of the specialties of the various state communities. A sampling, however, suggests that the concept of Main Street uniformity scarcely harmonizes with the economic variations of the state. It must be added that small towns have leagued capital with ideas and local resources to create and enlarge home-grown industries.

If, in viewing divergent developments in industry and business, one also takes into account the educational and cultural differences among scores of towns, the disparity between the conventional view of uniformity and the actuality becomes the more apparent. No single development is sufficient in itself to explain the special character or individuality of a community. But to many people Rochester is medicine, surgery, and research (in recent times International Business Machines); Northfield is colleges; the iron-range towns are red earth, Finns, and cooperatives; the north shore settlements are fishing, recreation, and vistas; Alexandria is lakes and Bellanca planes; New Ulm is Germans and Turners; and Excelsior is apples, berries, and boats.

American village and city life is admittedly uniform in many ways, and the expanding forces of communication and mobility tend to forward a creeping uniformity for rural as well as urban life. But in numerous ways the patterns of communities vary. They do so just as individuals and ideas vary, as land and resources are unlike, as the imaginations, energies, and cultural backgrounds of people differ, in truth as history itself lends color and character to place and the ways in which people live in place.

Farming and farm life of recent years have been characterized by agricultural diversification, surplusage of crops, intensive mechanization, increasing application of science to the cultivation of the soil, transition from rural isolation to participation in and identification with urban life, and rising standards in housing and the conveniences that have accompanied modernization in state and country. Accompanying these trends was a reduction in farm population and in the number of farms. At the

563

same time there was an increase in the average size of Minnesota farms. Notable has been the advance in farm cultivation by owners as compared with the high degree of tenancy in the mid-1930s.

An all-state view of the progress of agricultural diversification may be indicated by a few figures, but they must be looked at with awareness that, as cities and towns vary in their industry, the major sections of rural Minnesota differ in many ways. Nevertheless, statistics of production for the entire state furnish significant evidence of the spreading diversification, the backgrounds of which have been described. In 1961 the state produced 324,242,000 bushels of corn, 159,988,000 bushels of oats, and 53,843,000 bushels of soybeans. Flaxseed stood at more than 6,400,000 bushels, potatoes (in hundredweight) at more than 14,000,000, and sugar beets (measured in tons) at 1,262,000. In 1960 Minnesota had 145,662 farms with a total of nearly 31,000,000 acres (about 19,000,000 in cropland). Its cattle population was above 4,000,000. Expressing statistical findings in dollars, the 1960 agricultural income (to September 1 of that year) was $258,765,000 for crops and $791,685,000 for livestock and livestock products. The total thus ran beyond a billion dollars and ranked Minnesota fifth among the states of the country in its farm receipts.

Such statistics do not fill out the picture of farming diversification, however. How widely the state has departed from wheat specialization may be further indicated by noting its ranking in various fields. A recent tabulation places Minnesota first in butter, dry milk, dressed turkeys, sweet corn, and honey (for processing); second in flax, oats, and cheese; and high in milk, peas, feed corn, hay, and eggs (for processing).

Soybeans have become one of the major crops of the state, and they constitute a relatively new rural industry. The surge in American soybean production came in the 1940s when the war interrupted imports of soybeans from Asia, where they had been cultivated for centuries. Since World War II the "soybean acreage in the United States has shot up as miraculously as Jack's beanstalk." Minnesota farmers joined in the surge with enthusiasm. To them soybeans — highly useful for oil and meal and a fantastic number of products — proved a prime cash crop. The state produces about an eighth of the total American crop, and Minnesota manufacturers have not been slow to exploit it, notably at Mankato, where two great companies (Honeymead Products and Archer-Daniels-Midland) have large plants.

Wheat, though its acreage is only an eighth, or less, in comparison with that for corn, is not negligible, for the production in 1960 and 1961 was in the vicinity of 25,000,000 to 26,000,000 bushels a year. Since the Minnesota interest in apple culture has been mentioned in an earlier chapter, one should note that the apple crop of the state in 1961 was about 370,000 bushels.

As has been suggested, no view of the state farm picture can fail to take cognizance of regional differences — south, north, east, west. Census statistics may seem to some people to imply an even spread of products, though of course they are not so intended. One must remember, however, that Minnesota is prairies, forests, rivers, waterfalls, valleys, lakes, rolling country, iron ore, beds of glacial lakes, and differing temperatures, soil, and conditions that foster the growth of the soil. The state is no smooth table of farms and towns (or of statistics).

The southwestern and southeastern counties are alike in certain respects, notably in the predilection of the farmers for corn, oats, cattle, hogs, and soybeans. But the two areas are different in the problems they pose. The southwest is flat prairie country, with good sandy soil, whereas to the southeast are river valleys, hills, rolling country, rich soils. In the southeast the unevenness of the land has necessitated conservation, brush coverage of steep terrains to stay erosion, contour and strip cropping, and carefully planned scientific rotation.

The level southwest is the chief area for cattle, hogs, and corn, and soybeans are the main cash crop. But the southeast is also strong in cattle and hogs and it has the stimulus of proximity to the South St. Paul and Austin meat-packing plants. Both regions are rich in farming traditions. The southeast was first settled by farmers in the late 1840s and the 1850s. The southwest had its pioneering later when caravans of covered wagons, with settlers unafraid of the prairie lands, moved across the southern edge of the state in scenes that were later exploited by both novelists and historians.

Important for farming through more than a century, the southeastern counties comprise about a tenth of Minnesota but produce a fourth of its crops. They are noted, apart from their corn, cattle, and hog industry, for poultry, dairying, egg production, cheese making, truck gardening, and thriving apple orchards. Southeast and southwest, though dotted with cities, towns, and villages, and subject to ceaseless urban influences, are still in essence agricultural.

From northwestern Minnesota down and across the state north of the bending Minnesota River and reaching to the Wisconsin border on the east lies a broad stretch of lands of diverse geographical conditions and use, with many cities as marketing, industrial, and cultural centers. Much of Minnesota's agricultural strength is derived from these interrelated but differing regions.

The northwestern counties are part of the rich bottom of Glacial Lake Agassiz — the Minnesota side of the Red River Valley. Here wheat had its golden era as settlers swarmed onto the open lands. The valley has been farmed with persistent energy ever since the post-Civil War generation. The Red River country, as has been noted, was favored by Scandinavian, especially Norwegian, settlers who turned first to wheat and raised mighty crops before shifting into diversified farming. Spring wheat is still grown in considerable quantity in the valley, but it has yielded primacy to sugar beets. The region is also famed for its potatoes, which constitute approximately two-thirds of the entire state potato crop.

Unlike the corn and cattle country to the south and east, the Red River Valley, with its relatively short growing season, is predominantly a cash crop region. The growing of the beets is under supervision and control by companies managing the sugar industry, which has large establishments in the bustling nearby cities of Crookston, Moorhead, and East Grand Forks; and the potato industry has attracted "big farmers" — owners of extensive farm lands. Modern machinery and methods are used in harvesting and preparing the potatoes for marketing. In East Grand Forks alone there are some forty potato warehouses.

The Red River Valley has traveled the road of diversification, with specializations adjusted to its soil and seasons. This is not to say that the valley farms are restricted to sugar beets, wheat, and potatoes. They also produce flax — once a very important crop — as well as barley and, in the southern reaches of the valley, soybeans. But the region is not one of beef cattle or dairy farming on a large scale.

To the east is a solid block of central counties extending northward from the line of the Minnesota River as far as Otter Tail, Wadena, Cass, and Crow Wing counties and including a long and winding stretch of the Mississippi. In this area are lakes of perennial interest to tourists. It also includes many towns that figure prominently in the state's history — Sauk Centre of *Main Street* fame; Little Falls, where Colonel Lindbergh once lived; St. Peter, home city of one territorial and four state governors; the granite city of St. Cloud; the vacation (and runestone) town of Alexandria; and the market city of Willmar, noted for its turkey industry (and its devotion to afternoon coffee).

With all the specialties of the region in manufactures, plus its historical distinction, it still is fundamentally agricultural. No single crop dominates the scene, however. The prairie area is strong in livestock; dairying is important in the lake regions, and especially in Stearns County; butter, dried milk, cream, poultry, and eggs contribute to the prosperity of the farmers in much of the area; the raising of hogs is a significant industry; and in many communities corn, alfalfa, oats, soybeans, and vegetables are produced in quantity. In a word, the central region is vigorously agricultural, its varied products depending upon local conditions, nearness of markets, and other factors.

Farther to the east are a half dozen counties near or bordering upon the Wisconsin boundary. Some of these, notably Washington County, are famed in early and later Minnesota farming, with rich, rolling lands adjacent to rivers and streams. It is estimated that about 90 per cent of Washington County lends itself to profitable field-crop use. But the eastern section also includes old pine country, cutover areas not easy to clear for fields. The area as a whole, because of the quick transportation available to the Twin Cities, finds vegetable growing profitable. The Askov community (in Pine County) specializes in rutabagas, but most of the crop is sent to the South or to concerns in Chicago or its vicinity. Washington County contributes heavily to the state's apple production. Rivers, woods, and terrain give the region distinctive natural beauty, and much of the nonagricultural land has been turned into state forests and parks or hunting and fishing tracts. The unsightly cutover tracts are gradually being reforested, repairing the scars left by the lumber industry.

Minnesota lands to the north and northeast — the old forested areas, the mining country, the domain of the voyageurs, the north shore of Lake Superior — have been described by Lowry Nelson as the state's "rural problem area." His special interest centered in the difficulties of farmers (and part-time farmers) in cultivating the land, but he recognized the fact that much of this region is not farming land at all. No part of Minnesota, he wrote, "has a history which is garlanded with more romance or enlivened by greater adventure." He took due account of the beauty of the north country, its wild life, mines, modern paper mills, shipping, and the fact that every summer "tens of thousands of people" go north for rest and recreation. The region is one of parks and forests managed as a resource for the people.

Agriculture in the north country has been minor and unduly laborious, however. Farming has indeed been tried. Some farmers have remained long on their rugged lands. Many have combined farming with work in mines or woods. But the number of farms has declined, farm profits have been modest, and farm living standards have been meager.

If northern farming conditions contrast unfavorably with those in the lush acres of southern, western, and central Minnesota, the Emersonian law of compensation seems to operate. There are compensatory values to state and country in northern nature, with all its resources. Consolation there is also in the assurance that Americans are concerned about retaining for posterity some part of the primeval life woven into the natural history of the lands and waters of the north country.

St. Paul capitol approach in 1960

MINNESOTA STATE HIGHWAY DEPARTMENT

Social Currents, Politics, and Problems

THE contrasts of sections of Minnesota, the changing fruits of its soil, and the specialties of communities furnish clues to economic interests of recent years. They do not shed much light, however, on the social forces that have altered the pattern of rural — and urban — living. They do not explain what a perceptive sociologist has called the "desegregation" of farm and town.

The industries of both the larger and the smaller towns, making capital of the productivity of nearby farms, have forwarded cooperation and, in some instances, partnerships between country folk and town people. Thousands of farmers near urban centers, large or small, have identified themselves with urban trade and the social and cultural interests of the cities.

Such trends supply only part of the answer to the riddle of social change. One must go beyond them to other potent forces, including the modernizing of communication. This has had a pervasive influence on rural-town desegregation. The telephone has become nearly as universal in country districts as in towns — and its development in Minnesota is another version of the saga of small beginnings leading to great growth. Its backgrounds are both national and local. More than one man experimented with transmission of the voice by wire, but it was Alexander Graham Bell's invention that was patented in 1876 and exhibited to a curious public at the centennial exposition in Philadelphia. In Minnesota as early

571

as 1877 a telegrapher and former Civil War soldier, Richard H. Hankinson, after experimenting with a single line, found that it worked. And so he built the first Minnesota switchboard, placing it in the Minneapolis City Hall. It was a crude affair, set on an old sewing machine table, but through it he reached eleven telephones. This was the beginning. The invention was considered a luxury for the few, but Hankinson believed that it would become the handy servant of all — a dream that came true.

Telephone exchanges were built in Minneapolis and St. Paul in 1879 and in Duluth two years later. Hankinson took the lead in incorporating the Northwestern Telephone Exchange Company. Telephones spread rapidly; hundreds of small companies were formed; but in this field, as in many others, consolidations were effected. The Northwestern Bell Telephone Company emerged as the giant of the business in Minnesota and became itself a subsidiary of a greater giant — the American Telephone and Telegraph Company.

By the early 1960s much of the telephone business in the state was under the control of the Northwestern, and the number of telephones had mounted to more than a million. Invention kept pace with growth. Automatic telephones were everywhere. Fantastic improvements in speed of service and technical efficiency were climaxed by direct dialing to homes and offices in distant cities. The telephone brought together farm and farm as well as farm and town. It was a major force in breaking down isolation in rural areas and in promoting business and social contacts everywhere.

The spread of the radio became statewide soon after the early experimental years of earphones. Networks began in 1925. By the late 1950s the radio was very nearly universal in farm as well as city and town homes. And by 1960 sixty-five stations were located in more than fifty Minnesota towns and cities. From 1948, when the first Minnesota television station was established, this means of communication by word and scene had wide acceptance. Television stations to the number of ten, including one wholly devoted to educational programs, engaged in regular broadcasting. If radio coverage reached nearly all farm homes, television sets were in one-third of them, perhaps more. News, entertainment, sports, and advertising, and the educational and cultural programs of radio and television stations poured into homes in country and town alike.

Since 1849 the newspaper press has played a major role in the life of

Minnesota Territory and State. The beginnings, in the ebullient and combative James M. Goodhue's *Minnesota Pioneer*, were followed by an expansion that kept step — and more than step — with the rise of population. It is no exaggeration to say that newspapers have been Minnesota's most important medium of general communication through more than eleven decades.

By a process of competition and consolidation, influential daily (and Sunday) papers were developed in the Twin Cities and Duluth. But many of the smaller cities — including Winona, St. Cloud, Rochester, Mankato, Stillwater, and New Ulm — have long had daily newspapers of their own. Buttressing the daily papers have been hundreds of weeklies — a veritable statewide press. The early years of the twentieth century witnessed a cascade of approximately 700 newspapers in Minnesota, most of them weekly, devoted to little communities and their nearby farmer constituencies.

Through many years Minnesota's immigrant press continued to have vitality, with some excellent daily newspapers such as the *Svenska Amerikanska Posten* (Swedish-American Post), edited by Swan J. Turnblad, the *Budstikken* (Messenger), and the *Minneapolis Daglige Tidende* (Daily Times), the latter under the editorship of Carl G. O. Hansen. Such newspapers fell away as the second, third, and fourth generations succeeded the immigrants, and in recent years the number of foreign-language papers has dwindled to only a very few. Some were merged with weekly or semiweekly papers in other states, of which a few remain. At their best the immigrant newspapers presented, in addition to local news of special interest to their constituencies, reports from Europe that were more detailed and informing than those in the state press generally.

The metropolitan newspapers — in recent years the *Minneapolis Star* and *Tribune*, the *St. Paul Pioneer Press* and *Dispatch*, and the *Duluth News-Tribune* — have reached into the corners of the state and even beyond its borders, particularly with their Sunday issues. The chronicle of the press is one of many papers that no longer are published, of faded dreams and broken ambitions, of combinations, changes of names, and shifts in editorial and business management. Two trends are noteworthy. The number of newspapers has been much reduced, and there are now some 400 or so papers as compared with the much larger number a half century ago. And in the large cities ownership has tended to concentrate in one person or group (for each city).

573

Major newspapers of the present have great magnitude in capital, plant, staff, the scope of news services, and circulation. Competition is virtually ruled out. However excellent the news reporting, such control results in an absence of contending points of view on economic and political issues. This is the more noticeable since the clash of policy and opinion was traditional in city newspapers in earlier Minnesota journalism.

The American talent for organization, often emphasized in this narrative, found expression in the journalistic field. A league of editors and publishers has been the Minnesota Editorial Association (newly renamed the Minnesota Newspaper Association), directed through recent decades by Ralph W. Keller. It has dealt with problems of modern journalism, urban and rural, and among many services it has promoted professional interest and journalistic education through courses arranged at the university's School of Journalism and also in its Department of Agriculture.

No quick survey can encompass the reach and breadth of the newspapers of the state — their multiform service and their leadership in business and in public education. It may fairly be said that the people of Minnesota have had an enterprising and informing press through all the years since the day of Goodhue. Time has wrought changes. Other media of communication, emerging from man's inventiveness, have challenged the press as a purveyor of news, a forum of opinion, a protagonist of causes. But the press has been and now is one of the powerful social and cultural institutions of Minnesota.

Other circumstances eased rural isolation and flavored the amenities of farm life. The consolidated schools, the problems of township government, the management of school districts, and legislative, congressional, and gubernatorial politics — all these were areas beyond the fences of the farms. And the automobile, buses, and trucks spelled a mobility that contrasted dramatically with the slow-moving transportation of earlier days. Old farmers sometimes shook their heads sadly and predicted that the horse would come back. But the horse did not come back. The car meant quick trips to town and easy conveyance to neighbors. Even for those living far from the Twin Cities or Duluth it made journeys for pleasure and business in the big centers a commonplace — a routine kind of excursion. Sometimes whole communities would crowd into cars and buses to spend an afternoon or evening watching the Minnesota Twins play baseball or the Gophers play football. Shopping in the metropolitan centers was an occasional experience for many, and from both farms and villages large numbers departed for the lakes or the north shore or state parks or distant states.

In other respects rural living kept abreast of the advances in communication and transportation. Farm houses were modernized. After World War II, Minnesota farmers did not plunge their surplus moneys into additional land, as many had done after World War I. Instead, they improved their houses and conveniences. As late as 1940, notwithstanding the Rural Electrification Administration set in motion under Roosevelt in 1935, less than one-third of the Minnesota farms were equipped with electricity, whereas by the mid-1950s electrification had become nearly universal. This led to other changes: radios and television, modernized plumbing, refrigerators, freezers, and electric lighting of houses and barns.

The total scene reveals a swift lessening of old disparities between living in town and living on the farm. The traditional dichotomy of the two, emphasized in decennial statistics which separate rural and urban figures, was disappearing or at least losing some of its old-time relevance. As country life to some degree merged with that of town and city, city people took advantage of modern mobility to extend their experiences into the country. This was by no means a matter only of excursions or outings. In many rather large areas, beyond the borders of cities and of suburbs, urban people made homes for themselves — a phase of contemporary life not reflected in the usual statistics for town and country. As a consequence, not only the Twin Cities and Duluth, but many other cities and towns of smaller size, such as St. Cloud and Rochester, have been extended in actual fact — though not in terms of their municipal boundaries — many miles into rural districts. This has meant an increasing nonfarm population in farming country. Thanks to the automobile these urban-country families are within easy reach of the cities and towns. Normally jobs and professional work are less than an hour away.

This kind of urban spread is important in the relationships of town and country and may have significance for public policy in the future, educational and otherwise. But one must not carry generalizations too far — the farmers still farm their lands, and the essentially urban folk, unless living in retirement in country homes, still are, for the most part, townsmen in their business.

Other institutions and activities played roles in changing the character of country as well as city life. Social historians find that whereas the churches declined in number, church membership increased measurably. A generation ago about two-fifths of the Minnesota population held church membership, whereas by the mid-1950s such membership had increased to somewhere between 50 and 60 per cent. Actually, in the half century from 1906 to 1956, the number of churches declined from 4721 to 4343 — that is, a drop of 378. The explanation in part is that the divisive theological controversies of an earlier day were mitigated in various synods and other church bodies. There were tendencies in the direction of cooperation, merger, and a new spirit of toleration. This was notable among the Lutherans of Scandinavian backgrounds, who once had been much divided. During the past generation, they have unified their activities to a very considerable extent.

Travelers in Minnesota today will see, in town and country, hundreds of churches representing virtually all denominations. In their religious and social activities they are an integral part of the life of the state. Figures for 1956 indicate that at that time, 60 per cent of the Minnesota churchgoers were Protestant, 37 per cent Catholic, and 3 per cent (or a little less) Jewish. The influence of churches is beyond computation in statistics or appraisal in dependable generalizations, but they have played and today play a major role in the integration of the social life of the people, in the maintenance of traditional faiths, and in their interpretation of these faiths to the people in a new age of state and world.

Amid economic and social change, Minnesota in the 1950s was also the scene of another political turn. The Republican party had held the governorship without a break from 1939 to 1955. On the national front Minnesota Democrats and the Farmer-Labor party, from Olson's day onward, had generally supported Democrats for the presidency, and the Democratic tickets carried the state in five national elections beginning in 1932.

In the state arena, however, the Farmer-Labor party and the Democrats had each offered candidates for governor in twelve of the thirteen elections from 1918 to 1942 inclusive, notwithstanding some efforts to bring about a fusion. A commentator on the state party situation in the 1950s suggests that fusion presented difficulties because the Democrats, with their long traditions, had their major strongholds in urban centers such as St. Paul, Duluth, and St. Cloud. Their leaders, predominantly from the upper middle class, were at first reluctant to identify themselves with the more definitely liberal leadership of the Farmer-Labor party. That party had no little strength in the western rural areas and among workers in mines and factories. Another political factor, as has been indicated, was dissension and turmoil within the Farmer-Labor group during and following the Benson regime.

Toward the end of World War II, a fusion of the two parties was accomplished and soon thereafter there was a sharp intraparty struggle that eventuated in the pushing out of the more radical Benson wing. In this period new Democratic-Farmer-Labor leadership emerged in such personalities as Hubert H. Humphrey, Orville L. Freeman, Eugenie Anderson, Eugene J. McCarthy, Arthur E. Naftalin, Karl F. Rolvaag, and John A. Blatnik. Of the seven persons mentioned, one was eight years old when the United States entered World War I, two were six, one was four, one was a year old, one was born the year America entered the war, and one during the year the war ended. Thus they were as a group a "younger generation" — people whose ages as World War II came to an end ranged from twenty-seven to thirty-six. One sees a parallel in some respects with the rise of Stassen and the "young Republicans" in the 1930s.

These leaders and others joined in a determined move to unite Democrats and Farmer-Laborites. They took part in party organization and activity, in speaking, and in mobilizing popular support. Humphrey, a native of South Dakota, a pharmacist, scholar, college teacher, and politician, was the chief architect of the fusion. He realized, as did his followers, that if Democrats and Farmer-Laborites could present a united front, their chances of winning state elections would be enhanced. He also understood that, although the agrarian movement through many decades had encouraged political independence in Minnesota, the Republican traditions of the state were deep and strong, and that — even after fusion — victory at the polls was not likely to be immediate. And it was not. From Sibley's election as the first governor of Minnesota (before the Civil War) up to and including the election of 1952, the voters cast their ballots for governor in forty-eight successive elections and in thirty-eight of these Republicans triumphed. In the other ten elections Democrats won six times and Farmer-Labor candidates four times. Three of the six Democratic victories were won by one man, John A. Johnson, and three of the four Farmer-Labor victories by one man, Floyd B. Olson. In the early 1950s, however, Humphrey and his supporters probably looked less at the political panorama of nearly ninety years than at the eight state elections from 1938 to 1952. All these were carried decisively by the Republicans.

A man of versatile talents, a liberal, and a hard-hitting and rapid-fire speaker, Humphrey had tried, and failed, to win the position of mayor of Minneapolis in 1943. The next year he played a large role in the convention that united the two parties, and he managed the Democratic campaign in Minnesota for Roosevelt. With this background, he was elected mayor of Minneapolis in 1945 and served in that office until, in 1948, he was chosen senator.

Freeman, Minneapolis-born, a university graduate in arts and law, and a battle-tested veteran of the Marines in World War II, was an assistant to Humphrey in the mayor's office and an organizer for the fused party, of which he became state chairman. Effective in debate and a tough fighter for the party of his choice, he was chosen to run for governor in 1952. In that election he lost by a wide margin to Governor C. Elmer Anderson, but he ran again in 1954 and this time defeated Anderson by some 68,000 votes. Twice re-elected, he served as governor for six years.

Most of Humphrey's colleagues in the movement to unify the party went on to public office. Eugenie Anderson, active in many humane and political causes and in 1955 appointed chairman of the State Fair Employment Practices Commission, was chosen by President Truman to be United States ambassador to Denmark and served in that capacity from 1949 to 1953 — the first American woman to hold the rank of ambassador (and in 1962 she was appointed minister to Bulgaria). McCarthy, a man of university education, who had taught economics and sociology at St. Thomas College, after ten years of service as congressman from St. Paul was elected to the United States Senate in 1958. Rolvaag was lieutenant governor with Freeman through his three terms and then was re-elected again under a Republican governor. In 1962 he was chosen by his party to run for governor. Naftalin, a university-trained expert in political science, became the state's commissioner of administration under Freeman and thereafter was elected mayor of Minneapolis. Blatnik went to Congress in 1947. Humphrey himself, after unseating Joseph H. Ball in the election of 1948, twice has been re-elected to the United States Senate.

Freeman, as he assumed office in 1955, gave special emphasis to the world crisis, the cold war, and the responsibilities of Minnesota as an integral part of the nation. For the state he described four basic goals that were strikingly reminiscent of the four "broad but compelling objectives"

PHOTO BY DON BERG

The skylines of Minneapolis (above) and St. Paul

PHOTO BY ROBERT I. WARD

The Round Tower at Fort Snelling

The Sibley House at Mendota

The Lake Superior port of Duluth

Main Street, Sauk Centre

A modern Minnesota farm

Contour farming in Minnesota

that Youngdahl had advanced in 1947 — maximum development of human resources, "enhancement and conservation" of natural resources, an expanding economy, and efficiency in government. On human resources he underlined the importance of education in its range from primary and secondary schools to colleges and the university. He spoke of a welfare program, rehabilitation, the problems of older citizens, improvement in workmen's compensation, and fairness to minority groups. As to natural resources he stressed the need of a long-range program and the best scientific advice available. Business activity, farm prosperity, expanding payrolls, and a favorable "tax climate" were elements in his concept of an expanding economy. And on government, he asked for further administrative reorganization, study of the report of what was known as the "Little Hoover Commission," constitutional revision, legislative reapportionment, and the resumption of party designation in candidacies for the legislature.

In Freeman's second and third inaugural addresses (1957 and 1959) he returned to the goals that had seemed of major importance to him as he began. As a means of achieving them, he turned more and more to committees, commissions, conferences, and surveys to ascertain facts and clarify issues, and he called on citizens and professional experts for such services. An interim building commission; a committee to study and analyze the evolution of the state's tax policies; a vast self-survey of the state's governmental functions and operations (conducted under the leadership of Naftalin); studies of governmental ethics, consumer credit, even atomic-energy problems; and conferences on aging, higher education, youth, and retarded and gifted children — all these fitted into his conception of executive policy.

A Fair Employment Practices Law was passed in 1955. It embodied concepts that Humphrey had tried out as mayor of Minneapolis when he established a city Fair Employment Practices Commission. It also harked back to a proposal which Youngdahl had specifically recommended in his second inaugural address (1949) and had in effect endorsed in 1947, when he urged legislation to eliminate discrimination. The state law of 1955 was one for which many citizens had worked. It was designed to protect employment "regardless of race, color, creed, religion or national origin." To forward compliance with the law, a state commission of nine members was established, with appointment by the governor. The purposes underlying the act were not unrelated to those of the Human

Rights Commission, set up by Governor Thye through executive order, though that commission gave its primary attention to intergroup relations, housing, and citizenship rights.

A Water Resources Board, also authorized in 1955, has jurisdiction over watershed districts and concerns itself generally with state water policy and conservation. The federal Social Security system was extended to state and local governmental employees, and various benefits (old-age assistance, unemployment insurance, and workmen's compensation) were increased.

As governmental costs mounted, many additional taxes, including surtaxes on incomes and iron ore, were authorized in order to meet budgets. Among other items one may note that in 1957 a Seaway Port Authority Commission was established; state aid was given to the junior colleges; and a Korean bonus was authorized.

In this period the state's judicial system underwent some change. This was initiated by the legislature in 1955, and the next year the voters approved an amendment to Article VI of the state constitution — the most extensive revision of the basic formulation of the judiciary system since the adoption of the constitution.

When statehood was achieved in 1858, an orthodox court system was established under the constitution. It was headed by a supreme court (composed at first of Chief Justice Lafayette Emmett, an Ohio-born lawyer who had served as attorney-general of Minnesota Territory, and Associate Justices Charles E. Flandrau and Isaac Atwater, the latter a graduate of Yale College). With the rapid growth of Minnesota, it was found necessary in 1875 to remove constitutional restrictions on the number of state judicial districts and district judges, but not until 1930 was the number of associate justices on the supreme court increased to six from the maximum of four originally specified in the constitution. It is of interest to note that during the state's first forty-five years the federal district court system was represented in Minnesota by only one judge. Through thirty-eight of those years the incumbent was Rensselaer R. Nelson. A native of New York, he, like Atwater, was a graduate of Yale. He came to St. Paul in 1850, and in 1857 he was appointed a territorial judge by President Buchanan. Since 1891 Minnesota has been part of the Eighth Judicial Circuit served by a United States Court of Appeals.

The Minnesota constitution had authorized, in addition to the supreme and state district courts, a system of probate courts and justices of the peace. The constitutional amendment of 1956 provided for a reorganization of the state judicial system and even further reorganization when, in the judgment of the state legislature, it should be needed. One matter of dispute for some years concerned the justices of the peace, the officers of the lowest state courts. They received no regular salary, and since they were compensated by fees derived from cases brought before them, charges of abuses and inequities were not infrequently made. Under the revision of Article VI the justices of the peace are not specified as part of the state court system, and the legislature has authority to continue or abolish the office. In recent years one proposed reform has been that of requiring legal training as one of the qualifications for justice of the peace.

The state has ten judicial districts, and the chief judge of the supreme court is now required to supervise and coordinate the work of the courts in these districts. Nearly sixty district judges function, and each of the ten districts has a chief judge who coordinates the business of the courts in his area.

In response to the complexities of an increasing body of laws and the range of problems confronting the courts, including newer kinds of litigation, studies and proposals have been made in recent years looking toward further changes in the court system to improve and strengthen its effectiveness.

A new departure in state government during this period was an act passed in a special legislative session in 1958 authorizing the elongation of the terms of state executive officers (governor, lieutenant governor; secretary of state, treasurer, and attorney-general) from two to four years (the term of the other state executive officer, auditor, had been extended to four years in 1883). It was accepted by the voters on November 4, 1958, to take effect from and after the state elections of 1962. In 1959 the old question of a legislative reapportionment was again debated. As early as 1947 Governor Youngdahl had insisted that reapportionment was a legislative obligation — as indeed it was, for the state constitution requires it after each ten-year census. But legislators through the years had been unwilling to make changes in legislative districting as set up in 1913, and they blandly ignored the constitution. Now, in 1959, action was taken that looked to changes effective in 1962 based on close to a half century of population growth and of shifts in the relative proportions of rural and urban inhabitants.

Minnesotans through long experience were schooled in political turbulence, and it was not lacking in the 1950s. At the national level the popular Dwight D. Eisenhower had carried the state by a large majority over Adlai E. Stevenson in 1952. Four years later differences of opinion developed within state Democratic-Farmer-Labor circles with respect to the renomination of Stevenson — Freeman and Humphrey both supporting Stevenson, while another faction gave its support to Estes Kefauver of Tennessee, who in the primary campaign captured a majority of the state's district delegates to the national nominating convention. In the election that followed President Eisenhower once more carried Minnesota — his majority exceeding 100,000 votes. That voting preferences in the state do not necessarily follow the pattern of presidential choice was evidenced in the same election when Freeman won the governorship again, with a margin of some 45,000 votes over his Republican opponent.

The third term of Freeman (1959–61) was shadowed by economic and labor troubles, and he was the object of much criticism. The production of iron ore declined drastically in 1959 under the impact of a disastrous steel strike. Thousands of workers were unemployed, and state taxes on ore fell by about $18,000,000. Other strikes also darkened the state scene — one in the transit company serving the Twin Cities and another (and concurrently a lockout) in the Minneapolis grocery stores. But the one producing the widest political repercussions and the sharpest attacks on Freeman was a strike of packing-house workers in the city of Albert Lea. It began early in November. In December the governor, believing that the troubles would endanger human life, declared martial law, ordered national guardsmen to the scene, and closed the plant. Less than two weeks after these events, a federal court condemned the governor's action and ordered the packing plant reopened. A few days thereafter martial law came to an end. The administration of the governor also came under criticism following revelation of certain irregularities at the Stillwater state prison. The prison and its wardens had been in the newspaper headlines periodically during the 1950s, notably during a short-lived prison riot in 1953. In 1960 controversy over commissary withdrawals at the prison (as well as at some other state institutions) received wide publicity and added to Freeman's troubles.

Governor Freeman ran for a fourth term in 1960, but in this campaign he lost to the Republican candidate, Elmer L. Andersen of St. Paul. The shifting tides of politics find apt illustration in a comparison of 1956 with 1960. In 1956 Minnesotans gave their support to a Republican for President while re-electing a Democratic-Farmer-Labor governor, whereas in 1960 the state supported the election of a Democratic President while choosing a Republican governor. Andersen carried the state with a margin of 22,879 over Freeman while John F. Kennedy won the state's electoral votes by 22,018 over Richard M. Nixon.

Freeman was thereafter appointed secretary of agriculture in President Kennedy's Cabinet. Humphrey continued his senatorial career after challenging Kennedy unsuccessfully for the Democratic nomination for President in the primary elections. Minnesotans played important roles in both parties in the closely contested presidential election — Congressman Walter H. Judd of Minneapolis as the eloquent keynote speaker in the Republican convention and Governor Freeman and Senators McCarthy and Humphrey as influential figures (and speakers) in the Democratic convention.

Governor Elmer L. Andersen, a man of broad and humane interests and extensive experience in business and state affairs, took office in 1961. A native of Chicago, he was educated in Michigan schools and the University of Minnesota. He had taken a prominent part in civic activities and for more than a decade (1949–58) had been a member of the state Senate. By his own choice he did not run for re-election to the Senate in 1959.

In his inaugural address (January 4, 1961) Governor Andersen reviewed the needs and problems of the state. He gave attention to Minnesota's agricultural economy and the importance of continuing research in this field. He was concerned about industrial expansion, iron-ore production, forestry, and the tourist industry. Like many of his predecessors, he emphasized education, conservation, and the modern highway system; and he urged the adoption of measures to promote traffic safety. On the front of social welfare he asked for increased personnel in mental hospitals, intensification of short-time corrective care, even a new department of mental health. For the aged and disabled, he favored removal of maximum relief rates; and in the light of a scandal affecting the highly regarded Elizabeth Kenny Rehabilitation Institute, he recommended corrective legislation, including the filing of detailed accountings of funds by such institutions with the state's attorney-general. The governor gave support to human rights and emphasized housing, employment, civil liberties, and the needs of minorities, including the Indians, whose many and distressing problems and troubles had been the subject of several governmental studies, notably one by Governor Youngdahl's Interracial Commission in 1947.

The governor commended the Metropolitan Planning Commission (established in 1957). This commission was created by legislative action during the Freeman administration to forward understanding of the problems of the metropolitan area centered in the Twin Cities (Hennepin, Ramsey, Washington, Anoka, and Dakota counties — later Scott and Carver counties as well). The commission's range of interest included housing, water supply, transportation, sewers and drainage, health and safety, and land for industrial uses; recently it has given somewhat special attention to sewers. Governor Andersen advocated water and transportation studies and a review of public-utility regulation in the Twin City area; and he recommended the establishment by both houses of the legislature of committees on metropolitan affairs.

The legislative sessions of 1961, true to Minnesota political tradition, were stormy, with clashes between the conservatives, controlling the Senate, and the liberals, who had a majority in the House. Notwithstanding the absence of party labels in legislative elections, the cleavage generally implied a tug of war between Republicans and Democratic-Farmer-Labor adherents. There were scrambles for advantage, delays, and compromises, but not a few significant acts were passed and approved by the governor.

A tax change of major character was the establishment in 1961 of a system of "withholding" for the collection of the state income tax, a matter that had been before the legislature and the public for several years. The appropriations required for state expenditures resulted in a budget of $567,000,000 for the biennium 1961–63, the largest in the history of Minnesota. Within this total, education received $366,000,000, welfare $130,000,000, and buildings $33,000,000. Additional surtaxes and various other increases were employed to reach the needed budget sums. A move for a 3 per cent sales tax, strongly supported by the Minnesota Taxpayers Association and the Minnesota Farm Bureau, was defeated. No little public interest centered in three constitutional amendments passed by the legislature for ratification or rejection by the voters in November 1962. One of these was intended to open the way to investment of state funds in corporate securities as well as in government bonds. A second was aimed at setting aside a provision of the state constitution for a limitation of $250,000 on the aggregate state debt — a pioneer precaution that was thoroughly unrealistic in the light of modern conditions and had been evaded by the device of short-term certificate borrowing. The fate of future state building operations hinged upon the success of this amendment. The third proposed amendment concerned extending the regular session of the legislature from 90 to 120 days, a reform believed to be needed in the light of the increase of legislative business and the frequent necessity, under the earlier limitation, of special sessions. Alongside legislative approval of these amendments went a rejection of another proposed amendment intended to give assurance to the taconite industry that its taxes in the future would not be put above the levels applied to other manufacturing industries, though the legislature adopted a resolution of fair intent and urged future legislatures to deal fairly with the new industry of the north.

Neither the regular legislative session nor a special session that immediately followed it came to grips with the redistricting of Minnesota's congressional districts from nine to eight in consequence of the census of 1960. A reapportionment was finally worked out, however, in a second special session of two days called by Governor Andersen late in December.

Among other actions taken by the legislature and approved by the governor may be noted a statewide sanitary act authorizing two or more communities to cooperate in a sanitary district designed to meet their needs; a somewhat similar measure looking to cooperation of communities in fire and police protection; an "ethics-in-government" measure; an act extending the principle of fair employment to housing and forbidding the application of tests of race, national origin, or creed to those seeking to rent or purchase housing facilities.

Some advance was made in relation to traffic safety, notably through a so-called implied consent law, which authorized the forfeiture of driving licenses by drivers suspected of drunkenness who refuse to take an alcohol test. Several other proposed driving reforms were defeated, however, including one for the mandatory use of safety belts.

The election of 1962 was less noteworthy for its party issues and debates than for an almost even split in the statewide vote for governor. It was the closest election in the history of the state, and the indecisive initial outcome offered a test to the resourcefulness and common sense of a democratic people. The question was how to settle a political contest involving a difference in votes of a fraction of one per cent in a grand vote total of nearly a million and a quarter. Because of the dramatic test thus imposed, the election and the recount procedures that followed it warrant analysis in some detail.

The campaign was one of *outs* versus *ins,* or of *ins* versus *outs* — a struggle for power, with the Republican party endorsing and supporting Governor Andersen, and the Democratic-Farmer-Labor party, headed by Karl F. Rolvaag, attempting to unseat the incumbent, each documenting its policies with a detailed platform.

Each party of course wanted to win. It was a political fight, but one cannot review the platforms without realizing that both parties were earnestly concerned about the progress of the state. Both pledged support of agriculture, education, civil rights, labor, conservation, mental health and public welfare, highway development and improvement, road safety measures, law enforcement, amelioration of the distress of the Indians, aid to senior citizens, metropolitan planning, party designation in legislative elections, encouragement of the taconite industry, and the three constitutional amendments put before the electorate by the 1961 legislature. The DFL expressed its conviction that the "processes of government can be used to pursue a goal of continuing progress for the American people in science and the arts, in technology and in industry, in the improvement of our cities, farms and rural communities." The Republicans called for "expansion of opportunity, the creation of more jobs, the development of human and natural resources, the maintenance of a healthy climate for agriculture, business, and labor, and continuing adaptability to our changing times."

The platforms voiced a common concern for state progress and proposed not a few similar solutions of problems, but they were by no means identical, especially in their formulation of detail and in their political tone. The Republicans gave applause and commendation to the administration of Governor Andersen, whereas the DFL belabored the "timid conservatism" of the Republicans. The DFL asked for a "resources development agency" with a long-range program; the Republicans suggested expanding the business development department into one of "business and job development." The Republicans supported measures to improve "opportunities and economic conditions of all working people in Minnesota" and proposed adjustments in unemployment compensation. The DFL spelled out many details in a program for labor, including commitment to the principle of a minimum wage law calling for at least $1.25 per hour. The DFL urged the strengthening of farm credit programs, encouragement of cooperatives, and use of lands not needed in farming for recreation and wildlife, while the Republicans called for more market research and various other advances in the interest of agriculture. The Republicans wanted to improve the state's health program, give additional scope to the governor's council on aging, and promote low-cost housing, while the DFL called for hospital and nursing care for older citizens under the social security system — and also for the removal of the ceiling of $71 per month for recipients of old-age assistance. As to conservation, the DFL favored a ten-year "action program" for statewide management; the Republicans supported the governor's Minnesota Natural Resources Council and described it as "the first statewide natural resource development organization in America." On the question of taconite and its future, the Republicans gave their support to the earlier proposed taconite amendment, whereas the DFL endorsed "fair and equitable tax treatment to the taconite and other types of ore processing industries, by the legislative process" — without a constitutional amendment.

The campaign was spirited. It employed the full panoply of modern electioneering — speeches by candidates throughout the state, pamphlets, newspaper advertisements, television and radio, signs, placards, stickers on cars. The issues were probed, and charges, replies, and countercharges were made. DFL spokesmen emphasized the need of new leadership, as they believed, and their opponents upheld the governor's record. In the midst of the campaign the momentous Cuban crisis occurred and problems of national magnitude overshadowed the political struggle in the state, but as the President and the nation surmounted the international crisis, the Minnesota contest again claimed the major interest of voters. The leaders of both state parties had promptly given assurance to President Kennedy of their support of the United States in the face of international danger, and the influence, if any, of the Cuban crisis on the home election was impossible to appraise. Late in the campaign, DFL spokesmen made charges of improper construction procedures on a northern state highway. Indignant denials followed and there was a flurry of criticism, reply, and emotion. Thoroughgoing investigations obviously could not be completed until after the election, and the impact of the charges, one way or another, on the vote eluded objective measurement. Post-election state and federal findings with respect to the issue disclosed a few defects of a kind regularly checked and corrected by routine inspections. An influential state newspaper commented on the matter in an editorial entitled "Deflated Charges," while some DFL leaders still insisted that their allegations of "irregularities" had been sustained.

When the votes were counted, after November 6, it was found that all three of the constitutional amendments had been carried. DFL candidates were elected to three state offices, lieutenant governor (A. M. Keith), attorney-general (Walter F. Mondale), and secretary of state (Joseph L. Donovan), while Republicans were elected to two offices, state auditor (Stafford King) and state treasurer (Val Bjornson). The election resulted in a conservative majority in both House and Senate. In an upset, the oft-elected Republican congressman Dr. Judd was defeated in the Fifth Minnesota District by the DFL candidate, Donald M. Fraser.

Meanwhile, as votes were slowly tabulated, it was evident that the contest for the governorship probably would end in a virtual tie. Not until November 29 did the state canvassing board report Governor Andersen as the winner by 142 votes — 619,722 to Rolvaag's 619,580 (a third candidate, William Braatz, of the "Industrial Government" party, polled 7234 votes). The board's report was made only after intervention by the state supreme court, a move necessitated by a deadlock of the board over the issue of whether or not to accept amended returns submitted from ten counties. It had voted two for and two against acceptance of the amended returns, with one member taking no stand. This sent the dispute to the state's highest court, which held a hearing and announced its judgment that the amended returns had reflected the true votes in their respective counties. The amendments (or corrections), as the court pointed out, had been made before the state canvassing board met and perforce had to be accepted. Andersen was therefore declared the winner.

Because the margin was so slim, however, with the likelihood of various errors in tabulations or of defective ballots, a recount was inevitable, and the state had to adopt an appropriate procedure to ensure its fair handling and thereby achieve a decision reflecting the choice of the voters. Democracy is not centrally a matter of winning an election, but of determining, with safeguards, the will of the people as recorded in their votes, no matter how small the final and authenticated majority may be. In some countries of the world hairline elections can be preludes to revolutions — Minnesota had such an election in 1962, and its people turned for settlement, not to guns, but to orderly procedures under the aegis of the courts.

The first move toward a recount was made, as it had to be, by representatives of Rolvaag, who for tactical reasons tried to have the handling of procedures based in a southern county. The Andersen forces petitioned for a transfer of the case to Ramsey County and were sustained by the supreme court. Under the orders of the court, a panel of three district judges was set up (with a fourth judge as an alternate) by agreement between representatives of the contenders. The next step was that of selecting the personnel of one hundred inspection teams, each including a Republican, a Democratic-Farmer-Labor representative, and a neutral (the panel of neutrals decided by agreement between representatives of the two candidates). After preliminaries, the recount got under way on December 19. Ballots challenged as defective were to be submitted for settlement before the three designated district judges, in the Ramsey County district court, after the completion of the recount by the inspection teams. Since the number of challenges would go to many thousands, however, each party group appointed a panel of ten members, the two panels under agreement to sift the challenged ballots and thus to speed the final task of adjudication by the recount court of three judges.

The legislature met on January 6, 1963. The next day Governor Andersen addressed it, reviewing state progress and making recommendations. Later he presented a budget, and the lawmakers went forward with their hearings. Meanwhile the recount proceeded slowly. Many ballots were challenged (reportedly 96,000 or more), but the screening team drastically reduced the number. Those remaining were arranged in classes of irregularities. The judges began to hear arguments February 25, and each class of disputed ballots (in some 24 categories) was debated by lawyers. The final judges' ruling, March 15, assured Rolvaag of a majority of 91 (the revised totals: 619,842 to 619,751). After DFL spokesmen rested their case, the Republicans asked for a dismissal. This the judges denied (March 19), and two days later they directed the secretary of state to issue an election certificate to Rolvaag, at the same time author-

589

izing a stay of ten days to enable Andersen to appeal, if he so chose, to the supreme court.

Such an appeal the governor decided not to make (March 23). The judges had been "competent and fair," but the recount had centered in paper ballots, not machine votes. Andersen had many thousands more paper ballots than his opponent, and obviously the latter's chance of finding irregularities was thereby augmented. The governor doubted that anybody could know who had "the most voter support" on November 6, but he saw no likelihood of a supreme court reversal of the verdict and he desired no futile delay. So he waived the ten-day stay, and on March 25, Rolvaag — son of the novelist, St. Olaf graduate, veteran, party politician, and former lieutenant governor — was sworn in as governor. The public mood seemed tinged with apathy, but much concern was voiced for reforms to obviate in the future any similarly frustrating impasse.

Thus the election was brought to a conclusion. Various explanations, none of them conclusive, have been offered to account for the closeness of the results: the Cuban crisis, political uncertainties that made the off-year elections in 1962 difficult nationally for incumbents, the late highway allegations, the similarities in the platform declarations of the major state parties, the failure of many thousands of voters (though they went to the polls) to record choices for the governorship, the appeals by both parties employing the devices of modern political campaigning, and perhaps a tradition of independent voting so rooted that one historian described the "photo finish" of the 1962 election as a "further demonstration of Minnesota's role as a true maverick in politics — a place where the unexpected and improbable are likely to happen." These and other suggested factors may not, as historians look back to 1962 from the vantage point of several decades hence, yield an adequate explanation of what happened. Two conclusions were inescapable, however. The voters, for whatever reasons, were about evenly divided in their political and personal judgments of the candidates; and the state proved itself able to resolve in orderly fashion a political contest with a "photo finish."

Perspective is inevitably lacking in any review of contemporary history and appraisal must await the passing of time. On the other hand, it is evident that, as Minnesota moved forward in the second half of the twentieth century, its people were alert to basic problems that would have to be met during the coming years. Some had already been subjected to study and long-term planning.

One was education. It involved the increasing thousands of young people crowding the schools at every level. If, as has been suggested, the "little red schoolhouse" was obsolete, the truth was that at the beginning of the 1960s the state still had no fewer than a hundred single-room schoolhouses, although their day seemed to be nearing its end. Consolidation at the secondary level had made much progress, but Minnesota still had large numbers of relatively small public high schools. The problems they faced with respect to adequate staffs were particularly serious and urgent in view of rising educational standards and public acceptance of the imperative importance of good quality in secondary education. Urbanization and the interconnections of educational problems and policies in interrelated communities suggested to some leaders the need of a transition from local and county to some form of effective regional cooperation in the affairs of the public schools.

Meanwhile nearly everybody recognized the compelling need for post-secondary and advanced education in the specialized and professionalized society of the modern state. It needed no gift of prophecy to foresee that the resources of existing institutions would be strained in the years ahead or that costs would increase. In 1962 it was estimated that within the next ten years the college and university students in the state would number close to 116,000. The estimate, based upon dependable figures of population, assumed enrollments of 8721 students in junior colleges, 25,216 in private colleges, 26,188 in state colleges, and 55,700 (or 48.1 per cent of the total) in the University of Minnesota. It seemed not unlikely that additional junior colleges would be established, and the growth of some of the state colleges might stir local or regional ambitions to turn them into universities, with the almost incalculable costs involved in instituting university work of high quality. Whatever was done obviously would have to be done on the basis of a broadly considered statewide plan.

Conditions also presaged enlarged attention to adult education in its many forms and to technical education at post-secondary levels. It seemed certain too that television would take on new and larger dimensions in the educational programs for the future.

Rural-urban *rapprochement,* increasingly evident through a half century or more, may yet be in its early or intermediate stages. Minnesota's

591

industrialization and metropolitan growth almost certainly would continue to modify, and perhaps even reshape, the economic and social structure, with a plethora of attendant problems not yet solved or fully envisaged. The need for cooperative action, recognized in the establishment of the Metropolitan Planning Commission in 1957, will be felt more and more throughout the state. A trend toward reducing the number of governmental units in Minnesota is already clearly discernible. A decade ago the state counted more than 9000 such units, in a national total only a little above 116,000. Toward the end of the 1950s the number had been reduced to a few more than 6000, mainly as a result of school-district consolidation. But the state still ranked very high in its totals, and it seemed likely that there would be further moves toward centralization and integration, "a tightening of bonds" — in the words of a scholar who has made a thorough study of intergovernmental relations — "between governments, both vertically and horizontally." Dr. William Anderson pictures the layers of local government "piled one on top of another" and takes into account increases in the functions of government and the movement of such functions "toward larger and larger units." Similarly he discerns an "upward movement of tax-collecting activities," with modification through state and federal aids to localities. Cooperation and integration are not easily achieved, but they represent a realistic grappling with the problems of government in a society of evolving economic and social forces.

Long-continued scientific research has been devoted to the varied resources of the state — agricultural, mineral, business, and industrial. If anything is patent from past records, it is that these fields will challenge further study and ingenuity. Search will be made for new uses of known resources and for novel ways of using resources little tapped or even untapped. In 1962 the Minnesota Natural Resources Council pointed out that there was a limit to the wealth of the state's natural resources and it sounded a warning that the people might one day "wake up to find some of our precious resources diminishing in value, some languishing for want of development, some practically exhausted." The council took up in detail such matters as recreation, game and fish, land, water, forests, and minerals. It emphasized the importance of research, controls, and planning. The governor, endorsing the report, went so far as to propose a state department of planning backed by funds up to $20,000,000 for developing natural resources.

Concurrently an Upper Midwest Research and Development Council has been formed as a cooperative project that includes the University of Minnesota and eight other research and educational institutions. Its purpose as expounded by its president, J. Cameron Thompson of Minneapolis, is to take "a good hard look at the progress, problems and potentials of the region." It is nonpartisan and nonprofit in organization, with support from foundations, business, and individuals. It is gathering up information about the economy of the Upper Midwest, factors that may bring about change, and ways of meeting future problems. It has already underscored the importance of foreign trade to the region, citing census figures for 1960 which show the foreign trade of Minnesota alone as having a value of $176,400,000 with 107 companies in twenty-two cities and towns sharing in the business. Its challenge to the state is research and more research — an unwillingness to settle for things as they are.

The problems of taconite persistently confront the state as the reserves of marketable high-grade ores dwindle. The Natural Resources Council predicted that they would last only about ten years (from 1962). The prediction reminds one of the shrewd prophecy made by Floyd B. Olson in 1935, before taconite research came to fruition, that the iron-ore industry would become "decadent within the next forty or fifty years." Many proposals have been made of ways to forward taconite manufacture, especially in the domain of taxation. The industry wants a state tax policy that will encourage the processing of billions of tons of low-grade ore in the generations ahead. That the problem has had political repercussions is evidenced by the shunting aside of the "taconite amendment," but, as has been noted, the legislature in 1961 by resolution declared its concern for a policy of fairness. The problem of taconite will surely continue to stir public interest and concern. Minnesota presumably will not complacently allow its iron industry, with all the labor, productivity, and taxes involved, to sink into the status of a declining enterprise.

The general problem of taxation is perennial. It has been studied by successive state administrations, sometimes in depth. But every biennial legislature exhibits a scramble to fit together odds and ends of taxes, drawing on miscellaneous sources in sufficient amount to balance the steadily increasing budgets. Major sources of state revenue are taxes on income, personal and corporate, and gasoline. Together these produce more than a third of the total. Other taxes are on property, motor vehicles, iron ore, gross earnings of railroads and other communication companies, liquor, and cigarettes. Present in the political picture is the question of a sales tax, a subject of recurring difference of opinion and of spirited debate. The Democratic-Farmer-Labor side has opposed such a tax; the Republicans seem to be favorable to it but have not taken a forthright stand for it. By 1962, thirty-seven of the fifty states (74 per cent) had adopted sales taxes. In the Middle West, four states adopted the sales tax in 1933 — Iowa, Michigan, Illinois, and South Dakota. Ohio and Missouri followed suit in 1934, North Dakota in 1935, and Kansas in 1937. These actions were all taken in the depression years, when income was low and the problem of tax resources acute. Wisconsin became a sales-tax state in 1962 after prolonged controversy. Majority opinion in Minnesota, as appraised by polls in 1962, continued to run counter to this form of taxation. All taxation, of course, has to be paid with money — from savings, earnings, surplus, balances on hand. Whatever the tax, it must be met, not by services or the offering of goats or sheep as was customary in ancient times, but by dollars and cents, and however levied and collected, taxes depend upon the ability of people to pay in cash.

The costs of government have mounted enormously in recent decades. It has been estimated that from 1900 to mid-century the amount spent by the state and local units in Minnesota jumped by some 900 per cent. A striking aspect of the expenditures is the changing proportion between the state and the localities, with the state's part advancing from about 15 per cent in 1911 to more than 27 per cent forty years later. Such figures do not, of course, reveal the increasing responsibility taken by the state for purposes once considered mainly local. Much state money has been poured into the schools, agencies of public welfare, and highways, to the advantage of localities as well as state, and school districts in particular have benefited by state grants. The aphorism that nothing is certain but death and taxes is not less true today than when it was uttered by Benjamin Franklin in 1789. For Minnesota the tax problem will intensify for state and local units — perhaps in increasing degree for cities in this urbanizing age. As needs and demands for public services increase, governmental costs will rise to higher levels. What the people want and demand of their government in its manifold activities, they necessarily must pay for and they must do so in taxes.

594

Few trends of recent years have been more conspicuous, politically and socially, than public concern over humane advance, aid to the unfortunate, and the validation of civil rights in the face of bias.

Spokesmen for both parties — none more vigorously than Youngdahl — have lent support to social reform. Their efforts have included advocacy of measures to cope with the problems of youth, not just those of the delinquent and retarded, but also of the gifted and those in between. As medical science has increased the "average age," the problems of older people in retirement have invited increasing attention. The public realizes that modern life gives a larger place to leisure than was true in the past and that social welfare is tied in with the effective use of leisure time. Similarly, and in relation to the stresses of modern living, there has been a widening sense of public responsibility for adequate medical aid to the mentally ill.

On federal, state, and local levels society has recognized the necessity of assistance to people suffering from want in bad times or good. The fight for physical well-being, and against disease and infirmity, is being fought through public agencies and by private institutions and the professions. And the problem of guarantees of medical and fiscal protection against the onslaught of sickness among the aged is one of the acute questions of the time. At the same time, efforts to overcome racial discrimination are statewide and reflect the national and local concern for tolerance in an age darkened by racial persecution (in our own country and throughout the world).

No one can question the actuality of the progress achieved by the state in dealing with social problems or the sincerity of public and private efforts to cope with them. That they have not been fully met few will dispute. Nor will people disagree that in the years ahead more will be done or that, in all probability, approaches not yet attempted will be devised to grapple with the social dilemmas that perplex contemporary society. The realm of social legislation and social work will widen.

Interconnections with nation and world affect every period in Minnesota history, from the French explorers to the Iron Curtain and the Communist-democratic struggle to influence the destinies of nations. The interconnections have by no means been restricted to political and economic spheres, however. They have embraced ideas, faiths, culture, the very tenets of civilization. Neither Minnesota nor any other state — nor indeed any country of the world — has ever been an island of isolation. In no period could the ideas of men be kept from crossing boundaries and seas or the walls of tradition. But the modern age, however harassed by the conflict of ideologies, has been intimately knit by invention, communication, airplanes, and many other forces.

No review of Minnesota's past can fail to emphasize its involvement with societies, ideas, and problems that seem, at first glance, to be remote from its boundaries – a far cry from its Main Streets. But the world has impinged upon Minnesota (and Gopher Prairie) through a long sweep of time. The problems of the divided world will continue to be American problems and therefore Minnesota and Main Street problems for a future that no one can yet measure. But this is not all. Innumerable currents of knowledge, as in the past, will reach into and modify life in the region – in science, medicine, the arts, education, philosophy, social ideas, industry, and other areas in which man's mind, the world over, works its way beyond the hitherto known.

Paddles, wheels, steam, and wings symbolize changes in Minnesota transportation. The transition from Red River carts and covered wagons to the iron horse seems dramatic, but it pales in comparison with the advance to the automobile and airplane, not to speak of flight in space. Transportation is like a pageant, and changes have been almost incredibly accelerated in the twentieth century. After reviewing progress through a century, one can scarcely doubt that transportation in the future will unveil new devices, new scenes, new controls, and new impetus to the mobility characteristic of society in the past.

Not less startling have been changes in communication. The newspaper press, served by inventions that faithfully bring the news of the world to Minnesota doorsteps morning and evening, is an institution of strength and importance. But abutting it are radio, television, telephone, and recording tapes and disks, with techniques that know no pause in their advances. Few realize the full implications of these and related inventions as instruments of education and for the dissemination of knowledge in the future. It would be folly to assume that the technology of communication will not unfold new wonders for succeeding generations.

The saga of a state, like that of America, must necessarily deal with exploration; soils and crops; invention and machines; industry and business; institutions and buildings; parties and politics; government and law; peace and war; the play of economic and social forces; the universe

596

of ideas; the world of research and education and creative work in the arts and literature.

Confronting such a congeries of factors, one is tempted to fix the propulsions of change in a wholly impersonal frame of reference. If so, it is well to be reminded that history is people. It is the record of their doings, their hopes and dreams, their successes and failures. A student of human affairs has wisely suggested that physical resources are not resources at all until "acted upon by the mind and hand of man."

It is people who have built Minnesota. They started and bore its movements and parties and institutions. They created the actualities recorded in statistical tables. They ran the plows. They built the buildings in pioneer days. They founded and conducted the newspapers. They initiated the schools. They run the tractors and machines of modern times. They perform the operations in the hospitals and carry forward researches in laboratories and libraries. They direct the mechanical contraptions conceived by human minds. They pour vigor into ideas and causes and efforts to solve the problems of the days and years. Behind the façade of historical events are thousands of human beings. They include men and women of lustrous reputations, such as Ramsey and Sibley and Pillsbury, Folwell and Northrop, Whipple and Ireland, the Mayos, Lind and Olson and Youngdahl, Hill and Donnelly, Sinclair Lewis and O. E. Rölvaag, Maria Sanford and Clara Ueland. But they also include folk of little or no fame whose work and integrity gave substance to their communities.

Names symbolizing distinction are prominent, but an American statesman once reminded the country of the contributions made by everyday people. It was Woodrow Wilson who said that a nation draws its "power of renewal and enterprise" from "the ranks of the great body of unnamed men."

Whatever the sum total may be of the achievements and contributions — or of the foibles and mistakes of Minnesota — those who developed the state are the thousands of men and women whose lives figure in that total. Because of them, the people, the state's yesterdays are legacy on the one hand, prologue on the other. Of Minnesota — if the many actors in its past could speak — they might paraphrase Aeneas of old and say, "Part of it we are. We are the people who built Minnesota."

FOR FURTHER READING

✦ For Further Reading

THE materials for Minnesota history are as abundant as they are rich and varied in interest — histories, biographies, articles, manuscripts, newspapers, official records, and novels based on historical studies. I hope that some readers of this book — perhaps many — will want to go on independent journeys of exploration either in broad terrains of Minnesota history or in some of its many special fields, topical or biographical.

My purpose here is not to present a comprehensive bibliography, but instead to call attention to selected readings which will, I hope, open the way to the kind of exploration I have in mind. Those who wish a fuller listing of materials than I can offer here are referred to a book entitled *Minnesota History: A Guide to Reading and Study*, which Theodore L. Nydahl and I prepared for publication by the University of Minnesota Press (1960). In that volume of 223 pages we outlined the state's history in some forty or more sections, for each of which we listed numerous writings. I cannot repeat all the titles here. Nor can I assume that readers will have the *Guide* at their elbows. Copies of it are available in libraries, however, where they may be consulted by those whose curiosity runs beyond the limits of the suggestions made in these pages.

General Suggestions

At the outset it may be helpful to mention books or periodicals that grapple with the entire Minnesota story or with large segments of it.

First and foremost is Dr. William W. Folwell's four-volume *History of Minnesota*, originally published from 1921 to 1930. The first two volumes — most basic in value of the four — were reprinted by the Minnesota Historical Society in 1956 and 1961. The Folwell history was the culmination of the long career of Minnesota's revered educator-scholar and it set high standards by the quality of its research and writing.

Minnesota History, the quarterly magazine of the Minnesota Historical Society, is not a history in the sense of chapters arranged in sequence. But, published regularly since 1915 and in its thirty-seventh volume by 1962, it comprises a veritable library of articles and documents over the full compass of Minnesota history from the native Indians and early exploration to recent times. Its interest is varied, its coverage catholic, with solid research underlying its contents. Much of the good scholarship in the Minnesota field has been poured into its pages.

Of lively interest is the society's *Gopher Historian*, a magazine for younger readers but not lacking in value for mature readers. From its files two editors, A. H. Poatgieter and James T. Dunn, have drawn together a selection of articles in a charming volume entitled the *Gopher Reader* (1958).

Bertha L. Heilbron's *The Thirty-Second State* (1958) is a pictorial history of distinctive quality. It is an interweaving of narrative with nearly five hundred illustrations — a colorful and interesting survey of the Minnesota story from its beginnings to the centennial year of 1958. *Minnesota Heritage* (1960) is a cooperative work of uneven quality, but it includes several good contributions in such fields as geology, the prehistoric Indians, exploration, communication, education, and social advance. In 1938, under the auspices of the Works Progress Administration, *Minnesota: A State Guide* was issued. It has been reprinted twice and is useful notwithstanding many errors of fact. Probably few readers will find it possible to consult the files of the *Minnesota Alumni Weekly*, vols. 31–34 (1932–34), but they will repay the effort of looking them up. The *Alumni Weekly* published a series of more than forty brief articles on Minnesota history by many writers. These amount to a popular synthesis of the state's history representing informed scholarship.

Two former governors of Minnesota have written general histories of the state, Joseph A. A. Burnquist and Theodore Christianson. The Burnquist narrative (*Minnesota and Its People*) appeared in 1924, Christianson's (*A History of the State and Its People*) in 1935. In each work the narrative is presented in two volumes, to which are added volumes of biographies of the kind included in commercial histories. Though the scope of the historical narratives is general, special interest attaches to the surveys made by the governors of the periods in which they took leading parts in Minnesota politics.

The Minnesota Historical Society in its earlier years published seventeen volumes of *Collections* which contain important firsthand material and many articles and monographs of lasting value, though some of the volumes are miscellaneous in content. Through more than eleven decades the society has built up a priceless collection of manuscripts, a library unparalleled in its field, great newspaper and picture collections, and a museum that presents a modern and authentic documentation of the state's past. Taken together, the society's collections and exhibits are a treasure trove for all students of Minnesota's past. Some idea of the scope of the manuscript collection is afforded by two *Guides* — one published in 1935, the other twenty years later. Together they list more than 1600 separate collections of manuscripts, some of them running to many thousands of items. Not far from the Historical Society Building in St. Paul, the state maintains its official archives.

In reviewing historical resources, it is worth while to take note of books for younger readers, some of which merit adult attention. One is John R. Borchert's *Minnesota's Changing Geography* (1959). Its focus is the modern state and its approach is geographical, but it takes into account the past of Minnesota. Numerous other books for younger readers deserve mention for their maps and illustrations and for lucid and spirited narratives. A few among many (some in revised editions) may be mentioned: *Minnesota, the Story of a Great State* (1957) by Maude L. Lindquist and James W. Clark; *Exploring Minnesota* (1958) by Harold T. Hagg; *Minnesota: Its Geography, History, and Government* (1948) by Floyd E. Perkins and Dudley S. Brainard; *Minnesota's Government* (1956) by Joseph Kise; *Minnesota, Star of the North* (revised ed., 1961) by Antoinette E. Ford and Neoma Johnson; and *Building Minnesota* (1938) by Theodore C. Blegen.

A few collections of readings from firsthand sources and secondary writings are available. One is *With Various Voices: Recordings of North Star Life* (1949) edited by Philip D. Jordan and T. C. Blegen; and another is the interesting *Gopher Reader. Early Days and Ways in the Old Northwest* (1937) by Maude L. Lindquist and James W. Clark was prepared for younger readers. A mimeographed volume entitled *Readings in Early Minnesota History*, edited by T. C. Blegen in 1938, is now available chiefly in libraries. One hopes that an anthology of articles from the quarterly *Minnesota History* ultimately will be issued, for the best fruits of that highly interesting magazine are not readily available to general readers, though the quarterly is on file in many libraries.

Readers desiring summaries of the state's history may care to turn to articles on Minnesota in standard encyclopedias, including one in *Collier's Encyclopedia* by Russell W. Fridley and H. D. Cater, one in the current edition of the *Encyclopedia Americana* by Jeanne Sinnen, and one in the *World Book Encyclopedia* by T. C. Blegen. A good sketch of Minnesota history by Mr. Fridley appears as an introduction to *Who's Who in Minnesota* (1958); and the biennial editions of the state's *Legislative Manual* usually include broad surveys of Minnesota history. An interpretation of the state's past is T. C. Blegen's "What's Past Is Prologue" in *Minnesota Heritage*. A convenient calendar of Minnesota history is Roy Swanson's *The Minnesota Book of Days* (1949). One of the choicest of Minnesota literary interpretations is Glanville Smith's "Minnesota, Mother of Lakes and Rivers," in the *National Geographic Magazine* for March 1935. *American Heritage* (Winter 1950) contains a series of essays on Minnesota by Grace Lee Nute, Bertha L. Heilbron, Nora O'Leary Sorem, and others. In biographical sketches of earlier and later Minnesota figures, the *Dictionary of American Biography* is helpful for its summaries and its references to sources. Many more Minnesotans are included in *Who's Who in Minnesota*. Two regional books of interest are James Gray's *Pine, Stream and Prairie* (1945) and Graham Hutton's *Midwest at Noon* (1946). A striking collection of photographs appears in John Szarkowski's *The Face of Minnesota* (1958).

The Land and the Redmen (Chapters 1 and 2)

Geographers, geologists, historians, and anthropologists have taken a lively interest in the state's geographic conditions, geological backgrounds, and the native Indians — especially the Sioux and Chippewa.

Minnesota's Rocks and Waters: A Geological Story (1954) by George M. Schwartz and George A. Thiel is the best and most interesting treatment of its subject. The Science Museum of St. Paul issued in 1962 a highly informing and well-illustrated book by Edmund C. Bray entitled *A Million Years in Minnesota: The Glacial Story of the State*. Borchert's *Minnesota's Changing Geography* is packed with information presented in elementary form. The clearest short account of Minnesota geological backgrounds is J. Merle Harris, "Minnesota Heritage in the Making," in *Minnesota Heritage*. Louis H. Powell wrote a fascinating essay, "Around a Geologic Clock in Minnesota," in *Minnesota History*, 15:141–47 (June 1934); and the same magazine for August 1918 (2:443–53) has an article by C. J. Posey on "The Influence of Geographic Features in the Development of Minnesota." Edward Van Dyke Robinson in his *Early Economic Conditions and the Development of Agriculture in Minnesota* (1915) is factually informing on Minnesota's climate and physical features. The many bulletins of the Minnesota Geological Survey, including James H. Zumberge's *The Lakes of Minnesota* (1952), are the products of specialized scholarship. The University of Minnesota Press has published many books of interest for Minnesota natural backgrounds, notably Thomas S. Roberts' two-volume study on Minnesota birds and a later one-volume *Bird Portraits in Color* (1934; reprinted in 1960); C. O. Rosendahl's books on the trees and shrubs and flowers of Minnesota; a study of *The Mammals of Minnesota* (1953) by H. L. Gunderson and J. R. Beer; and Samuel Eddy and Thaddeus Surber's *Northern Fishes* (1943). For charm, description, and splendid illustrations *Canoe Country* (1938) and *Snowshoe Country* (1944) by Florence P. and Francis Lee Jaques are incomparable. Sigurd Olson presents sensitive interpretations of the north country in such books as *The Singing Wilderness* (1956) and *The Lonely Land* (1961). Two "river" books of interest are Walter

Havighurst, *Upper Mississippi* (revised ed., 1944), and Evan Jones, *The Minnesota: Forgotten River* (1962).

Writings on Minnesota Indian life are voluminous. Among the most informing are Frances Densmore's *Chippewa Customs* (1929) and her earlier two volumes on *Chippewa Music* (1910–13); Samuel W. Pond's firsthand account of the Sioux in 1834, in *Minnesota Historical Collections*, vol. 12 (1908); William W. Warren's study of the Ojibways in the same series, vol. 5 (1885); and Joseph A. Gilfillan's account of the Chippewa, vol. 9 (1901). Henry R. Schoolcraft, the explorer, was a prolific writer about the Indians and their myths. A convenient book in which some of his writings are brought together is *Indian Legends*, edited by Mentor L. Williams (1956). Yet another Schoolcraft volume of recent vintage (1962) is *The Literary Voyager or Muzzeniegun*, edited by Philip P. Mason, a series of essays, poems, and miscellaneous writings on Indian life and customs, with special attention to the Chippewa. John C. Ewer has written or edited many volumes of interest on western Indians and their portrayal by artists. One such work is the edition of Edwin T. Denig's *Five Indian Tribes of the Upper Missouri* (1961) which includes accounts of the Sioux and the Assiniboin Indians. A brilliant article by Everett E. Edwards tells of "American Indian Contributions to Civilization," in *Minnesota History*, 15:255–72 (September 1934); and Theodore L. Nydahl in the same magazine, 31:193–208 (December 1950), writes interestingly of the Pipestone quarries. Lloyd Wilford summarizes the results of recent archaeological studies in his account of "The First Minnesotans" in *Minnesota Heritage*. A minor classic is William Joseph Snelling's *Tales of the Northwest*, a collection of stories by a son of Colonel Snelling, reprinted and edited by John T. Flanagan in 1936; and Henry Hastings Sibley wrote the full-length story of a half-breed warrior, scout, and hunter named Jack Frazer, edited in 1950 by Sarah A. Davidson and T. C. Blegen under the title *Iron Face*. An early work is Newton H. Winchell's *The Aborigines of Minnesota* (1911), and Dr. Albert E. Jenks has told of *Pleistocene Man in Minnesota* (1936). An educated mixed-blood, Dr. Charles A. Eastman, has written about *Indian Boyhood* (1902) and the transition *From the Deep Woods to Civilization* (1916).

An extensive bibliography could be compiled for the controversy over the authenticity of the Kensington Runestone. It is sufficient here to call attention to H. R. Holand's *The Kensington Stone* (1932) and *Explorations in America before Columbus* (1956); and (for the negative side of the argument) to Erik Wahlgren's *The Kensington Stone: A Mystery Solved* (1958).

The French and British Regimes (Chapters 3, 4, and 5)

The French and British regimes offer unending interest in the narratives of explorers and fur traders. Here, to mention only a few, one thinks of Father Hennepin (a convenient reference is the English translation by Marion E. Cross, 1938, of his *Description of Louisiana*); the famous "Voyages" of Radisson (1885); the journals and letters of La Vérendrye (edited in 1927 by Lawrence J. Burpee); Jonathan Carver's *Travels* (1778 and reprinted from a third edition in 1956); the diary of Peter Pond; the journals kept by the two Alexander Henrys and David Thompson (edited by Elliott Coues, 1897); Thompson's narrative as edited by J. B. Tyrrell (1916); the diaries of *Five Fur Traders of the Northwest* (including Peter Pond), edited in 1933 by Charles M. Gates; Daniel W. Harmon's colorful journal of travel originally published in 1820 (edited in a new edition in 1911); and the *Voyages* of the great Alexander Mackenzie (1801). Louise P. Kellogg's *Early Narratives of the Northwest, 1634–1699* (1917) brings together many documents of the French regime. There is a growing library of books and documents relating to the Hudson's Bay Company — narratives, reports, minutes, and diaries. Of special value are the volumes that have appeared in recent years under the auspices of the Hudson's Bay Record Society of London. And one should not forget the majestic series of *Jesuit Relations and Allied Documents*, edited with French and English texts in 73 volumes by Reuben Gold Thwaites (1896–1901). Readers will find selections from this multi-volume work in Edna Kenton's *Jesuit Relations* (2 vols., 1925) and in her two additional volumes on *The Indians of North America* (1927).

For those who choose to read secondary accounts one cannot recommend too highly the books and articles by Grace Lee Nute. They include her delightful volume on *The Voyageur* (1931, reprinted in 1955); *The Voyageur's Highway* (1941); *Caesars of the Wilderness* (1943 — her biography of Radisson and Groseilliers); *Rainy River Country* (1950); and *Lake Superior* (1944 — the first two chapters on the French and British). Among her many articles, three especially call for mention: "Posts in the Minnesota Fur-Trading Area, 1660–1855," in *Minnesota History*, 11:353–85 (December 1930); in the same magazine, "Marin versus La Vérendrye," 32:226–38 (December 1951); and "By Minnesota Waters," in *Minnesota Heritage*.

As Dr. Nute is the outstanding Minnesota historian of the French and British regimes, so the late Louise Phelps Kellogg ranked for Wisconsin. Among her writings are two volumes on the French and British regimes in Wisconsin and the Northwest (1925 and 1935). Minnesota readers will enjoy especially her articles in *Minnesota History* on "Fort Beauharnois" and on "The French Regime in the Great Lakes Country" (8:232–46, September 1927; and 12:347–58, December 1931).

Other books and articles to be noted in relation to the French and British periods include Nellis M. Crouse's biography of La Vérendrye (1956); Solon J. Buck's *The Story of the Grand Portage* (1931); Wayne E. Stevens' *The Northwest Fur Trade, 1763–1800* (1928); Alfred L. Burt's *The Old Province of Quebec* (1933) for Canadian backgrounds;

606

Walter O'Meara's *The Savage Country* (1960), a narrative based largely on the diary kept by Alexander Henry the Younger, and also his article "Adventure in Local History," in *Minnesota History*, 31:1–10 (March 1950), in which he writes about Daniel Harmon. *Portage into the Past* (1960) by J. Arnold Bolz is the story of a modern-day canoe journey in northern waters with extensive use of historical references. A recent booklet (with maps) is Eric Morse's *Canoe Routes of the Voyageurs* (1962). Inevitably the early period has attracted the interest of novelists, as illustrated in *Northwest Passage* (1938) by Kenneth Roberts (the story of Robert Rogers and Jonathan Carver) and *The Grand Portage* (1951) by Walter O'Meara.

The Americans Arrive (Chapters 6, 7, 8, and 9)

Not less fascinating than the French and British diaries, narratives, and reports are those of explorers and traders in the American period from Zebulon M. Pike to Major Samuel Woods.

Pike's diary of his journey to Minnesota in 1805–6 was first published in 1807 but is conveniently available in vol. 1 of Elliott Coues, *The Expeditions of Zebulon Montgomery Pike* (1895). Henry R. Schoolcraft's *Narrative Journal* of the Cass expedition in 1820 appeared in print in 1821 (reprinted in 1953 by M. L. Williams, with additional documents). The Stephen H. Long expedition of 1823 was recorded in a *Narrative* by William H. Keating in 1824 (reprinted in 1959). And in 1824 Giacomo C. Beltrami's ecstatic story of his travels was brought out in French, to be followed four years later by an English version. A reprint of Beltrami's *Pilgrimage* (the English version) appeared in 1962.

One of the best documented American expeditions was Schoolcraft's second exploration, in 1832. He recorded it in a detailed *Narrative* in 1834 (edited and reprinted in 1958); his companion, the missionary Boutwell, kept a diary (parts of which appeared in the first volume of the *Minnesota Historical Collections*), and reports by the vaccinating physician, Dr. Houghton, and an army officer, Lieutenant Allen, are also available (along with Schoolcraft's account) in the volume well edited by Philip P. Mason in 1958.

A new edition of Frederick Marryat's *A Diary in America*, edited by Sydney Jackman, appeared in 1962. Two of its chapters, "Indian Country" and "The Wild West — Fort Snelling," report his Minnesota experiences and observations. The full records of the basic geographer of Minnesota, Joseph N. Nicollet, have not yet been published, but his fundamental map of the region, with a brief narrative, was made public in a governmental document in 1843. George Catlin's magnificent *Letters and Notes* on the North American Indians, published in 1841, includes his Minnesota visits; and the Woods-Pope expedition of 1849 is reported by Major Woods in a government document. These are major records, but many others can be tracked down through the Minnesota *Guide to Reading and Study* and by references in Dr. Folwell's first volume, which is detailed and informing on Minnesota exploration.

From the extensive literature on Fort Snelling, American exploration, Indian feuds, and the American fur trade, some items call for special note. Marcus Lee Hansen wrote the standard history of *Old Fort Snelling 1819–1858* (1918, reprinted in 1958 with an excellent introduction by Russell W. Fridley); and a supplement of interest is a pamphlet entitled *New Light on Old Fort Snelling: An Archaeological Exploration*, by John M. Callender (1959). W. E. Hollon has written an entertaining biography of Pike (1949).

A study of "The Army and the Westward Movement" by Edgar B. Wesley is in *Minnesota History*, 15:375–81 (December 1934); and he is also the author of a scholarly book on frontier defense in the period 1815–25 under the title *Guarding the Frontier* (1935). A charming book of reminiscences of early life at Fort Snelling is Charlotte O. Van Cleve's *"Three Score Years and Ten"* (1881). John T. Flanagan in his introduction to William J. Snelling's *Tales of the Northwest* writes interestingly about activities at Fort Snelling in the 1820s, and John F. McDermott includes an account of the fort in his biography of one of its commanders, *Seth Eastman: Pictorial Historian of the Indian* (1961). The origin of the name of Lake Itasca was solved by William J. Petersen in an article "Veritas Caput: Itasca," in *Minnesota History*, 18:180–85 (June 1937).

The American fur trade and early American relations with the Indians in the Minnesota area have attracted no little historical attention. Essays on Joseph Renville by Gertrude Ackermann, on Louis Provençalle by W. M. Babcock, on Alexander Faribault by Grace Lee Nute, on Sibley by W. P. Shortridge, and on Norman W. Kittson by C. W. Rife are in *Minnesota History*, vols. 12, 20, 8, 3, and 6. Sibley's writings are voluminous. Many are to be found in the *Minnesota Historical Collections* (especially vols. 1 and 3). His *Unfinished Autobiography*, together with some of his letters from early days, was edited by T. C. Blegen in a book published in 1932; and Sibley's career is the theme of Wilson P. Shortridge's book *The Transition of a Typical Frontier* (1922). Grace Lee Nute has published a calendar of the American Fur Company manuscripts and also an illuminating essay on the historical value of these papers in the *American Historical Review*, 32:519–38 (April 1927). The biography of *John Jacob Astor: Business Man* has been written in two volumes by Kenneth W. Porter (1931). And one should not omit mention of Maud Hart Lovelace's novel *Early Candlelight* (1929; reprinted 1949), with its ingratiating picture of Fort Snelling and Mendota in Sibley's time.

For the Indian story and the Indian governmental agency, an excellent reference is W. M. Babcock's article "Major Lawrence Taliaferro, Indian Agent," in the *Mississippi Valley Historical Review*, 11:358–75 (December 1924). The major's autobiography (written in 1864) is published in the *Minnesota Historical Collections*, vol. 6 (1894), but the extensive Taliaferro diaries preserved by the Minnesota Historical Society have not yet been published. An early record is that of Ezekiel G. Gear, edited (by T. C. Blegen) in "Armistice and War on the Minnesota Frontier," in *Minnesota History*, 24:11–25 (March 1943). William J. Snelling's account of "Running the Gauntlet" is in the *Minnesota Historical Collections*, vol. 1 (1902 edition).

The stirring missionary story is recorded both in contemporary and later writings by the missionaries themselves and in historical studies. Stephen R. Riggs recounts his experiences (and those of his wife) in an endearing book entitled *Mary and I* (1880); Augustin Ravoux's *Reminiscences* was published in 1890; a "Memoir of Rev. Lucian Galtier" by John Ireland, in vol. 3 of *Minnesota Historical Collections*, includes parts of Galtier's own account of his Minnesota mission; and Bishop Whipple tells the story of his life in *Lights and Shadows of a Long Episcopate* (1899). The Pond brothers wrote many articles for the *Minnesota Historical Collections*, notably Samuel W. Pond's account of the Sioux in 1834 (vol. 12). A long narrative by him was edited under the title "Two Missionaries in the Sioux Country" by T. C. Blegen for *Minnesota History*, 21:15–32, 158–75, 272–83 (March, June, September 1940); and his book *Two Volunteer Missionaries among the Dakota* (1893) narrates the experiences of himself and his brother Gideon.

Sister Mary Aquinas Norton has written the story of *Catholic Missionary Activities in the Northwest, 1818–1864* (1930); and Sister Grace McDonald has an interesting article on "Father Francis Pierz, Missionary," in *Minnesota History*, 10:107–25 (June 1929). Catholic missionary backgrounds are dealt with also in Colman J. Barry's book *Worship and Work* (1956), a history of St. John's Abbey and University during the century 1856–1956. A basic work of importance for the Catholic missionary enterprise in the Red River colony is Grace Lee Nute's *Documents Relating to Northwest Missions 1815–1827* (1942). In 1961 an illustrated, cooperative booklet on *Catholic Origins of Minnesota*, edited by the Reverend Vincent A. Yzermans, appeared, with accounts of Catholic missionaries and missions from French to American times.

Charles M. Gates is the author of an account of "The Lac qui Parle Indian Mission" in *Minnesota History*, 16:133–51 (June 1935); and Grace Lee Nute offers a survey of the Indian missions in *Minnesota Heritage*. One of the most perceptive of the essays on the missionaries is Dr. Nute's "Wilderness Marthas," in *Minnesota History*, 8:247–59 (September 1927). M. M. Hoffmann is the author of an interesting article, "New Light on Old St. Peter's and Early St. Paul," in *Minnesota History*, 8:27–51 (March 1927). Dr. Folwell took a lively interest in the early Indian missions and has a good chapter on this subject in vol. 1 of his *History of Minnesota*.

Of historical and pictorial interest are writings on the artists who recorded the Minnesota scene in early times — and on their paintings, sketches, and panoramas. Harold McCracken's *George Catlin and the Old Frontier* (1959) is a superbly illustrated book enhanced in value by the inclusion of a check list of writings by and about Catlin. Another interesting book is Bernard De Voto's *Across the Wide Missouri* (1947), notable for its writing and also for illustrations taken from the paintings of Catlin, Alfred J. Miller, and Charles Bodmer. Bertha L. Heilbron and John F. McDermott have written in *Minnesota History* and other magazines on Peter Rindisbacher, Seth Eastman, Paul Kane, Henry Lewis, Frank B. Mayer, Edwin Whitefield, J. C. Wild, J. O. Lewis, Adolf Hoeffler, Samuel Seymour, and others. Miss Heilbron is editing for publication an English version of *Das Illustrirte Mississippithal* by Henry Lewis; and among Professor McDermott's many works are *The Lost Panoramas of the Mississippi* (1958) and a beautifully illustrated book on *Seth Eastman: Pictorial Historian of the Indian* (1961), with a check list of Eastman's works. Of basic importance as a guide to pioneer artists of the West is P. T. Rathbone's richly illustrated *Westward the Way* (1954).

Territory and State (Chapters 10, 11, and 12)

Much of Minnesota's story in the 1840s and from the organization of the territory to the Civil War is recorded in articles and special documents rather than in one or more comprehensive books. There is no single work devoted to the full and absorbing history of the years 1849–60. Good surveys are offered in Folwell's vol. 1 and in Bertha L. Heilbron's *Thirty-Second State*; and several monographs deal authoritatively with large parts of the story, notably William Anderson (and Albert J. Lobb) in a *History of the Constitution of Minnesota* (1921). Mary W. Berthel in *Horns of Thunder* (1948) tells of Goodhue and the *Minnesota Pioneer* and quotes extensively from Goodhue's lively writings. Thomas Hughes writes of *Old Traverse des Sioux* (1929), and Bertha L. Heilbron presents the diary and sketches of Frank B. Mayer in her volume *With Pen and Pencil on the Frontier in 1851* (1932).

Margaret Snyder is the author of a charming book, *The Chosen Valley* (1948), about a southern Minnesota town, Chatfield. Hans Mattson's *Reminiscences: The Story of an Emigrant* (1891) is a very interesting pioneer autobiography. Much light on pioneer farming and social life is shed in Rodney C. Loehr's *Minnesota Farmers' Diaries* (1939), and Arthur J. Larsen gathers up the newspaper letters of Jane Grey Swisshelm in his *Crusader and Feminist* (1934). Health conditions are recorded in Philip D. Jordan's *The People's Health* (1953); and Merrill E. Jarchow's *The Earth Brought Forth* (1949) is informing on early agricultural history. Several essays on the pioneer era are in T. C. Blegen's *Grass Roots History* (1947), including "The Fashionable Tour," "Attic Inventory," and "Everyday Life as Advertised." In his *Land Lies Open* (1949) are chapters on "The Land Takers," "The Booming of Gopher Prairie," and "Yankees on the Land." An original contribution to Minnesota history in the 1850s is a volume on book, job, and ornamental printing by Marjorie Kreidberg under the title *Fragments of Early Printing* (1958). The period covered is 1849–60. A good biography of Edward D. Neill by Huntley Dupre was published in 1949. An interesting novel of pioneer life in the 1850s is *One Stayed at Welcome* (1934) by Maud and Delos Lovelace. The letters of Fredrika Bremer, prophet of the "glorious new Scandinavia," were originally published in 1853 in two volumes. A judicious selection drawn from the original is *America of the Fifties: Letters of Fredrika Bremer* (1924), edited by A. B. Benson. Her apostrophe to the new Scandinavia may be found on p. 234.

The *Minnesota History* quarterly contains many articles on the 1850s. Notable are those of Evadene A. Burris on pioneer food, building and furnishing frontier homes, and "keeping house" on the frontier — all four in vols. 14 and 15 of the magazine (1933 and 1934). Lucile M. Kane tells of "The Sioux Treaties and the Traders," 32:65–80 (June 1951); Ralph H. Brown of "Fact and Fancy in Early Accounts of Minnesota's Climate," 17:243–61 (September 1936); and Arthur J. Larsen of "Roads and Trails in the Minnesota Triangle, 1849–60," 11:387–411 (December 1930). Other essays of interest include Dudley S. Brainard's story of Nininger as a boom town, 13:127–51 (June 1932); William J. Petersen's article on Minnesota River steamboating, 11:123–44 (June 1930) and "The Rock Island Railroad Excursion of 1854," 15:405–20 (December 1934); Charles J. Ritchey's "Claim Associations and Pioneer Democracy in Early Minnesota," 9:85–95 (June 1928); and Alice F. Tyler's "William Pfaender and the Founding of New Ulm," 30:24–35 (March 1949). T. C. Blegen describes "Minnesota Pioneer Life as Revealed in Newspaper Advertisements," 7:99–121 (June 1926); and Charles M. Gates has a thoughtful essay on "Bridges Facing East," 16:22–34 (March 1935).

Bertha L. Heilbron writes entertainingly about "Christmas and New Year's on the Frontier," in *Minnesota History*, 16:373–90 (December 1935); and Zylpha S. Morton on "Harriet Bishop, Frontier Teacher," 28:132–41 (June 1947). Yet other articles in the society's magazine are William Anderson's "Minnesota Frames a Constitution," 36:1–12 (March 1958); R. J. Forrest's "Mythical Cities of Southwestern Minnesota," 14:243–62 (September 1933); and a study of territorial politics by Erling Jorstad, 36:259–71 (September 1959). The texts of the state constitution and other basic documents of Minnesota may be found in the various issues of the *Legislative Manual*. *Murder in Minnesota* by Walter N. Trenerry (1962) includes three cases from the 1850s, two of them with grisly filigrees of lynching.

Scores of other articles on the 1850s in *Minnesota History*, the *Gopher*

Historian, and other magazines are listed in the *Guide to Reading and Study* and in the notes accompanying the essays cited above.

The Civil and Sioux Wars (Chapters 13 and 14)

Dr. Folwell's vol. 2 is comprehensive and reliable as a general account of Minnesota in the Civil and Sioux wars, but recent years have witnessed renewed interest in this dramatic period for the state as they have for the United States. New books and recent articles have added much detail to the story as told by Dr. Folwell. A large volume on *The Indian Wars of Minnesota* by Louis H. Roddis was published in 1956, and three years later C. M. Oehler issued a book on *The Great Sioux Uprising*. Chapters on the Civil War and the Sioux War are included in Virginia B. Kunz's military history of Minnesota, *Muskets to Missiles* (1958).

Published in 1961 were dramatic books by Kenneth Carley on Minnesota in the Civil War and on the Sioux Uprising. An original volume is *Charles E. Flandrau and the Defense of New Ulm*, edited by Russell W. Fridley, Leota M. Kellett, and June D. Holmquist (1962); and an artist, Jerry Fearing, has prepared a volume of colored cartoons (1962) depicting the events of the Sioux War. A recent novel with the Sioux War as its setting is Bernard F. Ederer's *Birch Coulie* (1957). Frank H. Heck is the author of *The Civil War Veteran in Minnesota Life and Politics* (1941).

Nearly all the magazine articles to be cited on the Civil and Sioux wars postdate Folwell's vol. 2 (1924). Two exceptions are an able, analytical study by Lester B. Shippee of the social and economic effects of the Civil War on Minnesota, in *Minnesota History Bulletin*, 2:389–412 (May 1918), and a notable study by John D. Hicks of the organization of the volunteer army in 1861, in the same magazine, 2:324–68 (February 1918). Later articles in *Minnesota History* include Winfred A. Harbison's "President Lincoln and the Faribault Fire-Eater," 20:269–86 (September 1939); Solon J. Buck's essay on "Lincoln and Minnesota," 6:355–61 (December 1925); Frank Klement's "The Abolition Movement in Minnesota," 32:15–33 (March 1951); F. Paul Prucha's study of the Minnesota attitude with respect to the southern position on secession, 24:307–17 (December 1943); and Walter N. Trenerry's original analysis of "The Minnesota Rebellion Act of 1862," 35:1–10 (March 1956). T. C. Blegen has edited diaries and letters of interest in "Campaigning with Seward in 1860" and "Guri Endreson, Frontier Heroine," 8:150–71 (June 1927), and 10:425–30 (December 1929). The issues of *Minnesota History* and the *Gopher Historian* for the fall of 1962 are devoted to the Sioux War. Of special interest in the *Minnesota History* issue are articles on "Minnesota's Indian War" by W. M. Babcock; on the Sioux campaign as recorded in letters from General Sibley to his wife, by Kenneth Carley; and on the shooting of Little Crow, by Walter N. Trenerry, who uses as a subtitle "Heroism or Murder?" An interesting article by Alvin C. Gluek, Jr., deals with "The Sioux Uprising: A Problem in International Relations," *Minnesota History*, 34:317–24 (Winter 1955). Bertha L. Heilbron describes John Stevens' panorama of the Sioux War in her "Documentary Panorama," *Minnesota History*, 30:14–23 (March 1949). An illustrated article on the Sioux War by R. K. Andrist in the April 1962 issue of *American Heritage* includes some of the Stevens pictures in color.

Changes after the Civil War (Chapters 15, 16, and 17)

As one moves into the swirl of postwar changes, the Minnesota story becomes more complex, its records scattered, its books and articles often dealing with large themes that traverse broader ground than the particular chapters as numbered above. Notwithstanding difficulty in choosing a few among many titles, the books and articles to be mentioned can serve exploratory purposes. Their references in turn will open the way to varied sources of specialized character.

Dr. Folwell's third volume (1926) covers no small part of the ground, and many of the readings in the book entitled *With Various Voices* are relevant. A fundamental work is Robinson's *Early Economic Conditions and the Development of Agriculture in Minnesota*. Merrill E. Jarchow's more recent book, *The Earth Brought Forth* (1949), is a study of Minnesota agriculture to 1885, with appreciative attention given to social as well as economic factors. Henrietta M. Larson has written a basic account of *The Wheat Market and the Farmer in Minnesota* (1926). Agnes Larson is the author of an equally basic *History of the White Pine Industry in Minnesota* (1949), and William G. Rector, in his *Log Transportation in the Lake States Lumber Industry 1840–1918* (1953), has made a contribution of interest and value. Useful for background is R. G. Lillard, *The Great Forest* (1947).

Another standard and enduring work is Mildred L. Hartsough's *Development of the Twin Cities as a Metropolitan Market* (1925). Charles B. Kuhlmann has written on *The Development of the Flour-Milling Industry in the United States* (1929), with special attention to Minneapolis; and James Gray has told the story of General Mills in *Business without Boundary* (1954). Lowry Nelson deals understandingly with historical backgrounds in his book *The Minnesota Community: Country and Town in Transition* (1960); and Samuel T. Dana, John H. Allison, and R. N. Cunningham have made available a mass of information about the ownership, use, and management of *Minnesota Lands* (1960). Minnesota is the focus also of M. N. Orfield's monograph on *Federal Land Grants to the States* (1915).

We still await a scholarly life of James J. Hill and a history of the Great Northern Railroad, but no little information can be found in

Joseph G. Pyle's two-volume eulogistic life of Hill (1917); and a summary is given in a popular biography by Stewart H. Holbrook (1955). The agrarian movement has been recorded by Solon J. Buck in his *Agrarian Crusade* (1920) and *Granger Movement* (1913) and by John D. Hicks in his broad-ranging *Populist Revolt* (1931).

Much significant material on population and national elements is in articles, and not a few books are available. They include James P. Shannon's excellent *Catholic Colonization on the Western Frontier* (1957); Carlton C. Qualey's *Norwegian Settlement in the United States* (1938), with an informing chapter on Minnesota; W. G. Plaut's *The Jews in Minnesota* (1959); and Earl Spangler's *The Negro in Minnesota* (1961). A pamphlet by Lowry Nelson, C. E. Ramsey, and J. Toews, *A Century of Population Growth in Minnesota* (1954), has useful summaries of census data. James H. Moynihan's *Life of Archbishop John Ireland* (1953) includes information about Ireland as colonizer. O. E. Rölvaag's memorable novel *Giants in the Earth* deals chiefly with South Dakota, but it begins with Minnesota scenes and its total picture affords insight into immigrant pioneering generally. A number of Minnesota immigrant letters are presented in a chapter, "The Glorious New Scandinavia," in T. C. Blegen's *Land of Their Choice* (1955), pp. 419–46, and he also includes some Minnesota material in the two volumes of his *Norwegian Migration to America* (1931, 1940).

Background articles for Chapters 15–17 are numerous, especially those in the various volumes of *Minnesota History*. Thomas P. Christensen writes of Minnesota Danish settlements, 8:363–85 (December 1927); Carlton C. Qualey of pioneer Norwegian settlement and also, more generally, of Minnesota "national groups," 12:247–80 (September 1931) and 31:18–32 (March 1950); John Sirjamaki on "The People of the Mesabi Range," 27:203–15 (September 1946); James P. Shannon on "Bishop Ireland's Connemara Experiment," 35:205–13 (March 1957); Alice E. Smith on "The Sweetman Irish Colony," 9:331–46 (December 1928); and George M. Stephenson on Swedish immigrants and their letters in a brilliant article, "When America Was the Land of Canaan," 10:237–60 (September 1929). Stephenson's many writings also include a scholarly work on *The Religious Aspects of Swedish Immigration* (1932) in which due attention is given to the Swedish element in Minnesota.

Other articles of interest in *Minnesota History* include Esther Jerabek's "The Transition of a New-World Bohemia," 15:26–42 (March 1934); Hildegard B. Johnson on "Eduard Pelz and German Emigration," 31:222–30 (December 1950); John I. Kolehmainen on "The Finnish Pioneers of Minnesota," 25:317–28 (December 1944); William A. Marin on "Sod Houses and Prairie Schooners," 12:135–56 (June 1931); Grace Lee Nute on "The Lindbergh Colony," 20:243–58 (September 1939); and Arthur R. Moro on "The English Colony at Fairmont in the Seventies," 8:140–49 (June 1927). That colony also supplies the theme for Maud H. Lovelace's colorful novel *Gentlemen from England* (1937).

For other and varied fields a few articles call for mention. John D. Hicks has written about Ignatius Donnelly's political career in the *Mississippi Valley Historical Review,* 8:80–132 (June–September 1921); and more recently Martin Ridge has traced Donnelly's congressional career in *Minnesota History,* 36:173–83 (March 1959), and has studied Donnelly and the Granger movement in the *Mississippi Valley Historical Review,* 42:693–709 (March 1956). He is also the author of an extensive biography, *Ignatius Donnelly: The Portrait of a Politician,* published in 1962. John Haugland writes of "Politics, Patronage, and Ramsey's Rise to Power," in *Minnesota History,* 37:324–34 (December 1961). Verne E. Chatelain discusses federal land policy and early Minnesota politics, in *Minnesota History,* 22:227–48 (September 1941); and Harold F. Peterson has articles on Minnesota railroads and their colonization activities in the same magazine, 13:25–44 (March 1932), and 10:127–44 (June 1929). Lester B. Shippee tells of "The First Railroad between the Mississippi and Lake Superior," in the *Mississippi Valley Historical Review,* 5:121–42 (September 1918). An original study of merit is Hildegard B. Johnson's essay on "King Wheat in Southeastern Minnesota," in the Association of American Geographers, *Annals,* 47:350–62 (December 1957). This "case study" questions the traditional domination of "King Wheat."

On the lumber story, in addition to the book on the white pine industry in Minnesota by Agnes M. Larson, readers will find her essay "On the Trail of the Woodsman in Minnesota" delightful — *Minnesota History,* 13:349–66 (December 1932). In the same magazine Elizabeth M. Bachmann has written about "Minnesota Log Marks," 26:126–37 (June 1945); John A. Bardon on "Early Logging Methods," 15:203–6 (June 1934); Emma Glaser on Stillwater, 24:195–206 (September 1943); Harold T. Hagg on "The Lumberjack's Sky Pilot," 31:65–78 (June 1950); and Rodney C. Loehr on Caleb Dorr's role in the lumber story, 24:125–41 (June 1943). An article with the charm of recorded firsthand experience is that by a former lumberjack, Wright T. Orcutt, "The Minnesota Lumberjacks," *Minnesota History,* 6:3–19 (March 1925). A brief article by Lucile Kane on "Isaac Staples, Pioneer Lumberman," is in the *Gopher Historian,* 7:7–9 (January 1953); and several excellent essays on the lumber industry are in the *Gopher Reader,* including one of special value by George B. Engberg entitled "Where Did the Lumberjacks Come From?"

On flour milling, in addition to the books of James Gray and C. B. Kuhlmann, there is a good brief account by Kuhlmann of the Minneapolis flour mills in relation to the state's economic history, in *Minnesota History,* 6:141–54 (June 1925); and Paul R. Fossum writes of the Cannon

River Valley mills in the same magazine, 11:271–82 (September 1930). The Paul Bunyan literature is almost boundless. It is sufficient here to refer to a critical study of the legend by Richard M. Dorson in his book *American Folklore* (1959).

Iron Ore and Land (Chapters 18 and 19)

Folwell in his vol. 4 (1930) has a detailed account of the Minnesota iron mines. Though written more than three decades ago, it is still one of the best general reviews of the iron-ore story. Other books to be noted are *Iron Millionaire: Life of Charlemagne Tower* by L. H. Bridges (1952); Paul de Kruif's *Seven Iron Men* (1929); Grace Lee Nute's edition of *Mesabi Pioneer: Reminiscences of Edmund J. Longyear* (1951); and Fremont P. Wirth's *Discovery and Exploitation of the Minnesota Iron Lands* (1937). A pamphlet of interest is J. L. Morrill's *Taconite! Sleeping Giant of the Mesabi* (1948). A series of short articles on Minnesota iron by several authors appears in the *Gopher Historian* for April 1952. Edward W. Davis writes of "Pioneering with Taconite: The Birth of a Minnesota Industry," in *Minnesota History*, 34:269–83 (Autumn 1955). On early backgrounds Newton Winchell's account of the discovery and development of the iron ores is a useful source – in *Minnesota Historical Collections,* vol. 8 (1898). A pamphlet entitled *Facts about Minnesota Iron Mining* (1958) includes articles of interest, especially the text of an address on the iron story by the late L. A. Rossman of Grand Rapids. For detail on the later story one must turn to newspapers, official statistics, and reports by the iron companies and state commissions. Legislative commission reports on the taxation of iron ore appeared in 1955 and 1961. A *Mining Directory*, prepared for 1961 by Henry H. Wade and Mildred R. Alm, and issued by the Mines Experiment Station of the university, is packed with information on the Minnesota iron-ore industry. The publication appears annually.

On agricultural diversification, cooperatives, and conservation, reading materials are numerous. Reference may be made once more to Robinson's early study of the development of agriculture in Minnesota and to Jarchow's *The Earth Brought Forth*. Everett E. Edwards has written informingly about T. L. Haecker and Minnesota dairying in *Minnesota History*, 19:148–61 (June 1938), and, with H. H. Russell, about Wendelin Grimm and alfalfa in the same magazine, 19:21–33 (March 1938). A basic work on *Cooperation in Agriculture* was brought out in 1929 by H. C. Filley; a book of selected readings, *Agricultural Cooperation*, edited by M. A. Abrahamsen and C. L. Scroggs, appeared in 1957. The earlier history of the *Minnesota Agricultural Experiment Station, 1885–1935* has been sketched by Andrew Boss (1935). As mentioned in the present book, T. A. Erickson has told the story of the 4-H clubs in his book *My Sixty Years with Rural Youth* (1956). John D. Hicks in *The*

Populist Revolt tells of the Farmers' Alliance, and C. H. Chrislock has written excellent articles on the Alliance and the state legislature of 1891, and on Sidney M. Owen, in *Minnesota History*, 35:297–312, and 36:109–26 (September 1957 and December 1958). No adequate life of Knute Nelson is yet available, but a work by Martin W. Odland (1926) is useful. Arthur Naftalin writes on the rise of agrarian and labor organizations in an article in *Minnesota History*, 35:53–63 (June 1956).

The reports of the Minnesota State Horticultural Society and bulletins of the University of Minnesota document Minnesota's role in the horticultural fields. An important and authoritative source of information is W. H. Alderman's *Development of Horticulture on the Northern Great Plains* (1962), which includes an informing chapter on horticulture in Minnesota and interprets the western development of horticulture in a broad setting. On conservation, the *Recollections* of C. C. Andrews is invaluable. E. G. Cheyney and A. L. Nelson write on *Forestry in Minnesota* (1932); and the files of the *Conservation Volunteer*, published since 1940 by the Department of Conservation, are rich in articles on varied aspects of conservation. For detailed references, readers may consult the *Guide to Reading and Study*.

Education, Changing Times, Peace and War
(Chapters 20, 21, and 22)

Dr. Folwell's fourth volume (1930) is a series of essays, two of which deal with the University of Minnesota and public education; and in an appendix he writes a series of twelve biographical sketches which he calls "The Acts of the Apostles." Six of the twelve gave part or much of their lives to Minnesota education: T. L. Haecker, Charles N. Hewitt, Edward D. Neill, William S. Pattee, Maria Sanford, and Newton H. Winchell. The other six were C. C. Andrews, Hastings H. Hart, Charles M. Loring, LeGrand Powers, Henry B. Whipple, and Thomas B. Walker. These were persons who, in Folwell's opinion, stood out as vanguards of progress. Whether one agrees with Dr. Folwell's selection of "apostles" or not, he ferreted out a dozen distinguished Minnesotans who in their ideas and actions were, in Ibsen's phrase, "in league with the future."

A modern view of Minnesota education is offered in a series of chapters in *Minnesota Heritage*, beginning with elementary and secondary schools, going on to the private liberal-arts colleges, and concluding with a series of essays on public higher education (plus accounts of the Minnesota Historical Society and of Minnesota's first public libraries). There are separate essays on the twelve private colleges as well as sections on the public junior colleges, the state colleges, and the University of Minnesota. Many of the institutions, private and public, have had their histories written in book form: St. John's Abbey and University by Colman J. Barry (1956); St. Thomas College by Edward Keenan (1936);

St. Olaf College by W. C. Benson (1949); Carleton College by D. L. Leonard (1904); Gustavus Adolphus by Conrad Peterson (1953); Macalester College by H. D. Funk (1910) and also, as part of a biographical study of Edward D. Neill, by Huntley Dupre (1949), and similarly as part of the story by Edwin Kagin of James Wallace (1957). Hamline University has a volume edited by C. N. Pace (1939), and its early story, from 1854 to 1869, is effectively recorded in an article in *Minnesota History* by Hellen D. Asher, 9:363–78 (December 1928). The story of Augsburg has been told (in Norwegian) by Andreas Helland (1920), who is also the author of a biography (in English) of Georg Sverdrup (1947) and the editor of six volumes (also in Norwegian) of Sverdrup's writings (1909–12). The history of St. Catherine's and the Sisters of St. Joseph is related in Sister Helen Angela Hurley's *On Good Ground* (1951); and Sister Grace McDonald records the Convent and College of St. Benedict in her scholarly book *With Lamps Burning* (1957).

The basic history of the University of Minnesota from 1851 to 1951 is by James Gray (1951), and he has also written a briefer story of the institution in a book called *Open Wide the Door* (1958). The early period (1851–69) of the university is recorded in T. C. Blegen's *The Land Lies Open*, pp. 151–95.

From an array of other publications on educational history, only a few can be mentioned. They include O. C. Carmichael's thoughtful appraisal of "The Roots of Higher Education in Minnesota," in *Minnesota History*, 34:90–95 (Autumn 1954); Fred Engelhardt's *Minnesota Public Schools* (1934); Dr. Folwell's autobiography and letters, edited by S. J. Buck (1933); *Cyrus Northrop: A Memoir*, by Oscar Firkins (1925); Helen Whitney's *Maria Sanford* (1922); a comprehensive cooperative work on *Higher Education in Minnesota* issued by the Minnesota Commission on Higher Education (1950); Jean Talbot's book on Winona State College (1960); the rich files of the *Minnesota Journal of Education*; and *The Changing Educational World, 1905–1930*, edited by A. C. Eurich (1931). Readers may be interested in addresses by presidents of the University of Minnesota at different periods. Thus Dr. Folwell had a volume of *University Addresses* (1909); Cyrus Northrop, *Addresses, Educational and Patriotic* (1910); Lotus D. Coffman, *The State University* (1934); Guy Stanton Ford, *On and Off the Campus* (1938); and J. L. Morrill, *The Ongoing State University* (1960).

On the political side, George M. Stephenson has written a crisp biography of *John Lind of Minnesota* (1935); and readers may wish to see the text of Lind's biennial message to the state legislature in 1899, as printed in *With Various Voices*, pp. 345–72.

Of many documents having to do with social and humanitarian advance, Dr. Folwell's essay on "Hastings H. Hart, Apostle of Public Charities," in vol. 4 of his *History of Minnesota*, based largely on the published reports of the Board of Corrections and Charities, is interesting. A sample of Hart's own writing is included in *With Various Voices*, pp. 324–28 – a discussion from 1884 of "Conditions in Minnesota Jails." An informing modern survey of public welfare and social work is offered by John C. Kidneigh in *Minnesota Heritage*, pp. 344–70. Joseph Kise in *Minnesota's Government*, pp. 147–54, reviews the state's activities in the care of dependent and disabled persons.

For public health, medicine, dentistry, and hospitals, major works include Philip D. Jordan's *The People's Health* (1953); Helen Clapesattle's *The Doctors Mayo* (1941 and 1954); Netta Wilson's biography of *Alfred Owre* (1937); and Dr. J. Arthur Myers' study of tuberculosis in Minnesota in his book *Invited and Conquered* (1949). Dr. Robert Rosenthal surveys the story of the Minnesota State Medical Association in an article in *Minnesota Medicine*, vol. 36 (April 1953); and in the same journal, vol. 15, H. S. Diehl traces the rise of Minnesota medical education (December 1934). James Gray in his *Education for Nursing* (1960) tells about the University of Minnesota's School of Nursing. An article of lively interest is Helen Clapesattle's "When Minnesota Was Florida's Rival," in *Minnesota History*, 35:214–21 (March 1957). And one should not overlook Dr. Folwell's essay on "Charles N. Hewitt, Apostle of Public Health," in vol. 4 of *History of Minnesota*. The Minnesota hospital story is reviewed in a chapter, "From Cottage to Clinic," in T. C. Blegen's *Grass Roots History*.

On the rise of cities, Mildred L. Hartsough's book on the Twin Cities as a metropolitan market is valuable, as is an article by N. S. B. Gras on the significance of the Twin Cities, in *Minnesota History*, 7:3–17 (March 1926). A solid historical account of a smaller city is Edgar Wesley's *Owatonna: The Social Development of a Minnesota Community* (1938). George W. Lawson has written a *History of Labor in Minnesota* (1955); and George B. Engberg has articles on the Knights of Labor and the rise of organized labor in the state in *Minnesota History*, 22:367–90, and 21:372–94 (the December issues for 1941 and 1940). Fifteen Minnesota communities are studied in R. J. Holloway's *A City Is More Than People* (1954). Interesting information about Minneapolis is in the *Gopher Historian* (Spring 1956), and in later numbers of this magazine there are sketches of many Minnesota communities. An essay on "The Booming of Gopher Prairie" is in T. C. Blegen's *The Land Lies Open*, pp. 128–36. Lawrence M. Brings has edited a volume on *Minneapolis, City of Opportunity* (1956); and a comprehensive history of Minneapolis by Lucile Kane is in course of preparation. For other references, see the *Guide to Reading and Study*, pp. 126–28.

On the Spanish-American War, Dr. Folwell has an excellent chapter in his *History of Minnesota*, vol. 3; and George M. Stephenson deals with that period in his life of John Lind (pp. 105–91). A well-written biography touching the same era and the early years of the twentieth century is *John A. Johnson, the People's Governor*, by Winifred G. Helmes (1949). The adoption of the direct primary law in 1901 is the subject of a scholarly article by C. J. Hein in *Minnesota History*, 35:341–51 (December 1957).

The changing national social scene in the early 1900s is described colorfully in Walter Lord's *The Good Years* (1960). On modern transportation there are numerous readings of which a few may be mentioned. Several articles in the *Gopher Historian* for Spring 1957 are helpful, and some are reprinted in *The Gopher Reader*. The origins of the Greyhound Bus Company are described in the *Gopher Historian* for May 1951. A basic work is Mildred L. Hartsough's *From Canoe to Steel Barge on the Upper Mississippi* (1934). The state highway system is described in *Highway Transportation in Minnesota* (1954); and there is a quick sketch of "Great Lakes Ships and Shipping" by D. T. Bowen in *Minnesota History*, 34:9–16 (Spring 1954). Early automobiling in Minnesota is discussed by Dorothy V. Walters in the same magazine, 26:19–28 (March 1945); and there is a summary of "Minnesota in the World of Aviation," also in *Minnesota History*, 33:236–46 (Summer 1953). Much has been written about Colonel Lindbergh. A notable work is Kenneth S. Davis, *The Hero* (1959), a family saga of the Lindberghs, but many readers will want to consult Lindbergh's own firsthand account in *The Spirit of St. Louis* (1953).

On the Progressive movement, C. R. Adrian's article "The Origin of Minnesota's Nonpartisan Legislature," in *Minnesota History*, 33:155–63 (Winter 1952), is of interest. Lynn and Dora B. Haines tell the story of *The Lindberghs* in a volume published in 1931. The history of the Nonpartisan League is told by R. L. Morlan, *Political Prairie Fire* (1955); and he is also the author of an article on "The Nonpartisan League and the Minnesota Campaign of 1918," in *Minnesota History*, 34:221–32 (Summer 1955). The story of Minnesota in World War I is told in detail in a two-volume work by F. F. Holbrook and Livia Appel, *Minnesota in the War with Germany* (1928–32); and O. A. Hilton has recorded the mournful story of the Minnesota Commission of Public Safety in a *Bulletin* (1951) of the Oklahoma Agricultural and Mechanical College. World War I also comes in for a survey in Virginia B. Kunz, *Muskets to Missiles*, pp. 132–58. Governor Burnquist in his *Minnesota and Its People*, vol. 1, pp. 366–78, tells of the years 1916–23; and Theodore Christianson in the second volume of his history of the state includes much detail on politics in the period from 1918 to 1934. Dr. Folwell in his vol. 3, pp. 293–322, presents a survey of events in the period from 1909 to 1925. An appraisal of "Frank B. Kellogg's View of History and Progress" by Charles G. Cleaver appears in *Minnesota History*, 35:157–66 (December 1956), and a recent book by L. E. Ellis deals with his service in wider fields, *Frank B. Kellogg and American Foreign Relations* (1961). The readings thus cited will provide an introduction, but only an introduction, to a period crowded with events and personalities in this era of Minnesota's history.

The Flourishing of the Arts (Chapters 23 and 24)

A dependable and interesting book is *A History of the Arts in Minnesota*, edited by William Van O'Connor (1958). In it John Sherman tells of music and the theater, Grace Lee Nute writes about books and authors, and Donald R. Torbert deals with art and architecture. These essays are all by authoritative writers. To each section are appended relevant bibliographical aids. For most readers this book alone is satisfactory background reading for Chapters 23 and 24, but some special books and articles must be mentioned.

For Minnesota music John Sherman's very good history of the Minneapolis Symphony Orchestra, *Music and Maestros* (1952), is indispensable. Equally so is Leola N. Bergmann's biography of F. Melius Christiansen, *Music Master of the Middle West* (1944). E. E. Simpson has written a *History of St. Olaf Choir* (1921). Philip D. Jordan has told the story of the Hutchinson family in *Singin' Yankees* (1946), and Carol Ryrie Brink has dealt with this chapter of musical history in her *Harps in the Wind* (1947). The Andrews family is recorded by Cornelia A. DuBois in an article on "Operatic Pioneers," in *Minnesota History*, 33:317–25 (Winter 1953).

On painting, sculpture, and architecture, the best survey is Professor Torbert's chapter on "A Century of Art and Architecture in Minnesota," in *A History of the Arts in Minnesota*. Several readings on early artists are mentioned above (pp. 609–610). An excellent article on LeRoy S. Buffington by Muriel B. Christison is in *Minnesota History*, 23:219–32 (September 1942); and Robert A. Jones writes about Cass Gilbert in the *Northwest Architect* for November–December 1959. Dr. Folwell tells of Douglas Volk in the *Minnesotan* for May 1916; and in vol. 4 of his *History of Minnesota* he presents Thomas B. Walker as Minnesota's "Apostle of Art." Wanda Gág tells her own story in *Growing Pains* (1940) and her biography has been written by Alma Scott (1949). Luth Jaeger has an article on Jacob and Paul Fjelde in "Two American Sculptors," *American-Scandinavian Review*, 10:467–72 (August 1922). The story of Horace W. S. Cleveland, landscape architect, is told in an essay on "Pioneers of the Second Line," in T. C. Blegen's *The Land Lies Open*; and Dr. Folwell in his fourth volume describes Charles M. Loring as the state's "Apostle of Parks and Playgrounds." A pamphlet of distinction is Laurence Schmeckebier's *Art in Red Wing* (1946).

On books and writers, no attempt will be made here to repeat the names of Minnesota authors and titles of books already referred to in Chapter 24, but some special appraisals may be mentioned. Dr. Nute reviews the field in *A History of the Arts in Minnesota*, and such creative giants as Rölvaag, Sinclair Lewis, F. Scott Fitzgerald, and Thorstein Veblen have had their biographers, notably — and in the order named — Theodore Jorgenson and Nora Solum (1939); Mark Schorer (1961); Arthur Mizener (1951) and Andrew Turnbull (1962); and Joseph Dorfman (1934) and David Riesman (1953). Innumerable articles and other books have been written about these noted writers. Pamphlet-length studies of two of them have appeared in the University of Minnesota Press series on American writers — *F. Scott Fitzgerald* by Charles Shain (1961) and *Sinclair Lewis* by Mark Schorer (1963). Among articles of special interest are Henry S. Commager's "The Literature of the Pioneer West," on Rölvaag, and John T. Flanagan's "The Minnesota Backgrounds of Sinclair Lewis' Fiction," in *Minnesota History*, 8:319–28 (December 1927), and 37:1–13 (March 1960). Professor Flanagan has also written many other articles in *Minnesota History* on such writers (in their Minnesota connections) as William J. Snelling, Edward Eggleston, Hamlin Garland, and Knut Hamsun. One of his essays is on "The Middle Western Farm Novel," *Minnesota History*, 23:113–25 (June 1942); and he is the editor of an anthology of middle western literature in his book *America Is West* (1945). A critical reappraisal that controverts recent claims for Fitzgerald is Guy A. Cardwell's "The Lyric World of Scott Fitzgerald," in the *Virginia Quarterly Review*, Spring 1962. An excellent review of "The Public Library Movement in Minnesota, 1849–1900," by Ellworth Carlstedt is in *Minnesota Libraries* for September 1945; and an essay on "Frontier Bookshelves" is in T. C. Blegen's *Grass Roots History*, pp. 175–86. Autobiographical sketches by Minnesota authors are in Carmen Nelson Richards, *Minnesota Writers* (revised edition, 1961), with appraisals by Mrs. Richards and lists of their writings.

Recent Minnesota History (Chapters 25, 26, and 27)

The problem of selected readings becomes difficult as one moves into the era of Minnesota as presented in the final three chapters in this book. For much pertinent information, one must turn to the reports of departments and commissions; to yearbooks, notably those issued by the *Encyclopedia Britannica* and the *Encyclopedia Americana* (contemporary surveys, with emphasis on economic and political developments); to messages and speeches; to the *Legislative Manuals*; and to newspapers and other scattered sources.

No one has written a comprehensive book on Minnesota in the 1930s. There is no survey of Minnesota in World War II comparable with the two-volume work on World War I. And the period since 1945 is too recent to have produced an integrated study of its economic, social, and political aspects. Not a few references have already been offered, however, on developments in a number of fields, including education, agriculture, the iron-ore industry, social advance, and the arts.

622

On the political side, a scholarly book on *The Political Career of Floyd B. Olson* (1951) has been written by George H. Mayer. R. A. Esbjornson is the author of an exuberant biography of *A Christian in Politics: Luther Youngdahl* (1955). Selections from Harold E. Stassen's addresses are given in his book *Where I Stand!* (1947); and Michael Amrine has written *This Is Humphrey* (1960) — obviously a campaign document of 1960, when Senator Humphrey tried for the Democratic nomination for President. The inaugural addresses and messages of Minnesota's governors, from the territorial period and through the state's history to 1961, have been published and can be found in libraries, including that of the Minnesota Historical Society, as separate pieces or in governmental documents. Minnesota's political party platforms — like the governors' messages — are not available in modern compilations, though typewritten copies of the platforms from 1849 to 1938 were made some years ago by Sarah A. Davidson, William Anderson, and T. C. Blegen; and one copy of this document is in the manuscript division of the Minnesota Historical Society.

G. Theodore Mitau's *Politics in Minnesota* (1960) emphasizes twentieth-century politics, election law and party organization, the nonpartisan legislature, and lobbies. Of wider scope is a study of *Agricultural Discontent in the Middle West, 1900–1939* (1951) by Theodore Saloutos and John D. Hicks. Lloyd M. Short and C. W. Tiller have jointly written a monograph on *The Minnesota Commission of Administration and Finance, 1925–39* (1942).

Other sources for recent history are Lowry Nelson's book on *The Minnesota Community*; and Virginia B. Kunz's *Muskets to Missiles*, in which she devotes pp. 159–91 to "Peace — and the Second World War." Many articles in the *Gopher Historian*, especially for the years 1958–62, deal with agriculture and industry in the various sections of Minnesota and are a mine of information on small communities as well as on the large cities of the state. One of the leading industrial concerns of Minnesota is recorded by Virginia Huck in her book *Brand of the Tartan: The 3M Story* (1955).

For the depression of the 1930s, a publication on the *Works Progress Administration in Minnesota* was issued in 1936; and in 1934, Frank M. Rarig wrote an illuminating report, "Division of Relief," published by the State Board of Control. The Minnesota Department of Health has issued many valuable reports and surveys. One of interest is *Homes for Aged and Chronically Ill Persons in Minnesota*, prepared by Ethel McClure (December 1959). A more recent compilation is entitled *Minnesota State Plan for Hospitals, Public Health Centers and Related Medical Facilities* (1961). Those interested in sports will find good reading in George A. Barton, *My Lifetime in Sports* (1959), and Fred A. Sassé, *The Dan Patch Story* (1957). Recent urban problems are analyzed in a report of the Twin Cities Metropolitan Commission entitled *The Chal-*

lenge of Metropolitan Growth (1959). Ten publications in a series on Intergovernmental Relations as Observed in the State of Minnesota were issued from 1950 to 1960 under the editorship of William Anderson and Edward W. Weidner. They include many facts and figures on courts, highways, education, public health, social welfare, employment security, and government financing in Minnesota. *Aging in Minnesota* (1963), edited by Arnold M. Rose, looks closely at the state's "senior citizens."

Among many publications, the State Department of Business Development has issued a brochure on Minnesota's *Industrial Horizons,* and the Northwestern National Bank of Minneapolis has published an excellent summary of *Minnesota's Electronics and Related Science Industries* (1960). Covering much more than recent financial history are three important books. One is Charles S. Popple's *Development of Two Bank Groups in the Central Northwest* (1944). A second is a history of the Farmers and Mechanics Savings Bank of Minneapolis, *Pioneer Harvest* (1949), by Marion E. Cross. And the third is the story of the First National Bank of St. Paul, *The First through a Century* (1954). A standard fiscal study is Roy G. Blakey's *Taxation in Minnesota* (1932). A personal interpretation of *The Twin Cities* (1961) has been written by the novelist Carol Brink.

An informative series of a dozen pamphlets dealing with a representative Minnesota community — Red Wing — was published from 1944 to 1952 under the auspices of the Graduate School of the University of Minnesota with the general title "The Community Basis for Postwar Planning." This was a cooperative study, with many scholars joining hands. The separate pamphlets dealt with the economic impact of the war, community leadership and opinion, the schools, art, journalism, churches, public health, and other subjects. Five years after the first surveys were made, Roland S. Vaile wrote an appraisal of changes in this community during the half decade after the close of World War II. The series is a contribution of value to the understanding of the war period and the community problems it posed.

These are a few items that throw light on the Minnesota story for the past three or more decades. Others are listed in the *Guide to Reading and Study,* but the problem of drawing the story into sequence involves the use of many and scattered stray bits of information in sources that cannot be detailed in this sketch.

It is beyond the scope of these suggestions to list the books and articles needed to correlate Minnesota history with its North American and European backgrounds. As has been indicated, the interrelations of the state with region, nation, and world are integral to the history of Minnesota; and readers are urged to turn to books in their own collections or in public or other libraries to supply connections and backgrounds that have not been clarified in this book.

INDEX

Index

INDEX

Ames, Rev. Charles G., political activity of, 216

Ancker Hospital, in St. Paul, 442

Andahazy, Lorand, ballet school of, 506

Andersen, Elmer L. (governor, *1961–63*): in election of *1960*, 582; policies as governor, 583–84; and congressional redistricting, 585; in election of *1962*, 585–89

Andersen Corporation, World War II production of, 547

Anderson, Andrew G., and motor buses, 465–66

Anderson, C. Elmer (governor, *1951–55*), 536: in election of *1952*, 555, 578; in election of *1954*, 578

Anderson, Eugenie: Democratic-Farmer-Labor leader, 577; State Fair Employment Practices Commission chairman, 578; ambassador to Denmark, 578

Anderson, Frank M., historian, 424

Anderson, Maj. Robert, surrender of Fort Sumter, 238, 239

Anderson, William, political scientist: quoted, 225; publications of, 517, 610, 611, 623, 624; on reducing number of governmental units, 592

Andersonville Prison, 247

Andreani, Count Paolo, visit to Minnesota, 113

Andrews, Christopher C.: at Murfreesboro, 248; and Union party, 249; debates with Miller, 250; in election of *1868*, 290; and conservation, 324, 404–6; writings of, 509, 617; article on, 617

Andrews family: presents operas, 488; article on, 621

Andreyev, Leonid Nikolaevich, playwright, 505

Annuities to Indians, 129, 131, 140, 166, 173, 259, 260, 262, 265, 266, 281, 283

Anoka, Minn.: Sioux attack on Chippewa near, 132; railroad to, 296; hospital for insane at, 435

Anoka County, represented on Metropolitan Planning Commission, 584

Anthony Wayne, river steamer, 190

Anti-evolution bill, 482

Anti-isolationism, 538

Anti-loan-shark law, 537

Anzio, 542

Apollo Club, 489, 490

Appleby, W. R., educator, 424

Apples, 201, 392, 401–4, 563, 565: Wealthy, 401, 402; Haralson, 404; Beacon, 404; Washington County and, 567

Aquatennials, 533

Arbre Croche (Harbor Springs, Mich.), 152

Archaeology of Minnesota, 17–19, 20: publications on, 605

Archer-Daniels-Midland Company, 564

Archibald Mill, 348, 351

Architecture, 487, 496–98: suggested reading on, 621

Arese, Count Francesco, traveler, 120

Argonne, 475

Armistice Day, 475

Army, U.S., 104: contribution to knowledge about Minnesota, 121; Civil War recruiting problems, 242–43; Minnesota Civil War units, 243; in Sioux War, 271; Minnesota World War I recruits, 474; Minnesota World War II recruits, 542, 543

Arnest, Bernard, artist, 494

Arnold, H. V., on westward migration, 346–47

Arrowhead country, 13, 123

Art education, 412, 419, 493–94

Arthritis, 438

Artifacts, archaeological, 18, 19, 83

Arts, 487: in pioneer times, 102, 117–18, 121, 167, 176–77, 492, 610; panoramists, 121, 156–57, 492; folk art, 492; art schools, 493–94; amateur, 494; photography, 494; architecture, 496–98; landscape architecture, 498–500; WPA and, 527; publications on, 610, 621, 624

Ashburton, Lord Alexander, and boundary dispute, 122–23

Askov, Minn., rutabaga production at, 567

"Assiniboia," 92, 93, 282

Assiniboin Indians: dialect of, 20; councils with, 48, 58; friendly to French, 59

Assiniboine River: French fort established on, 60; Selkirk colony near, 93

Astor, John Jacob, fur merchant: and China trade, 85; enlargement of American Fur Company, 90, 96; monopoly of fur trade, 90, 132; use of liquor in fur trade, 130; retires from fur trade, 134; decline of fur trade, 134, 136; biography of, 608

Astoria, trading post, 77, 86

Athabasca region, 71

Athenaeum, Minneapolis, 506

629

geographic board, 536; special sessions of, 536, 585; passes anti-loan-shark law, 537; adopts civil service reform, 537; approves labor relations act, 537; authorizes state reorganization, 537; strengthens control of liquor traffic, 553; bans slot machines, 553; passes Fair Employment Practices Law, 579; takes action on legislative reapportionment, 581; sessions of *1961*, 584; approves withholding of state income tax, 584; approves constitutional amendments for popular vote, 584–85; and congressional redistricting, 585; and taconite amendment, 585, 587, 593; *Legislative Manuals*, 603, 611, 622; suggested reading on, 620

Legislature, territorial, 164: laws passed, 165; and Crystal Palace exhibit, 181; and normal schools, 187; and "blue laws," 205; and sale of liquor to Indians, 206; and St. Peter Company, 219; special session of, 221

Leipzig, Germany: fur auctions at, 78; Leipzig fair, 139

Lend-lease, 540

Lester, Col. Henry C., at Murfreesboro, 248

Le Sueur, Pierre Charles, fur trader and explorer, 52, 53

Le Sueur, Minn.: Dr. W. W. Mayo at, 198, 270; canning industry at, 562

Le Sueur County, flour milling at, 349

Levi, Werner, political scientist and writer, 517

Lewis, Henry, panoramist, 156–57, 492, 517, 610

Lewis, J. O., painter, article on, 610

Lewis, Meriwether, explorer, 46, 87

Lewis, Sinclair, 597: writings of, 512–13; biography of, 518, 622

Lewis, Dr. and Mrs. William, missionaries, 150

Lewis and Clark expedition, 87

Lewis and Clark fair, 461

Libby, Robert, quoted, on ore loading, 380

Libby Prison, 248

Liberal education, 415, 416, 417, 418, 419

Liberal Republicans, 292–93

Liberty loans, 471

Libraries, 415, 487, 506–8, 622: on frontier, 138, 506; library associations, 203, 472, 506, 507; of colleges, 419; of university, 421, 428; in World War I, 472; Athenaeum, 506; public, 506, 507, 530, 617, 622; of county historical societies, 508

Library subscription clubs, 506, 507

Licenses: fur trade, 36, 38, 51, 53, 61, 67, 72, 80, 133, 134; liquor, 206; saloon, 386; automobile, 464, 484; fishing, 533; drivers', 585

Liebling, Jerome, photographer, 494

Life expectancy, 447

Lillehei, Dr. C. Walton, pioneer in heart surgery, 447

Lincoln, Abraham, 262: vote on Sibley's status, 162; Lincoln-Douglas debates, 224; Shields' duel with, 227; elected President, 235–36; in Civil War, 239, 240, 243, 248, 249; quoted, 245, 250, 280, 476; dismissal of Colonel Lester, 248; in election of *1864*, 250; signs Homestead Act, 253; death of, 255, 504; and Sioux War, 274, 276, 279, 280; approves railroad land grant, 297; publications on, 612

Lincoln County, Danish settlers in, 310

Lind, John (governor, *1899–1901*), 457, 597: program as governor, 433–34, 436–37; on future population of state, 434, 483; withdraws from Commission of Public Safety, 473; biography of, 517, 518, 618, 619; text of *1899* message to legislature, 618

Lindbergh, Rep. Charles A.: opposes tariff, 467; defeated for senatorial nomination, 468; in election of *1918*, 476–77

Lindbergh, Col. Charles A., 566: *1927* flight of, 485; publications on, 620

Lippincott, Gertrude, dancer, 506

Liquor: use by Indians, 25, 28, 88, 99, 130, 134, 140, 144, 152, 154, 164, 167, 206, 262; effect on Indians, 77, 117, 127, 129–30, 132; use in fur trade, 77, 129, 134, 144–45, 152, 206; extent of liquor traffic, 129–30; smuggling by independent traders, 130; in oxcart traffic, 192; in early settlements, 202; "liquorary association," 204; temperance societies, 204, 206; and crime, 206; "Maine Law," 206; prohibitory law proposed, 217; in Sioux Uprising, 260, 262; Temperance party, 291; brewing industry, 308; in lumber camps, 332; saloon license fees, 386; regulation of, 471, 553; national prohibition of, 477,

packing in, 392; market gardening in, 401; colleges in, 416, 418; hospitals in, 442–43; medical schools in, 443; commerce in, 451; financial center, 451; industries in, 451; municipal problems of, 453; strikes in, 454, 527; labor in, 454, 455; streetcars in, 454, 462; government of, 461–62; newspapers of, 462, 573; automobiles in, 463–64; airmail flight starts in, 466; Loyalty League of, 470; Dunwoody Institute in, 475, 558; Ku Klux Klan in, 482; motion picture theaters in, 482; skyline of, 483; nine-foot channel project, 484; airport at, 485; orchestras of, 488; music societies of, 488–89; Symphony Orchestra, 490–91, 492, 518; museums of, 493–95, 508; parks in, 498–99; theater in, 503–6; ballet in, 506; libraries in, 506–8; sports in, 531, 532, 534; Aquatennial of, 533; World War II manufacturing in, 546–47, 548; vocational schools in, 557–58; electronics industry in, 558, 624; manufactures of, 559; department stores in, 560; barge traffic of, 560–61; first switchboard in, 572; Hubert Humphrey as mayor, 578; Fair Employment Practices Commission in, 579; suggested reading on, 619, 624

Minneapolis and Cedar Valley Railroad: land grant to, 195; renamed Minnesota Central, 296

Minneapolis and Duluth Railroad, 298

Minneapolis and St. Louis Railroad, 298, 356

Minneapolis Baseball Association, 531

Minneapolis Board of Park Commissioners, 499

Minneapolis Chamber of Commerce, 355

Minneapolis City Hall, first switchboard at, 572

Minneapolis College of Physicians and Surgeons, 443

Minneapolis Daglige Tidende, 573

Minneapolis Flour Manufacturing Company, 354

Minneapolis Harvester Works, 342

Minneapolis-Honeywell Regulator Company: World War II production of, 546; research by, 557

Minneapolis Institute of Fine Arts, 494–95

Minneapolis Journal, 462

Minneapolis Mill Company, 349

Minneapolis Millers' Association, 355

Minneapolis Moline, Inc., World War II production of, 546

Minneapolis Public Library, 506, 507, 508: Rood sculpture at, 494

Minneapolis Society of Fine Arts, 493, 494: art school, 493

Minneapolis Star and *Tribune*, 573

Minneapolis Symphony Orchestra, 490–91, 492: history of, 518

"Minneapolis-to-Gulf Day," 484

Minnehaha Falls, 13, 103: Stevens house at, 178; Fjelde statue at, 493; park at, 499

Minneota, Minn.: Irish settlers at, 309; Icelandic settlers at, 312

"Minnesota, The," flour mill, 348

Minnesota Agricultural Experiment Station, 392, 396, 402, 403, 425, 428: publication on, 616

"Minnesota and Northwestern Railroad," chartered, 194, 296

Minnesota and Ontario Paper Company, 329

"Minnesota and Pacific Railroad": chartered, 194; land grant to, 195; renamed St. Paul and Pacific, 296

Minnesota Arrowhead Association, 532

Minnesota Athletic Commission, 534

Minnesota Butter and Cheese Association, 393

Minnesota Central Railroad, 296, 298

Minnesota College Hospital, 443

Minnesota College of Homeopathic Medicine, 443

Minnesota Commission of Administration and Finance, 623

Minnesota Commission of Public Safety, 470

Minnesota Commission on Higher Education, 618

Minnesota Community, The, 556, 623

Minnesota Co-operative Dairies Association, 398

Minnesota Cooperative Oil Company, 399

Minnesota Corrections Association, 438

Minnesota Dairymen's Association, 393

Minnesota Editorial Association, 574

Minnesota Education Association, 413

Minnesota Farm Bureau, 584

Minnesota Farm Bureau Federation, 400

Minnesota Farmer and Gardener, 394

Minnesota Farmers' Union, 399

Minnesota Federation of Women's Clubs, 507

university, 188; political activity of, 216, 223; at constitutional convention, 223
North Dakota, 396: Nonpartisan League in, 468–69; sales tax in, 594
North Star Grange, founded, 292
North Star Woolen Mills, World War II production of, 548
North West Company, 67, 71, 72, 73, 86: trade with Sioux, 74; trading posts, 74; David Thompson's map-making for, 76; Alexander Henry the Younger's expeditions for, 77; international fur trade of, 78; collection of chansons, 80; competition to, 80, 81, 92; relinquishes posts, 81; XY Company merger, 81; merged with Hudson's Bay Company, 82, 93; trade with Astor, 85; Pike's visit to post of, 89–90; hostility to Selkirk colony, 93; use of liquor in fur trade, 129
Northern Lumber Company, 328
"Northern Outfit," 135
Northern Pacific Railroad, 298: chartered, 194; land grants to, 299, 300, 301, 327, 345; colonization program of, 304–6; in merger, 456–57
Northern Pump Company, World War II production of, 546
Northern Securities Company case, 456, 468
Northfield, Minn.: flour milling in, 348; colleges in, 416, 453, 563
Northland Transportation Company, 466
Northrop, Cyrus: educator, 423–24, 425, 518, 597; and peace crusade, 470; publication on, 618; addresses of, 618
Northrop Auditorium, 408, 427, 490–91
Northup, Anson, and steamboat on Red River, 192
Northwest Angle, 57, 94
Northwest Ordinance, 95, 224
Northwest Paper Company, 329
Northwest Passage, 38, 66, 73: search for, 67–69
Northwest Territory, states formed from, 95, 157
Northwestern Aeronautical Corporation, World War II production of, 547
Northwestern Bell Telephone Company, 572
Northwestern Chronicle, 309
Northwestern Conservatory of Music, 489
Northwestern Consolidated Milling Company, 354
Northwestern Hospital, 442

Northwestern Lancet, 442
Northwestern National Bank, Minneapolis, publication on, 624
Northwestern Telephone Exchange Company, 572
Norton, Sen. Daniel S., policy on South, 289–90
Norton, James L., in lumber industry, 321
Norton, Matthew G., in lumber industry, 321
Norwegian influence, 200, 201, 305, 306, 387, 477: settlers, 175, 193, 202, 305, 307, 309–11, 566, 614; Lutheran churches, 207, 311; in Civil War, 243; in Sioux War, 276–77; in education, 311, 414, 416, 417; in politics, 311, 387, 389, 390; lumberjacks, 330, 332; in iron mining, 377; in music, 491–92; in art, 492–93; in theater, 504; writers, 510–11, 512, 514, 518, 519; Norwegian-American Historical Association, 514; skiing, 533
Norwood, Dr. J. G., discovers iron ore, 361
Nova Scotia, British control of, 54
Nuclear weapons, 548
Nursing, 446: by Catholic nuns, 198; education for, 419, 423, 442, 546, 619; in World War I, 474
Nursing homes, 442–43: suggested reading on, 623
Nute, Grace Lee: quoted, 362, 365; work as historian, 516–17; writings of, 604, 606, 608, 609, 614, 616, 621

Oak Grove, 149
Oats, 100, 195, 200, 339, 346, 391, 564, 567
Oberhoffer, Emil, conductor, 489, 491, 492
Oberlin, Ohio, missionary work among Indians at, 144, 150
"Oberlin Band," 150
O'Brien, Dillon, writer, 309, 509
O'Connor, William Van, literary critic, 519, 621
Odd Fellows, 203
Oelrich, Ernest L., defense coordinator, 543
Oftedal, Sven, theologian, 417
Ohage, Dr. Justus, physician, 441
Ohio, 91, 307, 421: part of Northwest Territory, 95; influence on Minnesota, 326, 401; sales tax in, 594

cans, 91, 97; Fort Crawford established at, 97; *1825* Indian conclave at, 114, 128; council of *1830* at, 128; American Fur Company post at, 135; railroad reaches, 193

Prairie fires, 77, 195, 405

Prairie Island: trading post on, 52; friendly Sioux gathered on, 281

Pratte, Chouteau, and Company, 135: and land-cession treaties, 166

Pre-Cambrian era, 7

Pre-emption: act of *1841*, 173–74; act of *1855*, 178; rights, 178, 234; practices, 364

Preference primaries enacted, 467

Preparatory schools, 188, 410, 416

Preparedness, 470, 538, 540, 541

Presbyterians: missionary work with Indians, 144, 145, 147–48; church growth, 207; support college, 415, 416, 417. *See also* Neill, Edward D.

Prescott, Philander: visit to Pipestone, 118; death of, 269

Press, *see* Journalism; Newspapers

Preus, J. A. O. (governor, *1921–25*): policies as governor, 477–78, 481; in special election of *1923*, 478

Price, Richard, educator, 425

Prince Edward Island, 92

Pro-Germanism, charges made of, 471, 473, 476–77, 543

Proclamation of *1763*, 66, 67, 70

Production, in World War II, 546–48

Progressive party, 467, 620

Prohibition, 477, 478: Temperance party, 291; Prohibition party, 389; enforcement problems, 481–82; repeal of, 482, 535

Property, rights of, 164

Protective League, 473

Protestant churches, 530: support colleges, 416–17, 419; percentage of churchgoers, 576

Provençalle, Louis: at Traverse des Sioux, 133, 137; essay on, 608

Provencher, Joseph N., priest, 151

Public examiner, office established, 294

Public health, 421, 439–40, 458–59, 479, 517, 553, 584: publications on, 610, 619, 623, 624

Public lands, 165, 192, 221, 322, 344, 364

Public schools, *see* Education

Public services, increased demand for, 594–95

Public utilities, 528, 538: municipal ownership of, 457–58; regulation of, 584

Public welfare, 586: state aid to, 594. *See also* Social problems

Purcell, Dr. Edward, physician at Fort Snelling, 102

Pure Food and Drug Act, 440

Puritan influence, 205, 207, 217, 308: in Zumbrota, 201; New England settlers, 308

Pyle, Howard, artist, 497

Quakers, meeting house built, 207

Qualey, Carlton, historian, quoted, 313, 614

Quebec, 42, 151: founded, 31, 34; British conquest of, 35; fur-trade center, 37, 58; in French and Indian War, 61; Quebec Act, 66; suggested reading on, 606

Quebec Act of *1774*, 66

Queen Anne's War, 54, 62

Quigley, Harold S., political scientist, 517

Quirt, Walter, artist, 494

Race problems, 510, 552, 595: Fair Employment Practices Law, 553, 579, 583; in housing, 580, 583, 585; Interracial Commission, 583–84; with Indians, 583–84, 586

Racing, 167: steamboat, 189–90; horse, 200; at state fair, 403

Rackets, 481–82, 535

Radical Republicans, 290

Radio, 480, 483, 508, 532, 587, 596: university broadcasting, 428; development of stations, 572

Radisson, Pierre, 69, 71, 509, 516–17: expedition with Groseilliers, 36–38; importance of, 38–39; biography of, 606; "Voyages," 606

Rafts, 189: for lumber, 318, 320, 333

Railroad and Warehouse Commission, 344, 386, 388, 467

Railroads, 10, 180, 189, 248, 287, 293, 310, 318, 325, 341, 343, 349, 362, 462, 560, 562: reach Rock Island, 193; plans for, 193–95, 218; land grants for, 194–95, 220, 221, 252, 296–97, 299, 301, 324, 327, 341, 344, 345, 362; railroad lands, 194–95, 221, 301, 302, 306, 309, 327, 341, 344, 345, 362, 363; map of projected, 196; "Five Million Loan," 228, 252, 254, 294; rail fares, 252, 304; construction of, 252, 255, 287, 295–304,

CODA

PUBLISHER'S NOTE

Theodore Blegen had planned to revise the preceding narrative extensively in a second edition, bringing it up to date and modifying interpretations in the light of later developments. He died before he could do so. The University of Minnesota Press decided to let these chapters stand as he had written them to preserve the unity of his approach. In the chapter that follows Russell W. Fridley surveys the events and problems in Minnesota in the decade or so after the original publication of this history.

✱
"A State That Works"

by Russell W. Fridley

THE painful and turbulent 1960s will be remembered by Americans for the violent deaths of national leaders, an unpopular war in Southeast Asia, pollution of natural resources, racial tensions, a rising crime rate, development of a drug culture, changing life styles, continuing depopulation of rural areas while suburban sprawl increased, and alienation by many from conventions and traditional values. Positive achievements included man's landing on the moon, the Great Society's attack on poverty and its civil rights legislation, a rising affluence for a wider segment of America's people, and a higher level of formal education for its citizenry. Minnesotans shared with their countrymen the individual agonies of the Bay of Pigs fiasco in 1961, the Cuban missile crisis in 1962, President John F. Kennedy's assassination in 1963, escalation of the Vietnam War in 1964, the Arab-Israeli Six-Day War in 1967, the assassinations of Martin Luther King, Jr., and Robert F. Kennedy in 1968, and the riots that followed. The powerful currents in our national life that did much to disrupt and fragment our society during the 1960s left their indelible mark on Minnesota history. At the same time, Minnesotans assumed an ever-greater role in the life of the nation. It was these two pronounced trends — a nation in turmoil and the North Star State through its sons and daughters assuming a stronger place in the federal union — that shaped Minnesota history during the 1960s and early 1970s.

691

"To a remarkable extent," writes a chronicler of the post–World War II American scene, "historians and popular writers agreed on the mood of the 1950s: we had entered upon a placid age, economically secure and pleasantly dull. The affluent, even as they turned from public issues to the suburban pursuit of status, had surrendered their independence to corporations; Americans were absorbing from the media a bland popular culture — 'midcult,' its critics called it — that was neither vulgar nor serious but simply insipid; they filled churches but made the 'American way of life' their religion; and they raised children in amazing numbers. Commentators noted an increasingly complicated structure of corporation, government, military, and academic bureaucracies in which procedures and methods were more and more standard. America, they observed, was flattening into a single unit as the West gained population, the South industrialized, and indistinguishable suburbs sprang up from one end of the country to the other." The national media — television, radio, and newspapers — exerted their homogenizing influence through the daily diet of popular network shows and commercials and advertisements emanating from Madison Avenue agencies. Such widely consumed pap seemed to satisfy a desire on the part of Americans to become more and more like each other.

While Americans were homogenizing in certain matters, and a large part of the population (not so large as was then thought) had entered upon a remarkably comfortable economic existence, in other respects the American intellect was sharpening, the national conscience was becoming more acute, and society was fracturing into new sorts of antagonistic interests and persuasions.

A major object of social and cultural criticism was standardization; and yet standardization held conflicting possibilities. As people in increasing numbers moved to different sections of the country, from one suburb or urban development to another set of boxes in glass and brick, they were abandoning everything that could sentimentally be called their "roots." "The major institutions," an astute historian observed, "created a national and rootless class of managers and professionals; the corporations and the military moved their men about to teach them all phases of their work and to give them a national rather than a local orientation. Stripping away cluttered detail, cutting down the environment to its useful commodities and packaging those in neutral plastic, pulling families from neighborhoods and setting them in cubicles bare of personality, postwar technology

692

could throw suburbanites and apartment dwellers back upon themselves and upon the advanced professional skills that gave them the place and identity their surroundings could not provide." The repetitive institutions of the credit card, the chain store, and the quickly marketed fashions gave firmness of line to an unstable environment; the similar houses and shops and roads and name brands, the main streets of small towns with their monotonous rows of neon signs, were increasingly indistinguishable from one another. Technology and economics, together with an accelerating mobility — geographical and occupational — were shaping a society increasingly removed from its roots.

By the 1960s the enormous movement off the farms and into the cities had crested; the even larger contrary shift, from the central cities to the peripheries, continued unabated. These two migrations heightened the crisis of the city. The newcomers, who included impoverished rural blacks, country white southerners, Puerto Ricans, and Mexican-Americans, were poorly equipped culturally and economically for life in the metropolis; they put increasing pressure on housing and public services, while families able to cope with big-city conditions and solvent enough to bear the tax burdens were leaving in ever-growing numbers to enrich the school systems and the governments of the suburbs.

Suburban society was particularly child-centered. PTA meetings drew suburbanites together as few other purposes did. Churches emphasized family social services, reflecting the importance of an adolescent subsociety. The latter largely discovered and defined itself, though, not in its schooling, secular or religious, but in its leisure — which, paradoxically enough, was enlarging in possibilities at a period when the demands of education were also growing. This was perhaps the first generation with sufficient money at its disposal so that it could sustain a whole consumer market of its own. And an important part of that market was rock and roll.

Rock is artistically important in its own right. Forms once distinctive, such as the jazz of the twenties and the swing of the thirties and after, had become by the forties and early fifties simply the common currency of American culture: the show tunes, the popular ballads, the "rhythm" numbers, all retaining a distant relationship to their origins in Negro music but attenuated by decades of adaptation. During the forties and fifties, folk music remained largely the preserve of the small American Left, which had discovered this music in seeking replacements for the bourgeois values it rejected. Toward the end of the 1950s, a folk revival appeared, encouraged by the scholarly research of ethnomusicologists, and was thriving during the 1960s. A central figure in this revival was Duluth-born Bob Dylan, sometime resident of Hibbing, who sounded enough like the legendary balladeer Woody Guthrie to startle his audiences. Progressive rock music drew upon a wide heritage of folk, blues, and country music. Hard rock fused opposites. It grafted the modern technology of amplification and tone on songs chosen for their folkish quality, songs speaking of a simpler and rural past.

Rock provided a stimulating if at times disrupting infusion of energy and creative impulse. Rock concerts and festivals turned into quasi-political events, struggles for power between youth and local people. A Fourth of July celebration became, with semiofficial backing, a statement of an older culture against the new. In the colleges, avant-garde students denied the possibility of divorcing intellectual activity from politics.

Social scientists are fond of discovering in American history a political cycle, emerging in the 1790s, 1820s, 1850s, and 1930s, in which a stable coalition politics dissolves, then composes itself into a new coalition, correspondent to new issues, that maintains the political peace for another generation. All of these changes in American politics have had their violent side. At first glance the 1960s appeared to be of a like political nature. Perhaps a liberal coalition was forming, or possibly in a new era of policy and debate a liberal collapse would lead to a conservative politics. Instead the 1960 election, with its curious crosscurrents over Kennedy's Catholicism, led back into the politics of stalemate that had overtaken the New Deal coalition in the forties, a stalemate based upon a conservative leadership in Congress and a continuing alternation of the presidency among candidates frozen by their slender majorities into executive inaction. Then the death of Kennedy, Johnson's accession, and Goldwater's staggering defeat in 1964 seemed to settle American politics into a liberal course. Even before Johnson's re-election, however, his response to the Tonkin Gulf incident began a process that would prevent his solidifying the country around a new enduring liberal coalition in the spiritual lineage of the New Deal. In 1968 the Democratic party was driven from the presidency and a Republican put in office by a small margin. Richard M. Nixon's attempt to rally a new conservative coalition was unsuccessful. A Republican President faced a Democratic Congress, and both parties had already made their bid for a new politics and failed. In sum, the political vacillation that America had entered in the late Eisenhower years continued into the seventies. We achieved neither a stable politics of division between the parties as in the late nineteenth century nor a practical dominance by either party; nor did the new and ill-defined issues that had hovered at the edges of political debate manage to take full control, displacing the economic questions that had occupied American public discourse since the New Deal. Commentators talked of one or another "social issue" — crime, public order, the quality of life, the role of youth, even the basis of personality and community — but politicians, aided by the most careful analyses of public opinion, were unable to find the tone that would reach the anxieties of the nation.

The sixties did have their special pungencies of style. John F. Kennedy's polished rhetoric tried to cast the world in the form of a moral drama. Norman Mailer, who caught one spirit of the decade sooner than almost any other writer, believed that heroism of a cool new kind would be the temper of the period. Martin Luther King brought to his times a rare eloquence. At the extraordinary civil rights gathering at the Lincoln Memorial on August 28, 1963, King gave his "Free at Last" speech and articulated the dream black Americans like Frederick Douglass, Booker T. Washington, and W. E. B. DuBois had held down through the decades. The Cold War psychology worked itself out to a terrible denouement in Vietnam and lost its hold. A long tradition of liberalism reached its end and could no longer distinguish itself from the forces it had once tried to control. Young people moved from the interstices of American institutions into a measure of power. The fragmentation that had marked American life for some time found its own counterforce in the consolidation of subcultures, each with its own voice and view, in a way that enriched America even while it complicated our politics and our individual lives.

In presidential elections, Minnesotans voted Democratic throughout the 1960s. In 1960, John F. Kennedy narrowly carried the state while in 1964 and 1968 first Lyndon B. Johnson and then Hubert H. Humphrey won by landslide proportions. In 1972, President Nixon reclaimed the state for the Republicans. In 1964, Senator Eugene J. McCarthy easily won re-election. He chose not to run again in 1970. Walter F. Mondale, who was appointed to Humphrey's Senate seat in 1964 when the latter became Vice President, was elected and re-elected by large margins in 1966 and 1972.

The 1960s were truly years of triumph and tragedy for Hubert H. Humphrey. Humphrey, father of much pacesetting legislation, including Medicare, the Peace Corps, the Arms Control and Disarmament Agency, major parts of the National Defense Education Act, Food for Peace, and the Wilderness Act of 1964, was chosen by President Johnson as his running mate in 1964. He was the first Minnesotan to attain the second highest office in the nation. While Vice President, Humphrey maintained an unrelenting, rigid anticommunism. In 1967 he called the threat to peace in Vietnam "a militant, aggressive Asian communism with headquarters in Peking." Humphrey and McCarthy became estranged over President Johnson's Vietnam policy, and fate pitted them against each other in the contest for the 1968 Democratic presidential nomination. McCarthy joined forces with the peace movement — initially led by radical activists and pacifists (including the Catholic priests Daniel and Philip Berrigan, natives of towns on the Mesabi iron range) but lacking a prominent leader. While the cause of peace was faithfully served in Congress by Senators J. William Fulbright, Wayne Morse, George McGovern, and Ernest Gruening, none came forward to assume a national leadership role.

During the summer of 1967 McCarthy, a handsome, graying, and sardonically witty man of fifty-one, became increasingly disturbed by what he felt was a calculated isolation of Congress resulting from a dangerous and illegal seizure of power by the President. McCarthy decided in November 1967 to run in the Democratic presidential primaries as a challenge to the administration because of its "continued escalation and intensification of the war in Vietnam." The first test came early in March 1968, when an army of students and other young people carried the McCarthy message throughout New Hampshire. McCarthy made a strong showing, doubly impressive when one considers that he was running not only against an incumbent President but also against an American war while that war was still being waged. Three days later Senator Robert F. Kennedy indicated that he too would enter the primaries; and by the end of that month, President Johnson dramatically announced that he would not seek re-election in November, leaving the field open to McCarthy, Kennedy, and Humphrey. Although Republican spokesmen derided McCarthy's campaign and, to a lesser extent, that of Kennedy as "children's crusades," McCarthy's victory in Wisconsin provided clear proof of the willingness of young people to involve themselves, with effectiveness surprisingly disproportionate to their experience. The Wisconsin campaign

696

was significant, too, in focusing the attention of many voters on the war as an election issue. McCarthy's campaign later bogged down in the Nebraska and South Dakota primaries, and came to final defeat at the Democratic convention in Chicago. Yet it was a landmark — in two respects: for Minnesota, it was the first time that two of the state's sons had faced each other in a national presidential contest; and for the nation it marked the emergence of an active but independent movement of the student left, within the framework of the major party structure. The convention, however, revealed on the television screens of the nation the potential for violence in the growing antiwar militancy of college-age youth and their elders. Outside the convention hotel and at antiwar rallies in Grant Park, bloody clashes between protestors and Mayor Richard Daley's police led to extensive arrests and the long-drawn-out trial of the "Chicago Seven."

Robert Kennedy's assassination had left only the two Minnesotans as serious contenders. Humphrey received the nomination. In 1968, Hubert H. Humphrey became the first Minnesotan ever nominated by a major political party for President of the United States. Another record set that year was the largest number of Minnesota voters ever to poll at a state election — 1,606,307. As might have been expected, the Humphrey-Muskie ticket won in Minnesota with ease, but Nixon won the presidency in a close election.

Humphrey was overwhelmingly returned to the United States Senate in 1970. In 1972, he unsuccessfully sought to repeat as the Democratic nominee, losing out to Senator George McGovern of South Dakota. "Hubert Humphrey," wrote James Reston, "didn't lose the Democratic presidential nomination here in Miami Beach; he lost it in Chicago in 1968. And he lost in Chicago because he was more faithful to Lyndon Johnson on Vietnam than he was to his own deepest beliefs about the war, and that finished him, and in his heart he knew it."

Hubert Humphrey made a lasting imprint on Minnesota politics. He carried the Democratic-Farmer-Labor party from minority to majority party within twenty years after its formation in 1944. He helped found a political organization impressive for its vitality and talent. Notable indeed are the Minnesota Democratic-Farmer-Laborites who served in positions of national leadership in the 1960s — Humphrey, McCarthy, Orville L. Freeman, who held the post of secretary of agriculture throughout the presidencies of Kennedy and Johnson, Congressman Donald Fraser of Minneapolis, Ambassador Eugenie Anderson, Walter W. Heller (chairman of the President's Council of Economic Advisers), Charles L. Shultze (director of the United States Bureau of the Budget, 1965–68), and many others.

Minnesota Republicans, too, rose to prominence in this period in greater numbers than at any time since the 1920s. President Nixon nominated Warren E. Burger as chief justice of the United States in 1969. Burger, a native of St. Paul, graduate of the St. Paul College of Law, and veteran of the United States Court of Appeals, was the first Minnesotan to attain that position. President Nixon also appointed two Minnesotans to his cabinet in 1969 — Maurice H. Stans, born in Shakopee, as secretary of commerce; and James D. Hodgson, born in Dawson, as secretary of labor. Stans, who previously had served as director of the Bureau of the Budget in the Eisenhower administration, resigned in 1972 to become finance director of the Committee to Re-Elect the President. He later pleaded guilty to misdemeanors in connection with the Watergate scandal. Hodgson served throughout President Nixon's first term but was not reappointed to the cabinet. Harold E. Stassen, a perennial Republican candidate for President, made his last attempt in 1968, garnering but a handful of delegates.

In 1970 when there was another opening on the United States Supreme Court, Nixon, after abortive attempts to appoint two southerners, again turned to a Minnesotan, Harry A. Blackmun, a resident of Rochester and, like Burger, a judge from the Circuit Court of Appeals. Burger and Blackmun (dubbed the "Minnesota twins" by journalists), both considered strict constructionists, have agreed on the vast majority of Supreme Court decisions in which they have participated. One on which they disagreed was Blackmun's ruling on abortion in 1972. In a decision that has generated more comment — favorable and unfavorable — than any other issued by either Minnesotan on the Supreme Court, Justice Blackmun (supported by a majority of the other justices) held that abortion is legal and the province of a woman and her physician during the first trimester (three months) of pregnancy; that a state may regulate abortion during the second trimester to safeguard the mother's health; and that a state may prohibit abortion after "viability" at the beginning of the third trimester (seven months).

In state politics Karl F. Rolvaag proved a genial but ineffective governor. His hairline majority began to erode early in his term. It was reduced by the repercussions of his campaign attack on Governor Elmer L. Andersen for permitting defective workmanship on Interstate Highway 35, near Duluth, charges which (after the election) were proved to be groundless; and by his inaccurate forecast that falling state revenues would necessitate a 5 per cent reduction in school aids and state services. His public image was damaged, too, by the American Allied Insurance Co. scandal of 1965–66, culminating in indictment for fraud of, among others, the Rolvaag-appointed insurance commissioner. By mid-1966 it was clear that he did not possess the leadership qualities, energy, and political skills that marked the other Democratic-Farmer-Laborites who had come to power.

"One by one," editorialized *Time* magazine on July 1, 1966, the Democratic-Farmer-Labor party's "brightest luminaries — Humphrey, Agricultural Secretary Orville Freeman, Senators Eugene McCarthy and Walter Mondale — [had] gone off to Washington, leaving the party's fortunes in less gifted hands." Democratic-Farmer-Labor leaders exhibited increasing concern over the governor's declining position and its implications for the fall election. At a meeting of the Democratic-Farmer-Laborite state central committee at Sugar Hills, a resort in northern Minnesota, a decision was reached to recommend to the party convention the unprecedented step of not renominating an incumbent governor and in his place choosing the lieutenant governor, A. M. "Sandy" Keith of Rochester. The party's luminaries split — Fraser and Humphrey for Keith, McCarthy and Mondale for Rolvaag. Rolvaag was asked to step down but refused and fought back. At the party's convention Keith was nominated as its standardbearer on the twentieth ballot. Rolvaag stumped the state with the slogan "Let the people decide" and defeated Keith in the primary, 315,734 to 146,-926. Leading a deeply divided party in November, he was in turn defeated by Harold LeVander, the Republican candidate, 680,593 to 607,943 votes.

During his governorship Rolvaag was frequently at odds with the conservative-controlled legislature. Among the major pieces of legislation passed with his support, however, were the Natural Resources and Recreation Act, reform of the criminal code, laws against water pollution, and authorization (over the strong opposition of the dairy industry) of the sale of colored oleomargarine. Strong bipartisan support assured enactment of a taconite statute in 1963 which guaranteed the taconite industry would not be taxed higher than other industries; an amendment to the state constitution, approved by the voters in 1964, extended such protec-

699

tion to the taconite industry for twenty-five years. Organizing and leading a public campaign for passage of the amendment was Rolvaag's predecessor and foe in the 1962 gubernatorial election, Elmer L. Andersen. As lieutenant governor, Rolvaag had opposed special treatment for the new taconite industry but, as governor, he signed the legislation desired by the industry.

On occasion, Rolvaag did exercise leadership and independence. In 1965, for example, he vetoed the appropriation for bounties on predatory animals. His action ended a time-honored legislative practice of paying bounties on wolves and other animals, a reform welcomed and long advocated by the Conservation Department.

Harold LeVander, a South St. Paul attorney, emerged as the Republican standardbearer after defeating Elmer L. Andersen and John S. Pillsbury, Jr., a Minneapolis insurance executive, in a hard-fought battle at the state Republican convention in 1966. At the age of fifty-six, he — along with Samuel Van Sant — was the state's oldest governor. LeVander, a tall, striking man, had gained extensive knowledge of the state as an active Lutheran layman and through his work as legal counsel for numerous cooperatives. He entered office in 1967 with a vigorous program. Mistakenly thought to be a conservative Republican, he rapidly showed himself to be in the tradition of Progressive Republicanism. In his inaugural address he pushed new state programs on many fronts — education, environment, civil rights, and corrections. He called for a state-wide approach to problem-solving: "Because our most critical problems are really people problems, we are going to have to try to understand people. How do we encourage society to accept the former convict? How do we motivate underprivileged children? How do we create true harmony among races? How do we assure our senior citizens of a meaningful life? These concerns touch the individual personality. It's our own responsibility to dream the dreams that will ease the hurts of mankind. Our new problem-solvers must also be people willing to cooperate. The problems of a mature Minnesota stretch beyond our towns, counties, and districts — they are problems of all of us. Education, human rights, mental health, conservation, metropolitan sprawl, recreation — these aren't problems of Montevideo, Montgomery, or Monticello. These burdens lie before Minnesota."

His budget message was the first to urge budget expenditures of $1 billion for a biennium. Two legislative landmarks were achieved in the 1967 session: establishment of the first state Human Rights Department

700

and creation of the Metropolitan Council — the nation's most advanced form of regional government — for the seven-county Twin Cities area. Other important pieces of legislation were the Capitol Area Architectural and Planning Commission, a far-reaching measure protecting land use around the state capitol in St. Paul, and a Pollution Control Agency.

LeVander, a strong and successful governor during the first half of his term, began encountering difficulty in 1969. In Mankato, speaking on behalf of legislation designed to extend the regional government concept throughout the state, LeVander said, "Some towns will have to die." The rural backlash was fierce. By the close of the 1969 legislative session LeVander's leadership was further challenged. With sizable majorities in both houses, the conservatives enacted a 3 per cent sales tax, exempting food, clothing, and medicines. LeVander twice vetoed it (he had promised in his campaign for the governorship that no sales tax would be enacted without a public referendum), but defections from the liberal ranks overrode the veto. The sales tax issue, long a volatile one in Minnesota politics, was laid to rest. That this form of taxation had become a permanent element in the state's revenue system became clear in 1971 when it was increased to 4 per cent by the conservative-dominated legislature and signed into law by the newly elected Democratic-Farmer-Labor governor, Wendell R. Anderson.

LeVander was an impressive orator. But his speaking style was reminiscent of an earlier day. His public utterances frequently were characterized by verbosity. His personality was dignified but staid, and lacked warmth and color. That he brought to the office high-minded and ambitious goals for the state, however, there can be no doubt. As the gubernatorial campaign of 1970 began to take shape, LeVander was expected to run for re-election. And he was expected to be successful against any Democratic-Farmer-Labor opposition. It came as a surprise when he took himself out of the race. Sixty years of age, suffering from an arthritic hip, he seemed to lose his zest for the office during the latter half of his term. An example of this was the change in his attitude toward reorganization of the executive branch. His enthusiastic championing of reorganization had been largely successful: The 1969 legislature approved a reorganization plan, somewhat reducing the number of state agencies by merging several small units into larger ones. It also renamed some of the major agencies and granted the governor broad authority to implement reforms. Once LeVander had secured the enabling legislation, however, his interest in the problem seemed to wane and he failed to pursue reorganization of the state's executive branch. Among the other accomplishments of the 1969 legislature was the creation of a state zoological garden.

A number of veteran conservative senators went down to defeat in the elections for state offices in 1970. Foremost among these was Gordon Rosenmeier of Little Falls. A brilliant lawyer, an acknowledged expert on the state constitution, a consummate legislative strategist and tactician, a vigorous champion of nonpartisan legislative elections, and author of much progressive legislation during his thirty years in the state Senate, he had been the dominant figure in state government during the 1960s.

Possession of the governorship had alternated between the Republican and Democratic-Farmer-Labor parties during the 1960s. In 1970, Wendell Anderson, who defeated Republican Douglas Head, ushered in a new generation of political leadership. The thirty-seven-year-old St. Paul attorney, a former Olympic hockey player, had been a state legislator. In his inaugural address the new governor stressed the role of the state in equalizing social justice and promoting a richer life for all citizens. "Never," said Governor Anderson, "have our people been so aware of the needs and the possibilities of a free society. There is a vision, newly formed but already widely shared, that goes beyond the concept of a quantitative standard of living and concerns itself as well with the intrinsic quality of the life that each individual can lead. The anguish and dissatisfaction so evident in recent years are primarily the result of a greatly heightened awareness among our people — an awareness, as if for the first time, of the scope and the cost of injustice and inequity and delay."

Anderson, facing a legislature still under conservative control though by a small margin, proposed a bold and imaginative plan for reforming school financing and taxes. During the 1970 gubernatorial campaign Anderson had promised to bring about property tax equalization and an increased state share in financing school costs. His plan called for $700 million in new taxes. Anderson was successful in enlisting bipartisan support in the Senate, an effort in which he was aided by majority leader Stanley Holmquist, but he faced stiff opposition from the House conservatives. The longest special session in the state's history dragged on until October when an omnibus tax package of $580 million was agreed upon.

Historic changes in state policy toward local government were enacted by the 1971 Minnesota legislature. Formulas for distributing state tax revenues were dramatically altered to provide larger amounts than ever before to local governments. At the same time the legislature took over a more direct responsibility for levying and limiting taxes of all kinds on the state's cities, villages, townships, counties, and school districts. No longer were there to be two separate fiscal systems. Among the major actions taken by the .1971 legislature in changing its policy toward local government were these: (1) A comprehensive revision of the school-aid formula, designed to assure equality of opportunity for students throughout the state, regardless of their socioeconomic background or the wealth of the school districts where they live. (2) A comprehensive revision of the formulas for distribution of state aid to cities, villages, townships, and counties, with emphasis on providing funds for those units of government most in need of additional financing. (3) A large infusion of state nonproperty revenues to local government, accompanied by mandatory reductions in local property tax levies and by strict limits on local property taxes to guarantee property tax relief. (4) A new public employees bargaining law designed to assure orderly and equitable settlement of compensation negotiations between state and local governments and their employees. (5) A new seventeen-member Quality Education Council with a $750,-000 appropriation to fund local school district experimentation in "new approaches to the learning process, better utilization of professional staff and community resources, different requirements as to course offerings, course content, grading, graduation and school attendance." (6) An upgraded local government fiscal information system under the commissioner of taxation, working with a new Intergovernmental Information Services Advisory Council, designed to assure a complete, computerized, up-to-date record of local government receipts and expenditures. (7) A joint executive-legislative Tax Study Commission assigned, in part, to review causes and effects of intercommunity disparities, alternative sources of tax revenue for local government, and levy limits. (8) A formula to lessen metropolitan fiscal disparities by which all municipalities and townships in the seven-county Twin Cities area contribute 40 per cent of their net growth in commercial-industrial taxable valuation to an area-wide "pool" of valuations, with each municipality and township then receiving a proportionate share of this pool as determined by its population and the market value of its property per capita. The pool involves dollars of valuation, *not* taxes. After each municipality receives its share of the pool of valuations, the share becomes fully a part of the municipality's assessed valuation as if the property were physically located within its borders.

703

Then the municipality and all overlapping taxing districts levy taxes on this valuation. This so-called fiscal disparities law was the most controversial of the actions taken by the 1971 legislature in connection with local government. It was challenged in the courts and not until September 1974 was its constitutionality upheld by the state supreme court.

The growth in state government — in size, function, and cost — had been almost mind-boggling. In 1967, the biennial cost of state government reached $1 billion for the first time. In 1973, legislators approved a biennial budget of $4 billion in public funds. Sixty per cent of this amount was collected from various state taxes. Twenty per cent came from the federal government. The remaining 20 per cent was made up of state charges for services provided to specific users and by earnings from the investment of funds.

In 1973, the state Department of Administration published a comprehensive report on state expenditures, which showed two major trends. The first was an increased emphasis on social services and education. From 1970 to 1973, expenditures for education increased 94 per cent and expenditures for social services increased nearly 84 per cent. The second trend reflected a change in the manner by which the state spent its fiscal resources. In 1971, grants-in-aid to other units of government represented 59 per cent of total state expenditures. By the end of 1973, they increased to 67 per cent. Thus a greater percentage of the state's available resources was allocated to local units of government to administer. Both of these trends were influenced by the greater state contribution to the costs of public schools following the action of the 1971 legislature. These funds go directly to school districts. In the total "pie"'of state expenditures, 37 per cent went to education in the 1971–73 biennium, 21 per cent to social services, 18 per cent to local units of government, and 12 per cent to developing and maintaining the state's system of transportation. The remaining 12 per cent was disbursed to protect persons and property, manage the environment, provide health services, promote the state's economy, protect the consumer of goods and services, develop the state's manpower resources, and provide the necessary administrative and other supportive services required for the internal operations of state government.

A hot political issue that persisted throughout the decade was legislative reapportionment. The legislature had consistently lagged behind the population shift from rural to urban areas in reapportioning election districts and failed to comply with the "one man, one vote" ruling of the United States Supreme Court. In November 1971, Governor Anderson, following his predecessors, vetoed still another reapportionment bill enacted by the legislature, finding it inadequate on several grounds. The issue then went to a panel of three federal judges which devised its own reapportionment plan for Minnesota and in the process reduced the 202-member legislature by almost half. The plan was reviewed by the United States Supreme Court and the changes found to be "excessive." The case was remanded to the federal District Court, which then reduced the House of Representatives by one to 134 members and left the Senate at 67.

Among the measures approved by the 1973 legislature was one lowering the voting age to eighteen, thus adding 221,000 new voters to the state's electorate. The legislature repealed the sixty-year-old practice of electing legislators without party designation. An era ended with the repeal of this law. The question remains unsettled whether the nonpartisan system promoted or retarded the state's progressive political tradition. On the one hand, it may be contended that political parties in the state were weakened by nonpartisan elections and the actions of legislators were more subject to personal idiosyncrasy; on the other hand the nonpartisan system of electing legislators may be said not only to have reflected the independence of Minnesotans but to have contributed to the vitality and openness of Minnesota politics. The 1973 statute also authorized party designation on ballots for municipal elections in the state's three largest cities.

The 1973 legislature opened all its committee meetings — including those of the rules and conference committees — to the public and decreed that all public decision-making bodies in the state must open their deliberations as well. By this act Minnesota undoubtedly became one of the "most open" states — in a political sense — of the fifty United States. The law, and early interpretations of it by the state's attorney-general, also presented problems by calling into question the right, under any circumstances, of elected public officials to gather informally and out of view of the public.

New state Departments of Finance and Personnel were established in 1973 in a major reorganization of the executive branch that had been among the recommendations of a study group called Loaned Executives Action Program (LEAP). Governor Anderson had appointed LEAP to examine ways of improving the efficiency and accountability of the state government.

In 1974 the state legislature held its first annual session in modern times — authorized by a constitutional amendment in 1972 which retained 120 meeting days every two years for the legislature but permitted "flexible" sessions. It authorized statewide utility regulation, created a state energy agency, passed a no-fault insurance law to take effect in 1975, approved probate reform, adopted a campaign ethics law providing for partial public funding of political campaigns and requiring candidates for office to disclose the source of contributions, prohibited abortions during the second half of pregnancy (an act declared unconstitutional later in the year by the United States Supreme Court), and provided tax relief for the "working poor" — a law spearheaded by Senate majority leader Nicholas D. Coleman.

The fall 1974 election in Minnesota followed the national Democratic trend in the wake of Watergate, spiraling inflation, and the energy crisis. Governor Anderson became the state's first governor re-elected to a four-year term; polled 786,787 votes, the highest total ever cast in Minnesota for a gubernatorial candidate; defeated his opponent by 419,065 votes — also a record — and captured 63 per cent of the vote. For the first time in history, the Democratic-Farmer-Labor party elected its candidates for all six state constitutional offices. Attorney-General Warren Spannaus, a forthright champion of gun control — an inflammatory issue, for years shied away from by most politicians — was among those re-elected and led all Democratic-Farmer-Labor vote-getters, with a total of 786,857 votes. The party also elected an overwhelming three to one majority to the state House of Representatives.

Wendell Anderson began his second term with a seemingly bright future ahead. He had fashioned a popular public image. Though his public appearances were few in comparison with those of other governors, he exhibited an uncommon skill in communicating with the people over television. During his first term he had considerably strengthened and expanded the role of the executive branch of state government and established a firmer control on state finances through the School Finance Law of 1971. His only significant opposition in the legislative sessions of 1973 and 1974 emanated from the traditionally independent-minded state Senate, led by Nicholas D. Coleman, his chief foe for the Democratic-Farmer-Labor nomination for governor in 1970.

Senator Walter Mondale had been regarded as an almost certain candidate for the Democratic presidential nomination in 1976. But late in 1974 he surprised almost everyone by withdrawing. He continued to play an influential role in the Senate.

In officially nonpartisan elections for mayor of each of the Twin Cities at the turn of the decade, voters rejected candidates endorsed by the established parties. Independent Charles Stenvig, a policeman running on a law-and-order theme, was elected in 1969 as mayor of Minneapolis. In 1971, he was re-elected with 72 per cent of the vote, but in 1973 he was defeated by Al Hofstede, a Democratic-Farmer-Laborite, in the first election held under the new party designation law. The St. Paul voters' flirtation with an independent mayor proved even more ephemeral. Charles McCarty, colorful city hall gadfly, was elected mayor of that city in 1970. Two years later he was defeated by Democratic-Farmer-Laborite Lawrence Cohen, who was re-elected in 1974. A third-party movement — the Taxpayer's party — showed some strength in Minneapolis elections in 1971 and 1973, primarily in races for the school board.

At the mid-1970s, then, state administrative offices, the statehouse, and the city halls of both major cities in Minnesota were controlled by the Democratic-Farmer-Labor party, for the first time ever.

Minnesota, long a leader among the states in conservation, was strongly influenced in the 1960s and 1970s by the national movement to protect the environment. Hundreds of state organizations came into being during the 1960s to clean up the air we breathe and the water we drink, to check the growing problem of noise, to oppose threats to visual beauties of the St. Croix River, Fort Snelling, and other natural and historical sanctuaries, to regulate nuclear power plants, and to halt the dumping of taconite wastes into Lake Superior.

The Minnesota Natural Resources and Recreation Act, passed by the legislature in 1963, grew out of a citizens' committee appointed by Governor Elmer L. Andersen. The program embraced forests, wetlands, parks, and historic sites and provided for revenue to finance itself from a one-cent tax on each pack of cigarettes sold. Ten years later, the results were manifold and impressive. A hardwood forest atop the bluffs along the Mississippi River in southern Minnesota had been created; habitat areas for wildlife had been reclaimed and restored to the state's public domain; ninety thousand acres and a score of parks had been added to the state system by the Department of Natural Resources (successor to the Conservation Department); a historic sites program had been inaugurated under the direction of the Minnesota Historical Society with a full-scale restoration of Fort Snelling the major effort. Increasingly, the environmental movement focused on the most congested area of the state — the Twin Cities. In 1961 the state's first urban state park, Fort Snelling, had been established. Repeated battles were fought throughout the decade to preserve from federal office buildings and private developers the wilderness and the historical character of the scene at the confluence of the Mississippi and Minnesota rivers. In 1971, the state's most urban county, Ramsey, instituted an ambitious program to purchase open spaces. It was funded by $16 million in bonds authorized by the legislature. Determined citizen efforts blocked the construction of a highway in St. Paul and the building of a second airport at Ham Lake in Anoka County, north of the Twin Cities. Throughout the state, concern was exhibited for preserving the best of the natural and manmade environment as historical and community organizations labored to safeguard wilderness oases along with historical and architectural landmarks in Minnesota. Heritage preservation commissions were formed in Minneapolis and Fergus Falls. The University of Minnesota Landscape Arboretum attracted 150,000 visitors in 1974; other preserves and sanctuaries were similarly popular. In 1971 an environmental rights act was passed by the legislature, permitting citizens to sue anyone violating pollution control regulations.

In 1968 the St. Croix River was included in the new national system of wild rivers. In 1974 the lower section of the St. Croix was officially designated by Governor Anderson as the state's first "critical area" under a law enacted by the 1973 legislature designed to protect areas possessing unusual scenic and historical value.

A highly significant court case in the environmental field was initiated in Minnesota in 1973, when the United States government and the states of Minnesota, Wisconsin, and Michigan brought suit against the Reserve Mining Company of Silver Bay to force the company to halt disposal of taconite tailings in Lake Superior. It was alleged that the daily dumping of 67,000 tons of waste was polluting the lake and causing a serious public health hazard. The government cited the finding as far away as Duluth of asbestos fibers from the waste in drinking water taken from Lake Superior. In April 1974, after more than nine months of testimony,

The Minneapolis skyline in the 1970s, dramatically
changed by the freeway and the IDS tower

St. Paul's Osborn Building

The Guthrie Theater in 1974

The old Duluth railway depot, now the St. Louis County Heritage and Arts Center

One of the demonstrations that marked the 1960s and early 1970s — a peace march on the state capitol, May 9, 1970

Hubert H. Humphrey

Eugene J. McCarthy

Warren E. Burger

Wendell R. Anderson and
Elmer L. Andersen

Fishing remains an important industry on the Red Lake Indian Reservation

Snowmobiles on a winter trail

Charles A. Lindbergh, Jr., at Rainy Lake in 1969, part of the future Voyageurs National Park

District Court Judge Miles Lord ordered the company to stop its discharges immediately, but appeals stayed his order and the attempt to find a satisfactory on-land disposal site became mired in controversy. The Court of Appeals ruled in March 1975 that the company must shift to an on-land disposal site within a "reasonable time period." Essentially this was a conflict between environmentalists who feared irreparable damage to the lake, as well as danger to public health, and those concerned with the economy of the region, on which Reserve is estimated to have an annual impact of $50 million.

Significant federal legislation was passed in the 1960s that gave further protection to Minnesota's famous canoe country, the one-million-acre Boundary Waters Canoe Area (BWCA) in the Superior National Forest. A sustained battle had been waged since 1909 to preserve this unique wooded lakeland region. Leading the effort to protect the interlaced lakes and streams and forests on both sides of the international border (the historic Indian fur trade canoe route) was the Quetico-Superior Council, whose guiding spirit was Ernest Oberholtzer of International Falls. The early skirmishes pitted conservationists against commercial timber interests. By the 1960s, however, overuse by the public became a concern that paralleled any threat of commercial exploitation. The Thye-Blatnik Act of 1948 had granted the United States Forest Service authority to buy private lands for recreation, and an amendment to this act in 1956 permitted enlargement of the BWCA. Then in 1960 the Multiple Use Act recognized preservation of wilderness as one of many bona fide uses of United States Forest Service lands. A second amendment to the Thye-Blatnik Act in 1961 granted to the Forest Service the right to condemn private lands within the BWCA. In 1964 the Land and Water Conservation Act gave the Forest Service the power to purchase private lands for recreational purposes anywhere within or contiguous to a national forest; and in the same year the Wilderness Act further defined and extended federal protection for national wilderness areas, including the BWCA.

Perhaps the most striking achievement toward public enjoyment of the environment in the years after 1960 was the creation of a new national park, the thirty-sixth and the foremost lakeland park in the National Park System. As early as 1891 the state legislature had asked Congress to establish a national park in the Canadian border lakes area. But the coordinated, sustained, and successful push for the Voyageurs National

Park had to wait seventy-one years, until the governorship of Elmer Andersen. Determined to do all in his power to conserve the Kabetogama area, Andersen in 1962 obtained the support of the National Park Service. An eight-year legislative battle followed. Andersen's successors, Governors Rolvaag and LeVander, hesitantly endorsed the idea of a national park, but the effort to implement it was spearheaded by Andersen and the Voyageurs National Park Association, a voluntary citizens' organization. Among those who gave it wholehearted backing was Minnesota's native son Charles A. Lindbergh and Minnesota-born United States Supreme Court Justice William O. Douglas. Finally, in December of 1970 Congress passed the Voyageurs National Park bill and President Nixon signed it into law on January 8, 1971. With the unqualified support of incumbent Governor Wendell Anderson, the Minnesota legislature, with some bipartisan opposition, enacted a transfer enabling act.

The area of the Voyageurs National Park, near International Falls, is not only geologically and historically interesting but breathtaking in natural beauty and wild scenery. Lakes and forests interlock in a lacework of greens and blues, lush islands, frothy torrents, and deep gorges. The timber forts and other physical traces of the *couriers du bois* and the voyageurs have long since vanished, covered by forest, but the Minnesota Historical Society's underwater archaeologists have recovered a bonanza of artifacts from the area's waters — parts of voyageur canoes, muzzle-loading rifles, beads intended for fur trading with the Indians, and so on. Such exploration will no doubt continue under the aegis of the National Park Service.

Lindbergh, in a 1973 address at his boyhood home, now in Lindbergh State Park near Little Falls, challenged Minnesotans to carry forward their ongoing effort to preserve the natural environment: "I believe our civilization's latest advance is symbolized by the park rather than by satellites and space travel. In establishing parks and nature reserves, man reaches beyond the material values of science and technology. He recognizes the essential value of life itself, of life's natural inheritance irreplaceably evolved through earthly epochs, of the miraculous spiritual awareness that only nature in balance can maintain. As our civilization advances, if our follies permit it to advance, I feel sure we will realize that progress can be measured only by the quality of life — in all life, not human life alone. The accumulation of knowledge, the discoveries of science, the products of technology, our ideals, our art, our social structures, all the achievements of mankind have value only to the extent that they preserve and improve the quality of life. This is why I say that parks symbolize the greatest advance our civilization has yet made."

When O. Meredith Wilson became the ninth president of the University of Minnesota in 1961, student enrollment was 28,277 and the institution's budget was approximately $87 million. Wilson enjoyed harmonious relations with state officials, legislators, students, and faculty. He resigned in 1967 and was succeeded by Malcolm Moos, a political scientist and former speech writer for President Dwight D. Eisenhower. Moos, the first alumnus to head the university, resigned under pressure in 1974. While he had been praised for his handling of student unrest during his tenure and had emphasized excellence in all divisions of the institution, his administration was marred by faculty and student dissatisfaction, poor rapport with the legislature, and an unusual number of resignations by his aides. C. Peter McGrath was inaugurated as president in fall 1974, when student enrollment had reached a record 51,834 on the university's campuses. Inflationary economic pressures on faculty and staff, along with student demands for new programs, posed challenges of considerable magnitude.

The state college and junior college systems greatly expanded during the 1960s and early 1970s. Strong leadership was given the former by G. Theodore Mitau, a political science professor at Macalester College, who became chancellor of the state college system in 1968. Mitau, a vigorous and articulate advocate with a flair for publicity, significantly strengthened the role of state colleges in Minnesota's program for publicly supported higher education. A seventh state college, Metropolitan State, was authorized by the 1971 legislature. Located in St. Paul, it was modeled on the "college without walls" concept. While junior colleges — renamed community colleges in 1973 — had long received state financial aid, their governance traditionally was tied to a local area. State responsibility for them dates from 1964 when a state junior college board created by the 1963 legislature began functioning and total funding for these schools was assumed by the state. Since then eight new community colleges have been added, bringing the total in the community college system to eighteen.

Still another facet of Minnesota's impressive support of post–high school public educational institutions during the 1960s was the creation of area vocational and technical institutes. Between 1967 and 1974 thirty-four were established under the supervision of the state Board of Education. Between 1970 and 1974, enrollment increased 51 per cent, resulting in part from the tuition-free policy for students under twenty-one years of age.

Also experiencing growth in the early and middle 1960s were the private four-year liberal arts colleges. While their proportional share of student enrollment in the state perceptibly declined in comparison to public institutions, most gained in numbers. Extensive building programs were undertaken. However, the decade that began with unprecedented growth in program and buildings in the early 1960s shifted to retrenchment by the early 1970s. Higher costs and perhaps a lessening desire of young people for a college degree turned enrollments downward. Among the 150 private colleges closing their doors across the country between 1970 and 1975 was Lea College in Albert Lea. What was once viewed as a growth enterprise in Minnesota is now regarded as overbuilt and overstaffed for the recession-ridden times ushered in by inflation and the energy crisis. Minnesota's private colleges faced an uncertain future. Macalester presented an extreme and unusual case of the problems of a private liberal arts college. It had been the recipient of gifts totaling more than $36 million from DeWitt Wallace, publisher of *Reader's Digest*, and enjoyed a dramatic expansion. But, abruptly, Wallace's munificent financial support was terminated in 1971 as a result of his dissatisfaction with the college's program and policies in recent years.

Other institutions added to the higher educational system were medical schools at the Mayo Clinic in Rochester and the University of Minnesota campus at Duluth (both in 1972) and the Midwest School of Law at Hamline University, the latter attaining partial accreditation in 1975.

One of the state's outstanding educational leaders, James P. Shannon, a member of the Roman Catholic clergy, was appointed auxiliary archbishop of St. Paul in 1966 and shortly thereafter left the presidency of the College of St. Thomas. In 1969, he unexpectedly made known his differences with the Roman Catholic Church's official policy on birth control, resigned as a bishop of the church, and later married, the first American who had held his rank in the Catholic Church to do so.

During this period the position of the Twin Cities area as the cultural center of much of the Middle West was solidified. The outstanding

Guthrie Theater, designed by Ralph Rapson, which opened in Minneapolis in 1963, was only the first of a series of new buildings erected to house the arts. The following year the St. Paul Arts and Science Center brought under one roof Theatre St. Paul (succeeded by the Chimera Theatre), the St. Paul Art Center, the city's Civic Opera Company, and the Science Museum. An enlarged Walker Art Center building was completed in 1973; it adjoins the Guthrie. O'Shaughnessy Hall on the campus of the College of St. Catherine (1968–70) expanded opportunities for St. Paulites to enjoy major orchestras, including the Minnesota Orchestra, as the Minneapolis Symphony was renamed in 1968. The fall of 1974 found the Minnesota Orchestra in its new permanent home in Minneapolis, Orchestra Hall, and the remodeled Minneapolis Institute of Arts in the new setting of the Minneapolis Society of Fine Arts Park, designed by Japanese architect Kenzo Tange to house the Minneapolis College of Art and Design and the Children's Theatre Company as well as the Institute.

As interest in productions of the Guthrie repertory company grew, several other very competent professional or semiprofessional theater groups attracted audiences. The Children's Theatre and its director, John Clark Donahue, achieved national renown. Vocal music enjoyed a resurgence of interest too, with the Bach Society led by David La Berge one manifestation. The Metropolitan Opera Company played to full houses each spring, and around the year the Center Opera Company and the St. Paul Opera Company offered interesting seasons. The St. Paul Chamber Orchestra under Dennis Russell Davies provided full seasons of concerts and, in 1974, traveled to Europe.

The growth of art institutions in Minneapolis alone during the 1960s and early 1970s was spectacular. The city had no fewer than forty theaters, thirty-four music groups, and seventeen art centers of varying size. Because they required a continual subsidy for survival and most of that had come from private philanthropy, their success – in an institutional sense – seemed to contain the seeds of their potential decline as they confronted mounting deficits in the economic inflation-recession of the mid-1970s. "The arts in Minneapolis," wrote a close observer late in 1974, "are as vigorous as they've ever been, and closer to disaster than we suspect." A publicly funded Minneapolis City Arts Commission, the first in Minnesota, was created early in 1975, signifying that cultural institutions would increasingly be depending upon public funds in order to maintain their programs.

713

Writers — of poetry, fiction, plays, criticism — found outlets for their work both locally and nationally. Two Minnesota physicians were authors of widely read books about the medical profession: Ronald J. Glasser, of the University of Minnesota, who wrote *365 Days* (1971), a searing account of soldier-patients in Vietnam; and William Nolen of Litchfield, author of *The Making of a Surgeon* (1970) and *A Surgeon's World* (1972). Poet John Berryman, who taught at the University of Minnesota from 1955 until his death in 1972, won the Pulitzer Prize for poetry in 1965 and a National Book Award in 1969. Robert Bly, another Minnesota poet, who lives on a farm near Madison, Minnesota, received a National Book Award in 1968. The University of Minnesota Press and the Minnesota Historical Society, oldest of the state's book-publishing agencies, were joined over the years by a number of other publishing houses; scholarly studies, regional works, books for children, textbooks, general-reader volumes, all were issued with Minnesota imprints, for residents of the state and for a national book-reading public. (See Added Readings at the end of this chapter for titles by and about Minnesotans.)

Extensive urban renewal projects, made possible by infusions of federal funds, were undertaken in the core areas of Minneapolis and St. Paul. Notable was the revival of the "gateway" section of downtown Minneapolis. Not only was a blighted area restored to a thriving commercial area but new buildings enriched the quality of the city's architecture — the Northwestern National Life Insurance Company Building, designed by Minoru Yamasaki, and the Federal Reserve Bank, designed by Gunnar Birkert. Another important new structure in Minneapolis was the Investors Diversified Services building, designed by Philip Johnson. A fifty-one-story eight-sided tower, it drastically altered the skyline of the city, dwarfing the forty-five-year-old Foshay Tower and providing the visitor with a commanding view of the entire Twin Cities area. To attract shoppers Nicollet Avenue in downtown Minneapolis was converted to an attractive pedestrian mall. An outstanding architectural addition to the downtown area of St. Paul was the Osborn Building (completed in 1968), designed by Clark D. Wold.

Two imaginative new "towns" were started in Minnesota. The first was Jonathan, a completely planned community, in Carver County. The second — a "new town in town" — was an apartment complex in the Cedar-Riverside area of Minneapolis. After strong beginnings, both were financially troubled and their future in doubt in the mid-1970s.

Major league professional sports — baseball, football, and hockey — took root in Minnesota in the 1960s, although two basketball franchises and a tennis team were shortlived. With independence typical in the state, the teams bore in their titles, not the names of cities as such teams traditionally did, but "Minnesota." The Minnesota Twins, which had moved to Bloomington in 1961, won the American League pennant in 1965 but lost the World Series. The Twins' professional football counterpart, the Minnesota Vikings, who also played at the Bloomington Metropolitan Stadium, came equally close to a world championship three times, in the 1968, 1974, and 1975 Super Bowls but lost each time. "Tailgating" was developed to a fine art by the hardy Minnesota fans of the Vikings, who even in subzero weather gathered in the stadium parking lot for convivial picnics before National Football Conference games. The hockey Minnesota North Stars, performing in an arena adjacent to the football-baseball stadium, reached the semifinals of the Stanley Cup playoffs in their first season in the National Hockey League, 1968. The Fighting Saints hockey team, based in St. Paul, began operations in 1973 in the rival World Hockey League. A national hockey Hall of Fame was founded at Eveleth in 1973. The University of Minnesota collegiate hockey, basketball, and baseball teams periodically or regularly dominated their leagues, but the Gopher football team fell on hard times after trips to the Rose Bowl in 1961 and 1962. In 1971 All-American alumnus Paul Giel was appointed athletic director in an effort to revitalize the university's athletic program.

By the mid-1970s the dominance of male "spectator" sports was being questioned by increasingly vocal critics, notably women student groups at the university and colleges who called for greater equality between the sexes in athletic budgets. Winter participant sports like skiing enjoyed steadily increasing popularity; ski resorts and amateur hockey arenas proliferated in most parts of the state. In the sixties snowmobiling emerged as not only a major sport but an important industry, which gave an economic lift to northern Minnesota. Invented in its commercial manifestation by Al and Edgar Hetteen, the snowmobile became the basis of major firms at Roseau, Thief River Falls, and Crosby-Ironton. Seventy-five per cent of all the snowmobiles produced in the United States in the early seventies were made in Minnesota.

Minnesotans have shared with their countrymen strains on the social fabric of American society as blacks, Indians, Mexican-Americans, and other minorities struggled for civil rights and equal opportunity. In Minnesota, a strong civil rights movement, whose main strength was the liberal white community and black middle class, gained momentum in the late fifties and early sixties. A small state Fair Employment Practices Commission was succeeded by a larger and stronger state Department of Human Rights. Race riots in Minneapolis in 1966 and 1967 temporarily threatened community accord, but by the early 1970s, modest gains began to appear. Organizations such as the Urban Coalition (first in the country), concerned with social action in the inner city ghetto, emerged with financial support from the business community; blacks were elected to corporate boards of directors, to the University of Minnesota Board of Regents, and in 1972 to the state legislature for the first time since 1898.

The Indian rights movement emerged late in the decade. The most militant Indian organization, the American Indian Movement (AIM), was founded in Minneapolis in 1968. The number of people leaving reservations to take jobs in distant cities has steadily increased. In the Twin Cities, to which most of those leaving reservations have migrated, community centers have been established where problems are shared and help is given in finding jobs, housing, and medical care. These, along with the organizations like AIM that have been formed to defend the rights of Indians as a minority, are usually intertribal, for a Chippewa living in Minneapolis or St. Paul faces the same difficulties of discrimination and adjustment to city life as a Dakota, a Cree, or a Menominee. But although cooperation among Indians living in the white man's society has been achieved, tribal groups still treasure and preserve the distinctive features of their own cultures. The Chippewa, like others, find it hard to keep up from a distance the community ties that give meaning to their lives as Indians. In order to do so they return to their homes on reservations for weekends or a longer period of time to nourish their roots.

Tribal enterprises have added a new dimension to economic life on several Chippewa reservations. Whether it be a fishing cooperative or motel at Grand Portage, a commercial wild rice paddy or a "mini-mart" at Leech Lake, or an electronics component plant at Mille Lacs, these Indian-owned, tribally managed businesses employed Indian peoples on their own terms and kept alive the hope of economic independence. *Indian and Free*, a book-length photographic essay by Charles Brill, provides a unique glimpse of life — past and present — on the Indian reservation at

716

Red Lake. In 1974, a major publication on Indian culture — *The Ojibwe Resource Unit* — was a joint effort of the Minnesota Historical Society, the University of Minnesota's Department of Indian Studies, and the Ojibwe (Chippewa) Curriculum Committee. Indian Studies programs were inaugurated at the University of Minnesota (at both the Minneapolis and Duluth campuses) and at a number of state and private colleges.

In setting up an Indian Claims Commission in 1946, Congress specified that all Indian claims should be filed within five years and all cases decided within ten, when the commission would cease to exist. In 1972, twenty-six years later, the commission had made decisions in just over half the cases before it, and Congress had already extended its life three times. Nineteen of the sixty Chippewa claims had been dismissed, awards had been made in ten, and title had been fixed in nine cases; in twenty-two cases no decisions had yet been reached.

The most significant breakthrough for the restoration of traditional Indian rights in Minnesota came in 1972 when the Anderson administration reached an agreement with the Leech Lake Band of Chippewa after a three-year legal dispute over hunting, fishing, and ricing rights on the Leech Lake Indian reservation. Under the agreement, exclusive rights in the taking of rough fish were given to the Leech Lake Indians, who relinquished any right to commercial fishing within the boundaries of the Leech Lake Reservation; the taking of game and fish by Indians for their own consumption was to be regulated by the band's Tribal Conservation Committee; a licensing system was set up which allows the Leech Lake Indians to charge a one-dollar fee for non-Indian hunting and fishing within the reservation; and control of wild ricing, previously regulated by the state, was awarded to the Tribal Conservation Committee. The agreement received final approval by the 1973 legislature.

During 1974 the cause of Indian rights was dramatized in a United States District Court chamber in St. Paul. For eight months the "Wounded Knee" trial garnered national attention. The defendants, Russell Means and Dennis Banks, were charged with conspiracy and larceny in connection with the occupation of the South Dakota reservation village of Wounded Knee by AIM forces in 1973. In turn they claimed they had been justifiably protesting the government's failure to do anything about oppressive living conditions among the Indians and to live up to treaty provisions. The occupation was, their lawyer, activist William Kunstler, said, the start of a "social upheaval." All charges against the

717

two were dismissed as the result of what the trial judge termed gross misconduct by the federal government in the course of the trial.

An old cause, women's rights — long dormant — ignited in the 1970s. Women's liberation groups in Minnesota as elsewhere recruited a visible and vocal following, staged protests, and demanded equal rights. Although polls indicated that a substantial portion of the female population was not in sympathy with the manners and methods of the "new feminists," the movement drew attention to widespread inequality in employment opportunities and pay for women in schools, colleges, government, and business. In Minnesota women were modestly successful in seeking greater political representation. Of the 4359 persons elected to the state legislature between 1849 and 1970, only seventeen were women. More than that number entered legislative primaries in 1972. Six were elected — three conservatives and three liberals. In 1974 one of the women elected to the legislature in 1972, Joan Growe, was elected secretary of state, the second to hold a state constitutional office; the first was Mrs. Mike Holm, appointed secretary of state in 1952 and subsequently elected. In a special election in 1975 Nancy Brataas of Rochester became the second woman state senator in the history of Minnesota, the first being Laura E. Naplin of Thief River Falls, elected in 1927. In St. Paul, first Rosalie Butler and then Ruby Hunt served as president of the city council in the early 1970s.

Other conventions and institutions came under increased scrutiny. An ombudsman was established in the Department of Corrections to protect the human rights of inmates in penal institutions. A full-time parole board was set up. The effectiveness of prisons, mental hospitals, and the whole array of welfare programs and practices was investigated. The sixties witnessed a rethinking of institutions, mental habits, relationships in a remarkably brief span of time and on a vast scale. "If I understand the current state of the values of the young," Max Lerner told a graduating class in 1973 at one of the surviving women's colleges, "you are no longer focused on demonstrations and activisms for their own sake. But you have not become apathetic or acquiescent. You are, rather, part of a values shift from making a living to making a life, from acquisitive and power values to those of . . . fulfillment and wholeness."

The decade of the sixties experienced too what can be called an "ethnic renaissance." Following the thrust of the blacks and Indians to assert their self-identity and culture, Mexican-Americans and those of immi-

718

grant stock brought their cultural uniqueness and their accomplishments to the fore. The belief that Minnesota's vitality and character are based to a considerable extent on the special contributions of the thirty or more ethnic groups that form the tapestry of the state's past and present was reinforced.

Population is the key to understanding change in Minnesota during the 1960s and into the 1970s. Population changed in composition, in sheer numbers, and in location. It created or intensified urban and metropolitan problems, notably shortages of housing and inadequate transportation. A metropolitan consciousness was fostered among Twin Cities residents, with a concomitant fear of the Twin Cities among rural leaders and a revitalization of some rural towns and regional experiments in government.

Between 1960 and 1970, the population of Minnesota increased 11½ per cent. At the same time, over half of the eighty-seven counties had a net decline in population. Twelve counties had a population decline of more than 10 per cent. The state's nonfarm population expanded especially along the northwest-southeast major transportation routes. While the large central cities of Minneapolis and St. Paul lost population, smaller cities around them grew dramatically, one of them, Bloomington, becoming the fourth largest in the state. The predominant population thrust was toward the principal service centers but not into the older areas. The concentration of people continued to shift away from the railroads and moved toward the flatlands, rolling hills, lakes, and forests. There were belts of growth from Minneapolis to La Crescent, Rochester, Albert Lea, Mankato, Willmar, St. Cloud, Brainerd, around Mille Lacs, and from St. Paul up the St. Croix into Chisago County. By 1980, it is estimated that the state's population will be in excess of 4,077,000 persons, with at least 50 per cent of the state's population living in the Twin Cities metropolitan area.

Projections also indicate continued concentration of the state's population in nine urban clusters (three crossing state lines) with each of the following cities (or pair of cities) as a hub: Minneapolis–St. Paul, Duluth (and Superior, Wisconsin), Rochester, St. Cloud, Mankato, Moorhead (and Fargo, North Dakota), the cities along the Mesabi iron range, Winona, and East Grand Forks (and Grand Forks, North Dakota). The distinguishing characteristics of the clusters are these: Travel time within them is less than 100 minutes. They include multiple major shopping centers, serving separate trade areas within the urban cluster. They have large numbers of retail service trade centers and specialty businesses, principal industrial and wholesale zones, an array of public and higher education facilities, major medical centers, a network of newspaper and public broadcasting media that serve the region. There are two types of housing — scattered custom-built homes and concentrated mass housing provided by a few large developers. Suburban dwellers long resisted apartments in residential areas but this pattern changed in the late 1960s. The Twin Cities is still one of the two lowest density metropolitan areas in the United States in the million or more population category. A unique feature of the Twin Cities seven-county area is the 200 fishing and boating lakes and 1000 scenic lakes and ponds.

As the shift from farm trade to industry took place in the state, the older forms of local government proved inadequate to cope with such translocal issues as pollution control, highways, and education. Rural population, as well as urban, is highly mobile and no longer bound to a county. The legislature, recognizing the need for comprehensive planning and administration, took significant steps in 1967 and 1969 to coordinate both metropolitan and rural government.

In 1967 the Metropolitan Council was created, as noted earlier, to provide a new form of government for the seven-county Twin Cities area. The council controls planning for two million people and works with 321 political units. Its basic concerns are pollution, sewage, highway routes, and preservation of open space; control of police, schools, zoning, and taxation is left to the communities. Its members are appointed by the governor. It has its own tax base of 70 cents per $1000 taxable valuation — about $1 million a year — and a staff of fifty.

The Metropolitan Council was well conceived and skillfully promoted; the enabling legislation sailed through the legislature. Public acceptance was excellent. Two years later, in 1969, the concept was extended to the rest of the state in the form of a plan for ten regional governments, or commissions, all falling within the jurisdiction of the state-wide Regional Development Commission. Again, the legislature was sympathetic. The bill's author, Senator Gordon Rosenmeier, guided it through both houses, encountering only token opposition. Subsequently, two regions were subdivided, bringing the total to twelve. The public reaction was just the opposite of the reception accorded the Metropolitan Council: antagonism

720

from most of the regions, which reflected a feeling of further alienation from the Twin Cities area.

In 1973 Governor Anderson announced the formation of the last of the regional commissions, calling it "a major milestone in the history of state and local government and intergovernmental relations in Minnesota." "Completion of the regional commission formation process," said the governor, "coupled with the $800,000 appropriated by the 1973 legislature to support the activities of the commission, can result in a major strengthening of the planning partnership between state and local government . . . The truth is that we have to think in regional terms because no one municipality, no one town, no one county has the means to create programs adequate to its own needs — much less to the needs of the areas that surround it and are affected by it. What has to be done cannot be done by a single locality acting alone. If the trend toward the concentration of most of Minnesota's people in the Twin Cities area continues, outstate Minnesota will be further drained of its population — and of its ability to meet the needs of those who are left. At the same time, the Twin Cities will face increasing pressures from overcrowding, urban sprawl, traffic congestion and inadequate housing and public facilities. Unless we begin to think in regional terms in outstate Minnesota we're in great trouble."

By this time much of the fear and hostility and the volatile opposition aroused after the Minnesota legislature adopted the 1969 Regional Development Act had faded. The concept became ever more widely accepted as a way to stop rural population loss, to build rural Minnesota through intergovernmental cooperation, and to channel federal and state money to rural counties and municipalities.

At the same time the Metropolitan Council was running into some criticism from those who feared its emergence as another layer of government. Originally created as a planning and coordinating body, it enlarged its scope (as a result of action by the 1974 legislature) in the fields of parks, housing, health, and transit, and strengthened its control of the Metropolitan Transit Commission, the Metropolitan Airports Commission, the Metropolitan Sewer Board, and other boards serving the seven-county area. A serious impasse over what type of public transit system to build for the Twin Cities arose between the Metropolitan Transit Commission and the Metropolitan Council in 1973. The Metropolitan Transit Commission favored a fixed guideway, automated vehicle system, while the Metropolitan Council threw its weight behind a comprehensive system of busways. The likelihood of ever-higher prices for gasoline and the threat of severe shortages made solution of the public transportation problem an issue of considerable concern to the citizens of the metropolitan area.

The state, like the nation, faced in the 1960s and 1970s the complex problems engendered by an inflationary-recessive economy. But while unemployment, rising prices, and potential scarcities in sources of energy, along with increased costs for those available, were serious, Minnesota was not as hard hit generally as some other sections of the country. Its balanced economic mix — agriculture as well as manufacturing and services, varied businesses as well as a few giants — and its skilled work force (there were by the early 1970s more than 170 "brain-industries" in the state, making it a center of such activity) had strengths of significance.

Minnesota's third city, Duluth, familiar with frequent periods of economic depression over the years, experienced a veritable renaissance in the late 1960s with programs for urban renewal, growth as an inland port as a result of taconite and grain shipments, and development as a mecca for winter sports. Instrumental in this economic upturn was a strong civic leadership headed by Mayor Ben Boo, a Republican, and a sizable infusion of federal funds secured by the state's senior congressman (until his retirement in 1974), Democratic-Farmer-Laborite John Blatnik of the Eighth District, who chaired the public works committee of the United States House of Representatives. By the mid-1970s declining ore and grain shipments on the St. Lawrence Seaway had become a source of worry.

On the iron range to the west of Duluth mining employment decreased 23 per cent (18,000 to 14,000) during the decade of the 1960s, but the taconite industry increased its capacity for production; the state still produced 63 per cent of the nation's iron ore and taconite. And a new mining industry loomed on the horizon: copper and nickel. Explorations for deposits were carried out in the Duluth Gabbro area — north of Duluth and just south of Ely, containing at a conservative estimate, 14 million tons of copper, in some 6.5 billion tons of crude ore. A state interagency task force on base metal mining estimated the ore's worth at $55 billion and sufficient to meet the total needs of the United States for seventy years. Several environmental organizations and the State Pollution Control Agency staff, however, urged a moratorium on the starting of any mining until environmental concerns could be fully explored and satisfied.

Agricultural employment, like employment in mining, declined from 1960 to 1970, by 40 per cent, from 184,000 to 111,000, owing partly to consolidation of farms. But advances in technology resulted in a growth in agricultural output in this period and agriculture remained a strong element in the state's economy. The state continued to lead the nation in butter production, was second in dry milk and hay, third in meat, fourth in corn.

Corporate farming came under the scrutiny of the 1971 legislature. Fears of weakening the family farm and of absentee ownership led to passage of a law requiring that farms operating under a corporate structure register with the secretary of state. An investigation showed that 550 corporations operated farms within Minnesota, comprising 451,976 acres and 1.6 per cent of the state's farmland. Minnesota corporations controlled 420,720 acres, leaving only 31,256 acres under the control of out-of-state firms. The in-state corporations had average holdings of 890 acres while out-of-state firms had average holdings of 1041 acres per corporate farm. The distribution of corporate farms covered the entire state except for Cook and Lake counties, which had none. In 1973 the legislature went further, prohibiting off-farm corporations from engaging in farming. It also gave farmers the right to bargain collectively with agricultural processors.

The weather remained a challenge to state farmers, with floods, late springs, and early frosts ever-present threats. A blizzard on January 10–12, 1975, the most severe in thirty-five years, cost Minnesota farmers an estimated $25 million in livestock and poultry losses, as well as building damage. Hardest hit were seven southwestern counties — Rock, Nobles, Cottonwood, Jackson, Pipestone, Murray, and Redwood.

Employment in the transportation, communications, and utilities sector increased slightly over the decade, 93,000 to 96,000. In 1970 the Great Northern, Northern Pacific, and Chicago, Burlington, and Quincy railroads were merged into the Burlington Northern Railway Company, with headquarters in St. Paul, thus becoming the largest single railway system in the United States.

Employment also increased in manufacturing (248,000 to 309,000), trade (249,000 to 323,000), finance, insurance, and real estate (52,000

723

to 68,000), government (48,000 to 56,000) — and, most strikingly, in services (272,000 to 405,000). An important component of services is health care; while Minnesota remained one of the foremost areas in the country for quality health care, the availability of health services to the average citizen diminished. The inadequacy of private health insurance and the shortcomings of nursing home care for the elderly increasingly came under the scrutiny of legislative committees.

Forecasters in 1975 predicted that in the year 2000 Minnesota would have a work force of slightly more than 2 million, 29 per cent in services, 22 per cent in manufacturing, 21 per cent in trade, and 5 per cent in agriculture.

In the perspective of the long sweep of Minnesota history, what are the continuities that emerge from a study of Minnesota's past?

Geography has been a powerful force here. At the center of the North American continent, Minnesota is a composite of three distinct regions: North Woods, Great Plains, and Corn Belt. Etched into interlacing lakes and streams, rockbound shores, continental divides, river bluffs, rolling prairies, fertile valleys, marshes, and wooded sanctuaries are the headwaters of three great river systems. Rivers flowing to the Atlantic, to Hudson Bay, and to the Gulf of Mexico made Minnesota a crossroads not only for the great waterways but also for migrating peoples. Their diverse ideas led to social experimentation, volatile political activities, and innovative movements.

After the last glacier retreated 10,000 years ago, Asians crossed the Bering Strait and moved to the Great Lakes in search of plants and animals that spread over the region. Through successive millenniums there came Indian tribes and then white men drawn by a rich and rare combination of resources. Frenchmen seeking fur pelts were unrolling the map of Minnesota by 1650. Two hundred years later Yankee lumbermen from eastern states had replaced the French-Canadian voyageurs, and lumbering had replaced fur as the major industry. With the taking of Indian lands and the onrush of white settlement, waves and then tides of immigrants from Europe enriched and diversified the ethnic mix that is today's population.

Farming set Minnesota's life style through most of its first hundred years as a state, and in the second half of the twentieth century its foremost industry is still agriculture and agribusiness. The fabulous dimen-

724

sions of the iron ranges, particularly the Mesabi, became visible in the 1880s, and Minnesota emerged as the chief supplier of iron to feed the industrial hunger of a growing nation. In transportation canoe and steamboat gave way to roads that opened the back country to farmers and landseekers. The Red River ox cart, covered wagon, and stagecoach linked river towns to land-locked western Minnesota but were soon replaced by the railroad. Going all the way to the Pacific, the "iron horse" pushed the edge of the frontier westward, and Minnesota moved out of its frontier era. In the modern era a network of interstate highways, an international airport, and an international port brought Minnesota ever closer to its sister states and the nations of the world.

Conservative in government institutions but progressive in politics, Minnesota fashioned an independent tradition with a three-party system through part of its history. This nonconformity, flavored by farmer revolts and blended with advanced social legislation influenced by the state's Scandinavians, has produced a remarkable string of political leaders whose impact has been felt far beyond Minnesota's boundaries.

Now, what of the next hundred years? The immigrant tides have ebbed, but the drive continues for an ever-better life.

The state has industrialized and urbanized. Its great extractive industries — lumbering and mining — have been superseded by manufacturing. The Twin Cities are the metropolitan capital for a vast multistate region. But urbanization has brought problems. Family farms and small communities have withered. Decay eats away inner cities. Metropolitan growth is too often accompanied by urban blight. Developments in cheap and efficient public transportation have not kept pace with needs. Some Minnesotans have been left behind, too. Indians on reservations and in the core city; the increasing black population whose first members arrived during the Civil War; and migratory laborers — largely Mexican-American — are excluded from many community advantages. The increasing numbers of senior citizens find themselves disadvantaged in an inflationary economy. There are other Minnesotans, too, for whom the promises of the frontier have not been fulfilled: losers in the race to exploit resources and also those who see careless destruction of the environment as a threat to future generations.

Yet, despite problems, Minnesota is rated near the top of the nation in "quality of life," reflecting the benefits shared by most of its citizens. As it entered the last quarter of the twentieth century, it increasingly received accolades as a state "that works," one that is as "good a model as one can find in these United States and the successful society," a state whose leaders play an increasingly prominent role in the life of the nation, a state whose political structure is open, issue-oriented, clean, and responsive, a state that provides a high level of services to its people and recognizes the need to levy high taxes to pay for those services, and a state that excels in quality of education, health care, economic growth, industries that remain home-owned, and cultural leadership. "Among Twin Cities leaders," writes Neal R. Peirce in *The Great Plains States of America*, "one senses a deep orientation to change — and a determination not to be engulfed by that change, but rather to make it work constructively." That could be said of the state as a whole. Political innovation and leadership should continue, and this state should remain a fertile source of talent across the spectrum of human activity. Minnesota stands a good chance of retaining much of its picturesque beauty and little likelihood of losing its invigorating climate. By drawing strength from their environment, their past, and their ingrained independence, Minnesotans may look ahead with confidence.

What is it that invests Minnesota with a legacy from the past that invites continual rewriting and interpretation? Rene Dubos, the eminent microbiologist, put it well when he wrote, ". . . as human beings, we demand more of the environment than just providing health and economic prosperity; the quality of life includes emotional and spiritual values. These values come from our contacts with the spirit of the place. . . . Spirit of place implies fitness between man and nature. But this fitness does not just happen. It depends on active human participation. The catalyst that converts a physical locality into a 'place' is the process of experiencing it deeply, and of engaging with it in a symbiotic relationship." It is this "spirit of place" that animates the story of Minnesota. "Because of them, the people," wrote Theodore C. Blegen as he completed the first edition of this book over a decade ago, "the state's yesterdays are legacy on the one hand, prologue on the other."

✽

Added Readings

THERE is no lack of sources on Minnesota in the 1960s and 1970s. The difficulty in using them is the lack of collation and synthesis. There is a sore need of monographs that interpret this intensely interesting and highly significant period in the development of the state. In the absence of refined historical studies, one frequently has to fall back on scattered sources such as reports, newspapers, and speeches.

Helpful as always are the annual Minnesota articles in the yearbooks of the *Encyclopaedia Britannica*, the *Encyclopedia Americana*, and *Collier's Encyclopedia* as well as the *Legislative Manuals* for the period. The messages of the governors — inaugural, budget, and special — provide important data as well as insight into the marked growth, shifting priorities, and new programs of state government. A mountain of reports from state and regional agencies confronts the historian, who must attempt to sift through them in order to identify continuities and departures. While a great many of these are devoid of meaningful information and can be discarded as image-promoting pieces, the reports of a number of state departments and commissions are invaluable as one attempts to piece together the Minnesota story during the 1960s and 1970s. *Minnesota Settlement and Land Use 1985* (undated), prepared for the Minnesota State Planning Agency by John R. Borchert and Donald D. Carroll, illuminates the large population shifts during the 1960s that altered life styles, social fabrics, and political power bases during that decade. The *Minnesota Pocket Data Book* (1973), also published by the State Planning Agency, is a rich statistical reference source on Minnesota and includes an excellent bibliography of state agency reports. Also informative are the reports of the Citizens League, a private organization.

Particularly valuable for an understanding of the state's political and economic development during the period covered by the last chapter are the published summaries of papers presented at a symposium held for legislators at the beginning of the 1975 legislative session, entitled *Minnesota Horizons: A Legislative Symposium, January 14–16, 1975*. This compendium presents the views of sixteen social scientists and state officials on the condition of Minnesota in relation to population patterns, economy, environment, housing, transportation, energy, health, education, human services, and government. The increasing interaction of economy and government of the state was the subject of a paper given to that symposium by Russell W. Fridley, which was published as "Public Policy and Minnesota's Economy — A Historical View" in *Minnesota History*, Spring 1975. The Constitutional Study Commission was authorized by the 1971 legislature to recommend revisions of the state constitution; its *Report*, issued in 1973, contains a great many data about the contemporary structure and workings of state government.

Books that added to a knowledge of specific aspects of Minnesota history and politics were numerous. Michael Brooks's *Reference Guide to Minnesota History* (1974) is invaluable. The Minnesota Historical Society inaugurated a scholarly series of archaeological studies, foremost of which is *Prehistoric Peoples of Minnesota* (1969) by Elden Johnson. Theodore C. Blegen's *The Kensington Runestone: New Light on an Old Riddle* (1968) is a thoughtful assessment of the evidence on that historical problem. *Selections from "Minnesota History": A Fiftieth Anniversary Anthology*, edited by Rhoda R. Gilman and June D. Holmquist, was published in 1965. A long-awaited biography was *Ignatius Donnelly, Portrait of a Politician* (1962) by Martin Ridge. *Politics in Minnesota* (revised ed., 1970) by G. Theodore Mitau provides a concise sketch of the independent political tradition of Minnesota and an analysis of the workings of state government. Carl H. Chrislock's excellent study *The Progressive Era in Minnesota, 1899–1918* was issued in 1971. Abigail McCarthy's *Private Faces/Public Places* (1972) gives a well-written and perceptive view of the political life of St. Paul; particularly interesting is her account of the 1952 congressional campaign of her husband, Eugene J. McCarthy. *The 21st Ballot: A Political Party Struggle in Minnesota* (1969) by David Lebedoff is a detailed and lively account of the 1966 contest for the gubernatorial nomination in the Democratic-Farmer-Labor party and of the subsequent election. Lebedoff's *Ward Number Six* (1972) is a close look at the local tug-of-war between supporters of McCarthy and of Hubert H. Humphrey in one Minneapolis ward in 1968. A valuable addition to the literature that explains the increasing role of Minnesotans in the nation's affairs is Barbara Stuhler's

728

Ten Men of Minnesota and United States Foreign Policy, 1898–1968 (1973), particularly the final chapter devoted to the diverging political philosophies of Humphrey and McCarthy over the war in Vietnam. A book devoted to Humphrey's and McCarthy's struggle over the Democratic presidential nomination in 1968 is Albert Eisele's *Almost to the Presidency* (1972). There were a number of campaign biographies of Humphrey.

A comprehensive summary of the varied regions of the state — in terms of their geography, natural resources, ethnic makeup, industrial or agricultural base, urban and rural characteristics, and settlement patterns — is the focus of *Gopher Reader II* (1975), edited by A. Hermina Poatgieter and James Taylor Dunn, a second anthology drawn from articles published in the *Gopher Historian.* This volume also contains original and fresh material on Minnesota's ethnic minorities — Indians, blacks, and Mexican-Americans. Three significant publications on the state's Indian people are *Indians in Minnesota* (1962 and 1971), published by the League of Women Voters in Minnesota; *The Ojibwe Resource Unit* (1974), a joint effort of the Minnesota Historical Society, the University of Minnesota Department of Indian Studies, and the Ojibwe Curriculum Committee; and *Indian and Free* (1974) by Charles Brill, published by the University of Minnesota Press. An additional work of interest to any student of the state's ethnic composition is the English translation of Hans R. Wasastjerna's *History of the Finns in Minnesota* (1967). Behavioral studies of two communities with extensive German populations are Noel Iverson's *Germania, U.S.A.: Social Change in New Ulm, Minnesota* (1966) and Edward L. Henry's *Micropolis in Transition* (1971). The former is a sociological investigation that compares the attitudes and life styles of residents of New Ulm who were Turners with corresponding generations of non-Turner families in the community. The latter analyzes the changing demands confronting the rapidly growing city of St. Cloud, from the vantage point of a political scientist who had also served the city as its mayor. William Hoffman's *Tales of Hoffman* (1961) depicts the hardships Eastern European Jewish immigrants endured and overcame on St. Paul's West Side. Max Shulman's *Potatoes Are Cheaper* (1972) takes a comic look through fiction at Jewish life in the Selby-Dale area of St. Paul during the 1930s before it became a predominantly black section. Harold Allen's *The Linguistic Atlas of the Upper Midwest,* vol. 1 (1973) records speech patterns of Minnesotans as well as of residents of nearby states. A useful source for understanding the changes sweeping welfare programs at the state and local levels is Ethel McClure's *More Than a Roof: The Development of Minnesota Poor Farms and Homes for the Aged* (1968).

Delightfully reminiscent accounts came from the pens of two Minnesotans: Charles W. Mayo's *Mayo: The Story of My Family and Career*

(1968) and Charles A. Lindbergh's *Boyhood on the Upper Mississippi* (1972). Lindbergh's father, Charles A. Lindbergh, Sr., was the subject of a biography entitled *Lindbergh of Minnesota* (1973) by Bruce L. Larson.

Samuel Eliot Morison in *The Oxford History of the American People* (1965) gives a succinct summary (pages 965–966) of the twentieth-century effort by conservationists to preserve the Quetico-Superior country. A series of books by Sigurd F. Olson — *The Lonely Land* (1961), *Runes of the North* (1963), *Open Horizons* (1969), and *Wilderness Days* (1972) — offered philosophical prose portraits of the Quetico-Superior country, which the author knows intimately and has done so much to preserve. Other books about life in Minnesota's north woods were Helen Hoover's *The Long-Shadowed Forest* (1963), *The Gift of the Deer* (1966), *A Place in the Woods* (1969), and *The Years of the Forest* (1973). James Taylor Dunn wrote of *The St. Croix: Midwest Border River* (1965) in the Rivers of America Series. Henry Lewis's *The Valley of the Mississippi Illustrated* (1967) was edited by Bertha L. Heilbron and translated by A. Hermina Poatgieter. Florence Page Jaques, in *Francis Lee Jaques: Artist of the Wilderness World* (1973), provides a poignant and vivid tribute to her late husband with whom she collaborated on many memorable books and in aiding the cause of conservation in Minnesota and elsewhere. *A Flora of Northeastern Minnesota* (1965) by Olga Lakela, *Common Wild Flowers of Minnesota* (1971) by Wilma Monserud, illustrator, and Gerald Ownbey, author, and *Northern Fishes* (revised ed., 1974) by Samuel Eddy and James C. Underhill were additions to the shelf of books on Minnesota natural history.

A number of books reflect the increasing interest and effort in preserving the state's important historic sites and architectural landmarks: June D. Holmquist and Jean A. Brookins, *Minnesota's Major Historic Sites: A Guide* (1963); H. F. Koeper, *Historic St. Paul Buildings* (1964); Marilyn Ziebarth and Alan Ominsky, *Fort Snelling: Anchor Post of the Northwest* (1970); Neil B. Thompson, *Minnesota's State Capitol: The Art and Politics of a Public Building* (1974); and James Allen Scott, *Duluth's Legacy*, Volume I (1974). *The Twin Cities Explored: A Guide to Restaurants, Shops, Theaters, Museums, and Other Features* (1972) by Jean and John Ervin has a useful section on the architecture of Minneapolis and St. Paul. John Francis McDermott's *Seth Eastman: Pictorial Historian of the Indian* (1961) added an important book about an early and superb Minnesota artist. A scholarly commentary on fictional literature for the period, emphasizing the Twin Cities area, is Dorothy R. Dodge and Patricia L. Kane, *The Quality of Urban Life: Perceptions from Quantitative Data and Literature* (undated). The most complete source on nonfiction works is the book review section of *Minnesota History*, the quarterly magazine of the Minnesota Historical Society.

The 1960s produced solid works that are prime sources on Minnesota industries and institutions. Among the best examples are E. W. Davis's *Pioneering with Taconite* (1964), an autobiographical account of northeastern Minnesota's new industry that began to burgeon in the 1960s, told by the man who made the manufacture of taconite into magnetized pellets commercially feasible; Russell H. Bennett's autobiographical *Quest for Ore* (1963), the story of a Minneapolis mining engineer whose career embraced the Mesabi and Cuyuna iron ranges and the vast nickel mines at Sudbury, Ontario; Frank A. King's *The Missabe Road . . . The Duluth, Missabe and Iron Range Railway* (1972); *Timber and Men: The Weyerhaeuser Story* (1963) by Ralph W. Hidy, Frank Ernest Hill, and Allan Nevins, a comprehensive account — through corporate eyes — of one of the oldest families and one of the largest enterprises in the forest industry; Hiram M. Drache's *The Day of the Bonanza: A History of Bonanza Farming in the Red River Valley of the North* (1964); Lucile M. Kane's *The Waterfall That Built a City: The Falls of St. Anthony* (1966), a study of the harnessing of the waterpower that gave rise to the industrial growth of Minneapolis; and Herman J. Arnott's *Approaching the Centennial* (1974), an updated history of the Farmers and Mechanics Savings Bank of Minneapolis. A comprehensive study with individual histories of Minnesota's sixteen private liberal arts colleges is Merrill E. Jarchow's *Private Liberal Arts Colleges in Minnesota: Their History and Contribution* (1973). Also published were separate histories of two of the colleges: Leal A. Headley and Merrill E. Jarchow, *Carleton: The First Century* (1966) and Carl H. Chrislock, *From Fjord to Freeway: 100 Years, Augsburg College* (1969).

An overview of Minnesota, somewhat weighted toward the Twin Cities, is "Minnesota: The Successful Society" in Neal R. Peirce's *The Great Plains States of America* (1972). The author emerges with a highly favorable profile of the North Star State. A contemporary photographic portrait of the Minnesota scene is *Minnesota in Focus* (1974), with text by George Moses and photographs by *The Minneapolis Star* and the *Minneapolis Tribune*.

It is encouraging to witness a renewed and intensified interest in Minnesota history. The state of Minnesota has many faces and they invite endless and fascinating study. It is certain that the mosaic of peoples, places, and events that constitute Minnesota will receive greater scrutiny and analysis than ever before during the years ahead. Piecing together the multifarious links of this never-ending chain is the task of the Minnesota historians of the future.